DEFINING DOCUMENTS
IN AMERICAN HISTORY

Dissent & Protest
(1635–2017)

DEFINING DOCUMENTS
IN AMERICAN HISTORY

Dissent & Protest (1635-2017)

Editor

Aaron Gulyas

Volume 2

SALEM PRESS
A Division of EBSCO Information Services
Ipswich, Massachusetts

GREY HOUSE PUBLISHING

Cover Image: Declaration of Independence Signatures (istockphotos.com/duncan1890)
Copyright ©2017, by Schlager Group, Inc., and Grey House Publishing, Inc.

All rights reserved. No part of this work may be used or reproduced in any manner whatsoever or transmitted in any form or by any means, electronic or mechanical, including photocopy, recording, or any information storage and retrieval system, without written permission from the copyright owner.

∞ The paper used in these volumes conforms to the American National Standard for Permanence of Paper for Printed Library Materials, Z39.48 1992 (R2009).

Publisher's Cataloging-In-Publication Data
(Prepared by The Donohue Group, Inc.)

Names: Gulyas, Aaron John, 1975- editor.
Title: Dissent & protest (1635-2017) / editor, Aaron Gulyas.
Other Titles: Dissent and protest (1635-2017) | Defining documents in American history (Salem Press)
Description: [First edition]. | Ipswich, Massachusetts : Salem Press, a division of EBSCO Information Services ; [Amenia, New York] : Grey House Publishing, [2017] | Includes bibliographical references and index.
Identifiers: ISBN 978-1-68217-289-6 (set) | ISBN 978-1-68217-291-9 (v. 1) | ISBN 978-1-68217-292-6 (v. 2)
Subjects: LCSH: Protest movements--United States--History--Sources. | Social movements--United States--History--Sources. | Dissenters--United States--History--Sources. | United States--Social conditions--Sources.
Classification: LCC HM881 .D57 2017 | DDC 303.484/0973--dc23

FIRST PRINTING
PRINTED IN THE UNITED STATES OF AMERICA

Table of Contents

Publisher's Note vii
Editor's Introduction ix
Contributors xiii

Volume 1

From Colonies to Nation — 1

Excerpts from the Massachusetts Bay Colony Trial against Anne Hutchinson 3
Declaration of Protestant Subjects in Maryland 10
The Rights of the British Colonies Asserted and Proved 17
Declaration of Rights of the Stamp Act Congress 22
Letters from a Farmer in Pennsylvania 27
Boston Non-Importation Agreement 35
Samuel Adams Writing as Candidus 39
Rules by Which a Great Empire May Be Reduced to a Small One 43
Boston Massacre Oration 49
"Liberty or Death" Speech 56
Common Sense 62
Petition against the Excise Tax by Inhabitants of Western Pennsylvania 76

Slavery and Abolition — 81

A Minute against Slavery, From the Germantown Monthly Meeting, Addressed to the Monthly
    Meeting in Dublin 83
An Account of the Negroe Insurrection in South Carolina 90
Petition of Prince Hall and Other African Americans to the Massachusetts General Court 94
Petition to the Assembly of Pennsylvania against the Slave Trade 99
An Address to Those Who Keep Slaves, and Approve the Practice 101
Appeal to the Coloured Citizens of the World 105
The Confessions of Nat Turner 118
Declaration of Sentiments of the American Anti-Slavery Convention 129
Prejudices against People of Color, and Our Duties in Relation to This Subject 135
"An Address to the Slaves of the United States of America" 143
"What to the Slave is the Fourth of July?" 151
The Condition, Elevation, Emigration, and Destiny of the Colored People of the United States,
    Politically Considered 165

Twelve Years a Slave: Narrative of Solomon Northup	176
Provisional Constitution and Ordinances for the People of the United States	184
A Voice from Harper's Ferry	195
Incidents in the Life of a Slave Girl	209
"Under the Flag"	216
Valedictory Editorial of the *Liberator*	220

SECTIONAL CONFLICT, CIVIL WAR, AND RECONSTRUCTION — 225

South Carolina Ordinance of Nullification	227
Speech Opposing the Kansas-Nebraska Act	232
South Carolina Declaration of Causes of Secession	237
Farewell Address to the U.S. Senate	245
Speech on His Refusal to Take the Oath of Loyalty to the Confederacy	251
"Cornerstone Speech"	254
Speech on His Expulsion from the Georgia Legislature	263
"All That We Ask Is Equal Laws, Equal Legislation, and Equal Rights"	272
Preface to *The Rise and Fall of the Confederate Government*	281

NATIVE AMERICAN DISSENT — 287

Appeal to Choctaws and Chickasaws	289
Memorial to Congress	294
Battle of Sand Creek: Editorials and Congressional Testimony	298
Treaty of Fort Laramie	316
Dawes Severalty Act	325
Wounded Knee Massacre: Statements and Eyewitness Accounts	333
Indians of All Tribes Occupation of Alcatraz: Proclamation	343
Summary of Letter Requesting Further Review of the Dakota Access Pipeline (DAPL)	347

Volume 2

AFRICAN-AMERICAN CIVIL RIGHTS — 355

Atlanta Exposition Address	357
Niagara Movement Declaration of Principles	363
"Lynching: Our National Crime"	369

"Agitation" 375
William Monroe Trotter's Protest to Woodrow Wilson 378
"The Eruption of Tulsa" 383
"U.S. Department of (White) Justice" 390
"A Black Inventory of the New Deal" 397
Call to Negro America to March on Washington 405
An Appeal to the World 410
Student Nonviolent Coordinating Committee Statement of Purpose 416
Letter from Birmingham Jail 419
"I Have a Dream" 433
"Message to the Grass Roots" 439
"The Ballot or the Bullet" 446
What We Want 453
"Black Power" 461
"What We Want, What We Believe" 474

WOMEN'S RIGHTS   481

Seneca Falls Convention Declaration of Sentiments 483
Lecture on Constitutional Equality 488
"Is It a Crime for a Citizen of the United States to Vote?" 494
"The Status of Woman, Past, Present, and Future" 501
"Why Women Should Vote" 508
Testimony before the House Judiciary Committee 514
The SCUM Manifesto 520
Women's March on Washington 529

POLITICAL AND SOCIAL PROTEST   533

Ten Days in a Mad-House 535
How the Other Half Lives 545
"The Subjective Necessity for Social Settlements" 554
Editorial on the Pullman Strike 558
"Liberty" 562
The "Cross of Gold" Speech 566
Speech Opposing the League of Nations 574

Auto Workers Strike 579
"Share Our Wealth" Address 585
Southern Manifesto 590
The Port Huron Statement 595
Gay Power Comes to Sheridan Square 601
Steal This Book 606
Commonwealth Address 613

ANTI-WAR ACTIVISM 621

Speech against Conscription and War 623
Speech Opposing War with Germany 628
Antiwar Speech 633
"Beyond Vietnam: A Time to Break Silence" 638
Testimony of the Vietnam Veterans against the War 651
"The Emperor Has No Clothes" Speech 658

APPENDIXES 663

Chronological List 665
Web Resources 668
Bibliography 669
Index 683
Photo Credits 688

AFRICAN-AMERICAN CIVIL RIGHTS

Following the long-awaited abolition of slavery following the Civil War and the efforts of the Reconstruction process to recognize full civil and political rights for African-Americas, the late nineteenth century saw the emergence of the Jim Crow era—a time of legally sanctioned segregation that was accompanied by violent suppression of political rights in the southern states and subtler forms of discrimination (such as in housing, education, and employment) in the northern states. African-American leaders responded with different ideas and strategies to combat these developments and to work for change.

Booker T. Washington's strategy of "accommodation," expressed in his 1895 Atlanta Exposition Address, laid out a plan of economic self-improvement as the path to eventual social and political equality. Washington's moderate position served as a target for the opposition of a more active, forceful, and disruptive vision of dissent. These principles were put forward in the 1905 Niagara Movement "Declaration of Principles," this declaration was authored by W. E. B. Du Bois and William Monroe Trotter, who would go on to remain active forces in the civil rights movement of the early and mid twentieth century. Du Bois, in his 1910 piece "Agitation," would directly debate Washington's notions of accommodation, while Trotter's 1914 Protest to Woodrow Wilson directly attacked the President's policy of segregation in federal offices. Activists like Ida B. Wells called public attention to specific, horrific abuses of African-Americans, as she did in "Lynching: Our National Crime." Walter F. White undertook similar tasks in 1921 and 1935 when he exposed the outpouring of white violence presented to the media as a "race riot" in his article "The Eruption of Tulsa" and attempted to rekindle the movement for federal anti-lynching law in "U.S. Department of (White) Justice."

Despite the widespread transfer of African-American votes to the Democratic Party with the election of Franklin Roosevelt in 1932, civil rights activists continued to put pressure on the President to take action on behalf of his black supporters. In 1935, John P. Davis presented "A Black Inventory of the New Deal," which faulted the administration for policies and programs that in some cases actually worsened the situation of African-Americans. On the eve of the Second World War, as war production ramped up, A. Phillip Randolph issued a "Call to Negro America to March on Washington." While the march would not happen for another two decades, Randolph used the possibility as leverage in persuading Roosevelt to issue regulations for non-discrimination in hiring in the defense industries.

The Civil Rights movement of the 1950s, under the leadership of Martin Luther King Jr. distinguished itself through its adoption of the practice of nonviolent confrontation and protest, a view promoted also, initially, by the Student Nonviolent Coordinating Committee in their Statement of Purpose. King would expound on the need for active confrontation of discrimination and racism—within the bounds of nonviolence in his Letter from Birmingham Jail and present his vision for the future of the United States in his 1963 "I Have a Dream" Speech. At the same time, another trend was emerging that was less focused on nonviolence and equality and more on the development of political power, economic self-sufficiency, and the need for strong independent communities. Malcolm X in speeches like "Message to the Grass Roots" and "The Ballot or the Bullet" proposed a path for African-American activism that aimed to take the "passive" out of passive resistance. These ideas were developed in the mid-1960s by Stokely Carmichael. Carmichael coined the phrase Black Power and in What We Want advocated a movement that was focused entirely on the needs of the African American Community rather on political expediency or the sensibilities of white liberals. The Black Panther Party, in their 1966 statement of goals and beliefs, "What We Want, What We Believe" introduced Marxist political and economic goals into the conversation about racial equality.

Atlanta Exposition Address

Date: 1895
Author: Booker T. Washington
Genre: Speech

Summary Overview

The Atlanta Exposition Address, a speech that ran a little over ten minutes, propelled the previously unknown principal of Tuskegee Institute, a small black college in rural Alabama, into the national spotlight. The immediate response, both in Atlanta and across the country, was overwhelmingly positive, but over time both Washington and his address have been sharply criticized, especially by other African American intellectuals and leaders. These critics termed the Atlanta address the "Atlanta Compromise" and made Washington a symbol of accommodation and acquiescence to southern racism, segregation, and the political disenfranchisement of African Americans. Throughout much of the twentieth century Washington and his famous (or infamous) address were a defining element in the African American political debate.

Defining Moment

The 1890s were a difficult decade for African Americans. Many of the gains they had achieved during the Reconstruction period (1863-1877) both in securing their political and civil rights and in attaining a measure of physical security gave way to an assault on their rights as citizens and on their personal safety. In the late 1870s and 1880s these gains began to unravel. In *Plessy v. Ferguson* (163 U.S. 537 [1896]), the Supreme Court legitimized state-sponsored segregation as long as "separate but equal" facilities were provided for blacks, and in 1898 the Court ruled that literacy tests and other similar methods of restricting the right to vote did not violate the Fifteenth Amendment.

Against this background Atlanta businessmen conceived of an international exposition, a small-scale world's fair, which would highlight the emergence of a "New South," promote the city and the entire region as a progressive area, and attract new business and investment capital. They hoped to capture some of the positive press coverage and economic benefits that Chicago had received with the 1893 Columbian Exposition. In the spring of 1894 Washington and several other African Americans were asked to join a delegation of prominent southerners to lobby Congress for an appropriation to support the Atlanta Exposition. At some point, and after some controversy, exposition officials decided to involve African Americans in the opening ceremonies. On August 23, 1895, about three weeks before opening day, organizers of the exposition asked Washington to represent African Americans at this event.

Two years earlier black leaders had been unhappy with the way they were treated at the World's Columbian Exposition in Chicago. Their exhibits were segregated in Negro buildings. Consequently, a number of African American leaders were reluctant to support the Negro exhibits at this much smaller provincial event. Washington, however, cooperated with the organizers and urged others to do likewise, even though blacks had to fund their own exhibits and these exhibits would be housed in a separate building. Appreciation of Washington's assistance with Congress and his support of the event brought him to the podium on opening day.

Author Biography

Booker Taliaferro Washington was born on a farm Franklin County, Virginia. While his exact birth date is not clear, most authorities place it on April 5, 1856. Washington spent the first eight years of his childhood as a slave. Following emancipation he moved with his mother, brother, and sister to join his stepfather, who had found employment in the saltworks in Malden, West Virginia. Emancipation did not significantly raise the economic well-being of the family. The young Washington alternated between working in the saltworks and attending school. In 1867 his situation improved dramatically when he took a job in the home of General Lewis Ruffner, one of Malden's wealthiest citizens, serving as houseboy and companion for Viola Ruffner, the general's New England wife. Washington later credited Mrs. Ruffner for much of his early education and especially with preparing him for college.

At age sixteen Washington left home to further his education at Hampton Institute, which allowed impoverished black students to work at the school to pay the costs of their education. Three years later he graduated as one of its top students. After a short stint as a schoolteacher in Malden, he returned to Hampton to teach and to acquire additional education. In May 1881 the board of a recently authorized Alabama state normal school for black students accepted Washington to head the school.

When Washington arrived in Tuskegee, he discovered that the school existed only on paper—he literally had to find land, build buildings, and recruit faculty. It is to Washington's credit that in spite of his youth and inexperience, he mastered the political, administrative, and financial skills he needed to create a black institution in the inhospitable hills of northern Alabama. By the early 1890s Tuskegee had become a success.

The Atlanta Exposition Address transformed Washington from a southern educator to the most influential and powerful African American in the United States. He consulted with presidents and corporate leaders, and headed a political machine that dispersed funds from white philanthropists and political patronage throughout the black community. In the early twentieth century opposition to Washington's leadership increased, especially that organized around Du Bois. The founding of the NAACP in 1910 and Du Bois's prominent role in that organization deflected some white support from Washington. Nevertheless, at the time of his death in November 1915, Washington was still the most widely known and respected African American leader in the United States.

HISTORICAL DOCUMENT

Mr. President and Gentlemen of the Board of Directors and Citizens:

One-third of the population of the South is of the Negro race. No enterprise seeking the material, civil, or moral welfare of this section can disregard this element of our population and reach the highest success. I but convey to you, Mr. President and Directors, the sentiment of the masses of my race when I say that in no way have the value and manhood of the American Negro been more fittingly and generously recognized than by the managers of this magnificent Exposition at every stage of its progress. It is a recognition that will do more to cement the friendship of the two races than any occurrence since the dawn of our freedom.

Not only this, but the opportunity here afforded will awaken among us a new era of industrial progress. Ignorant and inexperienced, it is not strange that in the first years of our new life we began at the top instead of at the bottom; that a seat in Congress or the state legislature was more sought than real estate or industrial skill; that the political convention or stump speaking had more attractions than starting a dairy farm or truck garden.

A ship lost at sea for many days suddenly sighted a friendly vessel. From the mast of the unfortunate vessel was seen a signal, "Water, water; we die of thirst!" The answer from the friendly vessel at once came back, "Cast down your bucket where you are." A second time the signal, "Water, water; send us water!" ran up from the distressed vessel, and was answered, "Cast down your bucket where you are." And a third and fourth signal for water was answered, "Cast down your bucket where you are." The captain of the distressed vessel, at last heeding the injunction, cast down his bucket, and it came up full of fresh, sparkling water from the mouth of the Amazon River. To those of my race who depend on bettering their condition in a foreign land or who underestimate the importance of cultivating friendly relations with the Southern white man, who is their next-door neighbor, I would say: "Cast down your bucket where you are"—cast it down in making friends in every manly way of the people of all races by whom we are surrounded.

Cast it down in agriculture, mechanics, in commerce, in domestic service, and in the professions. And in this connection it is well to bear in mind that whatever other sins the South may be called to bear, when it comes to business, pure and simple, it is in the South that the Negro is given a man's chance in the commercial world, and in nothing is this Exposition more eloquent than in emphasizing this chance. Our greatest danger is that in the great leap from slavery to freedom we may overlook the fact that the masses of us are to live by the productions of our hands, and fail to keep in mind that we shall prosper in proportion as we learn to dignify and glorify common labour, and put brains and skill into the common occupations of life; shall prosper in proportion as we learn to draw the line between the superficial and the substantial, the ornamental gewgaws of life and the useful. No race can prosper till it learns that there is as much dignity in tilling a field as in writing a poem. It is at the bottom of life we must begin, and not at the top. Nor should we permit our grievances to overshadow our opportunities.

To those of the white race who look to the incoming of those of foreign birth and strange tongue and habits for the prosperity of the South, were I permitted I would repeat what I say to my own race, "Cast down your bucket where you are." Cast it down among the eight millions of Negroes whose habits you know, whose fidelity and love you have tested in days when to have proved treacherous meant the ruin of your firesides. Cast down your bucket among these people who have, without strikes and labour wars, tilled your fields, cleared your forests, builded your railroads and cities, and brought forth treasures from the bowels of the earth, and helped make possible this magnificent representation of the progress of the South. Casting down your bucket among my people, helping and encouraging them as you are doing on these grounds, and to education of head, hand, and heart, you will find that they will buy your surplus land, make blossom the waste places in your fields, and run your factories. While doing this, you can be sure in the future, as in the past, that you and your families will be surrounded by the most patient, faithful, law-abiding, and unresentful people that the world has seen. As we have proved our loyalty to you in the past, in nursing your children, watching by the sick-bed of your mothers and fathers, and often following them with tear-dimmed eyes to their graves, so in the future, in our humble way, we shall stand by you with a devotion that no foreigner can approach, ready to lay down our lives, if need be, in defense of yours, interlacing our industrial, commercial, civil, and religious life with yours in a way that shall make the interests of both races one. In all things that are purely social we can be as separate as the fingers, yet one as the hand in all things essential to mutual progress.

There is no defense or security for any of us except in the highest intelligence and development of all. If anywhere there are efforts tending to curtail the fullest growth of the Negro, let these efforts be turned into stimulating, encouraging, and making him the most useful and intelligent citizen. Effort or means so invested will pay a thousand per cent interest. These efforts will be twice blessed—blessing him that gives and him that takes. There is no escape through law of man or God from the inevitable:

The laws of changeless justice bind Oppressor with oppressed;

And close as sin and suffering joined We march to fate abreast...

Nearly sixteen millions of hands will aid you in pulling the load upward, or they will pull against you the load downward. We shall constitute one-third and more of the ignorance and crime of the South, or one-third [of] its intelligence and progress; we shall contribute one-third to the business and industrial prosperity of the South, or we shall prove a veritable body of death, stagnating, depressing, retarding every effort to advance the body politic.

Gentlemen of the Exposition, as we present to you our humble effort at an exhibition of our progress, you must not expect overmuch. Starting thirty years ago with ownership here and there in a few quilts and pumpkins and chickens (gathered from miscellaneous sources), remember the path that has led from these to the inventions and production of agricultural implements, buggies, steam-engines, newspapers, books, statuary, carving, paintings, the management of drug stores and banks, has not been trodden without contact with thorns and thistles. While we take pride in what we exhibit as a result of our independent efforts, we do not for a moment forget that our part in this exhibition would fall far short of your expectations but for the constant help that has come to our educational life, not only from the Southern states, but especially from Northern philanthropists, who have made their gifts a constant stream of blessing and encouragement.

The wisest among my race understand that the agitation of questions of social equality is the extremest folly, and that progress in the enjoyment of all the privileges that will come to us must be the result of severe and constant struggle rather than of artificial forcing. No race that has anything to contribute to the markets of the world is long in any degree ostracized. It is important and right that all privileges of the law be ours, but it is vastly more important that we be prepared for the exercise of these privileges. The opportunity to earn a dollar in a factory just now is worth infinitely more than the opportunity to spend a dollar in an opera-house.

In conclusion, may I repeat that nothing in thirty years has given us more hope and encouragement, and drawn us so near to you of the white race, as this opportunity offered by the Exposition; and here bending, as it were, over the altar that represents the results of the struggles of your race and mine, both starting practically empty-handed three decades ago, I pledge that in your effort to work out the great and intricate problem which God has laid at the doors of the South, you shall have at all times the patient, sympathetic help of my race; only let this he constantly in mind, that, while from representations in these buildings of the product of field, of forest, of mine, of factory, letters, and art, much good will come, yet far above and beyond material benefits will be that higher good, that, let us pray God, will come, in a blotting out of sectional differences and racial animosities and suspicions, in a determination to administer absolute justice, in a willing obedience among all classes to the mandates of law. This, coupled with our material prosperity, will bring into our beloved South a new heaven and a new earth.

GLOSSARY

animosities: hostilities; bitter anger

body politic: the people as a whole in a state or a nation

fidelity: faithfulness to one's duties and obligations; loyalty

letters: literature

mandates: authoritative demands or requirements

ostracized: systematically excluded or discriminated against

philanthropists: persons who contribute to the betterment of others, usually by charitable donations of money

sectional: related to one part or state of a country over another

Document Analysis

In the first paragraph Washington emphasizes the significance of African Americans to the South and observes that no enterprise for the development of the South that ignores that element of the population will "reach the highest success." Washington concludes this paragraph by praising the leaders of the exposition for recognizing the "value and manhood of the American Negro" throughout the planning and staging of the event, which contrasted considerably with the World's Columbian Exposition of 1893.

The second paragraph Washington feeds negative racial stereotypes when he essentially apologizes for the ignorance and inexperience that led newly emancipated blacks to make unwise choices, seeking political office rather than land or industrial skills and prizing political activity over entrepreneurship. Critics cite this paragraph as evidence that Washington acquiesced to white efforts to deprive blacks of their political rights. In truth, Washington consistently opposed both publicly and privately the disenfranchisement of southern blacks. However, Washington did feel that blacks should place greater emphasis on their economic betterment.

The third paragraph centers on one of Washington's best-known homilies. This is the story of the ship lost at sea, its crew dying of thirst and sending out a desperate cry for water, only to be told, "Cast down your bucket where you are." Washington uses this story to admonish the blacks in his audience to remain in the South rather than attempt to better their condition in a "foreign land," whether that be the western frontier or a northern city. As discrimination and racial violence intensified, many considered Washington's advice to be misguided, binding blacks to a new slavery.

Still addressing the African Americans in the audience, in the fourth paragraph Washington lays out his economic agenda. While he is usually cited for promoting only low-skilled, working-class, and agricultural labor for blacks, here he is quite specific—his list of occupations includes commerce and the professions. Washington acknowledges that initially, lacking skills, capital, and education, most blacks will survive by the labor "of [their] hands," and he warns blacks not to denigrate the dignity and importance of this type of work and not to sacrifice the habits of thrift. Finally, he warns blacks not to let discrimination and injustice blind them to the opportunities that surround them.

In paragraph 5, Washington advises white southerners to employ African Americans, rather than immigrants. He refers to the numerous "strikes and labour wars," in the industrial north and reminds whites that during the Civil War, blacks did not strike down the families Confederate soldiers left behind. He goes on to detail the contributions of the African American people made to the region. Washington concludes paragraph 5 with his most famous statement: "In all things that are purely social we can be as separate as the fingers, yet one as the hand in all things essential to mutual progress." This sentence is at the heart of the criticism of Washington and the Atlanta Exposition Address. He goes on to discuss the connectedness of blacks and whites, urging whites to invest in the advancement of African Americans for the betterment of all.

In paragraph 7, Washington quotes from the poem "At Port Royal," written by the abolitionist poet John Greenleaf Whittier in 1862 to celebrate the November 1861 Union victory over the South and the occupation of the Port Royal area on the Georgia and South Carolina coasts. This battle was significant because the Union army liberated a number of slaves. It was one of the earliest steps towards emancipation. For those in the audience who might not know the poem or understand its message, Washington repeats it in very clear, unambiguous language in paragraph 8. Either blacks and whites cooperate for the betterment of the South, or blacks will work against whites and slow future progress. Washington warns white southerners of economic and social catastrophe unless they are willing to work with blacks and allow blacks to share appropriately in southern progress and development.

Washington then turns to humor to defuse the tension. He begins paragraph 9 with a reference that caters to the white stereotype of blacks as petty thieves—much to the dismay of his critics and describes the advances and accomplishments that African Americans had made in the thirty years since emancipation and the assistance from southern states and northern philanthropists that made this progress possible.

Paragraph 10 consists of three often-quoted sentences in which Washington discusses is view of "agitation in questions of social equality." He ends this paragraph by asserting that at the current time, it is more important that blacks achieve the right to work in a factory than to buy a seat in the opera house. Again Washington expresses his belief that in the short term, economic priority should be the highest priority for African Americans.

In the final paragraph, Washington ends where he began, praising the organizers of the exhibition and observing the tremendous progress blacks and whites have made, the former starting as slaves with nothing and the latter coming out of a war in which they lost everything. He again links the destiny of the two races and adds a religious component. It is God who has laid before the South the task of creating a just society, free of "sectional differences and racial animosities and suspicions." If whites, with the support of blacks, resolve this problem, they will bring into the South a "new heaven and a new earth," a reference drawn from Revelation 21:1.

Essential Themes

One of the key themes in Washington's address is that the destinies and well-being of African American southerners and white southerners are inextricably linked. He returns to this theme again and again. In the context of this particular address, Washington often describes this destiny as being rooted in economic growth and development, both for African Americans and for the South as a whole. His approach is practical—not dismissing the need for social and political equality but, rather, placing a higher priority on economic engagement of African Americans; a goal to which his largely white audience might prove more amenable.

The immediate response, both in Atlanta and across the country, was overwhelmingly positive, but over time both Washington and his address have been sharply criticized, especially by other African American intellectuals and leaders. These critics termed the Atlanta address the "Atlanta Compromise" and made Washington a symbol of accommodation and acquiescence to southern racism, segregation, and the political disenfranchisement of African Americans. Throughout much of the twentieth century Washington and his famous (or infamous) address were a defining element in the African American political debate.

The assessment of Washington's Atlanta Exposition Address is clouded by the problem that Washington's actual words are less known than the responses and the analysis of those words by Washington's allies and especially by his opponents. As soon as the news of Washington's triumph at Atlanta spread across the country, friends and foes began to dissect his words and to interpret various phrases or images that he utilized. As a result, the speech itself quickly faded from memory, while discrete segments of the speech became permanently imbedded in American racial discourse, both within the African American community and among white Americans. The original context of the address, as well as its complex and nuanced arguments, gave way to the overly simplified and largely inaccurate view that Washington had surrendered the rights that African Americans had won during the Civil War and Reconstruction.

——Cary D. Wintz, PhD

Bibliography and Additional Reading

Brundage, W. Fitzhugh, ed. *Booker T. Washington and Black Progress: Up from Slavery 100 Years Later.* Gainesville: University of Florida Press, 2003.

Harlan, Louis R. *Booker T. Washington: The Making of a Black Leader, 1856–1901.* New York: Oxford University Press, 1972.

———. *Booker T. Washington: The Wizard of Tuskegee, 1901–1915.* New York: Oxford University Press, 1983.

———, et al., eds. *The Booker T. Washington Papers.* 14 vols. Urbana: University of Illinois Press, 1972–1989.

Meier, August. *Negro Thought in America, 1880–1915: Racial Ideologies in the Age of Booker T. Washington.* Ann Arbor: University of Michigan Press, 1968.

Moore, Jacqueline H. *Booker T. Washington, W. E. B. Du Bois, and the Struggle for Racial Uplift.* Wilmington, Del. Scholarly Resources, 2003.

West, Michael Rudolph. *The Education of Booker T. Washington: American Democracy and the Idea of Race Relations.* New York: Columbia University Press, 2006.

Wolters, Raymond. *Du Bois and His Rivals.* Columbia: University of Missouri Press, 2002.

"The Booker T. Washington Papers." University of Illinois Press Web site. http://www.historycooperative.org/btw/info.html. Accessed on October 17, 2007.

"Booker T. Washington National Monument, Virginia." National Park Service Web site. http://www.nps.gov/bowa/index.htm. Accessed on October 17, 2007.

Niagara Movement Declaration of Principles

Date: 1905
Authors: W. E. B. Du Bois and William Monroe Trotter
Genre: Public declaration

Summary Overview

The Niagara Movement Declaration of Principles outlined a philosophy and political program designed to address racial inequality in the United States. The document had its origin on July 11, 1905, when twenty-nine African American men began deliberations at the Erie Beach Hotel in Fort Erie, Ontario, just across the border from Buffalo and Niagara, New York. When they adjourned three days later, the Niagara Movement had been born. The Niagara Movement had a limited impact on race relations in the United States. Within five years it would cease to exist, and in the history of the struggle for equal rights it has long been overshadowed by the more successful, long-lived, biracial National Association for the Advancement of Colored People (NAACP). Nevertheless, the Niagara Movement was an important landmark in U.S. and African American history.

Several factors distinguish the movement. First, it was a purely African American effort to address discrimination and racial inequality. No whites were involved in its creation, organization, or operation. Second, it enunciated a clearly defined philosophy and political program, embodied in the Declaration of Principles that was drafted and approved at the 1905 meeting. While rephrased and modified somewhat, the sentiments and tone of the Declaration of Principles would outlive the Niagara Movement and help define the agenda of the NAACP and the civil rights movement of the 1950s and early 1960s. Finally, the gathering in Fort Erie pointedly excluded the most prominent African America leader of the day, Booker T. Washington, as well as anyone perceived to be allied with him, challenging Washington's leadership.

Defining Moment

In 1896, the Supreme Court's the *Plessy v. Ferguson* decision legitimized "separate but equal facilities" and provided the legal basis for segregation for the next half-century. At the same time, southern states began to place limits on the right of African American to vote, using tactics such as the grandfather clause, white primaries, literacy tests, residency requirements, and poll taxes to prevent blacks from voting. In 1898 the Supreme Court upheld so-called race-neutral restrictions on black suffrage in *Williams v. Mississippi*. The effect was virtually to eliminate black voting in the states of the South. African Americans did not fare much better in the North, where segregation, if not disenfranchisement, grew increasingly common.

Accompanying segregation and disenfranchisement was a resurgence in racial violence. The late nineteenth century and early twentieth century experienced an unprecedented wave of racially motivated lynchings and riots. During the first decade of the twentieth century, between fifty-seven and 105 African Americans were lynched by white mobs each year. Lynch mobs targeted blacks almost exclusively, and any pretense of legalism and due process vanished. Furthermore, blacks more and more became victims of the more generalized racial violence of race riots.

As the racial scene deteriorated, African Americans faced a transition in leadership. In 1895, Booker T. Washington rose to national prominence with his speech at the Cotton States and International Exposition in Atlanta. Washington believed that rational argument and an appeal to southerners' self-interest would defeat prejudice. As time passed many blacks, especially college-educated northerners, grew impatient with Washington's leadership. Critics as William Monroe Trotter had become increasingly outspoken about Washington's failures. After 1903 W. E. B. Du Bois emerged as the most respected opponent of Washington and his Tuskegee political machine, the loose coalition of friends and allies through which Washington exercised his political influence on the African American community.

Author Biographies

While the Declaration of Principles would be approved by the twenty-nine delegates at the Fort Erie meeting, the actual drafting of the declaration was a collaboration between Du Bois and William Monroe Trotter.

W. E. B. Du Bois was born February 23, 1868, in Great Barrington, Massachusetts, and raised by his mother in an environment characterized by varying degrees of poverty. In spite of this, Du Bois excelled in school and achieved one of the most impressive educations of his generation, including a PhD in history from Harvard in 1895. In 1903 he published *The Souls of Black Folk*, his third book and the one that propelled him to the forefront of African American intellectuals; shortly thereafter he emerged as the most respected critic of Booker T. Washington. In 1905 he made his first major foray into racial politics when he assumed a major role in the creation and operation of the Niagara Movement.

William Monroe Trotter was born on April 7, 1872, in Chillicothe, Ohio, but was raised in Boston among the city's black elite. He attended Harvard, where he met Du Bois. After graduating, he worked in insurance and real estate. In 1901 he cofounded and became editor of the *Guardian*, a Boston newspaper noted for its militant support of African American civil rights and racial justice and for its criticism and attacks on Booker T. Washington. While Du Bois was the leading African American intellectual of his day, Trotter was the race's most outspoken polemicist.

Du Bois and Trotter worked well together on the Declaration of Principles. The document combined Du Bois's more scholarly approach with Trotter's more polemical style. The partnership did not last long. The two clashed over leadership issues, especially the role that whites should play in the Niagara Movement. Trotter withdrew from the organization and founded the National Equal Rights League in 1908. Although he participated in the creation of the NAACP, he objected to the dominant roles whites played in the organization.

HISTORICAL DOCUMENT

Progress: The members of the conference, known as the Niagara Movement, assembled in annual meeting at Buffalo, July 11th, 12th and 13th, 1905, congratulate the Negro-Americans on certain undoubted evidences of progress in the last decade, particularly the increase of intelligence, the buying of property, the checking of crime, the uplift in home life, the advance in literature and art, and the demonstration of constructive and executive ability in the conduct of great religious, economic and educational institutions.

Suffrage: At the same time, we believe that this class of American citizens should protest emphatically and continually against the curtailment of their political rights. We believe in manhood suffrage; we believe that no man is so good, intelligent or wealthy as to be entrusted wholly with the welfare of his neighbor.

Civil Liberty: We believe also in protest against the curtailment of our civil rights. All American citizens have the right to equal treatment in places of public entertainment according to their behavior and deserts.

Economic Opportunity: We especially complain against the denial of equal opportunities to us in economic life; in the rural districts of the South this amounts to peonage and virtual slavery; all over the South it tends to crush labor and small business enterprises; and everywhere American prejudice, helped often by iniquitous laws, is making it more difficult for Negro-Americans to earn a decent living.

Education: Common school education should be free to all American children and compulsory. High school training should be adequately provided for all, and college training should be the monopoly of no class or race in any section of our common country. We believe that, in defense of our own institutions, the United States should aid common school education, particularly in the South, and we especially recommend concerted agitation to this end. We urge an increase in public high school facilities in the South, where the Negro-Americans are almost wholly without such provisions. We favor well-equipped trade and technical schools for the training of artisans, and the need of adequate and liberal endowment for a few institutions of higher education must be patent to sincere well-wishers of the race.

Courts: We demand upright judges in courts, juries selected without discrimination on account of color and the same measure of punishment and the same efforts at reformation for black as for white offenders. We need orphanages and farm schools for dependent children, juvenile reformatories fox delinquents, and the abolition of the dehumanizing convict-lease system.

Public Opinion: We note with alarm the evident retrogression in this land of sound public opinion on the subject of manhood rights, republican government and human brotherhood, arid we pray God that this nation will not degenerate into a mob of boasters and oppressors, but rather will return to the faith of the fathers, that all men were created free and equal, with certain unalienable rights.

Health: We plead for health—for an opportunity to live in decent houses and localities, for a chance to rear our children in physical and moral cleanliness.

Employers and Labor Unions: We hold up for public execration the conduct of two opposite classes of men: The practice among employers of importing ignorant Negro-American laborers in emergencies, and then affording them neither protection nor permanent employment; and the practice of labor unions in proscribing and boycotting and oppressing thousands of their fellow-toilers, simply because they are black. These methods have accentuated and will accentuate the war of labor and capital, and they are disgraceful to both sides.

Protest: We refuse to allow the impression to remain that the Negro-American assents to inferiority, is submissive under oppression and apologetic before insults. Through helplessness we may submit, but the voice of protest of ten million Americans must never cease to assail the ears of their fellows, so long as America is unjust.

Color-Line: Any discrimination based simply on race or color is barbarous, we care not how hallowed it be by custom, expediency or prejudice. Differences made on account of ignorance, immorality, or disease are legitimate methods of fighting evil, and against them we have no word of protest; but discriminations based simply and solely on physical peculiarities, place of birth, color of skin, are relics of that unreasoning human savagery of which the world is and ought to be thoroughly ashamed.

"Jim Crow" Cars: We protest against the "Jim Crow" car, since its effect is and must be to make us pay first-class fare for third-class accommodations, render us open to insults and discomfort and to crucify wantonly our manhood, womanhood and self-respect.

Soldiers: We regret that this nation has never seen fit adequately to reward the black soldiers who, in its five wars, have defended their country with their blood, and yet have been systematically denied the promotions which their abilities deserve. And we regard as unjust, the exclusion of black boys from the military and naval training schools.

War Amendments: We urge upon Congress the enactment of appropriate legislation for securing the proper enforcement of those articles of freedom, the thirteenth, fourteenth and fifteenth amendments of the Constitution of the United States.

Oppression: We repudiate the monstrous doctrine that the oppressor should be the sole authority as to the rights of the oppressed. The Negro race in America stolen, ravished and degraded, struggling up through difficulties and oppression, needs sympathy and receives criticism; needs help and is given hindrance, needs protection and is given mob-violence, needs justice and is given charity, needs leadership and is given cowardice and apology, needs bread and is given a stone. This nation will never stand justified before God until these things are changed.

The Church: Especially are we surprised and astonished at the recent attitude of the church of Christ—of an increase of a desire to bow to racial prejudice, to narrow the bounds of human brotherhood, and to segregate black men to some outer sanctuary. This is wrong, unchristian and disgraceful to the twentieth century civilization.

Agitation: Of the above grievances we do not hesitate to complain, and to complain loudly and insistently. To ignore, overlook, or apologize for these wrongs is to prove ourselves unworthy of freedom. Persistent manly agitation is the way to liberty, and toward this goal the Niagara Movement has started and asks the cooperation of all men of all races.

Help: At the same time we want to acknowledge with deep thankfulness the help of our fellowmen from the Abolitionist down to those who today still stand for equal opportunity and who have given and still give of their wealth and of their poverty for our advancement.

Duties: And while we are demanding, and ought to demand, and will continue to demand the rights enumerated above, God forbid that we should ever forget to urge corresponding duties upon our people:

The duty to vote.
The duty to respect the rights of others.
The duty to work.
The duty to obey the laws.
The duty to be clean and orderly.
The duty to send our children to school.
The duty to respect ourselves, even as we respect others.

This statement, complaint and prayer we submit to the American people, and Almighty God.

GLOSSARY

artisans: skilled craftsmen or workers

convict-lease system: a system of labor in which prisoners are leased to an employer by the court or the prison system

"Jim Crow" car: a segregated railroad coach, usually of inferior quality, set aside for African Americans

peonage: a system of agricultural labor in which workers are bound to their job, often against their will, by economic debt or other means; virtual bondage

suffrage: the right to vote

Document Analysis

The first section of the declaration, "Progress," comments on the gathering of the Niagara Movement and congratulates African Americans on progress they had achieved in the preceding ten years. The Niagarites viewed this as a period of failed leadership and a decline in the rights of African Americans.

The next three paragraphs the declaration lists grievances for the first time and evokes protest as an appropriate response. The declaration notes that black political rights have been curtailed and that blacks cannot afford to place their political fate in the hands of others. The declaration calls on blacks to protest as long as their political rights are violated, a theme that runs through the declaration.

The declaration defines civil liberty as civil rights including the right to "equal treatment in places of public entertainment," that is, restaurants, theaters, hotels, and other places of public accommodation. Exclusion from such places must not be based on race or color but on the individual's behavior and demeanor.

As it turns to economic opportunity, the Declaration of Principles directly confronts Washington's ideas. Washington believed that the acquisition of property and prosperity would earn blacks the respect of whites and equal rights and that this prosperity could most easily be achieved in the South. The declaration rejects this, noting that African Americans are denied equal economic opportunity in the South and provides examples of the prejudice and inequity in the law in that region undermine black economic efforts.

The declaration recognizes the need for all forms of education in the African American community. It focuses its complaints on the lack of equal access to education for blacks, especially in the South. It calls for blacks to have access to education at all levels, and calls for the U.S. government to aid education. The statement does not call for the desegregation of education but for an increase in the number of public high schools in the South and for white philanthropists to provide adequate endowments for black institutions of higher education. The language of this section is also much more conciliatory; agitation is suggested only to pressure the U.S. government to provide aid to black common schools.

The statement on courts begins with a "demand" for fair and honest judges, the inclusion without discrimination of blacks on juries, and fair and equitable sentencing procedures. It then lists additional needed reforms ranging from social-service institutions such as orphanages and reformatories and an end to the convict-lease system. There was a connection between this issue and that of "Health" issues. Reforming the criminal justice system extended to providing a decent environment for orphans, dependent children, and children in the court system; health was extended to include a healthy environment, both physically and morally, in which to raise children.

The paragraph on public opinion introduces a new concern, a perceived shift away from the ideals of democracy that were voiced in the eighteenth century by the Founding Fathers. The Niagara delegates were not ignorant of the slavery and racial prejudice that were central to the founding of the United States, but their alarm over the "retrogression" was justified by the increasing racial violence in the United States.

Turning to economic opportunity in the North, the declaration addresses the abuses blacks have suffered at the hands of racially prejudiced labor unions and the practice of white employers exploiting blacks by using them as strike breakers. The declaration denounces the practices of both employers and unions in strong terms and blames them for contributing to class warfare.

Protest, along with agitation, were central tenets of the Niagara Movement's strategy for achieving racial justice, and both terms appear frequently in the Declaration of Principles and are presented as necessary tools to combat injustice. However, the language and tone in the section specifically discussing protest are exceptionally mild. There is little power or threat in this language beyond the assurance that although blacks may of necessity submit to oppression, they must continue to raise their voices in protest.

"Color-Line" discusses legitimate and illegitimate discrimination. The former included discrimination based on intelligence, immorality, and disease (for example, quarantining someone with a highly infectious disease to protect public health). In contrast, discrimination based on physical conditions such as place of birth (immigrants) and race was never justified. The color line—segregation and discrimination based on race or skin color or both—is described in harsh terms, as barbarous and as a relic of unreasoning human savagery, regardless of whether or not it is sanctioned by law.

The issue of Jim Crow segregation on railroads was the subject of the *Plessy v. Ferguson* case; the Supreme Court ruling legitimizing separate-but-equal segregation provided the legal basis for segregation in schools, parks, public accommodations, and almost all areas of life. The Declaration of Principles condemns Jim Crow cars as effectively crucifying "wantonly our manhood, womanhood and self-respect." "Soldiers" puts the Niagara Movement on record protesting the systematic discrimination and mistreatment experienced by African Americans serving in the armed forces. The Declaration then calls for is legislation from Congress to enforce the provisions of the 13th, 14th, and 15th amendments.

In examining the broad issue of oppression, the Declaration presents a broad litany of crimes perpetrated on African Americans and place blame on African American leadership for providing in the face of oppression only cowardice and apology. The Declaration also charges churches and organized religion with acquiescence to racial oppression. Following this litany of grievances, the Declaration of Principles reaffirms its commitment to protest and agitation. As in the section on "Protest," the language is clear but measured and temperate rather than threatening.

The Declaration of Principles concludes with a section recognizing with gratitude the valuable assistance that African Americans had received from white allies. It then lists eight duties that it expects blacks to follow as they pursue their rights. These last two sections softened the impact of the declaration and were intended to assure whites that the Niagara Movement was neither revolutionary nor antiwhite. The final sentence of the Declaration notes that the document, characterized as a "statement, complaint and prayer," is being submitted to the American people and to God.

Essential Themes
Taken as a whole, the Declaration of Principles is both an interesting and a compelling document. It is a comprehensive list of issues, concepts, grievances, and statements about the conditions confronting blacks at the beginning of the last century. What is compelling is that this was the most successful effort to date to express all of this in one place and do so in language that was pointed and uncompromising yet restrained. At the same time, the declaration is interesting for what it did not say. By the standards of the twenty-first century it is not a particularly radical document. Although the Niagara Movement was an all-black organization, there is no hint of black

nationalism or separatism in its Declaration of Principles. Rather, it serves as a restrained, moderate document outlining a program of desegregation, equal rights, and racial justice. It praises white friends and allies for their support, and it reminds blacks that they have the duty and responsibility to be hardworking and law-abiding citizens who embody the values and habits of middle-class America. Despite the anti–Booker T. Washington nature of the Niagara Movement and its members and Washington's open hostility to both the Niagara Movement and its Declaration of Principles, there is little in the document with which the Tuskegeean could take issue.

——*Cary D. Wintz, PhD*

Bibliography and Additional Reading

Fox, Stephen R. *The Guardian of Boston: William Monroe Trotter*. (New York: Atheneum, 1970).

Harlan, Louis R. *Booker T. Washington: The Wizard of Tuskegee, 1901–1915*. (New York: Oxford University Press, 1983).

Lewis, David Levering. *W. E. B. Du Bois: Biography of a Race, 1868–1919*. (New York: Henry Holt, 1993).

Marable, Manning. *W. E. B. Du Bois: Black Radical Democrat*. Boston: Twayne, 1986.

Moore, Jacqueline M. *Booker T. Washington, W. E. B. Du Bois, and the Struggle for Racial Uplift*. (Wilmington, Delaware: Scholarly Resources, 2003).

Wolters, Raymond. *Du Bois and His Rivals*. (Columbia: University of Missouri Press, 2002).

Web Site

"The Niagara Movement." African American History of Western New York Web site. http://www.math.buffalo.edu/~sww/0history/hwny-niagara-movement.html. Accessed on January 27, 2017.

■ "Lynching: Our National Crime"

Date: 1909
Author: Ida B. Wells
Genre: Speech

Summary Overview

In "Lynching: Our National Crime," her address before the convention that led to the creation of the National Association for the Advancement of Colored People (NAACP), she labels lynching a national crime and calls for federal intervention.

Ida Wells was deeply affected by racism and the violence inflicted by whites upon blacks in the United States in the late nineteenth and early twentieth centuries. In an attempt to arouse the nation to confront its racial prejudices and barbaric actions, she began to write articles and pamphlets and to lecture widely both in this country and in Great Britain. Her vivid depictions of the horrors of lynching and her statistically supported discussion of that practice began the slow, arduous process toward public rejection of those crimes. Pulling no punches in her comments, Wells criticized both blacks and whites. Black elites, shielded by their wealth from many of the indignities of discrimination, ignored the problems of others in their communities. Black clergymen did not speak out strongly enough against segregation. Black politicians betrayed their race to seek the favor of whites. Whites accepted social myths and cultural stereotypes that allowed them to excuse inexcusable crimes against humanity.

Wells took it upon herself to wage a public crusade against the sufferings, indignities, and wrongs of an oppressed race.

Defining Moment

When William Monroe Trotter and W. E. B. Du Bois, two other dissenters from Booker T. Washington's point of view, joined efforts to form a new organization for racial protest in 1905, Ida Wells quickly joined it. Known as the Niagara Movement, the association condemned segregation, the disenfranchisement of black voters, lynching, and any suggestion that the demand for immediate civil rights be deferred. This new body gained strength as a result of a race riot in Springfield, Illinois, in the summer of 1908.

The riot had started when a white woman accused a black man of trying to rape her. That charge triggered two nights of violence. Eventually, local officials had to call in the state militia to restore order. Several days after the riot, the white woman recanted her charge.

That a major race riot could occur in a northern city that also happened to be the hometown of Abraham Lincoln showed that racially motivated white mob violence was not a problem unique to the South.

One of those who had been shocked by the violence in Springfield was William English Walling, a noted social activist. In the aftermath of the riot, Walling concluded that a new national organization was needed to fight racial oppression. His idea quickly caught the attention of white liberals. In 1909 Walling and his supporters sent out an invitation known as "The Call" to other like-minded individuals of both races to attend a conference for the discussion of ways in which social and political equality might be obtained for African Americans. The petition, issued on the one-hundredth anniversary of Abraham Lincoln's birth, contained the signatures of sixty activists, including Wells. The conference, which took place in New York City on May 31 and June 1, 1909, led to the creation of the NAACP.

Given an opportunity to speak at the conference, Wells gave a short address entitled "Lynching: Our National Crime."

Author Biography

Ida B. Wells was born a slave in Holly Springs, Mississippi, on July 16, 1862. When her parents and a younger brother died in a yellow fever epidemic in 1878, she accepted the first of several jobs as a rural schoolteacher to help support her six younger brothers and sisters. Success as a freelance writer eventually led to a career as a newspaper journalist and editor. Through newspaper articles and lectures, she quickly gained fame as a crusader against lynching. In addition to numerous newspaper and magazine articles, Wells is known for two pamphlets published in the 1890s—*Southern Horrors* and *The Red Record*. After marrying Ferdinand Lee Barnett, a Chicago newspaperman and civil rights advocate in 1895, Wells devoted much of her time to civic reform work. She also gained notoriety as an investigator into the causes of race riots.

Defiant and confrontational throughout her life, Wells challenged the racial policies of both the Woman's

SOUTHERN HORRORS.

LYNCH LAW

IN ALL

ITS PHASES

Miss IDA B. WELLS.

Price, - - - Fifteen Cents.

THE NEW YORK AGE PRINT,
1892.

Christian Temperance Union and the National American Woman Suffrage Association, openly debated Booker T. Washington on the proper course for black progress, and withdrew from the NAACP because she was not comfortable with its liberal white leadership. During the 1920s, a decade that saw a rebirth of the Ku Klux Klan, Wells became increasingly disillusioned with the state of race relations in America. Never a black separatist, she was drawn to Marcus Garvey's Universal Negro Improvement Association during the 1920s because of his call for black self-help and economic independence and for instilling a new racial consciousness among African Americans. Feeling that she had lost her influence as a spokesperson for racial issues, Wells began writing her *Autobiography*. She was at work on the project when she died on March 25, 1931.

HISTORICAL DOCUMENT

The lynching record for a quarter of a century merits the thoughtful study of the American people. It presents three salient facts:

First: Lynching is color line murder.
Second: Crimes against women is the excuse, not the cause.
Third: It is a national crime and requires a national remedy.

Proof that lynching follows the color line is to be found in the statistics which have been kept for the past twenty-five years. During the few years preceding this period and while frontier lynch law existed, the executions showed a majority of white victims. Later, however, as law courts and authorized judiciary extended into the far West, lynch law rapidly abated and its white victims became few and far between.

Just as the lynch law régime came to a close in the West, a new mob movement started in the South. This was wholly political, its purpose being to suppress the colored vote by intimidation and murder. Thousands of assassins banded together under the name of Ku Klux Klans, "Midnight Raiders," "Knights of the Golden Circle," etc., spread a reign of terror, by beating, shooting and killing colored people by the thousands. In a few years, the purpose was accomplished and the black vote was suppressed. But mob murder continued.

From 1882, in which year 52 were lynched, down to the present, lynching has been along the color line. Mob murder increased yearly until in 1892 more than 200 victims were lynched and statistics show that 3,284 men, women and children have been put to death in this quarter of a century. During the last ten years from 1899 to 1908 inclusive the number lynched was 959. Of this number 102 were white while the colored victims numbered 857. No other nation, civilized or savage, burns its criminals; only under the stars and stripes is the human holocaust possible. Twenty-eight human beings burned at the stake, one of them a woman and two of them children, is the awful indictment against American civilization—the gruesome tribute which the nation pays to the color line.

Why is mob murder permitted by a Christian nation? What is the cause of this awful slaughter? This question is answered almost daily—always the same shameless falsehood that "Negroes are lynched to protect womanhood." Standing before a Chautauqua assemblage, John Temple Graves, at once champion of lynching and apologist for lynchers, said: "The mob stands to-day as the most potential bulwark between the women of the South and such a carnival of crime as would infuriate the world and precipitate the annihilation of the Negro race." This is the never varying answer of lynchers and their apologists. All know it is untrue. The cowardly lyncher revels in murder, then seeks to shield himself from public execration by claiming devotion to woman. But truth is mighty and the lynching record discloses the hypocrisy of the lyncher as well as his crime.

The Springfield, Illinois, mob rioted for two days, the militia of the entire state was called out, two men were lynched, hundreds of people driven from their homes, all because a white woman said a Negro had assaulted her. A mad mob went to the jail, tried to lynch the victim of her charge and, not being able to find him, proceeded to pillage and burn the town and to lynch two innocent men. Later, after the police had found that the woman's charge was false, she published a retraction, the indictment was dismissed and the intended victim discharged. But the lynched victims were dead. Hundreds were homeless and Illinois was disgraced....

Various remedies have been suggested to abolish the lynching infamy, but year after year, the butchery of men, women and children continues in spite of plea and protest....

The only certain remedy is an appeal to law. Lawbreakers must be made to know that human life is sacred and that every citizen of this country is first a citizen of the United States and secondly a citizen of the state in which he belongs. This nation must assert itself and defend its federal citizenship at home as well as abroad. The strong arm of the government must reach across state lines whenever unbridled lawlessness defies state laws....

Federal protection of American citizenship is the remedy for lynching....

[This]...has been more than once suggested in Congress. Senator Gallinger of New Hampshire in a resolution introduced in Congress called for an investigation "with the view of ascertaining whether there is a remedy for lynching which Congress may apply." The Senate Committee has under consideration a bill drawn by A. E. Pillsbury, formerly Attorney-General of Massachusetts, providing for federal prosecution of lynchers in cases where the state fails to protect citizens or foreigners. Both of these resolutions indicate that the attention of the nation has been called to this phase of the lynching question....

In a multitude of counsel there is wisdom. Upon the grave question presented by the slaughter of innocent men, women and children there should be an honest, courageous conference of patriotic, law-abiding citizens anxious to punish crime promptly, impartially and by due process of law, also to make life, liberty, and property secure against mob rule.

Time was when lynching appeared to be sectional, but now it is national—a blight upon our nation, mocking our laws and disgracing our Christianity. "With malice toward none but with charity for all" let us undertake the work of making the "law of the land," effective and supreme upon every foot of American soil—a shield to the innocent and to the guilty punishment swift and sure.

GLOSSARY

Chautauqua: an educational institution, founded in New York State, that provides nontraditional educational opportunities and forums for discussion of public issues

Gallinger: Jacob Harold Gallinger, a U.S. senator

holocaust: mass murder, usually directed against a racial, ethnic, or religious group

John Temple Graves: newspaper editor and politician from Georgia

Ku Klux Klan: a white supremacist organization, formed in 1866, that mounted a campaign of violence and intimidation against African Americans, Jews, and others

"With malice toward none but with charity for all" : a quotation from President Abraham Lincoln's Second Inaugural Address

Document Analysis
In her address, she emphasizes the arguments that lynching is "color line murder" and that crimes committed or supposedly committed against women are the excuses rather than the causes of such actions. On this occasion, in light of the Springfield riot, Wells calls lynching a national crime that requires a national solu-

tion, in essence, urging the Congress to produce federal anti-lynching legislation.

She then cites statistics about the decline of lynching in the west as legitimate courts and law enforcement became established in the west. However, despite gains against extra-judicial executions on the frontier, lynching increased in the south. Wells attributes this to the political motivations of groups like the Ku Klux Klan, which wished to intimidate African Americans and suppressing their electoral power. Despite black voting rates falling dramatically in the years following Reconstruction (after 1877) Wells points out that the "mob murder" of lynching continued. Detailing her argument that lynching in the United States has increasingly become "color line murder," Wells cites statistics such as the lynching numbers from 1899 to 1908, demonstrating that nearly 90 percent of lynchings were against African Americans.

Wells then asks the audience a pair of rhetorical questions, "Why is mob murder permitted by a Christian nation? What is the cause of this awful slaughter?" In answering, she moves on to explicate her second point, refuting lynching supporters' reasoning that lynching is the result of African American male victimization of white women, encapsulated in the "shameless falsehood that 'Negroes are lynched to protect womanhood.'" This was a stereotypical view of the supposed danger that African American men posed to white women that extended far back into the days of slavery. Wells uses, as her case-in-point, the then-recent riot in Springfield, Illinois. Wells points out that despite the fact that the rioting mob in that city was not able to find the man black man accused of assaulting a white woman, they continued to destroy property in Springfield and lynch two men who, apparently, had nothing to do with the alleged crime. Further, the "victim" retracted her statement and the accused man was set free. That justice was, eventually, done, did not erase the deaths or destruction that the mob caused.

Here, she returns to the question of the role the federal government must play in stopping the practice of lynching. She maintains that a person's citizenship lies first with the United States and only secondarily with the individual state. The federal government, she explains thus has a responsibility for the "protection of American citizenship." Wells is invoking the fourteenth amendment, which guarantees that none of the states can "deprive any person of life, liberty, or property, without due process of law; nor deny to any person within its jurisdiction the equal protection of the laws." The continued failure of the federal government to prevent lynching is a failure to enforce the constitution.

While people have suggested, she goes on to say, different ways to halt the spread of lynching and mob violence against African Americans, protests and discussion have been ineffective. Agitation to stop lynching has to be supported by the force of antilynching legislation that would provide for federal prosecution of offenders in cases where states fail to act. She cites a number of politicians, from northern states such as Massachusetts and New Hampshire, who have introduced such legislation. Wells claims that these proposed laws demonstrate that public interest in and opposition to lynching has reached a critical point. Such legislation is necessary "to make life, liberty, and property secure against mob rule."

Wells closes her speech by explaining that—as in the case of Springfield, Illinois, lynching of African Americans is spreading beyond the south, proving to be "a blight" upon the entire nation, not just one region. Only the national enforcement of a law prevent lynching will protect the innocent and punish the guilty.

Essential Themes

Wells had been working to bring public attention to the evils of lynching for years. Here, she does so but she focuses on specific issues and a specific call to action. Crucial to her message is the spread of the lynching of African Americans to northern states such as Illinois. The calamity is expanding rather than contracting. She also emphasizes the increasingly racial nature of lynching and mob violence in recent decades, arguing that this the horror of lynching is concentrated against African Americans. Her evidence is sophisticated, employing a blend of statistics as well as a critique of the argument that lynching is the only protection white women have against the depredations of black men. This dual argument blends numerical data with a racist cultural context that has a deep history. This history—especially in the south—makes local or state protection of potential lynching victims highly unlikely.

Her solution, then, is to apply legal pressure from a federal, national authority rather than rely on the power of individual state governments or local law enforcement and judicial systems. In making this argument she both calls back to the idols and goals of the radical Republican politicians of the Reconstruction era who framed the fourteenth amendment as well as anticipates the growing power of the federal government to enforce civil rights in the mid-to-late twentieth century.

——*Steven L. Piott, PhD*
with additional material by Aaron Gulyas, MA

Bibliography and Additional Reading

Bay, Mia. *To Tell the Truth Freely: the life of Ida B. Wells.* (New York: Hill & Wang, 2009).

Giddings, P. J. *Ida, A Sword Among Lions: Ida B. Wells and the Campaign Against Lynching* (New York: Amistad/HarperCollins, 2008).

Shay, Allison. "Remembering Ida B. Wells-Barnett". University of North Carolina at Chapel Hill. https://lcrm.lib.unc.edu/blog/index.php/2012/07/16/remembering-ida-b-wells-barnett/ Retrieved 1-23-201

Schechter, Patricia A. Ida B. Wells-Barnett and American Reform, 1880-1930. (Chapel Hill: University of North Carolina Press, 2001)

Wells, Ida B. Alfreda M. Duster. ed. *Crusade For Justice: The Autobiography of Ida B. Wells*. Negro American Biographies and Autobiographies Series. John Hope Franklin, Series Editor. (Chicago: University of Chicago Press, 1970).

■ "Agitation"

Date: 1910
Author: W. E. B. Du Bois
Genre: Essay

Summary Overview

W. E. B. Du Bois came of age during the nadir of race relations in the United States. The gains that African Americans had achieved during Reconstruction were undone as segregation became the standard across the country, southern states denied blacks the right to vote or participate in the political process, and the nation was swept by an epidemic of racial violence, especially in the form of lynching. Du Bois himself, despite his superior education and record of scholarship, could not obtain a faculty position in a "white" college or university. This was the reality that Du Bois confronted as he began his career as a professor and intellectual, and he chose to address the era's racial injustice with his pen. Various documents trace the development and evolution of his political thought from the beginning of his career in the late nineteenth century to his resignation from the NAACP in 1934. In 1910 Du Bois published the essay "Agitation," arguing for the active confrontation of racism and inequality.

Defining Moment

The African American civil rights movement in the late nineteenth and early twentieth centuries underwent a split between the ideas and goals of Booker T. Washington, which focused on economic and educational development for black Americans as a prelude to eventual political activism and a younger generation of black leaders who positioned themselves to take a more active stand. In 1905, W. E. B. Du Bois joined with other more militant African Americans to establish the Niagara Movement and push their civil rights agenda. However, they lacked the financial resources to successfully challenge Washington's political power or to pursue their goals. In 1909 Du Bois joined with white liberals to create the National Negro Committee, which would found the National Association for the Advancement of Colored People in 1910. That year Du Bois became the only African American on the NAACP board and launched the organization's monthly magazine, the *Crisis*. Du Bois now had a position with a well-funded civil rights organization that shared his political views and was editing a journal that provided him with an outlet through which to expound on his views. In the first issue of the *Crisis*, Du Bois published the essay "Agitation," arguing for the active confrontation of racism and inequality.

Author Biography

William Edward Burghardt Du Bois was born on February 23, 1868, in Great Barrington, Massachusetts, and raised by his mother. In spite of the poverty of his childhood, Du Bois excelled in school and achieved one of the most impressive educations of his generation. He received bachelor degrees from Fisk University and Harvard University, pursued graduate work at Harvard and Germany's University of Berlin, and earned his PhD in history from Harvard in 1895. He received a faculty appointment at Wilberforce University in 1894, worked for the University of Pennsylvania on a study of blacks in Philadelphia in 1896, and joined the faculty of Atlanta University in 1897. In 1910 he left Atlanta and took a paid position as the director of publishing and research for the newly founded National Association for the Advancement of Colored People (NAACP). He served in that position and also as the founding editor of the NAACP journal, the *Crisis*, subtitled *A Record of the Darker Races*, until 1934.

Following his departure from the NAACP, Du Bois returned to Atlanta University, retiring in 1943 and returning to the NAACP. Du Bois was clearly out of step with the civil rights organization; his increasingly leftist, pro-Soviet politics and his criticism both of U.S. foreign policy and of the NAACP director Walter White cost him his job in 1948. Du Bois became involved in leftist organizations, continued condemning the United States and its foreign policy while praising the Soviet Union, making him a target of the post–World War II "Red Scare" inspired by Senator Joseph McCarthy. He would make highly publicized visits to East Germany, the Soviet Union, and Communist China. In 1961, disillusioned with the United States, Du Bois formally joined the U.S. Communist Party before relocating to the newly independent nation of Ghana, becoming a citizen in 1963. On August 27, 1963, he died at the age of ninety-five.

HISTORICAL DOCUMENT

Some good friends of the cause we represent fear agitation. They say: "Do not agitate—do not make a noise; *work*." They add, "Agitation is destructive or at best negative—what is wanted is positive constructive work."

Such honest critics mistake the function of agitation. A toothache is agitation. Is a toothache a good thing? No. Is it therefore useless? No. It is supremely useful, for it tells the body of decay, dyspepsia and death. Without it the body would suffer unknowingly. It would think: All is well, when lo! danger lurks.

The same is true of the Social Body. Agitation is a necessary evil to tell of the ills of the Suffering. Without it many a nation has been lulled to false security and preened itself with virtues it did not possess.

The function of this Association is to tell this nation the crying evil of race prejudice. It is a hard duty but a necessary one—a divine one. It is Pain; Pain is not good but Pain is necessary. Pain does not aggravate disease—Disease causes Pain. Agitation does not mean Aggravation—Aggravation calls for Agitation in order that Remedy may be found.

GLOSSARY

agitation: disruption; uncomfortable irritation

dyspepsia: literally, indigestion; often used to suggest ill humor or disgruntlement

Social Body: society

Document Analysis

Du Bois begins his very short essay by acknowledging the concern that some civil rights activists have for the more radical agenda of "agitation" that he and his colleagues at the NAACP had been promoting. His characterization of their position as "Do not agitate…work" is probably directed at Booker T. Washington, whose vision for African American activism was strongly predicated on economic development and building vocational skills rather than on more political and judicial activities. They take the position, according to Du Bois that agitation is destructive and negative.

Du Bois asserts that the critics, while honest, misunderstand the purpose of agitation. While harmful and disruptive (like a toothache, in his example), it is a warning of other more dangerous conditions. Without the "agitation" of the toothache pain, someone might think they were well when they were not. Society, he explains, is much the same way. "Agitation is a necessary evil to tell of the ills of the Suffering." The agitation undertaken by groups such as the NAACP are necessary to prevent the United States from accepting the racial status quo.

He concludes this brief defense of agitation by explains that the purpose of the NAACP ("this Association") is to reveal the evil of racial prejudice to the nation. This is painful and pain, while necessary, is not good. Pain however, is the result of the underlying disease or condition. In the same way, agitation is the product of the "aggravation" of racial conditions in the United States. Only by suffering through the agitation, as painful as it may be, will a cure eventually be found.

Essential Themes

"Agitation" was one of the shortest essays that Du Bois wrote but clearly communicated his point. As a political approach, agitation was central to the tactics of the *Crisis* and the NAACP. Du Bois remarks, "The function of this Association is to tell this nation the crying evil of race prejudice. It is a hard duty but a necessary one—a divine one." Agitation, he argues, is an essential means of forcing awareness of social evils into the public consciousness; it is particularly necessary to prevent the public from turning a blind eye to the social evils faced by African Americans. Du Bois thus justifies the use of agitation to combat racial injustice. It is significant that Du Bois chose the topic of agitation for one of his first editorials in the *Crisis*. While Booker T. Washington did speak out on issues like segregation, voting rights, and lynching and was not the accommodationist he often is accused of being, he did avoid direct confrontation with southern racists and southern leaders. Du Bois did not take his civil rights battles to the streets, but he was confrontational in his writing and in the positions he took, and he made sure that agitation defined the tone of the NAACP.

——Cary D. Wintz, PhD
with additional material by Aaron Gulyas, MA

Bibliography and Additional Reading

Lewis, David Levering. *W. E. B. Du Bois: Biography of a Race, 1868–1919*. (New York: Henry Holt, 1993).

Marable, Manning. *W. E. B. Du Bois: Black Radical Democrat*. Boston: Twayne, 1986.

Moore, Jacqueline M. *Booker T. Washington, W. E. B. Du Bois, and the Struggle for Racial Uplift*. (Wilmington, Delaware: Scholarly Resources, 2003).

Wolters, Raymond. *Du Bois and His Rivals*. (Columbia: University of Missouri Press, 2002).

William Monroe Trotter's Protest to Woodrow Wilson

Date: 1914
Author: William Monroe Trotter
Genre: Speech

Summary Overview

In 1914, *Boston Guardian* editor William Monroe Trotter delivered a stinging protest to Woodrow Wilson concerning segregation in the federal bureaucracy. As a candidate for the presidency of the United States in 1912, Wilson had proposed a platform based on what he characterized as "new freedom." In doing so, Wilson had made promises to African Americans that he could be counted on to provide fairness if elected. However, upon his election, Wilson reneged on his original promise and instituted a policy of racial segregation in both the Department of the Treasury and the Post Office Department. The National Association for the Advancement of Colored People (NAACP), the leading civil rights group in the nation at that time, forwarded a letter of protest to Wilson, but their efforts were ignored. On November 6, 1913, and again on November 12, 1914, President Wilson met with a delegation of African American leaders from the National Independent Equal Rights League. Their spokesman, the uncompromising Trotter, challenged Wilson in his opening remarks at the second meeting to live up to his promises to provide equality for African Americans. Trotter's message was characteristically direct, even blunt. It led to a tense encounter that garnered much public attention.

Defining Moment

The 1910s were a time of racial volatility in the United States, evidenced by numerous urban race riots, notably in East St. Louis and Chicago. Terrifying violence against African Americans included numerous lynchings and other hostile attacks. Racial segregation had become entrenched in American life. The doctrine of "separate but equal" had even obtained legal status in the Supreme Court's *Plessy v. Ferguson* decision of 1896. A broader effect of southern violence was the northward migration of black Americans. Beginning in earnest in 1910, this persistent shift saw millions of African Americans move to the industrial north in search of jobs and, they hoped, a better life. To assist in meeting the numerous social, economic, cultural, and political challenges posed by the recently arriving black southerners, the National Urban League was formed in New York City in 1910.

In 1912, Woodrow Wilson, a Democrat, had appealed to blacks (who were mainly Republicans) for their votes, offering promises of equal treatment should he be elected president. Frustrated with the incursion of segregation into the federal bureaucracy, Trotter requested meetings with Wilson in November 1913 and again in November 1914. In this time of great travail, the election of Wilson to the presidency of the United States offered hope for African Americans. In fact, a number of black leaders, including Trotter, publicly supported Wilson's candidacy, breaking with their traditional Republican allegiance. Wilson was known in many circles as a progressive, but his concerns did not extend to African Americans and their condition. Like his early foreign policy, Wilson's approach to African American demands for equality could well be described as noninterventionist. Adding to the tensions that flared in the meeting, Wilson was still grieving at the time over the death of his wife, Ellen Axson Wilson, on August 6.

Author Biography

William Monroe Trotter was born on April 7, 1872 and raised in a middle-class neighborhood in Boston. He graduated from Harvard with Phi Beta Kappa honors in 1895 and earned his master's there the following year. Primarily known as a journalist, he served in various activist organizations and, in 1901, founded (along with George W. Forbes) the influential newspaper the *Boston Guardian*, which served as an important news vehicle promoting equal rights for African Americans. Defiant and uncompromising on issues of race, he went on to become a militant civil rights advocate and one of the most influential African American leaders of the early twentieth century. He accomplished much in his career before the age of forty.

Along with W. E. B. Du Bois, Trotter also played a leading role in the founding of the Niagara Movement in 1905 and played a leading role in the NAACP, attending the founding meeting in 1909 and maintaining contact with the group until disputes occurred with leaders such as Oswald Garrison Villard and Du Bois. During these years, Trotter was also an important figure in the National Independent Equal Rights League. Trotter's death is still somewhat of a mystery. On his sixty-second birthday, he reportedly fell (or, some say, jumped) from a window of his home to his death.

HISTORICAL DOCUMENT

One year ago we presented a national petition, signed by Afro-Americans in thirty-eight states, protesting against the segregation of employees of the National government whose ancestry could be traced in whole or in part to Africa, as instituted under your administration in the treasury and postoffice departments. We then appealed to you to undo this race segregation in accord with your duty as president and with your pre-election pledges. We stated that there could be no freedom, no respect from others, and no equality of citizenship under segregation for races, especially when applied to but one of many racial elements in the government employ. For such placement of employes means a charge by the government of physical indecency or infection, or of being a lower order of beings, or a subjection to the prejudices of other citizens, which constitutes inferiority of status. We protested such segregation as to working conditions, eating tables, dressing rooms, rest rooms, lockers and especially public toilets in government buildings. We stated that such segregation was a public humiliation and degradation, entirely unmerited and far-reaching in its injurious effects, a gratuitous blow against ever-loyal citizens and against those many of whom aided and supported your elevation to the presidency of our common country.

At that time you stated you would investigate conditions for yourself. Now, after the lapse of a year, we have come back having found that all the forms of segregation of government employes of African extraction are still practiced in the treasury and postoffice department buildings, and to a certain extent have spread into other government buildings.

Under the treasury department, in the bureau of engraving and printing there is segregation not only in dressing rooms, but in working positions, Afro-American employes being herded at separate tables, in eating, and in toilets. In the navy department there is herding at desks and separation in lavatories. In the post-office department there is separation in work for Afro-American women in the alcove on the eighth floor, of Afro-American men in rooms on the seventh floor, with forbidding even of entrance into an adjoining room occupied by white clerks on the seventh floor, and of Afro-American men in separate rooms just instituted on the sixth floor, with separate lavatories for Afro-American men on the eighth floor; in the main treasury building in separate lavatories in the basement; in the interior department separate lavatories, which were specifically pointed out to you at our first hearing; in the state and other departments separate lavatories; in marine hospital service building in separate lavatories, though there is but one Afro-American clerk to use it; in the war department in separate lavatories in the postoffice department building separate lavatories; in the sewing and bindery divisions of the government printing office on the fifth floor there is herding at working positions of Afro-American women and separation in lavatories, and new segregation instituted by the division chief since our first audience with you This lavatory segregation is the most degrading, most insulting of all. Afro-American employes who use the regular public lavatories on the floors where they work are cautioned and are then warned by superior officers against insubordination.

We have come by vote of this league to set before you this definite continuance of race segregation and to renew the protest and to ask you to abolish segregation of Afro-American employes in the executive department.

Because we cannot believe you capable of any disregard of your pledges we have been sent by the alarmed American citizens of color. They realize that if they can be segregated and thus humiliated by the national government at the national capital the beginning is made for the spread of that persecution and prosecution which makes property and life itself insecure in the South, the foundation of the whole fabric of their citizenship is unsettled.

They have made plain enough to you their opposition to segregation last year by a national anti-segregation petition, this year by a protest registered at the polls, voting against every Democratic candidate save those outspoken against segregation. The only Democrat elected governor in the eastern states, was Governor Walsh of Massachusetts, who appealed to you by letter to stop segregation. Thus have the Afro-Americans shown how they detest segregation.

In fact, so intense is their resentment that the movement to divide this solid race vote and make peace with the national Democracy, so suspiciously revived when you ran for the presidency, and which some of our families for two generations have been risking all to promote, bids fair to be undone.

Only two years ago you were heralded as perhaps the second Lincoln, and now the Afro-American leaders who supported you are hounded as false leaders and traitors to their race. What a change segregation has wrought!

You said that your "Colored fellow citizens could depend upon you for everything which would assist in advancing the interests of their race in the United States." Consider this pledge in the face of the continued color segregation! Fellow citizenship means congregation. Segregation destroys fellowship and citizenship. Consider that any passerby on the streets of the national capital, whether he be black or white, can enter and use the public lavatories in government buildings while citizens of color who do the work of the government are excluded.

As equal citizens and by virtue of your public promises we are entitled at your hands to freedom from discrimination, restriction, imputation and insult in government employ. Have you a "new freedom" for white Americans and a new slavery for your Afro-American fellow citizens? God forbid!

We have been delegated to ask you to issue an executive order against any and all segregation of government employes because of race and color, and to ask whether you will do so. We await your reply, that we may give it to the waiting citizens of the United States of African extraction.

GLOSSARY

bureau of engraving and printing: a federal agency, part of the Treasury Department, that produces paper currency, government bonds, postage stamps, and various other official documents

Governor Walsh: David Ignatius Walsh, the isolationist governor of Massachusetts who argued for film censorship in his state in response to The Birth of a Nation, a film glorifying the Ku Klux Klan that Wilson had approved of

this league: the National Independent Equal Rights League

Document Analysis

In the first paragraph, Trotter reminds the president that, a year earlier, he and other black leaders had presented a petition, signed by persons from thirty-eight states. The focus of the group's concerns was segregation at the U.S. Treasury and Post Office. Trotter reminds Wilson that the group had urged him to undo this racial segregation and highlights the social, political, and personal damage of such an arrangement. Trotter then proceeds to list the segregated areas of the federal government, drawing specific attention to facilities for dining, dressing, and washing. This policy has far-reaching consequences. He also notes that segregation persists in all the areas of initial concern and has, in fact, spread to other federal buildings despite Wilson's promises to investigate.

In the third paragraph, Trotter details the specifics of racial segregation in federal government buildings. Segregated facilities then existed in the Treasury Department, the Bureau of Engraving and Printing, and the Navy Department for dressing rooms, working positions, eating arrangements, and even lavatories.

That such high hopes were followed by such worsening outcomes a year later was too much for the delegation, especially Trotter, to stomach. To the fiery activist it was unbearable that African American employees who dared to use the public facilities on the floors where they worked would be accused of "insubordination." In Trotter's mind there seemed to be no rational or substantial explanation for such debased and mortifying treatment for any human beings, especially for African Americans who had staunchly pledged their support for the nation, and (in many cases) for Wilson himself, at the behest of Trotter.

Such matters were not petty for Trotter. The overt and underlying message they sent to African Americans all around the country was indicative of the value that their federal government placed on them. Black citizens were already devastated by the degree to which the party of Abraham Lincoln had abandoned its forthright championing of the interests of African Americans for nearly two decades, even while African Americans remained loyal to the Republicans. Now, searching for some sense of hope in Wilson as emblematic of a new Democratic Party, black people were intensely disappointed. That African Americans were undergoing one of the worst periods in their history at this time, owing to the rampant harassment, violence, and lynchings, made the added insult of toilet segregation too much to bear. Trotter unequivocally states, in paragraph 4, that the delegation has come to "renew the protest," asking the president once again to "abolish segregation of Afro-American employees in the executive department."

In paragraph 5, Trotter predicts that if the government of the United States of America can be allowed to segregate African Americans, it will encourage the rest of the nation to continue to do the same, permitting segregation to spread from the White House to every part of the nation. In this policy Trotter foresaw danger for the entire nation, potentially leading to its unraveling. American citizenship thus would become extremely precarious, even to the point of placing into question the promises of the founding documents and the structure of American democracy itself.

Trotter proceeds in paragraph 6 to recount the delegation's strategy to date, reminding Wilson of the serious and organized manner of their protest. That protest had graduated from the national antisegregation petition offered in 1913 to protests at the voting polls. Trotter noted that David Walsh of Massachusetts, the only Democrat elected governor in the eastern part of the country, had publicly appealed to Wilson to end segregation. Only tangible, concerted actions by governmental leaders would do that. The clear message to the president was that he should reverse course and make good on his promise or else potentially face the same fate as many of his Democratic colleagues around the nation. With the next presidential election just two years away, this message was no idle threat.

Trotter underscores the power of the African American vote in the recent shift of black political allegiance that helped to elect Wilson. Here the race leader demonstrates that the shift was not a matter that blacks took lightly. African Americans were not wedded to Wilson or the Democrats any more than they were to the Republican Party, should either turn its back on African American efforts for equality. Wilson may have been touted as the "second Lincoln," says Trotter, but his actions and inactions placed African American representatives, like Trotter himself, in the compromising position of being labeled as false leaders and race traitors.

In the final sections of his address, Trotter reminds the president of the promise he made to African American people. Then, in paragraph 9, comes an argument linking fellow citizenship with "congregation," by which he means a united community, one that is subverted by segregation.

Trotter's parting shot that surely rang throughout the entire room asks if Wilson had instituted a "new freedom for white Americans and new slavery for your Afro-American fellow citizens." Trotter concludes with the delegation's specific policy proposal: that the president issue an executive order banning all racial segregation of government employees "We await your reply."

Essential Themes

That reply would come quickly. According to an article published that day in the Philadelphia *Evening Ledger*, Wilson reportedly replied to Trotter that he had spoken "as no other man has spoken since I assumed the Presidency" and said that he would no longer receive him as part of a future delegation. Much has been made of Trotter's militant tone during this meeting. However, this opening statement to the president evidences a degree of decorum and respect. He maintains a reasonable attitude in expressing the hope that Wilson will be a man of his word. But Trotter and the delegation also offered a warning that the people whom they represented were greatly alarmed at the lack of progress, especially the further encroachment upon their movement for equality. Furthermore, the symbolism of the president of the United States seeming to condone racial segregation in the very citadel of democracy could not go unchallenged. Neither could Wilson's professed dedication to making the world "safe for democracy" while he directly and indirectly denied African Americans their rights and full citizenship.

———Zachery Williams

Bibliography and Additional Reading

"President Resents Negro's Criticism." *New York Times*, November 13, 1914, p. 11.

Bartlett, Bruce. *Wrong on Race: The Democratic Party's Buried Past*. New York: Palgrave Macmillan, 2008.

Bennett, Lerone, Jr. *Pioneers in Protest*. Baltimore, Md. Penguin, 1969.

Cooper, John Milton. *Reconsidering Woodrow Wilson: Progressivism, Internationalism, War, and Peace*. Baltimore, Md. Johns Hopkins University Press, 2008.

———. *Woodrow Wilson: A Biography*. New York: Alfred A. Knopf, 2009.

Fox, Stephen R. *The Guardian of Boston: William Monroe Trotter*. New York: Atheneum, 1970.

———. "William Monroe Trotter." In *Dictionary of American Negro Biography*, ed. Rayford W. Logan and Michael R. Winston. New York: W. W. Norton, 1982.

Logan, Rayford W. *The Betrayal of the Negro: From Rutherford B. Hayes to Woodrow Wilson*. New York: Da Capo Press, 1997.

Lunardini, Christine. "Standing Firm: William Monroe Trotter's Meetings with Woodrow Wilson, 1913–1914." *Journal of Negro History* 64, no. 3 (Summer 1979): 244–264.

Maynard, William Barksdale. *Woodrow Wilson: Princeton to the Presidency*. New Haven, Conn. Yale University Press, 2008.

Smith, Jessie Carney. "William Monroe Trotter." In *Notable Black American Men*. Detroit: Gale Research, 1999.

■ "The Eruption of Tulsa"

Date: 1921
Author: Walter F. White
Genre: Magazine article

Summary Overview

The race riot in Tulsa, Oklahoma, of May 31–June 1, 1921, "the night Tulsa died," stands as one of the more disgraceful episodes in American history. Among its first chroniclers was Walter F. White, whose article "The Eruption of Tulsa" appeared in *The Nation* magazine on July 29 that year. The riot was sparked by a rumor of a sexual assault that was picked up by a city newspaper. Events quickly spiraled out of control as mobs gathered. On the night of May 31 and continuing until noon the following day, gangs of white and black citizens waged open warfare on one another, with white gangs shooting black citizens in public and torching and vandalizing homes and businesses in Tulsa's black Greenwood district. Roughly thirty-five blocks in Greenwood, including more than twelve hundred homes and numerous businesses, were destroyed by fire, and some ten thousand people were left homeless. Although the official death toll was put at thirty-nine, few who have studied the event, including White, believe this figure. According to an American Red Cross investigation, the number was at least three hundred, and some investigators place the number much higher, perhaps in the thousands. Suspicions remain that many of those killed in the rioting were buried in mass graves.

Defining Moment

Several specific developments conspired to create the conditions that would erupt in violence in Tulsa. White alludes to many of these conditions in his article. One development was the reemergence of the Ku Klux Klan. In Tulsa, numerous judges, lawyers, and other community and business leaders were Klan members. Another was the powerful anti-immigrant and anti-radical sentiment that followed World War One, as radical labor organizations often targeted disaffected African Americans for recruitment.

The crisis began on May 30. A nineteen-year-old shoe shiner named Dick Rowland needed to use a restroom. The only one available for a "colored" person was on the top floor of the nearby Drexel Building in downtown Tulsa. He entered an elevator operated by seventeen-year-old Sarah Page, who was white. It is unclear what exactly happened in the elevator, since no copy of Page's statement to the police exists. The police did not regard the incident as serious, but the following morning they pursued Rowland to his mother's home in Greenwood and took him to the Tulsa County Courthouse for questioning.

Matters might have ended there, but in its afternoon edition of May 31 the *Tulsa Tribune* ran a story with the headline "Nab Negro for Attacking Girl in an Elevator." In response, a crowd of white people began gathering at the courthouse. Many were just curious onlookers, but many others were outraged at what they believed had been an assault on a white woman by a black man. By early evening the growing crowd had all the earmarks of a lynch mob.

Gunfire began at 10:00 PM and bands of whites pursued blacks to the Greenwood section. Throughout the night, groups of whites and blacks fired on each other across the railroad tracks that separated Greenwood from the white part of town. Fires were set in two dozen black-owned businesses at the edge of Greenwood. In the early morning of June 1, white gangs fired indiscriminately on any blacks who had not yet fled. There were reports that planes were dropping firebombs into the community, and throughout the early morning, fires spread throughout Greenwood. People in the city's white section were threatened with violence and vandalism if they did not turn over black cooks and housekeepers to the rioters.

Finally, at about 9:00 am on June 1, Oklahoma National Guard troops began arriving from Oklahoma City. Tulsa was placed under martial law, and by noon the violence had come to an end. Many white Tulsans were horrified by what had been wrought in their city and opened their homes to homeless blacks, and the American Red Cross provided food and tents for the homeless. But a sense of shame settled over the city, and the Tulsa riot became a largely forgotten event until the 1990s.

Author Biography

Walter Francis White, one of the most prominent civil rights leaders of the first half of the twentieth century, was born on July 1, 1893, in Atlanta, Georgia. He joined the staff of the NAACP in New York City in 1918. Working as the NAACP's assistant national secretary until 1931, when he became the executive director—a position he held until his death.

He was the motivating force behind President Harry Truman's order to desegregate the military after World War II, and under his direction the Legal Defense Fund led the efforts to erase segregated schooling that culminated in the 1954 U.S. Supreme Court case *Brown v. Board of Education*.

White was the author of numerous essays that appeared in national magazines. During his early years in the NAACP, he investigated lynchings and riots, often traveling incognito to the sites of these events and putting himself in great personal danger in the process, though his ability to "pass" as white because of his light complexion helped gain him access to the police, politicians, and others. In 1919, for example, he traveled to Arkansas to investigate the riot that had taken place in Elaine in October of that year—and fled the town in the face of threats. Seventy-nine African Americans were arrested, tried, and convicted for their role in that riot. As a result of White's efforts, the U.S. Supreme Court eventually overturned the convictions on the ground that armed observers in the courtroom and an armed mob outside the courthouse had a tendency to intimidate the jury.

White was also a prominent figure in the Harlem Renaissance, the flowering of black culture and art that was centered in the Harlem neighborhood of New York City in the 1920s and 1930s. he died on March 21, 1955, in New York City.

HISTORICAL DOCUMENT

A hysterical white girl related that a nineteen-year-old colored boy attempted to assault her in the public elevator of a public office building of a thriving town of 100,000 in open daylight. Without pausing to find whether or not the story was true, without bothering with the slight detail of investigating the character of the woman who made the outcry (as a matter of fact, she was of exceedingly doubtful reputation), a mob of 100-per-cent Americans set forth on a wild rampage that cost the lives of fifty white men; of between 150 and 200 colored men, women and children; the destruction by fire of $1,500,000 worth of property; the looting of many homes; and everlasting damage to the reputation of the city of Tulsa and the State of Oklahoma.

This, in brief, is the story of the eruption of Tulsa on the night of May 31 and the morning of June 1. One could travel far and find few cities where the likelihood of trouble between the races was as little thought of as in Tulsa. Her reign of terror stands as a grim reminder of the grip mob violence has on the throat of America, and the ever-present possibility of devastating race conflicts where least expected.

Tulsa is a thriving, bustling, enormously wealthy town of between 90,000 and 100,000. In 1910 it was the home of 18,182 souls, a dead and hopeless outlook ahead. Then oil was discovered. The town grew amazingly. On December 29, 1920, it had bank deposits totaling $65,449,985.90; almost $1,000 per capita when compared with the Federal Census figures of 1920, which gave Tulsa 72,076. The town lies in the center of the oil region and many are the stories told of the making of fabulous fortunes by men who were operating on a shoe-string. Some of the stories rival those of the "forty-niners" in California. The town has a number of modern office buildings, many beautiful homes, miles of clean, well-paved streets, and aggressive and progressive business men who well exemplify Tulsa's motto of "The City with a Personality."

So much for the setting. What are the causes of the race riot that occurred in such a place?

First, the Negro in Oklahoma has shared in the sudden prosperity that has come to many of his white brothers, and there are some colored men there who are wealthy. This fact has caused a bitter resentment on the part of the lower order of whites, who feel that these colored men, members of an "inferior race," are exceedingly presumptuous in achieving greater economic prosperity than they who are members of a divinely ordered superior race. There are at least three colored persons in Oklahoma who are worth a million dollars each; J. W. Thompson of Clearview is worth $500,000; there are a number of men and women worth $100,000; and many whose possessions are valued at $25,000 and $50,000 each. This was particularly true of Tulsa, where there were two colored men worth $150,000 each; two worth $100,000; three $50,000; and four who were assessed at $25,000. In one case where a colored man owned and operated a printing plant with $25,000 worth of printing machinery in it, the leader of the mob that set fire to and destroyed the plant was a linotype operator employed for years by the colored owner at $48 per week. The white man was killed while attacking the plant. Oklahoma is largely populated by pioneers from other States. Some of the white pioneers are former residents of Mississippi, Georgia, Tennessee, Texas, and other States more typically southern than Oklahoma. These have brought with them their anti-Negro prejudices. Lethargic and unprogressive by nature, it sorely irks them to see Negroes making greater progress than they themselves are achieving.

One of the charges made against the colored men in Tulsa is that they were "radical." Questioning the whites more closely regarding the nature of this radicalism, I found it means that Negroes were uncompromisingly denouncing "Jim-Crow" [railroad] cars, lynching, peonage; in short, were asking that the Federal constitutional guaranties of "life, liberty, and the pursuit of happiness" be given regardless of color. The Negroes of Tulsa and other Oklahoma cities are pioneers; men and women who have dared, men and women who have had the initiative and the courage to pull up stakes in other less-favored States and face hardship in a newer one for the sake of greater eventual progress. That type is ever less ready to submit to insult. Those of the whites who seek to maintain the old white group control naturally do not relish seeing Negroes emancipating themselves from the old system.

A third cause was the rotten political conditions in Tulsa. A vice ring was in control of the city, allowing open operation of houses of ill fame, of gambling joints, the illegal sale of whiskey, the robbing of banks and stores, with hardly a slight possibility of the arrest of the criminals, and even less of their conviction. For fourteen years Tulsa has been in the absolute control of this element. Most of the better element, and there is a large percentage of Tulsans who can properly be classed as such, are interested solely in making money and getting away. They have taken little or no interest in the election of city or county officials, leaving it to those whose interest it was to secure officials who would protect them in their vice operations. About two months ago the State legislature assigned two additional judges to Tulsa County to aid the present two in clearing the badly clogged dockets. These judges found more than six thousand cases awaiting trial. Thus in a county of approximately 100,000 population, six out of every one hundred citizens were under indictment for some sort of crime, with little likelihood of trial in any of them.

Last July a white man by the name of Roy Belton, accused of murdering a taxicab driver, was taken from the county jail and lynched. According to the statements of many prominent Tulsans, local police officers directed traffic at the scene of the lynching, trying to afford every person present an equal chance to view the event. Insurance companies refuse to give Tulsa merchants insurance on their stocks; the risk is too great. There have been so many automobile thefts that a number of companies have canceled all policies on care in Tulsa. The net result of these conditions was that practically none of the citizens of the town, white or colored, had very much respect for the law.

So much for the general causes. What was the spark that set off the blaze? On Monday, May 30, a white girl by the name of Sarah Page, operating an elevator in the Drexel Building, stated that Dick Rowland, a nineteen-year-old colored boy, had attempted criminally to assault her. Her second story was that the boy had seized her arm as he entered the elevator. She screamed. He ran. It was found afterwards that the boy had stepped by accident on her foot. It seems never to have occurred to the citizens of Tulsa that any sane person attempting criminally to assault a woman would have picked any place in the world rather than an open elevator in a public building with scores of people within calling distance. The story of the alleged assault was published Tuesday afternoon by the Tulsa Tribune, one of the two local newspapers. At four o'clock Commissioner of Police J. M. Adkison reported to

Sheriff [Willard] McCullough that there was talk of lynching Rowland that night. Chief of Police John A. Gustafson, Captain Wilkerson of the Police Department, Edwin F. Barnett, managing editor of the Tulsa Tribune, and numerous other citizens all stated that there was talk Tuesday of lynching the boy.

In the meantime the news of the threatened lynching reached the colored settlement where Tulsa's 15,000 colored citizens lived. Remembering how a white man had been lynched after being taken from the same jail where the colored boy was now confined, they feared that Rowland was in danger. A group of colored men telephoned the sheriff and proffered their services in protecting the jail from attack. The sheriff told them that they would be called upon if needed. About nine o'clock that night a crowd of white men gathered around the jail, numbering about 400 according to Sheriff McCullough. At 9:15 [pm] the report reached "Little Africa" that the mob had stormed the jail. A crowd of twenty-five armed Negroes set out immediately, but on reaching the jail found the report untrue. The sheriff talked with them, assured them that the boy would not be harmed, and urged them to return to their homes. They left, later returning, 75 strong. The sheriff persuaded them to leave. As they complied, a white man attempted to disarm one of the colored men. A shot was fired, and then—in the words of the sheriff—"all hell broke loose." There was a fusillade of shots from both sides and twelve men fell dead—two of them colored, ten white. The fighting continued until midnight when the colored men, greatly outnumbered, were forced back to their section of the town.

Around five o'clock Wednesday morning the [white] mob, now numbering more than 10,000, made a mass attack on Little Africa. Machine-guns were brought into use; eight aeroplanes were employed to spy on the movements of the Negroes and according to some were used in bombing the colored section. All that was lacking to make the scene a replica of modern "Christian" warfare was poison gas. The colored men and women fought gamely in defense of their homes, but the odds were too great. According to the statements of onlookers, men in uniform, either home guards or ex-service men or both, carried cans of oil into Little Africa, and, after looting the homes, set fire to them. Many are the stories of horror told to me—not by colored people—but by white residents. One was that of an aged colored couple, saying their evening prayers before retiring in their little home on Greenwood Avenue. A mob broke into the house, shot both of the old people in the backs of their heads, blowing their brains out and spattering them over the bed, pillaged the home, and then set fire to it.

Another was that of the death of Dr. A. C. Jackson, a colored physician. Dr. Jackson was worth $100,000; had been described by the Mayo brothers "the most able Negro surgeon in America"; was respected by white and colored people alike, and was in every sense a good citizen. A mob attacked Dr. Jackson's home. He fought in defense of it, his wife and children and himself. An officer of the home guards who knew Dr. Jackson came up at that time and assured him that if he would surrender he would be protected. This Dr. Jackson did. The officer sent him under guard to Convention Hall, where colored people were being placed for protection. En route to the hall, disarmed, Dr. Jackson was shot and killed in cold blood. The officer who had assured Dr. Jackson of protection stated to me, "Dr. Jackson was an able, clean-cut man. He did only what any red-blooded man would have done under similar circumstances in defending his home. Dr. Jackson was murdered by white ruffians."

It is highly doubtful if the exact number of casualties will ever be known. The figures originally given in the press estimate the number at 100. The number buried by local undertakers and given out by city officials is ten white and twenty-one colored. For obvious reasons these officials wish to keep the number published as low as possible, but the figures obtained in Tulsa are far higher. Fifty whites and between 150 and 200 Negroes is much nearer the actual number of deaths. Ten whites were killed during the first hour of fighting on Tuesday night. Six white men drove into the colored section in a car on Wednesday morning and never came out. Thirteen whites were killed between 5:30 am and 6:30 am Wednesday. O. T. Johnson, commandant of the Tulsa Citadel of the Salvation Army, stated that on Wednesday and Thursday the Salvation Army fed thirty-seven Negroes employed as grave diggers and twenty on Friday and Saturday. During the first two days these men dug 120 graves in each of which a dead Negro was buried. No coffins were used. The bodies were dumped into the holes and covered over with dirt. Added to the number accounted for were numbers of others—men, women, and children—who were incinerated in the burning houses in the Negro settlement. One story was told me by an eye-witness of five colored men trapped in a burning house. Four burned to death. A fifth attempted to flee, was shot to death as he emerged from the burning structure, and his body was thrown back into the flames. There was an unconfirmed rumor afloat in Tulsa of two truck loads of dead Negroes being dumped into the Arkansas River, but that story could not be confirmed.

What is America going to do after such a horrible carnage—one that for sheer brutality and murderous anarchy cannot be surpassed by any of the crimes now being charged to the Bolsheviki in Russia? How much longer will America allow these pogroms to continue unchecked? There is a lesson in the Tulsa affair for every American who fatuously believes that Negroes will always be the meek and submissive creatures that circumstances have forced them to be during the past three hundred years. Dick Rowland was only an ordinary bootblack with no standing in the community. But when his life was threatened by a mob of whites, every one of the 15,000 Negroes of Tulsa, rich and poor, educated and illiterate, was willing to die to protect Dick Rowland. Perhaps America is waiting for a nationwide Tulsa to wake her. Who knows?

GLOSSARY

Bolsheviki: usually spelled Bolsheviks, referring to the political party in Russia regarded as synonymous with Communism

Citadel: the name given to any church building used by the Salvation Army

forty-niners: gold prospectors who migrated to California during the gold rush of 1849

Mayo brothers: Charles and William Mayo, famous as the founders of the Mayo Clinic

peonage: a system that requires debtors to work for their creditors until the debt is discharged

pogroms: organized or spontaneous rioting directed against a religious or ethnic group, usually associated with Communist Russia

Document Analysis
White begins his article by sketching in broad strokes the events that happened in Tulsa. He notes that the incident was sparked by the report of a "hysterical white girl" and suggests that her account of what happened in the elevator was dubious, given that she was of "doubtful reputation" and that the alleged attack occurred in "open daylight" in a city of one hundred thousand people (though he later acknowledges the 1920 U.S. Census figure of seventy-two thousand). White ironically refers to "100-per-cent Americans" who acted on the report without bothering to verify it, causing death and destruction (one of the slogans of the Ku Klux Klan in this era was "100 percent Americanism"). In the second paragraph, White laments the "grip" that mob violence can have on the "throat of America," where that violence can break out anywhere and at any time.

Beginning with the third paragraph, White provides statistics on Tulsa, including its dramatic population growth and its prosperity as a result of the state's oil boom. In the fifth paragraph he notes that African Americans had shared in the prosperity, to the "bitter resentment" of "the lower order of whites," who believed that the city's African Americans were "presumptuous" in their prosperity. Many of these whites, immigrants from southern states, were themselves "lethargic and unprogressive by nature." White then proceeds to detail that prosperity, noting that Tulsa was home to at least three black millionaires and several others with substantial assets. Because of changes in the value of the dollar from inflation, $25,000 in 1921 is equivalent to about $287,000 today.

White goes on to discuss the supposed "radical" views of Tulsa's black population—and dismisses this belief by noting that the community simply wanted an end to "'Jim-Crow' [railroad] cars, lynching, peonage." "Jim Crow" is the informal name given to laws designed to keep African Americans in subservient positions, such as laws requiring them to ride in separate railroad cars. "Peonage" refers to a system that requires debtors to work for their creditors until the debt is discharged. White asserts that black efforts to emancipate themselves from these conditions fostered resentment on the part of whites.

The seventh paragraph details the rough-and-tumble nature of life in Tulsa at that time, where justice was as likely to be enacted at the end of a gun or noose as in the courtroom. White notes that corruption and vice permeated the city and that large numbers of people were interested not in the community's civic life but in making money and getting away with illegal activities. White provides further startling facts in the eighth paragraph. When a white man charged with murder was lynched, the police directed traffic so that onlookers could get a view of the event. Insurance companies refused to do business in Tulsa because the risk was too great. All of this, in White's view, fostered disrespect for the law among both blacks and whites.

Paragraphs 9 through 12 detail the events of the riot: the incident in the elevator, the newspaper account of the alleged assault, the gathering of a lynch mob and the fears in the black community that Rowland would fall into the hands of the mob, and the escalating violence. White repeats the claim that airplanes were used to drop incendiary bombs on the Greenwood community, a charge that would later be investigated and found to likely have been true. White makes his account more graphic and dramatic by focusing on the fates of individuals, such as an aged couple who were shot in their home and a prominent doctor who was shot to death while being taken to a detention center. This man had been described by the "Mayo brothers" (Charles and William Mayo, famous as the founders of the Mayo Clinics) as "the most able Negro surgeon in America."

In the thirteenth paragraph, White addresses the number of casualties. He rejects the official body count and calls attention to the activities of gravediggers, which suggest that the death toll was much greater than that given by the authorities. He notes that at least some victims of the riot were "incinerated" in their homes and that there were reports of truckloads of bodies being dumped in the nearby Arkansas River, though he acknowledges that this rumor could not be confirmed. In more recent years, some efforts have been made to investigate the matter using archaeological methods, but no systematic search for these graves has been made, and the results have been inconclusive.

In the final paragraph White grows more rhetorical. He refers to the riot's "horrible carnage" and suggests that it was worse than the crimes being ascribed to the "Bolsheviki," or Bolsheviks, referring to the political party in Russia regarded as synonymous with Communism. He uses the word "pogroms," referring to organized or spontaneous rioting directed against a religious or ethnic group and again associated with Russia. White concludes by noting the willingness of Tulsa's black population to come to the defense of Dick Rowland, and he suggests that a "nationwide Tulsa" might be necessary to "wake" the United States to racial injustice.

Essential Themes

One of the key themes that emerges from Walter F. White's discussion of the Tulsa Race Riot is that the explosion of violence was the result not only of the same racism that permeated the United States at the time but also an astonishingly violent and corrupt. Theft, murder, lynching, and political corruption were a fact of life in Tulsa. One comes away from reading White's account thinking that it, perhaps, would have been shocking these events (or something very much like them) *didn't* happen.

Of course, the root cause of all of this violence was the racism pervaded Tulsa and, in White's view, the prosperity of African American Tulsans which fueled white envy. This envy and fear—further fueled by the nationwide sentiments of anti-radicalism and the desire for "100 percent Americanism." Another factor in the "riot" that White addresses—if obliquely—is that applying the term "race riot" to this is misleading. His detailing of the assault of whites against the Little Africa district of Tulsa makes it very clear that this was no "riot" of a city's black residents—it was a quasi-military assault with automatic weapons and aerial bombardment. After reading White's report from Tulsa, it was clear that white america had declared war.

——*Michael J. O'Neal, PhD*

Bibliography and Additional Reading

Brophy, Alfred L. *Reconstructing the Dreamland: The Tulsa Race Riot of 1921: Race, Reparations, and Reconciliation.* (New York: Oxford University Press, 2002).

Ellsworth, Scott. *Death in a Promised Land: The Tulsa Race Riot of 1921.* (Baton Rouge: Louisiana State University Press, 1982).

Halliburton, R. *The Tulsa Race War of 1921.* (San Francisco: R and E Research Associates, 1975).

Hirsch, James S. *Riot and Remembrance: The Tulsa Race War and Its Legacy.* (Boston: Houghton Mifflin, 2002).

Hower, Bob, and Maurice Willows. *1921 Tulsa Race Riot and the American Red Cross, "Angels of Mercy."* (Tulsa: Homestead Press, 1993).

Johnson, Hannibal B. *Black Wall Street: From Riot to Renaissance in Tulsa's Historic Greenwood District.* (Austin: Eakin Press, 1998).

Madigan, Tim. *The Burning: Massacre, Destruction, and the Tulsa Race Riot of 1921.* (New York: St. Martin's Press, 2001).

Parrish, Mary E. Jones. *Race Riot 1921: Events of the Tulsa Disaster.* (Tulsa: Out on a Limb Publishers, 1998).

Williams, Lee E., and Lee E. Williams II. *Anatomy of Four Race Riots: Racial Conflict in Knoxville, Elaine (Arkansas), Tulsa, and Chicago, 1919–1921.* (Hattiesburg: University and College Press of Mississippi, 1972).

Web Sites

"Tulsa Race Riot." Oklahoma Historical Society "Encyclopedia of Oklahoma History and Culture" Web site. http://digital.library.okstate.edu/encyclopedia/entries/T/TU013.html

University of Tulsa, McFarlin Library, "Tulsa Race Riot of 1921 Archive—Photographs" Web site. http://www.lib.utulsa.edu/Speccoll/collections/RaceRiot/indexphotos.htm

■ "U.S. Department of (White) Justice"

Date: 1935
Author: Walter F. White
Genre: Magazine article

Summary Overview

During the 1920s and 1930s, Walter White published dozens of essays to rally public opposition to lynching, including the 1935 article "U.S. Department of (White) Justice." As the executive secretary of the National Association for the Advancement of Colored People (NAACP), White called on the federal government to enact laws to prevent mob violence and punish its perpetrators. Published in *The Crisis*, the NAACP's monthly journal, this particular essay focused on the reluctance of federal law enforcement officials to intervene in southern lynching cases.

The antilynching movement was one of the first civil rights causes to emerge on the national political scene. Walter White and the NAACP spearheaded a diverse alliance of churchwomen, labor unions, progressive activists, and southern liberals united in their opposition to lynching. Their crusade forced a showdown with southern politicians, who resisted any effort by the federal government to intervene in their affairs. While the national crusade against mob violence failed to enact federal antilynching laws, White's efforts to publicize the horrors of lynching were a crucial step in the emergence of civil rights as a national issue.

Defining Moment

By the 1930s American lynch mobs had murdered nearly five thousand documented victims since the end of Reconstruction. Lynchings had occurred across the country during the late nineteenth century, claiming men and women of various racial and ethnic backgrounds. Yet as mob violence peaked at the turn of the century, lynching became an increasingly regional and racial phenomenon. White supremacists condoned or explicitly endorsed vigilante violence as a means of discouraging black political participation and resisting any semblance of racial equality. By the early twentieth century, the vast majority of lynchings occurred in the South, and nearly all the victims were black. While lynching is often associated with hanging, vigilantes frequently shot, stabbed, burned, and tortured their victims as well.

As lynchings surged in the early 1930s (after a brief decline during the 1920s), the antilynching movement gained momentum. In 1918 Republican congressman Leonidas Dyer sponsored the first antilynching bill in American history. Four years later, the House of Representatives passed the Dyer bill despite the nearly unanimous opposition of its southern members. In the Senate however, southerners filibustered the bill into oblivion. After the election of Franklin D. Roosevelt, there was hope for passage of antilynching legislation. FDR, however, was reluctant to endorse any legislation that would alienate southern Democrats. "If I come out for the anti-lynching bill now," Roosevelt admitted, as recalled by White in *A Man Called White*, "they will block every bill I ask Congress to pass to keep America from collapsing. I just can't take that risk."

Despite White's and others' mounting frustration with the federal government, the antilynching movement was gaining momentum by 1935, as the NAACP was working alongside civil rights groups, organized labor, and white southern women to rally public opposition to lynching. Gruesome exposés and scholarly studies of lynching fed public indignation. Contemporary polls revealed that even a significant percentage of white southerners favored legislation to stamp out lynching. But such promising shifts in public attitudes were meaningless without government action. By publishing articles like "U.S. Department of (White) Justice," Walter White hoped to spotlight governmental apathy and pressure federal authorities to stamp out lynching once and for all.

Author Biography

Walter White was an influential journalist and civil rights activist who led the NAACP from 1929 until his death in 1955. Born on July 1, 1893, to a light-skinned Atlanta mail collector and his equally fair-complexioned wife, White enjoyed a relatively privileged upbringing among the city's black middle class. But this did not shield White from the racial violence that swept Atlanta in 1906. During the three-day race riot, White watched as marauding whites assaulted hundreds of African Americans and destroyed black property.

White never forgot that mob. After graduating from Atlanta University in 1916, the young insurance salesman threw himself into a local campaign to increase funding for black schools. Later that year, White wrote directly to the national headquarters of the NAACP, asking for its help in organizing an Atlanta chapter. Impressed by the young leader's energy and organizing skills, the NAACP executive secretary James Weldon Johnson invited White to join the national staff.

Less than two weeks after moving to New York to work at the national headquarters, White traveled south to investigate a lynching firsthand. Posing as a traveling salesman, White gathered gruesome details from local whites who had no idea they were speaking with a man of African ancestry. Over the next decade, White investigated dozens of lynchings and race riots at great personal risk. By the late 1920s he was one of the country's foremost authorities on lynching. He recounted his investigations in northern newspapers and national magazines. White published both a novel and a nonfiction book based on his firsthand investigations of southern lynchings.

In 1929, White assumed leadership of the NAACP. During his long tenure as executive secretary, White enlisted powerful allies in NAACP campaigns against racial violence, discrimination, and segregation. The antilynching campaign was always close to White's heart, and he spent much of the 1930s lobbying Congress and federal officials to take action against mob violence. White died on March 21, 1955, after leading the NAACP for nearly three decades.

HISTORICAL DOCUMENT

The Department of Justice in Washington may lay claim to a 100 per cent performance in at least one branch of its activities—the evasion of cases involving burning questions of Negro rights. It sidestepped the issue of the exclusion of Negroes from southern elections on the ground that it was loaded with political dynamite. Other legalistic reasons were later added but the first orders to "Go Slow" were placed on purely political grounds. On the lynching issue the department has set a new record for its ability to dodge from one excuse to another.

On June 6, 1933, a white girl was murdered near Tuscaloosa, Alabama, and shortly thereafter three Negro boys were thrown in jail on suspicion of the murder. On August 12, 1933, the sheriff of Tuscaloosa county unlawfully under color of authority took it upon himself to order their removal from Tuscaloosa to Birmingham "for safekeeping." The sheriff's deputies started at night for Birmingham in two automobiles: two deputies and the boys in the leading car, and a car full of deputies trailing behind. The sheriff ordered the convoy to take a back road because, as the deputies later testified, he did not want to risk the convoy being overtaken by a mob on the highway. When the convoy reached the Tuscaloosa county line, the trailing car turned back, leaving the first car with the boys in it to make the rest of the journey alone. Two miles across the county line the car with the boys in it was *met*, not overtaken, by other cars full of masked men. The boys were taken out, riddled with bullets, and two of them killed. The Southern Association for the Prevention of Lynching made an investigation which found the sheriff culpable.

A delegation made up of representatives from several national organizations on August 24 called at the Department of Justice pursuant to an appointment made with William Stanley, executive assistant to Attorney General Homer S. Cummings, who had promised to receive it in the absence of the attorney general, to request the department to investigate the lynching and prosecute the offending sheriff under Revised Statutes 5510 which makes it a federal offense to deprive an inhabitant of any state of any rights, privileges or immunities secured or protected by the federal Constitution under color of law or custom. But although Stanley had made the appointment himself, when the delegation arrived at the department, Stanley was not present, had sent no excuse for his absence, and investigation disclosed that he had not even entered the appointment on his calendar pad.

The delegation was so indignant that the officials of the department four hours later carried them in to see the attorney general himself. The attorney general was suave; he would make no commitment;

he called for a brief. Accordingly a thorough brief was filed with the department October 13, 1933, and Stanley stated that he would let the delegation know the decision of the department by November 1. Actually he kept the delegation in suspense until March 5, 1934, although months before both he and the attorney general had told Roger N. Baldwin of the American Civil Liberties Union that the department did not intend to take any action in the case.

In the meanwhile a bill amending the original Lindbergh kidnaping law of 1932 had been introduced in Congress. The 1932 act had made kidnaping a federal offense where the kidnaped person was knowingly transported in interstate or foreign commerce and "held for ransom or reward." The amendment to the 1932 act proposed to broaden the scope of federal jurisdiction and make kidnaping a federal offense when the person kidnaped was knowingly transported in interstate or foreign commerce and "held for ransom or reward *or otherwise*" (italics ours). It also proposed that there should be a prima facie presumption that the person kidnaped had been carried across the state line unless released within three days.

While the bill was before the Senate judiciary committee the attorney general submitted a memorandum to the committee in support of the amendment as follows:

"This amendment adds thereto (to the Lindbergh Act of 1932) the word 'otherwise'....The object of the word 'otherwise' is to extend the jurisdiction of this act to persons who have been kidnaped and held, not only for reward *but for any other reason*.

"In addition this bill adds a proviso to the Lindbergh Act that in the absence of the return of the person kidnaped...during a period of three days *the presumption arises* that such person has been transported in interstate or foreign commerce, but such presumption is not conclusive.

"*I believe that this is a sound amendment which will clear up border line cases*, justifying federal investigation in most of such cases and assuring the validity of federal prosecution in numerous instances in which such prosecution would be questionable under the present form of this act" (italics ours).

In other words, at this stage the attorney general placed the Department of Justice squarely behind the amendment, giving to its provisions the broadest possible interpretation. But as soon as questions of lynching were raised, the attorney general abandoned his broad construction and began hopping from one position to another to avoid taking jurisdiction.

The bill passed Congress and became enacted into law June 22, 1934, with all the provisions of the amendment adopted except that the time within which a kidnaped person had to be held for presumption of an interstate transportation to arise was increased from three days to seven; and certain other changes not here material.

On October 4, 1934, one Curtis James' house was broken into near Darien, Georgia, about fifty miles from the Florida line, and James, a Negro, shot and abducted by a mob. In spite of an intensive search he was not found. After waiting more than the seven days provided by the amended Lindbergh law, the National Association for the Advancement of Colored People on October 15 wrote the Department of Justice asking whether the abductors of James could not be prosecuted under the amended Lindbergh law. Under date of October 20 the department replied:

"...there is nothing to indicate that the person alleged to have been kidnaped was transported in interstate commerce and was held for ransom, reward or otherwise. In the absence of these facts establishing these elements it would seem that the matter would be one entirely for the authorities of the State of Georgia..."

It is interesting that in the James case the Department of Justice recognized that a lynching case might be covered under the words "or otherwise" of the amended Lindbergh act, but it dodged jurisdiction by repudiating the presumption. In short the department deliberately ignored the fact that not returning James within seven days created a presumption that there had been an interstate kidnaping, and thereby gave the federal government jurisdiction over the crime. It demanded that the N.A.A.C.P. substitute itself for the department's own Bureau of Investigation and produce the *facts* establishing an interstate kidnaping.

Then on October 26, 1934, a Negro named Claude Neal was kidnaped from the jail in Brewton,

Alabama, by a mob which came to the scene in automobiles bearing Florida licenses. Neal was transported across the Alabama line into Florida, held for fifteen hours and then murdered after unspeakable barbarities near Marianna, Florida. The N.A.A.C.P. felt that at last it had a perfect case for federal prosecution, but before it could even get a letter to the Department of Justice requesting an investigation, the department had issued a public statement that the words "or otherwise" in the amended Lindbergh law did not cover the case of lynching. Faced by the indisputable fact of an interstate kidnaping, the department was forced to the position that the amended Lindbergh law covered kidnaping for purposes of gain, but not for purposes of murder.

With loud fan-fare and carefully staged publicity, on November 7, 1934, the attorney general announced to the country a National Crime Conference called by him in Washington, December 10-13, 1934, "to give broad and practical consideration to the problem of crime" including causes and prevention of crime; investigation; detection and apprehension of crime and criminals. A comprehensive and distinguished list of delegates, including bar associations, was invited; but no Negro associations. On November 9 the N.A.A.C.P. wrote the attorney general asking whether lynching would be placed on the conference agendum. On November 16 the department replied:

"...the program for the conference has not as yet been completed, obviously it will be impossible to cover all the phases of the crime problem in the short space of three days. No definite decision has been made with reference to the subject of lynching. I wish to thank you, however, for bringing this matter to our attention."

The crime of lynching was not even within the range of the department's vision.

No word came from the department concerning its decision whether to place lynching on the conference agendum, so on November 22 the N.A.A.C.P. wired the attorney general inquiring whether the decision had been made, and what. The department replied November 27 that "it was not probable that the subject of lynching will be given place on program of Crime Conference." Repeated efforts were made by local representatives of N.A.A.C.P. to see the Department of Justice in an attempt to obtain a reconsideration of the decision not to place lynching on the agendum, but the department remained unmoved.

Finally on the opening night of the conference when President Roosevelt made his key-note speech and roundly denounced lynching as one of the major crimes confronting this country, another wire was sent the attorney general asking in view of the President's pronouncement whether he would not at that date place lynching on the agendum. No reply was received the following morning, so at 12:30 P. M. that day the District of Columbia branch of the N.A.A.C.P. began to picket the Crime Conference.

The pickets were arrested almost as soon as they appeared and charged with violation of the District of Columbia sign law and parading without a permit. But that afternoon at 2:25 P. M. the branch received a telegram from the attorney general stating that although there was no room for a discussion of lynching on the formal agendum of the conference, there was a discussion period after each session and that if a discussion period were free, he hoped that the subject of lynching would be taken up on the floor. He further invited a delegation consisting of representatives of the local colored bar association to membership in the conference.

In spite of this action by the attorney general however, the chairman of the conference announced that the discussion period would be limited to the papers read on the formal agendum at the particular session. Under the circumstances the District of Columbia branch of the N.A.A.C.P. decided to resume the picketing.

On the last day of the conference, December 13, just before the morning session adjourned, about sixty pickets suddenly appeared on the sidewalk in front of the convention hall, and silently took up pre-arranged stations about ten feet apart, stretching all the way from the entrance of the hall about three squares along the street the delegates had to use in leaving the conference. To avoid the sign law which prohibited signs twelve inches or over, the pickets carried signs across their breasts eleven inches wide. Ropes were looped around their necks to symbolize lynching. To avoid the charge of parading, each picket remained silent and stationary. The police were taken completely by surprise. To add to the confusion of the police the pickets were provided with a mimeographed sheet of instructions, one of which read that if anybody bothered them they were to call on the police for protection, as the police would not arrest them if they were not violating any law, since to do so would subject the police to an action for damages. The police fumed; an attorney for the Department of Justice hurriedly left to consult the law and find grounds for arresting the pickets, but never returned. That afternoon the conference, smoked out beyond the point of endurance, adopted a completely inane and harmless resolution condemning the use of illegal means in disposing of matters arousing racial antagonisms. The attorney general held both his peace and his hand.

Finally March 12, 1935, a Negro, Ab Young, was lynched near Slayden, Mississippi, allegedly for shooting a white man. Young had been seized in Tennessee, and taken across the line into Mississippi for the ceremonies. Memphis news reporters were on hand either by accident or previous notice.

The N.A.A.C.P. telegraphed both the attorney general and the President of the United States asking for investigation and prosecution under the amended Lindbergh law. To date it is still awaiting a reply. The coroner's jury returned a verdict that Young had died at the hands of parties unknown.

The attorney general continues his offensive against crime—except crimes involving the deprivation of life and liberty and citizenship to Negroes.

GLOSSARY

color: as a legal term, pretense, as in "under color of authority, law, or custom"

Lindbergh kidnapping law: a law passed in 1932 in response to the highly publicized kidnapping and murder of the son of the aviation hero Charles Lindbergh in New Jersey

***prima facie*:** a legal term from the Latin for "at first sight," referring to a fact presumed to be true unless rebutted by evidence

Document Analysis

White opens by stating that the Department of Justice has failed to protect African Americans from violence and discrimination. White contends that federal agencies are moving slowly on civil rights because the Roosevelt administration is unwilling to do anything that would offend its white southern supporters. To illustrate the gravity of the issue, in the second paragraph, White discusses the horrific details of several recent lynchings. By revealing the gruesome details, the motives behind the murders, and the generally callous attitude of local authorities toward the killings, White hoped to convince the American public and federal officials that outside intervention was necessary to eliminate lynching.

In paragraphs 3 and 4, White reveals that he and fellow activists have repeatedly lobbied the Department of Justice to investigate lynchings. White, however, could not persuade a Justice Department official to meet with his delegation. Undeterred, White and his colleagues refused to leave the building until officials escorted them to see the attorney general in person, but never received a commitment from the department about their demands. The fifth paragraph reveals activists' methods using the legal system to their advantage. With no antilynching laws, the only way to justify federal prosecution of mob violence was to cite other laws that lynch mobs had violated. White had hoped that a revised version of a federal interstate kidnapping law would be broad enough to cover lynchings in which a mob carried a victim across state lines. In paragraphs 6–10, White reveals that the same attorney general who had refused to investigate the Tuscaloosa lynching had agreed in principle to broader laws against interstate kidnapping. But when civil rights activists cited this revised law to urge the Department of Justice to investigate lynchings, the attorney general once again refused to take action. White's discussion of the Lindbergh kidnapping law reveals the importance of litigation in the NAACP's civil rights activism. By using test cases, like the Curtis James lynching described in paragraph 12, the NAACP hoped to force the federal government to apply existing laws to civil rights violations.

In paragraphs 11–14, White describes how the Department of Justice evaded the NAACP's claim that the James lynching violated the expanded language of the recently revised Lindbergh law and argues that Department of Justice officials are willfully misrepresenting existing laws and making excuses to justify their inaction. In paragraph 15, White mentions the lynching of Claude Neal. White saw in this incident an opportunity to rally public support for the antilynching campaign. But he also recognized that the Neal lynching was an ideal test case for the interstate kidnapping law. Authorities had apprehended the suspect in Florida and carried him to Alabama, but before the NAACP could even request a federal investigation, the Department of Justice announced publicly that the Lindbergh law did not apply to lynching cases.

In paragraphs 16–22, White describes the NAACP's reaction to a highly publicized crime conference sponsored by the Department of Justice. Despite White's intensive lobbying and the upsurge in lynchings during the early 1930s, the Department of Justice refused to include mob violence on the agenda.

Despite this setback, President Roosevelt spoke out forcefully against lynching. Faced with mounting pressure from antilynching activists, the president could not ignore lynching altogether. As Roosevelt rallied support for his New Deal programs, he walked a fine line between alienating his powerful southern allies and offending his growing number of African American supporters. His lynching statement at the crime conference was intended to reassure his black supporters without committing himself to any actions that would anger southern Democrats.

When the Department of Justice denied repeated requests to address the lynching problem, civil rights activists took to the streets. Local police responded by arresting the picketers outside the Justice Department, but the protest yielded tangible results. The attorney general invited African American representatives to participate in the conference and suggested that they could bring up lynching during an informal discussion session. When the conference coordinators backed off this promise, the local NAACP resumed its protest outside of the conference.

The willingness of the NAACP to stage peaceful protests reveals another dimension to the antilynching campaign. Decades before nonviolent protests hit the television screens, civil rights activists employed nonviolent measures to publicize their cause. In the antilynching protests outside the 1934 crime conference, activists carefully planned a public action that would dramatize the lynching problem. Because policemen had arrested early picketers under sign and parade laws, the second round of protestors planned a perfectly legal public action. Standing silently with lynching ropes looped around their necks and small signs pinned to their chests, the protestors forced the conference delegates to confront the reality of lynching even if they refused to discuss it. The spectacle finally forced the conference participants to adopt a vague resolution that did not name lynching specifically but conceded that racial violence was illegal and wrong.

In the closing three paragraphs, White makes clear that the moral victory at the crime conference did little to ease the bitterness and frustration of the antilynching movement. Less than three months after the conference, another lynching occurred that involved an interstate abduction. White concludes his article with the bitter admission that the Department of Justice remained reluctant to use its enforcement powers to protect African Americans from mob violence.

Essential Themes

White's account of the NAACP's efforts to persuade the federal government to adopt antilynching laws or, at the very least, prosecute perpetrators of lynchings for other crimes they committed in the process, such as kidnapping, is a valuable study in the politics of civil rights. The political implications that limited even sympathetic politicians' desire to take concerted action are an oft overlooked factor during this period. As White describes it, President Roosevelt was not "pro lynching," but, rather, did not view it as a significant enough problem to risk derailing the New Deal legislation he believed was necessary "to keep America from collapsing." In addition to the President's inaction, White's piece demonstrates that he (and others) were clearly skeptical that the Department of Justice would suddenly reverse its stance on lynching. He firmly believed, however, that the campaign against mob violence depended on publicity and propaganda. Every piece of literature he produced was meant to turn up the heat on government officials by increasing the public outcry against lynching.

While this particular article appeared in an African American publication, White knew that it would also be quoted or reprinted in other newspapers and magazines. Earlier in his career, many white publications had refused to publish White's articles on lynching. But by 1935 White had recruited influential white allies. Mainstream newspapers and magazines followed suit, publishing articles similar to this one. Walter White did more than any other activist to bring about this slow but significant transformation in public attitudes toward mob violence. No single person was more influential in making lynching a national political issue, and articles like "U.S. Department of (White) Justice" were a crucial part of White's crusade.

———*Jason Morgan Ward*

Bibliography and Additional Reading

Dray, Philip. *At the Hands of Persons Unknown: The Lynching of Black America.* (New York: Random House, 2002).

Dyja, Thomas. *Walter White: The Dilemma of Black Identity in America.* (Chicago: Ivan R. Dee, 2008).

Pfeifer, Michael J. *Rough Justice: Lynching and American Society, 1874–1947.* (Urbana: University of Illinois Press, 2004).

Pfeifer, Michael J. (ed.), *Lynching Beyond Dixie: American Mob Violence Outside the South.* (Urbana, IL: University of Illinois Press, 2013).

Sitkoff, Harvard. *A New Deal for Blacks: The Emergence of Civil Rights as a National Issue during the Depression Decade.* New York: Oxford University Press, 1978.

White, Walter. *A Man Called White: The Autobiography of Walter White.* (Athens, Georgia: University of Georgia Press, 1995).

Web Sites

Without Sanctuary: Photographs and Postcards of Lynching in America Web site. http://www.withoutsanctuary.org/main.html

"Jim Crow Stories: Walter White." PBS "The Rise and Fall of Jim Crow" Web site. http://www.pbs.org/wnet/jimcrow/stories_people_white.html

"A Black Inventory of the New Deal"

Date: 1935
Author: John P. Davis
Genre: Essay

Summary Overview

John Preston Davis's essay "A Black Inventory of the New Deal" is a scathing indictment of President Franklin Delano Roosevelt's early programs to combat the economic woes of the Great Depression. Published in May of 1935 in *The Crisis*, the magazine of the National Association for the Advancement of Colored People (NAACP), this essay challenged African Americans to create their own solutions to their dire economic situation rather than relying on a government that had systematically failed to come through for them.

Davis's essay was published at the time of a conference held at Howard University in Washington, D.C., titled "The Position of the Negro in Our National Economic Crisis." The conference was organized by Davis and Ralph Bunche, who was a professor of political science at Howard University and would later become a key architect of the United Nations. Like Davis, most of the participants in the conference were highly critical of Roosevelt's New Deal, noting that the government programs had severely negative impacts on African Americans. "A Black Inventory of the New Deal" serves as a reminder that oft-celebrated historical achievements have not always included all Americans.

Davis's critique of Roosevelt's New Deal programs gained him increased recognition as a black activist and leader. It also positioned him at odds with the more conservative African American figures who sought to work within the Roosevelt administration to effect change.

Defining Moment

African Americans suffered immensely during the great depression. Black tenant farmers in the South languished as crop prices fell, and black workers in the industrial North were the first to be let go as the unemployment rate climbed. President Franklin D. Roosevelt's Democratic administration showed signs of promise for the plight of African Americans. In the summer of 1933, Roosevelt created a position for a special adviser on "the economic status of negroes" to serve under the secretary of the Department of the Interior. The government also initiated programs to provide direct relief to the public. Two of these important programs were initiated, respectively, by the Agricultural Adjustment Act (AAA) and the National Industrial Recovery Act (NIRA), both passed in 1933.

It soon became apparent, however, that these two programs had considerable flaws. One component of the NIRA was to develop industry-specific standards that would govern competition, pricing, wages, and work hours in each industry. However, as business leaders worked with government representatives, it became clear that African Americans were being systematically discriminated against. Black workers in Atlanta, Georgia, protested against the industrial codes in August of 1933. Southern business interests, however, won concessions from the government that perpetuated racial discrimination.

Similarly, the AAA harmed black farmers, who farmed as tenants, or sharecroppers who did not own their own land. In order to increase farmers' income, the government paid farmers incentives to leave land unfarmed. Unfortunately, southern landowners fired their black tenant farmers first, as fewer crops grown meant fewer farmers needed. Just as black workers in the North protested against the NIRA, tenant farmers in the South, black and white, joined together to form the Southern Tenant Farmers Union in 1934, bringing the plight of African American farmers to the public's attention.

In 1935 unemployment was a staggering 20 percent, and the promises of the Roosevelt administration appeared unfulfilled.

Author Biography

John Preston Davis was born on January 19, 1905, and grew up in Washington, D.C. Davis participated in the artistic and literary movement known as the Harlem Renaissance, replacing W. E. B. Du Bois as editor of *The Crisis* magazine. Davis received a master's degree in journalism from Harvard University in 1927 and served as Fisk University's director of publicity until 1928. He went on to earn a law degree from Harvard in 1933.

Davis and several of his peers at Harvard grew increasingly concerned with the U.S. government's response to the deepening economic crisis that was the Great Depression. In the summer of 1933 Davis and his colleague Robert Weaver traveled back to their hometown of Washington, D.C., in order to give voice to the plight of African Americans. They created the Negro Industrial League to call for equitable treatment of black Americans in New Deal programs. Davis and Weaver's example led many civil rights organizations to form the Joint Committee on National Recovery, an organization dedicated to exposing racial injustice in the implementation of federal programs. In 1934 the NAACP sent Davis to the South to interview black farmers, an experience that exposed Davis to the inequalities of the New Deal program that resulted from the AAA.

In 1935, Davis became executive secretary of the National Negro Congress, which he had helped found. The organization sought to unite African Americans across class lines and involved the support of the Communist Party. This affiliation became a political liability following the Nazi-Soviet Nonaggression Pact of 1939, and more conservative organizations withdrew from the National Negro Congress. Davis remained its executive secretary until 1942. The next year he filed the first lawsuit in Washington, D.C., to challenge the district's segregated school system. Later in life, Davis turned to the literary world once again, founding *Our World*—a magazine dedicated to the African American community—in 1946, and publishing *The American Negro Reference Book* in 1964. He died on September 11, 1973.

HISTORICAL DOCUMENT

It is highly important for the Negro citizen of America to take inventory of the gains and losses which have come to him under the "New Deal." The Roosevelt administration has now had two years in which to unfold itself. Its portents are reasonably clear to anyone who seriously studies the varied activities of its recovery program. We can now state with reasonable certainty what the "New Deal" means for the Negro.

At once the most striking and irrefutable indication of the effect of the New Deal on the Negro can be gleaned from relief figures furnished by the government itself. In October, 1933, six months after the present administration took office, 2,117,000 Negroes were in families receiving relief in the United States. These represented 17.8 per cent of the total Negro population as of the 1930 census. In January, 1935, after nearly two years of *recovery measures*, 3,500,000 Negroes were in families receiving relief, or 29 per cent of our 1930 population. Certainly only a slight portion of the large increase in the number of impoverished Negro families can be explained away by the charitable, on the grounds that relief administration has become more humane. As a matter of fact federal relief officials themselves admit that grave abuses exist in the administration of rural relief to Negroes. And this is reliably borne out by the disproportionate increase in the number of urban Negro families on relief to the number of rural Negro families on relief. Thus the increase in the number of Negroes in relief families is an accurate indication of the deepening of the economic crisis for black America.

The promise of N.R.A. to bring higher wages and increased employment to industrial workers has glimmered away. In the code-making process occupational and geographical differentials at first were used as devices to exclude from the operation of minimum wages and maximum hours the bulk of the Negro workers. Later, clauses basing code wage rates on the previously existing wage differential between Negro and white workers tended to continue the inferior status of the Negro. For the particular firms, for whom none of these devices served as an effective means of keeping down Negro wages, there is an easy way out through the securing of an exemption specifically relating to the *Negro* worker in the plant. Such exemptions are becoming more numerous as time goes on. Thus from the beginning relatively few Negro workers were even theoretically covered by N.R.A. labor provisions.

But employers did not have to rely on the code-making process. The Negro worker not already discriminated against through code provisions had many other gauntlets to run. The question of importance to him as to all workers was, "as a result of all of N.R.A.'s maneuvers will I be able to buy more?" The answer has been "No." A worker cannot eat a wage rate. To determine what this wage rate means to him we must determine a number of other factors. Thus rates for longshoremen seem relatively high. But when we realize that the average amount of work a longshoreman receives during the year is from ten to fifteen weeks, the wage rate loses much of its significance. When we add to that fact the increase in the cost of living—as high as 40 per cent in many cases—the wage rate becomes even more chimerical. For other groups of industrial workers increases in cost of living, coupled with the part time and irregular nature of the work, make the results of N.R.A. negligible. In highly mechanized industries speed-up and stretch-out nullify the promised result of N.R.A. to bring increased employment through shorter hours. For the workers are now producing more in their shorter work periods than in the longer periods before N.R.A. There is less employment. The first sufferer from fewer jobs is the Negro worker. Finally the complete break-down of compliance machinery in the South has cancelled the last minute advantage to Negro workers which N.R.A.'s enthusiasts may have claimed.

The Agricultural Adjustment Administration has used cruder methods in enforcing poverty on the Negro farm population. It has made violations of the rights of tenants under crop reduction contracts easy; it has rendered enforcement of these rights impossible. The reduction of the acreage under cultivation through the government rental agreement rendered unnecessary large numbers of tenants and farm laborers. Although the contract with the government provided that the land owner should not reduce the number of his tenants, he did so. The federal courts have now refused to allow tenants to enjoin such evictions. Faced with this Dred Scott decision against farm tenants, the A.A.A. has remained discreetly silent. Farm laborers are now jobless by the hundreds of thousands, the conservative government estimate of the decline in agricultural employment for the year 1934 alone being a quarter of a million. The larger portion of these are unskilled Negro agricultural workers—now without income and unable to secure work or relief.

But the unemployment and tenant evictions occasioned by the crop reduction policies of the A.A.A. is not all. For the tenants and sharecroppers who were retained on the plantations the government's agricultural program meant reduced income. Wholesale fraud on tenants in the payment of parity checks occurred. Tenants complaining to the Department of Agriculture in Washington have their letters referred back to the locality in which they live and trouble of serious nature often results. Even when this does not happen, the tenant fails to get his check. The remainder of the land he tills on shares with his landlord brings him only the most meagre necessities during the crop season varying from three to five months. The rest of the period for him and his family is one of "root hog or die."

The past year has seen an extension of poverty even to the small percentage (a little more than 20 per cent) of Negro farmers who own their own land. For them compulsory reduction of acreage for cotton and tobacco crops, with the quantum of such reduction controlled and regulated by local boards on which they have no representation, has meant drastic reduction of their already low income. Wholesale confiscation of the income of the Negro cotton and tobacco farmer is being made by prejudiced local boards in the South under the very nose of the federal government. In the wake of such confiscation has come a tremendous increase in land tenantry as a result of foreclosures on Negro-owned farm properties.

Nor has the vast public works program, designed to give increased employment to workers in the building trades, been free from prejudice. State officials in the South are in many cases in open rebellion against the ruling of P.W.A. that the same wage scales must be paid to Negro and white labor. Compliance with this paper ruling is enforced in only rare cases. The majority of the instances of violation of this rule are unremedied. Only unskilled work is given Negroes on public works projects in most instances. And even here discrimination in employment is notorious. Such is bound to be the case when we realize that there are only a handful of investigators available to seek enforcement.

Recently a move has been made by Negro officials in the administration to effect larger employment of Negro skilled and unskilled workers on public works projects by specifying that failure of a contractor to pay a certain percentage of his payroll to Negro artisans will be evidence of racial discrimination. Without doubting the good intentions of the sponsors of this ingenious scheme, it must nevertheless be pointed out that it fails to meet the problem in a number of vital particulars. It has yet to face a test in the courts, even if one is willing to suppose that P.W.A. high officials will bring it to a test. Percentages thus far experimented with are far too low and the number of such experiments far too few to make an effective dent in the unemployment conditions of Negro construction industry workers. Moreover the scheme gives aid and comfort to employer-advocates of strike-breaking and the open shop; and, while offering, perhaps, some temporary relief to a few hundred Negro workers, it establishes a dangerous precedent which throws back the labor movement and the organization of Negro workers to a considerable degree. The scheme, whatever its Negro sponsors may hope to contrary, becomes therefore only another excuse for their white superiors maintaining a "do-nothing" policy with regard to discrimination against Negroes in the Public Works Administration.

The Negro has no pleasanter outlook in the long term social planning ventures of the new administration. Planning for subsistence homesteads for industrially stranded workers has been muddled enough even without consideration of the problem of integrating Negroes into such plans. Subsistence Homesteads projects are overburdened with profiteering prices for the homesteads and foredoomed to failure by the lack of planning for adequate and permanent incomes for prospective homesteaders.

In callous disregard of the interdiction in the constitution of the United States against use of federal funds for projects which discriminate against applicants solely on the ground of color, subsistence homesteads have been planned on a strictly "lily-white" basis. The more than 200 Negro applicants for the first project at Arthurdale, West Virginia were not even considered, Mr. Bushrod Grimes (then in charge of the project) announcing that the project was to be open only to "native white stock." As far north as Dayton, Ohio, where state laws prohibit any type of segregation against Negroes, the federal government has extended its "lily-white" policy. Recently it has established two Jim-Crow projects for Negroes. Thus the new administration seeks in its program of social planning to perpetuate ghettoes of Negroes for fifty years to come.

An even more blatant example of this policy of "lily-white" reconstruction is apparent in the planning of the model town of Norris, Tennessee, by the Tennessee Valley Authority. This town of 450 model homes is intended for the permanent workers on Norris Dam. The homes are rented by the federal government, which at all times maintains title to the land and dwellings and has complete control of the town management. Yet officials at T.V.A. openly admit that no Negroes are allowed at Norris.

T.V.A. has other objectionable features. While Negro employment now approaches an equitable proportion of total employment, the payroll of Negro workers remains disproportionately lower than that of whites. While the government has maintained a trade school to train workers on the project, no Negro trainees have been admitted. Nor have any meaningful plans matured for the future of the several thousand Negro workers who in another year or so will be left without employment, following completion of work on the dams being built by T.V.A.

None of the officials of T.V.A. seems to have the remotest idea of how Negroes in the Tennessee Valley will be able to buy the cheap electricity which T.V.A. is designed to produce. They admit that standards of living of the Negro population are low, that the introduction of industry into the Valley is at present only a nebulous dream, that even if this eventuates there is no assurance that Negro employment will result. The fairest summary that can be made of T.V.A. is that for a year or so it has furnished bread to a few thousand Negro workers. Beyond that everything is conjecture which is most unpleasant because of the utter planlessness of those in charge of the project.

Recovery legislation of the present session of Congress reveals the same fatal flaws which have been noted in the operation of previous recovery ventures. Thus, for example, instead of genuine unemployment insurance we have the leaders of the administration proposing to exclude from their plans domestic and agricultural workers, in which classes are to be found 15 out of every 23 Negro workers. On every hand the New Deal has used slogans for the same raw deal.

The sharpening of the crisis for Negroes has not found them unresponsive. Two years of increasing hardship has seen strange movement among the masses. In Chicago, New York, Washington and Baltimore the struggle for jobs has given rise to action on the part of a number of groups seeking to boycott white employers who refuse to employ Negroes. "Don't Buy Where You Can't Work" campaigns are springing up everywhere. The crisis has furnished renewed vigor to the Garvey Movement. And proposals for a 49th State are being seriously considered by various groups.

In sharp contrast with these strictly racial approaches to the problem, have been a number of interracial approaches. Increasing numbers of unemployed groups have been organized under radical leadership and have picketed relief stations for bread. Sharecroppers unions, under Socialist leadership in Arkansas, have shaken America into a consciousness of the growing resentment of southern farm tenants and the joint determination of the Negro and white tenants to do something about their intolerable condition.

In every major strike in this country Negro union members have fought with their white fellow workers in a struggle for economic survival. The bodies of ten Negro strikers killed in such strike struggles offer mute testimony to this fact. Even the vicious policies of the leaders of the A. F. of L. in discrimination against Negro workers is breaking down under the pressure for solidarity from the ranks of whites.

This heightening of spirit among all elements of black America and the seriousness of the crisis for them make doubly necessary the consideration of the social and economic condition of the Negro at this time. It was a realization of these conditions which gave rise to the proposal to hold a national conference on the economic status of Negroes under the New Deal at Howard University in Washington, D.C., on May 18, 19 and 20. At this conference, sponsored by the Social Science Division of Howard University and the Joint Committee on National Recovery, a candid and intelligent survey of the social and economic condition of the Negro will be made.

Unlike most conference it will not be a talk-rest. For months nationally known economists and other technicians have been working on papers to be presented. Unlike other conferences it will not be a one-sided affair. Ample opportunity will be afforded for high government officials to present their views of the "New Deal." Others not connected with the government, including representatives of radical political parties, will also appear to present their conclusions. Not the least important phase will be the appearance on the platform of Negro workers and farmers themselves to offer their own experience under the New Deal. Out of such a conference can and will come a clear-cut analysis of the problems faced by Negroes and the nation.

But a word of caution ought to be expressed with regard to this significant conference. In the final analysis it cannot and does not claim to be representative of the mass opinion of Negro citizen[s] in America. All it can claim for itself is that it will bring together on a non-representative basis well informed Negro and white technicians to discuss the momentous problem it has chosen as its topic. It can furnish a base for action for any organization which chooses to avail itself of the information developed by it. It cannot act itself.

Thus looking beyond such a conference one cannot fail to hope that it will furnish impetus to a national expression of black America demanding a tolerable solution to the economic evils which it suffers. Perhaps it is not too much to hope that public opinion may be moulded by this conference to such an extent that already existing church, civic, fraternal, professional and trade union organizations will see the necessity for concerted effort in forging a mighty arm of protest against injustice suffered by the Negro. It is not necessary that such organizations agree on every issue. On the problem of relief of Negroes from poverty there is little room for disagreement. The important thing is that throughout America as never before Negroes awake to the need for a unity of action on vital economic problems which perplex us.

Such a hope is not lacking in foundation upon solid ground. Such an instance as the All India Congress of British India furnishes an example of what repressed groups can do to better their social and economic status. Perhaps a *"National Negro Congress"* of delegates from thousands of Negro organizations (and white organizations willing to recognize their unity of interest) will furnish a vehicle for channeling public opinion of black America. One thing is certain: the Negro may stand still but the depression will not. And unless there is concerted action of Negroes throughout the nation the next two years will bring even greater misery to the millions of underprivileged Negro toilers in the nation.

GLOSSARY

A.F. of L.: the American Federation of Labor, an umbrella organization for labor unions

Agricultural Adjustment Administration: a federal agency created by the Agricultural Adjustment Act that paid farmers to reduce crop production to raise prices

All India Congress of British India: the All India Congress Committee, which led the struggle for Indian independence from British rule

code-making process: a reference to Title I, Section 3, of the National Industrial Recovery Act, which permitted trade or industrial associations to seek presidential approval of codes of fair competition

Dred Scott decision: a reference to the 1858 U.S. Supreme Court decision in *Dred Scott v. Sandford*, which denied citizenship rights to African Americans

Garvey Movement: a reference to the black nationalism of Marcus Garvey, the founder of the United Negro Improvement Association

homestead: land acquired from U.S. public lands by filing a record and living on and cultivating it

New Deal: the name given to the legislative programs of the Franklin Roosevelt administration to alleviate the effects of the Great Depression

N.R.A. the National Recovery Administration, created by the National Industrial Recovery Act; enacted changes in the American economy but was declared unconstitutional in 1935

open shop: place of employment where the employee is not required to join or pay dues to a labor union as a condition of hiring or continued employment

P.W.A. Public Works Administration: a New Deal agency created to provide funds for public-works projects to increase employment during the Great Depression

relief: welfare payments

Document Analysis

Davis begins by systematically evaluating key measures enacted by the government, showing how they have had mostly negative effects on black Americans. Davis cites government statistics demonstrating that the number of black families receiving aid increased during Roosevelt's time in office, arguing that the administration's policies have created more poverty among African Americans.

Davis states that the National Recovery Administration as yet failed to improve wages and hiring conditions arguing that during the development of the industrial "code," companies in the South were excluding black workers from the protective features of the labor codes, fighting the idea of national wage standards. While the federal intent behind the codes was to eliminate racial bias in wages and hours for each industry, its implementation resulted in the continuation of "the inferior status of the Negro." Even with an increased wage, African American workers were still disproportionately affected by layoffs or the reduction of work hours. The rising cost of living (one of the by-products of the codes was that the prices for food and other necessities were set above market value) disproportionately affected poor Americans, including African Americans.

Davis next turns his attention to the Agricultural Adjustment Act and Agency. The act allowed the secretary of agriculture to reduce the production of a given commodity through the use of incentives. The goal of the program was to prop up the prices of agricultural products and thus help raise the income and buying power of farmers. Davis argues that it actually worsened the farmers' plight. Uncultivated land meant fewer farmers were needed to tend to crops, and black sharecroppers were the first to be turned out. In the South, implementation of these policies was often corrupt. The government mandated that landowners pay a portion of the government incentive for crop reduction to its tenants, but many landowners simply kept all of the money for themselves. Local authorities refused to enforce the law.

Davis then takes up the Public Works Administration (PWA), a job-creation program designed to put people to work building roads, dams, bridges, and other infrastructure. While all PWA contracts had to include a nondiscrimination clause, southern interests found ways to circumvent this. The quota system developed to aid in enforcement, under which PWA contract recipients would be required to hire a minimum percentage of black skilled workers based on the proportion of such workers in the local population, had several problems. These included the tensions placed on unions.

The PWA and other New Deal programs also funded public housing. Most of these housing projects were segregated, upholding the status quo of racial inequality in America. Davis criticizes two specific programs: the Subsistence Homestead projects and the Tennessee Valley Authority (TVA) model towns. Part of the NIRA, the Subsistence Homesteads were designed to be communities based on the older American idea of the family subsistence farm, where families grew enough to sustain themselves but not to bring cash crops to market. However, the earliest communities were designated for whites only. In particular, the Arthurdale project in West Virginia, mentioned by Davis in paragraph 11, aroused virulent protest from civil rights activists.

The TVA also built segregated communities. Part of the TVA's development program included the creation of housing in planned communities based on a social vision similar to that of the Subsistence Homestead program. The TVA model communities were to be examples of self-contained, self-sustaining rural towns tied to cooperative industries. Norris, Tennessee, was one such community. As Davis notes, Norris functioned more as a "company town" for workers building the Norris Dam; the government supplied housing and power, ran the town store, and controlled all aspects of town life, not to mention providing the monthly paycheck. While the all-black Dayton communities were "ghettoes," Norris was "lily-white," designated as a whites-only town.

Davis refers to the debates over the new Social Security legislation and contends that parts of these laws that would exclude certain workers (such as agricultural workers) would unfairly target the black population.

Davis discusses how the black community has responded to this litany of injustice, such as the "Don't Buy Where You Can't Work" campaigns, which began in Chicago in 1929 but spread to many cities by the mid-1930s which encouraged African Americans to boycott establishments that refused to hire blacks. He also mentions the Garvey Movement and The National Movement for Establishment of a 49th State, both early examples of black separatism. He also goes on to highlight interracial protests, often backed by the Communist Party, which organized Unemployed Councils, radical groups that employed a variety of tactics to demand relief. Bread riots, street demonstrations, and rent strikes were commonplace in cities such as New

York and Detroit. He also notes the interracial nature of labor activism.

At the end of his essay, Davis points to the future. He comments on the upcoming conference at Howard University and calls for existing organizations from a variety of sectors to come together. He uses the All India Congress as an example of such an organization. Divided by caste and religious differences, India overcame such differences to achieve independence and serve as a model for other repressed groups. Davis pointedly states that African Americans are responsible for overcoming their own divisions and must take responsibility for solving the economic and social problems that face them.

Essential Themes

While African Americans might have supported Roosevelt and his party, many were growing more and more disillusioned with the administration's unproductive policies. John P. Davis's "A Black Inventory of the New Deal" gave voice to the increasingly urgent demand from the black community for tangible strides to be made in America's move toward racial equality. It is with historical hindsight that Davis's essay has become important for a wider American audience. This document catalogs what are now well-established negative effects of New Deal programs on the African American community, effects that were minimized by many in the government and the public in 1935. One of the lasting impacts of this essay is its reminder to modern audiences that even the most well intentioned of public policies can sometimes have negative consequences for some citizens.

——*Karen Linkletter*

Bibliography and Additional Reading

Fishel, Leslie H., Jr. "The Negro in the New Deal Era." *Wisconsin Magazine of History* 8, no. 2 (Winter 1964–1965): 111–126.

Hamilton, Donna Cooper. "The National Association for the Advancement of Colored People and New Deal Reform Legislation: A Dual Agenda." *Social Service Review* 68, no. 4 (December 1994): 488–502.

Sitkoff, Harvard. *A New Deal for Blacks: The Emergence of Civil Rights as a National Issue: The Depression Decade.* (New York: Oxford University Press, 1981).

Sullivan, Patricia. *Days of Hope: Race and Democracy in the New Deal Era.* (Chapel Hill: University of North Carolina Press, 1996).

Call to Negro America to March on Washington

Date: 1941
Author: A. Phillip Randolph
Genre: Press release

Summary Overview

In the May 1941 issue of Black Worker, A. Philip Randolph, a prominent civil rights leader in his capacity as president of the National Negro Congress and head of the Brotherhood of Sleeping Car Porters labor union, issued a "Call to Negro America to March on Washington" to demand an end to discrimination in the defense industry and in the military. His call, made in cooperation with the civil rights leaders Bayard Rustin and A. J. Muste, initiated the March on Washington Movement, which lasted until 1947. This movement influenced future civil rights leaders such as Martin Luther King, Jr., who joined with Randolph in 1963 to organize the historic March on Washington for Jobs and Freedom (where King made his famous "I Have a Dream" speech). Randolph's "call to Negro America" took place in the context of America's transition from the Great Depression of the 1930s to the wartime economy that would employ millions of industrial workers during World War II.

Ultimately, the march Randolph envisioned never took place. Under pressure from civil rights leaders and out of his recognition that the United States would need all the manpower it could muster in the coming years, President Franklin Delano Roosevelt issued an executive order banning racial discrimination in the defense industries and in the federal government. Accordingly, the number of African Americans employed in defense industries and government swelled, although the armed forces remained segregated throughout World War II. It would fall to Roosevelt's successor, President Harry S. Truman, to desegregate the military by executive order in 1948—in large part because of the efforts of the Committee against Jim Crow in Military Service and Training, which Randolph founded.

Defining Moment

During the Great Depression of the 1930s, African Americans were initially skeptical of President Franklin Roosevelt's "New Deal," Various provisions in these laws and the agencies they created continued a pattern of discrimination against African AmericansOver the course of the decade, though, some progress was made.

By 1939 African Americans were beginning to benefit from New Deal programs, and their income from public sector employment was almost as large as their income in the private sector. Helping to spur this modest growth in black income was the union movement.

The position of unemployed African American workers in the late 1930s, however, remained dire. As the nation was emerging from the depression, white workers were able to return to full-time employment, but black workers continued to rely on relief programs and public sector jobs, primarily in construction and infrastructure building. However, war clouds were gathering over the horizon. On September 1, 1939, World War II began in Europe when Nazi Germany invaded Poland. In preparation for the possibility of war, the United States instituted a peacetime draft, and under the Lend-Lease program, begun in 1941, the U.S. government began sending military supplies to England, China, Russia, and Brazil.

As the nation mobilized for the possibility of war, the unemployment rate fell below 10 percent for the first time since 1932. Industrial output was up in a variety of defense-related industries such as ship-building. African Americans, however, were getting only a handful of the new jobs being created. Accordingly, on January 15, 1941, labor and civil rights leader A. Philip Randolph issued a press release in which he called on African Americans to protest this inequity by marching on Washington.

The date of the proposed march was to be July 1, 1941. The Roosevelt administration, alarmed by the prospect of tens of thousands of protesters descending on the nation's capital, tried to dissuade Randolph from this course of action and call off the march. Randolph, however, remained steadfast, and in May of that year he redoubled his efforts with his "Call to Negro America to March on Washington for Jobs and Equal Participation in National Defense," published in the journal *Black Worker*.

Author Biography

Asa Philip Randolph was born on April 15, 1889, in Crescent City, Florida, the son of a Methodist minister. After graduating as valedictorian of his high school class in 1907, he moved to New York City with the early goal of becoming an actor; in Harlem, he organized a Shakespearean society and performed the lead role in several of Shakespeare's plays. During the 1910s he became a Socialist and began his earliest involvement in trade unionism. Along with his close friend and collaborator, Chandler Owen, he founded and edited *The Messenger*, a radical journal that espoused Socialism and trade unionism and urged African Americans to resist the military draft after the United States entered World War I.

During the 1920s Randolph's involvement in trade unionism intensified, and in 1925 he organized the Brotherhood of Sleeping Car Porters, the first black trade union. By the mid-1930s the union had over seven thousand members. For a decade Randolph and the union carried on bitter negotiations with the Pullman Company, which operated the sleeping and dining railroad cars on which black porters and maids worked—often for low wages, with no overtime pay. Finally, in 1935, the Brotherhood of Sleeping Car Porters was certified as the union that would represent the Pullman employees. Two years later the union reached an agreement with Pullman that provided workers with significant wage increases, overtime pay, and a shorter work week. Meanwhile, in 1936, Randolph was named the first president of the National Negro Congress.

In January 1941, as U.S. industrial output was increasing with the growing threat of American involvement in World War II, Randolph issued a call for a march on Washington, D.C., to demand equality of opportunity in the defense industries and in the U.S. military. He met with President Franklin Roosevelt in June of that year; as a result of that meeting, Roosevelt issued Executive Order 8802, which desegregated the defense industries and the federal government.

HISTORICAL DOCUMENT

We call upon you to fight for jobs in National Defense.

We call upon you to struggle for the integration of Negroes in the armed forces....

We call upon you to demonstrate for the abolition of Jim-Crowism in all Government departments and defense employment.

This is an hour of crisis. It is a crisis of democracy. It is a crisis of minority groups. It is a crisis of Negro Americans.

What is this crisis?

To American Negroes, it is the denial of jobs in Government defense projects. It is racial discrimination in Government departments. It is widespread Jim-Crowism in the armed forces of the Nation.

While billions of the taxpayers' money are being spent for war weapons, Negro workers are finally being turned away from the gates of factories, mines and mills—being flatly told, "Nothing Doing." Some employers refuse to give Negroes jobs when they are without "union cards," and some unions refuse Negro workers union cards when they are "without jobs."

What shall we do?
What a dilemma!
What a runaround!
What a disgrace!
What a blow below the belt!

Though dark, doubtful and discouraging, all is not lost, all is not hopeless. Though battered and bruised, we are not beaten, broken, or bewildered.

Verily, the Negroes' deepest disappointments and direst defeats, their tragic trials and outrageous oppressions in these dreadful days of destruction and disaster to democracy and freedom, and the rights of minority peoples, and the dignity and independence of the human spirit, is the Negroes' greatest opportunity to rise to the highest heights of struggle for freedom and justice in Government, in industry, in labor unions, education, social service, religion, and culture.

With faith and confidence of the Negro people in their own power for self-liberation, Negroes can break down the barriers of discrimination against employment in National Defense. Negroes can kill the deadly serpent of race hatred in the Army, Navy, Air and Marine Corps, and smash through and blast the Government, business and labor-union red tape to win the right to equal opportunity in vocational training and re-training in defense employment.

Most important and vital of all, Negroes, by the mobilization and coordination of their mass power, can cause President Roosevelt to Issue an Executive Order Abolishing Discriminations in All Government Department, Army, Navy, Air Corps and National Defense Jobs.

Of course, the task is not easy. In very truth, it is big, tremendous and difficult.

It will cost money.

It will require sacrifice.

It will tax the Negroes' courage, determination and will to struggle. But we can, must and will triumph.

The Negroes' stake in national defense is big. It consists of jobs, thousands of jobs. It may represent millions, yes, hundreds of millions of dollars in wages. It consists of new industrial opportunities and hope. This is worth fighting for.

But to win our stakes, it will require an "all-out," bold and total effort and demonstration of colossal proportions.

Negroes can build a mammoth machine of mass action with a terrific and tremendous driving and striking power that can shatter and crush the evil fortress of race prejudice and hate, if they will only resolve to do so and never stop, until victory comes.

Dear fellow Negro Americans, be not dismayed by these terrible times. You possess power, great power. Our problem is to harness and hitch it up for action on the broadest, daring and most gigantic scale.

In this period of power politics, nothing counts but pressure, more pressure, and still more pressure, through the tactic and strategy of broad, organized, aggressive mass action behind the vital and important issues of the Negro. To this end, we propose that ten thousand Negroes MARCH ON WASHINGTON FOR JOBS IN NATIONAL DEFENSE AND EQUAL INTEGRATION IN THE FIGHTING FORCES OF THE UNITED STATES.

An "all-out" thundering march on Washington, ending in a monster and huge demonstration at Lincoln's Monument will shake up white America.

It will shake up official Washington.

It will give encouragement to our white friends to fight all the harder by our side, with us, for our righteous cause.

It will gain respect for the Negro people.

It will create a new sense of self-respect among Negroes.

But what of national unity?

We believe in national unity which recognizes equal opportunity of black and white citizens to jobs in national defense and the armed forces, and in all other institutions and endeavors in America. We condemn all dictatorships, Fascist, Nazi and Communist. We are loyal, patriotic Americans all.

But if American democracy will not defend its defenders; if American democracy will not protect its protectors; if American democracy will not give jobs to its toilers because of race or color; if American democracy will not insure equality of opportunity, freedom and justice to its citizens, black and white, it is a hollow mockery and belies the principles for which it is supposed to stand....

Today we call on President Roosevelt, a great humanitarian and idealist, to...free American Negro citizens of the stigma, humiliation and insult of discrimination and Jim-Crowism in Government departments and national defense.

The Federal Government cannot with clear conscience call upon private industry and labor unions to abolish discrimination based on race and color as long as it practices discrimination itself against Negro Americans.

GLOSSARY

Fascist: a reference to right-wing authoritarian rule at the time in such places as Italy under Benito Mussolini

Jim-Crowism: from "Jim Crow," the term commonly used to refer to laws and social systems that kept African Americans in disadvantaged positions

Document Analysis

Randolph's "Call to Negro America to March on Washington for Jobs and Equal Participation in National Defense" is a highly rhetorical document consisting of a large number of short paragraphs and sentences that make his purpose absolutely clear. He sweeps his reader along with repetition and exclamations ("What a dilemma! What a runaround! What a disgrace!") and such literary devices as alliteration ("deepest disappointments and direst defeats…dreadful days of destruction and disaster to democracy")—all perhaps reflecting his early theatrical background. He announces his purpose in the opening paragraph of his address, where he says, "We call upon you to fight for jobs in National Defense. We call upon you to struggle for the integration of Negroes in the armed forces." He then condemns "Jim-Crowism," a reference to the pattern of discrimination and segregation that had existed since the nineteenth century and that kept African Americans in inferior social and economic positions; the phrase *Jim Crow* was taken from the name of a character in a popular nineteenth-century minstrel show.

Randolph stresses his view of the black employment situation as a "crisis," indeed, a "crisis of democracy." He goes on to note that African Americans are being systematically denied employment in the defense industries and that they are segregated in the U.S. military. Randolph was, of course, correct. In the early decades of the twentieth century, African Americans served primarily in menial and service jobs in the military. In the U.S. Navy and Marine Corps, for example, African Americans were pushed into the Steward's Branch, where they worked as cooks and waiters in officers' mess halls. During World War II they fought in segregated units; the few black officers commanded segregated African American units. Many military officers argued that integrating units, and thus having blacks and whites serve side by side, would result in conflict and low morale. Randolph then goes on to point out that African American workers were caught on the horns of a dilemma: They could not get jobs because there were not members of unions, and they could not gain union membership because they were without jobs.

Midway into the essay, Randolph begins to express hope that the situation can be remedied; he foresees black Americans rising from their current position to new heights of achievement in the "struggle for freedom and justice in Government, in industry, in labor unions, education, social service, religion, and culture." He then asserts that African Americans, through "their own power for self-liberation," can break down "barriers of discrimination" and slay the "deadly serpent of race hatred" in the military, government, labor unions, and industry. Here, Randolph calls for efforts to provide unskilled African American workers with job training that will enable them to make a contribution.

Randolph also takes up a potential objection to the proposed march on Washington. Critics would argue that such a march at such a time, with war looming, might affect national unity. Randolph rejects this argument, arguing instead that "we believe in national unity which recognizes equal opportunity of black and white citizens." The paragraph goes on to reject all forms of dictatorship, including Fascism, Nazism, and Communism, and to emphasize that African Americans are "loyal, patriotic Americans all." Interestingly, early in his career, during World War I, Randolph had been arrested for breaking the 1917 Espionage Act because of the left-wing Socialist ideals he espoused in the journal he founded, *The Messenger*. By the late 1930s Randolph was muting his Socialist beliefs, and here he makes clear that he regards the Communist Soviet Union as a dictatorship.

In the final paragraphs Randolph sums up his views. He states that American democracy would be a "hollow mockery" if it failed to protect its protectors and to extend equality of opportunity to all citizens, black and white. He again calls on President Roosevelt to end "Jim-Crowism" in the military and in the defense industry and closes by stating that if the federal government is guilty of discrimination, it has forfeited the right to take industry and the labor unions to task for the same discrimination.

Essential Themes

Randolph is explicit in explaining what he wants: not just an end to discrimination in all areas of the national defense establishment. This encompasses equitable hiring practices, pay, and working conditions in America's industrial "Arsenal of Democracy" but also an end to discrimination within the fighting forces of the United States. Crucial to Philips's efforts his specific call for an executive order from the president that will put an end to discrimination in the defense industry and the military. In the latter part of the essay, he notes that efforts on the part of the black community to gain jobs will not be easy and will require money and sacrifice.

He calls on African Americans to take action, urging them to "build a mammoth machine of mass action" and to "harness and hitch" their power. He then arrives at his key goal: the organization of a march on Washington to demand economic equality. Randolph asserts that such a march will "shake up white America" and "shake up official Washington." Further, the massing of thousands of black demonstrators will give encouragement not only to African Americans but also to "our white friends" who fight for justice by the side of African Americans.

As noted earlier, while the march did not take place, the Roosevelt and Truman administrations did issue executive orders that spoke to Randolphs's concerns. While these efforts were, in many ways, flawed in the limited ways they could be implemented and enforced, this essay prefigures not only the civil rights gains that would be made in the 1940s and early 1950s within the national defense establishment, but also the wider story of the civil rights movement.

———Michael J. O'Neal, PhD

Bibliography and Additional Reading

Barnhill, J. Herschel. "Civil Rights in the 1940s." *Negro History Bulletin* 45, no. 1 (January–March 1982): 21–22.

Anderson, Jervis. *A. Philip Randolph: A Biographical Portrait*. Berkeley: University of California Press, 1986.

Garfinkel, Herbert. *When Negroes March: The March on Washington Movement in the Organizational Politics for FEPC*. New York: Atheneum, 1969.

Harris, William H. *The Harder We Run: Black Workers since the Civil War*. New York: Oxford University Press, 1982.

Kersten, Andrew E. *A. Philip Randolph: A Life in the Vanguard*. Lanham, Md. Rowman and Littlefield, 2007.

Miller, Calvin Craig. *A. Philip Randolph and the African American Labor Movement*. Greensboro, N.C. Morgan Reynolds, 2005.

Pfeffer, Paula F. *A. Philip Randolph, Pioneer of the Civil Rights Movement*. Baton Rouge: Louisiana State University Press, 1996.

Sternsher, Bernard, ed. *The Negro in Depression and War: Prelude to Revolution, 1930–1945*. Chicago, Ill. Quadrangle Books, 1969.

Taylor, Cynthia. *A. Philip Randolph: The Religious Journey of an African American Labor Leader*. New York: New York University Press, 2006.

Wolters, Raymond. *Negroes and the Great Depression: The Problem of Economic Recovery*. Westport, Conn. Greenwood Press, 1970.

Wright, Sarah E. *A. Philip Randolph: Integration in the Workplace*. Englewood Cliffs, N.J. Silver Burdett Press, 1990.

Web sites

Chenoweth, Karin. "Taking Jim Crow Out of Uniform: A. Philip Randolph and the Desegregation of the U.S. Military: Special Report: The Integrated Military—50 Years." *Diverse Issues in Higher Education* Web site. http://diverseeducation.com/article/8291/

"Executive Order 8802." TeachingAmericanHistory.org. http://teachingamericanhistory.org/library/index.asp?document=547

Randolph, A. Philip. "'The March on Washington Movement': Excerpts from Keynote Address to the Policy Conference of the March on Washington Movement, Detroit, Michigan, September 26, 1942." University of Maryland Web site. http://www.aasp.umd.edu/chateauvert/mowmcall.htm

An Appeal to the World

Date: 1947
Author: W. E. B. Du Bois
Genre: Petition

Summary Overview

In 1947, the National Association for the Advancement of Colored People sought the intervention of the United Nations in the ongoing condition of racial oppression against African Americans in the United States. In his groundbreaking introduction to the petition, W. E. B. Du Bois unequivocally outlines the ill treatment and oppression of blacks in America in detail and cites similar examples in other parts of the world. He emphasizes the hypocrisy of white America's so-called ideals of politics, philanthropy, and religion. Du Bois sounds a note of warning, saying that America's attitude could provoke a dangerous consequence in encouraging the aggression of smaller nations against their minorities. He states that these issues are not problems restricted to the United States but, indeed, are basic problems of humanity. It is this discussion of the effects of America's racial discrimination and legal segregation on the wider world that sets this appear apart from many other civil rights efforts that had taken place in previous years. The NAACP petition made this into a geopolitical issue as well as inserting the United States into the rapidly growing and contentious conversation about colonization and imperial exploitation of African and Asian nations by European powers. One result of the appeal was President Harry Truman's subsequent creation of the Committee on Civil Rights.

Defining Moment

The immediate postwar years of 1946–1948 witnessed the growth of vibrant African American groups, seeking ways for their grievances to be addressed by the Truman Administration. In May 1946 the National Negro Congress took the first initiative when the historian Herbert Aptheker was employed to write a brief description (in the form of a petition) of the political, social, and economic oppression African Americans faced domestically, in the hope that the United Nations would address the petition. The petition was dismissed on the ground that the United Nations lacked the authority to act in U.S. domestic affairs and could not accept petitions from non-state actors.

Du Bois, who was then the director of special research for the NAACP, made his own attempt to petition the UN General Assembly. Du Bois's words were not the first time that activists for racial justice had appealed to the broader international world. The abolition movement, for example, had strong connections to Great Britain in the nineteenth century and, as discussed above, the National Negro Congress had made a similar attempt just a year before. The NAACP petition, however, appeared at a time of significant change and transition. The Second World War had ended with the United States and the Soviet Union positioned as the two remaining major powers with other states—particularly the nations of Europe—coming under their diplomatic, military, and economic sway. Although the shape of the coming Cold War was not fully formed at this time, there was a greater fear of a collision between the east and west than even in 1946. In doing so, he assembled a team of legal experts to each write a chapter for a book-length petition covering the historical and current grievances of African Americans, which he himself edited. By September 1947, the NAACP's petition, formally titled *An Appeal to the World: A Statement on the Denial of Human Rights to Minorities and an Appeal to the United Nations for Redress*, was completed and approved by the NAACP board. Du Bois wrote the introduction to the petition.

Author Biography

William Edward Burghardt Du Bois was born on February 23, 1868, in Great Barrington, Massachusetts, and raised by his mother. In spite of the poverty of his childhood, Du Bois excelled in school and achieved one of the most impressive educations of his generation. He received bachelor degrees from Fisk University and Harvard University, pursued graduate work at Harvard and Germany's University of Berlin, and earned his PhD in history from Harvard in 1895. He received a faculty appointment at Wilberforce University in 1894, worked for the University of Pennsylvania on a study of blacks in Philadelphia in 1896, and joined the faculty of Atlanta University in 1897. In 1910 he left Atlanta and took a paid position as the director of publishing and research for the newly founded National Association for the Advancement of Colored People (NAACP).

He served in that position and also as the founding editor of the NAACP journal, the *Crisis*, subtitled *A Record of the Darker Races*, until 1934.

Following his departure from the NAACP, Du Bois returned to Atlanta University, retiring in 1943 and returning to the NAACP. Du Bois was clearly out of step with the civil rights organization; his increasingly leftist, pro-Soviet politics and his criticism both of U.S. foreign policy and of the NAACP director Walter White cost him his job in 1948. Du Bois became involved in leftist organizations, continued condemning the United States and its foreign policy while praising the Soviet Union, making him a target of the post–World War II "Red Scare" inspired by Senator Joseph McCarthy. He would make highly publicized visits to East Germany, the Soviet Union, and Communist China. In 1961, disillusioned with the United States, Du Bois formally joined the U.S. Communist Party before relocating to the newly independent nation of Ghana, becoming a citizen in 1963. On August 27, 1963, he died at the age of ninety-five.

HISTORICAL DOCUMENT

There are in the Unites States of America, fifteen millions or more of native-born citizens, something less than a tenth of the nation, who form largely a segregated caste, with restricted legal rights, and many illegal disabilities. They are descendants of the Africans brought to America during the sixteenth, seventeenth, eighteenth, and nineteenth centuries and reduced to slave labor. This group has no complete biological unity, but varies in color from white to black, and comprises a great variety of physical characteristics, since many are the offspring of white European-Americans as well as of Africans. Similarly, there is an equal and perhaps even larger number of white Americans who also descend from Negroes but who are not counted in the colored group nor subject to caste restrictions because the preponderance of white blood conceals their descent.

The so-called American Negro group, therefore, while it is in no sense absolutely set off physically from its fellow Americans, has nevertheless a strong, hereditary cultural unity, born of slavery, of common suffering, prolonged prescription and curtailment of political and civil rights; and especially because of economic and social disabilities. Largely from this fact have arisen their cultural gifts to America—their rhythm, music and folk-song; their religious faith and customs; their contribution to American art and literature; their defense of their country in every war, on land and sea; and especially the hard, continuous toil upon which the prosperity and wealth of this continent has largely been built.

The group has long been internally divided by dilemma as to whether its striving upward, should be aimed at strengthening its inner cultural and group bonds, both for intrinsic progress and for offensive power against caste; or whether it should seek escape wherever and however possible into the surrounding American culture. Decision in this matter has been largely determined by outer compulsion rather than inner plan; for rabid and prolonged policies of segregation and discrimination have involuntarily welded the mass almost into a nation within a nation with its own schools, churches, hospitals, newspapers, and often other business enterprises.

The result has been to make American Negroes to a wide extent provincial, introvertive, self-conscious, and narrowly race loyal; but it has also inspired them to frantic and often successful effort to achieve, to deserve, to show the world their capacity to share modern civilization. As a result there is almost no area of American civilization in which the Negro has not made credible showing in the face of all his handicaps.

If however the effect of the color caste system on the American Negro has been both good and bad, its effect on white America has been disastrous. It has repeatedly led the greatest modern attempt at democratic government to deny its political ideals, to falsify its philanthropic assertions, and to make its religion a vast hypocrisy. A nation which boldly declared "All men equal," proceeded to build its economy on chattel slavery; masters who declared race-mixture impossible, sold their own children into slavery and left a mulatto progeny which neither law nor science can today disentangle; churches which excused slavery as calling the heathen to God, refused to recognize the freedom of converts or admit them to equal communion. Sectional strife over the vast profits of slave labor and conscientious revolt against making human beings real estate led to bloody civil war, and to a partial emancipation of slaves which nevertheless even to this day is not complete. Poverty, ignorance, disease, and crime have been forced on these unfortunate victims of greed to an extent far beyond any social necessity; and a great nation, which today ought to be in the forefront of the march toward peace and democracy, finds itself continuously making common cause with race hate, prejudiced exploitation and oppression of the common man. Its high and noble words are tuned against it, because they are contradicted in every syllable by the treatment of the American Negro for three hundred and twenty-seven years.

In the Constitution of the United States, Negroes are referred to as fellows although the word "slave" is carefully avoided before the thirteenth amendment. Article I (1787) Section 2, apportionment of members of the House of Representatives: "Representatives and direct taxes shall be apportioned among the several States which may be included within this Union, according to their respective numbers, which shall be determined by adding to the whole number of free persons, including those bound to service for a term of years, and excluding Indians not taxed, three-fifths of all other persons." "Other persons" means Negro slaves. Article I, Section, 9 "The migration or importation of such persons as any of the States now existing shall think proper to admit, shall not be prohibited by the Congress prior to the year one thousand eight hundred and eight, but a tax or duty may be imposed on such importation, not exceeding ten dollars for each person." "Each person" refers to Negro slaves. Article IV, (1787) Section 2, "No person held to service or labor in one State, under the laws thereof, escaping into another, shall, in consequence of any law or regulation therein, be discharged from such service or labor, but shall be delivered upon claim of the party to whom such service or labor may be due." This refers particularly to fugitive slaves. Article XIII (1865) Section 1. "Neither slavery nor involuntary servitude, except as a punishment for crime, whereof the party shall have been duly convicted, shall exist within the United States, or any place subject to their jurisdiction. Section 2. Congress shall have power to enforce this article by appropriate legislation." Article XIV, (1868) Section 1. "All persons born or naturalized in the United States, and subject to the jurisdiction thereof, are citizens of the United States and of the State wherein they reside. No State shall make or enforce any law which shall abridge the privileges or immunities of citizens of the United States; nor shall any State deprive any person of life, liberty or property, without due process of law, not deny to any person within its jurisdiction the equal protection of the laws. Section 2. Representatives shall be apportioned among the several States according to their respective numbers, counting the whole number of persons in each State, excluding Indians not taxed. But when the right to vote at any election for the choice of electors for President and Vice-President of the United States, representatives in Congress, the executive or judicial offers of a State, or the members of the Legislature thereof, is denied to any of the male inhabitants of such State, being twenty-one years of age, and citizens of the United States, or in any way abridged, except for participation in rebellion or other crime, the basis of representation therein shall be reduced in the proportion which the number of such male citizens shall bear to the whole number of male citizens twenty-one years of age in such State. Section 3. No person shall be a senator or representative in Congress, or elector of President or Vice-President, or hold any office, civil or military, under the United States, or under any State, who having previously taken an oath as a member of Congress, or as an officer of the United States, or as a member of any State Legislature, or as an executive or judicial officer of any State, to support the Constitution of the United States, shall have engaged in insurrection or rebellion against the same, or given aid or comfort to the enemies thereof. But Congress may, by a vote of two-thirds of each house, remove such disability. Section 4. The validity of the public debt of the United States, authorized by law, including debts incurred for payment of pensions and bounties for services in suppressing insurrection or rebellion, shall not be questioned. But neither the United States nor any State shall assume or pay any debt or obligation incurred in aid of insurrection or rebellion against the

United States, or any claim for the loss or emancipation of any slave; but all such debts, obligations, and claims shall be held illegal and void. Section 5. The Congress shall have power to enforce, by appropriate legislation, the provisions of this article." Article XV, (1870) Section 1. "The rights of citizens of the United States to vote shall not be denied or abridged by the United States, or by any State, on account of race, color or previous condition of servitude. Section 2. The Congress shall have power to enforce this article by appropriate legislation."

We appeal to the world to witness that this attitude of America is far more dangerous to mankind than the Atom bomb; and far, far more clamorous for attention than disarmament or treaty. To disarm the hidebound minds of men is the only path to peace; and as long as Great Britain and the United States profess democracy with one hand and deny it to millions with the other, they convince none of their sincerity, least of all themselves. Not only that, but they encourage the aggression of smaller nations: so long as the Union of South Africa defends Humanity and lets two million whites enslave ten million colored people, its voice spells hypocrisy. So long as Belgium holds in both economic and intellectual bondage, a territory seventy-five times her own size and larger in population, no one can sympathize with her loss of dividends based on serf labor at twenty-five to fifty cents a day. Seven million "white" Australians cannot yell themselves into championship of democracy for seven hundred million Asiatics.

Therefore, Peoples of the World, we American Negroes appeal to you; our treatment in America is not merely an internal question of the United States. It is a basic problem of humanity; of democracy; of discrimination because of race and color; and as such it demands your attention and action. No nation is so great that the world can afford to let it continue to be deliberately unjust, cruel and unfair toward its own citizens.

This is our plea to the world; and to show its validity; we are presenting you with the proof. The National Association for the Advancement of Colored People, with more than a half million members, has asked four scholars under my editorship to present chapters showing in detail the status of American Negroes in the past and today, in law, administration and social condition; and the relation of this situation to the Charter of the United Nations.

GLOSSARY

caste: a legally defined system of hereditary classes

chattel slavery: a system of slavery in which slaves were considered the legal property of their masters

hidebound: conservative, unchanging

progeny: descendents

serf labor: work that is paid at a wage that is insufficient for workers to support themselves

Document Analysis

Du Bois begins his introduction to *An Appeal to the World* by outlining the basic situation in which African Americans found themselves in the late 1940s. While this opening paragraph may seem obvious, it is important to remember that the audiences for this was the United Nations. The various delegates from the member nations might not have a full or complete understanding of the history of racial discrimination in the United State nor the role that the legacy of slavery played in that history. He also highlights an important inconsistency in American segregation—that there are white Americans who have people of African descent in their ancestry but who, because of their skin color—are not subject to the same discrimination.

In the second paragraph, Du Bois explains that despite the physical diversity of the "American Negro group" there is a strong sense of cultural unity that stems from the common background of slavery and oppression. Ironically, this oppression has let to a number of cultural achievements as well as the steadfast and dedicated service—both military and economic—rendered by the descendants of America's slaves.

In the next paragraph, Du Bois explains the internal conflicts within the African American community non the best way to proceed. Should efforts be directed as developing cultural bonds "both for intrinsic progress and for offensive power" or to escaping into "the surrounding American culture"? Du Bois asserts that the rapid pace and thoroughness of the segregation agenda has force the creation of a "nation within a nation" as African Americans struggle to sustain separate businesses and cultural institutions. This oppression and segregation, according to Du Bois, has driven African Americans to demonstrate that they deserve political, economic, and social equality, leading to significant contributions to "American civilization."

Du Bois then turns to the effects of the "color caste system" on "white America." He argues that it has been disastrous, undermining the nation's political and religious ideals. Seizing on Jefferson's language of equality from the Declaration of Independence, Du Bois highlights the hypocrisy of the nation's developing its economy on the backs of slaves. The hypocrisy extended to the churches and led, eventually, to the Civil War and what Du Bois characterizes as a "partial emancipation of slaves which nevertheless even to this day is not complete." Poverty and crime affect African Americans in disproportionately great numbers.

Du Bois ends this paragraph with a final example of the hypocrisy engendered by the oppression and legal segregation of African Americans that would have been deeply familiar to the delegates to the United Nations General Assembly in 1947. Du Bois argues that the United States is "a great nation, which today ought to be in the forefront of the march toward peace and democracy." What is particularly telling about this is the word "ought." Certainly, in 1947, the leaders of the United States were certainly presenting themselves to the world as being "in the forefront" of democracy, presenting itself to both its western allies and potential allies such as Turkey and Greece as the democratic and peaceful alternative to the totalitarian and aggressive Soviet Union. Despite this Assertion, the nation "finds itself continuously making common cause with race hate, prejudiced exploitation and oppression of the common man. Its high and noble words are tuned against it, because they are contradicted in every syllable by the treatment of the American Negro for three hundred and twenty-seven years." What Du Bois is doing, in this section, is publicly undermining the American image of its role in the post-war world by exposing the lie at the heart of the American dream of equality and justice.

In the next—very long—paragraph, Du Bois explicates the treatment of race and slavery in the US Constitution and its amendments. He begins with the original document, with its requirement that Congress enact a fugitive slave law and the three-fifths clause which allowed southern states to take advantage of their slave ownership to receive political power. He moves then into the 13th, 14th, and 15th amendments—ratified following the Civil War that ended slavery (13), granted citizenship regardless of race (14) and guaranteed the right to vote to all adults regardless of "race, color or previous condition of servitude."

This recitation of constitutional language leads into Du Bois's conclusion, asking the world to pay heed to the injustice in the United States, which he characterized as "more dangerous to mankind than the Atom bomb." His reasoning is that the injustice in America will encourage the aggression of smaller nations." He also draws parallels between the American treatment of African Americans and the colonial and racial oppression practiced by nations such as Great Britain, South Africa, Belgium, and Australia.

Du Bois ends by telling the UN delegates that this is not an American problem, but a human problem and that the remainder of the petition will provide ample evidence of oppression of "American Negroes in the past and today, in law, administration and social condition; and the relation of this situation to the Charter of the United Nations."

Essential Themes

The key theme presented in Du Bois's introduction to this petition to the United Nations is not only that the continued racial oppression of African Americans is a violation of the nation's own laws and constitutional principles but that it represents a hypocrisy that is geopolitically dangerous and could destabilize other parts of the world. Hence, the United Nations—an organization formed for the purpose of maintaining global peace—had a vested interest in correcting what Du Bois presents as a potentially threatening situation. The very presentation of the racial injustices of the United States to an international governing body also indicates the development of a significant strand of the civil rights movement in the United States. During the 1950s and 1960s, some African American activists would come to see the plight of African Americans increasingly in terms of colonization and the need for a "decolonization" effort in the United States akin to those in Africa and nations like Vietnam. Here, as Du Bois explicitly connects the United States to Belgium, whose colony in the Congo had a well-earned reputation for vicious exploitation and oppression, he casts America's racial past and present in a new light.

—— *Aaron Gulyas, with additional material by Mary A. Afolabi*

Bibliography and Additional Reading

Lewis, David Levering. *W. E. B. Du Bois: Biography of a Race, 1868–1919*. (New York: Henry Holt, 1993).

Marable, Manning. *W. E. B. Du Bois: Black Radical Democrat*. Boston: Twayne, 1986.

Moore, Jacqueline M. *Booker T. Washington, W. E. B. Du Bois, and the Struggle for Racial Uplift*. (Wilmington, Delaware: Scholarly Resources, 2003).

Wolters, Raymond. *Du Bois and His Rivals*. (Columbia: University of Missouri Press, 2002).

Student Nonviolent Coordinating Committee Statement of Purpose

Date: 1960
Author: James Lawson, Jr.
Genre: Public declaration

Summary Overview

The Student Nonviolent Coordinating Committee Statement of Purpose, written by theology student and civil rights activist James Lawson, Jr., and dated April 1960, emphasizes the organization's commitment to nonviolence in efforts to defeat racial segregation during the civil rights era. Members of the SNCC strictly adhered to the principle of nonviolence at sit-ins and demonstrations, a principle reflected in the Student Nonviolent Coordinating Committee Statement of Purpose. The hope was that pacifism would enable student demonstrators to occupy the moral high road and win converts to their cause. Nonviolence was often a challenge. At sit-ins, students were often taunted and even struck. Later, when members engaged in community organizing in the segregated South, they were sometimes greeted with bullets, and many members of the organization were beaten or jailed, if not both. Accordingly, the SNCC relaxed its standards and allowed members to carry guns strictly for self-defense.

Defining Moment

On April 15–17, 1960, the Student Nonviolent Coordinating Committee (SNCC) was formed on the campus of Shaw University in Raleigh, North Carolina. The SNCC was the product, in large part, of the Southern Christian Leadership Conference, led by Martin Luther King, Jr. That organization's executive director, Ella Baker, organized a conference on the Shaw University campus with a view to bringing together student groups participating in the civil rights movement.

Sparking the movement was the first "sit-in," which took place at a segregated lunch counter at a Woolworth store in Greensboro, North Carolina. That February, students from nearby North Carolina Agricultural and Technical College, a predominantly black institution, sat at the whites-only lunch counter and refused to leave. Soon, students throughout the nation were taking part in sit-ins, "kneel-ins" (at churches), and even "wade-ins" (at segregated public swimming pools). The SNCC was a "coordinating committee" because its purpose was to coordinate and encourage these kinds of protests.

Continued violence against African Americans created strains in the civil rights movement. The Southern Christian Leadership Conference maintained its nonviolent position, but the SNCC became more militant, particularly after 1966, when the activist Stokely Carmichael, credited with coining the phrase *Black Power*, became the SNCC's chairman. Under his leadership, whites were expelled from the SNCC. Members of the organization began openly to arm themselves. Carmichael's public pronouncements were increasingly inflammatory. The SNCC was attracting the attention of police and the Federal Bureau of Investigation. In the late 1960s financial support for the SNCC began to disappear, and the organization disbanded in the 1970s.

Author Biography

James Lawson, Jr., born September 22, 1928, was the author of the Student Nonviolent Coordinating Committee Statement of Purpose. He was born in Pennsylvania and raised in Ohio, and studied at Ohio's Baldwin Wallace College. It was here that he became involved in the African American civil rights movement, joining the Congress of Racial Equality (CORE). Through is work with CORE, Lawson came to advocate nonviolent resistance to oppression. It was this stance that led him to serve 14 months in prison rather than report for the draft in 1951.

After this, he travelled to India as a Methodist missionary and studied nonviolent resistance of the kind used by Ghandi in the Indian independence movement. After his 1956 return to the United States and introduction to Martin Luther King, Jr., moved to Nashville working for CORE. Here, he trained students in nonviolent resistance methods, using their training to undertake sittings in downtown Nashville stores to protest segregation.

In 1960, a number of student civil rights activists, as well as delegate from major civil rights organizations like CORE, the Southern Christian Leadership Conference and others led to the formation of the student Nonviolent Coordinating Committee. Lawson served as a sort of mentor to the group, including crafting this statement of purpose.

HISTORIAL DOCUMENT

We affirm the philosophical or religious ideal of nonviolence as the foundation of our purpose, the presupposition of our faith, and the manner of our action. Nonviolence as it grows from the Judaeo-Christian tradition seeks a social order of justice permeated by love. Integration of human endeavor represents the crucial first step towards such a society.

Through nonviolence, courage displaces fear; love transforms hate. Acceptance dissipates prejudice; hopes ends despair. peace dominates war; faith reconciles doubt. Mutual regard cancels enmity. Justice for all overcomes injustice. The redemptive community supersedes systems of gross social immorality.

Love is the central motif of nonviolence. Love is the force by which God binds man to himself and man to man. Such love goes to the extreme; it remains loving and forgiving even in the midst of hostility. It matches the capacity of evil to inflict suffering with an even more enduring capacity to absorb evil, all the while persisting in love.

By appealing to conscience and standing on the moral nature of human existence, nonviolence nurtures the atmosphere in which reconciliation and justice become actual possibilities.

GLOSSARY

Emnity: Hostility

Judaeo-Christian: Sometimes spelled "Judeo-Christian," this term refers to the ethical teachings of Judaism and Christianity.

Motif: defining characteristic

Presupposition: A first principle; something that is assumed to be true

Document Analysis

At just 182 words, the Student Nonviolent Coordinating Committee Statement of Purpose is brief and relatively simple. It begins with an affirmation of the "philosophical or religious ideal of nonviolence." The devotion to nonviolence is stated in unequivocal terms, referred to as the "presupposition" of the group's "faith," that is to say the groups first and foundational principle. Reference is made to the nonviolent tradition of Judaeo-Christianity, which is erected on the foundation of a just society "permeated by love."

The second paragraph of the statement pairs a number of opposites to assert that, for example, "love transforms hate" and "justice for all overcomes injustice." The religious roots of the SNCC—Shaw University, the oldest of the historically black colleges in the South, was affiliated with the Baptist Church—are emphasized in the third paragraph, which takes the position that "love is the force by which God binds man to himself and man to man." The single sentence of the final paragraph expresses the hope that nonviolence can bring about reconciliation and justice.

Essential Themes

The Student Nonviolent Coordinating Committee Statement of Purpose, while short, encapsulates the essence of nonviolent resistance during the civil rights movement of the 1950s and 1960s. The tactic was rooted in love, as modeled in the "Judeo-Christian" tradition, coming to the movement through its religious foundations in institutions like the Baptist church. The pairs of opposed forces in the second paragraph illustrates the optimism of the movement as well, with the firm assurance that love and justice will overcome the forces of oppression. While SNCC, as discussed above, would drift from the strict nonviolence of groups like the SCLC, that core would remain a strong part of the civil rights movement as a whole.

———*Michael J. O'Neal, PhD*

Bibliography and Additional Reading

Carson, Clayborne. *In Struggle : SNCC and the Black Awakening of the 1960s* (Cambridge: Harvard University Press, 1995).

Halberstam, David. *The Children.* (New York: Fawcett, 1999).

Holsaert, Faith S., et al, ed. Hands on the Freedom Plow: Personal Accounts by Women in SNCC (Urbana-Champaign: University of Illinois Press, 2010).

Zinn, Howard. *SNCC: The New Abolitionists.* Reprint Edition (Chicago: Haymarket Books, 2013).

Letter from Birmingham Jail

Date: 1963
Author: Martin Luther King, Jr.
Genre: Letter

Summary Overview

Written in April 1963, Martin Luther King, Jr.'s "Letter from Birmingham Jail" delivered an important statement on civil rights and civil disobedience. The 1963 racial crisis in Birmingham, Alabama, was a critical turning point in the struggle for African American civil rights. Although King's letter was not published until after the Birmingham crisis was resolved, it is widely regarded as the most important written document of the modern civil rights movement and a classic text on civil disobedience.

In Birmingham, nonviolent protestors led by King faced determined opposition from hard-core segregationists. King and his organization, the Southern Christian Leadership Conference (SCLC), needed a victory to sustain the momentum of their movement. The integration of downtown stores and lunch counters was the primary focus of SCLC's "Project C"—the "C" stood for *confrontation*. Demonstrations began one day after a new city government was elected. Many observers criticized King for protesting at a time when Birmingham's race relations appeared to be moving in a more positive direction. These critics included eight prominent white clergymen who published a statement characterizing these protests as "unwise and untimely" and asking African Americans to withdraw their support from King's efforts.

The SCLC timed its campaign to coincide with the Easter shopping season. Its strategy involved using economic pressure to force white businesses to remove segregated facilities, extend more courteous treatment to African American customers, and hire black salespeople. King was arrested on Good Friday in 1963 and remained imprisoned for eight days. He used his jail time to compose a response to the clergymen. In his "Letter from Birmingham Jail," King articulated a moral and philosophical defense of his tactics and delivered a stinging rebuke to those who counseled caution on civil rights.

Defining Moment

Birmingham had long had a reputation as one of the most racist and violent cities in the South. Terrorists struck churches and the homes of civil rights leaders. Because no one was apprehended for any of the more than fifty explosions, Birmingham blacks concluded that the police were in league with the bombers. Public Safety Commissioner Eugene "Bull" Connor, an outspoken segregationist, used all resources at his disposal to preserve segregation in the city.

In January 1963 the SCLC decided to make Birmingham the site of its next major civil rights drive. The SCLC had suffered a serious setback the previous year in Albany, Georgia, where, despite months of nonviolent struggle and hundreds of arrests, African Americans were unable to win any concessions. Leaders believed Connor could be counted on to react in his usual heavy-handed fashion. King also had a larger objective in mind: He hoped that by creating a crisis in Birmingham, he could force President John F. Kennedy to take much-needed action on civil rights.

Protests began on April 3 with sit-ins and picketing at downtown department stores. On April 10 Judge W. A. Jenkins issued an injunction prohibiting King and other civil rights leaders from participating in or encouraging any civil disobedience. King decided to defy the court order, and on Good Friday, April 12, he and more than fifty other demonstrators were arrested. They were taken to the Birmingham City Jail, where King was placed in solitary confinement.

On April 12 a statement by eight white clergymen appeared in the *Birmingham News* under the title "A Call for Unity." They characterized the demonstrations as "unwise and untimely" and would "incite…hatred and violence" and urged blacks to withdraw their support from King's efforts. They implied that King should return to Atlanta and allow local residents to resolve their differences without outside interference. King's letter was directed at these clergy but released as an open letter to the nation's press.

Author Biography

Martin Luther King, Jr., was born and raised in Atlanta, Georgia, where both his father and grandfather pastored the Ebenezer Baptist Church. At the age of fifteen he entered Morehouse College to study sociology. He prepared for the ministry at Crozier Theological Seminary, in Pennsylvania, and then earned a doctorate

420 • AFRICAN-AMERICAN CIVIL RIGHTS

in philosophy from Boston University. While in Boston he met and married Coretta Scott, an aspiring concert singer from Marion, Alabama.

In 1953 King returned to the South to become pastor of the Dexter Avenue Baptist Church in Montgomery, Alabama. When Rosa Parks was arrested in 1955 for refusing to give up her seat to a white passenger, King emerged as the leader of a year-long boycott of city buses. His application of Gandhian nonviolent resistance to fight Jim Crow laws and the successful outcome of the Montgomery protest thrust him into the national spotlight. In 1957 he founded the Southern Christian Leadership Conference to carry his fight for civil rights to other southern communities. Over the next decade King remained at the forefront of the rapidly growing civil rights movement. In 1963 he led a campaign of civil disobedience against segregation in Birmingham, Alabama—one of the most violent southern cities. His "Letter from Birmingham Jail," written following his arrest while leading a demonstration, is an eloquent defense of his nonviolent tactics.

King's "I Have a Dream" Speech at the March on Washington helped build public support for the landmark Civil Rights Act that was passed by Congress in 1964. In turn, the Voting Rights Act that became law the following year was enacted largely because of his efforts to dramatize the disenfranchisement of African American citizens in Selma, Alabama. In 1966 King turned his attention to the North, where he attacked slum conditions and segregated housing in Chicago. King's growing opposition to the Vietnam War put him in the front ranks of the antiwar movement. At the time of his assassination in 1968, he was preparing to lead the Poor People's Campaign, a multiracial effort to spur government action against poverty.

King received the Nobel Peace Prize in 1964. In the United States, his birthday is commemorated by a national holiday, and his bust stands in the U.S. Capitol.

HISTORICAL DOCUMENT

My Dear Fellow Clergymen:

While confined here in the Birmingham city jail, I came across your recent statement calling my present activities "unwise and untimely." Seldom do I pause to answer criticism of my work and ideas. If I sought to answer all the criticisms that cross my desk, my secretaries would have little time for anything other than such correspondence in the course of the day, and I would have no time for constructive work. But since I feel that you are men of genuine good will and that your criticisms are sincerely set forth, I want to try to answer your statements in what I hope will be patient and reasonable terms.

I think I should indicate why I am here In Birmingham, since you have been influenced by the view which argues against "outsiders coming in." I have the honor of serving as president of the Southern Christian Leadership Conference, an organization operating in every southern state, with headquarters in Atlanta, Georgia. We have some eighty-five affiliated organizations across the South, and one of them is the Alabama Christian Movement for Human Rights. Frequently we share staff, educational and financial resources with our affiliates. Several months ago the affiliate here in Birmingham asked us to be on call to engage in a nonviolent direct-action program if such were deemed necessary. We readily consented, and when the hour came we lived up to our promise. So I, along with several members of my staff, am here because I was invited here I am here because I have organizational ties here.

But more basically, I am in Birmingham because injustice is here. Just as the prophets of the eighth century B.C. left their villages and carried their "thus saith the Lord" far beyond the boundaries of their home towns, and just as the Apostle Paul left his village of Tarsus and carried the gospel of Jesus Christ to the far corners of the Greco-Roman world, so am I compelled to carry the gospel of freedom beyond my own home town. Like Paul, I must constantly respond to the Macedonian call for aid.

Moreover, I am cognizant of the interrelatedness of all communities and states. I cannot sit idly by in Atlanta and not be concerned about what happens in Birmingham. Injustice anywhere is a threat to justice everywhere. We are caught in an inescapable network of mutuality, tied in a single garment of destiny. Whatever affects one directly, affects all indirectly. Never again can we afford to live with the narrow, provincial "outside agitator" idea. Anyone who lives inside the United States can never be considered an outsider anywhere within its bounds.

You deplore the demonstrations taking place in Birmingham. But your statement, I am sorry to say, I fails to express a similar concern for the conditions that brought about the demonstrations. I am sure that none of you would want to rest content with the superficial kind of social analysis that deals merely with effects and does not grapple with underlying causes. It is unfortunate that demonstrations are taking place in Birmingham, but it is even more unfortunate that the city's white power structure left the Negro community with no alternative.

In any nonviolent campaign there are four basic steps: collection of the facts to determine whether injustices exist; negotiation; self-purification; and direct action. We have gone through all these steps in Birmingham. There can be no gainsaying the fact that racial injustice engulfs this community. Birmingham is probably the most thoroughly segregated city in the United States. Its ugly record of brutality is widely known. Negroes have experienced grossly unjust treatment in the courts. There have been more unsolved bombings of Negro homes and churches in Birmingham than in any other city in the nation. These are the hard, brutal facts of the case. On the basis of these conditions, Negro leaders sought to negotiate with the city fathers. But the latter consistently refused to engage in good-faith negotiation.

Then, last September, came the opportunity to talk with leaders of Birmingham's economic community. In the course of the negotiations, certain promises were made by the merchants—for example, to remove the stores' humiliating racial signs. On the basis of these promises, the Reverend Fred Shuttlesworth and the leaders of the Alabama Christian Movement for Human Rights agreed to a moratorium on all demonstrations. As the weeks and months went by, we realized that we were the victims of a broken promise. A few signs, briefly removed, returned; the others remained.

As in so many past experiences, our hopes had been blasted, and the shadow of deep disappointment settled upon us. We had no alternative except to prepare for direct action, whereby we would present our very bodies as a means of laying our case before the conscience of the local and the national community. Mindful of the difficulties involved, we decided to undertake a process of self-purification. We began a series of workshops on nonviolence, and we repeatedly asked ourselves: "Are you able to accept blows without retaliating?" "Are you able to endure the ordeal of jail?" We decided to schedule our direct-action program for the Easter season, realizing that except for Christmas, this is the main shopping period of the year. Knowing that a strong economic withdrawal program would be the by-product of direct action, we felt that this would be the best time to bring pressure to bear on the merchants for the needed change.

Then it occurred to us that Birmingham's mayoralty election was coming up in March, and we speedily decided to postpone action until after election day. When we discovered that the Commissioner of Public Safety, Eugene "Bull" Connor, had piled up enough votes to be in the run-off, we decided again to postpone action until the day after the run-off so that the demonstrations could not be used to cloud the issues. Like many others, we waited to see Mr. Connor defeated, and to this end we endured postponement after postponement. Having aided in this community need, we felt that our direct-action program could be delayed no longer.

You may well ask: "Why direct action? Why sit-ins, marches and so forth? Isn't negotiation a better path?" You are quite right in calling for negotiation. Indeed, this is the very purpose of direct action. Nonviolent direct action seeks to create such a crisis and foster such a tension that a community which has constantly refused to negotiate is forced to confront the issue. It seeks so to dramatize the issue that it can no longer be ignored. My citing the creation of tension as part of the work of the nonviolent-resister may sound rather shocking.

But I must confess that I am not afraid of the word "tension." I have earnestly opposed violent tension, but there is a type of constructive, nonviolent tension which is necessary for growth. Just as Socrates felt that it was necessary to create a tension in the mind so that individuals could rise from the bondage of myths and half-truths to the unfettered realm of creative analysis and objective appraisal, so must we see the need for nonviolent gadflies to create the kind of tension in society that will help men rise from the dark depths of prejudice and racism to the majestic heights of understanding and brotherhood.

The purpose of our direct-action program is to create a situation so crisis-packed that it will inevitably open the door to negotiation. I therefore concur with you in your call for negotiation. Too long has our beloved Southland been bogged down in a tragic effort to live in monologue rather than dialogue.

One of the basic points in your statement is that the action that I and my associates have taken in Birmingham is untimely. Some have asked: "Why didn't you give the new city administration time to act?" The only answer that I can give to this query is that the new Birmingham administration must be prodded about as much as the outgoing one, before it will act. We are sadly mistaken if we feel that the election of Albert Boutwell as mayor will bring the millennium to Birmingham. While Mr. Boutwell is a much more gentle person than Mr. Connor, they are both segregationists, dedicated to maintenance of the status quo. I have hope that Mr. Boutwell will be reasonable enough to see the futility of massive resistance to desegregation. But he will not see this without pressure from devotees of civil rights. My friends, I must say to you that we have not made a single gain in civil rights without determined legal and nonviolent pressure. Lamentably, it is an historical fact that privileged groups seldom give up their privileges voluntarily. Individuals may see the moral light and voluntarily give up their unjust posture; but, as Reinhold Niebuhr has reminded us, groups tend to be more immoral than individuals.

We know through painful experience that freedom is never voluntarily given by the oppressor; it must be demanded by the oppressed. Frankly, I have yet to engage in a direct-action campaign that was "well timed" in the view of those who have not suffered unduly from the disease of segregation. For years now I have heard the word "Wait!" It rings in the ear of every Negro with piercing familiarity. This "Wait" has almost always meant "Never." We must come to see, with one of our distinguished jurists, that "justice too long delayed is justice denied."

We have waited for more than 340 years for our constitutional and God-given rights. The nations of Asia and Africa are moving with jetlike speed toward gaining political independence, but we still creep at horse-and-buggy pace toward gaining a cup of coffee at a lunch counter. Perhaps it is easy for those who have never felt the stinging darts of segregation to say, "Wait." But when you have seen vicious mobs lynch your mothers and fathers at will and drown your sisters and brothers at whim; when you have seen hate-filled policemen curse, kick and even kill your black brothers and sisters; when you see the vast majority of your twenty million Negro brothers smothering in an airtight cage of poverty in the midst of an affluent society; when you suddenly find your tongue twisted and your speech stammering as you seek to explain to your six-year-old daughter why she can't go to the public amusement park that has just been advertised on television, and see tears welling up in her eyes when she is told that Funtown is closed to colored children, and see ominous clouds of inferiority beginning to form in her little mental sky, and see her beginning to distort her personality by developing an unconscious bitterness toward white people; when you have to concoct an answer for a five-year-old son who is asking: "Daddy, why do white people treat colored people so mean?"; when you take a cross-county drive and find it necessary to sleep night after night in the uncomfortable corners of your automobile because no motel will accept you; when you are humiliated day in and day out by nagging signs reading "white" and "colored"; when your first name becomes "nigger," your middle name becomes "boy" (however old you are) and your last name becomes "John," and your wife and mother are never given the respected title "Mrs."; when you are harried by day and haunted by night by the fact that you are a Negro, living constantly at tiptoe stance, never quite knowing what to expect next, and are plagued with inner fears and outer resentments; when you are forever fighting a degenerating sense of "nobodiness"—then you will understand why we find it difficult to wait. There comes a time when the cup of endurance runs over, and men are no longer willing to be plunged into the abyss of despair. I hope, sirs, you can understand our legitimate and unavoidable impatience.

You express a great deal of anxiety over our willingness to break laws. This is certainly a legitimate concern. Since we so diligently urge people to obey the Supreme Court's decision of 1954 outlawing segregation in the public schools, at first glance it may seem rather paradoxical for us consciously to break laws. One may well ask: "How can you advocate breaking some laws and obeying others?" The answer lies in the fact that there are two types of laws: just and unjust. I would be the first to advocate obeying just laws. One has not only a legal but a moral responsibility to obey just laws. Conversely, one has a moral responsibility to disobey unjust laws. I would agree with St. Augustine that "an unjust law is no law at all."

Now, what is the difference between the two? How does one determine whether a law is just or unjust? A just law is a man-made code that squares with the moral law or the law of God. An unjust law is a code that is out of harmony with the moral law. To put it in the terms of St. Thomas Aquinas: An unjust law is a human law that is not rooted in eternal law and natural law. Any law that uplifts human personality is just. Any law that degrades human personality is unjust. All segregation statutes are unjust because segregation distorts the soul and damages the personality. It gives the segregator a false sense of superiority and the segregated a false sense of inferiority.

Segregation, to use the terminology of the Jewish philosopher Martin Buber, substitutes an "I-it" relationship for an "I-thou" relationship and ends up relegating persons to the status of things. Hence segregation is not only politically, economically and sociologically unsound, it is morally wrong and sinful. Paul Tillich has said that sin is separation. Is not segregation an existential expression of man's tragic separation, his awful estrangement, his terrible sinfulness? Thus it is that I can urge men to obey the 1954 decision of the Supreme Court, for it is morally right; and I can urge them to disobey segregation ordinances, for they are morally wrong.

Let us consider a more concrete example of just and unjust laws. An unjust law is a code that a numerical or power majority group compels a minority group to obey but does not make binding on itself. This is *difference* made legal. By the same token, a just law is a code that a majority compels a minority to follow and that it is willing to follow itself. This is *sameness* made legal.

Let me give another explanation. A law is unjust if it is inflicted on a minority that, as a result of being denied the right to vote, had no part in enacting or devising the law. Who can say that the legislature of Alabama which set up that state's segregation laws was democratically elected? Throughout Alabama all sorts of devious methods are used to prevent Negroes from becoming registered voters, and there are some counties in which, even though Negroes constitute a majority of the population, not a single Negro is registered. Can any law enacted under such circumstances be considered democratically structured?

Sometimes a law is just on its face and unjust in its application. For instance, I have been arrested on a charge of parading without a permit. Now, there is nothing wrong in having an ordinance which requires a permit for a parade. But such an ordinance becomes unjust when it is used to maintain segregation and to deny citizens the First-Amendment privilege of peaceful assembly and protest.

I hope you are able to see the distinction I am trying to point out. In no sense do I advocate evading or defying the law, as would the rabid segregationist. That would lead to anarchy. One who breaks an unjust law must do so openly, lovingly, and with a willingness to accept the penalty. I submit that an individual who breaks a law that conscience tells him is unjust, and who willingly accepts the penalty of imprisonment in order to arouse the conscience of the community over its injustice, is in reality expressing the highest respect for law.

Of course, there is nothing new about this kind of civil disobedience. It was evidenced sublimely in the refusal of Shadrach, Meshach and Abednego to obey the laws of Nebuchadnezzar, on the ground that a higher moral law was at stake. It was practiced superbly by the early Christians, who were willing to face hungry lions and the excruciating pain of chopping blocks rather than submit to certain unjust laws of the Roman Empire. To a degree, academic freedom is a reality today because Socrates practiced civil disobedience. In our own nation, the Boston Tea Party represented a massive act of civil disobedience.

We should never forget that everything Adolf Hitler did in Germany was "legal" and everything the Hungarian freedom fighters did in Hungary was "illegal." It was "illegal" to aid and comfort a Jew in Hitler's Germany. Even so, I am sure that, had I lived in Germany at the time, I would have aided and comforted my Jewish brothers. If today I lived in a Communist country where certain principles dear to the Christian faith are suppressed, I would openly advocate disobeying that country's antireligious laws.

I must make two honest confessions to you, my Christian and Jewish brothers. First, I must confess that over the past few years I have been gravely disappointed with the white moderate. I have almost reached the regrettable conclusion that the Negro's great stumbling block in his stride toward freedom is not the White Citizens Counciler or the Ku Klux Klanner, but the white moderate, who is more devoted to "order" than to justice; who prefers a negative peace which is the absence of tension to a positive peace which is the presence of justice; who constantly says: "I agree with you in the goal you seek, but I cannot agree with your methods of direct action"; who paternalistically believes he can set the timetable for another man's freedom; who lives by a mythical concept of time and who constantly advises the Negro to wait for a "more convenient season." Shallow understanding from people of good will is more frustrating than absolute misunderstanding from people of ill will. Lukewarm acceptance is much more bewildering than outright rejection.

I had hoped that the white moderate would understand that law and order exist for the purpose of establishing justice and that when they fail in this purpose they become the dangerously structured dams that block the flow of social progress. I had hoped that the white moderate would understand that the present tension in the South is a necessary phase of the transition from an obnoxious negative peace, in which the Negro passively accepted his unjust plight, to a substantive and positive peace, in which all men will respect the dignity and worth of human personality Actually, we who engage in nonviolent direct action are not the creators of tension. We merely bring to the surface the hidden tension that is already alive. We bring it out in the open, where it can be seen and dealt with. Like a boil that can never be cured so long as it is covered up but must be opened with all its ugliness to the natural medicines of air and light, injustice must be exposed, with all the tension its exposure creates, to the light of human conscience and the air of national opinion before it can be cured.

In your statement you assert that our actions, even though peaceful, must be condemned because they precipitate violence. But is this a logical assertion? Isn't this like condemning a robbed man because his possession of money precipitated the evil act of robbery? Isn't this like condemning Socrates because his unswerving commitment to truth and his philosophical inquiries precipitated the act by the misguided populace in which they made him drink hemlock? Isn't this like condemning Jesus because his unique God-consciousness and neverceasing devotion to God's will precipitated the evil act of crucifixion? We must come to see that, as the federal courts have consistently affirmed, it is wrong to urge an individual to cease his efforts to gain his basic constitutional rights because the quest may precipitate violence. Society must protect the robbed and punish the robber.

I had also hoped that the white moderate would reject the myth concerning time in relation to the struggle for freedom. I have just received a letter from a white brother in Texas. He writes: "All Christians know that the colored people will receive equal rights eventually, but it is possible that you are in too great a religious hurry. It has taken Christianity almost two thousand years to accomplish what it has. The teachings of Christ take time to come to earth." Such an attitude stems from a tragic misconception of time, from the strangely irrational notion that there is something in the very flow of time that will inevitably cure all ills. Actually, time itself is neutral; it can be used either destructively or constructively. More and more I feel that the people of ill will have used time much more effectively than have the people of good will. We will have to repent in this generation not merely for the hateful words and actions of the bad people but for the appalling silence of the good people. Human progress never rolls in on wheels of inevitability; it comes through the tireless efforts of men willing to be co-workers with God, and without this hard work, time itself becomes an ally of the forces of social stagnation. We must use time creatively, in the knowledge that the time is always ripe to do right. Now is the time to make real the promise of democracy and transform our pending national elegy into a creative psalm of brotherhood. Now is the time to lift our national policy from the quicksand of racial injustice to the solid rock of human dignity.

You speak of our activity in Birmingham as extreme At first I was rather disappointed that fellow clergymen would see my nonviolent efforts as those of an extremist. I began thinking about the fact that I stand in the middle of two opposing forces in the Negro community. One is a force of complacency, made up in part of Negroes who, as a result of long years of oppression, are so drained of self-respect and a sense of "somebodiness" that they have adjusted to segregation; and in part of a few middle-class Negroes who, because of a degree of academic and economic security and because in some ways they profit by segregation, have become insensitive to the problems of the masses. The other force is one of bitterness and hatred, and it comes perilously close to advocating violence. It is expressed in the various black nationalist groups that are springing up across the nation, the largest and best-known being Elijah Muhammad's Muslim movement. Nourished by the Negro's frustration over the continued existence of racial discrimination, this movement is made up of people who have lost faith in America, who have absolutely repudiated Christianity, and who have concluded that the white man is an incorrigible "devil."

I have tried to stand between these two forces, saying that we need emulate neither the "do-nothingism" of the complacent nor the hatred and despair of the black nationalist. For there is the more excellent way of love and nonviolent protest I am grateful to God that, through the influence of the Negro church, the way of nonviolence became an integral part of our struggle.

If this philosophy had not emerged, by now many streets of the South would, I am convinced, be flowing with blood. And I am further convinced that if our white brothers dismiss as "rabble-rousers" and "outside agitators" those of us who employ nonviolent direct action, and if they refuse to support our nonviolent efforts, millions of Negroes will, out of frustration and despair, seek solace and security in black-nationalist ideologies—a development that would inevitably lead to a frightening racial nightmare.

Oppressed people cannot remain oppressed forever. The yearning for freedom eventually manifests itself, and that is what has happened to the American Negro. Something within has reminded him of his birthright of freedom, and something without has reminded him that it can be gained. Consciously or unconsciously, he has been caught up by the *Zeitgeist* and with his black brothers of Africa and his brown and yellow brothers of Asia, South America and the Caribbean, the United States Negro is moving with a sense of great urgency toward the promised land of racial justice. If one recognizes this vital urge that has engulfed the Negro community, one should readily understand why public demonstrations are taking place. The Negro has many pent-up resentments and latent frustrations, and he must release them. So let him march; let him make prayer pilgrimages to the city hall; let him go on freedom rides—and try to understand why he must do so. If his repressed emotions are not released in nonviolent ways, they will seek expression through violence; this is not a threat but a fact of history. So I have not said to my people: "Get rid of your discontent." Rather, I have tried to say that this normal and healthy discontent can be channeled into the creative outlet of nonviolent direct action. And now this approach is being termed extremist.

But though I was initially disappointed at being categorized as an extremist, as I continued to think about the matter I gradually gained a measure of satisfaction from the label. Was not Jesus an extremist for love: "Love your enemies, bless them that curse you, do good to them that hate you, and pray for them which despitefully use you, and persecute you." Was not Amos an extremist for justice: "Let justice roll down like waters and righteousness like an ever-flowing stream." Was not Paul an extremist for the Christian gospel: "I bear in my body the marks of the Lord Jesus." Was not Martin Luther an extremist: "Here I stand; I cannot do otherwise, so help me God." And John Bunyan: "I will stay in jail to the end of my days before I make a butchery of my conscience." And Abraham Lincoln: "This nation cannot survive half slave and half free." And Thomas Jefferson: "We hold these truths to be self-evident, that an men are created equal. ..." So the question is not whether we will be extremists, but what kind of extremists we will be. Will we be extremists for hate or for love? Will we be extremist for the preservation of injustice or for the extension of justice? In that dramatic scene on Calvary's hill three men were crucified. We must never forget that all three were crucified for the same crime—the crime of extremism. Two were extremists for immorality, and thus fell below their environment. The other, Jesus Christ, was an extremist for love, truth and goodness, and thereby rose above his environment. Perhaps the South, the nation and the world are in dire need of creative extremists.

I had hoped that the white moderate would see this need. Perhaps I was too optimistic; perhaps I expected too much. I suppose I should have realized that few members of the oppressor race can understand the deep groans and passionate yearnings of the oppressed race, and still fewer have the vision to see that injustice must be rooted out by strong, persistent and determined action. I am thankful, however, that some of our white brothers in the South have grasped the meaning of this social revolution and committed themselves to it. They are still too few in quantity, but they are big in quality. Some—such as Ralph McGill, Lillian Smith, Harry Golden, James McBride Dabbs, Ann Braden and Sarah Patton Boyle—have written about our struggle in eloquent and prophetic terms. Others have marched with us down nameless streets of the South. They have languished in filthy, roach-infested jails, suffering the abuse and brutality of policemen who view them as "dirty nigger-lovers" Unlike so many of their moderate brothers and sisters, they have recognized the urgency of the moment and sensed the need for powerful "action" antidotes to combat the disease of segregation.

Let me take note of my other major disappointment. I have been so greatly disappointed with the white church and its leadership. Of course, there are some notable exceptions. I am not unmindful of the fact that each of you has taken some significant stands on this issue. I commend you, Reverend Stallings, for your Christian stand on this past Sunday, in welcoming Negroes to your worship service on a nonsegregated basis. I commend the Catholic leaders of this state for integrating Spring Hill College several years ago.

But despite these notable exceptions, I must honestly reiterate that I have been disappointed with the church. I do not say this as one of those negative critics who can always find something wrong with the church. I say this as a minister of the gospel, who loves the church; who was nurtured in its bosom; who has been sustained by its spiritual blessings and who will remain true to it as long as the cord of life shall lengthen.

When I was suddenly catapulted into the leadership of the bus protest in Montgomery, Alabama, a few years ago, I felt we would be supported by the white church. I felt that the white ministers, priests and rabbis of the South would be among our strongest allies.

Instead, some have been outright opponents, refusing to understand the freedom movement and misrepresenting its leaders; all too many others have been more cautious than courageous and have remained silent behind the anesthetizing security of stained-glass windows.

In spite of my shattered dreams, I came to Birmingham with the hope that the white religious leadership of this community would see the justice of our cause and, with deep moral concern, would serve as the channel through which our just grievances could reach the power structure. I had hoped that each of you would understand. But again I have been disappointed.

I have heard numerous southern religious leaders admonish their worshipers to comply with a desegregation decision because it is the law, but I have longed to hear white ministers declare: "Follow this decree because integration is morally right and because the Negro is your brother." In the midst of blatant injustices inflicted upon the Negro, I have watched white churchmen stand on the sideline and mouth pious irrelevancies and sanctimonious trivialities. In the midst of a mighty struggle to rid our nation of racial and economic injustice, I have heard many ministers say: "Those are social issues, with which the gospel has no real concern." And I have watched many churches commit themselves to a completely other-worldly religion which makes a strange, un-Biblical distinction between body and soul, between the sacred and the secular.

I have traveled the length and breadth of Alabama, Mississippi and all the other southern states. On sweltering summer days and crisp autumn mornings I have looked at the South's beautiful churches with their lofty spires pointing heavenward. I have beheld the impressive outlines of her massive religious-education buildings. Over and over I have found myself asking: "What kind of people worship here? Who is their God? Where were their voices when the lips of Governor Barnett dripped with words of interposition and nullification? Where were they when Governor Wallace gave a clarion call for defiance and hatred? Where were their voices of support when bruised and weary Negro men and women decided to rise from the dark dungeons of complacency to the bright hills of creative protest?"

Yes these questions are still in my mind. In deep disappointment I have wept over the laxity of the church. But be assured that my tears have been tears of love. There can be no deep disappointment where there is not deep love. Yes, I love the church. How could I do otherwise? I am in the rather unique position of being the son, the grandson and the great-grandson of preachers. Yes, I see the church as the body of Christ. But oh! How we have blemished and scarred that body through social neglect and through fear of being nonconformists.

There was a time when the church was very powerful—in the time when the early Christians rejoiced at being deemed worthy to suffer for what they believed. In those days the church was not merely a thermometer that recorded the ideas and principles of popular opinion; it was a thermostat that transformed the mores of society. Whenever the early Christians entered a town, the people in power became disturbed and immediately sought to convict the Christians for being "disturbers of the peace" and "outside agitators.'" But the Christians pressed on, in the conviction that they were "a colony of heaven," called to obey God rather than man. Small in number, they were big in commitment. They were too God-intoxicated to be "astronomically intimidated." By their effort and example they brought an end to such ancient evils as infanticide and gladiatorial contests.

Things are different now. So often the contemporary church is a weak, ineffectual voice with an uncertain sound. So often it is an archdefender of the status quo. Far from being disturbed by the presence of the church, the power structure of the average community is consoled by the church's silent—and often even vocal—sanction of things as they are.

But the judgment of God is upon the church as never before. If today's church does not recapture the sacrificial spirit of the early church, it will lose its authenticity, forfeit the loyalty of millions, and be dismissed as an irrelevant social club with no meaning for the twentieth century. Every day I meet young people whose disappointment with the church has turned into outright disgust.

Perhaps I have once again been too optimistic. Is organized religion too inextricably bound to the status quo to save our nation and the world? Perhaps I must turn my faith to the inner spiritual church, the church within the church, as the true *ekklesia* and the hope of the world. But again I am thankful to God that some noble souls from the ranks of organized religion have broken loose from the paralyzing chains of conformity and joined us as active partners in the struggle for freedom. They have left their secure congregations and walked the streets of Albany, Georgia, with us. They have gone down the highways of the South on tortuous rides for freedom. Yes, they have gone to jail with us. Some have been dismissed from their churches, have lost the support of their bishops and fellow ministers. But they have acted in the faith that right defeated is stronger than evil triumphant. Their witness has been the spiritual salt that has preserved the true meaning of the gospel in these troubled times. They have carved a tunnel of hope through the dark mountain of disappointment.

I hope the church as a whole will meet the challenge of this decisive hour. But even if the church does not come to the aid of justice, I have no despair about the future. I have no fear about the outcome of our struggle in Birmingham, even if our motives are at present misunderstood. We will reach the goal of freedom in Birmingham and all over the nation, because the goal of America is freedom.

Abused and scorned though we may be, our destiny is tied up with America's destiny. Before the pilgrims landed at Plymouth, we were here. Before the pen of Jefferson etched the majestic words of the Declaration of Independence across the pages of history, we were here. For more than two centuries our forebears labored in this country without wages; they made cotton king; they built the homes of their masters while suffering gross injustice and shameful humiliation—and yet out of a bottomless vitality they continued to thrive and develop. If the inexpressible cruelties of slavery could not stop us, the opposition we now face will surely fail. We will win our freedom because the sacred heritage of our nation and the eternal will of God are embodied in our echoing demands.

Before closing I feel impelled to mention one other point in your statement that has troubled me profoundly. You warmly commended the Birmingham police force for keeping "order" and "preventing violence." I doubt that you would have so warmly commended the police force if you had seen its dogs sinking their teeth into unarmed, nonviolent Negroes. I doubt that you would so quickly commend the policemen if you were to observe their ugly and inhumane treatment of Negroes here in the city jail; if you were to watch them push and curse old Negro women and young Negro girls; if you were to see them slap and kick old Negro men and young boys; if you were to observe them, as they did on two occasions, refuse to give us food because we wanted to sing our grace together. I cannot join you in your praise of the Birmingham police department.

It is true that the police have exercised a degree of discipline in handling the demonstrators. In this sense they have conducted themselves rather "nonviolently" in public. But for what purpose? To preserve the evil system of segregation. Over the past few years I have consistently preached that nonviolence demands that the means we use must be as pure as the ends we seek. I have tried to make clear that it is wrong to use immoral means to attain moral ends. But now I must affirm that it is just as wrong, or perhaps even more so, to use moral means to preserve immoral ends. Perhaps Mr. Connor and his policemen have been rather nonviolent in public, as was Chief Pritchett in Albany, Georgia, but they have used the moral means of nonviolence to maintain the immoral end of racial injustice. As T. S. Eliot has said: "The last temptation is the greatest treason: To do the right deed for the wrong reason."

I wish you had commended the Negro sit-inners and demonstrators of Birmingham for their sublime courage, their willingness to suffer and their amazing discipline in the midst of great provocation. One day the South will recognize its real heroes. They will be the James Merediths, with the noble sense of purpose that enables them to face jeering, and hostile mobs, and with the agonizing loneliness that characterizes the life of the pioneer. They will be old, oppressed, battered Negro women, symbolized in a seventy-two-year-old woman in Montgomery, Alabama, who rose up with a sense of dignity and with her people decided not to ride segregated buses, and who responded with ungrammatical profundity to one who inquired about her weariness: "My feets is tired, but my soul is at rest." They will be the young high school and college students, the young ministers of the gospel and a host of their elders, courageously and nonviolently sitting in at lunch counters and willingly going to jail for conscience' sake. One day the South will know that when these disinherited children of God sat down at lunch counters, they were in reality standing up for what is best in the American dream and for the most sacred values in our Judaeo-Christian heritage, thereby bringing our nation back to those great wells of democracy which were dug deep by the founding fathers in their formulation of the Constitution and the Declaration of Independence.

Never before have I written so long a letter. I'm afraid it is much too long to take your precious time. I can assure you that it would have been much shorter if I had been writing from a comfortable desk, but what else can one do when he is alone in a narrow jail cell, other than write long letters, think long thoughts and pray long prayers?

I have said anything in this letter that overstates the truth and indicates an unreasonable impatience, I beg you to forgive me. If I have said anything that understates the truth and indicates my having a patience that allows me to settle for anything less than brotherhood, I beg God to forgive me.

I hope this letter finds you strong in the faith. I also hope that circumstances will soon make it possible for me to meet each of you, not as an integrationist or a civil rights leader but as a fellow clergyman and a Christian brother. Let us all hope that the dark clouds of racial prejudice will soon pass away and the deep fog of misunderstanding will be lifted from our fear-drenched communities, and in some not too distant tomorrow the radiant stars of love and brotherhood will shine over our great nation with all their scintillating beauty.

Yours for the cause of Peace and Brotherhood,
Martin Luther King, Jr.

Reprinted by arrangement with The Heirs to the Estate of Martin Luther King Jr., c/o Writers House as agent for the proprietor New York, NY. Copyright © 1963 Dr. Martin Luther King Jr.; Copyright © renewed 1991 Coretta Scott King.

GLOSSARY

black nationalism: the belief that blacks should live separately from whites

concoct: to invent

cognizant: aware

complacency: a feeling of contentment or self-satisfaction

ekklesia: Greek term for a congregation of believers

gainsaying: contradicting

inevitability: the impossibility of avoiding or preventing

lamentably: with regret

latent: hidden; unseen

moratorium: a temporary halt or cessation of activity

query: a question

paradoxical: inconsistent; contradictory

paternalistically: in a fatherly manner exercised authoritatively

precipitate: to cause to happen suddenly

reiterate: to repeat

sanctimonious: pretending to be pious or righteous

Zeitgeist: German term for "spirit of the times"

Document Analysis

To explain his presence in Birmingham, King compares himself to the apostle Paul, who spread the Christian faith among the Gentiles. He asserts that people living outside Alabama cannot ignore blatant racism in Birmingham. Every citizen has an obligation to act against injustice wherever it may be found.

King takes the clergymen to task for their statement deploring the Birmingham demonstrations. Instead of worrying about threats to public order, they should be concerned about racism and inequality in their city. King contends that black citizens of Birmingham had "no alternative" other than to take to the streets.

King goes on to outline the stages of his nonviolent crusade. Fact finding was the first phase, uncovering Birmingham's long history of unpunished attacks on its black citizens and the failure of leaders to negotiate in good faith with civil rights advocates.

The second stage was negotiation. King claims that like his critics, he desires negotiation but explains that sometimes pressure must be applied to bring reluctant parties to the bargaining table.

King next rejects the accusation that the protests were "untimely." He maintains that those in positions of power rarely surrender their privileges voluntarily; they must be persuaded forcefully to do the right thing. King points out that any action disrupting the status quo is likely to be considered poorly timed by those who are comfortable with existing arrangements. Change, however, cannot come soon enough for the oppressed.

King next addresses the most difficult question raised by the Birmingham clergymen: How can he encourage his followers to violate some laws and at the same time urge whites to observe such legal decisions as *Brown v. Board of Education*? Here he draws on the concept of "natural law" developed by Saint Thomas Aquinas and other Catholic philosophers. A man-made law is just if it accords with the divinely established code to uplift the human spirit. All such laws should be obeyed. Segregation laws are immoral and therefore should not be obeyed. Other examples of unjust laws are those that are unequally applied or those that violate constitutional rights.

King maintains that those who advocate civil disobedience do not contribute to anarchy. In the tradition of Henry David Thoreau and Mahatma Gandhi, he asserts that those who violate unjust laws must do so "openly, lovingly, and with a willingness to accept the penalty."

The longest section of the letter addresses the role of the white moderate in the struggle for civil rights. King expresses his frustration with liberals who claimed to support the goal of equal rights while objecting to the methods of the movement. Many detractors denounced civil rights activists for precipitating violence from those opposed to integration. According to King, they should defend those being attacked and condemn their attackers. King also refutes the argument that that civil rights advocates like King were pressing too hard to transform southern society and should be more patient.

The eight clergymen had described the Birmingham protestors as extremists. King at first repudiates this label. Rather than viewing himself as an extremist, he claims that he is a moderate caught between Uncle Toms who have acquiesced to segregation and the Black Muslims who charge that the white man is "the devil." In this context, the true extremists are those advocating separation from American society. Believers in nonviolent, direct action seek inclusion in the larger community, not its destruction.

After considering the extremist label, however, King reverses course and embraces it. "Was not Jesus an extremist?" he asks. He then recites a long list of heroic figures who could be considered extremists including Martin Luther and Abraham Lincoln. All of these men were seen as extremists in their time. King implies that the United States needs more visionaries of this sort.

Although King harshly criticizes those moderates who had failed to defend the civil rights movement and praises those southern whites who risked persecution and ostracism by their public support of the movement.

King then launches a sustained critique of established religion in the South. He squarely embraces the Social Gospel tradition that calls upon Christians to work for the welfare of their fellow humans. Nevertheless, despite the opposition of organized religion, King expresses confidence that the movement he leads eventually will be victorious.

King's final paragraphs dwell on the clergymen's ironic praise of the Birmingham police force for keeping order during the demonstrations. Three weeks after their statement was published, Connor ordered his men to turn police dogs and fire hoses on peaceful demonstrators. He faults the ministers for not praising the discipline and courage of the African American protestors, who remained nonviolent in the face of great provocation.

King closes his letter on a brotherly note, apologizing for the length of his missive and asking for understanding. He expresses the hope that one day they may be able to meet person to person without the antagonism and misunderstanding that currently surround them.

Essential Themes

Although the "Letter from Birmingham Jail" was nominally addressed to the eight white clergymen who had publicly urged African Americans to curtail their Birmingham demonstrations, King had a much wider audience in mind; his letter was produced for national consumption. Specifically, his letter was intended to answer his critics, especially white liberals who questioned the timing of his decision to initiate sit-ins, pickets, and marches following the electoral defeat of Connor. More generally, King hoped to explain the religious and philosophical foundations of nonviolent, direct action to all who shared his Judeo-Christian beliefs.

King's "Letter from Birmingham Jail" has been hailed as the most important written document of the modern civil rights struggle. In it King set forth in prophetic language the aspirations of African Americans to be accepted as human beings entitled to the same respect and rights as other Americans. He articulated the objectives of his movement and offered an eloquent defense of civil disobedience and nonviolent, direct action. His letter has been included in anthologies alongside the classic works of Thoreau and Gandhi. King's words and example have inspired people fighting for freedom around the world, from workers in Poland's Solidarity movement to Chinese students in Beijing's Tiananmen Square.

——Paul T. Murray

Bibliography and Additional Reading

Bass, S. Jonathan. *Blessed Are the Peacemakers: Martin Luther King, Jr., Eight White Clergymen, and the "Letter from Birmingham Jail."* Baton Rouge: Louisiana State University Press, 2001.

Branch, Taylor. *Parting the Waters: America in the King Years, 1954–63.* New York: Simon & Schuster, 1988.

Colaiaco, James A. "The American Dream Unfulfilled: Martin Luther King, Jr., and the 'Letter from Birmingham Jail.'" *Phylon* 45 (1984): 1–18.

Durham, Michael S. *Powerful Days: The Civil Rights Photography of Charles Moore.* New York: Stewart, Tabori & Chang, 1991.

Eskew, Glenn T. *But for Birmingham: The Local and National Movements in the Civil Rights Struggle.* Chapel Hill: University of North Carolina Press, 1997.

Garrow, David J. *Bearing the Cross: Martin Luther King, Jr., and the Southern Christian Leadership Conference, 1955–1968.* New York: William Morrow, 1986.

———, ed. *Birmingham, Alabama, 1956–1963: The Black Struggle for Civil Rights.* New York: Carlson Publishing, 1989.

Manis, Andrew M. *A Fire You Can't Put Out: The Civil Rights Life of Birmingham's Reverend Fred Shuttlesworth.* Tuscaloosa: University of Alabama Press, 1999.

McWhorter, Diane. *Carry Me Home: Birmingham, Alabama—The Climactic Battle of the Civil Rights Revolution.* New York: Simon & Schuster, 2001.

Mott, Wesley T. "The Rhetoric of Martin Luther King, Jr. Letter from Birmingham Jail." *Phylon* 36 (1975): 411–421.

Washington, James M., ed. *A Testament of Hope: The Essential Writings of Martin Luther King, Jr.* San Francisco: Harper & Row, 1986.

Web Sites

"King Encyclopedia: Birmingham Campaign." Stanford University "Martin Luther King, Jr., Papers Project" Web site. http://www.stanford.edu/group/King/about_king/encyclopedia/birmingham_campaign.htm. Accessed on January 26, 2017.

■ "I Have a Dream"

Date: 1963
Author: Martin Luther King, Jr.
Genre: Speech

Summary Overview

On August 28, 1963, nearly a quarter of a million people arrived in the District of Columbia for the March on Washington for Jobs and Freedom. The marchers on that day in 1963 had been summoned by the veteran African American labor leader A. Philip Randolph to urge the federal government to broaden economic opportunities for low-income families and to pressure Congress to pass the Civil Rights Act, which was then being debated. Delegations of civil rights supporters from cities across the United States thus joined together for a massive one-day protest. Amid the day's various events and speeches, one stood out: Martin Luther King, Jr.'s speech "I Have a Dream." His oration eclipsed the remarks of all other speakers that day and is among the most quoted American public addresses. "I Have a Dream" has come to epitomize the aspirations of the modern civil rights movement. In it, King reminded his listeners of African Americans' legitimate grievances and promised that they would not rest until full equality was won. As he neared the end of his speech, King departed from his prepared text to deliver his most memorable words: "I have a dream," he thundered, in the powerful preaching cadence of the black Baptist tradition. Using a series of riveting images, King shared his vision of a country free of racial hatred, in which black and white Americans would live as equals.

Defining Moment

In 1941 A. Philip Randolph, the president of the Brotherhood of Sleeping Car Porters, threatened to lead one hundred thousand African Americans down Pennsylvania Avenue, forcing President Franklin D. Roosevelt to act against racial discrimination in defense industries.

As civil rights protests gained momentum in the early 1960s, Randolph revived the idea of a march on Washington. He maintained that a massive assembly of black citizens was needed to prod a reluctant President Kennedy into action. Randolph's idea initially drew a lukewarm response from other black leaders—until Martin Luther King, Jr., lent his support.

King had just finished a successful campaign to desegregate stores and lunch counters in Birmingham, Alabama. Nationally televised scenes of police dogs and fire hoses battering youthful demonstrators roused public sympathy behind the crusade for equal rights. After Kennedy submitted his civil rights bill to Congress, the event was renamed the "March for Jobs and Freedom," the emphasis shifted from economic issues to support for the proposed legislation.

President Kennedy tried to convince march organizers that a mass protest could create opposition to the bill. When Randolph and King declared their determination to go ahead with the demonstration, the president offered the assistance of federal agencies to ensure that the march proceeded smoothly. In the weeks leading up to the event, Randolph's chief aide, Bayard Rustin, worked around the clock to nail down the smallest details.

As the huge crowd congregated on either side of the memorial's Reflecting Pool, the speakers took their turns at the podium in the shadow of the Great Emancipator's statue. John Lewis, the young head of the Student Nonviolent Coordinating Committee, delivered the day's most militant address, calling for a "great revolution" to "splinter the segregated south into a thousand pieces." Then, Randolph introduced King, whose address sounded the climactic final note for the day's celebration

Author Biography

Martin Luther King, Jr., was born and raised in Atlanta, Georgia, where both his father and grandfather pastored the Ebenezer Baptist Church. At the age of fifteen he entered Morehouse College to study sociology. He prepared for the ministry at Crozier Theological Seminary, in Pennsylvania, and then earned a doctorate in philosophy from Boston University. While in Boston he met and married Coretta Scott, an aspiring concert singer from Marion, Alabama.

In 1953 King returned to the South to become pastor of the Dexter Avenue Baptist Church in Montgomery, Alabama. When Rosa Parks was arrested in 1955 for refusing to give up her seat to a white passenger, King emerged as the leader of a year-long boycott of city buses. His application of Gandhian nonviolent resistance to fight Jim

Crow laws and the successful outcome of the Montgomery protest thrust him into the national spotlight. In 1957 he founded the Southern Christian Leadership Conference to carry his fight for civil rights to other southern communities. Over the next decade King remained at the forefront of the rapidly growing civil rights movement. In 1963 he led a campaign of civil disobedience against segregation in Birmingham, Alabama—one of the most violent southern cities. His "Letter from Birmingham Jail," written following his arrest while leading a demonstration, is an eloquent defense of his nonviolent tactics.

King's "I Have a Dream" Speech at the March on Washington helped build public support for the landmark Civil Rights Act that was passed by Congress in 1964. In turn, the Voting Rights Act that became law the following year was enacted largely because of his efforts to dramatize the disenfranchisement of African American citizens in Selma, Alabama. In 1966 King turned his attention to the North, where he attacked slum conditions and segregated housing in Chicago. King's growing opposition to the Vietnam War put him in the front ranks of the antiwar movement. At the time of his assassination in 1968, he was preparing to lead the Poor People's Campaign, a multiracial effort to spur government action against poverty.

King received the Nobel Peace Prize in 1964. In the United States, his birthday is commemorated by a national holiday, and his bust stands in the U.S. Capitol.

HISTORICAL DOCUMENT

I am happy to join with you today in what will go down in history as the greatest demonstration for freedom in the history of our nation.

Fivescore years ago, a great American, in whose symbolic shadow we stand today, signed the Emancipation Proclamation. This

momentous decree came as a great beacon light of hope to millions of Negro slaves who had been seared in the flames of withering injustice. It came as a joyous daybreak to end the long night of their captivity.

But one hundred years later, the Negro still is not free. One hundred years later, the life of the Negro is still sadly crippled by the manacles of segregation and the chains of discrimination. One hundred years later, the Negro lives on a lonely island of poverty in the midst of a vast ocean of material prosperity. One hundred years later the Negro is still languished in the corners of American society and finds himself an exile in his own land. And so we've come here today to dramatize a shameful condition.

In a sense we've come to our nation's capital to cash a check. When the architects of our republic wrote the magnificent words of the Constitution and the Declaration of Independence, they were signing a promissory note to which every American was to fall heir. This note was a promise that all men, yes, black men as well as white men, would be guaranteed the "unalienable Rights of Life, Liberty, and the pursuit of Happiness." It is obvious today that America has defaulted on this promissory note insofar as her citizens of color are concerned. Instead of honoring this sacred obligation, America has given the Negro people a bad check, a check which has come back marked "insufficient funds."

But we refuse to believe that the bank of justice is bankrupt. We refuse to believe that there are insufficient funds in the great vaults of opportunity of this nation. And so we've come to cash this check, a check that will give us upon demand the riches of freedom and the security of justice.

We have also come to this hallowed spot to remind America of the fierce urgency of now. This is no time to engage in the luxury of cooling off or to take the tranquilizing drug of gradualism. Now is the time to make real the promises of democracy. Now is the time to rise from the dark and desolate valley of segregation to the sunlit path of racial justice. Now is the time to lift our nation from the quicksands of racial injustice to the solid rock of brotherhood. Now is the time to make justice a reality for all of God's children.

It would be fatal for the nation to overlook the urgency of the moment. This sweltering summer of the Negro's legitimate discontent will not pass until there is an invigorating autumn of freedom and equality. Nineteen sixty-three is not an end, but a beginning. And those who hope that the Negro needed to blow off steam and will now be content will have a rude awakening if the nation returns to business as usual, There will be neither rest nor tranquility in America until the Negro is granted his citizenship rights. The whirlwinds of revolt will continue to shake the foundations of our nation until the bright day of justice emerges.

But there is something that I must say to my people, who stand on the warm threshold which leads into the palace of justice: In the process of gaining our rightful place, we must not be guilty of wrongful deeds. Let us not seek to satisfy our thirst for freedom by drinking from the cup of bitterness and hatred. We must forever conduct our struggle on the high plane of dignity and discipline. We must not allow our creative protest to degenerate into physical violence. Again and again, we must rise to the majestic heights of meeting physical force with soul force. The marvelous new militancy which has engulfed the Negro community must not lead us to a distrust of all white people, for many of our white brothers, as evidenced by their presence here today, have come to realize that their destiny is tied up with our destiny. And they have come to realize that their freedom is inextricably bound to our freedom. We cannot walk alone.

And as we walk, we must make the pledge that we shall always march ahead. We cannot turn back. There are those who are asking the devotees of civil rights, "When will you be satisfied?"

We can never be satisfied as long as the Negro is the victim of the unspeakable horrors of police brutality. We can never be satisfied as long as our bodies, heavy with the fatigue of travel, cannot gain lodging in the motels of the highways and the hotels of the cities. We cannot be satisfied as long as the Negro's basic mobility is from a smaller ghetto to a larger one. We can never be satisfied as long as our children are stripped of their selfhood and robbed of their dignity by signs stating "for whites only." We cannot be satisfied as long as a Negro in Mississippi cannot vote and a Negro in New York believes he has nothing for which to vote. No, no, we are not satisfied and we will not be satisfied until "justice rolls down like waters and righteousness like a mighty stream."

I am not unmindful that some of you have come here out of great trials and tribulations. Some of you have come fresh from narrow jail cells. Some of you have come from areas where your quest for freedom left you battered by the storms of persecution and staggered by the winds of police brutality. You have been the veterans of creative suffering.

Continue to work with the faith that unearned suffering is redemptive. Go back to Mississippi, go back to Alabama, go back to South Carolina, go back to Georgia, go back to Louisiana, go back to the slums and ghettos of our northern cities, knowing that somehow this situation can and will be changed. Let us not wallow in the valley of despair.

I say to you today, my friends so even though we face the difficulties of today and tomorrow, I still have a dream. It is a dream deeply rooted in the American dream. I have a dream that one day this nation will rise up and live out the true meaning of its creed: "We hold these truths to be self-evident, that all men are created equal."

I have a dream that one day on the red hills of Georgia, the sons of former slaves and the sons of former slave owners will be able to sit down together at the table of brotherhood.

I have a dream that one day even the state of Mississippi, a state sweltering with the heat of injustice, sweltering with the heat of oppression, will be transformed into an oasis of freedom and justice.

I have a dream that my four little children will one day live in a nation where they will not be judged by the color of their skin but by the content of their character. I have a dream today.

I have a dream that one day down in Alabama, with its vicious racists, with its governor having his lips dripping with the words of "interposition" and "nullification," one day right there in Alabama little black boys and black girls will be able to join hands with little white boys and white girls as sisters and brothers. I have a dream today.

I have a dream that one day "every valley shall be exalted, and every hill and mountain shall be made low; the rough places will be made plain, and the crooked places will be made straight; and the glory of the Lord shall be revealed, and all flesh shall see it together."

This is our hope. This is the faith that I go back to the South with. With this faith we will be able to hew out of the mountain of despair a stone of hope. With this faith we will be able to transform the jangling discords of our nation into a beautiful symphony of brotherhood. With this faith we will be able to work together, to pray together, to struggle together, to go to jail together, to stand up for freedom together, knowing that we will be free one day. This will be the day, this will be the day when all of God's children will be able to sing with new meaning:

> My Country, 'tis of thee, sweet land of liberty, of thee I Sing.
> Land where my fathers died, land of the pilgrim's pride
> From every mountainside, let freedom ring!
> And if America is to be a great nation, this must become true.
> And so let freedom ring from the prodigious hilltops of New Hampshire.
> Let freedom ring from the mighty mountains of New York.
> Let freedom ring from the heightening Alleghenies of Pennsylvania.
> Let freedom ring from the snowcapped Rockies of Colorado.
> Let freedom ring from the curvaceous slopes of California.
> But not only that: Let freedom ring from Stone Mountain of Georgia.
> Let freedom ring from Lookout Mountain of Tennessee.
> Let freedom ring from every hill and molehill of Mississippi.
> From every mountainside, let freedom ring.

And when this happens, when we allow freedom ring, when we let it ring from every village and every hamlet, from every state and every city; we will be able to speed up that day when all of God's children, black men and white men, Jews and Gentiles, Protestants and Catholics, will be able to join hands and sing in the words of the old Negro spiritual:

> Free at last! Free at last!
> Thank God Almighty, we are free at last!

GLOSSARY

curvaceous: endowed with ample curves, such as an attractive woman

hallowed: sacred

interposition and nullification: a discredited legal theory holding that states can nullify federal laws that they consider unconstitutional, as used by segregationists trying to reverse the Supreme Court's *Brown v. Board of Education* decision

promissory note: a written promise to pay a specific amount on demand or at a specific time

fivescore: one hundred—a "score" being twenty

Document Analysis

After a brief salutation, King reminds his listeners of the symbolic importance of the ground they occupy. King's use of the archaic "fivescore years ago" is an obvious echo of Lincoln's Gettysburg Address. He briefly mentions the triple problems of segregation, discrimination, and poverty that face black Americans and emphasizes the long gap between the Emancipation Proclamation's promise of equality and the lingering reality of pervasive racism.

Using the words of the Declaration of Independence, King says African Americans are seeking only the rights guaranteed to all citizens. He accuses the United States of bad faith in delivering its pledge of freedom. He concludes this passage on a hopeful note, stating his belief that the United States will soon honor its commitment to its black citizens.

King asserts that America cannot afford to wait any longer. Many critics were accusing the civil rights movement of impatience, of pressing too hard for reform. King rejects this argument, underscoring the urgency of African American demands for equal rights by reiterating "now is the time" four times. He threatens that "there will be neither rest nor tranquility" until these demands are granted.

King also admonishes his fellow African Americans to refrain from bitterness and a desire for revenge and emphasizes the need for continued nonviolent tactics. He acknowledges the presence of white supporters, estimated to be about 10 percent of the march's participants. He insists white allies are essential for the movement's success.

King then resumes a more militant tone, listing some of the top priorities of the civil rights movement: an end to police brutality, access to public accommodations, the elimination of housing segregation, the removal of Jim Crow signs, voting rights, and meaningful participation in political affairs. He ends this litany by paraphrasing the Old Testament prophet Amos in saying that blacks will not be satisfied until "justice rolls down like waters and righteousness like a mighty stream."

King next turns his attention to those battle-scarred veterans of the civil rights movement in the audience, saluting their sacrifices and courage. Some of them have questioned the effectiveness of Gandhian civil disobedience, but King encourages them to keep faith in nonviolence.

King then begins the most well-known portion of the speech, in which he outlines his dream for America. In the first glimpse of his dream, King refers again to the Declaration of Independence, asserting his belief that one day Americans truly will honor the words "all men are created equal." He foresees a society where the barriers of segregation dividing the races no longer will be enforced—where blacks and whites will be able to sit down and eat together.

King's dream also extends to the state of Mississippi, home to some of the most violent defenders of white supremacy, asserting that Mississippi will become "an oasis of freedom and justice."

King next makes the dream very personal by including his four young children. He maintains that one day, instead of being considered inferior beings and denied opportunities to develop their full human potential because of the color of their skin, they will be judged by "the content of their character."

Alabama will also be transformed in this renewed nation, offering a vision of a time when "little black boys and black girls" will not be isolated from their white peers. Not only will they see each other as equals, but they will also join hands "as sisters and brothers." The physical intimacy King suggests by this simple act was no doubt offensive to rabid racists but presented a powerful image of innocent fraternity to those in his audience.

Quoting the book of Isaiah, he recalls the prophet's description of the kingdom of God. King embraces the prophetic role, testifying that the quest for civil rights is part of God's divine plan for America and equating the coming victory over segregation with the arrival of the millennium.

At this point King briefly returns to his prepared text for a few sentences affirming his faith in this vision; it gives him confidence that America can overcome its bitter divisions. Then, improvising again, he claims that the knowledge that "we will be free one day" is enough to sustain him and other civil rights activists through the difficult battles that undoubtedly lie ahead.

King continues spontaneously, describing a coming era when "all of God's children" will win their freedom. On that day, African Americans will be able to sing the patriotic hymn "America the Beautiful," confident at last that the verses apply to them. He summons a vision of the day when freedom will ring "from every village and every hamlet" and when this message will be embraced by "all of God's children." He offers a closing image of blacks and whites, Jews and Gentiles, Protestants and Catholics all joining hands in brotherhood. Finally King invokes an African American spiritual for his benediction: "Free at last, free at last, thank God Almighty, we are free at last."

Essential Themes

The final seven minutes of this speech made King's speech a triumph of American oratory. These are the words that schoolchildren memorize, because, in author Drew Hanson's words, King "added something completely fresh to the way that Americans thought about race and civil rights. He gave the nation a vision of what it could look like if all things were made new." There was little in King's rhetoric about the need for civil rights that was truly new. Activists, for a over a century, dating back to the days of the abolition movement, had pointed out the disparity between the nation's ideals and the reality of slavery and racial inequality. However, coming on the heels of the Birmingham campaign, as well as sit-ins and boycotts, and marches around the country, the familiar rhetoric took on a new urgency.

The immediate audience for King's speech was the approximately 250,000 people gathered on August 28, 1963, in front of the Lincoln Memorial and around the nearby Reflecting Pool. Additional millions listened on the radio and watched on television. King's words were aimed at all Americans. For black listeners they carried a message of hope with the promise that the goals of freedom and equality were within reach. For whites, King articulated the aspirations of African Americans, placing them squarely in the context of the American dream. Each year, on the national holiday commemorating his life, King's message is passed on to new generations.

———*Paul T. Murray*

Bibliography and Additional Reading

Alvarez, Alexandra. "Martin Luther King's 'I Have a Dream': The Speech Event as Metaphor." *Journal of Black Studies* 18, no. 3 (March 1988): 337–357.

Bennett, Lerone. *Confrontation: Black and White.* (Chicago: Johnson Publishing, 1965).

Garrow, David J. *Bearing the Cross: Martin Luther King, Jr., and the Southern Christian Leadership Conference.* (New York: Vintage Books, 1986).

Garrow, David J. "King: The Man, the March, the Dream." *American History* 38, no. 3 (August 2003): 26–35.

Hansen, Drew D. *The Dream: Martin Luther King, Jr., and the Speech That Inspired a Nation.* (New York: HarperCollins, 2003).

Johnson, Charles, and Bob Adelman. *King: The Photobiography of Martin Luther King, Jr.* (New York: Viking Studio, 2000).

Lischer, Richard. *The Preacher King: Martin Luther King, Jr. and the Word That Moved America.* (New York: Oxford University Press, 1995).

Miller, Keith D. *Voice of Deliverance: The Language of Martin Luther King, Jr., and Its Sources.* (New York: Free Press, 1992).

Mills, Nicholas. "Heard and Unheard Speeches: What Really Happened at the March on Washington?" *Dissent* 35 (Summer 1988): 285–291.

Powers, Richard Gid. "The FBI Marches on the Dreamer." *American History* 38, no. 3 (August 2003): 42–47.

Reed, Harry A. "Martin Luther King, Jr. History and Memory, Reflections on Dreams and Silences." *Journal of Negro History* 84, no. 2 (Spring 1999): 150–166.

Web Site

"March on Washington for Jobs and Freedom (1963)." King Encyclopedia Web site. http://www.stanford.edu/group/King/about_king/encyclopedia/march_washington.html. Accessed on March 5, 2008.

"Message to the Grass Roots"

Date: 1963
Author: Malcolm X
Genre: Speech

Summary Overview

Malcolm X's "Message to the Grass Roots," delivered in a Detroit church on November 10, 1963, is typically direct, blunt, and uncompromising. Malcolm X gained great fame in his own lifetime largely as the result of his provocative—and some would say inflammatory—speeches. He created the persona of an angry black man, critical of mainstream civil rights leaders such as Martin Luther King, Jr. Malcolm X rejected the doctrine of nonviolence and the Christian tradition that inspired King and many of his followers. It seemed especially sinister to some that he advocated African American self-defense "by any means necessary" (a term he used in several speeches). It did not seem to be the case that he was preaching revolution, however, because as a minister of the Nation of Islam, he was committed to supporting a program of self-help within the African American community. Unlike radical groups such as the Black Panthers, Black Muslims did not engage in confrontations with the police; on the contrary, Black Muslims believed that African Americans should police themselves. But the Nation of Islam rejected the drive for integration and the gradual acceptance of African Americans into a white-dominated society. In this speech, Malcolm X advocates militancy in fighting for civil rights.

Defining Moment

During the early 1960s, the African American civil rights movement began the process of moving in different directions. To the approach of the NAACP, using the court system to enforce equal rights and the peaceful, nonviolent philosophies and practices of Martin Luther King, Jr. and the Southern Christian Leadership Council were added an increasingly independent strand of the movement that, within a few years, would adopt the slogan "black power." In general, the adherents of this segment of the movement were younger and, often, more politically radical.

When Malcolm X delivered this speech on November 10, 1963, much of the focus of the civil rights movement had been on the city of Birmingham, Alabama, which Martin Luther King Jr. had characterized the most segregated city in America. Months of sit-ins, marches, boycotts and other nonviolent demonstrations had resulted in mass arrests and police brutality. Compounding the public interest and concern was the civil rights leadership's decision to deploy children (some elementary school aged) as a significant part of their demonstrators. By May, 1963, the sheer volume of prisoners in the city jail brought the system to a halt. The city government began the process of making concessions but violence continued. The home of King's brother, and the hotel where King himself was staying were bombed and police who arrived to investigate were met with violent resistance from an African American crowd. President Kennedy responded by sending troops (as many as 18,000) to the Birmingham area to restore order.

Despite the agreements between the city and civil rights leaders, unrest continued—particularly from white residents who resented the concessions by the city. The most violent example of this was the bombing of the 16th Street Baptist Church on September 15, 1963, which killed four young girls. Two months later, Malcolm X would be in Detroit, delivering this speech which, in part, critiqued the methods used in the Birmingham campaign.

Author Biography

Malcolm X was born Malcolm Little on May 19, 1925, in Omaha, Nebraska. The family soon moved to Lansing, Michigan, where the six-year-old Malcolm's father was killed in 1931—possibly murdered by members a local Ku Klux Klan group. A good student, Malcolm nevertheless got into trouble early and soon became involved with the numbers racket and drugs. It did not help that his mother was committed to a mental institution and that having lost both parents he was placed in foster care. Living with his sister failed to provide enough stability for the unruly teenager, and at the age of twenty-one he was sent to prison for burglary, larceny, breaking and entering, and carrying a firearm.

Prison life provided Malcolm with the time to reflect on his criminal behavior and absorb the teachings of the Nation of Islam. Malcolm came to see much of his lawbreaking as a response to a repressive white society, however he did not absolve himself of responsibility for his actions. Malcolm left prison with a new name, Malcolm X, jettisoning the last name he associated with his race's slave heritage. He became a preacher for the Nation of Islam, which called upon African Americans to develop their own independence and not base their sense of self-worth on the dictates of the white power structure.

Although his rhetoric against whites could seem quite harsh, he could be hard on the black community and its leaders as well. His speeches—particularly "Message to the Grass Roots" bristle with dynamism that make change seem not merely desirable but inevitable. Not afraid to dramatize the consequences of racial strife, Malcolm X also called for African Americans to scrutinize their own collaboration in second-class citizenship. By noting just how far America had fallen short of its democratic ideals, he also drew the support of many white critics of society.

That Malcolm X eventually broke free from Elijah Muhammad, who had assumed leadership of the Nation of Islam in 1931, can be seen as an extension of his quest to develop a style of leadership entirely his own. His assassination on February 21, 1965, was viewed, in part, as the result of his unwillingness to submit to Elijah Muhammad's authority.

HISTORICAL DOCUMENT

America's problem is us....The only reason she has a problem is she doesn't want us here. And every time you look at yourself, be you black, brown, red, or yellow—a so-called Negro—you represent a person who poses such a serious problem for America because you're not wanted. Once you face this as a fact, then you can start plotting a course that will make you appear intelligent, instead of unintelligent.

What you and I need to do is learn to forget our differences. When we come together, we don't come together as Baptists or Methodists. You don't catch hell 'cause you're a Baptist, and you don't catch hell 'cause you're a Methodist. You don't catch hell 'cause you're a Methodist or Baptist. You don't catch hell because you're a Democrat or a Republican. You don't catch hell because you're a Mason or an Elk. And you sure don't catch hell 'cause you're an American; 'cause if you was an American, you wouldn't catch no hell. You catch hell 'cause you're a black man....All of us catch hell, for the same reason.

So we are all black people, so-called Negroes, second-class citizens, ex-slaves. You are nothing but an ex-slave. You don't like to be told that. But what else are you?...You didn't come here on the "Mayflower." You came here on a slave ship—in chains, like a horse, or a cow, or a chicken. And you were brought here by the people who came here on the "Mayflower." You were brought here by the so-called Pilgrims, or Founding Fathers. They were the ones who brought you here.

We have a common enemy. We have this in common: We have a common oppressor, a common exploiter, and a common discriminator. But once we all realize that we have this common enemy, then we unite on the basis of what we have in common. And what we have foremost in common is that enemy—the white man. He's an enemy to all of us. I know some of you all think that some of them aren't enemies. Time will tell.

In Bandung back in, I think, 1954, was the first unity meeting in centuries of black people. And once you study what happened at the Bandung conference, and the results of the Bandung conference, it actually serves as a model for the same procedure you and I can use to get our problems solved. At Bandung all the nations came together. There were dark nations from Africa and Asia. Some of them were Buddhists. Some of them were Muslim. Some of them were Christians. Some of them were Confucianists; some were atheists. Despite their religious differences, they came together. Some were communists; some were socialists; some were capitalists. Despite their economic and political differences, they came together. All of them were black, brown, red, or yellow.

The number-one thing that was not allowed to attend the Bandung conference was the white man.

He couldn't come. Once they excluded the white man, they found that they could get together. Once they kept him out, everybody else fell...fell in line. This is the thing that you and I have to understand. And these people who came together didn't have nuclear weapons; they didn't have jet planes; they didn't have all of the heavy armaments that the white man has. But they had unity.

They were able to submerge their little petty differences and agree on one thing:...who their enemy was. The same man that was colonizing our people in Kenya was colonizing our people in the Congo. The same one in the Congo was colonizing our people in South Africa, and in Southern Rhodesia, and in Burma, and in India, and in Afghanistan, and in Pakistan. They realized all over the world where the dark man was being oppressed, he was being oppressed by the white man; where the dark man was being exploited, he was being exploited by the white man. So they got together under this basis—that they had a common enemy....Instead of us airing our differences in public, we have to realize we're all the same family....Put the white man out of our meetings...and then sit down and talk shop with each other....

You haven't got a revolution that doesn't involve bloodshed. And you're afraid to bleed. I said, you're afraid to bleed....How are you going to be nonviolent in Mississippi, as violent as you were in Korea? How can you justify being nonviolent in Mississippi and Alabama, when your churches are being bombed, and your little girls are being murdered, and at the same time you're going to get violent with Hitler, and Tojo, and somebody else that you don't even know?

If violence is wrong in America, violence is wrong abroad. If it's wrong to be violent defending black women and black children and black babies and black men, then it's wrong for America to draft us and make us violent abroad in defense of her. And if it is right for America to draft us, and teach us how to be violent in defense of her, then it is right for you and me to do whatever is necessary to defend our own people right here in this country....

There's been a revolution, a black revolution, going on in Africa. In Kenya, the Mau Mau were revolutionaries; they were the ones who made the word "Uhuru." They were the ones who brought it to the fore....They believed in scorched earth. They knocked everything aside that got in their way, and their revolution also was based on land, a desire for land. In Algeria, the northern part of Africa, a revolution took place. The Algerians were revolutionists; they wanted land. France offered to let them be integrated into France. They told France: to hell with France. They wanted some land, not some France. And they engaged in a bloody battle.

So I cite these various revolutions, brothers and sisters, to show you—you don't have a peaceful revolution. You don't have a turn-the-other-cheek revolution. There's no such thing as a nonviolent revolution. The only kind of revolution that's nonviolent is the Negro revolution. The only revolution based on loving your enemy is the Negro revolution. The only revolution in which the goal is a desegregated lunch counter, a desegregated theater, a desegregated park, and a desegregated public toilet....That's no revolution. Revolution is based on land. Land is the basis of all independence. Land is the basis of freedom, justice, and equality.

The white man knows what a revolution is. He knows that the black revolution is world-wide in scope and in nature....A revolution is bloody. Revolution is hostile. Revolution knows no compromise. Revolution overturns and destroys everything that gets in its way. And you, sitting around here like a knot on the wall, saying, "I'm going to love these folks no matter how much they hate me." No, you need a revolution. Whoever heard of a revolution where they lock arms, as Reverend Cleage was pointing out beautifully, singing "We Shall Overcome"? Just tell me. You don't do that in a revolution. You don't do any singing; you're too busy swinging....

When you want a nation, that's called nationalism....A revolutionary is a black nationalist. He wants a nation. I was reading some beautiful words by Reverend Cleage, pointing out why he couldn't get together with someone else here in the city because all of them were afraid of being identified with black nationalism. If you're afraid of black nationalism, you're afraid of revolution. And if you love revolution, you love black nationalism.

To understand this, you have to go back to what the young brother here referred to as the house Negro and the field Negro—back during slavery. There was two kinds of slaves. There was the house Negro and the field Negro. The house Negroes…lived in the house with master. They dressed pretty good; they ate good 'cause they ate his food.…They lived in the attic or the basement, but still they lived near the master; and they loved their master more than the master loved himself. They would give their life to save the master's house quicker than the master would. The house Negro, if the master said, "We got a good house here," the house Negro would say, "Yeah, we got a good house here." Whenever the master said "we," he said "we." That's how you can tell a house Negro.…

This modern house Negro loves his master. He wants to live near him. He'll pay three times as much as the house is worth just to live near his master, and then brag about "I'm the only Negro out here." "I'm the only one on my job." "I'm the only one in this school."…Just as the slavemaster of that day used Tom, the house Negro, to keep the field Negroes in check, the same old slavemaster today has Negroes who are nothing but modern Uncle Toms, 20th-century Uncle Toms, to keep you and me in check, keep us under control, keep us passive and peaceful and nonviolent.…

The white man do the same thing to you in the street,…put knots on your head and take advantage of you and don't have to be afraid of your fighting back. To keep you from fighting back, he gets these old religious Uncle Toms to teach you and me,… suffer peacefully. Don't stop suffering—just suffer peacefully. As Reverend Cleage pointed out, "Let your blood flow In the streets." This is a shame. And you know he's a Christian preacher. If it's a shame to him, you know what it is to me.

There's nothing in our book, the Quran …that teaches us to suffer peacefully. Our religion teaches us to be intelligent. Be peaceful, be courteous, obey the law, respect everyone; but if someone puts his hand on you, send him to the cemetery. That's a good religion. In fact, that's that old-time religion. That's the one that Ma and Pa used to talk about: an eye for an eye, and a tooth for a tooth, and a head for a head, and a life for a life: That's a good religion. And doesn't nobody resent that kind of religion being taught but a wolf, who intends to make you his meal.

This is the way it is with the white man in America. He's a wolf and you're sheep. Any time a shepherd, a pastor, teach you and me not to run from the white man and, at the same time, teach us not to fight the white man, he's a traitor to you and me. Don't lay down our life all by itself. No, preserve your life. It's the best thing you got. And if you got to give it up, let it be even-steven.

The slavemaster took Tom and dressed him well, and fed him well, and even gave him a little education …; gave him a long coat and a top hat and made all the other slaves look up to him. Then he used Tom to control them. The same strategy that was used in those days is used today, by the same white man. He takes a Negro…and make him prominent, build him up, publicize him, make him a celebrity. And then he becomes a spokesman for Negroes— and a Negro leader.

I would like to just mention just one other thing else quickly, and that is the method that the white man uses, how the white man uses these "big guns," or Negro leaders, against the black revolution. They are not a part of the black revolution. They're used against the black revolution.

When Martin Luther King failed to desegregate Albany, Georgia, the civil-rights struggle in America reached its low point. King became bankrupt almost, as a leader.…Even financially, the Southern Christian Leadership Conference was in financial trouble; plus it was in trouble, period, with the people when they failed to desegregate Albany, Georgia.…

As soon as King failed in Birmingham, Negroes took to the streets.…And as these Negroes of national stature began to attack each other, they began to lose their control of the Negro masses.

And Negroes was out there in the streets. They was talking about how we was going to march on Washington. By the way, right at that time Birmingham had exploded, and the Negroes in Birmingham—remember, they also exploded. They began to stab the crackers in the back and bust them upside their head—yes, they did. That's when Kennedy sent in the troops, down in Birmingham. So, and right after that, Kennedy got on the television and said "this is a moral issue." That's when he said he was going to put out a civil-rights bill. And when he mentioned civil-rights bill and the Southern crackers started talking about how they were going to boycott or filibuster it, then the Negroes started talking — about what? We're going to march on Washington, march on the Senate, march on the White House, march on the Congress, and tie it up, bring it to a halt; don't let the government proceed. They even said they was going out to the airport and lay down on the runway and don't let no airplanes land. I'm telling you what they said. That was revolution. That was revolution. That was the black revolution.

It was the grass roots out there in the street. It scared the white man to death, scared the white power structure in Washington, D.C. to death; I was there....The same white element that put Kennedy in power—labor, the Catholics, the Jews, and liberal Protestants; the same clique that put Kennedy in power, joined the march on Washington.

It's just like when you've got some coffee that's too black, which means it's too strong. What you do? You integrate it with cream; you make it weak. If you pour too much cream in, you won't even know you ever had coffee. It used to be hot, it becomes cool. It used to be strong, it becomes weak. It used to wake you up, now it'll put you to sleep. This is what they did with the march on Washington. They joined it. They didn't integrate it; they infiltrated it. They joined it, became a part of it, took it over. And as they took it over, it lost its militancy. They ceased to be angry. They ceased to be hot. They ceased to be uncompromising. Why, it even ceased to be a march. It became a picnic, a circus. Nothing but a circus, with clowns and all.

No, it was a sellout. It was a takeover....And every one of those Toms was out of town by sundown. Now I know you don't like my saying this. But I can back it up. It was a circus, a performance that beat anything Hollywood could ever do, the performance of the year.

GLOSSARY

crackers: an insulting term for whites, especially southern whites

filibuster: the technique of obstructing a bill in a legislature by indefinitely prolonging debate

Mason or an Elk: reference to members of two fraternal and civic organizations

Mau Mau: secret terrorist organization that battled British colonial rule in Kenya from 1952 to 1960

Mayflower: the name of the ship that brought the Pilgrims, a group of religious separatists, to America in 1620

Quran: the sacred scripture of Islam

Reverend Cleage: Albert Cleage, an African American minister famous for arguing that Jesus was a black revolutionary leader

Tojo: Hideki Tojo, the Japanese prime minister during World War II

Uncle Tom: a central character in Harriet Beecher Stowe's 1852 novel *Uncle Tom's Cabin*; a character symbolic of black subservience to whites

Document Analysis

Malcolm X's "Message to the Grass Roots" was delivered in Detroit in a Christian church and addressed to an audience of African Americans. "America's problem is us," he tells his audience, emphasizing that African Americans cannot begin to act properly until they confront racism by recognizing that to be black is to be rejected in the United States. What hinders African Americans, he reiterates, is their blackness. Any other differences between blacks and blacks or blacks and whites hardly matter. Life for African Americans would not get better, he implies, until they came to realize that their blackness is their bond, which should cause them to unite.

Blacks did not like to acknowledge their history as slaves, he argues, and yet the crucial fact is that they were brought to this country in bondage by its very founders. He argues that only when people of color unite could they solve their problems. His illustration is the Bandung Conference, a 1955 meeting of delegates from twenty-nine Asian and African states in Bandung, Indonesia, to discuss the effects of colonialism and cold war tensions on the East. But this unity was achieved only by excluding whites from participating. Until the "dark man" realized that he belonged to a family of dark peoples oppressed by whites, the dark man would never be free.

Malcolm X asserts that freedom would have to be obtained through revolution. Blacks would have to bleed for their freedom instead of bleeding for the white man's wars. Black churches, he concludes, were being bombed in the South, and yet blacks were afraid to shed blood in their own cause.

Malcolm X challenges his audience to take action by critically examining the black community's failings. African Americans have as much right to defend themselves as other nations have, including the new (at that time) African states. Just as Kenya and Algeria violently rejected the terms and ideology of their colonial oppressors and established their own governments. African Americans should expect to do nothing less.

From this militant position, Malcolm goes on to reject the civil rights revolution. He implies that its goals are too modest, for it is not good enough to be able to coexist on the same level with whites in public spaces. Without land and control over their own lives in the form of their own government, blacks would never be self-determining. Malcolm X contends that blacks wanted exactly what whites wanted when making revolutions: a sense of nationality and unity.

In this speech Malcolm X also attacked traditional black civil rights leaders, accusing them of being house slaves, those members of the slave community who were closest to whites and imbibed white values. He refers to these black collaborators with the white power structure as "Uncle Toms," the character in Harriet Beecher Stowe's 1852 antislavery novel *Uncle Tom's Cabin* whose name became synonymous with black subservience to whites.

As a Black Muslim, Malcolm X preached that Christianity was a slave religion emphasizing suffering and the need to bleed rather than rebel. Christian black civil rights leaders, he says, have capitulated to whites, preaching that it is virtuous to turn the other cheek. Instead, Malcolm X argues for the superiority of the Muslim religion, which teaches self-defense and striking out for one's rights. Those black Christian preachers who taught nonviolence were traitors to the black cause. Indeed, they have been groomed by whites to stifle the strivings of the black community just as slave masters housed and indoctrinated their house slaves into the values of white supremacy. Malcolm X suggests that such leaders actually prided themselves on their influence with white people. In effect, they were the dupes of whites.

At this point, Malcolm engages in a full assault on the history of white oppression and the black collaboration in slavery as well as the role Christianity has played in subduing African Americans. Even Martin Luther King, Jr., is treated as a failure with a bankrupt organization, who did not succeed as a leader in areas of the South where he campaigned for desegregation. Only when violence and the threat of more violence caught the attention of President John F. Kennedy did the white power structure begin to take the black revolution seriously. But as usual, that revolution was co-opted, infiltrated by several white leaders, so that in the end revolutionary action became impossible.

Malcolm X explains this adulterating of black revolution in his vivid metaphor of too much cream diluting coffee, making it cold and weak. By making the movement acceptable to white America, activists rob it of its potency.

He concludes by suggesting that the 1963 March on Washington that King led was nothing more than a spectacle, a show, a movie with black leaders ultimately playing the part the "white power structure" had organized for them. He questions the black leadership's level of commitment, and he challenges his audience to make history the only way it can be made: by exercising their power at the grass roots.

Essential Themes

In this speech, Malcolm X presented himself, Islam, and black nationalism as an alternative to the civil rights movement led by Martin Luther King, Jr. and other ministers steeped in the Christian tradition. In this speech as opposed to later ones Malcolm X is particularly strident in his condemnation of Christianity as a source not only of slavery in the United States but as an ongoing tool of white oppressors—a tool that is unwittingly supported by the mainstream civil rights movement. To take this view in late 1963, after the struggles and violence of the Birmingham campaign was a bold step. Characteristically, Malcom X draws a different conclusion from the events of Birmingham. While most of the movement, government officials, press, and public were focused on the suffering and eventual success of the nonviolent portion of the campaign—lamenting the violent confrontations that did take place—Malcolm X seems to assert that the violent confrontations were the part of the entire sequence of events that got results. He uses this to bolster his support of aggressive, revolutionary tactics: "That was revolution. That was the black revolution."

Another key theme that Malcolm X addresses is the increasing identification of the black nationalist movement with the ongoing struggles of African and Asian nations breaking away from their European colonizers. Revolution in Kenya or Algeria might be a better model for African Americans rather than the nonviolence of Ghandi in India.

——*Carl Rollyson, PhD*

Bibliography and Additional Reading

Abernethy, Graeme. *The Iconography of Malcolm X.* (Lawrence, Kan.: University Press of Kansas, 2013).

Assensoh, A. B.; Alex-Assensoh, Yvette M. *Malcolm X and Africa*. (Amherst, N.Y.: Cambria Press, 2016).

Conyers Jr., James L.; Smallwood, Andrew P., eds. *Malcolm X: A Historical Reader.* (Durham, N.C.: Carolina Academic Press, 2008).

Goldman, Peter. *The Death and Life of Malcolm X* (2nd ed.). (Urbana, Ill.: University of Illinois Press, 1979).

■ "The Ballot or the Bullet"

Date: 1964
Author: Malcolm X
Genre: Speech

Summary Overview

Malcolm X's speech "The Ballot or the Bullet," delivered on April 12, 1964, in Detroit, Michigan, is one of the provocative—and some would say inflammatory—speeches through which the man born Malcolm Little gained great fame in his own lifetime. In speeches such as this, Malcolm X created the persona of an angry black man, critical of mainstream civil rights leaders such as Martin Luther King, Jr. Malcolm X rejected the doctrine of nonviolence and the Christian tradition that inspired King and many of his followers. It seemed especially sinister to some that he advocated African American self-defense "by any means necessary" (a term he used in several speeches). While Malcolm X initially scorned the tactics of nonviolence and advocated self-defense in a revolutionary cause, at the same time—as is evident in his speech "The Ballot or the Bullet"—he was seeking ways to unite all African Americans in recognizing their oppression and urge them to create their own strong, self-governing communities.

Defining Moment

During the early 1960s, the African American civil rights movement began the process of moving in different directions. To the approach of the NAACP, using the court system to enforce equal rights and the peaceful, nonviolent philosophies and practices of Martin Luther King, Jr. and the Southern Christian Leadership Council were added an increasingly independent strand of the movement that, within a few years, would adopt the slogan "black power." In general, the adherents of this segment of the movement were younger and, often, more politically radical.

Much was made of Malcolm X's adherence to the theology of the Nation of Islam. Under the leadership of Elijah Muhammad, the Black Muslims developed a religion that cast the white race as an evil oppressor of the black man. Integration of the races was deemed impossible, and therefore collaboration with whites was rejected because it could only abet the white power structure. The Nation of Islam, a separatist organization, was spurned by many—even within the black community—as outside the mainstream of American life and inimical to the dreams and ambitions of African Americans. It was in this context that Malcolm X made his appeal to black congregations. He did not minimize the theological differences between Black Muslims and Christian black leaders, but as in this speech, given at the Cory Methodist Church in Cleveland, Ohio, and sponsored by the Congress on Racial Equality, he emphasized that as people of color African Americans could unite around a common experience of subjugation stemming from slavery. In other words, whatever might divide blacks in terms of religion and politics, the black nationalist movement held a set of principles that every African American could adopt.

Author Biography

Malcolm X was born Malcolm Little on May 19, 1925, in Omaha, Nebraska. The family soon moved to Lansing, Michigan, where the six-year-old Malcolm's father was killed in 1931—possibly murdered by members a local Ku Klux Klan group. A good student, Malcolm nevertheless got into trouble early and soon became involved with the numbers racket and drugs. It did not help that his mother was committed to a mental institution and that having lost both parents he was placed in foster care. Living with his sister failed to provide enough stability for the unruly teenager, and at the age of twenty-one he was sent to prison for burglary, larceny, breaking and entering, and carrying a firearm.

Prison life provided Malcolm with the time to reflect on his criminal behavior and absorb the teachings of the Nation of Islam. Malcolm came to see much of his lawbreaking as a response to a repressive white society, however he did not absolve himself of responsibility for his actions. Malcolm left prison with a new name, Malcolm X, jettisoning the last name he associated with his race's slave heritage. He became a preacher for the Nation of Islam, which called upon African Americans to develop their own independence and not base their sense of self-worth on the dictates of the white power structure.

Although his rhetoric against whites could seem quite harsh, he could be hard on the black community and its leaders as well. His speeches bristle with dynamism that make change seem not merely desirable but inevitable. Not afraid to dramatize the consequences of racial strife, Malcolm X also called for African Americans to scrutinize their own collaboration in second-class citizenship. By noting just how far America had fallen short of its democratic ideals, he also drew the support of many white critics of society.

That Malcolm X eventually broke free from Elijah Muhammad, who had assumed leadership of the Nation of Islam in 1931, can be seen as an extension of his quest to develop a style of leadership entirely his own. His assassination on February 21, 1965, was viewed, in part, as the result of his unwillingness to submit to Elijah Muhammad's authority.

HISTORICAL DOCUMENT

So today, though Islam is my religious philosophy, my political, economic, and social philosophy is Black Nationalism....If we bring up religion we'll have differences...but when we come out here, we have a fight that's common to all of us against an enemy who is common to all of us.

The political philosophy of Black Nationalism only means that the black man should control the politics and the politicians in his own community.... The time when white people can come in our community and get us to vote for them so that they can be our political leaders and tell us what to do and what not to do is long gone. By the same token, the time when that same white man, knowing that your eyes are too far open, can send another negro into the community and get you and me to support him so he can use him to lead us astray—those days are long gone too.

The political philosophy of Black Nationalism only means that if you and I are going to live in a Black community—and that's where we're going to live, 'cause as soon as you move into one of their— soon as you move out of the Black community into their community, it's mixed for a period of time, but they're gone and you're right there all by yourself again....So the political philosophy of Black Nationalism only means that we will have to carry on a program, a political program, of re-education to open our people's eyes, make us become more politically conscious, politically mature, and then we will—whenever we get ready to cast our ballot, that ballot will be—will be cast for a man of the community who has the good of the community of heart.

The economic philosophy of Black Nationalism only means that we should own and operate and control the economy of our community....You can't open up a black store in a white community. White men won't even patronize you. And he's not wrong. He's got sense enough to look out for himself. You the one who don't have sense enough to look out for yourself....The white man is too intelligent to let someone else come and gain control of the economy of his community. But you will let anybody come in and take control of the economy of your community, control the housing, control the education, control the jobs, control the businesses, under the pretext that you want to integrate. No, you're out of your mind....

And you and I are in a double-track, because not only do we lose by taking our money someplace else and spending it, when we try and spend it in our own community we're trapped because we haven't had sense enough to set up stores and control the businesses of our community. The man who's controlling the stores in our community is a man who doesn't look like we do. He's a man who doesn't even live in the community. So you and I, even when we try and spend our money in the block where we live or the area where we live, we're spending it with a man who, when the sun goes down, takes that basket full of money in another part of the town...

So our people not only have to be reeducated to the importance of supporting black business, but the black man himself has to be made aware of the importance of going into business. And once you and I go into business, we own and operate at least the businesses in our community. What we will be doing is developing a situation wherein we will actually be able to create employment for the people in the community....

We're all in the same bag, in the same boat. We suffer political oppression, economic exploitation, and social degradation—all of them from the same enemy. The government has failed us; you can't deny that. Anytime you live in the twentieth century, 1964, and you walkin' around here singing "We Shall Overcome," the government has failed us.

This is part of what's wrong with you—you do too much singing. Today it's time to stop singing and start swinging. You can't sing up on freedom, but you can swing up on some freedom. Cassius Clay can sing, but singing didn't help him to become the heavyweight champion of the world; swinging helped him become the heavyweight champion....

And once we see that all these other sources to which we've turned have failed, we stop turning to them and turn to ourselves....Before we can get a self-help program started we have to have a self-help philosophy.

Black Nationalism is a self-help philosophy. What's so good about it? You can stay right in the church where you are and still take Black Nationalism as your philosophy. You can stay in any kind of civic organization that you belong to and still take black nationalism as your philosophy. You can be an atheist and still take black nationalism as your philosophy. This is a philosophy that eliminates the necessity for division and argument. 'Cause if you're black you should be thinking black, and if you are black and you not thinking black at this late date, well I'm sorry for you....

As long as you gotta sit-down philosophy, you'll have a sit-down thought pattern, and as long as you think that old sit-down thought you'll be in some kind of sit-down action. They'll have you sitting in everywhere. It's not so good to refer to what you're going to do as a "sit-in." That right there castrates you. Right there it brings you down....Well you and I been sitting long enough, and it's time today for us to start doing some standing, and some fighting to back that up.

When we look...at other parts of this earth upon which we live, we find that black, brown, red, and yellow people in Africa and Asia are getting their independence. They're not getting it by singing "We Shall Overcome." No, they're getting it through nationalism....And it will take black nationalism...to bring about the freedom of 22 million Afro-Americans here in this country where we have suffered colonialism for the past 400 years.

America is just as much a colonial power as England ever was. America is just as much a colonial power as France ever was. In fact, America is more so a colonial power than they because she's a hypocritical colonial power behind it....What do you call second class citizenship? Why, that's colonization....They try and make you think they set you free by calling you a second class citizen. No, you're nothing but a 20th-century slave.

Just as it took nationalism...to remove colonialism from Asia and Africa, it'll take black nationalism today to remove colonialism from the backs and the minds of 22 million Afro-Americans here in this country.

And 1964 looks like it might be the year of the ballot or the bullet....

Because Negroes have listened to the trickery, and the lies, and the false promises of the white man now for too long. And they're fed up. They've become disenchanted. They've become disillusioned. They've become dissatisfied, and all of this has built up frustrations in the black community that makes the black community throughout America today more explosive than all of the atomic bombs the Russians can ever invent....

And in 1964 this seems to be the year, because what can the white man use now to fool us after he put down that march on Washington? And you see all through that now. He tricked you, had you marching down to Washington. Yes, had you marching back and forth between the feet of a dead man named Lincoln and another dead man named George Washington singing "We Shall Overcome." He made a chump out of you....

And in 1964 you'll see this young black man, this new generation asking for the ballot or the bullet. That old Uncle Tom action is outdated. The young generation don't want to hear anything about the odds are against us. What do we care about odds?

When this country here was first being founded there were 13 colonies....The whites were colonized. They were fed up with this taxation without representation, so some of them stood up and said "liberty or death." Though I went to a white school over here in Mason, Michigan, the white man made the mistake of letting me read his history books. He made the mistake of teaching me that Patrick Henry was a patriot, and George Washington, wasn't nothing non-violent about old Pat or George Washington.

Liberty or death was what brought about the freedom of whites in this country from the English. They didn't care about the odds. Why they faced the wrath of the entire British Empire. And in those days they used to say that the British Empire was so vast and so powerful when the sun—the sun would never set on it. This is how big it was, yet these 13 little scrawny states, tired of taxation without representation, tired of being exploited and oppressed and degraded, told that big British Empire "liberty or death."

And here you have 22 million Afro-American black people today catching more hell than Patrick Henry ever saw....I'm here to tell you in case you don't know it—that you got a new...generation of black people in this country who don't care anything whatsoever about odds. They don't want to hear you old Uncle Tom handkerchief heads talking about the odds....

This is the year when all of the white politicians are going to come into the Negro community. You never see them until election time. You can't find them until election time. They're going to come in with false promises, and as they make these false promises they're gonna feed our frustrations and this will only serve to make matters worse....

I speak as a victim of America's so-called democracy....We don't see any American dream; we've experienced only the American nightmare. We haven't benefited from America's democracy; we've only suffered from America's hypocrisy. And the generation that's coming up now can see it and are not afraid to say it....

If you go to jail, so what? If you black, you were born in jail. If you black, you were born in jail, in the North as well as the South....

You're in a position to determine who will go to the White House and who will stay in the dog house. You're the one who has that power. You can keep Johnson in Washington D.C., or you can send him back to his Texas cotton patch. You're the one who sent Kennedy to Washington. You're the one who put the present Democratic Administration in Washington D.C. The whites were evenly divided. It was the fact that you threw 80 percent of your votes behind the Democrats that put the Democrats in the White House.

When you see this, you can see that the Negro vote is the key factor. And despite the fact that you are in a position...to be the determining factor, what do you get out of it? The Democrats have been in Washington D.C. only because of the Negro vote. They've been down there four years, and...all other legislation they wanted to bring up they brought it up and gotten it out of the way, and now they bring up you. And now, they bring up you. You put them first, and they put you last, 'cause you're a chump, a political chump....

I was in Washington a couple weeks ago while the Senators were filibustering, and I noticed in the back of the Senate a huge map, and on this map it showed the distribution of Negroes in America, and surprisingly the same Senators that were involved in the filibuster were from the states where there were the most Negroes. Why were they filibustering the civil rights legislation? Because the civil rights legislation is supposed to guarantee voting rights to Negroes in those states, and those senators from those states know that if the Negroes in those states can vote, those senators are down the drain....

These Northern Democrats are in cahoots with the Southern Democrats. They're playing a giant con game, a political con game. You know how it goes....One of them comes to you and makes believe he's for you, and he's in cahoots with the other one that's not for you. Why? Because neither one of them is for you, but they got to make you go with one of them or the other....

Now you take your choice. You going to choose a Northern dog or a Southern dog? Because either dog you choose I guarantee you you'll still be in the dog house.

This is why I say it's the ballot or the bullet. It's liberty or it's death....A revolution is bloody, but America is in a unique position. She's the only country in history in a position actually to become involved in a blood-less revolution....All she's got to do is give the black man in this country everything that's due him—everything.

I hope that the white man can see this, 'cause if he don't see it you're finished. If you don't see it you're going to be coming—you're going to become involved in some action in which you don't have a chance. And we don't care anything about your atomic bomb;...it's useless because other countries have atomic bombs. When two or three different countries have atomic bombs, nobody can use them, so it means that the white man today is without a weapon....If you want some action, you gotta come on down to Earth. And there's more black people on Earth than there are white people on Earth....

The strategy of the white man has always been divide and conquer. He keeps us divided in order to conquer us. He tells you I'm for separation and you're for integration to keep us fighting with each other. No, I'm not for separation and you're not for integration. What you and I is for is freedom. Only you think that integration will get you freedom, I think separation will get me freedom. We both got the same objective. We just got different ways of getting at it....

But when you go to a church and you see the pastor of that church with a philosophy and a program that's designed to bring black people together and elevate black people—join that church....If you see where the NAACP is preaching and practicing that which is designed to make Black Nationalism materialize—join the NAACP. Join any kind of organization—civic, religious, fraternal, political, or otherwise that's based on lifting the black man up and making him master of his own community....

Anything that I can ever do, at any time, to work with anybody in any kind of program that is sincerely designed to eliminate the political, the economic, and the social evils that confront all of our people, in Detroit and elsewhere, all they got to do is give me a telephone call and I'll be on the next jet right on into the city.

GLOSSARY

Cassius Clay: American boxer who later converted to Islam and adopted the name Muhammad Ali

filibustering: a way of obstructing a bill in a legislature by indefinitely prolonging debate

Johnson: President Lyndon B. Johnson

Kennedy: President John F. Kennedy

NAACP: the National Association for the Advancement of Colored People, a civil rights organization

Patrick Henry: American Revolutionary, most famous for his statement "Give my Liberty, or give me Death!"

Uncle Tom: a central character in Harriet Beecher Stowe's 1852 novel *Uncle Tom's Cabin*; a character symbolic of black subservience to whites

Document Analysis

Malcolm X begins this speech by clarifying that although he is, by religious belief, a Muslim, his political ideology is black nationalism which meant, above all, self-government—taking control of the black community's resources. Malcolm X believed that a new era in African American experience had emerged, so that the black community would no longer defer to white leadership or to traditional civil rights leaders. In effect, he accuses the previous generation of black leaders of duplicity, seeming to act on behalf of African Americans while in fact serving only the interests of the dominant Caucasian culture.

In this speech he clearly suggests that by understanding how the black community has been serving interests of the white master class, they could ultimately achieve independence and equality through peaceful means (the ballot). But this could be achieved only through reeducation and control over both the politics and the economy of black communities. Malcolm X discusses the lack of black business owners in black communities and insists that blacks have to own their means of production, as Black Muslims had done in their own communities.

All African Americans were subject to the same fate: a government that had failed them. This failure was more than a political and economic catastrophe. When he speaks here of "social degradation," he is describing a people who have been deprived of their self-respect. They could regain a sense of self-worth only by asserting authority over their own communities. Malcolm X references Cassius Clay, soon to take the name Muhammad Ali, a convert to the Nation of Islam. Like Clay, the African American community, Malcolm X says, should start "swinging," that is, behave aggressively. Malcolm's direct and even harsh words are a wake-up call, demanding that his listeners understand the failure of black leaders and the black community's collaboration in its own oppression.

Malcolm X then criticizes the program of nonviolence led by Martin Luther King, Jr. Sit-ins, which often lead to arrests and police beatings of black demonstrators, are ineffective in Malcolm X's opinion. He argues that despite their differences, member of the black community should be "thinking black"— holding a view of the common interests of African Americans in. To him the absence of a black nationalist mentality meant that his people would continue to be oppressed. A nonviolent philosophy of passive resistance, of sitting down, was to him a form of emasculation, depriving black men of their manhood and the black nation of its energy and conviction.

Referring to black independence movements around the world, Malcolm X notes that none have been achieved through nonviolent resistance, by singing or sitting in. Even though he suggests in this speech and in earlier public talks that violence seemed to be the only way to attain independence, freedom, and equality, this speech marks a departure in indicating that blacks might yet achieve autonomy and self-respect by exercising the ballot (the vote). Frustration in the black community was so profound and had built to such a peak that an explosion was ready to erupt with the force of an atomic bomb.

At the same time, Malcolm X attacks King's historic March on Washington. It was not the ethic of nonviolence that would prevail but rather the aroused militancy of a new generation of blacks with a combustible energy that would ignite the nation if its force were not reflected in a new government obtainable through the ballot. True revolutionaries, he says, are not daunted by the odds against them. Malcolm X concludes that this new generation understood that blacks have experienced not the American dream but the American "nightmare," and this is why the old generation of black leaders and their white liberal masters could no longer take the African American community for granted.

Malcolm X argues that if blacks united and used their political power to elect the next president and made him accountable to their support, then the ballot, not the bullet, might ultimately benefit black people. But they had to realize that they could not count on northern Democrats, who had collaborated with southern Democrats in oppressing African Americans. He cautions that these same politicians had to realize that their old tactics would not work: They could not simply placate blacks. Whites had to understand that worldwide they were outnumbered by people of color and that acknowledging and enforcing equal rights for black people was mandatory. If African Americans united around the black nationalist agenda, the white strategy to divide and conquer the black community would not succeed. For his part, Malcolm X pledges to collaborate with every organization regardless of its religious and political principles so long as it works to "eliminate the political, the economic, and the social evils that confront all of our people."

Essential Themes

As his public speeches show his appeal was not merely to audiences of Black Muslims or those who might wish to convert to the Nation of Islam but to African Americans of all creeds. Malcolm X presented himself as an alternative to the civil rights movement led by Martin Luther King, Jr., and other ministers steeped in the Christian tradition. While Malcolm X initially scorned the tactics of nonviolence and advocated self-defense in a revolutionary cause, at the same time—as is evident in his speech "The Ballot or the Bullet"—he was seeking ways to unite all African Americans in recognizing their oppression and urge them to create their own strong, self-governing communities.

As discussed above, in this speech, Malcolm X moves away from an emphasis on violent revolution and toward the exercise of peaceful political power. This sudden and seemingly bold departure from his previous argument in favor of revolution is, in fact, signaled near the beginning of the speech when he suggests that the consciousness of the African American community has been altered and that a process of reeducation is under way.

———*Carl Rollyson, PhD*

Bibliography and Additional Reading

Abernethy, Graeme. *The Iconography of Malcolm X*. (Lawrence, Kan.: University Press of Kansas, 2013).

Assensoh, A. B.; Alex-Assensoh, Yvette M. *Malcolm X and Africa*. (Amherst, N.Y.: Cambria Press, 2016).

Conyers Jr., James L.; Smallwood, Andrew P., eds. *Malcolm X: A Historical Reader*. (Durham, N.C.: Carolina Academic Press, 2008).

Goldman, Peter. *The Death and Life of Malcolm X* (2nd ed.). (Urbana, Ill.: University of Illinois Press, 1979).

What We Want

Date: 1966
Author: Stokely Carmichael
Genre: Magazine article

Summary Overview

This article shares many of the same ideas and examples as the speech Carmichael would give in October, 1966 at the University of California at Berkley. This article, however, goes more deeply into the role and philosophy of SNCC (the Student Nonviolent Coordinating Committee). Carmichael highlights SNCC's role as a focal point for a younger group of activists than more established organizations like Martin Luther King Jr.'S Southern Christian Leadership Council or the NAACP. The article also discusses SNCC's goals of obtaining not only equal rights but also the need for the African American community to gain political power. It is in connection with this that we see Carmichael use the phrase "Black Power" as well as discuss the activities of the developing Black Panther party.

There is also, in Carmichael's article, indications of the eventual turn away from the pacifistic, non-confrontational methods that typified the methods of the SCLC. He also discusses the need for civil rights organizations not only to work fully and exclusively for the needs and benefit of the communities which they represent but also to "speak in the tone of that community." Carmichael also speaks to specific efforts to gain political gains and power in southern states as well as the development of the emerging Black Panther party in northern and western urban centers like Los Angeles, New York, and other cities.

Defining Moment

The year 1966 was pivotal for both of Carmichael's major concerns: civil rights and the Vietnam War. This article was written when the political and social climate of the country was being shaped by the assassinations of three major figures. President John F. Kennedy had been assassinated on November 22, 1963, and the black civil rights activist Malcolm X had been killed on February 21, 1965. Prior to this articles publication, Carmichael had taken part in the March against Fear from Memphis, Tennessee, to Jackson, Mississippi. The march had been organized by James Meredith, the first African American student at the University of Mississippi, where he had been subject to constant harassment. After graduation he organized the march, which began on June 5, 1966, in order to bring attention to black voting rights issues in the South and to help blacks overcome fear of violence. During the march he was shot in an assassination attempt by Aubrey James Norvell, but he survived. Several civil rights leaders, including Carmichael, joined the march after the shooting. Carmichael was arrested in Greenwood, Mississippi, while participating in the march. When he rejoined the marchers, he galvanized them with a speech at a rally; that speech has also been referred to as his "Black Power" speech.

When this article was published in the early autumn of 1966, Carmichael was still not only a member of SNCC but also in many ways its public face and certainly its most charismatic speaker. He was particularly highly regarded as a speaker on college campuses. SNCC, formed in 1960, was a major force in the civil rights movement. It organized voter registration drives throughout the South and events such as the 1963 March on Washington. Leaders of the organization included such notables of the civil rights movement as Julian Bond, John Lewis, Marion Barry, and Carmichael's successor as chairman, H. Rap Brown. In addition to its "Black Power" focus, SNCC was also involved in protests against the Vietnam War.

Author Biography

Stokely Carmichael, later in life known also as Kwame Ture, was born on June 29, 1941, in Port-of-Spain, Trinidad and Tobago. Carmichael eventually joined his parents, who had emigrated to New York. In 1960 he began attending Howard University, where he became involved with the newly formed SNCC. While he was a member of SNCC in 1965, Carmichael played a lead role in increasing the number of registered black voters in Lowndes County, Alabama, from seventy to twenty-six hundred. As a representative of the militant wing of SNCC, Carmichael rose to become the organization's chairman in 1966.

While Carmichael was at first supportive of the work of Martin Luther King, he would later repudiate King's nonviolent stance. He would, however, continue to join King in speaking out against the Vietnam War. Through the force of his rhetoric, Carmichael became a celebrity, but others in SNCC resented his prominence and he was soon formally expelled from the organization. He joined the more militant Black Panther Party and as "honorary prime minister" of the Panthers, he became an even more forceful critic of the Vietnam War, lecturing around the world (often on college campuses).

After the assassination of King on April 4, 1968, Carmichael was in Washington, D.C., and, although he was no longer officially a member of SNCC, led members of that organization in trying to maintain order. In 1969 he left the United States and the Panthers to live in the Republic of Guinea. From his base in Guinea, Carmichael wrote and spoke, advocating pan-Africanism and Socialism.

Carmichael died of prostate cancer on November 15, 1998, at the age of fifty-seven, Before his death, he had claimed that the Federal Bureau of Investigation had infected him with a strain of cancer in order to assassinate him. It was later learned that he had been the subject of surveillance by the FBI and the Central Intelligence Agency since 1968.

HISTORICAL DOCUMENT

One of the tragedies of the struggle against racism is that up to now there has been no national organization which could speak to the growing militancy of young black people in the urban ghetto. There has been only a civil rights movement, whose tone of voice was adapted to an audience of liberal whites. It served as a sort of buffer zone between them and angry young blacks. None of its so-called leaders could go into a rioting community and be listened to. In a sense, I blame ourselves—together with the mass media—for what has happened in Watts, Harlem, Chicago, Cleveland, Omaha. Each time the people in those cities saw Martin Luther King get slapped, they became angry; when they saw four little black girls bombed to death, they were angrier; and when nothing happened, they were steaming. We had nothing to offer that they could see, except to go out and be beaten again. We helped to build their frustration.

For too many years, black Americans marched and had their heads broken and got shot. They were saying to the country, "Look, you guys are supposed to be nice guys and we are only going to do what we are supposed to do—why do you beat us up, why don't you give us what we ask, why don't you straighten yourselves out?" After years of this, we are at almost the same point—because we demonstrated from a position of weakness. We cannot be expected any longer to march and have our heads broken in order to say to whites: come on, you're nice guys. For you are not nice guys. We have found you out.

An organization which claims to speak for the needs of a community—as does the Student Nonviolent Coordinating Committee—must speak in the tone of that community, not as somebody else's buffer zone. This is the significance of black power as a slogan. For once, black people are going to use the words they want to use—not just the words whites want to hear. And they will do this no matter how often the press tries to stop the use of the slogan by equating it with racism or separatism.

An organization which claims to be working for the needs of a community—as SNCC does—must work to provide that community with a position of strength from which to make its voice heard. This is the significance of black power beyond the slogan.

Black power can be clearly defined for those who do not attach the fears of white America to their questions about it. We should begin with the basic fact that black Americans have two problems: they are poor and they are black. All other problems arise from this two-sided reality: lack of education, the so-called apathy of black men. Any program to end racism must address itself to that double reality.

Almost from its beginning, SNCC sought to address itself to both conditions with a program aimed at winning political power for impoverished Southern blacks. We had to begin with politics because black Americans are a propertyless people in a country where property is valued above all. We had to work for power, because this country does not function by morality, love, and nonviolence, but by power. Thus we determined to win political power, with the idea of moving on from there into activity that would have economic effects. With power, the masses could *make or participate in making* the decisions which govern their destinies, and thus create basic change in their day-to-day lives.

But if political power seemed to be the key to self-determination, it was also obvious that the key had been thrown down a deep well many years earlier. Disenfranchisement, maintained by racist terror, makes it impossible to talk about organizing for political power in 1960. The right to vote had to be won and SNCC workers devoted their energies to this from 1961 to 1965. They set up voter registration drives in the Deep South. They created pressure for the vote by holding mock elections in Mississippi in 1963 and by helping to establish the Mississippi Freedom Democratic Party (MFDP) in 1964. That struggle was eased, though not won, with the passage of the 1965 Voting Rights Act SNCC workers could then address themselves to the question: "Who can we vote for, to have our needs met—how do we make our vote meaningful?"

SNCC had already gone to Atlantic City for recognition of the Mississippi Freedom Democratic Party by the Democratic convention and been rejected; it had gone with the MFDP to Washington for recognition by Congress and been rejected. In Arkansas, SNCC helped thirty Negroes to run for School Board elections; all but one were defeated, and there was evidence of fraud and intimidation sufficient to cause their defeat. In Atlanta, Julian Bond ran for the state legislature and was elected—twice—and unseated—twice. In several states, black farmers ran in elections for agricultural committees which make crucial decisions concerning land use, loans, etc. Although they won places on a number of committees, they never gained the majorities needed to control them.

All of the efforts were attempts to win black power. Then, in Alabama, the opportunity came to see how blacks could be organized on an independent party basis. An unusual Alabama law provides that any group of citizens can nominate candidates for county office and, if they win 20 percent of the vote, may be recognized as a county political party.

The same then applies on a state level. SNCC went to organize in several counties such as Lowndes, where black people—who form 80 per cent of the population and have an average annual income of $943—felt they could accomplish nothing within the framework of the Alabama Democratic Party because of its racism and because the qualifying fee for this year's elections was raised from $50 to $500 in order to prevent most Negroes from becoming candidates. On May 3, five new county "freedom organizations" convened and nominated candidates for the offices of sheriff, tax assessor, members of the school boards. These men and women are up for election in November—if they live until then. Their ballot symbol is the black panther a bold, beautiful animal, representing the strength and dignity of black demands today. A man needs a black panther on his side when he and his family must endure—as hundreds of Alabamians have endured—loss of job, eviction, starvation, and sometimes death, for political activity. He may also need a gun and SNCC reaffirms the right of black men everywhere to defend themselves when threatened or attacked. As for initiating the use of violence, we hope that such programs as ours will make that unnecessary; but it is not for us to tell black communities whether they can or cannot use any particular form of action to resolve their problems. Responsibility for the use of violence by black men, whether in self-defense or initiated by them, lies with the white community.

This is the specific historical experience from which SNCC's call for "black power" emerged on the Mississippi march last July. But the concept of "black power" is not a recent or isolated phenomenon: It has grown out of the ferment of agitation and activity by different people and organizations in many black communities over the years. Our last year of work in Alabama added a new concrete possibility. In Lowndes County, for example, black power will mean that if a Negro is elected sheriff, he can end police brutality. If a black man is elected tax assessor, he can collect and channel funds for the building of better roads and schools serving black people—thus advancing the move from political power into the economic arena. In such areas as Lowndes, where black men have a majority, they will attempt to use it to exercise control. This is what they seek: control. Where Negroes lack a majority, black power means proper representation and sharing of control. It means the creation of power bases from which black people can work to change statewide or nationwide patterns of oppression through pressure from strength—instead of weakness. Politically, black power means what it has always meant to SNCC: the coming-together of black people to elect representatives and *to force those representatives to speak to their needs*. It does not mean merely putting black faces into office. A man or woman who is black and from the slums cannot be automatically expected to speak to the needs of black people. Most of the black politicians we see around the country today are not what SNCC means by black power. The power must be that of a community, and emanate from there.

SNCC today is working in both North and South on programs of voter registration and independent political organizing. In some places, such as Alabama, Los Angeles, New York, Philadelphia, and New Jersey, independent organizing under the black panther symbol is in progress. The creation of a national "black panther party" must come about: it will take time to build, and it is much too early to predict its success. We have no infallible master plan and we make no claim to exclusive knowledge of how to end racism; different groups will work in their own different ways. SNCC cannot spell out the full logistics of self-determination but it can address itself to the problem by helping black communities define their needs, realize their strength, and go into action along a variety of lines which they must choose for themselves. Without knowing all the answers, it can address itself to the basic problem of poverty: to the fact that in Lowndes County, 86 white families own 90 percent of the land. What are black people in that county going to do for jobs, where are they going to get money? There must be reallocation of land and money.

Ultimately, the economic foundations of this country must be shared if black people are to control their lives. The colonies of the United States—and this includes the black ghettoes within its borders, north and south—must be liberated. For a century, this nation has been like an octopus of exploitation, its tentacles stretching from Mississippi and Harlem to South America, the Middle East, southern Africa, and Vietnam; the form of exploitation varies from area to area but the essential result has been the same—a powerful few have been maintained and enriched at the expense of the poor and voiceless colored masses. This pattern must be broken. As its grip loosens here and there around the world, the hopes of black Americans become more realistic. For racism to die, a totally different America must be born.

This is what the white society does not wish to face; this is why that society prefers to talk about integration. But integration speaks not at all to the problem of poverty, only to the problem of blackness. Integration today means the man who "makes it," leaving his black brothers behind in the ghetto as fast as his new sports car will take him. It has no relevance to the Harlem wino or to the cotton-picker making three dollars a day. As a lady I know in Alabama once said, "the food that Ralph Bunche eats doesn't fill my stomach."

Integration, moreover, speaks to the problem of blackness in a despicable way. As a goal, it has been based on complete acceptance of the fact that *in order to have* a decent house or education, blacks must move into a white neighborhood or send their children to a white school. This reinforces, among both black and white, the idea that "white" is automatically better and "black" is by definition inferior. This is why integration is a subterfuge for the maintenance of white supremacy. It allows the nation to focus on a handful of Southern children who get into white schools, at great price, and to ignore the 94 percent who are left behind in unimproved all-black schools. Such situations will not change until black people have power—to control their own school boards, in this case. Then Negroes become equal in a way that means something, and integration ceases to be a one-way street. Then integration doesn't mean draining skills and energies from the ghetto into white neighborhoods; then it can mean white people moving from Beverly Hills into Watts, white people joining the Lowndes County Freedom Organization. Then integration becomes relevant....

To most whites, black power seems to mean that the Mau Mau are coming to the suburbs at night. The Mau Mau are coming, and whites must stop them. Articles appear about plots to "get Whitey," creating an atmosphere in which "law and order must be maintained." Once again, responsibility is shifted from the oppressor to the oppressed. Other whites chide, "Don't forget—you're only 10 percent of the population; if you get too smart, we'll wipe you out." If they are liberals, they complain, "what about me?—don't you want my help any more?" These are people supposedly concerned about black Americans, but today they think first of themselves, of their feelings of rejection. Or they admonish, "you can't get anywhere without coalitions," without considering the problems of coalition with whom?; on what terms (coalescing from weakness can mean absorption, betrayal)?; when? Or they accuse us of "polarizing the races" by our calls for black unity, when the true responsibility for polarization lies with whites who will not accept their responsibility as the majority power for making the democratic process work....

Whites will not see that I, for example, as a person oppressed because of my blackness, have common cause with other blacks who are oppressed because of blackness. This is not to say that there are no white people who see things as I do, but that it is black people I must speak to first. It must be the oppressed to whom SNCC addresses itself primarily, not to friends from the oppressing group.

From birth, black people are told a set of lies about themselves. We are told that we are lazy—yet I drive through the Delta area of Mississippi and watch black people picking cotton in the hot sun for fourteen hours. We are told, "If you work hard, you'll succeed"—but if that were true, black people would own this country. We are oppressed because we are black—not because we are ignorant, not because we are lazy, not because we're stupid (and got good rhythm), but because we're black....

The need for psychological equality is the reason why SNCC today believes that blacks must organize in the black community. Only black people can convey the revolutionary idea that black people are able to do things themselves. Only they can help create in the community an aroused and continuing black consciousness that will provide the basis for political strength. In the past, white allies have furthered white supremacy without the whites involved realizing it—or wanting it, I think. Black people must do things for themselves; they must get poverty money they will control and spend themselves, they must conduct tutorial programs themselves so that black children can identify with black people. This is one reason Africa has such importance: The reality of black men ruling their own nations gives blacks elsewhere a sense of possibility, of power, which they do not now have.

This does not mean we don't welcome help, or friends. But we want the right to decide whether anyone is, in fact, our friend. In the past, black Americans have been almost the only people whom everybody and his momma could jump up and call their friends. We have been tokens, symbols, objects—as I was in high school to many young whites, who liked having "a Negro friend." We want to decide who is our friend, and we will not accept someone who comes to us and says: "If you do X, Y, and Z, then I'll help you." We will not be told whom we should choose as allies. We will not be isolated from any group or nation except by our own choice. We cannot have the oppressors telling the oppressed how to rid themselves of the oppressor....

There is a vital job to be done among poor whites. We hope to see, eventually, a coalition between poor blacks and poor whites. That is the only coalition which seems acceptable to us, and we see such a coalition as the major internal instrument of change in American society. SNCC has tried several times to organize poor whites; we are trying again now, with an initial training program in Tennessee. It is purely academic today to talk about bringing poor blacks and whites together, but the job of creating a poor-white power bloc must be attempted. The main responsibility for it falls upon whites. Black and white can work together in the white community where possible; it is not possible, however, to go into a poor Southern town and talk about integration. Poor whites everywhere are becoming more hostile—not less—partly because they see the nation's attention focused on black poverty and nobody coming to them. Too many young middle-class Americans, like some sort of Pepsi generation, have wanted to come alive through the black community; they've wanted to be where the action is—and the action has been in the black community.

Black people do not want to "take over" this country. They don't want to "get whitey"; they just want to get him off their backs, as the saying goes. It was for example the exploitation by Jewish landlords and merchants which first created black resentment toward Jews—not Judaism. The white man is irrelevant to blacks, except as an oppressive force. Blacks want to be in his place, yes, but not in order to terrorize and lynch and starve him. They want to be in his place because that is where a decent life can be had....

As for white America, perhaps it can stop crying out against "black supremacy," "black nationalism," "racism in reverse," and begin facing reality. The reality is that this nation, from top to bottom, is racist; that racism is not primarily a problem of "human relations" but of an exploitation maintained—either actively or through silence—by the society as a whole. Camus and Sartre have asked, can a man condemn himself? Can whites, particularly liberal whites, condemn themselves? Can they stop blaming us, and blame their own system? Are they capable of the shame which might become a revolutionary emotion?

We have found that they usually cannot condemn themselves, and so we have done it. But the rebuilding of this society, if at all possible, is basically the responsibility of whites—not blacks. We won't fight to save the present society, in Vietnam or anywhere else. We are just going to work, in the way we see fit, and on goals we define, not for civil rights but for all our human rights.

GLOSSARY

"Four little black girls bombed to death": a reference to the victims killed in the bombing of Birmingham, Alabama's 16th Street Baptist Church on September 15, 1963.

Lowndes County: County in Georgia where, in 1965 the Lowndes County Freedom Organization was formed. This organization would be the basis for the Black Panther Party.

Mau Mau: Anti-colonial rebels in Kenya, Africa who staged an uprising against the British during the 1950s

Mississippi Freedom Democratic Party: Splinter of the Democratic party focused on registering African American voters in Mississippi in 1964.

Ralph Bunche: Nobel Peace Prize winning political scientist and diplomat who was active in the civil rights movement of the 1950s ad 1960s.

"Watts, Harlem, Chicago…": Sites of rioting or violent demonstrations during the mid-1960s

Document Analysis

Carmichael begins by recognizing that traditional civil rights organizations did not address "the growing militancy of young black people in the urban ghetto" but, rather, address themselves to largely white, northern liberals. he also notes that no "so-called" civil rights leaders would be able to get "a rioting community" to listen to them. Such a situation occurred after the Watts riot in Los Angeles, when Martin Luther King Jr. was heckled by some when he delivered a speech there. The strategy of nonviolence, Carmichael claims, offers these young people nothing but the opportunity to be repeatedly brutalized by the authorities and asserts that African Americans have been making demands equality from a position of weakness.

Carmichael then, in the third paragraph, argues that organizations that claim to speak for the community must serve that community and speak its language, not serve the needs or present themselves as acceptable for other groups (as he claims other civil rights organizations and leaders have done). This, he explains, is the origin of the term "black power." Despite the discomfort the term may cause, the term is significant for it is an example of African Americans using "the words they want to use—not just the words whites wants to hear." In other words, Black Power is an expression of black activists defining their own goals and parameters rather than tailoring their aims or methods to be acceptable to white America.

He goes on to define the "two-sided reality" facing African Americans, "they are poor and they are black." Racism and economic inequality are the core crises from which other problems. African Americans are "a propertyless people in a country where property is valued above all." To remedy this, Carmichael explains, black Americans must work to achieve and exercise power, since "this country does not function by morality, love, and nonviolence." Political power would make movement toward economic equality possible.

In the sixth paragraph, Carmichael explains that political power has been out of reach for African Americans due to "disenfranchisement, maintained by racist terror." He goes on to detail the efforts of the Mississippi Freedom Democratic Party to register voters in 1964 and the passage of the Voting Rights Act in 1965. The question then became, "who can we vote for to save our needs met—how to we make our vote meaningful?" Carmichael describes the successful efforts of African Americans to seek political office and how these efforts have been met with intimidation and defeat. This was due, at least partially, to efforts within the Democratic party to suppress black candidates—particularly in the south.

The solution to this issue, he explains, is to organize African Americans as an independent political party. This first happened in Lowndes County, Alabama when the state's Democratic party took measures to keep African Americans from running for office. Known as "freedom organizations," these groups symbol was a black panther. In 1966, the groups had several candidates who would be on the ballot in the November elections-"if they live until then.

Carmichael then discusses how SNCC "reaffirms the right of black men everywhere to defend themselves when threatened or attacked" and while they hope their plans will prevent the need for violence, "responsibility for the use of violence by black men, whether in self-defense or initiated by them, lies with the white community." Increasingly, as this article goes on, Carmichael is moving away from the rhetoric of nonviolence—not toward a rhetoric of revolutionary violence but, rather, a realistic appraisal of the threats faced by African Americans.

After detailing more voter registration efforts and discussing the national growth of the black panther party, Carmichael discusses his view of the "black ghettoes" within the United States as being colonized territories, placing them in the same category of colonial territories in that, during the 1960s, were fighting for liberation from western powers. He argues that liberation from economic exploitation is as necessary for African Americans as for those in places like Vietnam. Integration, he asserts will not fully address the economic inequalities in American society. He also denounces integration of neighborhoods and schools, claiming that "integration is a subterfuge for the maintenance of white supremacy" that "allows the nation to focus on a handful of Southern children who get into white schools, at great price, and to ignore the 94 percent who are left behind in unimproved all-black schools." Black Americans in positions of political power can bring real, lasting change.

He also clarifies the idea of "Black Power," refuting the idea that it is synonymous with black supremacy or similar to the revolutionary violence that had taken place in colonial Africa (he references the Mau Mau uprising in Kenya in this regard). He concludes by explaining that rather than black supremacy, SNCC has attempted to organize poor whites and that a "coalition" between poor whites and poor blacks is the only force that will fundamentally affect economic exploitation of all Americans.

Essential Themes

In this article, Stokely Carmichael refined the meaning of the term "Black Power," repositioning the Student Nonviolent Coordinating Committee as something more than a young people's version of traditional civil rights groups like the NAACP or the Southern Christian Leadership Council. He does this in two ways. One way is by pushing back against the unqualified promotion of nonviolence in the face of police brutality, asserting that self defense is acceptable. The other way Carmichael and SNCC distinguished themselves was by actively promoting not only equal rights but the seizure—through democratic means—of political power. Its was this latter goal that led to the creation of the groups that, eventually, would form the basis of the Black Panther Party. This was connected to Carmichael's rejection of the perceived need for civil rights organizations to make themselves acceptable to white political leaders and the public. Carmichael also emphasized the theme of economic inequality and injustice, linking it to both American racism and as a problem that cannot be remedied by "equal rights" but, rather by political power.

——*Aaron Gulyas, with additional material by Keith E. Sealing*

Bibliography and Additional Reading
Asante, Molefi Kete. *100 Greatest African Americans: A Biographical Encyclopedia.* Amherst, N.Y. Prometheus Books, 2002.
Carmichael, Stokely. *Stokely Speaks: Black Power Back to Pan-Africanism.* New York, Random House, 1971.
———, and Charles V. Hamilton. *Black Power: The Politics of Liberation in America.* New York: Random House, 1967.
———, and Ekwueme Michael Thelwell. *Ready for Revolution: The Life and Struggles of Stokely Carmichael.* New York: Scribner, 2003.
Carson, Clayborne. *In Struggle: SNCC and the Black Awakening of the 1960s.* Cambridge, Mass. Harvard University Press, 1981. Cwiklik, Robert. *Stokely Carmichael and Black Power.* Brookfield, Conn. Millbrook Press, 1993.
Johnson, Jacqueline. *Stokely Carmichael: The Story of Black Power.* Englewood Cliffs, N.J. Silver Burdett, 1990.
Sellers, Cleveland, and Robert Terrell. *The River of No Return: The Autobiography of a Black Militant in the Life and Death of SNCC.* New York: Morrow, 1973.
Zinn, Howard. *SNCC: The New Abolitionists.* Boston: Beacon Press, 1964.

Websites
Kaufman, Michael T. "Stokely Carmichael, Rights Leader Who Coined 'Black Power,' Dies at 57." *New York Times*, November 16, 1998. http://www.interchange.org/Kwameture/nytimes111698.html
"Stokely Carmichael." Federal Bureau of Investigation Web site. http://foia.fbi.gov/foiaindex/carmichael_stokely.htm

■ "Black Power"

Date: 1966
Author: Stokely Carmichael
Genre: Speech

Summary Overview

On October 29, 1966, Stokely Carmichael addressed an audience consisting primarily of college students at the University of California at Berkeley in a speech that has become known as "Black Power." Carmichael touched on a broad range of issues in his "Black Power" speech, including SNCC's condemnation of white America's "institutional racism" (a term he has been credited with coining) and fear of the term "Black Power." He also discussed the relationship between the American civil rights movement and unrest in much of the postcolonial world, the need for white activists to organize in white communities, nonviolence versus self-defense in the face of racial oppression, and the evil of the Vietnam War.

Carmichael was talking to an audience of largely left-leaning students on one of the most liberal, even radical, campuses in the country at a time when the civil rights movement had begun to hit its stride. He was speaking as a representative of SNCC and cited the positions taken as those of SNCC, whose platform he was largely responsible for developing and articulating. Although SNCC espoused nonviolence at the time and included whites in its membership, Carmichael was already moving away from white inclusion in SNCC, calling instead for whites to organize nonracist whites in their own communities. He was also questioning the workability of nonviolence in the face of violence against peaceful African American demonstrators by whites in positions of power.

Defining Moment

The year 1966 was pivotal for both of Carmichael's major concerns: civil rights and the Vietnam War. His address was delivered at a time when the political and social climate of the country was being shaped by the assassinations of three major figures. President John F. Kennedy had been assassinated on November 22, 1963, and the black civil rights activist Malcolm X had been killed on February 21, 1965. Several months before the UC Berkeley speech, Carmichael had taken part in the March against Fear from Memphis, Tennessee, to Jackson, Mississippi. The march had been organized by James Meredith, the first African American student at the University of Mississippi, where he had been subject to constant harassment. After graduation he organized the march, which began on June 5, 1966, in order to bring attention to black voting rights issues in the South and to help blacks overcome fear of violence. During the march he was shot in an assassination attempt by Aubrey James Norvell, but he survived. Several civil rights leaders, including Carmichael, joined the march after the shooting. Carmichael was arrested in Greenwood, Mississippi, while participating in the march. When he rejoined the marchers, he galvanized them with a speech at a rally; that speech has also been referred to as his "Black Power" speech.

At the time of his speech at UC Berkeley, Carmichael was still not only a member of SNCC but also in many ways its public face and certainly its most charismatic speaker. He was particularly highly regarded as a speaker on college campuses. SNCC, formed in 1960, was a major force in the civil rights movement. It organized voter registration drives throughout the South and events such as the 1963 March on Washington. Leaders of the organization included such notables of the civil rights movement as Julian Bond, John Lewis, Marion Barry, and Carmichael's successor as chairman, H. Rap Brown. In addition to its "Black Power" focus, SNCC was also involved in protests against the Vietnam War.

Author Biography

Stokely Carmichael, later in life known also as Kwame Ture, was born on June 29, 1941, in Port-of-Spain, Trinidad and Tobago. Carmichael eventually joined his parents, who had emigrated to New York. In 1960 he began attending Howard University, where he became involved with the newly formed SNCC. While he was a member of SNCC in 1965, Carmichael played a lead role in increasing the number of registered black voters in Lowndes County, Alabama, from seventy to twenty-six hundred. As a representative of the militant wing of SNCC, Carmichael rose to become the organization's chairman in 1966.

While Carmichael was at first supportive of the work of Martin Luther King, he would later repudiate King's nonviolent stance. He would, however, continue to join King in speaking out against the Vietnam War. Through the force of his rhetoric, Carmichael became a celebrity, but others in SNCC resented his prominence and was soon formally expelled from the organization. He joined the more militant Black Panther Party and as "honorary prime minister" of the Panthers, he became an even more forceful critic of the Vietnam War, lecturing around the world)often on college campuses).

After the assassination of King on April 4, 1968, Carmichael was in Washington, D.C., and, although he was no longer officially a member of SNCC, led members of that organization in trying to maintain order. In 1969 he left the United States and the Panthers to live in the Republic of Guinea. From his base in Guinea, Carmichael wrote and spoke, advocating pan-Africanism and Socialism.

Carmichael died of prostate cancer on November 15, 1998, at the age of fifty-seven, Before his death, he had claimed that the Federal Bureau of Investigation had infected him with a strain of cancer in order to assassinate him. It was later learned that he had been the subject of surveillance by the FBI and the Central Intelligence Agency since 1968.

HISTORICAL DOCUMENT

Thank you very much. It's a privilege and an honor to be in the white intellectual ghetto of the West. We wanted to do a couple of things before we started. The first is that, based on the fact that SNCC, through the articulation of its program by its chairman, has been able to win elections in Georgia, Alabama, Maryland, and by our appearance here will win an election in California, in 1968 I'm going to run for President of the United States. I just can't make it, 'cause I wasn't born in the United States. That's the only thing holding me back.

We wanted to say that this is a student conference, as it should be, held on a campus, and that we're not ever to be caught up in the intellectual masturbation of the question of Black Power. That's a function of people who are advertisers that call themselves reporters.

Oh, for my members and friends of the press, my self-appointed white critics, I was reading Mr. Bernard Shaw two days ago, and I came across a very important quote which I think is most apropos for you. He says, "All criticism is a[n] autobiography." Dig yourself. Okay.

The philosophers Camus and Sartre raise the question whether or not a man can condemn himself. The black existentialist philosopher who is pragmatic, Frantz Fanon, answered the question. He said that man could not. Camus and Sartre does not. We in SNCC tend to agree with Camus and Sartre that a man cannot condemn himself. Were he to condemn himself, he would then have to inflict punishment upon himself. An example would be the Nazis. Any prisoner who—any of the Nazi prisoners who admitted, after he was caught and incarcerated, that he committed crimes, that he killed all the many people that he killed, he committed suicide. The only ones who were able to stay alive were the ones who never admitted that they committed crimes against people—that is, the ones who rationalized that Jews were not human beings and deserved to be killed, or that they were only following orders.

On a more immediate scene, the officials and the population—the white population—in Neshoba County, Mississippi—that's where Philadelphia is—could not—could not condemn [Sheriff] Rainey, his deputies, and the other fourteen men that killed three human beings. They could not because they elected Mr. Rainey to do precisely what he did and that for them to condemn him will be for them to condemn themselves.

In a much larger view, SNCC says that white America cannot condemn herself. And since we are liberal, we have done it: You stand condemned. Now, a number of things that arises from that answer of how do you condemn yourselves. Seems to me that the institutions that function in this country are clearly racist, and that they're built upon racism. And the question, then, is how can black people inside of this country move? And then how can white people who say they're not a part of those institutions begin to move? And how then do we begin to clear away the obstacles that we have in this society, that make us live like human beings? How can we begin to build institutions that will allow people to relate with each other as human beings? This country has never done that, especially around the country of white or black.

Now, several people have been upset because we've said that integration was irrelevant when initiated by blacks, and that in fact it was a subterfuge, an insidious subterfuge, for the maintenance of white supremacy. Now we maintain that in the past six years or so, this country has been feeding us a "thalidomide drug of integration" and that some negroes have been walking down a dream street talking about sitting next to white people and that that does not begin to solve the problem, that when we went to Mississippi we did not go to sit next to Ross Barnett; we did not go to sit next to Jim Clark; we went to get them out of our way and that people ought to understand that; that we were never fighting for the right to integrate, we were fighting against white supremacy.

Now, then, in order to understand white supremacy we must dismiss the fallacious notion that white people can give anybody their freedom. No man can give anybody his freedom. A man is born free. You may enslave a man after he is born free, and that is in fact what this country does. It enslaves black people after they're born, so that the only acts that white people can do is to stop denying black people their freedom; that is, they must stop denying freedom. They never give it to anyone.

Now we want to take that to its logical extension, so that we could understand, then, what its relevancy would be in terms of new civil rights bills. I maintain that every civil rights bill in this country was passed for white people, not for black people. For example, I am black. I know that. I also know that while I am black I am a human being, and therefore I have the right to go into any public place. White people didn't know that. Every time I tried to go into a place they stopped me. So some boys had to write a bill to tell that white man, "He's a human being; don't stop him." That bill was for that white man, not for me. I knew it all the time. I knew it all the time.

I knew that I could vote and that that wasn't a privilege; it was my right. Every time I tried I was shot, killed or jailed, beaten or economically deprived. So somebody had to write a bill for white people to tell them, "When a black man comes to vote, don't bother him." That bill, again, was for white people, not for black people; so that when you talk about open occupancy, I know I can live anyplace I want to live. It is white people across this country who are incapable of allowing me to live where I want to live. You need a civil rights bill, not me. I know I can live where I want to live.

So that the failures to pass a civil rights bill isn't because of Black Power, isn't because of the Student Nonviolent Coordinating Committee; it's not because of the rebellions that are occurring in the major cities. It is incapability of whites to deal with their own problems inside their own communities. That is the problem of the failure of the civil rights bill.

And so in a larger sense we must then ask, How is it that black people move? And what do we do? But the question in a greater sense is, How can white people who are the majority—and who are responsible for making democracy work—make it work? They have miserably failed to this point. They have never made democracy work, be it inside the United States, Vietnam, South Africa, Philippines, South America, Puerto Rico. Wherever American has been, she has not been able to make democracy work; so that in a larger sense, we not only condemn the country for what it's done internally, but we must condemn it for what it does externally. We see this country trying to rule the world, and someone must stand up and start articulating that this country is not God, and cannot rule the world.

Now, then, before we move on we ought to develop the white supremacy attitudes that were either conscious or subconscious thought and how they run rampant through the society today. For example, the missionaries were sent to Africa. They went with the attitude that blacks were automatically inferior. As a matter of fact, the first act the missionaries did, you know, when they got to Africa was to make us cover up our bodies, because they said it got them excited. We couldn't go bare-breasted anymore because they got excited.

Now when the missionaries came to civilize us because we were uncivilized, educate us because we were uneducated, and give us some literate studies because we were illiterate, they charged a price. The missionaries came with the Bible, and we had the land. When they left, they had the land, and we still have the Bible. And that has been the rationalization for Western civilization as it moves across the world and stealing and plundering and raping everybody in its path. Their one rationalization is that the rest of the world is uncivilized and they are in fact civilized. And they are un-civil-ized.

And that runs on today, you see, because what we have today is we have what we call "modern-day Peace Corps missionaries," and they come into our ghettos and they Head Start, Upward Lift, Bootstrap, and Upward Bound us into white society, 'cause they don't want to face the real problem which is a man is poor for one reason and one reason only: 'cause he does not have money—period. If you want to get rid of poverty, you give people money—period.

And you ought not to tell me about people who don't work, and you can't give people money without working, 'cause if that were true, you'd have to start stopping Rockefeller, Bobby Kennedy, Lyndon Baines Johnson, Lady Bird Johnson, the whole of Standard Oil, the Gulf Corp, all of them, including probably a large number of the Board of Trustees of this university. So the question, then, clearly, is not whether or not one can work; it's Who has power? Who has power to make his or her acts legitimate? That is all. And that in this country, that power is invested in the hands of white people, and they make their acts legitimate. It is now, therefore, for black people to make our acts legitimate.

Now we are now engaged in a psychological struggle in this country, and that is whether or not black people will have the right to use the words they want to use without white people giving their sanction to it; and that we maintain, whether they like it or not, we gonna use the word "Black Power"—and let them address themselves to that; but that we are not going to wait for white people to sanction Black Power. We're tired waiting; every time black people move in this country, they're forced to defend their position before they move. It's time that the people who are supposed to be defending their position do that. That's white people. They ought to start defending themselves as to why they have oppressed and exploited us.

Now it is clear that when this country started to move in terms of slavery, the reason for a man being picked as a slave was one reason—because of the color of his skin. If one was black one was automatically inferior, inhuman, and therefore fit for slavery; so that the question of whether or not we are individually suppressed is nonsensical, and it's a downright lie. We are oppressed as a group because we are black, not because we are lazy, not because we're apathetic, not because we're stupid, not because we smell, not because we eat watermelon and have good rhythm. We are oppressed because we are black.

And in order to get out of that oppression one must wield the group power that one has, not the individual power which this country then sets the criteria under which a man may come into it. That is what is called in this country as integration: "You do what I tell you to do and then we'll let you sit at the table with us." And that we are saying that we have to be opposed to that. We must now set up criteria and that if there's going to be any integration, it's going to be a two-way thing. If you believe in integration, you can come live in Watts. You can send your children to the ghetto schools. Let's talk about that. If you believe in integration, then we're going to start adopting us some white people to live in our neighborhood.

So it is clear that the question is not one of integration or segregation. Integration is a man's ability to want to move in there by himself. If someone wants to live in a white neighborhood and he is black, that is his choice. It should be his rights. It is not because white people will not allow him. So vice versa: If a black man wants to live in the slums, that should be his right. Black people will let him. That is the difference. And it's a difference on which this country makes a number of logical mistakes when they begin to try to criticize the program articulated by SNCC.

Now we maintain that we cannot afford to be concerned about 6 percent of the children in this country, black children, who you allow to come into white schools. We have 94 percent who still live in shacks. We are going to be concerned about those 94 percent. You ought to be concerned about them too. The question is, Are we willing to be concerned about those 94 percent? Are we willing to be concerned about the black people who will never get to Berkeley, who will never get to Harvard, and cannot get an education, so you'll never get a chance to rub shoulders with them and say, "Well, he's almost as good as we are; he's not like the others"? The question is, How can white society begin to move to see black people as human beings? I am black, therefore I am; not that I am black and I must go to college to prove myself. I am black, therefore I am. And don't deprive me of anything and say to me that you must go to college before you gain access to X, Y, and Z. It is only a rationalization for one's oppression.

The political parties in this country do not meet the needs of people on a day-to-day basis. The question is, How can we build new political institutions that will become the political expressions of people on a day-to-day basis? The question is, How can you build political institutions that will begin to meet the needs of Oakland, California? And the needs of Oakland, California, is not 1,000 policemen with submachine guns. They don't need that. They need that least of all. The question is, How can we build institutions where those people can begin to function on a day-to-day basis, where they can get decent jobs, where they can get decent houses, and where they can begin to participate in the policy and major decisions that affect their lives? That's what they need, not Gestapo troops, because this is not 1942, and if you play like Nazis, we playing back with you this time around. Get hip to that.

The question then is, How can white people move to start making the major institutions that they have in this country function the way it is supposed to function? That is the real question. And can white people move inside their own community and start tearing down racism where in fact it does exist? Where it exists. It is you who live in Cicero and stop us from living there. It is white people who stop us from moving into Grenada. It is white people who make sure that we live in the ghettos of this country. it is white institutions that do that. They must change. In order for America to really live on a basic principle of human relationships, a new society must be born. Racism must die, and the economic exploitation of this country of non-white peoples around the world must also die—must also die.

Now there are several programs that we have in the South, most in poor white communities. We're trying to organize poor whites on a basis where they can begin to move around the question of economic exploitation and political disfranchisement. We know—we've heard the theory several times—but few people are willing to go into there. The question is, Can the white activist not try to be a Pepsi generation who comes alive in the black community, but can he be a man who's willing to move into the white community and start organizing where the organization is needed? Can he do that? The question is, Can the white society or the white activist disassociate himself with two clowns who waste time parrying with each other rather than talking about the problems that are facing people in this state? Can you dissociate yourself with those clowns and start to build new institutions that will eliminate all idiots like them.

And the question is, If we are going to do that when and where do we start, and how do we start? We maintain that we must start doing that inside the white community. Our own personal position politically is that we don't think the Democratic Party represents the needs of black people. We know it don't. And that if, in fact, white people really believe that, the question is, if they're going to move inside that structure, how are they going to organize around a concept of whiteness based on true brotherhood and based on stopping exploitation, economic exploitation, so that there will be a coalition base for black people to hook up with? You cannot form a coalition based on national sentiment. That is not a coalition. If you need a coalition to redress itself to real changes in this country, white people must start building those institutions inside the white community. And that is the real question, I think, facing the white activists today. Can they, in fact, begin to move into and tear down the institutions which have put us all in a trick bag that we've been into for the last hundred years?

I don't think that we should follow what many people say that we should fight to be leaders of tomorrow. Frederick Douglass said that the youth should fight to be leaders today. And God knows we need to be leaders today, 'cause the men who run this country are sick, are sick. So that can we on a larger sense begin now, today, to start building those institutions and to fight to articulate our position, to fight to be able to control our universities—we need to be able to do that—and to fight to control the basic institutions which perpetuate racism by destroying them and building new ones? That's the real question that faces us today, and it is a dilemma because most of us do not know how to work, and that the excuse that most white activists find is to run into the black community.

Now we maintain that we cannot have white people working in the black community, and we mean it on a psychological ground. The fact is that all black people often question whether or not they are equal to whites, because every time they start to do something, white people are around showing them how to do it. If we are going to eliminate that for the generation that comes after us, then black people must be seen in positions of power, doing and articulating for themselves, for themselves.

That is not to say that one is a reverse racist; it is to say that one is moving in a healthy ground; it is to say what the philosopher Sartre says: One is becoming an "antiracist racist." And this country can't understand that. Maybe it's because it's all caught up in racism. But I think what you have in SNCC is an anti-racist racism. We are against racists. Now if everybody who is white see themself [*sic*] as a racist and then see us against him, they're speaking from their own guilt position, not ours, not ours.

Now then, the question is, How can we move to begin to change what's going on in this country. I maintain, as we have in SNCC, that the war in Vietnam is an illegal and immoral war. And the question is, What can we do to stop that war? What can we do to stop the people who, in the name of our country, are killing babies, women, and children? What can we do to stop that? And I maintain that we do not have the power in our hands to change that institution, to begin to recreate it, so that they learn to leave the Vietnamese people alone, and that the only power we have is the power to say, "Hell no!" to the draft.

We have to say to ourselves that there is a higher law than the law of a racist named McNamara. There is a higher law than the law of a fool named Rusk. And there's a higher law than the law of a buffoon named Johnson. It's the law of each of us. It's the law of each of us. It is the law of each of us saying that we will not allow them to make us hired killers. We will stand pat. We will not kill anybody that they say kill. And if we decide to kill, we're going to decide who we going to kill. And this country will only be able to stop the war in Vietnam when the young men who are made to fight it begin to say, "Hell, no, we ain't going."

Now then, there's a failure because the Peace Movement has been unable to get off the college campuses where everybody has a 2S and not going to get drafted anyway. And the question is, How can you move out of that into the white ghettos of this country and begin to articulate a position for those white students who do not want to go. We cannot do that. It is something, sometimes ironic that many of the peace groups [are] beginning to call us violent and say they can no longer support us, and we are in fact the most militant organization [for] peace or civil rights or human rights against the war in Vietnam in this country today. There isn't one organization that has begun to meet our stance on the war in Vietnam, 'cause we not only say we are against the war in Vietnam; we are against the draft. We are against the draft. No man has the right to take a man for two years and train him to be a killer. A man should decide what he wants to do with his life.

So the question then is it becomes crystal clear for black people because we can easily say that anyone fighting in the war in Vietnam is nothing but a black mercenary, and that's all he is. Any time a black man leaves the country where he can't vote to supposedly deliver the vote for somebody else, he's a black mercenary. Any time a black man leaves this country, gets shot in Vietnam on foreign ground, and returns home and you won't give him a burial in his own homeland, he's a black mercenary, a black mercenary.

And that even if I were to believe the lies of Johnson, if I were to believe his lies that we're fighting to give democracy to the people in Vietnam, as a black man living in this country I wouldn't fight to give this to anybody. I wouldn't give it to anybody. So that we have to use our bodies and our minds in the only way that we see fit. We must begin like the philosopher Camus to come alive by saying "No!" That is the only act in which we begin to come alive, and we have to say "No!" to many, many things in this country.

This country is a nation of thieves. It has stole everything it has, beginning with black people, beginning with black people. And that the question is, How can we move to start changing this country from what it is—a nation of thieves. This country cannot justify any longer its existence. We have become the policeman of the world. The marines are at our disposal to always bring democracy, and if the Vietnamese don't want democracy, well dammit, "We'll just wipe them the hell out, 'cause they don't deserve to live if they won't have our way of life."

There is then in a larger sense, What do you do on your university campus? Do you raise questions about the hundred black students who were kicked off campus a couple of weeks ago? Eight hundred? Eight hundred? And how does that question begin to move? Do you begin to relate to people outside of the ivory tower and university wall? Do you think you're capable of building those human relationships, as the country now stands? You're fooling yourself. It is impossible for white and black people to talk about building a relationship based on humanity when the country is the way it is, when the institutions are clearly against us.

We have taken all the myths of this country and we've found them to be nothing but downright lies. This country told us that if we worked hard we would succeed, and if that were true we would own this country lock, stock, and barrel—lock, stock, and barrel—lock, stock, and barrel. It is we who have picked the cotton for nothing. It is we who are the maids in the kitchens of liberal white people. It is we who are the janitors, the porters, the elevator men; we who sweep up your college floors. Yes, it is we who are the hardest workers and the lowest paid, and the lowest paid.

And that it is nonsensical for people to start talking about human relationships until they're willing to build new institutions. Black people are economically insecure. White liberals are economically secure. Can you begin to build an economic coalition? Are the liberals willing to share their salaries with the economically insecure black people they so much love? Then if you're not, are you willing to start building new institutions that will provide economic security for black people? That's the question we want to deal with. That's the question we want to deal with.

We have to seriously examine the histories that we have been told. But we have something more to do than that. American students are perhaps the most politically unsophisticated students in the world. Across every country in this world, while we were growing up, students were leading the major revolutions of their countries. We have not been able to do that. They have been politically aware of their existence. In South America our neighbors down below the border have one every 24 hours just to remind us that they're politically aware.

And we have been unable to grasp it because we've always moved in the field of morality and love while people have been politically jiving with our lives. And the question is, How do we now move politically and stop trying to move morally? You can't move morally against a man like Brown and Reagan. You've got to move politically to put them out of business. You've got to move politically.

You can't move morally against Lyndon Baines Johnson because he is an immoral man. He doesn't know what it's all about. So you've got to move politically. You've got to move politically. And that we have to begin to develop a political sophistication—which is not to be a parrot: "The two-party system is the best party in the world." There is a difference between being a parrot and being politically sophisticated.

We have to raise questions about whether or not we do need new types of political institutions in this country, and we in SNCC maintain that we need them now. We need new political institutions in this country. Any time Lyndon Baines Johnson can head a Party which has in it Bobby Kennedy, Wayne Morse, Eastland, Wallace, and all those other supposed-to-be-liberal cats, there's something wrong with that Party. They're moving politically, not morally. And that if that party refuses to seat black people from Mississippi and goes ahead and seats racists like Eastland and his clique, it is clear to me that they're moving politically, and that one cannot begin to talk morality to people like that.

We must begin to think politically and see if we can have the power to impose and keep the moral values that we hold high. We must question the values of this society, and I maintain that black people are the best people to do that because we have been excluded from that society. And the question is, we ought to think whether or not we want to become a part of that society. That's what we want to do.

And that that is precisely what it seems to me that the Student Nonviolent Coordinating Committee is doing. We are raising questions about this country. I do not want to be a part of the American pie. The American pie means raping South Africa, beating Vietnam, beating South America, raping the Philippines, raping every country you've been in. I don't want any of your blood money. I don't want it—don't want to be part of that system. And the question is, How do we raise those questions? How do we begin to raise them?

We have grown up and we are the generation that has found this country to be a world power, that has found this country to be the wealthiest country in the world. We must question how she got her wealth? That's what we're questioning, and whether or not we want this country to continue being the wealthiest country in the world at the price of raping everybody else across the world. That's what we must begin to question. And that because black people are saying we do not now want to become a part of you, we are called reverse racists. Ain't that a gas?

Now, then, we want to touch on nonviolence because we see that again as the failure of white society to make nonviolence work. I was always surprised at Quakers who came to Alabama and counseled me to be nonviolent, but didn't have the guts to start talking to James Clark to be nonviolent. That is where nonviolence needs to be preached—to Jim Clark, not to black people. They have already been nonviolent too many years. The question is, Can white people conduct their nonviolent schools in Cicero where they belong to be conducted, not among black people in Mississippi. Can they conduct it among the white people in Grenada?

Six-foot-two men who kick little black children—can you conduct nonviolent schools there? That is the question that we must raise, not that you conduct nonviolence among black people. Can you name me one black man today who's killed anybody white and is still alive? Even after rebellion, when some black brothers throw some bricks and bottles, ten thousand of them has to pay the crime, 'cause when the white policeman comes in, anybody who's black is arrested, "'cause we all look alike."

So that we have to raise those questions. We, the youth of this country, must begin to raise those questions. And we must begin to move to build new institutions that's going to speak to the needs of people who need it. We are going to have to speak to change the foreign policy of this country. One of the problems with the peace movement is that it's just too caught up in Vietnam, and that if we pulled out the troops from Vietnam this week, next week you'd have to get another peace movement for Santo Domingo. And the question is, How do you begin to articulate the need to change the foreign policy of this country—a policy that is decided upon race, a policy on which decisions are made upon getting economic wealth at any price, at any price.

Now we articulate that we therefore have to hook up with black people around the world; and that that hookup is not only psychological, but becomes very real. If South America today were to rebel, and black people were to shoot the hell out of all the white people there—as they should, as they should—then Standard Oil would crumble tomorrow. If South Africa were to go today, Chase Manhattan Bank would crumble tomorrow. If Zimbabwe, which is called Rhodesia by white people, were to go tomorrow, General Electric would cave in on the East Coast. The question is, How do we stop those institutions that are so willing to fight against "Communist aggression" but closes their eyes to racist oppression? That is the question that you raise. Can this country do that?

Now, many people talk about pulling out of Vietnam. What will happen? If we pull out of Vietnam, there will be one less aggressor in there—we won't be there, we won't be there. And so the question is, How do we articulate those positions? And we cannot begin to articulate them from the same assumptions that the people in the country speak, 'cause they speak from different assumptions than I assume what the youth in this country are talking about.

That we're not talking about a policy or aid or sending Peace Corps people in to teach people how to read and write and build houses while we steal their raw materials from them. Is that what we're talking about? 'Cause that's all we do. What underdeveloped countries need—information on how to become industrialized, so they can keep their raw materials where they have it, produce them and sell it to this country for the price it's supposed to pay; not that we produce it and sell it back to them for a profit and keep sending our modern day missionaries in, calling them the sons of Kennedy. And that if the youth are going to participate in that program, how do you raise those questions where you begin to control that Peace Corps program? How do you begin to raise them?

How do we raise the questions of poverty? The assumptions of this country is that if someone is poor, they are poor because of their own individual blight, or they weren't born on the right side of town; they had too many children; they went in the army too early; or their father was a drunk, or they didn't care about school, or they made a mistake. That's a lot of nonsense. Poverty is well calculated in this country. It is well calculated, and the reason why the poverty program won't work is because the calculators of poverty are administering it. That's why it won't work.

So how can we, as the youth in the country, move to start tearing those things down? We must move into the white community. We are in the black community. We have developed a movement in the black community. The challenge is that the white activist has failed miserably to develop the movement inside of his community. And the question is, Can we find white people who are going to have the courage to go into white communities and start organizing them? Can we find them? Are they here and are they willing to do that? Those are the questions that we must raise for the white activist.

And we're never going to get caught up in questions about power. This country knows what power is. It knows it very well. And it knows what Black Power is 'cause it deprived black people of it for 400 years. So it knows what Black Power is. That the question of, Why do black people—Why do white people in this country associate Black Power with violence? And the question is because of their own inability to deal with "blackness." If we had said "Negro power" nobody would get scared. Everybody would support it. Or if we said power for colored people, everybody'd be for that, but it is the word "black"—it is the word "black" that bothers people in this country, and that's their problem, not mine—their problem, their problem.

Now there's one modern day lie that we want to attack and then move on very quickly and that is the lie that says anything all black is bad. Now, you're all a college university crowd. You've taken your basic logic course. You know about a major premise and minor premise. So people have been telling me anything all black is bad. Let's make that our major premise.

Major premise: Anything all black is bad.

Minor premise or particular premise: I am all black.

Therefore ...

I'm never going to be put in that trick bag; I am all black and I'm all good, dig it. Anything all black is not necessarily bad. Anything all black is only bad when you use force to keep whites out. Now that's what white people have done in this country, and they're projecting their same fears and guilt on us, and we won't have it, we won't have it. Let them handle their own fears and their own guilt. Let them find their own psychologists. We refuse to be the therapy for white society any longer. We have gone mad trying to do it. We have gone stark raving mad trying to do it.

I look at Dr. King on television every single day, and I say to myself: "Now there is a man who's desperately needed in this country. There is a man full of love. There is a man full of mercy. There is a man full of compassion." But every time I see Lyndon on television, I said, "Martin, baby, you got a long way to go."

So that the question stands as to what we are willing to do, how we are willing to say "No" to withdraw from that system and begin within our community to start to function and to build new institutions that will speak to our needs. In Lowndes County, we developed something called the Lowndes County Freedom Organization. It is a political party. The Alabama law says that if you have a Party you must have an emblem. We chose for the emblem a black panther, a beautiful black animal which symbolizes the strength and dignity of black people, an animal that never strikes back until he's back so far into the wall, he's got nothing to do but spring out. Yeah. And when he springs he does not stop.

Now there is a Party in Alabama called the Alabama Democratic Party. It is all white. It has as its emblem a white rooster and the words "white supremacy for the right." Now the gentlemen of the Press, because they're advertisers, and because most of them are white, and because they're produced by that white institution, never called the Lowndes County Freedom Organization by its name, but rather they call it the Black Panther Party. Our question is, Why don't they call the Alabama Democratic Party the "White Cock Party"? (It's fair to us.) It is clear to me that that just points out America's problem with sex and color, not our problem, not our problem. And it is now white America that is going to deal with those problems of sex and color.

If we were to be real and to be honest, we would have to admit that most people in this country see things black and white. We have to do that. All of us do. We live in a country that's geared that way. White people would have to admit that they are afraid to go into a black ghetto at night. They are afraid. That's a fact. They're afraid because they'd be "beat up," "lynched," "looted," "cut up," et cetera, et cetera. It happens to black people inside the ghetto every day, incidentally, and white people are afraid of that. So you get a man to do it for you—a policeman. And now you figure his mentality, when he's afraid of black people. The first time a black man jumps, that white man going to shoot him. He's going to shoot him. So police brutality is going to exist on that level because of the incapability of that white man to see black people come together and to live in the conditions. This country is too hypocritical and that we cannot adjust ourselves to its hypocrisy.

The only time I hear people talk about nonviolence is when black people move to defend themselves against white people. Black people cut themselves every night in the ghetto. Don't anybody talk about nonviolence. Lyndon Baines Johnson is busy bombing the hell of out Vietnam. Don't nobody talk about nonviolence. White people beat up black people every day. Don't nobody talk about nonviolence. But as soon as black people start to move, the double standard comes into being.

You can't defend yourself. That's what you're saying, 'cause you show me a man who would advocate aggressive violence that would be able to live in this country. Show him to me. The double standards again come into itself. Isn't it ludicrous and hypocritical for the political chameleon who calls himself a Vice President in this country to stand up before this country and say, "Looting never got anybody anywhere"? Isn't it hypocritical for Lyndon to talk about looting, that you can't accomplish anything by looting and you must accomplish it by the legal ways? What does he know about legality? Ask Ho Chi Minh, he'll tell you.

So that in conclusion we want to say that number one, it is clear to me that we have to wage a psychological battle on the right for black people to define their own terms, define themselves as they see fit, and organize themselves as they see it. Now the question is, How is the white community going to begin to allow for that organizing, because once they start to do that, they will also allow for the organizing that they want to do inside their community. It doesn't make a difference, 'cause we're going to organize our way anyway. We're going to do it. The question is, How are we going to facilitate those matters, whether it's going to be done with a thousand policemen with submachine guns, or whether or not it's going to be done in a context where it is allowed to be done by white people warding off those policemen. That is the question.

And the question is, How are white people who call themselves activists ready to start move into the white communities on two counts: on building new political institutions to destroy the old ones that we have? And to move around the concept of white youth refusing to go into the army? So that we can start, then, to build a new world. It is ironic to talk about civilization in this country. This country is uncivilized. It needs to be civilized. It needs to be civilized.

And that we must begin to raise those questions of civilization: What it is? And who do it? And so we must urge you to fight now to be the leaders of today, not tomorrow. We've got to be the leaders of today. This country is a nation of thieves. It stands on the brink of becoming a nation of murderers. We must stop it. We must stop it. We must stop it. We must stop it.

And then, therefore, in a larger sense there's the question of black people. We are on the move for our liberation. We have been tired of trying to prove things to white people. We are tired of trying to explain to white people that we're not going to hurt them. We are concerned with getting the things we want, the things that we have to have to be able to function. The question is, Can white people allow for that in this country? The question is, Will white people overcome their racism and allow for that to happen in this country? If that does not happen, brothers and sisters, we have no choice but to say very clearly, "Move over, or we're going to move on over you."

Thank you.

GLOSSARY

Berkeley: the University of California at Berkeley, the flagship campus of the University of California system

Brown: Governor Edmund G. "Pat" Brown of California

Eastland: James Eastland, a conservative U.S. senator from Mississippi

Frederick Douglass: the preeminent abolitionist during the nineteenth century

Gestapo: the official secret police of Nazi Germany

Head Start, Upward Lift, Bootstrap, and Upward Bound: all programs designed to provide educational and economic opportunities for the poor

Jim Clark: the sheriff of Dallas County, Alabama, who authorized the violent assaults and arrests of activists during the Selma-to-Montgomery march of 1965

Rockefeller: Nelson Rockefeller, the governor of New York and heir to the Standard Oil fortune

Ross Barnett: an earlier segregationist governor of Mississippi

Rusk: Dean Rusk, the U.S. secretary of state under Presidents John Kennedy and Lyndon Johnson

Sheriff Rainey: Lawrence Rainey, sheriff of Neshoba County, Mississippi, referring to the murder in 1964 of three civil rights workers through the collusion of local law enforcement agencies and the Ku Klux Klan

thalidomide: a drug given to pregnant women later found to cause severe birth defects

2S: II-S, a draft classification that deferred military service for students

Wayne Morse: a U.S. senator from Oregon who was one of only two U.S. senators to vote against the Gulf of Tonkin Resolution, deepening U.S. involvement in Vietnam

Document Analysis

Carmichael begins his speech by stating that he would not get caught up in questions about the meaning of "Black Power"—leaving that to the press—mocking them as "advertisers." Carmichael then turns to his first major point, the question of "whether or not a man can condemn himself." In breaking down this question, he turns to the thought of three intellectuals. Albert Camus and Jean-Paul Sartre were both French intellectuals and writers of the early- to mid-twentieth century. Frantz Fanon was a writer, philosopher, and revolutionary who was born in Martinique and whose works were key to the anticolonial movement.

Carmichael asserts that since "white America cannot condemn herself," SNCC has condemned it. He then mentions Sheriff Lawrence Rainey in Neshoba County, Mississippi; this is a reference to the notorious murder in 1964 of three civil rights workers, two of them white and one black, through the collusion of local law enforcement agencies and the Ku Klux Klan.

Carmichael then argues that integration is an "insidious subterfuge" that maintains white supremacy. Referring to incidents of law enforcement violence against activists, he argues that American institutions are racist and then asks rhetorically what whites who are not racists can do to change the system.

Carmichael rejects the idea that whites can give anybody their freedom, that civil rights legislation, passed by white people, is ultimately for the benefit of white people. Laws regarding public accommodations and the right to vote, he argues, show white people that African Americans have certain rights; however, African Americans should already be aware that they are entitled to those rights.

Carmichael next discusses white failures at democracy in the international sphere, condemning missionary efforts in Africa as well as more militaristic efforts. He rejects the notion that people are poor simply because they do not work. If this were actually the criterion for poverty, then powerful Americans should be poor, for in Carmichael's view, they do not work.

Carmichael argues, in paragraph 16, that the debate over the use of the term *Black Power* is part of a psychological struggle over whether African Americans can use terms without white approval. He draws attention to the continuing extent of segregation and draws his listeners' attention to the heavy-handed police presence in Oakland, California, and then asks what the nation's political parties can do to create institutions that "will become the political expressions of people on a day-to-day basis."

Carmichael then discusses true integration as being a two-way street. He argues that white activists must organize in the white community to change white society. He rejects the idea of whites working in the African American community as damaging on a psychological basis and concludes that his position on this is not "reverse racist." Carmichael also asserts that SNCC did not believe that the Democratic Party represents the needs of black people. He argues that what was needed was a new coalition of voters who would start building new political and social institutions that would meet the needs of all people.

Carmichael then turns to an attack on the Vietnam War as an "illegal and immoral war" and rhetorically asks the audience how it could be stopped. His answer is resistance to the draft. The peace movement, he argues, has been ineffective because it consists of college students who are exempt from the draft anyway. He calls attention to the irony of referring to black militancy as violent when black militant groups were fighting for human rights and the end of violence in places like Vietnam. Carmichael next challenges students on university campuses.

He notes, in paragraph 34, that it is impossible for whites and blacks to form "human relationships" given the nature of the country's institutions. He suggests that a form of social hypocrisy has become manifest in the economic insecurity of many African Americans and the unwillingness of most affluent whites to share their relative economic security with the black community. He calls on his listeners to follow the example of politically engaged, radical students in other parts of the world and again lambastes the Democratic political establishment. Only the seizure of power by revolution would put the political establishment out of business.

Carmichael then turns specifically to a discussion of SNCC. He notes that a central purpose of SNCC was to raise questions. One of these questions was how the United States had come to be a world power and the world's wealthiest nation. He thus segues into a discussion of nonviolence at a time when he was coming to reject his initial stance in favor of advocating violent social change. Groups like SNCC and the Quakers are not the ones who need to espouse nonviolence, he argues; rather, white supremacists need to be persuaded to act without violence toward peaceful demonstrators.

Carmichael returns to the relationship between the American civil rights struggle and the international movement Western domination of a postcolonial world largely inhabited by people of color, making glancing references to hot spots in the world other than Vietnam. He notes that the United States had tolerated oppression in these and other places as a way of opposing Communist expansion and aggression. He urges (in paragraph 51) the white community "to have the courage to go into white communities and start organizing them." He also discusses the fear that many white people have of anything black and the association of blackness with evil. He concludes his speech by stating that the chief issue facing African Americans was the psychological battle to define themselves and organize themselves as they saw fit. An important question related to this issue was how white activists could build new political institutions to destroy the old racist ones.

Essential Themes

Stokely Carmichael's 1966 address at the University of California at Berkley illustrates a transitional point in the American Civil Rights movement. One consistent theme that shines through is Carmichael's insistence on linking the struggles of African Americans to the struggles of other groups throughout the world. His outspoken criticism of American policy and military action in Vietnam (in which he would, later, be joined by Martin Luther King Jr.) is combined with a critique of American policy throughout the postcolonial world, condemning the support of tyrannical regimes and the exploitation of natural and economic resources. He even includes seemingly-benign US government initiatives such as the Peace Corps in his criticism. While Stokely's international perspective was not unheard of in the Civil Rights movement, he was one of the significant voices bringing it to the fore.

Similarly significant, Carmichael is moving away from the unwavering devotion to non-violence that characterized much of the Civil Rights movement to that point, asserting that non-violence would be a better policy for other groups, such as white supremacists with a history of brutalizing rights activists. This shift away from nonviolence goes hand in hand with his questioning of integration. The movement was changing and, in a way, fragmenting; Carmichael's speech is a clear indicator of new directions.

——Keith E. Sealing

Bibliography and Additional Reading

Asante, Molefi Kete. *100 Greatest African Americans: A Biographical Encyclopedia.* Amherst, N.Y. Prometheus Books, 2002.

Carmichael, Stokely. *Stokely Speaks: Black Power Back to Pan-Africanism.* New York, Random House, 1971.

———, and Charles V. Hamilton. *Black Power: The Politics of Liberation in America.* New York: Random House, 1967.

———, and Ekwueme Michael Thelwell. *Ready for Revolution: The Life and Struggles of Stokely Carmichael.* New York: Scribner, 2003.

Carson, Clayborne. *In Struggle: SNCC and the Black Awakening of the 1960s.* Cambridge, Mass. Harvard University Press, 1981. Cwiklik, Robert. *Stokely Carmichael and Black Power.* Brookfield, Conn. Millbrook Press, 1993.

Johnson, Jacqueline. *Stokely Carmichael: The Story of Black Power.* Englewood Cliffs, N.J. Silver Burdett, 1990.

Sellers, Cleveland, and Robert Terrell. *The River of No Return: The Autobiography of a Black Militant in the Life and Death of SNCC.* New York: Morrow, 1973.

Zinn, Howard. *SNCC: The New Abolitionists.* Boston: Beacon Press, 1964.

Websites

Kaufman, Michael T. "Stokely Carmichael, Rights Leader Who Coined 'Black Power,' Dies at 57." *New York Times*, November 16, 1998. http://www.interchange.org/Kwameture/nytimes111698.html

"Stokely Carmichael." Federal Bureau of Investigation Web site. http://foia.fbi.gov/foiaindex/carmichael_stokely.htm

■ "What We Want, What We Believe"

Date: 1966
Author: The Black Panther Party
Genre: Public declaration

Summary Overview

Although the Black Panthers instituted a variety of social programs aimed at improving conditions and in inner city neighborhoods throughout the country, they were perhaps best known for instituting armed citizens' patrols and carrying out acts of violence. The Panthers exploited a California law that made it legal to carry loaded rifles and shotguns in plain sight as long as they were not pointed at anyone. Between 1967 and 1970, nine police officers were killed, and fifty-six were wounded; ten Panthers were killed in a series of confrontations. Their reputation for violence captured the attention of then Federal Bureau of Investigation director J. Edgar Hoover, who instituted a widespread campaign of surveillance and infiltration. Some FBI informants were allegedly killed by the Panthers.

The Panthers had an extensive list of rules of behavior and in 1966 published "What We Know, What We Believe," (commonly known as the Ten-Point Program), which detailed the Black Panther Party's grievances and demands. One rule was that Panthers were expected to know this manifesto by heart. By the early 1980s the Panthers had dissolved, in large part owing to internal policy disputes but also because of continued police and FBI activity. In 1989 the New Black Panther Party was formed in Texas, but Panthers co-founder Seale does not consider the organization to be a legitimate heir to the Panther name and original organization.

Defining Moment

The nonviolent confrontation and protest, as well as the practice of passive resistance in the face of brutalization by police and the public, had been part of the civil rights movement's playbook since the 1950s. A new generation of activists however began to question the wisdom and effectiveness of these practices. Figures such as Malcolm X and Stokely Carmichael promoted a more aggressive, proactive stance. The right and responsibility to defend oneself against attack was an idea promoted by this new wave of activists. In addition to a skepticism about a passive resistance, this new generation of activists also questioned the viability of African-Americans aspiring only to be tolerated by white society. Perhaps, some wondered, it would be better for the black community to sustain and govern itself independently of the whims of white Americans.

Formed in the San Francisco Bay Area by Huey Newton and Bobby Seale in 1966, the Black Panther Party for Self-Defense was originally constituted with the avowed purpose of protecting African American neighborhoods from police violence, which was endemic at the time—a situation that had not improved in the midst of the urban unrest that swept the nation during the mid-1960s. The Panthers spread throughout the country and, with a membership of 10,000 at their peak in 1969 and circulation of 250,000 for the *Black Panther*, their newspaper edited by Eldridge Cleaver, the Panthers were an internationally recognized part of the Black Power movement and the counterculture. The organization was Marxist-Socialist and originally espoused black nationalism but moved away from this position and became more focused on Socialism without regard to race.

Author Biography

The Black Panther Party, and the ten point program presented here, were developed by two men in the San Francisco Bay area: Huey P. Newton and Bobby Seale.

Bobby Seale was born in 1936 in Texas. The Seale family, searching for economic opportunities not available in Texas, moved to Oakland, California when Seale was a child. After three years in the US Air Force, Seale received a bad conduct discharge for fighting with an officer. He worked in the aerospace industry and attended community college in the early 1960s. In college, he joined the Afro-American Association, a group which promoted black separatism rather than the racial integration that was the focus of much of the civil rights movement at the time. It was as part of this group that Seale met Huey P. Newton.

Newton was born in 1942 to a sharecropping family in Louisiana. Like the Seale family, the Newton family moved west to the Bay area to escape the poverty of the deep south. Newton got in trouble with the law a number of times as a teenager but graduated from high school (although he had to teach himself how to read) and enrolled at Merritt College, where he met Bobby Seale.

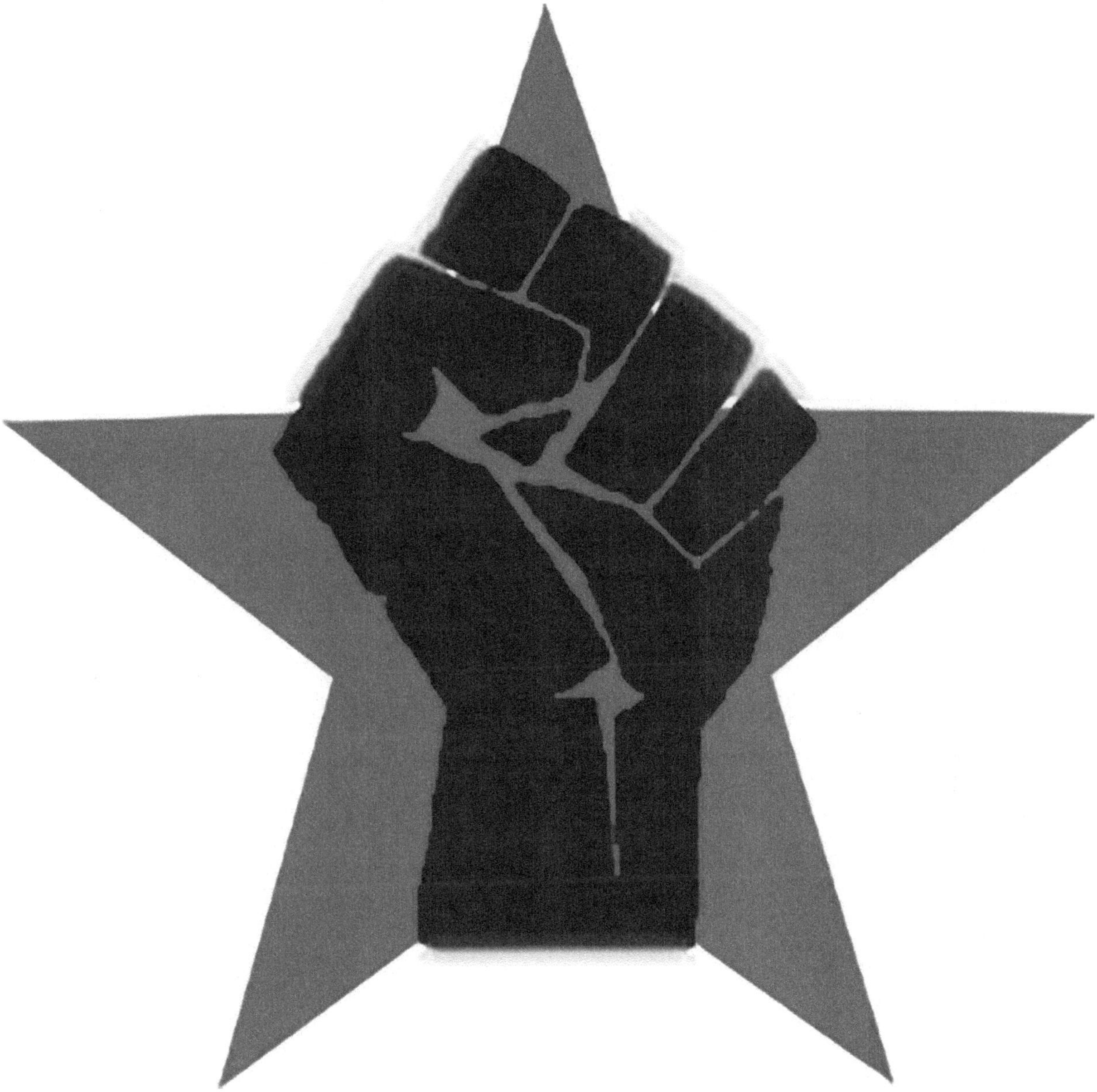

During this time, Seale and Newton became acquainted with the works and ideas of a number of leftist and revolutionary thinkers including Marx, Lenin, Mao Zedong, and Che Guevara. As a response to police brutality in the area, and influenced by their revolutionary studies, the pair formed the Black Panther Party for Self Defense in 1966, with Seale taking the role of Chairman and Newton the position of Minister of Defense. Soon after founding the organization, they developed the Ten-Point Program.

HISTORICAL DOCUMENT

1. *We want freedom. We want power to determine the destiny of our Black Community.*

We believe that black people will not be free until we are able to determine our destiny.

2. *We want full employment for our people.*

We believe that the federal government is responsible and obligated to give every man employment or a guaranteed income. We believe that if the white American businessmen will not give full employment, then the means of production should be taken from the businessmen and placed in the community so that the people of the community can organize and employ all of its people and give a high standard of living.

3. *We want an end to the robbery by the white man of our Black Community.*

We believe that this racist government has robbed us and now we are demanding the overdue debt of forty acres and two mules. Forty acres and two mules was promised 100 years ago as restitution for slave labor and mass murder of black people. We will accept the payment as currency which will be distributed to our many communities. The Germans are now aiding the Jews in Israel for the genocide of the Jewish people. The Germans murdered six million Jews. The American racist has taken part in the slaughter of over twenty million black people; therefore, we feel that this is a modest demand that we make.

4. *We want decent housing, fit for shelter of human beings.*

We believe that if the white landlords will not give decent housing to our black community, then the housing and the land should be made into cooperatives so that our community, with government aid, can build and make decent housing for its people.

5. *We want education for our people that exposes the true nature of this decadent American society. We want education that teaches us our true history and our role in the present-day society.*

We believe in an educational system that will give to our people a knowledge of self. If a man does not have knowledge of himself and his position in society and the world, then he has little chance to relate to anything else.

6. *We want all black men to be exempt from military service.*

We believe that Black people should not be forced to fight in the military service to defend a racist government that does not protect us. We will not fight and kill other people of color in the world who, like black people, are being victimized by the white racist government of America. We will protect ourselves from the force and violence of the racist police and the racist military, by whatever means necessary.

7. *We want an immediate end to police brutality and murder of black people.*

We believe we can end police brutality in our black community by organizing black self-defense groups that are dedicated to defending our black community from racist police oppression and brutality. The Second Amendment to the Constitution of the United States gives a right to bear arms. We therefore believe that all black people should arm themselves for self defense.

8. *We want freedom for all black men held in federal, state, county and city prisons and jails.*

We believe that all black people should be released from the many jails and prisons because they have not received a fair and impartial trial.

9. *We want all black people when brought to trial to be tried in court by a jury of their peer group or people from their black communities, as defined by the Constitution of the United States.*

We believe that the courts should follow the United States Constitution so that black people will receive fair trials. The 14th Amendment of the U.S. Constitution gives a man a right to be tried by his peer group. A peer is a person from a similar economic, social, religious, geographical, environmental, historical and racial background. To do this the court will be forced to select a jury from the black community from which the black defendant came. We have been, and are being tried by all-white juries that have no understanding of the "average reasoning man" of the black community.

10. *We want land, bread, housing, education, clothing, justice and peace. And as our major political objective, a United Nations–supervised plebiscite to be held throughout the black colony in which only black colonial subjects will be allowed to participate for the purpose of determining the will of black people as to their national destiny.*

When in the course of human events, it becomes necessary for one people to dissolve the political bands which have connected them with another, and to assume, among the powers of the earth, the separate and equal station to which the laws of nature and nature's God entitle them, a decent respect to the opinions of mankind requires that they should declare the causes which impel them to the separation.

We hold these truths to be self evident, that all men are created equal; that they are endowed by their Creator with certain unalienable rights; that among these are life, liberty, and the pursuit of happiness. *That, to secure these rights, governments are instituted among men, deriving their just powers from the consent of the governed; that, whenever any form of government becomes destructive of these ends, it is the right of the people to alter or to abolish it, and to institute a new government, laying its foundation on such principles, and organizing its powers in such form, as to them shall seem most likely to effect their safety and happiness.* Prudence, indeed, will dictate that governments long established should not be changed for light and transient causes; and accordingly, all experience hath shown, that mankind are more disposed to supper, while evils are sufferable, than to right themselves by abolishing the forms to which they are accustomed. *But, when a long train of abuses and usurpations, pursuing invariable the same object, evinces a design to reduce them under absolute despotism, it is their right, it is their duty, to throw off such government, and to provide new guards for their future security.*

GLOSSARY

cooperatives: a real estate agreement in which a group of people cooperatively own property, such as an apartment building.

decadent: moral decline

Plebiscite: a direct vote of the population on a major decision such as fundamental changes in government

prudence: caution

"the black colony": a phrase which characterizes African Americans as a colonized people under the imperialist domination of the United States

Document Analysis

Each of the ten points in this manifesto is accompanied by a brief explanation of the deeper meaning of the demand. In Black Panther Party publications, these were often organized as two separate lists: "What We Want Now!" and "What We Believe."

The first point is closely tied to the wider Black Power movement, a term coined by Stokely Carmichael. Here, the explanation is ver similar to the "We want" portion, basically restating the need for African Americans need political and economic power in order to control their own future.

The second point gives the first indication of the Marxist direction that the Black Panther Party would take. Their demand of "full employment" or "a guaranteed income" for "every man" (note that they do not specify a race here) is connected to a consequence of the "means of production" being seized and handed over to the community at large.

The third point demands financial restitution for the legacy of slavery in the United States. The reference to "forty acres and two mules" refers to attempts by some Union generals (such as William Tecumseh Sherman) during the Civil War to redistribute captured plantation land to the slaves of the plantation owner. Congress, however, refused to fully support the orders in the field by military officials to enable that redistribution and plantation land was, in almost all cases, restored to the original owners. This item also addresses the fact that the Federal Republic of Germany was financially contributing to the future of the Jewish people following the Holocaust, using the fact to shame the United States over its failure to provide recompense to the descendants of slaves.

The fourth point continues the theme of potential collective ownership of property, proposing that "housing and the land" should be organized into community owned housing cooperatives. The fifth section demands reforms to the education system that emphasizes the "true history" of African-Americans, emphasizing the role that the white establishment of the United States has played in oppressing them as a means of helping develop pride and cohesion.

The sixth point demands an end to compulsory military service for African-American men. The reference to killing "other people of color" relates to the Vietnam War; a war in which a disproportionate number of draftees were African-American. Here, the Black Panthers express solidarity with those people of color dying at the hands of American soldiers. This point declares that the community "will protect ourselves from the force and violence of the racist police and the racist military, by whatever means necessary." This connects closely to the next, seventh, demand which calls for an end to police brutality against African-Americans. It also uses the Second Amendment as the basis for a call for African-Americans to "arm themselves for self defense" presumably against police officers.

Points eight and nine both address the racial inequalities in the American criminal justice system. Demand eight calls for the the release of all black inmates on the ground that the trials that convinced them were not "fair and impartial." There reason for this judicial inequality is addressed by point nine, which demands that juries for black defendants be comprised of black citizens based on the requirement that defendants must be judged by a jury of their peers.

Demand ten is a summary. The call for "land" and "bread" echoes the call of the Russian Communists during the Bolshevik revolution. It also calls for a plebiscite under that authority of the United Nations. A plebiscite, in this context, is a vote on the question of whether a group within a nation should become a separate nation.

The remainder of the document is a recitation of parts of the beginning of the Declaration of Independence, establishing the idea that African0Americans in the United states are a colonized people whose rights have been violated by a government that does not share their values.

Essential Themes

"What We Want, What We Believe" took the emerging rhetoric and ideas of "Black Power" and united them with revolutionary politics and Black Nationalism, a school of thought that had been present in African-American activism throughout the twentieth century. Many of the concerns expressed in the Ten-Point Program developed by the Black Panthers are closely related to specific issues that were prevalent at the time. Demands that African-American men not be compelled to serve in the military were related directly to the disproportionate number of African-American men who were subject to the draft and being sent to Vietnam in combat roles. The demand that African-American men be released from jail and prisons as well as the call for juries consisting of the black defendant's "peer group or people from their black communities" was connected to instances of all white juries convicting African-Americans without sufficient evidence and, in some cases, with little regard to due process.

Other issues raised by the Ten-Point Program are more general in nature and less directly related to the historical context of the time. Calls for housing and employment, For adequate food and wages that are acceptable are less directly associated strictly with the plight of African-Americans. Rather, these are concerns that orbit around broader issues of class consciousness in class conflict. The revolutionary Marxism of the Black

Panther Party's list of demands and beliefs was a departure for the civil rights movement that is illustrated the growing radicalization of protest movements in the United States.

— *Aaron Gulyas, with additional material by Keith E. Sealing*

Bibliography and Additional Reading

Austin, Curtis J. *Up Against the Wall: Violence in the Making and Unmaking of the Black Panther Party.* Fayetteville: University of Arkansas Press, 2006).

Alkebulan, Paul. *Survival Pending Revolution: The History of the Black Panther Party* (Tuscaloosa: University of Alabama Press, 2007).

Lazerow, Jama and Yohuru Williams, Yohuru, ed. *In Search of the Black Panther Party: New Perspectives on a Revolutionary Movement.* (Durham, North Carolina: Duke University Press, 2006).

Murch, Donna. *Living for the City: Migration, Education, and the Rise of the Black Panther Party in Oakland, California* (Chapel Hill: University of North Carolina Press, 2010).

WOMEN'S RIGHTS

From colonial times through the liberty-infused era of the American Revolution, women in the colonies and in the early republic penned essays and letters that promoted the ideal of greater legal, economic, or political rights for women. It was in 1848, however, that the organized women's rights movement began in the United States. Until 1920, the primary focus of this movement was obtaining the right to vote nationwide. Beginning in the late nineteenth century, women's suffrage was the law of the land in many western states. However, even there, women's ability to affect national elections—such as the Presidential election—was limited. The documents in this section, fittingly, often focus on arguments for granting women the right to vote nationwide.

Appropriately, the first document in this section is the Declaration of Sentiments issued at the Seneca Falls Convention in 1848, which articulated he movement's ultimate goal of suffrage, along with other legal and social goals. Key figures in the women's rights movement such as Susan B. Anthony asked It a Crime for a Citizen of the United States to Vote? in 1873, and faced arrest and trial when she exercised what she believed to be her right under the Constitution. Anthony, a generation later, presented her ideas not only on the right to vote but also other issues of legal and economic importance. Anthony's 1897 article on "The Status of Woman, Past, Present, and Future" for example, examines the much-improve, but not yet ideal, situation women face in employment and, crucially, the legal right to own and inherit property. The right to vote was only part of the spectrum of rights and liberties that women's rights advocates sought. Voting brings with it political power. That political power—embodied in the ability to support or defeat candidates or parties and even to run for office if necessary—would enable women to pursue a political agenda that relieved the economic and legal inequalities they faced. The power to vote would also put women in a position to support politicians and policies that would serve the needs of society. This is one of the key points that prominent social reformer Jane Addams makes in her 1910 article "Why Women Should Vote."

The notion of women seeking political power rather than just political equality is prominent in several of these documents. Victoria Woodhull, in her 1871 Lecture on Constitutional Equality, pledges support for the idea of political separation from the United States if equality and a political voice for women are not forthcoming. In her 1915 Testimony before the House Judiciary Committee, Alice Paul was very clear (and her audience of Congressmen were very concerned) about the ability of women to vote for those who were friendly to their cause in those states where suffrage had been granted. Equality brought with it power, and that power could be used to influence the system for the benefit of women as well as men.

This section—like the selection of documents on Native American dissent—closes with a piece form the revolutionary era of the 1960s. The 1968 SCUM Manifesto, composed by Valerie Solanas, represents one of the most outrageous and extreme expressions of the women's rights movement in the United States. Solanas rails not just just against legal, economic, and political inequality but against the power of the patriarchy and the gendered nature of power in western society. Whether or not she was sincere in her claim that the recommendations of anti-male violence in the manifesto were not to be taken seriously, Solanas's radical positions provide an evocative bookend for this collection of documents on the women's rights movement.

Seneca Falls Convention Declaration of Sentiments

Date: 1848
Author: Elizabeth Cady Stanton
Genre: Public declaration

Summary Overview

The Declaration of Sentiments was written by Elizabeth Cady Stanton and was presented to the participants at a convention in Seneca Falls, New York, on July 19–20, 1848. Modeling her work on the Declaration of Independence, the author sought to address the wrongs perpetrated against womankind and called for redress of those wrongs. The Seneca Falls meeting was the first convention specifically devoted to the issue of women's rights. Organized by Stanton, Lucretia Coffin Mott, Mary Ann McClintock, Martha Wright, and Jane Hunt, the convention's goal was to address "the social, civil and religious rights of women," according to the *Seneca County Courier* of July 14, 1848. The Declaration of Sentiments summed up the current state of women's rights in the United States and served notice that women would no longer stand for being treated inequitably.

While antebellum reformers, many of whom were abolitionists, connected the situation of women with that of slaves, in that neither could vote, hold office, sit on juries, or have property rights, the Seneca Falls Convention marked the first time that men and women publicly discussed the issue of women's rights. The people who gathered at Seneca Falls realized that they were taking an unprecedented—not to mention controversial—step in calling for full citizenship for American women. The Declaration of Sentiments was considered radical for its time, especially in the clause calling for suffrage of women. In the context of antebellum America, this document is indeed a radical one. While it took seventy-two years for women to get the vote and even longer to abolish other forms of discrimination, the Declaration of Sentiments marked the first step in the long struggle for women's rights.

Defining Moment

The United States in the 1840s seethed with a variety of reform movements, inspired by the religious upheaval known as the Second Great Awakening as well as the rise of transcendentalism. Reformers thought they could improve American society by changing some of the ills they perceived as plagues upon the nation. Some of the reformers' causes included better treatment of the mentally ill, opposition to capital punishment and war, temperance, and most notably, abolitionism.

Men of conscience, however, were not the only ones who wanted to free the enslaved. Female abolitionists played a number of roles in the fight to end slavery, circulating petitions to Congress, holding antislavery fairs, contributing articles to antislavery publications, and organizing antislavery societies. Some even took the daring step of speaking out publicly against slavery.

The seed for what became the Seneca Falls Convention in 1848 was actually planted several years earlier at the 1840 World Anti-Slavery Convention in London. Lucretia Mott and Elizabeth Cady Stanton met for the first time at the London convention. Stanton was accompanying her husband, Henry, who was a delegate to the convention. Mott was actually a delegate herself but, because of her gender, was denied a seat at the convention. This blatant discrimination forced the women to rethink their treatment in American society and call for their rights as free citizens of the United States.

The immediate impetus for the Seneca Falls Convention was the impending passage of a married women's property law in New York State, which would give married women some property rights. The convention's organizers hoped that by meeting they would bring awareness to the inequitable treatment of women and gain support for passage of the law. Mott's husband, James, chaired the convention; the participants feared that having a woman preside would only increase hostility toward their cause. The Declaration of Sentiments was one of two documents produced at the convention. The other was a preamble followed by a series of eleven resolutions making various demands for women's rights, including the right to vote. All eleven resolutions passed, ten of them unanimously. Only the demand for the vote was not passed unanimously. Indeed, even Lucretia Mott felt that asking for votes for women would harm their cause.

Author Biography

Elizabeth Cady Stanton was born on November 12, 1815, in Johnstown, New York, the daughter of Margaret

Livingstone and Daniel Cady. Young Elizabeth received tutoring in Greek and mathematics; she also became an accomplished equestrian. By reading her father's law books, she learned that women were accorded a second-class status in the legal realm, planting the seed that eventually matured into her campaign for women's rights.

She became involved in the abolition movement, where she met Henry Stanton, whom she married in 1840. Stanton accompanied her husband to London in that year, where he was a delegate to the World Anti-Slavery Convention. She met another American delegate, Lucretia Coffin Mott, who, because of her gender, could not take her seat at the convention. All the female delegates were allowed only to observe the proceedings in silence. This fateful meeting eventually culminated in the Seneca Falls Convention.

In 1847 the Stantons left Boston for Seneca Falls, in Upstate New York, because of Henry's health. As she became involved in her new home, Stanton made the acquaintance of women who agreed that something needed to be done to improve the rights of women. Stanton, Lucretia Mott, Jane Hunt, Martha Wright, and Mary Ann McClintock organized a convention to discuss the rights of women. The Seneca Falls Convention, where Stanton presented her Declaration of Sentiments, gave birth to other women's rights conventions around the country, including the first national convention, in Worcester, Massachusetts, in 1850. The conventions continued until the outbreak of the Civil War.

Until her death on October 26, 1902, Stanton worked tirelessly for women's rights. Her ideas were often considered too radical for the mainstream, and eventually it was Susan B. Anthony who received most of the adulation from young suffragists, whose primary goal was the vote. In a great disservice to Stanton, the Nineteenth Amendment is also referred to as the "Susan B. Anthony amendment." With the revitalization of the feminist movement in the 1960s, Stanton has been restored to her proper place of importance as a founding mother of modern feminism.

HISTORICAL DOCUMENT

When, in the course of human events, it becomes necessary for one portion of the family of man to assume among the people of the earth a position different from that which they have hitherto occupied, but one to which the laws of nature and of nature's God entitle them, a decent respect to the opinions of mankind requires that they should declare the causes that impel them to such a course.

We hold these truths to be self-evident: that all men and women are created equal; that they are endowed by their Creator with certain inalienable rights; that among these are life, liberty, and the pursuit of happiness; that to secure these rights governments are instituted, deriving their just powers from the consent of the governed. Whenever any form of government becomes destructive of these ends, it is the right of those who suffer from it to refuse allegiance to it, and to insist upon the institution of a new government, laying its foundation on such principles, and organizing its powers in such form, as to them shall seem most likely to effect their safety and happiness. Prudence, indeed, will dictate that governments long established should not be changed for light and transient causes; and accordingly all experience hath shown that mankind are more disposed to suffer, while evils are sufferable, than to right themselves by abolishing the forms to which they are accustomed. But when a long train of abuses and usurpations, pursuing invariably the same object, evinces a design to reduce them under absolute despotism, it is their duty to throw off such government, and to provide new guards for their future security. Such has been the patient sufferance of the women under this government, and such is now the necessity which constrains them to demand the equal station to which they are entitled. The history of mankind is a history of repeated injuries and usurpations on the part of man toward woman, having in direct object the establishment of an absolute tyranny over her. To prove this, let facts be submitted to a candid world.

The history of mankind is a history of repeated injuries and usurpations on the part of man toward woman, having in direct object the establishment of an absolute tyranny over her. To prove this, let facts be submitted to a candid world.

He has never permitted her to exercise her inalienable right to the elective franchise.

He has compelled her to submit to laws, in the formation of which she had no voice.

He has withheld from her rights which are given to the most ignorant and degraded men—both natives and foreigners.

Having deprived her of this first right of a citizen, the elective franchise, thereby leaving her without representation in the halls of legislation, he has oppressed her on all sides.

He has made her, if married, in the eye of the law, civilly dead.

He has taken from her all right in property, even to the wages she earns.

He has made her, morally, an irresponsible being, as she can commit many crimes with impunity, provided they be done in the presence of her husband. In the covenant of marriage, she is compelled to promise obedience to her husband, he becoming, to all intents and purposes, her master—the law giving him power to deprive her of her liberty, and to administer chastisement.

He has so framed the laws of divorce, as to what shall be the proper causes, and in case of separation, to whom the guardianship of the children shall be given, as to be wholly regardless of the happiness of women—the law, in all cases, going upon a false supposition of the supremacy of man, and giving all power into his hands.

After depriving her of all rights as a married woman, if single, and the owner of property, he has taxed her to support a government which recognizes her only when her property can be made profitable to it.

He has monopolized nearly all the profitable employments, and from those she is permitted to follow, she receives but a scanty remuneration. He closes against her all the avenues to wealth and distinction which he considers most honorable to himself. As a teacher of theology, medicine, or law, she is not known.

He has denied her the facilities for obtaining a thorough education, all colleges being closed against her.

He allows her in church, as well as state, but a subordinate position, claiming apostolic authority for her exclusion from the ministry, and, with some exceptions, from any public participation in the affairs of the church.

He has created a false public sentiment by giving to the world a different code of morals for men and women, by which moral delinquencies which exclude women from society, are not only tolerated, but deemed of little account in man.

He has usurped the prerogative of Jehovah himself, claiming it as his right to assign for her a sphere of action, when that belongs to her conscience and to her God.

He has endeavored, in every way that he could, to destroy her confidence in her own powers, to lessen her self-respect, and to make her willing to lead a dependent and abject life.

Now, in view of this entire disfranchisement of one-half the people of this country, their social and religious degradation—in view of the unjust laws above mentioned, and because women do feel themselves aggrieved, oppressed, and fraudulently deprived of their most sacred rights, we insist that they have immediate admission to all the rights and privileges which belong to them as citizens of the United States.

GLOSSARY

candid: impartial

chastisement: discipline, especially physical punishment

covenant: formal agreement of legal validity

disfranchisement: denial of a right, especially the right to vote

franchise: the right to vote

remuneration: payment or consideration received for services or employment

sufferance: capacity to endure hardship

Document Analysis

The opening of the Declaration of Sentiments justifies the actions of those who support women's rights and prepares the reader for the litany of the wrongs perpetrated against womankind. Stanton uses the religious language of the Declaration of Independence when she refers to "nature's God" and points out that the rights women are demanding come not from government but from "nature" as well as the Supreme Being.

Stanton goes on to state, "We hold these truths to be self-evident: that all men and women are created equal." This ringing proclamation comes directly from the Declaration of Independence, with only the words "and women" added. Women, like men, are entitled to "life, liberty, and the pursuit of happiness," and the government was instituted to make sure that all people are guaranteed these rights. Stanton states that people who have been denied their rights have the right to "refuse allegiance" to their government and "insist upon the institution of a new government." In fact, those who are abused in this way have a responsibility and duty "to throw off such government." These are the words Thomas Jefferson used to justify the American people's break from Great Britain and formation of a new government. Stanton added, however, language stating that women have suffered patiently under the current government, which has denied them their full rights, and "such is now the necessity which constrains them to demand the equal station to which they are entitled."

A statement that the "history of mankind is a history of repeated injuries and usurpations on the part of man toward woman" introduces the lengthy portion of the document that lists the wrongs visited upon womankind. The first five focus on women's lack of political rights, beginning with the fact that women are denied the vote. Logically, from lacking the vote, women are subject to laws that they had no say in making. The next item argues that women have been denied simple rights possessed by even the "most ignorant and degraded" men, not only native-born but even foreign. This statement was an appeal to the nativist element that was emerging in the late nineteenth century. The next statement again makes mention of the denial of "the elective franchise" in the context of denying women "representation in the halls of the legislation."

The next set of wrongs deals with marriage and property rights. Stanton observes that the institution of marriage has been particularly destructive to women, given that married women are defined outright as "civilly dead" in the eyes of the law. Because of that, married women have no rights to property, even their own wages. The next clause states that because of the usurpation of these rights, the law has essentially rendered woman "an irresponsible being" who can commit any crime without fear of punishment, as long as it is done "in the presence of her husband." Stanton further notes that women must obey their husbands unquestioningly and that the law gives him the power "to deprive her of her liberty" and physically and emotionally abuse her without recourse. Divorce is the next topic, and here women are denied the guardianship of their children, no matter what the cause for ending the marriage. Single women are mentioned in the next clause, which points out that if a single woman is a property owner, then she is subject to taxes; thus the government "recognizes her only when her property can be made profitable to it."

Clauses on employment, education, and religion make up the next set. Stanton states that men have "monopolized nearly all the profitable employments." Not only that, but in the professions women could enter, they were not equitably paid. The next clause focuses on education, noting that all colleges are "closed against her." Stanton actually slightly exaggerates in this clause, as Oberlin College did admit women equally with men by 1848, but that was the exception rather than the rule. Organized religion comes under attack next, for it keeps women "in a subordinate position," barring them from the ministry and generally from any "public participation in the affairs of the church." Not only are women discriminated against by "the church," but also in the realm of morals they are subjected to a double standard; as the clause puts it, there is "a different code of morals for men and women." The penultimate clause makes reference to God and states that man has "usurped" the Lord's "prerogative" by assigning woman a sphere of action "when that belongs to her conscience and to her God." Finally, the last clause states that man has decreed women should be submissive and dependent, destroying "her confidence in her own powers" and lessening "her self-respect."

The last paragraph sums up the entire document. Stanton states that in light of the aforementioned grievances, including "the disenfranchisement of one-half the people of this country," American women "insist that they have immediate admission to all the rights and privileges which belong to them as citizens of the United States."

Essential Themes

The Declaration of Sentiments was revolutionary and echoed the ideology behind America's own Revolution. By changing the language of the Declaration of Independence, the basic document proclaiming America's independence from tyranny, Stanton brought focus to the failure of that document to provide rights for half of America's citizens: women.

The Declaration of Sentiments was written for several audiences. The first audience was the men and women who participated in the Seneca Falls Convention. Following the form and adapting many of the key concepts of the Declaration of Independence, the Declaration of Sentiments sought to set forth the wrongs done to women and offer a redress of those wrongs. Thus, another audience was the men who served as the lawmakers of the United States, both in the federal government and in each state and territory. These people made the laws and needed to be aware that women were treated as second-class citizens and were not granted all the rights of other American citizens. The last audience was the people of the United States. The document was intended to raise the awareness of all Americans regarding the treatment of women in the nation that proclaimed that "all men are created equal."

———Donna M. DeBlasio, with additional material by Marcia B. Dinneen

Bibliography and Additional Reading

Baker, Jean H., ed. *Votes for Women: The Struggle for Suffrage Revisited*. (New York: Oxford University Press, 2002).

DuBois, Ellen Carol. *Feminism and Suffrage: The Emergence of an Independent Women's Movement in the United States, 1848–1869*. Revised edition. (Ithaca, N.Y. Cornell University Press, 1999).

Flexner, Eleanor, and Ellen Fitzpatrick. *Century of Struggle: The Woman's Rights Movement in the United States*. Enlarged edition. (Cambridge, Mass. Belknap Press of Harvard University Press, 1996).

Ginzberg, Lori. *Untidy Origins: A Story of Woman's Rights in Antebellum New York*. (Chapel Hill: University of North Carolina Press, 2005).

Griffith, Elisabeth. *In Her Own Right: The Life of Elizabeth Cady Stanton*. (New York: Oxford University Press, 1985).

Isenberg, Nancy. *Sex and Citizenship in Antebellum America*. (Chapel Hill: University of North Carolina Press, 1998).

Wellman, Judith. *The Road to Seneca Falls: Elizabeth Cady Stanton and the First Woman's Rights Convention*. (Urbana: University of Illinois Press, 2004).

Lecture on Constitutional Equality

Date: 1871
Author: Victoria Woodhull
Genre: Speech

Summary Overview

In January 1871, Victoria Woodhull became the first women to appear before a congressional committee when she addressed the House Judiciary Committee in a bid to persuade Congress to enact female suffrage, or the right to vote. Benjamin Butler—a high-ranking Massachusetts Republican who would later chair the panel—allowed her to deliver her plea in person. Woodhull based her arguments on her belief that women already had the right to vote, in that the Fourteenth and Fifteenth Amendments to the Constitution implicitly granted that right to all citizens, not just men. The majority of the Representatives on the committee did not accept her arguments and voted to dismiss the request, but the minority report written by just two of the committee's members, Butler and William Loughridge, supported the cause, saying that women were "competent voters." Woodhull went on to deliver fiery lectures on the constitutional enfranchisement of women, notably at Lincoln Hall in Washington, D.C. in February of 1871. This expansion of her argument was published that same year in pamphlet form as *Lecture on Constitutional Equality*.

Defining Moment

With her *Lecture on Constitutional Equality*, Woodhull announced and expanded upon the address she had presented to Congress in January 1871 on the subject of woman suffrage. She had been given the privilege of a congressional audience mostly because she had gained a celebrity status shunned by other suffragettes. Woodhull was regularly featured in sensationalist newspaper stories relating to her roles as a newspaper publisher, as the first female owner of a stock brokerage, and as an announced presidential candidate. The scandal attached to her background made her more interesting to reporters than the staid personas of respectable middle-class suffragettes like Susan B. Anthony and Elizabeth Cady Stanton. In fact, a wide variety of suffragettes looked to Woodhull to make their case to the public and government. One advantage that Woodhull possessed as a spokeswoman for the woman suffrage movement was that, as an outsider, she had not taken part in the contentious split over the Fifteenth Amendment. The movement for woman suffrage had always been closely aligned with that for the abolition of slavery. When the Fifteenth Amendment, granting the right to vote to freed slaves, was being written, some more radical suffragettes, such as Anthony, campaigned for the same amendment to explicitly grant women the right to vote also, a position eventually advocated by the National Woman Suffrage Association. Meanwhile, conservatives such as Lucy Stone, a founder of the American Woman Suffrage Association, did not want to risk losing suffrage for former slaves by trying to then gain suffrage for all.

Author Biography

Victoria Claflin Woodhull was born on September 23, 1838, on an Ohio farm. She married to the physician Canning Woodhull (an alcoholic and poor provider) when she was fourteen. By the time of the Civil War, Woodhull's parents were in the business of promoting her younger sister, Tennessee Claflin, claiming that she could cure disease through mesmerism, or hypnosis. Claflin was indicted for manslaughter following the death a patient she was treating for breast cancer. The sisters practiced in various cities, with Woodhull providing consultations as a spirit medium, connecting clients with dead relatives. Remarrying, Woodhull moved to New York City in 1868.

In 1870, shipping and railroad tycoon Cornelius Vanderbilt consulted the sisters, probably in the hope of contacting his dead son. Vanderbilt came to establish the two as heads of a brokerage firm he capitalized, making them the first female stockbrokers in America. Using their new income, the sisters started a newspaper to promote suffrage for women. In 1870 she announced her candidacy for the presidency of the United States in the 1872 election. She would be formally nominated by the Equal Rights Party in 1872, with the abolitionist and former slave Frederick Douglass as her running mate.

By 1872 it had become clear that Woodhull had become too radical for her own good; she was damaging the public image of her causes, forfeiting the support of

Vanderbilt and her political allies. Acting on instructions from the spirit world, so she claimed, Woodhull attacked prominent Protestant preacher Henry Ward Beecher. Woodhull published evidence of Beecher's adultery in her newspaper, leading to perhaps the greatest scandal in nineteenth-century America. Woodhull spent many weeks in prison and saw her personal finances ruined by prosecution brought about by the postal censor Anthony Comstock over the publication of the Beecher story, though the case against her was thrown out on a technicality. After these proceedings, Woodhull was viewed as a martyr and was able to begin a national lecture tour that largely restored her fortunes. She died on June 9, 1927.

HISTORICAL DOCUMENT

I have no doubt it seems strange to many of you that a woman should appear before the people in this public manner for political purposes, and it is due both to you and myself that I should give my reasons for so doing.

On the 19th of December, 1870, I memorialized Congress, setting forth what I believed to be the truth and right regarding Equal Suffrage for all citizens. This memorial was referred to the Judiciary Committees of Congress. On the 12th of January I appeared before the House Judiciary Committee and submitted to them the Constitutional and Legal points upon which I predicated such equality. January 20th Mr. Bingham, on behalf of the majority of said Committee, submitted his report to the House in which, while he admitted all my basic propositions, Congress was recommended to take no action....I assumed and recommended that Congress *should* pass a Declaratory Act, forever settling the mooted question of suffrage.

Thus it is seen that equally able men differ upon a simple point of Constitutional Law, and it is fair to presume that Congress will also differ *when* these Reports come up for action. That a proposition involving such momentous results as this, should receive a one-third vote upon first coming before Congress has raised it in importance, which spreads alarm on all sides among the opposition. So long as it was not made to appear that women were denied Constitutional rights, no opposition was aroused; but now that new light is shed, by which it is seen that such is the case, all the Conservative weapons of bitterness, hatred and malice are marshalled in the hope to extinguish it, before it can enlighten the masses of the people, who are always true to freedom and justice.

Public opinion is against Equality, but it is simply from prejudice, which requires but to be informed to pass away. No greater prejudice exists against equality than there did against the proposition that the world was a globe. This passed away under the influence of better information, so also will present prejudice pass, when better informed upon the question of equality....

I come before you, to declare that my sex are entitled to the inalienable right to life, liberty and the pursuit of happiness. The first two I cannot be deprived of except for cause and by due process of law; but upon the last, a right is usurped to place restrictions so general as to include the whole of my sex, and for which no reasons of public good can be assigned. I ask the right to pursue happiness by having a voice in that government to which I am accountable. I have not forfeited that right, still I am denied. Was assumed arbitrary authority ever more arbitrarily exercised? In practice, then, our laws are false to the principles which we profess. I have the right to life, to liberty, unless I forfeit it by an infringement upon others' rights, in which case the State becomes the arbiter and deprives me of them for the public good. I also have the right to pursue happiness, unless I forfeit it in the same way, and am denied it accordingly. It cannot be said, with any justice, that my pursuit of happiness in voting for any man for office, would be an infringement of one of his rights as a citizen or as an individual. I hold, then, that in denying me this right without my having forfeited it, that departure is made from the principles of the Constitution, and also from the true principles of government, for I am denied a right born with me, and which is inalienable....

If freedom consists in having an *actual share* in appointing those who frame the laws, are not the women of this country in absolute *bondage*, and can government, in the face of the XV Amendment, assume to deny them the right to vote, being in this "condition of servitude?" According to Franklin we are absolutely enslaved, for there *are* "governors set over us by other men," and we are "subject to the laws" they make. Is *not* Franklin good authority in matters of freedom? Again, rehearsing the arguments that have emanated from Congress and applying them to the present case, we learn that "It is idle to show that, in certain instances, the fathers failed to apply the sublime principles which they declared. Their failure can be *no* apology for those on whom the duty is now cast." Shall it be an apology *now*? Shall the omission of others to do justice keep the government from measuring it to those who now cry out for it?…

I *am* subject to tyranny! I am taxed in every conceivable way. For publishing a paper I must pay—for engaging in the banking and brokerage business I must pay—of what it is my fortune to acquire each year I must turn over a certain per cent—I must pay high prices for tea, coffee and sugar: to *all* these must I submit, that *men's* government may be maintained, a government in the administration of which I am denied a voice, and from its edicts there is no appeal. I must submit to a heavy advance upon the first cost of *nearly everything I wear* in order that industries in which I have no interest may exist at my expense. I am compelled to pay extravagant rates of fare wherever I travel, because the franchises, extended to gigantic corporations, enable them to *sap* the vitality of the country, to make their *managers money kings*, by means of which they boast of being able to control not only legislators but even a State judiciary.

To be compelled to submit to *these* extortions that *such* ends may be gained, upon *any* pretext or under *any* circumstances, is bad enough: but to be compelled to submit to them, and also denied the right to cast my vote *against* them, is a tyranny *more* odious than that which, being rebelled against, gave this country independence.…

Therefore it is, that instead of growing in republican liberty, we are departing from it. From an unassuming, acquiescent part of society, woman has gradually passed to an individualized human being, and as she has advanced, one after another evident right of the common people has been accorded to her. She has now become so *much* individualized as to demand the full and unrestrained exercise of *all* the rights which can be predicated of a people constructing a government based on individual sovereignty. She asks it, and shall Congress deny her?

The formal abolition of slavery created several millions of male negro citizens, who, a portion of the acknowledged citizens assumed to say, were *not* entitled to equal rights with themselves. To get over this difficulty, Congress in its wisdom saw fit to propose a XIV Amendment to the Constitution, which passed into a law by ratification by the States. Sec. I. of the Amendment declares: "All persons, born or naturalized in the United States, and subject to the jurisdiction thereof, are citizens of the United States and of the State wherein they reside. No State shall make or enforce any law which shall abridge the privileges and immunities of citizens of the United States. Nor shall any State deprive any person of life, liberty and property without due process of law, nor deny any person within its jurisdiction the equal protection of the law."…

After the adoption of the XIV Amendment it was found that still more legislation [XV Amendment] was required to secure the exercise of the right to vote to all who by it were declared to be citizens, and the following comprehensive amendment was passed by Congress and ratified by the States: "The right of citizens of the United States to vote shall not be denied or abridged by the United States or by any State on account of race, color or previous condition of servitude." Nothing could be more explicit than this language, and nothing more comprehensive. "But," says the objector, ever on the alert, "it may be denied on account of sex." It must be remembered "that is law which is written," and that all *inferences* drawn must be in accord with the *general intent* of the instrument involved by the inference. *If* the right to vote cannot be denied on account of race, *how* can it be denied on account of a constituent part of race, unless the power of denial is specially *expressed*. The larger *always* includes the smaller, which, if reserved, the reservation that it has no *broader* application. Whoever it may include, under logical construction, to them the right to vote shall not be denied. Take the African race and the black color and the previous slaves out of the way, and what application would this Amendment then have? This is the way to test these things, the way to arrive at what they mean. *Who* will pretend to say this Amendment would mean nothing were there no negroes, and there had been no Southern slaves? Who will pretend to say that the Amendment would mean nothing in the coming election, provided that there never before had been an election under the Constitution? If you provide a Constitutional amendment, having *one* race specially in view, it must not be forgotten that there are *other* races besides. Thirty-seven States constitute the United States. If you speak of the United States you speak of all the States, for they are all included. If you speak of a *part* of the United States, you must designate *what* part, in order that it may be known what you mean. A race is composed of two sexes. If you speak of a race you include both sexes. If you speak of a *part* of a race, you must designate *which* part in order to make yourselves intelligible....

I make the plain and broad assertion, that the women of this country are as *much* subject to men as the slaves were to their masters. The extent of the subjection may be less and its severity milder, but it is a complete subjection nevertheless. What can women do that men deny them? What could not the slave have done if not denied?

It is not the women who are happily situated, whose husbands hold positions of honor and trust, who are blessed by the bestowal of wealth, comforts and ease that I plead for. These do not feel their condition of servitude any more than the happy, well-treated slave felt her condition. Had slavery been of this kind it is at least questionable if it would not still have been in existence; but it was not all of this kind. Its barbarities, horrors and inhumanities roused the blood of some who were free, and by their efforts the male portion of a race were elevated by Congress to the exercise of the rights of citizenship. Thus would I have Congress regard woman, and shape their action, *not* from the condition of those who are so well cared for as not to wish a change to enlarge their sphere of action, but for the *toiling female millions*, who have human rights which should be respected....

We are now prepared to dispose of the sex argument. If the right to vote shall not be denied to any person of any race, how shall it be denied to the female part of all races? Even if it could be denied on account of sex, I ask, what warrant men have to presume that it is the *female* sex to whom such denial can be made instead of the *male* sex? Men, you are wrong, and you stand convicted before the world of denying me, a woman, the right to vote, not by any right of law, but simply because you have usurped the power so to do, just as all other tyrants in all ages have, to rule their subjects. The extent of the tyranny in either case being limited only by the power to enforce it....

Under such glaring inconsistencies, such unwarrantable tyranny, such unscrupulous despotism. What is there left women to do but to become the mothers of the future government.

We will have our rights. We say no longer by your leave. We have besought, argued and convinced, but we have failed; *and we will not* fail.

We will try you *just once more*. If the very next Congress refuse women all the legitimate results of citizenship; if they indeed merely so much as fail by a proper declaratory act to withdraw every obstacle to the most ample exercise of the franchise, then we give here and now, deliberate notification of what we will do next.

There is one alternative left, and we have resolved on that. This convention is for the purpose of this declaration. As surely as one year passes, from this day, and this right is not fully, frankly and unequivocally considered, we shall proceed to call another convention expressly to frame a new constitution and to erect a new government, complete in all its parts, and to take measures to maintain it as effectually as men do theirs.

If for people to govern themselves is so unimportant a matter as men now assert it to be, they could not justify themselves in interfering. If, on the contrary, it is the important thing we conceive it to be, they can but applaud us for exercising our right.

We mean treason; we mean secession, and on a thousand times grander scale than was that of the South. We are plotting revolution; we will overthrow this bogus republic and plant a government of righteousness in its stead, which shall not only profess to derive its power from the consent of the governed, but shall do so in reality.

> **GLOSSARY**
>
> **besought:** asked for, begged for
>
> **Bingham:** John Bingham, Ohio congressman
>
> **Franklin:** Benjamin Franklin, one of the nation's founders
>
> **mooted:** having no legal significance, already settled

Document Analysis

The argument that Woodhull delivered to Congress and later reprised for popular consumption in New York (even after her proposals had been rejected by a two-thirds vote of Congress's joint Judiciary Committee) was essentially based on traditional suffragist thought going back to the 1848 Seneca Falls Convention on women's rights. Woodhull begins the main part of her argument by adapting the language of the Declaration of Independence: "I come before you, to declare that my sex are entitled to the inalienable right to life, liberty and the pursuit of happiness." This pattern of adaptation had been established by the Declaration of Sentiments produced at Seneca Falls. The essence of Woodhull's argument is that the right to personal freedom attaches to the condition of being human and that if the full exercise of freedom, including the right to vote, is denied women, it is a tyranny worse than that exercised by George III over the American colonies or by slave owners over slaves. In particular, Woodhull considers the legal position of women in America up until 1871 to be a "previous condition of servitude," which, according to the newly passed Fifteenth Amendment, could not be used as a bar to voting rights.

Again following the Declaration of Sentiments, Woodhull moves on to a specific list of grievances against women's freedoms, also based insofar as possible on the Declaration of Independence. Women are subject to laws over whose making they have no control because they neither vote for nor serve as legislators. In particular, women must pay taxes that they have no role in levying, a point echoing the colonial American grievance against taxation without representation. Woodhull moves on to the main part of her argument, an analysis of the Fourteenth and Fifteenth Amendments to the Constitution, which after the Civil War established the newly freed slaves as citizens and specifically granted them the right to vote. She contends that if there was any doubt about the equality of women's citizenship before, the broadly inclusive language of the Fourteenth Amendment should settle it: "All persons, born or naturalized in the United States, and subject to the jurisdiction thereof, are citizens of the United States and of the State wherein they reside." She does not, however, directly address the second clause of the amendment, which expressly prohibits states from denying suffrage to any male citizens only. Yet she insists that the inclusive language must be read in the broadest possible meaning, to comprehend everyone not specifically excluded. In such a reading, the specific mention of males indicates nothing about females.

It was the very brief and general language of the Fifteenth Amendment, however, that was the main support of suffragette hopes. Woodhull quotes the text in full: "The right of citizens of the United States to vote shall not be denied or abridged by the United States or by any State on account of race, color or previous condition of servitude." She regards this text as clearly supporting her cause: "Nothing could be more explicit than this language, and nothing more comprehensive." She presents two arguments for the inclusion of women within the language of the amendment. Since gender is a larger and more inclusive category than any of those specifically mentioned in the amendment, she supposes that it must be inferred that gender also cannot be used to deny the right to vote. Her second, and more powerful, argument, is actually the opposite of the first. She quite rightly reads the amendment as not referring exclusively to the "black" race but as applying equally to all races and to people of all colors. Since, insofar as race is a legal category, all women belong to some race, the guarantee of rights to members of any race includes the female members of the races unless, as the amendment does not do, they are specifically excluded. As she reasons, "A race is composed of two sexes. If you speak of a race you include both sexes. If you speak of a *part* of a race, you must designate *which* part in order to make yourselves intelligible."

The remainder of Woodhull's address departs from the mainstream of the suffrage movement. Most suffragettes were middle-class women from conservative backgrounds, and while they thought it just that women be granted the vote and other legal rights of citizens, they distanced themselves from the more radical political ideologies embraced by Woodhull (such as Socialism), both because they did not find them appealing and because they did not want their movement to be perceived as a general threat to the existing social order. Woodhull had no such scruples, and her further proposals here are of a piece with her radical decision to run for the presidency. She states that if women are not granted full equality by Congress to elect and be elected in 1872, women will start a new American revolution and create a new constitution based on freedom rather than tyranny.

Essential Themes

Victoria Woodhull's 1871 address to the House of Representatives Judiciary Committee came at a time when the initial wave of th women's movement in the United States began to break on the rocks of reconstruction. As the movement split over whether to push for women's suffrage along with black male suffrage during the debate over the 15th amendment, the coalition that had emerged from the abolition movement and solidified at the 1848 Seneca Falls Convention began to fragment. Here, Woodhull uses the traditional—for the time—method of arguing for women's suffrage: a generous reading of the 14th and 15th amendments. Woodhull, however, did not confine her self to this line of reasoning. A key component of her speech comes near the end. She had already announced her intention to run for the Presidency in 1872 and, here, she calls for a new nation to come forth if the demands of the women's suffrage movement are not met by that time. We mean treason," she proclaims. "We mean secession, and on a thousand times grander scale than was that of the South. We are plotting revolution; we will overthrow this bogus republic and plant a government of righteousness in its stead." This call for revolution heralded a new age not just in American gender politics but for American politics in general, as radical movements like socialism, communism, and anarchism would rear their heads in the coming decades.

———Bradley A. Skeen, PhD.

Bibliography and Additional Reading

Caplan, Sheri J. *Petticoats and Pinstripes: Portraits of Women in Wall Street's History*. (Westport, Connecticut: Praeger, 2013).

Fitzpatrick, Ellen. *The Highest Glass Ceiling : Women's Quest for the American Presidency*. (Cambridge: Harvard University Press, 2016).

Gabriel, Mary. *Notorious Victoria: The Life of Victoria Woodhull Uncensored*. (Chapel Hill: Algonquin Books, 1998)

Goldsmith, Barbara. *Other Powers: The Age of Suffrage, Spiritualism, and the Scandalous Victoria Woodhull*. (New York: Harper Perennial, 1998).

"Is It a Crime for a Citizen of the United States to Vote?"

Date: 1873
Author: Susan B. Anthony
Genre: Speech

Summary Overview

In all her speeches and writings, Susan B. Anthony displayed her single-minded devotion to the cause of women's rights—particularly the right to vote. Over the years she honed her arguments until the success of the cause of suffrage and women's rights became inevitable. This major shift in public opinion was the result in large part of Anthony's carefully crafted arguments.

In Rochester, New York, on November 5, 1872, Anthony cast her ballot for the Republican ticket in the presidential election. She had claimed the right to register to vote on the basis of the Fourteenth Amendment, which gave the vote to "all persons born or naturalized in the United States" as a privilege of citizenship (with no gender qualification). In response to her arrest and trial for illegally casting a ballot, Anthony launched a speaking tour throughout New York State. The address she delivered, which was included in the records of the trial, was titled "Is It a Crime for a Citizen of the United States to Vote?" Although she invoked the Declaration of Independence, the Constitution, James Madison, Thomas Paine, the Supreme Court, and the Civil War Amendments as justification for a woman's right to vote, she was convicted of the crime of voting in June of 1873.

Defining Moment

After the Civil War and the abolition of slavery, Anthony other suffragist leaders were hopeful that the Fifteenth Amendment to the Constitution, which granted voting rights to African Americans, would extend the same rights to women—and were bitterly disappointed that it did not. In 1868 Anthony launched a weekly journal called the *Revolution* under the motto "The true republic—men, their rights and nothing more; women, their rights and nothing less." For the next four decades Anthony devoted her life to writing and speaking in support of women's rights, particularly the right to vote.

After Anthony and several other women cast ballots in Rochester in the 1872 presidential election, she was arrested, tried, found guilty, and fined, though she never paid the fine and was never jailed. In response to her arrest, Anthony launched a statewide speaking tour in 1873, during which she delivered the address "Is It a Crime for a Citizen of the United States to Vote?" During the legal proceedings, she recorded her reactions in various letters she wrote in 1872 and 1873. Throughout the final decades of the nineteenth century, Anthony wrote articles and delivered speeches on issues affecting women and the suffragist cause.

Author Biography

Susan Brownell Anthony, who devoted more than a half century to women's suffrage and other social issues, was born in Adams, Massachusetts, on February 15, 1820. She received her education at a Quaker boarding school in Philadelphia, where she trained as a teacher, an occupation she pursued for three years beginning in 1846. After the family moved to Rochester, New York, in 1845, she became active in a range of social causes, including abolition of slavery, temperance, the rights of labor, education reform, and particularly women's rights. She signed the Declaration of Sentiments produced by the 1848 Seneca Falls Convention in New York, the first women's rights convention held in the United States. In the early 1850s she met her lifelong friend and fellow suffragist, Elizabeth Cady Stanton—although in later years some tension emerged between the two, with Stanton adopting a more radical approach to women's rights and Anthony a more moderate position.

Anthony is often regarded as the author of the Nineteenth Amendment to the U.S. Constitution recognizing the right of women to vote. She originally wrote the amendment in 1877, using the Fifteenth Amendment ("The right of citizens of the United States to vote shall not be denied or abridged by the United States or by any State on account of race, color, or previous condition of servitude") as a model. The amendment, which came to be referred to as the Anthony Amendment, was submitted to Congress by a sympathetic senator, Aaron Sargent, and while Congress did not act on it, it was submitted in every session of Congress until 1919. Just one month before her death on March 13, 1906, Anthony concluded her last public speech, delivered at a meeting of the National American Women Suffrage

Association, with the words "Failure is impossible"—her final public utterance and a phrase that survived as a rallying cry for women's rights proponents throughout the twentieth century. Her words proved to be prophetic, for Congress approved the Nineteenth Amendment in 1919, and the amendment was ratified in 1920.

HISTORICAL DOCUMENT

Friends and Fellow-citizens: I stand before you under indictment for the alleged crime of having voted at the last presidential election, without having a lawful right to vote. It shall be my work this evening to prove to you that in thus voting, I not only committed no crime, but instead simply exercised my citizen's right, guaranteed to me and all United States citizens by the National Constitution beyond the power of any State to deny.

Our democratic-republican government is based on the idea of the natural right of every individual member thereof to a voice and a vote in making and executing the laws. We assert the province of government to be to secure the people in the enjoyment of their inalienable rights. We throw to the winds the old dogma that governments can give rights. No one denies that before governments were organized each individual possessed the right to protect his own life, liberty and property. When 100 or 1,000,000 people enter into a free government, they do not barter away their natural rights; they simply pledge themselves to protect each other in the enjoyment of them through prescribed judicial and legislative tribunals. They agree to abandon the methods of brute force in the adjustment of their differences and adopt those of civilization. Nor can you find a word in any of the grand documents left us by the fathers which assumes for government the power to create or to confer rights. The Declaration of Independence, the United States Constitution, the constitutions of the several states and the organic laws of the territories, all alike propose *to protect* the people in the exercise of their God-given rights. Not one of them pretends to bestow rights.

"All men are created equal, and endowed by their Creator with certain inalienable rights. Among these are life, liberty and the pursuit of happiness. That to secure these [rights], governments are instituted among men, deriving their just powers from the consent of the governed."

Here is no shadow of government authority over rights, or exclusion of any class from their full and equal enjoyment. Here is pronounced the right of all men, and "consequently," as the Quaker preacher said, "of all women," to a voice in the government. And here, in this very first paragraph of the declaration, is the assertion of the natural right of all to the ballot; for how can "the consent of the governed" be given, if the right to vote be denied. Again:

"Whenever any form of government becomes destructive of these ends, it is the right of the people to alter or abolish it, and to institute a new government, laying its foundations on such principles, and organizing its powers in such forms as to them shall seem most likely to effect their safety and happiness."

Surely, the right of the whole people to vote is here clearly implied. For however destructive to their happiness this government might become, a disfranchised class could neither alter nor abolish it, nor institute a new one, except by the old brute force method of insurrection and rebellion. One-half of the people of this nation today are utterly powerless to blot from the statute books an unjust law, or to write there a new and a just one....

The preamble of the federal constitution says:

"We, the people of the United States, in order to form a more perfect union, establish justice, insure domestic tranquility, provide for the common defence, promote the general welfare and secure the blessings of liberty to ourselves and our posterity, do ordain and established this Constitution for the United States of America."

It was we, the people, not we, the white male citizens, nor we, the male citizens; but we, the whole people, who formed this Union. We formed it not to give the blessings of liberty but to secure them; not to the half of ourselves and the half of our posterity, but to the whole people—women as well as men. It is downright mockery to talk to women of their enjoyment of the blessings of liberty while they are denied the only means of securing them provided by this democratic-republican government—the ballot....

James Madison said;

> "Under every view of the subject, it seems indispensable that the mass of the citizens should not be without a voice in making the laws which they are to obey, and in choosing the magistrates who are to administer them.... Let it be remembered, finally, that it has ever been the pride and the boast of America that the rights for which she contended were the rights of human nature."

These assertions by the framers of the United States Constitution of the equal and natural right of all the people to a voice in the government, have been affirmed and reaffirmed by the leading statesmen of the nation, throughout the entire history of our government....

The clauses of the United States Constitution cited by our opponents as giving power to the States to disfranchise any classes of citizens they shall please are contained in Sections 2 and 4 of Article I. The second says:

> "The House of Representatives shall be composed of members chosen every second year by the people of the several States; and the electors in each State shall have the qualifications requisite for electors of the most numerous branch of the State legislature."

This cannot be construed into a concession to the States of the power to destroy the right to become an elector, but simply to prescribe what shall be the qualification, such as competency of intellect, maturity of age, length of residence, that shall be deemed necessary to enable them to make an intelligent choice of candidates. If, as our opponents assert, the last clause of this section makes it the duty of the United States to protect citizens in the several States against higher or different qualifications for electors for representatives in Congress than for members of the Assembly, then it must be equally imperative for the national government to interfere with the States, and forbid them from arbitrarily cutting off the right of one-half of the people to become electors altogether. Section 4 says:

> "The times, places and manner of holding elections for senators and representatives shall be prescribed in each State by the legislature thereof; but Congress may at any time, by law, make or alter such regulations, except as to the places of choosing Senators."

Here is conceded to the States the power only to prescribe times, places and manner of holding the elections; and even with these Congress may interfere in all excepting the mere place of choosing senators. Thus, you see, there is not the slightest permission in either section for the States to discriminate against the right of any class of citizens to vote. Surely, to regulate cannot be to annihilate; to qualify cannot be wholly to deprive....

For any State to make sex a qualification, which must ever result in the disfranchisement of one entire half of the people, is to pass a bill of attainder, or an ex post facto law, and is therefore a violation of the supreme law of the land. By it, the blessings of liberty are forever withheld from women and their female posterity. For them, this government has no just powers derived from the consent of the governed. For them this government is not a democracy. It is not a republic. It is the most odious aristocracy ever established on the face of the globe. An oligarchy of wealth, where the rich govern the poor; an oligarchy of learning, where the educated govern the ignorant; or even an oligarchy of race, where the Saxon rules the African, might be endured; but this oligarchy of sex, which makes father, brothers, husband, sons, the oligarchs over the mother and sisters, the wife and daughters of every household; which ordains all men sovereigns, all women subjects, carries dissension, discord and rebellion into every home of the nation. This most odious aristocracy exists, too, in the face of Section 4, of Article IV, which says:

> "The United States shall guarantee to every State in the Union a republican form of government."

What, I ask you, is the distinctive difference between the inhabitants of a monarchical and those of a republican form of government, save that in the monarchical the people are subjects, helpless, powerless, bound to obey laws made by political superiors—while in the republican, the people are citizens, individual sovereigns, all clothed with equal power, to make and unmake both their laws and law makers. The moment you deprive a person of his right to a voice in the government, you degrade him from the status of a citizen of the republic to that of a subject. It matters very little to him whether his monarch be an individual tyrant, as is the Czar of Russia, or a 15,000,000 headed monster, as here in the United States; he is a powerless subject, serf or slave; not in any sense a free and independent citizen.

It is urged that the use of the masculine pronouns *he*, *his* and *him*, in all the constitutions and laws, is proof that only men were meant to be included in their provisions. If you insist on this version of the letter of the law, we shall insist that you be consistent, and accept the other horn of the dilemma, which would compel you to exempt women from taxation for the support of the government and from penalties for the violation of laws....

Though the words persons, people, inhabitants, electors, citizens, are all used indiscriminately in the national and State constitutions, there was always a conflict of opinion, prior to the war, as to whether they were synonymous terms, but whatever there was for a doubt, under the old regime, the adoption of the Fourteenth Amendment settled that question forever, in its first sentence:

> "All persons born or naturalized in the United States and subject to the jurisdiction thereof, are citizens of the United States and of the state wherein they reside."

The second settles the equal status of all citizens:

> "No State shall make or enforce any law which shall abridge the privileges or immunities of citizens of the United States; nor shall any State deprive any person of life, liberty or property, without due process of law, nor deny to any person within its jurisdiction the equal protection of the laws."

The only question left to be settled, now, is: Are women persons? I scarcely believe any of our opponents will have the hardihood to say they are not. Being persons, then, women are citizens, and no State has a right to make any new law, or to enforce any old law, which shall abridge their privileges or immunities. Hence, every discrimination against women in the constitutions and laws of the several States, is today null and void, precisely as is every one against negroes....

If the Fourteenth Amendment does not secure to all citizens the right to vote, for what purpose was the grand old charter of the fathers lumbered with its unwieldy proportions? The Republican party, and Judges Howard and Bingham, who drafted the document, pretended it was to do something for black men; and if that something were not to secure them in their right to vote and hold office, what could it have been? For, by the Thirteenth Amendment, black men had become people, and hence were entitled to all the privileges and immunities of the government, precisely as were the women of the country, and foreign men not naturalized....

Thus, you see, those newly-freed men were in possession of every possible right, privilege and immunity of the government, except that of suffrage, and hence, needed no constitutional amendment for any other purpose. What right in this country has the Irishman the day after he receives his naturalization papers that he did not possess the day before, save the right to vote and hold office? The Chinamen now crowding our Pacific coast are in precisely the same position. What privilege or immunity has California or Oregon the right to deny them, save that of the ballot? Clearly, then if the Fourteenth Amendment was not to secure to black men their right to vote it did nothing for them, since they possessed everything else before. But if it was intended to prohibit the states from denying or abridging their right to vote, then it did the same for all persons, white women included, born or naturalized in the United States; for the amendment does not say that all male persons of African descent, but that all persons are citizens.

However much the doctors of the law may disagree, as to whether people and citizens, in the original Constitution, were one and the same, or whether the privileges and immunities in the Fourteenth Amendment include the right of suffrage, the question of the citizen's right to vote is forever settled by the Fifteenth Amendment. "The right of citizens of the United States to vote shall not be denied or abridged by the United States or by any State on account of race, color, or previous condition of servitude." How can the State deny or abridge the right of the citizen, if the citizen does not possess it? There is no escape from the conclusion that to vote is the citizen's right, and the specifications of race, color, or previous condition of servitude can in no way impair the force of the emphatic assertion that the citizen's right to vote shall not be denied or abridged.

The political strategy of the second section of the Fourteenth Amendment, failing to coerce the rebel States into enfranchising their negroes, and the necessities of the Republican party demanding their votes throughout the South, to ensure the re-election of Grant in 1872, that party was compelled to place this positive prohibition of the Fifteenth Amendment upon the United States and all the States thereof....

If, however, you will insist that the Fifteenth Amendment's emphatic interdiction against robbing United States citizens of their suffrage "on account of race, color, or previous condition of servitude" is a recognition of the right of either the United States or any State to deprive them of the ballot for any or all other reasons, I will prove to you that the class of citizens for whom I now plead are by all the principles of our government, and many of the laws of the States, included under the term "previous condition of servitude."

Consider first married women and their legal status. What is servitude? "The condition of a slave." What is a slave? "A person who is robbed of the proceeds of his labor; a person who is subject to the will of another." By the laws of Georgia, South Carolina, and all the States of the South, the negro had no right to the custody and control of his person. He belonged to his master. If he were disobedient, the master had the right to use correction. If the negro did not like the correction and ran away, the master had a right to use coercion to bring him back. By the laws of almost every State in this Union today, North as well as South, the married woman has no right to the custody and control of her person. The wife belongs to the husband; and if she refuse obedience, he may use moderate correction, and if she do not like his moderate correction and leave his "bed and board," the husband may use moderate coercion to bring her back. The little word "moderate," you see, is the saving clause for the wife, and would doubtless be overstepped should her offended husband administer his correction with the "cat-o'-nine-tails," or accomplish his coercion with blood-hounds.

Again, the slave had no right to the earnings of his hands, they belonged to his master; no right to the custody of his children, they belonged to his master; no right to sue or be sued, or to testify in the courts. If he committed a crime, it was the master who must sue or be sued....

I submit the question, if the deprivation by law of the ownership of one's own person, wages, property, children, the denial of the right as an individual to sue and be sued and testify in the courts, is not a condition of servitude most bitter and absolute, even though under the sacred name of marriage?

GLOSSARY

Chinamen: a term for Asians in general and persons of Chinese origin in particular common at the time and not considered a racial slur

doctors of the law: lawyers

enfranchising: giving people the vote

ex post facto: Latin for "after the fact," a term for a retroactive law, or a law that changes the consequences for specific acts that occurred prior to the time the law was adopted

horn of the dilemma: the position of being forced to choose between two equally unacceptable alternatives

interdiction: prohibition

lumbered with its unwieldy proportions: cluttered up so much that it became too wordy to be useful or effective

magistrates: government officials

odious aristocracy: a terrible system of rule by the wealthy and powerful

old regime: the U.S. government prior to the Civil War and the freeing of slaves

organic laws: original, fundamental laws

prescribed...tribunals: legally and formally chosen courts of review

suffrage: the right to vote

Document Analysis

In the opening paragraphs of her address, Anthony expresses the view that as a citizen of the United States, she possesses a "natural right" to participate in the nation's political affairs by voting. Anthony thus draws a distinction between rights that are granted by the state and those that any human being possesses by virtue of being a citizen. Anthony then cites the U.S. Constitution, noting that it begins with the words "We, the people," not "we, the white male citizens" or "we, the male citizens." She notes that even James Madison, who earlier in his career had expressed fear of the rabble, came around to a belief in universal suffrage, a view that he expressed in the 1787 debates at the Constitutional Convention and that Anthony quotes.

Anthony refers to the first article of the Constitution, which, her opponents asserted, disenfranchised women because it turned over to the states the power to regulate elections. Anthony replies to this view by noting that all the Constitution does is prescribe what are in effect procedural matters to ensure that electors are qualified; these stipulations in no way imply that half the population is to be disenfranchised. She then turns to the distinction between a democratic republic and a monarchy. She argues that disenfranchisement on the basis of sex amounts to a "bill of attainder." This phrase is a reference to English common law, which said that a legislature or monarch could declare persons or classes of persons guilty of violating a law without giving them the benefit of a trial. A person thus found guilty was "attainted"—that is, "tainted"—and forfeited his or her civil rights, including the right to own and pass property and to vote. She notes that under current U.S. law, a "monarchy," or at best an "oligarchy" of males rules females, in direct violation of the Constitution, which requires every state to guarantee to its citizens a "republican" form of government, with the concomitant right to vote.

On this basis, Anthony takes up the issue of the language of the law, in the process making an ingenious argument. She notes that laws routinely use the pronouns *he* and *his*, suggesting that women are excluded, just as they are excluded from the voting booth. If that is the case, then, women should be exempted from *all* laws in which *he* and *his* are used, including criminal laws and laws applying to taxation. Anthony extends her discussion of the language of the law to the indiscriminant use of words such as "persons, people, inhabitants, electors," and "citizens" and raises the question of who is included in these terms. She notes that under the Fourteenth Amendment, all "persons" who are born or naturalized in the United States are "citizens." If "persons" are "citizens," and if the under the Fourteenth Amendment "No State shall make or enforce any law which shall abridge the privileges or immunities of citizens of the United States," and further if women are "persons," then denying women the right to vote is a violation of the federal Constitution.

Making a transition to the third major argument of her address, Anthony draws an analogy between the status of African Americans and that of women, making the argument that the law as it applies to black men should also apply to women. She begins with a reference to the Fourteenth Amendment, Section 1 of the amendment reads:

> All persons born or naturalized in the United States, and subject to the jurisdiction thereof, are citizens of the United States and of the State wherein they reside. No State shall make or enforce any law which shall abridge the privileges or immunities of citizens of the United States; nor shall any State deprive any person of life, liberty, or property, without due process of law; nor deny to any person within its jurisdiction the equal protection of the laws.

Although Section 1 of the amendment does not mention race, the effect of the amendment was to make African Americans "citizens," deny to the states the right to "abridge" the rights of any citizens, and give all citizens due process and equal protection under the law. Anthony makes the argument that the earlier Thirteenth Amendment, which banned slavery, in effect already made African Americans citizens of the nation, giving them the right to vote. The Fourteenth Amendment, Anthony suggests, was unnecessary, except for the purpose of granting African Americans equal protection under the law, among other provisions. She concludes the argument by explaining that "the amendment does not say that all male persons of African descent, but that all persons are citizens."

Anthony turns to the Fifteenth Amendment, which specifically states that the right to vote cannot be denied or abridged on the basis of "race, color, or previous condition of servitude," the last of the three items prohibiting states from denying the vote to former slaves. Then Anthony makes yet another ingenious argument, asserting that women, like African Americans, lived under the condition of servitude, drawing parallels between the lives of slaves and legal restrictions placed on women. If the Fifteenth Amendment granted the right to vote despite "previous condition of servitude," then it granted women the right to vote.

Essential Themes

One of the earliest themes that Anthony integrates into this speech is that of "natural rights" and their relationship to voting rights and full citizenship. In support of her view, Anthony cites the Declaration of Independence, which enshrines the Enlightenment concept of natural rights with its statement that "life, liberty and the pursuit of happiness" are "inalienable rights"—that is to say, rights that cannot be alienated, or taken away. Rights, then, are not granted by the state, nor can the state deny to citizens their full enjoyment of their rights. People possess rights by virtue of being human. She goes on to say that the Declaration's avowal of the "right of the people to alter or abolish" a government that is "destructive of these ends" clearly implies the right to vote. Voting is the only civilized way to form and alter governments; the only alternative is brute force. Disenfranchising half of the population—women—compels them to obey laws to which they have never consented.

Anthony also spends a great deal of time in illustrating the ways that women, by law, carry the penalties and burdens of government and therefore should also be allowed to enjoy its privileges. She notes that even citizenship laws, including the section of the federal code that deals with the naturalization of citizens, grants women citizenship without the concurrence of their husbands, even in cases where the husband has applied for citizenship but dies before it is granted. If a naturalized woman is entitled to all the rights and privileges of citizenship, should not, Anthony asks, women born in the United States enjoy the same rights and privileges?

———Michael J. O'Neal, PhD

Bibliography and Additional Reading

Barry, Kathleen. *Susan B. Anthony: A Biography of a Singular Feminist.* (New York: Ballantine Books, 1988).

Dudden, Faye E. *Fighting Chance: The Struggle over Woman Suffrage and Black Suffrage in Reconstruction America.* (New York: Oxford University Press, 2011).

Graham, Sara Hunter. *Woman Suffrage and the New Democracy.* (New Haven: Yale University Press, 1996).

Hull, N. E. H. *The Woman Who Dared to Vote: The Trial of Susan B. Anthony.* (University Press of Kansas, 2012).

Ward, Geoffrey C., with essays by Martha Saxton, Ann D. Gordon and Ellen Carol DuBois. *Not for Ourselves Alone: The Story of Elizabeth Cady Stanton and Susan B. Anthony.* (New York: Alfred Knopf, 1999).

■ "The Status of Woman, Past, Present, and Future"

Date: 1897
Author: Susan B. Anthony
Genre: Magazine article

Summary Overview

In all her speeches and writings, Susan B. Anthony displayed her single-minded devotion to the cause of women's rights—particularly the right to vote. Over the years, she honed her arguments until the success of the cause of suffrage and women's rights became inevitable. This major shift in public opinion was the result in large part of Anthony's carefully crafted arguments. She crafted these arguments within the context of a rapidly changing United States. In her 1897 article for *Arena* magazine, "The Status of Woman, Past, Present, and Future," Anthony reflects on the efforts to change the status of women that had taken place since the Seneca Falls Convention of 1848, noting that various fields, such as education, had become much more open to women but that the political arena remained largely closed. She emphasizes the continued disparity and encourages women to continue to work together to gain the vote.

Defining Moment

By 1897, when she penned this article, Anthony was in a position to look back on decades of activity in the pursuit of women's rights. She was engaged in the writing and publication of the four-volume *History of Woman Suffrage* and was collaborating with Ida Husted Harper in a three-volume biography, *The Life and Work of Susan B. Anthony*. She was in a unique position, then, to reflect on the status of women and how it had changed during her lifetime. The fact that the *Arena* journal asked her to write the article suggests that already Anthony was regarded as an icon of women's rights. Here, near the dawn of the twentieth century, there had been some strides made in women's fight for equality. For example, beginning with Wyoming in 1869, women in western states and territories could vote. In the following decades, states would begin to adopt a constitutional amendments granting women the right to vote, with Colorado being the first in 1893. Outside the political realm, educational opportunities for women had been expanding as well, with publicly funded state universities admitting more women.

There was still, however, the challenge of winning the right to vote for women in the entire United States. In 1872, Anthony and several other women in New York voted in the Presidential election. Although arrested, tried, and convicted for the crime of voting illegally, she used the incident as a platform to continue her efforts to win suffrage for women . More than two decades later, the fight for suffrage continued, and Anthony highlights this struggle as key to American women's progress.

Author Biography

Susan Brownell Anthony, who devoted more than a half century to women's suffrage and other social issues, was born in Adams, Massachusetts, on February 15, 1820. She received her education at a Quaker boarding school in Philadelphia, where she trained as a teacher, an occupation she pursued for three years beginning in 1846. After the family moved to Rochester, New York, in 1845, she became active in a range of social causes, including abolition of slavery, temperance, the rights of labor, education reform, and particularly women's rights. She signed the Declaration of Sentiments produced by the 1848 Seneca Falls Convention in New York, the first women's rights convention held in the United States. In the early 1850s she met her lifelong friend and fellow suffragist, Elizabeth Cady Stanton—although in later years some tension emerged between the two, with Stanton adopting a more radical approach to women's rights and Anthony a more moderate position.

Anthony is often regarded as the author of the Nineteenth Amendment to the U.S. Constitution recognizing the right of women to vote. She originally wrote the amendment in 1877, using the Fifteenth Amendment ("The right of citizens of the United States to vote shall not be denied or abridged by the United States or by any State on account of race, color, or previous condition of servitude") as a model. The amendment, which came to be referred to as the Anthony Amendment, was submitted to Congress by a sympathetic senator, Aaron Sargent, and while Congress did not act on it, it was submitted in every session of Congress until 1919. Just one month before her death on March 13, 1906, Anthony concluded her last public speech, delivered at a meeting of the National American Women Suffrage Association, with the words "Failure is impossible"—her final public utterance and a phrase that survived as a rallying cry for women's rights proponents throughout the twentieth century. Her words proved to be prophetic, for Congress approved the Nineteenth Amendment in 1919, and the amendment was ratified in 1920.

HISTORICAL DOCUMENT

Fifty years ago woman in the United States was without a recognized individuality in any department of life. No provision was made in public or private schools for her education in anything beyond the rudimentary branches. An educated woman was a rarity, and was gazed upon with something akin to awe. The women who were known in the world of letters, in the entire country, could be easily counted upon the ten fingers. Margaret Fuller, educated by her father, a Harvard graduate and distinguished lawyer, stood preeminently at the head, and challenged the admiration of such men as Emerson, Channing, and Greeley.

In those days the women of the family were kept closely at home, carding, spinning, and weaving, making the butter and cheese, knitting and sewing, working by day and night, planning and economizing, to educate the boys of the family. Thus the girls toiled so long as they remained under the home roof, their services belonging to the father by law and by custom. Any kind of career for a woman was a thing undreamed of. Among the poorer families the girls might go about among the neighbors and earn a miserable pittance at housework or sewing. When the boy was twenty-one, the father agreed to pay him a fixed sum per annum, thenceforth, for his services, or, in default of this, he was free to carry his labor where it would receive a financial reward. No such agreement ever was made with the girls of the family. They continued to work without wages after they were twenty-one, exactly as they did before. When they married, their services were transferred to the husband, and were considered to be bountifully rewarded by food, shelter, and usually a very scanty supply of clothes. Any wages the wife might earn outside of the home belonged by law to the husband. No matter how drunken and improvident he might be; no matter how great her necessities and those of the children, if the employer paid the money to her he could be prosecuted by the husband and compelled to pay it again to him.

Cases were frequent where fathers willed all of their property to the sons, entirely cutting the daughters out. Where, however, the daughters received property, it passed directly into the sole possession of the husband, and all the rents and profits belonged to him to use as he pleased. At his death he could dispose of it by will, dispose of it by will, depriving the wife of all but what was called the "widow's dower," a life interest in one-third of that which was by right her own property. She lost not only the right to her earnings and her property, but also the right to the custody of her person and her children. The husband could apprentice the children at an early age, in spite of the mother's protest, and at his death could dispose of the children by will, even an unborn child. The wife could neither sue nor be sued, nor testify in the courts. The phrase in constant use in legal decisions was, "The wife is dead in law," or, "Husband and wife are one, and that one the husband." According to the English common law, which then prevailed in every State in the Union except Louisiana, a man might beat his wife up to the point of endangering her life, without being liable to prosecution.

Fifty years ago no occupations were open to women except cooking, sewing, teaching, and factory work. Very few women were sufficiently educated to teach, but those who could do so received from $4 to $8 a month and "boarded 'round," while men, for exactly the same service, received $30 a month and board. Every woman must marry, either with or without love, for the sake of support, or be doomed to a life of utter dependence, living, after the death of parents, in the home of a married brother or sister, the drudge and burden-bearer of the family, without any financial recompense, and usually looked upon with disrespect by the children.

Women might work like galley slaves for their own relatives, receiving only their board and clothes, and hold their social position in the community; but the moment they stepped outside of the home and became wage-earners, thus securing pecuniary independence, they lost caste and were rigidly barred out from the quilting bees, the apple-parings, and all the society functions of the neighborhood. Is it any wonder that a sour and crabbed disposition was universally ascribed to spinsterhood, or that those women should be regarded as most unfortunate, doomed to a loveless, aimless, and dependent existence,—universally considered as having made a failure of life?...

Such was the helpless, dependent, fettered condition of women when the first Women's Rights Convention was called just forty-nine years ago, at Seneca Falls, N. Y., by Elizabeth Cady Stanton and Lucretia Mott. Half a century before this, Mary Wollstonecraft had written her "Vindication of the Rights of Women," that matchless plea for the equality of the sexes. A quarter of century before, Frances Wright, in connection with addresses upon other subjects, demanded equal rights for women. In 1835, Ernestine L. Rose and Paulina Wright Davis circulated the first petition for property rights for women, and during the next ten years Mrs. Rose addressed the New York Legislature a number of times asking political equality. Mrs. Stanton also had circulated petitions and addressed the Legislature during this period. In 1847, Lucy Stone, on her return from Oberlin College, made her first women's rights address in her brother's church in Gardner, Mass.

While there had been individual demands, from time to time, the first organized body to formulate a declaration of the rights of women was the one which met at Seneca Falls, July 19–20, 1848, and adjourned to meet at Rochester two weeks later. In the Declaration of Sentiments and the Resolutions there framed, every point was covered that, down to the present day, has been contended for by the advocates of equal rights for women. Every inequality of the existing laws and customs was carefully considered and a thorough and complete readjustment demanded. The only resolution that was not unanimously adopted was the one urging the elective franchise for women. Those who opposed it did so only because they feared it would make the movement ridiculous. But Mrs. Stanton and Frederick Douglass, seeing that the power to make laws and choose rulers was the right by which all others could be secured, persistently advocated the resolution and at last carried it by a good majority....

There is not space to follow the history of the last fifty years and study the methods by which these victories have been gained, but there is not one foot of advanced ground upon which women stand today that has not been obtained through the hard-fought battles of other women. The close of this nineteenth century finds every trade, vocation, and profession open to women, and every opportunity at their command for preparing themselves to follow these occupations. The girls as well as the boys of a family now fit themselves for such careers as their tastes and abilities permit. A vast amount of the household drudgery, that once monopolized the whole time and strength of the mother and daughters, has been taken outside and turned over to machinery in vast establishments. A money value is placed upon the labor of women. The ban of social ostracism has been largely removed from the woman wage-earner. She who can make for herself a place of distinction in any line of work receives commendation instead of condemnation. Woman is no longer compelled to marry for support, but may herself make her own home and earn her own financial independence.

With but few exceptions, the highest institutions of learning in the land are as freely opened to girls as to boys, and they may receive their degrees as legal, medical, and theological colleges, and practise their professions without hindrance. In the world of literature and art women divide the honors with men; and our civil-service rules have secured for them many thousands of remunerative positions under the Government....

There has been a radical revolution in the legal status of women. In most States the old common law has been annulled by legislative enactment, through which partial justice, at least, has been done to married women. In nearly every State they may retain and control property owned at marriage and all they may receive by gift or inheritance thereafter, and also their earnings outside the home.

They may sue and be sued, testify in the courts, and carry on business in their own name, but in no State have wives any ownership in the joint earnings. In six or seven State have equal guardianship of the children. While in most States the divorce laws are the same for men and women, they never can bear equally upon both while all the property earned during marriage belongs wholly to the husband. There has been such a modification in public sentiment, however, that, in most cases, courts and juries show a marked leniency toward women.

The department of politics has been slowest to give admission to women. Suffrage is the pivotal rights, and if it could have been secured at the beginning, women would not have been half a century in gaining the privileges enumerated above, for privileges they must be called so long as others may either give or take them away. If women could make the laws or elect those who make them, they would be in the position of sovereigns instead of subjects. Were they the political peers of man they could command instead of having to beg, petition, and pray. Can it be possible it is for this reason that men have been so determined in their opposition to grant to women political power?

But even this stronghold is beginning to yield to the long and steady pressure. In twenty-five States women possess suffrage in school matters; in four States they have a limited suffrage in local affairs; in one State they have municipal suffrage; in four States they have full suffrage, local, State, and national. Women are becoming more and more interested in political questions and public affairs. Every campaign sees greater numbers in attendance at the meetings, and able woman speakers are now found upon the platforms of all parties. Especial efforts are made by politicians to obtain the support of women, and during the last campaign one of the Presidential candidates held special meetings for women in the large cities throughout the country. Some of the finest political writing in the great newspapers of the day is done by women, and the papers are extensively read by women of all classes. In many of the large cities women have formed civic clubs and are exercising a distinctive influence in municipal matters. In most of the States of the Union woman are eligible for many offices, State and County Superintendents, Registers of Deeds, etc. They are Deputies to State, County, and City officials, notaries public, State Librarians, and enrolling and engrossing clerks in the Legislatures.

It follows, as a natural result, that in the States where women vote they are eligible to all offices. They have been sent as delegates to National Conventions, made Presidential electors, and are sitting to-day as members in both the Upper and Lower Houses of the Legislatures. In some towns all the offices are filled by women. These radical changes have been effected without any social upheaval or domestic earthquakes, family relations have suffered no disastrous changes, and the men of the States where women vote furnish the strongest testimony in favor of woman suffrage....

From that little convention at Seneca Falls, with a following of a handful of women scattered through half-a-dozen different States, we have now the great National Association, with headquarters in New York City, and auxiliaries in almost every State in the Union. These State bodies are effecting a thorough system of county and local organizations for the purpose of securing legislation favorable to women, and especially to obtain amendments to their State Constitutions. As evidence of the progress of public opinion, more than half of the Legislatures in session, during the past winter, have discussed and voted upon bills for the enfranchisement of women, and in most of them they were adopted by one branch and lost by a very small majority in the other. The Legislatures of Washington and South Dakota have submitted woman-suffrage amendments to their electors for 1898, and vigorous campaigns will be made in those States during the next two years. For a quarter of a century Wyoming has stood as a conspicuous object-lesson in woman suffrage, and is now reinforced by the three neighboring States of Colorado, Utah, and Idaho. With this central group, standing on the very crest of the Rocky Mountains, the spirit of justice and freedom for women cannot fail to descend upon all the Western and Northwestern States. No one who makes a careful study of this question can help but believe that, in a very few years, all the States west of the Mississippi river will have enfranchised their women.

While the efforts of each State are concentrated upon its own Legislature, all of the States combined in the national organization are directing their energies toward securing a Sixteenth Amendment to the Constitution of the United States. The demands of this body have been received with respectful and encouraging attention from Congress. Hearings have been granted by the Committees of both Houses, resulting, in a number of instances, in favorable reports. Upon one occasion the question was brought to a discussion in the Senate, and received the affirmative vote of one-third of the members.

Until woman has obtained "that right protective of all other rights—the ballot," this agitation must still go on, absorbing the time and the energy of our best and strongest women. Who can measure the advantages that would result if the magnificent abilities of these women could be devoted to the needs of government, society, home, instead of being consumed in the struggle to obtain their birthright of individual freedom? Until this be gained we can never know, we cannot even prophesy, the capacity and power of woman for the uplifting of humanity. It may be delayed longer than we think, it may be here sooner than we expect, but the day will come when man will recognize woman as his peer, not only at the fireside, but in the councils of the nation. Then, and not until then, will there be the perfect comradeship, the ideal union between the sexes, that shall result in the highest development of the race. What this shall be we may not attempt to define, but this we know, that only good can come to the individual or the nation through the rendering of exact justice.

GLOSSARY

carding: brushing fabric in order to disentangle fibers

common law: law based primarily on past legal judgments, rather than on statutes passed by a legislative body such as the U.S. Congress

electors: elected representatives from each state whose vote, in the Electoral College, decides presidential elections

engrossing: preparing official documents according to precise legal procedures

Mary Wollstonecraft: prominent English feminist (1759–1797) whose daughter, Mary Wollstonecraft Shelley, wrote Frankenstein

spinsterhood: a term, common in the time before the sexual revolution of the 1960s, for the situation of a woman who will never be married

suffrage: the right to vote

the race: not a reference to "race" as it is commonly understood today but rather to the human race

the world of letters: the world of literature

Upper and Lower Houses of the Legislature: common divisions within parliamentary democracies such as the United States, in which the Senate and House of Representatives are the upper and lower house, respectively

Document Analysis

Anthony begins by focusing on the past status of women, noting that a half century earlier a woman "was without a recognized individuality in any department of life." Women rarely if ever enjoyed the benefits of education, and the nation boasted few women of letters. A person such as Margaret Fuller was an exception. Fuller was associated with the Transcendental movement of Ralph Waldo Emerson. "Channing" is a reference to William Henry Channing, also associated with the Transcendental movement.

Anthony then presents a grim picture of the status of women earlier in the century. The details of the picture are clear. Young women worked at domestic tasks, while their brothers were educated. Women had no opportunities to pursue a career. Young men received income from their fathers; women enjoyed no such privilege. Women were in effect the property of their fathers and then were turned over to husbands. If a woman earned wages outside the home, the wages were paid to the husband. Fathers willed their property to sons, generally not their daughters; in the few cases when women inherited property, that property became her husband's on marriage. Even widows were left in a dependent position through a "widow's dower." A widow generally retained an interest in a third of her deceased husband's property until she died, when the property would pass to a son. Anthony makes reference to English common law, which allowed husbands to beat their wives without fear of prosecution; *common law* refers to law developed through court decisions rather than statutes. Louisiana, because of its French roots, applies a system of statutory law rather than common law.

Women fifty years earlier could pursue few occupations outside the home. Teaching was perhaps the most attractive option, except that women were paid a fraction of what men were for the same work. Worse, women teachers remained dependent on members of their community for bed and board, while male teachers were given extra stipends for their room and board. Unmarried women had no social standing. Women who worked outside the home were regarded as peculiar, as bitter spinsters, and were excluded from social gatherings.

Anthony paints a picture of significant improvement in the status of women. She marks the beginning of this improvement with the women's rights convention at Seneca Falls, New York, in 1848—though she also notes that the issue of women's rights had begun to percolate with the 1792 publication of *Vindication of the Rights of Woman* by Mary Wollstonecraft and with the agitation of the Scottish reformer and freethinker Frances Wright. Paulina Wright Davis was a vigorous antislavery and women's rights activist and writer, as were Ernestine Rose and Lucy Stone, who was the first woman in Massachusetts ever to hold a college degree. In the intervening five decades most of the proposals made in the Seneca Falls convention's "Declaration of Sentiments" have become a reality. Women can pursue occupations outside the home, girls are being educated, household drudgery has been lessened, and women have opportunities to become more self-supporting. In particular, Anthony notes that institutions of higher learning are now open to women, although Anthony's picture is perhaps rosier than the reality, as higher education for women was still regarded as secondary to that of men.

Anthony speaks of improvements in the legal status of women. She says that women can now own their own property and businesses. They can retain ownership of property they have inherited. They can testify in court and sue; perversely, they can also be sued, suggesting that now they have a measure of wealth that a plaintiff can claim. Anthony points out, though, that wives have no claim on their husband's earnings, putting them at a disadvantage in divorce—though she also notes that courts are becoming more lenient in their treatment of women.

Anthony then turns to the fact that despite these successes, women still do not have the vote. She does, though, state that even in this matter the "steady pressure" of women has led to some success. Women can vote on school matters in twenty-five states. In some states, women can vote on other local matters. And four states have already acknowledged the right of women to vote in all elections, including federal ones. She goes on to detail the myriad ways in which women influenced political issues and advanced agendas.

In the final paragraphs of the article, Anthony strikes a note of optimism about the future. She points out the existence of such organizations as the National American Women Suffrage Association, and reviews the progress of women's suffrage efforts in states such as Washington and South Dakota. In paragraph 13, Anthony calls for a Sixteenth Amendment to the Constitution to give women the right to vote; she could not have known that such an amendment would be the Nineteenth. In the final paragraph, Anthony expresses optimism that sooner or later women will be granted the right to vote: "The day will come when man will recognize woman as his peer, not only at the fireside, but in the councils of the nation."

Essential Themes

One consistent theme within Anthony's history of the women's movement in the United States is that, despite the continuing struggle for voting rights, a remarkable amount of progress had been made during the nineteenth century. This progress laid the groundwork for the ongoing fight for suffrage. A crucial thing to keep in mind about her discussion of this progress is the fact that improvements to women's status with regard to education, property rights, employment opportunities, standing within the legal system and other areas often occurred without even the limited voting rights that women possessed even in 1897.

When she connects these gains to the persistence of women's political activism, participation in civic organizations and the formation of groups like that National American Women Suffrage Association she is positioning women's activism in a way that points to the future. The massive gains during the nineteen century, to Anthony, is a clear indicator that full suffrage would not remain forever out of reach. As she says near the end of this article, "It may be delayed longer than we think, it may be here sooner than we expect, but the day will come when man will recognize woman as his peer, not only at the fireside, but in the councils of the nation.

———*Michael J. O'Neal, PhD.*

Bibliography and Additional Reading

Barry, Kathleen (1988). *Susan B. Anthony: A Biography of a Singular Feminist*. New York: Ballantine Books.

Kerber, Linda K. No Constitutional Right to Be Ladies: Women and the Obligations of Citizenship. (New York: Hill and Wang, 1998).

Tetrault, Lisa. *The Myth of Seneca Falls: Memory and the Women's Suffrage Movement, 1848-1898*. University of North Carolina Press, 2014.

Troncale, Jennifer M., and Jennifer Strain. "Marching with Aunt Susan: Susan B. Anthony and the Fight for Women's Suffrage." *Social Studies Research & Practice* (2013) 8#2.

Ward, Geoffrey C., with essays by Martha Saxton, Ann D. Gordon and Ellen Carol DuBois (1999). *Not for Ourselves Alone: The Story of Elizabeth Cady Stanton and Susan B. Anthony*. New York: Alfred Knopf.

"Why Women Should Vote"

Date: 1910
Author: Jane Addams
Genre: Editorial

Summary Overview

Addams's essay on women's suffrage, "Why Women Should Vote," published as an editorial in the *Ladies' Home Journal* in January 1910, inscribes itself in the intense debate on the topic that took place at the beginning of the twentieth century in America. The women's movement was a crucial part of Progressivism, and one of its most pressing questions was how women could attain equality with men and reform a society dominated by them. Many women's rights advocates claimed that voting was essential for women to achieve their reformist goals. Addams shared this belief. Yet, contrary to other women's rights campaigners, she rooted her support for female suffrage within the values of domesticity. While many within the movement argued that suffrage would be instrumental in helping women move beyond the narrow boundaries of the home, Addams begins her essay by situating women's place firmly within the home. She finds that no social change will release women from their domestic obligations. However, for women to fulfill such obligations, it is crucial that they can vote so that they can "take part in the slow upbuilding of that code of legislation which is alone sufficient to protect the home from the dangers incident to modern life."

Defining Moment

Jane Addams was part of the Progressive movement, a broad and diverse middle-class coalition that, at the turn of the twentieth century, tried to reform American society and reconcile democracy with capitalism. The steady industrialization and urbanization of the 1880s and 1890s had deeply transformed American society, spurring harsh conflicts between labor and management. The middle class had supported the process of industrialization by espousing the Victorian values of laissez-faire individualism, domesticity, and self-control. Yet by the 1890s it was apparent that these values had trapped the middle class between the warring demands of big business and the working classes. Growing consumerism, a new wave of immigration, and tensions between the sexes further challenged bourgeois existence. In the face of these confrontations, the Progressives tried to reform the American capitalist system and its institutions from within, seeking to strike a compromise between radical demands and the preservation of established interests.

While the women's suffrage movement ("suffrage" meaning the right to vote) predated the progressive movement by several decades, the effort to gain increased political rights and participation for women fit in well with the broader aims of the movement. In her editorial, Addams connects women's fight for the right to vote to the wider political aims of progressivism.

Author Biography

Jane Addams was born on September 6, 1860, in Cedarville, Illinois. She earned a bachelor's degree in 1881 from Rockford Female Seminary, in Illinois. In the 1880s Addams began studying medicine, but she had to suspend her work because of poor health. Despite her poor health, she visited Europe several times. During one of her voyages, Addams and her companion, Ellen Gates Starr, visited London's original settlement house of Toynbee Hall, established in 1884. The visit led the two women to establish the Chicago settlement house of Hull House in 1889, the second such house to be established in America. Through Hull House, Addams found a vocation for her adult life.

Addams campaigned for every major reform issue of her era, such as fairer workplace conditions for men and women, tenement regulation, juvenile-court law, women's suffrage, and women's rights. While in the first part of her life Addams was mainly involved in social work in Hull House, in the twentieth century she used her notoriety to advance political causes and became a well-known public figure. In 1910 she was the first woman president of the National Conference of Social Work, and in 1912 she actively campaigned for the Progressive presidential candidate, Theodore Roosevelt, becoming the first woman to give a nominating speech at a party convention. Addams was also a founding member of the National Association for the Advancement of Colored People.

In the 1920s, Addams concentrated many of her efforts on antiwar efforts, she became the president of the Woman's Peace Party in 1915 and chaired the

KAISER WILSON
HAVE YOU FORGOTTEN YOUR SYMPATHY WITH THE POOR GERMANS BECAUSE THEY WERE NOT SELF-GOVERNED?
20,000,000 AMERICAN WOMEN ARE NOT SELF-GOVERNED.
TAKE THE BEAM OUT OF YOUR OWN EYE.

International Women's Congress for Peace and Freedom at The Hague, Netherlands. Americans were not unanimous in their praise for Addams's campaigning for peace. Despite her unpopular views in the US, Addams's antiwar efforts won her the Nobel Peace Prize, which she shared with Nicholas Murray Butler. Addams died in Chicago on May 21, 1935, three days after being diagnosed with cancer.

HISTORICAL DOCUMENT

For many generations it has been believed that woman's place is within the walls of her home, and it is indeed impossible to imagine the time when her duty there shall be ended or to forecast any social change which shall release her from that paramount obligation....

Many women today are failing to discharge their duties to their own households properly simply because they do not perceive that as society grows more complicated it is necessary that woman shall extend her sense of responsibility to many things outside of her own home if she would continue to preserve the home in its entirety....A woman's simplest duty, one would say, is to keep her house clean and wholesome and to feed her children properly. Yet if she lives in a tenement house...she cannot fulfill these simple obligations by her own efforts because she is utterly dependent upon the city administration for the conditions which render decent living possible. Her basement will not be dry, her stairways will not be fireproof, her house will not be provided with sufficient windows to give light and air, nor will it be equipped with sanitary plumbing, unless the Public Works Department sends inspectors who constantly insist that these elementary decencies be provided. Women who live in the country sweep their own dooryards and may either feed the refuse of the table to a flock of chickens or allow it innocently to decay in the open air and sunshine. In a crowded city quarter, however, if the street is not cleaned by the city authorities no amount of private sweeping will keep the tenement free from grime; if the garbage is not properly collected and destroyed a tenement-house mother may see her children sicken and die of diseases from which she alone is powerless to shield them, although her tenderness and devotion are unbounded. She cannot even secure untainted meat for her household, she cannot provide fresh fruit, unless the meat has been inspected by city officials, and the decayed fruit, which is so often placed upon sale in the tenement districts, has been destroyed in the interests of public health. In short, if woman would keep on with her old business of caring for her house and rearing her children she will have to have some conscience in regard to public affairs lying quite outside of her immediate household. The individual conscience and devotion are no longer effective....

In other words, if women would effectively continue their old avocations they must take part in the slow upbuilding of that code of legislation which is alone sufficient to protect the home from the dangers incident to modern life....

The more extensively the modern city endeavors on the one hand to control and on the other hand to provide recreational facilities for its young people the more necessary it is that women should assist in their direction and extension. After all, a care for wholesome and innocent amusement is what women have for many years assumed. When the reaction comes on the part of taxpayers women's votes may be necessary to keep the city to its beneficent obligations toward its own young people....

Ever since steam power has been applied to the processes of weaving and spinning woman's traditional work has been carried on largely outside of the home. The clothing and household linen are not only spun and woven, but also usually sewed, by machinery; the preparation of many foods has also passed into the factory and necssarily a certain number of women have been obliged to follow their work there, although it is doubtful, in spite of the large numbers of factory girls, whether women now are doing as large a proportion of the world's work as they used to do. Because many thousands of those working in factories and shops are girls between the ages of fourteen and twenty-two there is a necessity that older women should be interested in the conditions of industry. The very fact that these girls are not going to remain in industry permanently makes it more important that someone should see to it that they shall not be incapacitated for their future family life because they work for exhausting hours and under insanitary conditions.

If woman's sense of obligation had enlarged as the industrial conditions changed she might naturally and almost imperceptibly have inaugurated the movements for social amelioration in the line of factory legislation and shop sanitation. That she has not done so is doubtless due to the fact that her conscience is slow to recognize any obligation outside of her own family circle, and because she was so absorbed in her own household that she failed to see what the conditions outside actually were. It would be interesting to know how far the consciousness that she had no vote and could not change matters operated in this direction. After all, we see only those things to which our attention has been drawn, we feel responsibility for those things which are brought to us as matters of responsibility. If conscientious women were convinced that it was a civic duty to be informed in regard to these grave industrial affairs, and then to express the conclusions which they had reached by depositing a piece of paper in a ballot box, one cannot imagine that they would shirk simply because the action ran counter to old traditions....

To turn the administration of our civic affairs wholly over to men may mean that the American city will continue to push forward in its commercial and industrial development, and continue to lag behind in those things which make a city healthful and beautiful. After all, woman's traditional function has been to make her dwelling-place both clean and fair. Is that dreariness in city life, that lack of domesticity which the humblest farm dwelling presents, due to a withdrawal of one of the naturally co-operating forces? If women have in any sense been responsible for the gentler side of life which softens and blurs some of its harsher conditions, may they not have a duty to perform in our American cities?

In closing, may I recapitulate that if woman would fulfill her traditional responsibility to her own children; if she would educate and protect from danger factory children who must find their recreation on the street; if she would bring the cultural forces to bear upon our materialistic civilization; and if she would do it all with the dignity and directness fitting one who carries on her immemorial duties, then she must bring herself to the use of the ballot—that latest implement for self government. May we not fairly say that American women need this implement in order to preserve the home?

GLOSSARY

dooryards: small front yards

incident to: related to, or following from

tenement house: a slum dwelling

this implement: the vote

Document Analysis

Addams begins her editorial by reiterating the common sentiment that "woman's place is within the walls of her home." Addams agrees that it is likely that women will be tied to their home-making role for the foreseeable future. There is no sense of irony or sarcasm here—Addams did focus more than other women's rights and suffrage figures on the importances of women's domestic role.

However, as she continues in the first long paragraph, Addams explains that as American society—particularly in cities—grows more complex and complicated, women will have to "extend" their "sense of responsibility" to what was consider the "public sphere" rather than only the domestic one. This is not because women will be forced to abandon their domestic tasks and duties but, rather, because the complexities of modern society will require a broader perspective in order to carry out that domestic role successfully.

This is because women do not live in equal domestic situations. Addams uses the example of a woman's "simplest duty," to maintain a clean home and properly feed her children. This job, however simple, became nearly impossible for women who live in tenement buildings that are unfit for habitation. The onus for maintaining building safety, she explains, lies with a city's Public Works Department. Women in rural areas have more freedom to control their own environment than do women living "in a crowded city quarter." At the end of this paragraph, Addams presents her argument for women's involvement in the public sphere, saying "if woman would keep on with her old business of caring for her house and rearing her children she will have to have some conscience in regard to public affairs lying quite outside of her immediate household. The individual conscience and devotion are no longer effective." Modern urban society means that the personal, domestic life is intricately bound with public affairs. They must contribute to "the slow upbuilding" of legislation that will defend that domestic sphere.

Another example are opportunities for young people (and laws that limit their activities). Women must play a role in shaping government policy on these issues, Addams explains, because that is the sort of nurturing work that women have done throughout human history. "When the reaction comes on the part of taxpayers," Addams says, "women's votes may be necessary to keep the city to its beneficent obligations toward its own young people." By possessing the vote, Addams argues, women will provide a necessary bulwark against the short-sightenedness of male voters who might not understand or appreciate the need for governmental measures that affect the domestic sphere.

Addams traces these developments to the industrial revolution, with steam power and other developments moving things like textile manufacturing out of the home. Later, food production became industrialized and women were "obliged to follow their work there," with a huge number of young women working as "factory girls." Thus, she explains, older women have an obligation to ensure that their working environments are safe so they are healthy "for their future family life." Women, Addams asserts, have been slow to recognize their obligations that exist outside their domestic worlds. Women—particularly middle class women—were focused on their own homes and families, only recently recognizing the issues faces by women and youth in America's factories and cities. The process of taking fuller responsibility for their communities relies on women gaining the right to vote.

Allowing control of governments to remain solely in the hands of men may, Addams explains, improve industry and the economy but the urban issues—"those things which make a city healthful and beautiful"—may continue to take second place. Women's voice in government is necessary to maintain the proper balance. Women, she asserts, have a "duty" toward American cities and those who live in them.

Addams closes by encouraging women who have been active in social issues such as educating and protecting working children and caring for their own families have an obligation to work for voting rights, arguing that voting is necessary in order for women "to preserve the home."

Essential Themes

To Addams, the quest for women's suffrage represents an opportunity to hear women's voices in matters that are fundamental to the improvement of family life and to the struggle against urban vices. In its focus on the enhancement of living conditions within the urban environment, "Why Women Should Vote" ties the question of women's suffrage to the larger Progressive agenda, clearly stating that the two mutually reinforce each other. Because women have deep knowledge of the needs of youth, they can provide unique insights into effective ways "on the one hand to control and on the other hand to provide recreational facilities for its young people." Defining voting rights for women as a potential service toward the entire community, the essay is typical of the Progressives' affirmation of collective over individual concerns. As Brown writes, Addams assigns domesticity a crucial place in women's life not to "placate the patriarchs," but "because her daily experience taught her that domesticity was…a utilitarian reality for her working-class neighbors, and one that could be powerful if deployed in the political arena against America's individualistic patriarchs."

———*Luca Prono PhD*

Bibliography and Additional Reading

Brown Victoria Bissell, *The Education of Jane Addams* (Philadelphia: University of Pennsylvania Press, 2007).

DuBois, Ellen Carol. *Women's Suffrage and Women's Rights* (New York: New York University Press, 1998).

Knight, Louise W. *Citizen: Jane Addams and the Struggle for Democracy* (Chicago: University of Chicago Press, 2005).

——*Jane Addams: Spirit in Action* (New York: W.W. Norton, 2010).

McGerr, Michael. *A Fierce Discontent: The Rise and Fall of the Progressive Movement in America, 1870-1920*. (New York: Oxford University Press, 2005).

Testimony before the House Judiciary Committee

Date: 1915
Author: Alice Paul
Genre: Congressional testimony

Summary Overview

Alice Paul did not produce a large body of written documents. Modern students of the woman's suffrage and early feminist movements can gain insight into Paul's values and beliefs from oral sources, including her Testimony to the House Judiciary Committee on the question of female suffrage. Along with three of her fellow suffragists, Paul appeared before the committee on December 16, 1915, to speak on behalf of the Congressional Union for Woman Suffrage in support of an amendment to the U.S. Constitution granting voting rights to women.

Earlier that month, the so-called Anthony Amendment (named for Susan B. Anthony) had been introduced (not for the first time) in the House by Franklin Wheeler Mondell and in the Senate by George Sutherland. In the ensuing years, the amendment was repeatedly tabled, postponed, or rejected. It was not until June of 1919 that Congress voted 56 to 25 to pass the Nineteenth Amendment. It took effect on August 18, 1920, when Tennessee became the thirty-sixth state to ratify it.

Defining Moment

The suffrage movement at the end of the nineteenth century and during the first two decades of the twentieth century was an amalgam of high ideals of justice and equality and more practical, mundane politics. The mainstream suffrage organization was the National American Woman Suffrage Association, formed in 1890. The leaders of this group included such towering figures as Susan B. Anthony, Carrie Chapman Catt, Elizabeth Cady Stanton, and Frances Willard. Many of these women, however, had been fighting in the trenches for decades—Susan B. Anthony, for example, died in 1906 at the age of eighty-six—and a new generation of suffragists was growing impatient with the slow pace of progress. Among them was Alice Paul, who had absorbed the more radical tactics of militant feminists during the years she lived and studied in England, where she joined the Women's Social and Political Union. As a member, Paul urged the National American Woman Suffrage Association to adopt more militant tactics, but the more conservative organization resisted her pleas and forced her and her protégées out. Accordingly, Paul joined forces with such women as Lucy Burns, Olympia Brown, Mabel Vernon, Belle La Follette, Mary Ritter Beard, Maria Montessori, Doris Stevens, and Crystal Eastman to form the Congressional Union for Woman Suffrage (CUWS) in 1913.

During these years one of the principal issues faced by the suffragist movement was whether to pursue voting rights on a state-by-state basis or to seek an amendment to the Constitution. Already a number of states, led by Colorado, Idaho, Utah, and Wyoming and followed by Washington, California, Kansas, Oregon, Arizona, Montana, Nevada, and the Alaska Territory, had granted suffrage to women not only in municipal and state elections but in federal elections as well. Various other states had considered suffrage amendments to their state constitutions at different times. Approaching the matter one state at a time, though, was exhausting work, and it was generally believed that extending the franchise to women in the states of the highly conservative South would be next to impossible, particularly because of fears among many southerners that doing so would give black women the vote. For this reason, the new generation of suffragists focused on an amendment to the national Constitution. Paul's 1915 testimony here was one of the

Author Biography

Alice Paul, one of the nation's most outspoken suffragists and feminists in the early twentieth century and beyond, was born to a Quaker family at their Paulsdale estate in Mount Laurel, New Jersey, on January 11, 1885. Her religious background is relevant because the Hicksite Quakerism the family practiced placed a great deal of emphasis on gender equality. Paul earned a bachelor's degree in biology in 1905 from Swathmore College and, after attending the New York School of Philanthropy, earned a master's degree from the University of Pennsylvania in 1907. Paul then went on to study in England before returning to the University of Pennsylvania, where she earned a PhD in sociology in 1912.

In England, she came under the influence of the militant feminists Emmeline Pankhurst and her daughters, Christabel and Sylvia, participating in demonstrations and suffering arrests, imprisonment, hunger strikes, and force-feeding. On her return to the United States, she enlisted in the suffrage movement, founding the Congressional Union for Woman Suffrage in 1913. The purpose of the new organization was to seek a federal constitutional amendment granting women the right to vote.

In 1916 the Congressional Union evolved into the National Woman's Party. Paul and her followers, dubbed the Silent Sentinels, gained notoriety by launching a two-and-a-half-year picket (with Sundays off) of the White House, urging President Woodrow Wilson to support a suffrage amendment. Public opinion began to sway in favor of the suffragists when it was learned that more than 150 picketers had been arrested and sentenced to jail, usually on thin charges of obstructing traffic, and that the conditions the jailed women endured were often brutal. Paul, in particular, was subjected to inhuman treatment and launched a hunger strike in protest until she and the other protestors were released after a court of appeals ruled the arrests illegal.

Meanwhile, the National Woman's Party continued to campaign against U.S. legislators who opposed the suffrage amendment.

After the passage by Congress (1919) and successful ratification (1920) of the Nineteenth Amendment recognizing the right of women to vote, Paul remained active in the woman's rights movement. In 1921 she wrote an equal rights amendment in the face of opposition from more conservative women's groups, who feared that such an amendment might strip women of protective legislation—in such areas as labor conditions—that had been passed during the Progressive Era. Nevertheless, she campaigned to make an equal rights amendment a plank in the platforms of both major political parties, which she succeeded in doing by 1944. In November 1972 and May 1973 she shared her reflections on the women's movement with an interviewer as part of an oral history project conducted by the University of California, Berkeley. She lived long enough to see Congress approve the Equal Rights Amendment in 1972, though the amendment was not ratified by enough states to allow it to become part of the Constitution. Paul died on July 9, 1977.

HISTORICAL DOCUMENT

In closing the argument before this committee, may I summarize our position? We have come here to ask one simple thing: that the Judiciary Committee refer this Suffrage Amendment, known as the Susan B. Anthony Amendment, to the House of Representatives. We are simply asking you to do what you can do—that you let the House of Representatives decide this question. We have tried to bring people to this hearing from all over the United States to show the desire of women that this should be done.

I want to emphasize just one point, in addition, that we are absolutely non-partisan. We are made up of women who are strong Democrats, women who are strong Republicans, women who are Socialists, Progressives—every type of women. We are all united on this one thing—that we put Suffrage before everything else. In every election, if we ever go into any future elections, we simply pledge ourselves to this—that we will consider the furtherance of Suffrage and not our party affiliations in deciding what action we shall take.

Mr. Williams, of Illinois: Is it your policy to fight this question out only as a national issue? Do you make any attempt to secure relief through the States?

Miss Paul: The Congressional Union is organized to work for an Amendment to the National Constitution. We feel that the time has come, because of the winning of so many Suffrage States in the West, to use the votes of women to get Suffrage nationally. In the earlier days in this country, all the Suffrage work was done in the States, but the winning of the Western States has given us a power which we did not have before, so we have now turned from State work to national work. We are concentrating on the national government.

Mr. Gard: Miss Paul, is it true that you prefer to approach this through the State legislatures than to approach it directly through the people?

Miss Paul: We prefer the quickest way, which we believe is by Congressional action.

Mr. Taggart: Why did you oppose the Democrats in the last election?

Miss Paul: We came into existence when the administration of President Wilson first came in. We appealed to all members of Congress to have this Amendment put through at once. We did get that measure out upon the floor of the House and Senate, but when it came to getting a vote in the House we found we were absolutely blocked. We went again and again, week after week, and month after month to the Democratic members of the Rules Committee, who controlled the apportioning of the time of the House, and asked them to give us five or ten minutes for the discussion of Suffrage. Every time they refused. They told us that they were powerless to act because the Democrats had met in caucus and decided that Suffrage was a matter to be decided in the States and should not be brought up in Congress. (Here Miss Paul, moving the papers in front of her, deftly extracted a letter.) I have here a letter from Mr. Henry, Chairman of the Rules Committee, in which he says: "It would give me great pleasure to report the Resolution to the House, except for the fact that the Democratic caucus, by its direct action, has tied my hands and placed me in a position where I will not be authorized to do so unless the caucus is reconvened and changes its decision. I am sure your good judgment will cause you to thoroughly understand my attitude."…

After we had been met for months with the statement that the Democratic Party had decided in caucus not to let Suffrage come up in Congress, we said, "We will go out to the women voters in the West and tell them how we are blocked in Washington, and ask them if they will use their vote for the very highest purpose for which they can use it—to help get votes for other women."

We campaigned against every one of the forty-three men who were running for Congress on the Democratic ticket in any of the Suffrage States; and only nineteen of those we campaigned against came back to Washington. In December, at the close of the election, we went back to the Rules Committee. They told us then that they had no greater desire in the world than to bring the Suffrage Amendment out. They told us that we had misunderstood them in thinking that they were opposed to having Suffrage come up in Congress. They voted at once to bring Suffrage upon the floor for the first time in history. The whole opposition of the Democratic Party melted away and the decision of the party caucus was reversed.

The part we played in the last election was simply to tell the women voters of the West of the way the Democratic Party had blocked us at Washington and of the way the individual members of the Party, from the West, had supported their Party in blocking us. As soon as we told this record they ceased blocking us and we trust they will never block us again.

Question: But what about next time?

Miss Paul: We hope we will never have to go into another election. We are appealing to all Parties and to all men to put this Amendment through this Congress and send it on to the State Legislatures. What we are doing is giving the Democrats their opportunity. We did pursue a certain policy which we have outlined to you as you requested. As to what we may do we cannot say. It depends upon the future situation.

Question: But we want to know what you will do in the 1916 election?

Miss Paul: Can you possibly tell us what will be in the platform of the Democratic Party in 1916?

Mr. Webb: I can tell one plank that will not be there, and that is a plank in favor of Woman Suffrage.

Question: If conditions are the same, do you not propose to fight Democrats just the same as you did a year ago?

Miss Paul: We have come to ask your help in this Congress. But in asking it we have ventured to remind you that in the next election one-fifth of the vote for President comes from Suffrage States. What we shall do in that election depends upon what you do.

Mr. Webb: We would know better what to do if we knew what you were going to do.

Mr. Gard: We should not approach this bearing in any partisan sense. What I would like is to be informed about some facts. I asked Mrs. Field what reason your organization had for asking Congress to submit this question to States that have already acted upon it. Why should there be a resubmission to the voters by national action in States which have either voted for or against it, when the machinery exists in these same States to vote for it again?

Miss Paul: They have never voted on the question of a National Amendment.

Mr. Gard: The States can only ratify it. You would prefer that course to having it taken directly to the people?

Miss Paul: Simply because we have the power of women's votes to back up this method.

Mr. Gard: You are using this method because you think you have power to enforce it?

Miss Paul: Because we know we have power.

Mr. Taggart: The women who have the vote in the West are not worrying about what women are doing in the East. You will have to get more States before you try this nationally.

Miss Paul: We think that this repeated advice to go back to the States proves beyond all cavil that we are on the right track.

Mr. Taggart: Suppose you get fewer votes this time? Do you think it is fair to those members of Congress who voted for Woman Suffrage and have stood for Woman Suffrage, to oppose them merely because a majority of their Party were not in favor of Woman Suffrage?

Miss Paul: Every man that we opposed stood by his Party caucus in its opposition to Suffrage.

Mr. Volstead: This inquiry is absolutely unfair and improper. It is cheap politics, and I have gotten awfully tired listening to it.

Mr. Taggart: Have your services been bespoken by the Republican committee of Kansas for the next campaign?

Miss Paul: We are greatly gratified by this tribute to our value.

Mr. Moss: State just whether or not it is a fact that the question is, What is right? and not, What will be the reward or punishment of the members of this committee? Is not that the only question that is pending before this committee?

Miss Paul: Yes, as we have said over and over today. We have come simply to ask that this committee report this measure to the House, that the House may consider the question.

Mr. Moss: Can you explain to the committee what the question of what you are going to do to a member of this committee or a Congressman in regard to his vote has to do with the question of what we should do as our duty?

Miss Paul: As I have said, we don't see any reason for discussing that.

Mr. Webb: You have no blacklist, have you, Miss Paul?

Miss Paul: No.

Mr. Taggart: You are organized, are you not, for the chastisement of political Parties that do not do your bidding at once?

Miss Paul: We are organized to win votes for women and our method of doing this is to organize the women who have the vote to help other women to get it.

GLOSSARY

bring the Suffrage Amendment out: the act whereby legislators vote a bill, in this case the one on woman suffrage, out of committee for a vote

caucus: any group of members in the House of Representatives who meet to pursue common legislative interests

Congressional Union: the Congressional Union for Woman Suffrage, founded in 1913 by Alice Paul and her associates

Mrs. Field: Sara Bard Field, prominent suffragist and feminist orator

plank: a figure of speech referring to a goal expressed in a political party's platform, or agenda

Document Analysis

It was in this context that Alice Paul testified before the House Judiciary Committee on the suffrage question on December 16, 1915. In her remarks she summarizes the position of the CUWS—simply that its members wanted the House Judiciary Committee to refer the Anthony Amendment to the floor of the House of Representatives for a vote. (Congressional procedure dictates that any bill has to be referred by an appropriate committee for consideration on the floor.) Paul adds that her organization was "absolutely non-partisan," even though it had targeted Democrats in the previous year's election. She emphasizes that women of all political parties supported the goal of suffrage.

At this point the Democrat William Ezra Williams of Illinois interrupted the proceedings and asked Paul about the issue of pursuing suffrage through the states rather than nationally. Paul makes clear in her remarks that the goal of the Congressional Union was to pursue an amendment to the federal Constitution, noting that the western states, where suffrage was a reality, gave women a power base from which to urge a national amendment. She emphasizes the same point in a brief exchange with the Democratic Representative Warren Gard of Ohio.

Then the Democrat Joseph Taggart of Kansas asked Paul a pointed question—why the group opposed Democrats in the last election. In her reply Paul puts forward the position of the CUWS. The organization, she says, tried repeatedly, "again and again, week after week, and month after month," to bring the matter of suffrage to a vote in Congress. Repeatedly the effort was blocked. The culprits, in Paul's view, were congressional Democrats on the Rules Committee who refused to vote the measure out of committee and onto the floor of the House. These Democrats argued that the matter was one for the individual states to decide. Accordingly, the CUWS took a bold step: The organization went to the women of the West—the states where suffrage had been granted were all in the Midwest, the Rocky Mountain region, and the West Coast—and persuaded them that they could use their votes to defeat Democrats. The campaign was successful in defeating twenty-four of the forty-three Democratic candidates who were up for reelection in those states. This campaign, Paul notes, had the desired effect. When Congress reconvened, the Rules Committee, claiming that it had been "misunderstood," voted to bring the suffrage amendment to the floor of the House, and Democratic opposition to the measure "melted away."

The remainder of the committee's proceedings betrayed a certain level of irritation on the part of some members of the committee—irritation that Paul met with clear, measured responses. When asked about the CUWS's plans for the next election, Paul says that the answer to that depended on the actions of Congress and on the Democratic Party's platform in 1916. The Democrat Edwin Webb of North Carolina flatly gave his opinion that the platform would not include a suffrage amendment. In reply, Paul pointedly mentions that one-fifth of the vote in the next year's presidential election would come from states with woman's suffrage and says that "what we shall do in that election depends upon what you do." Congressman Gard questioned why the suffrage issue should come up for a vote in states that already had a suffrage amendment. Paul replies that those states "had never voted on the question of a National Amendment." Congressman Taggart suggested that the best way for the CUWS to proceed was to increase its power base by getting suffrage amendments passed in more states. Paul answers that the organization had repeatedly been given this advice, proving "beyond all cavil" that the organization was "on the right track." Taggart then raised the question of whether it was fair to target men from the party who had supported women's suffrage; Paul replies that in every case these men had stood by their party in blocking efforts to bring the amendment to a vote.

After the committee's chairman, Minnesota Republican Andrew Volstead, expressed the view that the inquiry was improper, Taggart and the Indiana Democrat Ralph Moss attempted to pin Paul down on her motives and future plans, including the question of whether the CUWS had a "blacklist." Paul, a slender, delicate woman who on this occasion appeared in a violet dress, refused to buckle under this interrogation and insisted that her only motive was to win the vote for women.

Essential Themes

One of the tactics the CUWS pursued was to target and defeat members of Congress who were up for reelection in 1914. Since 1878 the so-called Anthony Amendment had been proposed in every session of Congress. This was the original suffrage amendment formulated by Susan B. Anthony and other suffrage leaders in that year and which in 1920 would be ratified as the Nineteenth Amendment to the Constitution. In the intervening years, however, the amendment had been blocked, primarily by members of the Democratic Party, a party that was particularly strong in the South. In such states as Alabama, Georgia, and Louisiana every senator and congressman was a Democrat. Although Democrats also represented states in which suffrage had been granted, the CUWS targeted them in the 1914 election because, according to Paul, they had stood with the party in blocking efforts to bring a national amendment up for a vote on the floor of the Senate and House. The CUWS wanted to demonstrate that in states where women had the vote, they could use that power to chastise their congressional representatives and to demonstrate support for a national amendment. This demonstration of women's political power (in states which had granted women suffrage) and the implications for politicians who's party opposed the Anthony Amendment are an important component of Paul's testimony and the committee's questioning. As such, this testimony—and the entire history of civil rights in the United States—illustrates the balacne between ideology and political reality that leaders and activists had to navigate to secure ratification of the Nineteenth Amendment.

——*Michael J. O'Neal, PhD*

Bibliography and Additional Reading

Adams, Katherine H.; Keene, Michael L. *Alice Paul and the American Suffrage Campaign*. Chicago: University of Illinois Press, 2008.

Evans, Sara M. *Born for Liberty: A History of Women in America.* New York: The Free Press, 1989.

Walton, Mary. *A Woman's Crusade: Alice Paul and the Battle for the Ballot.* New York: Palgrave Macmillan, 2010

Ware, Susan (2012). "The book I couldn't write: Alice Paul and the challenge of feminist biography". *Journal of Women's History.* 24 (2): 13–36.

Zahniser, J. D.; Fry, Amelia R. (2014). *Alice Paul: Claiming Power.* New York: Oxford University Press, 2014.

The SCUM Manifesto

Date: 1968
Author: Valerie Solanas
Genre: Political manifesto

Summary Overview

Published in 1968, "The SCUM Manifesto" by Valerie Solanas, a scathing attack on men and patriarchy, attracted attention within the radical feminist movement. Although the document itself never explains the meaning of "SCUM," it is widely believed that it was an acronym for "Society for Cutting Up Men." The document pulls no punches. It is an unabashed call to "overthrow the government, eliminate the money system, institute complete automation and destroy the male sex." The document expresses utter contempt for men, often in language that some would regard as shocking and obscene.

Defining Moment

Valerie Solanas's SCUM Manifesto was a product of the radical feminist movement that developed in the 1960s. While earlier examples of the women's liberation movement had focused more narrowly on political rights (such as the right to vote) or economic equality and opportunity, radical feminism addressed a broader array of social, political, cultural, and economic concerns. One source of this new iteration of the women's movement was the civil rights activism of the 1950s and 1960s. Women activists, seeing the discrimination the was exercised against African Americans, began to work on behalf of many woman's rights issues such as the legal protection of the right to abortion, equal pay efforts, and ratification of the Equal Rights Amendment. While groups such as the National Organization of Women (NOW) pushed for advances on these fronts other, smaller, groups and individuals began to look at the oppression of women through different lenses.

Traditional feminist groups had often concentrated on political or legal solutions. In the late 1960s and early 1970s, socialist and communist feminist thinkers began to look at the oppression of women through the framework of class conflict. The radical feminists, meanwhile, sought to disrupt the entire concept of "patriarchy," the male-dominated power structure that had kept women subservient throughout history. It was this power structure that dictated the political, social, cultural, and economic inequalities to which women were subject. Connected to this concept of the patriarchy as being the source of women's oppression was the radical lesbian feminist view of heterosexuality being a political structure perpetuated by the hierarchy.

While this radical vision is present in the SCUM Manifesto is the suggestion of revolution and, accordingly, revolutionary violence as being justified as a means to create a new society. While Solanas would later claim that the violence advocated in the Manifest should not be taken literally, there were groups (such as the Weather Underground Organization) who followed through with violent revolutionary acts. Solanas promoted violence in an outrageous manner, but revolutionary violence certainly was not unheard of at this time.

Author Biography

Born in New Jersey on April 9, 1936, Solanis had a troubled relationship with her mother and stepfather and was abused by her grandfather, an alcoholic, with whom she lived after leaving her mother's home. By age fifteen, she was living on the streets, but she managed to graduate from high school, earn a degree from the University of Maryland, and do graduate work in psychology at the University of Minnesota. From the mid-1950s to the mid-1960s she lived an itinerant life and supported herself by prostitution and begging. Perhaps her biggest claim to fame is that in 1968, she shot the pop artist Andy Warhol, believing that he had stolen from her a play she had written called *Up Your Ass*. She also, at this time, shot art critic Mario Amaya. Her paranoid vendetta against Warhol was connected, tangentially, to her efforts to have the SCUM Manifesto published. In 1967, as she was self-publishing versions of the Manifesto, Solanis was approached by Maurice Girodias, the owner of Olympia Press, who offered to publish Solanas's work. She believed this offer was partially an attempt by the publisher to claim ownership of future writings. She suspected Girodias, like Warhol, of wanting to steal her work.

Under the conditions of a plea bargain, Solanas served three years in prison, as well as receiving treatment for paranoid schizophrenia.

Warhol never fully recovered from his gunshot wound, and after Solanas was released from prison in 1971, she continued to stalk Warhol and was arrested again in November of that year. During the remaining years of her life, Solanas fell from the public's notice and drifted in and out of mental hospitals. In a 1977 interview with the *Village Voice*, she claimed that "The SCUM Manifesto" was not to be taken literally. She died of pneumonia on April 25, 1988, in San Francisco's Tenderloin District.

HISTORICAL DOCUMENT

Life in this society being, at best, an utter bore and no aspect of society being at all relevant to women, there remains to civic-minded, responsible, thrill-seeking females only to overthrow the government, eliminate the money system, institute complete automation and destroy the male sex.

It is now technically feasible to reproduce without the aid of males (or, for that matter, females) and to produce only females. We must begin immediately to do so. Retaining the male has not even the dubious purpose of reproduction. The male is a biological accident: the Y (male) gene is an incomplete X (female) gene, that is, it has an incomplete set of chromosomes. In other words, the male is an incomplete female, a walking abortion, aborted at the gene stage. To be male is to be deficient, emotionally limited; maleness is a deficiency disease and males are emotional cripples.

The male is completely egocentric, trapped inside himself, incapable of empathizing or identifying with others, or love, friendship, affection of tenderness. He is a completely isolated unit, incapable of rapport with anyone. His responses are entirely visceral, not cerebral; his intelligence is a mere tool in the services of his drives and needs; he is incapable of mental passion, mental interaction; he can't relate to anything other than his own physical sensations. He is a half-dead, unresponsive lump, incapable of giving or receiving pleasure or happiness; consequently, he is at best an utter bore, an inoffensive blob, since only those capable of absorption in others can be charming. He is trapped in a twilight zone halfway between humans and apes, and is far worse off than the apes because, unlike the apes, he is capable of a large array of negative feelings—hate, jealousy, contempt, disgust, guilt, shame, doubt—and moreover, he is aware of what he is and what he isn't.

Although completely physical, the male is unfit even for stud service. Even assuming mechanical proficiency, which few men have, he is, first of all, incapable of zestfully, lustfully, tearing off a piece, but instead is eaten up with guilt, shame, fear and insecurity, feelings rooted in male nature, which the most enlightened training can only minimize; second, the physical feeling he attains is next to nothing; and third, he is not empathizing with his partner, but is obsessed with how he's doing, turning in an A performance, doing a good plumbing job. To call a man an animal is to flatter him; he's a machine, a walking dildo. It's often said that men use women. Use them for what? Surely not pleasure.

Eaten up with guilt, shame, fears and insecurities and obtaining, if he's lucky, a barely perceptible physical feeling, the male is, nonetheless, obsessed with screwing; he'll swim through a river of snot, wade nostril-deep through a mile of vomit, if he thinks there'll be a friendly pussy awaiting him. He'll screw a woman he despises, any snaggle-toothed hag, and furthermore, pay for the opportunity. Why? Relieving physical tension isn't the answer, as masturbation suffices for that. It's not ego satisfaction; that doesn't explain screwing corpses and babies.

Completely egocentric, unable to relate, empathize or identify, and filled with a vast, pervasive, diffuse sexuality, the male is psychically passive. He hates his passivity, so he projects it onto women, defines the make as active, then sets out to prove that he is ("prove that he is a Man"). His main means of attempting to prove it is screwing (Big Man with a Big Dick tearing off a Big Piece). Since he's attempting to prove an error, he must "prove" it again and again. Screwing, then, is a desperate compulsive, attempt to prove he's not passive, not a woman; but he *is* passive and *does* want to be a woman.

Being an incomplete female, the male spends his life attempting to complete himself, to become female. He attempts to do this by constantly seeking out, fraternizing with and trying to live through an fuse with the female, and by claiming as his own all female characteristics—emotional strength and independence, forcefulness, dynamism, decisiveness, coolness, objectivity, assertiveness, courage, integrity, vitality, intensity, depth of character, grooviness, etc.—and projecting onto women all male traits—vanity, frivolity, triviality, weakness, etc. It should be said, though, that the male has one glaring area of superiority over the female—public relations. (He has done a brilliant job of convincing millions of women that men are women and women are men). The male claim that females find fulfillment through motherhood and sexuality reflects what males think they'd find fulfilling if they were female....

Incapable of a positive state of happiness, which is the only thing that can justify one's existence, the male is, at best, relaxed, comfortable, neutral, and this condition is extremely short-lived, as boredom, a negative state, soon sets in; he is, therefore, doomed to an existence of suffering relieved only by occasional, fleeting stretches of restfulness, which state he can only achieve at the expense of some female. The male is, by his very nature, a leech, an emotional parasite and, therefore, not ethically entitled to live, as no one as the right to life at someone else's expense.

Just as humans have a prior right to existence over dogs by virtue of being more highly evolved and having a superior consciousness, so women have a prior right to existence over men. The elimination of any male is, therefore, a righteous and good act, an act highly beneficial to women as well as an act of mercy.

However, this moral issue will eventually be rendered academic by the fact that the male is gradually eliminating himself. In addition to engaging in the time-honored and classical wars and race riots, men are more and more either becoming fags or are obliterating themselves through drugs. The female, whether she likes it or not, will eventually take complete charge, if for no other reason than that she will have to—the male, for practical purposes, won't exist.

Accelerating this trend is the fact that more and more males are acquiring enlightened self-interest; they're realizing more and more that the female interest is in *their* interest, that they can live only through the female and that the more the female is encouraged to live, to fulfill herself, to be a female and not a male, the more nearly *he* lives; he's coming to see that it's easier and more satisfactory to live *through* her than to try to *become* her and usurp her qualities, claim them as his own, push the female down and claim that she's a male. The fag, who accepts his maleness, that is, his passivity and total sexuality, his femininity, is also best served by women being truly female, as it would then be easier for him to be male, feminine. If men were wise they would seek to become really female, would do intensive biological research that would lead to me, by means of operations on the brain and nervous system, being able to be transformed in psyche, as well as body, into women.

Whether to continue to use females for reproduction or to reproduce in the laboratory will also become academic: what will happen when every female, twelve and over, is routinely taking the Pill and there are no longer any accidents? How many women will deliberately get or (if an accident) remain pregnant? No, Virginia, women don't just adore being brood mares, despite what the mass of robot, brainwashed women will say. When society consists of only the fully conscious the answer will be none. Should a certain percentage of men be set aside by force to serve as brood mares for the species? Obviously this will not do. The answer is laboratory reproduction of babies.

As for the issue of whether or not to continue to reproduce males, it doesn't follow that because the male, like disease, has always existed among us that he should continue to exist. When genetic control is possible—and soon it will be—it goes without saying that we should produce only whole, complete beings, not physical defects of deficiencies, including emotional deficiencies, such as maleness. Just as the deliberate production of blind people would be highly immoral, so would be the deliberate production of emotional cripples.

Why produce even females? Why should there be future generations? What is their purpose? When aging and death are eliminated, why continue to reproduce? Why should we care what happens when we're dead? Why should we care that there is no younger generation to succeed us.

Eventually the natural course of events, of social evolution, will lead to total female control of the world and, subsequently, to the cessation of the production of males and, ultimately, to the cessation of the production of females.

But SCUM is impatient; SCUM is not consoled by the thought that future generations will thrive; SCUM wants to grab some thrilling living for itself. And, if a large majority of women were SCUM, they could acquire complete control of this country within a few weeks simply by withdrawing from the labor force, thereby paralyzing the entire nation. Additional measures, any one of which would be sufficient to completely disrupt the economy and everything else, would be for women to declare themselves off the money system, stop buying, just loot and simply refuse to obey all laws they don't care to obey. The police force, National Guard, Army, Navy and Marines combined couldn't squelch a rebellion of over half the population, particularly when it's made up of people they are utterly helpless without.

If all women simply left men, refused to have anything to do with any of them—ever, all men, the government, and the national economy would collapse completely. Even without leaving men, women who are aware of the extent of their superiority to and power over men, could acquire complete control over everything within a few weeks, could effect a total submission of males to females. In a sane society the male would trot along obediently after the female. The male is docile and easily led, easily subjected to the domination of any female who cares to dominate him. The male, in fact, wants desperately to be led by females, wants Mama in charge, wants to abandon himself to her care. But this is not a sane society, and most women are not even dimly aware of where they're at in relation to men.

The conflict, therefore, is not between females and males, but between SCUM—dominant, secure, self-confident, nasty, violent, selfish, independent, proud, thrill-seeking, free-wheeling, arrogant females, who consider themselves fit to rule the universe, who have free-wheeled to the limits of this "society" and are ready to wheel on to something far beyond what it has to offer—and nice, passive, accepting "cultivated," polite, dignified, subdued, dependent, scared, mindless, insecure, approval-seeking Daddy's Girls, who can't cope with the unknown, who want to hang back with the apes, who feel secure only with Big Daddy standing by, with a big strong man to lean on and with a fat, hairy face in the White House, who are too cowardly to face up to the hideous reality of what a man is, what Daddy is, who have cast their lot with the swine, who have adapted themselves to animalism, feel superficially comfortable with it and know no other way of "life," who have reduced their minds, thoughts and sights to the male level, who, lacking sense, imagination and wit can have value only in a male "society," who can have a place in the sun, or, rather, in the slime, only as soothers, ego boosters, relaxers and breeders, who are dismissed as inconsequents by other females, who project their deficiencies, their maleness, onto all females and see the female as worm.

But SCUM is too impatient to wait for the de-brainwashing of millions of assholes. Why should the swinging females continue to plod dismally along with the dull male ones? Why should the fates of the groovy and the creepy be intertwined? Why should the active and imaginative consult the passive and dull on social policy? Why should the independent be confined to the sewer along with the dependent who need Daddy to cling to? A small handful of SCUM can take over the country within a year by systematically fucking up the system, selectively destroying property, and murder:

SCUM will become members of the unwork force, the fuck-up force; they will get jobs of various kinds an unwork. For example, SCUM salesgirls will not charge for merchandise; SCUM telephone operators will not charge for calls; SCUM office and factory workers, in addition to fucking up their work, will secretly destroy equipment. SCUM will unwork at a job until fired, then get a new job to unwork at.

SCUM will forcibly relieve bus drivers, cab drivers and subway token sellers of their jobs and run buses and cabs and dispense free tokens to the public.

SCUM will destroy all useless and harmful objects—cars, store windows, "Great Art," etc.

Eventually SCUM will take over the airwaves—radio and TV networks—by forcibly relieving of their jobs all radio and TV employees who would impede SCUM's entry into the broadcasting studios.

SCUM will couple-bust—barge into mixed (male-female) couples, wherever they are, and bust them up.

SCUM will kill all men who are not in the Men's Auxiliary of SCUM. Men in the Men's Auxiliary are those men who are working diligently to eliminate themselves, men who, regardless of their motives, do good, men who are playing pall with SCUM. A few examples of the men in the Men's Auxiliary are: men who kill men; biological scientists who are working on constructive programs, as opposed to biological warfare; journalists, writers, editors, publishers and producers who disseminate and promote ideas that will lead to the achievement of SCUM's goals; faggots who, by their shimmering, flaming example, encourage other men to de-man themselves and thereby make themselves relatively inoffensive; men who consistently give things away—money, things, services; men who tell it like it is (so far not one ever has), who put women straight, who reveal the truth about themselves, who give the mindless male females correct sentences to parrot, who tell them a woman's primary goal in life should be to squash the male sex (to aid men in this endeavor SCUM will conduct Turd Sessions, at which every male present will give a speech beginning with the sentence: "I am a turd, a lowly abject turd," then proceed to list all the ways in which he is. His reward for doing so will be the opportunity to fraternize after the session for a whole, solid hour with the SCUM who will be present. Nice, clean-living male women will be invited to the sessions to help clarify any doubts and misunderstandings they may have about the male sex; makers and promoters of sex books and movies, etc., who are hastening the day when all that will be shown on the screen will be Suck and Fuck (males, like the rats following the Pied Piper, will be lured by Pussy to their doom, will be overcome and submerged by and will eventually drown in the passive flesh that they are); drug pushers and advocates, who are hastening the dropping out of men.

Being in the Men's Auxiliary is a necessary but not a sufficient condition for making SCUM's escape list; it's not enough to do good; to save their worthless asses men must also avoid evil. A few examples of the most obnoxious or harmful types are: rapists, politicians and all who are in their service (campaigners, members of political parties, etc); lousy singers and musicians; Chairmen of Boards; Breadwinners; landlords; owners of greasy spoons and restaurants that play Muzak; "Great Artists"; cheap pikers and welchers; cops; tycoons; scientists working on death and destruction programs or for private industry (practically all scientists); liars and phonies; disc jockies; men who intrude themselves in the slightest way on any strange female; real estate men; stock brokers; men who speak when they have nothing to say; men who sit idly on the street and mar the landscape with their presence; double dealers; flim-flam artists; litterbugs; plagiarisers; men who in the slightest way harm any female; all men in the advertising industry; psychiatrists and clinical psychologists; dishonest writers, journalists, editors, publishers, etc.; censors on both the public and private levels; all members of the armed forces, including draftees (LBJ and McNamara give orders, but servicemen carry them out) and particularly pilots (if the bomb drops, LBJ won't drop it; a pilot will). In the case of a man whose behavior falls into both the good and bad categories, an overall subjective evaluation of him will be made to determine if his behavior is, in the balance, good or bad.

It is most tempting to pick off the female "Great Artists," liars and phonies etc. along with the men, but that would be inexpedient, as it would not be clear to most of the public that the female killed was a male. All women have a fink streak in them, to a greater or lesser degree, but it stems from a lifetime of living among men. Eliminate men and women will shape up. Women are improvable; men are no, although their behavior is. When SCUM gets hot on their asses it'll shape up fast.

Simultaneously with the fucking-up, looting, couple-busting, destroying and killing, SCUM will recruit. SCUM, then, will consist of recruiters; the elite corps—the hard core activists (the fuck-ups, looters and destroyers) and the elite of the elite—the killers.

Dropping out is not the answer; fucking-up is. Most women are already dropped out; they were never in. Dropping out gives control to those few who don't drop out; dropping out is exactly what the establishment leaders want; it plays into the hands of the enemy; it strengthens the system instead of undermining it, since it is based entirely on the non-participating, passivity, apathy and non-involvement of the mass of women. Dropping out, however, is an excellent policy for men, and SCUM will enthusiastically encourage it.

Looking inside yourself for salvation, contemplating your navel, is not, as the Drop Out people would have you believe, the answer. Happiness likes outside yourself, is achieved through interacting with others.

Self-forgetfulness should be one's goal, not self-absorption. The male, capable of only the latter, makes a virtue of irremediable fault and sets up self-absorption, not only as a good but as a Philosophical Good, and thus gets credit for being deep.

SCUM will not picket, demonstrate, march or strike to attempt to achieve its ends. Such tactics are for nice, genteel ladies who scrupulously take only such action as is guaranteed to be ineffective. In addition, only decent, clean-living male women, highly trained in submerging themselves in the species, act on a mob basis. SCUM consists of individuals; SCUM is not a mob, a blob. Only as many SCUM will do a job as are needed for the job. Also SCUM, being cool and selfish, will not subject to getting itself rapped on the head with billy clubs; that's for the nice, "privileged, educated," middle-class ladies with a high regard for the touching faith in the essential goodness of Daddy and policemen. If SCUM ever marches, it will be over the President's stupid, sickening face; if SCUM ever strikes, it will be in the dark with a six-inch blade.

SCUM will always operate on a criminal as opposed to a civil disobedience basis, that is, as opposed to openly violating the law and going to jail in order to draw attention to an injustice. Such tactics acknowledge the rightness overall system and are used only to modify it slightly, change specific laws. SCUM is against the entire system, the very idea of law and government. SCUM is out to destroy the system, not attain certain rights within it. Also, SCUM—always selfish, always cool—will always aim to avoid detection and punishment. SCUM will always be furtive, sneaky, underhanded (although SCUM murders will always be known to be such).

Both destruction and killing will be selective and discriminate. SCUM is against half-crazed, indiscriminate riots, with no clear objective in mind, and in which many of your own kind are picked off. SCUM will never instigate, encourage or participate in riots of any kind or other form of indiscriminate destruction. SCUM will coolly, furtively, stalk its prey and quietly move in for the kill. Destruction will never me such [sic] as to block off routes needed for the transportation of food or other essential supplies, contaminate or cut off the water supply, block streets and traffic to the extent that ambulances can't get through or impede the functioning of hospitals.

SCUM will keep on destroying, looting, fucking-up and killing until the money-work system no longer exists and automation is completely instituted or until enough women co-operate with SCUM to make violence unnecessary to achieve these goals, that is, until enough women either unwork or quit work, start looting, leave men and refuse to obey all laws inappropriate to a truly civilized society. Many women will fall into line, but many others, who surrendered long ago to the enemy, who are so adapted to animalism, to maleness, that they like restrictions and restraints, don't know what to do with freedom, will continue to be toadies and doormats, just as peasants in rice paddies remain peasants in rice paddies as one regime topples another. A few of the more volatile will whimper and sulk and throw their toys and dishrags on the floor, but SCUM will continue to steamroller over them.

A completely automated society can be accomplished very simply and quickly once there is a public demand for it. The blueprints for it are already in existence, and it's construction will take only a few weeks with millions of people working on it. Even though off the money system, everyone will be most happy to pitch in and get the automated society built; it will mark the beginning of a fantastic new era, and there will be a celebration atmosphere accompanying the construction.

The elimination of money and the complete institution of automation are basic to all other SCUM reforms; without these two the others can't take place; with them the others will take place very rapidly. The government will automatically collapse. With complete automation it will be possible for every woman to vote directly on every issue by means of an electronic voting machine in her house. Since the government is occupied almost entirely with regulating economic affairs and legislating against purely private matters, the elimination of money wand with it the elimination of males who wish to legislate "morality" will mean there will be practically no issues to vote on.

After the elimination of money there will be no further need to kill men; they will be stripped of the only power they have over psychologically independent females. They will be able to impose themselves only on the doormats, who like to be imposed on. The rest of the women will be busy solving the few remaining unsolved problems before planning their agenda for eternity and Utopia—completely revamping educational programs so that millions of women can be trained within a few months for high level intellectual work that now requires years of training (this can be done very easily once out educational goal is to educate and not perpetuate an academic and intellectual elite); solving the problems of disease and old age and death and completely redesigning our cities and living quarters. Many women will for a while continue to think they dig men, but as they become accustomed to female society and as they become absorbed in their projects, they will eventually come to see the utter uselessness and banality of the male.

The few remaining men can exist out their puny days dropped out on drugs or strutting around in drag or passively watching the high-powered female in action, fulfilling themselves as spectators, vicarious livers or breeding in the cow pasture with the toadies, or they can go off to the nearest friendly suicide center where they will be quietly, quickly, and painlessly gassed to death.

Prior to the institution of automation, to the replacement of males by machines, the male should be of use to the female, wait on her, cater to her slightest whim, obey her every command, be totally subservient to her, exist in perfect obedience to her will, as opposed to the completely warped, degenerate situation we have now of men, not only not only not existing at all, cluttering up the world with their ignominious presence, but being pandered to and groveled before by the mass of females, millions of women piously worshiping the Golden Calf, the dog leading the master on a leash, when in fact the male, short of being a drag queen, is least miserable when his dogginess is recognized—no unrealistic emotional demands are made of him and the completely together female is calling the shots. Rational men want to be squashed, stepped on, crushed and crunched, treated as the curs, the filth that they are, have their repulsiveness confirmed.

The sick, irrational men, those who attempt to defend themselves against their disgustingness, when they see SCUM barreling down on them, will cling in terror to Big Mama with her Big Bouncy Boobies, but Boobies won't protect them against SCUM; Big Mama will be clinging to Big Daddy, who will be in the corner shitting in his forceful, dynamic pants. Men who are rational, however, won't kick or struggle or raise a distressing fuss, but will just sit back, relax, enjoy the show and ride the waves to their demise.

GLOSSARY

be rendered academic: made irrelevant

"LBJ and McNamara": Lyndon B. Johnson was President of the United States from 1963-1969; Robert McNamara was Secretary of Defense from 1961 to 1968.

"the Pill": birth control medication

usurp: to take over or replace

visceral: existing on a sensory level

Document Analysis
Two excerpts from "The SCUM Manifesto" are reproduced here. In the first excerpt—the first six paragraphs of which are presented here—Solanas announces the document's thesis. She explains that "this society" is irrelevant to women and, because of this, the onion option for "responsible, thrill-seeking females" is to topple the US government, eliminate the monetary system, and "institute complete automation." She also calls for gendercide, or the elimination of the male sex. She then notes a biological fact, one that was often cited by the radical feminist movement at the time—the notion that a male can be regarded biologically as an incomplete female, based on the idea that "the Y (male) gene is an incomplete X (female) gene, that is, it has an incomplete set of chromosomes. In other words, the male is an incomplete female, a walking abortion." Solanas then states her belief that males are "completely egocentric," unable to feel genuine empathy or human emotion. Rather, she says, males are ruled entirely by their "drives and needs," primarily sexual drives. Despite this enslavement to their physical drives, Solanas argues that men are "unfit even for stud service," that is to say that despite their "mechanical proficiency," men are not even fit for use as sexual use, as they are psychologically unfit to do so. Regardless of their unfitness, she says, men are "obsessed with screwing. She asserts that men are "psychically passive" and attempt to project their own inadequacies onto women. In the close of this first section, Solanas reiterates that men are, in reality, incomplete females, claiming ownership of traits that are, in reality, "female characteristics." The only thing men are capable of are "public relations," persuading women that motherhood is their natural role.

The second excerpt consists of the essay's final paragraphs. Solanas here asserts that men are "incapable of a positive state of happiness" and are fundamentally bored, turning them into leeches and parasites that are "not ethically entitled to live." Solanas further justifies the ethics of eliminating men by drawing the comparison between humans and dogs—since humans have a "superior consciousness" to dogs, humans are entitled to live. Since women have a higher consciousness than men, the "elimination" of men is "an act highly beneficial to women as well as an act of mercy." Although she calls for the elimination of men, she also suggests that men are eliminating themselves through war (the document was written at the height of the war in Vietnam), riots (the 1960s were a time of race riots in numerous American cities), drugs, and homosexuality. Further, advances in artificial reproduction would eventually eliminate the need for men, for all babies could be produced in a laboratory. Eventually, Solanas says, "the natural course of events... will lead to total female control of the world and, subsequently, to the cessation of the production of males and, ultimately, to the cessation of the production of females."

In the meantime, she calls for women to simply decline to participate in the social and economic system that exists by refusing, for example, to obey laws or to participate in the labor force. Rather, women will be part of the "unworkable force, the fuck-up force," disrupting the economy and In her view, "A small handful of SCUM can take over the country within a year by systematically fucking up the system, selectively destroying property, and murder." Meanwhile, a "Men's Auxiliary" can be allowed to exist; these men would recognize their inadequacies, work toward the elimination of men, and further the aims of women. Solanas emphasizes the revolutionary and active approach promoted by her ideas, arguing that "dropping out" (separating oneself from society, a popular notion in some parts of the 1960s counterculture) is not the answer. The reason for this is that the women cannot truly drop out because they have always been prevented from truly being "in." Dropping out, Solanas argues, is exactly what the male hierarchy wants. She also stresses that the movement launched by the SCUM Manifesto will not be a traditional protest movement: their disobedience will be criminal, not civil. Ultimately, women "will be busy solving the few remaining unsolved problems before planning their agenda for eternity and Utopia"—a world in which women perform intellectual work (all other work being automated) and solve the world's economic and social problems.

Essential Themes
Beneath the outrageous, often offensive language and imagery of the SCUM Manifesto, is a current of revolutionary thought and a call to action that transcends the gender conflict that dominates the piece. Solanas takes issue not only with the patriarchy but also targets the monetary system as well as the broader economy. It also rejects the once-dominant tactic of civil disobedience with a vehemence that is chilling in its implications and intent. Again, regardless of her claim

that she did not intend for the calls to violent action to be taken literally, Solanis's warning that "Both destruction and killing will be selective and discriminate" and that her followers "will coolly, furtively, stalk its prey and quietly move in for the kill does not sound like hyperbole.

Alongside the broader revolutionary aspects of the SCUM Manifesto is a cogent critique of women's place in the patriarchy. This is most apparent in the portion of the essay in which Solanis denounces the notion of women "dropping out" for the simply reason that women are not in a position of enough authority or importance where their dropping out would have an effect upon the power structure of the United States.

——Michael J. O'Neal, PhD

Bibliography and Additional Reading

Buchanan, Paul D. *Radical Feminists: A Guide to an American Subculture*. (Santa Barbara: Greenwood, 2011).

Heller, Dana (2008). "Shooting Solanas: radical feminist history and the technology of failure". In Victoria Hesford & Lisa Diedrich. *Feminist Time against Nation Time: Gender, Politics, and the Nation-State in an Age of Permanent War*. (Lanham, Maryland: Lexington Books, 2008). pp. 151–168.

Rich, B. Ruby (1993). "Manifesto destiny: drawing a bead on Valerie Solanas". *Voice Literary Supplement*. New York, NY: The Village Voice. 119: 16–17.

Third, Amanda (2006). "'Shooting from the hip': Valerie Solanas, SCUM and the apocalyptic politics of radical feminism". *Hecate*. 32 (2): 104–132.

■ Women's March on Washington

Date: January 21, 2017
Author: Angela Davis
Genre: Speech

Summary Overview

Controversial, world-renowned scholar and activist Angela Davis delivered this speech on September 21, 2017 during the Women's March on Washington. This event, organized in response and opposition to the incoming presidential administration of Donald J. Trump, was accompanied by marches around the United States as well as protests around the world and was the largest political demonstration in the nation's capital city since the protests of the Vietnam War era.

There are a number of important concepts and ideas in Davis's speech that give us some insight into the concerns of progressive activists in the second decade of the twenty-first century. One of the most important concepts is that of the "intersectional" aspects of feminism. Both Davis and the organizers of the march recognized that the structural aspects of American society, politics, economics and culture that placed women at a disadvantage also had similar effects on racial, ethnic, and religious minorities, people with disabilities, immigrants, and others in the United States. Thus, Davis's speech not only addresses issues of gender equality but homophobia and transphobia, economic inequality, environmental justice—particularly access to safe water—and other issues that "intersect" with feminist concerns.

In this speech, Angela Davis also calls for continued resistance throughout the coming years of the Trump administration, emphasizing that opposition to the proposed policies of the Trump White House (and the ideological and cultural factors that had contributed to his election) should not end with this post-inauguration event.

Defining Moment

The 2016 US Presidential election between Democrat Hillary Clinton and Republican Donald Trump was remarkably divisive. With heated rhetoric, Trump targeted immigrants (particularly Muslims and immigrants from Mexico) and promised severe restrictions on immigration. Numerous Trump comments surfaced that many considered to be degrading to women. While some were alienated by Trump's words, other Americans saw his forthrightness as a welcome response to what they considered to be a growing atmosphere of "political correctness." Donald Trump's Vice Presidential running mate, Indiana governor Mike Pence had supported legislation in Indiana that his critics charged limited women's access to reproductive health care as well as signing into law the 2015 Religious Freedom Restoration Act, which opponents asserted opened the door to discrimination against members of the LGBT community being protected as a "religious liberty." Trump's rhetoric and Pence's gubernatorial record proved troubling to civil rights advocates.

Following Trump's election, a number of activists organized nationwide protests and marches to take place on January 21, 2017, following Trump's inauguration. While the main march occurred in Washington, D.C., similar demonstrations were organized not only throughout the United States but around the world. The organizers, in their "Mission & Vision" statement, characterized the circumstances which inspired the protest as resulting from "he rhetoric of the past election cycle" which "insulted, demonized, and threatened many of us - immigrants of all statuses, Muslims and those of diverse religious faiths, people who identify as LGBTQIA, Native people, Black and Brown people, people with disabilities, survivors of sexual assault - and our communities are hurting and scared." While having as a starting point the concerns about women's rights under the new administration, the communities and causes addressed by the march broadened beyond gender, with the group's "Unity Principles" citing the following issues:

Ending violence
Reproductive rights
LGBTQIA [Lesbian, Gay, Bisexual, Transgender and Transsexual, Queer, Intersex, Asexual] rights
Worker's rights
Civil rights
Disability rights
Immigrant rights
Environmental justice

This broadened vision of concerns and causes illustrates the notion of, as Angela Davis says in her speech, of a feminism that is "inclusive and intersectional" and provides a window into the wide community of progressive activism in the twenty-first century.

Author Biography

Angela Y. Davis was born on January 26, 1944 in Alabama. As a child in Birmingham, Davis got involved in civil rights issues, taking part in anti-segregation marches. Her mother as involved in an organization called the Southern Negro Youth Congress, which was a civil rights organization that, from its inception in 1937, was suspected of some connection with the Communist Party. During the 1940s and 1950s, in fact, the organization was under surveillance by the FBI. In a 1989 interview, Davis recalled how she became acquainted with the Communist Party as a child through friends of her parents. This connection would continue when Davis was in high school. She earned a place in a program that provided for African American students from the south to attend school in the north. Davis attended school in Greenwich Village, New York City and became involved in a Communist-affiliated student organization called Advance.

Davis's political activism would continued as a student at Brandeis University, leading to her being interviewed about her attendance at a Communist-organized youth festival. Graduating from Brandeis, Davis continued her schooling at the University of Frankfurt in Germany, and the University of California, San Diego where she earned a Master's degree, and Humboldt University in East Berlin, where she earned a doctorate in philosophy. She began teaching in the philosophy department of the University of California at Los Angeles in 1969, where she was known for her radical feminist activism and membership in the Communist Party USA. She was briefly removed from the position by the University's ruling board—at the suggestion of Governor Ronald Reagan—because of her Communist Party membership. While rehired, she was fired again in 1970 for speeches in which, among other things, she referred to the police as "pigs."

In August, 1970, a California court house hostage situation resulted in the deaths of a judge and three others. Davis was put on the FBI most-wanted fugitive list due to charges of aggravated kidnapping and first degree murder for her role in the situation, alleged to be purchasing the guns used in the hostage taking. Davis was apprehended in October of that year. After a highly publicized trial, Davis was acquitted in June, 1972. Throughout the decade she visited Cuba, the Soviet Union, and East Germany delivering public speeches. During the 1980s and 1990s and into the twenty-first century, Davis continued her academic career teaching and writing at various institutions as well as her progressive political activism.

HISTORICAL DOCUMENT

At a challenging moment in our history, let us remind ourselves that we the hundreds of thousands, the millions of women, trans-people, men and youth who are here at the Women's March, we represent the powerful forces of change that are determined to prevent the dying cultures of racism, hetero-patriarchy from rising again.

We recognize that we are collective agents of history and that history cannot be deleted like web pages. We know that we gather this afternoon on indigenous land and we follow the lead of the first peoples who despite massive genocidal violence have never relinquished the struggle for land, water, culture, their people. We especially salute today the Standing Rock Sioux.

The freedom struggles of black people that have shaped the very nature of this country's history cannot be deleted with the sweep of a hand. We cannot be made to forget that black lives do matter. This is a country anchored in slavery and colonialism, which means for better or for worse the very history of the United States is a history of immigration and enslavement. Spreading xenophobia, hurling accusations of murder and rape and building walls will not erase history.

No human being is illegal.

The struggle to save the planet, to stop climate change, to guarantee the accessibility of water from the lands of the Standing Rock Sioux, to Flint, Michigan, to the West Bank and Gaza. The struggle to save our flora and fauna, to save the air—this is ground zero of the struggle for social justice.

This is a women's march and this women's march represents the promise of feminism as against the pernicious powers of state violence. And inclusive and intersectional feminism that calls upon all of us to join the resistance to racism, to Islamophobia, to anti-Semitism, to misogyny, to capitalist exploitation.

Yes, we salute the fight for 15. We dedicate ourselves to collective resistance. Resistance to the billionaire mortgage profiteers and gentrifiers. Resistance to the health care privateers. Resistance to the attacks on Muslims and on immigrants. Resistance to attacks on disabled people. Resistance to state violence perpetrated by the police and through the prison industrial complex. Resistance to institutional and intimate gender violence, especially against trans women of color.

Women's rights are human rights all over the planet and that is why we say freedom and justice for Palestine. We celebrate the impending release of Chelsea Manning. And Oscar López Rivera. But we also say free Leonard Peltier. Free Mumia Abu-Jamal. Free Assata Shakur.

Over the next months and years we will be called upon to intensify our demands for social justice to become more militant in our defense of vulnerable populations. Those who still defend the supremacy of white male hetero-patriarchy had better watch out.

The next 1,459 days of the Trump administration will be 1,459 days of resistance: Resistance on the ground, resistance in the classrooms, resistance on the job, resistance in our art and in our music.

This is just the beginning and in the words of the inimitable Ella Baker, 'We who believe in freedom cannot rest until it comes.' Thank you.

GLOSSARY

Ella Baker: African American civil rights activist who lived from 1903 to 1986.

ground zero: a point of impact or origination

hetero-patriarchy: the dominance of maleness and heterosexuality in the socio-political hierarchy

misogyny: hatred, fear, and oppression of women

"the fight for 15": the movement to increase the federal minimum wage to $15 per hour

Document Analysis
Davis begins her speech by highlighting the large number of participants at the march, which she numbers as "hundreds of thousands" and "millions." The Washington Post estimated the number of Marchers in Washington as around half a million, but the number who participated around the United States as between 3.3 and 4.6 million. Davis point out the diverse group of "women, trans-people, men and youth" participating in the march and points to both the numbers and the make-up of the marchers as the force that will ensure the continued decline of "racism, hetero-patriarchy."

Davis then describes herself and the marchers as "agents of history" and that history cannot be erased or "deleted." She invokes the indigenous, Native American possession of the land on which Washington, D.C. is located. Davis then draws a parallel between the centuries-long resistance of Native American groups to White American encroachment on land and resources and the goals and persistence of the marchers. Davis also takes this opportunity to recognize the efforts of the Standing Rock Sioux who had been protesting—both on the scene and through the court system—the construction of the Dakota Access oil pipeline as a danger to their religious sites as well as their drinking water supply.

In the third paragraph, Davis uses the rallying cry of the Black Lives Matter movement, which emerged in 2013 after George Zimmerman was acquitted in the death of Trayvon Martin, as a reminder that the United States has its roots in "slavery and colonialism" and explains that the history of the country "is a history of immigration and enslavement." Building on this theme of immigration, she asserts that "Spreading xenophobia, hurling accusations of murder and rape and building walls will not erase history." This is a reference to several comments and proposals from Donald Trump during the 2016 Presidential campaign, in which he alleged that immigrants—particularly from Mexico—were rapists and murders and his pledge to build "a wall" to prevent further illicit immigration. Her next statement, that human beings are not "illegal" is a broader condemnation of anti-immigration sentiment in the United States.

Davis then, again broadening the scope of the activism she sees represented by those marching and the causes for which they stand, addresses environmental concerns such as climate change but also narrower environmental concerns. She again mentions the Standing Rock protest, but also invokes the water crisis in Flint, Michigan where government mismanagement led to water contaminated with lead and other harmful substances. Her water concerns—which are also political issues—extend to issues of water access in Gaza and the West Bank, part of the ongoing Israeli-Palestinian conflict. In the next paragraph, Davis discusses the "inclusive and intersectional" nature of the feminism represented at the march; a feminism that recognizes the connections between feminism and racism as well as other issues.

She goes on to address issues of economic equality, such as the drive to raise the federal minimum wage, opposition to corporate profiteering—including that going in the health care sector. Davis then adds to the abuses the marchers will resist, scubas violent attacks on immigrants and the disabled. She also condemns the police and prison structures of the United States and promotes continued resistance to violence based on gender. She speaks to issues of gender and violence outside the United States, calling for "freedom and justice" for Palestine. She praises the release of Chelsea Manning (a transgender women convicted by court-martial in 2013 of violating the Espionage Act, and Oscar López Rivera, the Puerto Rican independence activist convicted of seditious conspiracy in 1981. Davis urges the release of others in prison for controversial, politically-charged reasons such as American Indian Movement activist Leonard Peltier and African American activists Mumia Abu-Jamal and Assata Shakur.

Davis closes her speech by calling for an intensification of protest and foresees an increased militancy as well. She declares that the entirety of the Trump administration will be focused on resistance in all areas of American life, culture, and society.

Essential Themes
In her 2017 speech to the Women's March on Washington, Angela Davis highlights the persistent and important theme that the march, as well as the resistance to the ideology and goals of the incoming Trump administration that the march symbolizes, is not a fight only by and for women. The march, rather, represents a wide array of progressive causes. This connection between feminism and other struggles, such as those against racism, economic inequality, homophobia or other is what Davis means when she discusses the feminism presented at the march as being "inclusive and intersectional." As discussed in "Defining Moment," above, the concerns of women in the face of the challenges presented by the Trump administration in areas such as reproductive rights, access to medical care, and economic equality, including the gender gap in pay, hiring, and benefits are central to the march organizers. Other issues of social justice, however, are also part of the unifying principles behind the march. Davis takes the opportunity bring the marchers' (and the world's) attention to a number of social justice issues that focused not only on gender but also on economic equality. Discussing causes like a $15 minimum wage, concerns about urban gentrification, and "billionaire mortgage profiteers" is in keeping with Davis's long-standing concerns, reaching back to the 1960s and 1970s as well.

—Aaron Gulyas, MA

Bibliography and Further Reading
Bhavnani, Kum-Kum, and Angela Y. Davis. "Complexity, Activism, Optimism: An Interview with Angela Y. Davis." *Feminist Review*, no. 31, 1989, pp. 66–81.

Davis, Angela Y. *Angela Davis: An Autobiography* (New York: International Publishers, 2013).

—— Freedom Is a Constant Struggle: Ferguson, Palestine, and the Foundations of a Movement (Chicago: Haymarket Books, 2016).

Ferree, Myra Marx and Alli Mari Tripp, eds., *Global Feminism: Transnational Women's Activism, Organizing, and Human Rights* (New York: New York University Press, 2006).

"Mission and Vision," Women's March on Washington https://www.womensmarch.com/mission/

"Unity Principles," Women's March on Washington https://www.womensmarch.com/principles/

POLITICAL AND SOCIAL PROTEST

"Political and social protest" is a vast category of American dissent and the documents in this section stretch from the late nineteenth century to the late twentieth. Despite the wide range of topics these documents address and the broad timeline they inhabit, they share a common target. These documents all, in one way or another, express opposition to entrenched political and social forces, economic and cultural paradigms that threaten (or are perceived to threaten) the wellbeing or livelihood of a great number of Americans for the unfair benefit of others.

During the late nineteenth century, as the so-called Gilded Age was drawing to a close and an era of "Progressive" organizations, movements and activists began to dawn, investigative journalists, writers, artists, photographers, and speakers used the newspapers, magazines, and other publishing outlets of the day to expose the victimization, abuse, or neglect of American urban society's most vulnerable members. Nellie Bly's *Ten Days in a Mad-House* presented a horrifying vision of women's lives in insane asylums while the photography and writing of Jacob Riis presented Americans with insight into *How the Other Half Lives*. Other writers and activists presented their ideas for solving these and other social crises. Jane Addams presents "The Subjective Necessity for Social Settlements" Labor leaders Samuel Gompers and Eugene V. Debs offer complementary but distinct visions of labor activism in the rapidly growing and industrializing United States. Closing out the nineteenth century, Democratic and Populist Presidential candidate William Jennings Bryan, in his Cross of Gold speech from the 1896 Democratic Party Convention advocates for the vitality of a rural, agrarian America and urges the adoption of radical financial policies that would benefit the workers on farms as well as in factories.

The 1930s, an era of economic disaster in the form of the Great Depression as well as untried and unprecedented actions by the federal government to reform broken financial systems and restore economic prosperity saw dissent and activism by those who believe the actions taken did not go far enough. Labor activist Walter Reuther provides his account of the 1933 Auto Workers Strike against Detroit's Briggs Manufacturing Company. Louisiana politician Huey Long, in his Share the Wealth Address, boldly calls for the wide scale retribution of wealth, promoting the goal of economic equality and long-term stability and prosperity. The work of labor activists is revisited at the end of the section with the 1984 Commonwealth Address by United Farm Workers leader César Chávez.

The political and social upheavals of the 1960s and early 1970s were not limited to protests against the ongoing war in Vietnam. The Port Huron Statement of the Students for a Democratic Society, originally presented in 1962, Tom Hayden's manifesto updated progressive politics for the new generation of Americans that came of age in the depth of the Cold War, striking out against economic inequality, racism and the conformity-imposing establishment of the time. The civil rights revolution that began with African-Americans in the 1950s, that informed the new Women's movement and revitalized Native American activism in the 1960s also spread to the gay and lesbian community during the decade. Gay Power Comes to Sheridan Square, Lucian Truscott's 1969 account of the Stonewall Riots in New York City, demonstrates that the goal of "power" as well as equality typified protest and dissent in the post-war era. An excerpt from Abbie Hoffman's *Steal This Book* gives us a glimpse into the street-level manifestation of fighting the establishment, with instructions and guidance for making one's way in the world at the expense of the government and corporations that had been exploiting the people for decades.

Two of the documents in this section come from a conservative, even reactionary, point of view. Senator Henry Cabot Lodge's 1919 Speech Opposing the

League of Nations was an emphatic effort to apply the brakes to the surge of internationalism that typified the Wilson administration's approach to foreign affairs. The Southern Manifesto, the 1956 declaration signed by dozens of Congressmen and Senators from the American south, threw down the gauntlet of opposition to what they saw as unprecedented and unwarranted federal interference as a result of the Supreme Court's order to desegregate public school in *Brown vs. Board of Education*.

Ten Days in a Mad-House

Date: 1887
Author: Nellie Bly
Genre: Book excerpt

Summary Overview

Nellie Bly's *Ten Days in a Mad-House* was published in book form in 1887, collecting her writing for the New York World newspaper. Bly's reporting was an audacious undercover operation in which she went undercover at the Women's Lunatic Asylum on Blackwell's Island in New York. *Ten Days in a Mad-House* told the story of Bly's successful attempt to convince fellow residents of a boarding house that she was mentally unbalanced, and then to keep up that presence throughout the process of being examined and committed to the asylum. Her investigation and reporting on what she experienced at the Women's Lunatic Asylum uncovered a remarkable range of abuse and neglect. It also revealed troubling stories of the ways in which women found themselves imprisoned in the asylum despite no discernible mental disorder. The excerpts presented here details some of those stories as well as Bly's account of her participation in a grand jury investigation into the conditions at the asylum.

Bly's account is emotional and moving but not melodramatic, and her determination that her efforts contribute to the attempts to correct the dangerous errors and abuses she experienced and witnessed place *Ten Days in a Mad-House* firmly in the emerging journalistic trend of muckraking and addressed issues not only the treatment of mental health disorders but also broader issues of women's legal and personal rights and liberties.

Defining Moment

Mental health treatment had been an ongoing concern of reformers in the United States and Europe throughout the nineteenth century. Psychology was, in many ways, in its infancy during this time and institutions like Bly investigated were not always staffed with experts who were fully informed about the latest treatments and standards of care. Reformer Dorothea Dix (1802-1887) had worked or the establishment of mental hospitals after witnessing mentally ill men and women imprisoned in jail as though they were criminals. The establishment of separate asylums, however, was not a cure-all. Social and legal issues surrounding mental illness complicated matters, with some states authorizing the commitment of women to insane asylums on the testimony of their husband or father, rather than on the judgment of a physician or psychologist.

Ten Days in a Mad-House is part of the "muck-raking" journalism tradition that became prominent in the late nineteenth and early twentieth centuries. These journalists worked to uncover corruption, unsafe working conditions and, as we see from Nellie Bly's work, abuses taking place within mental health facilities like the Women's Lunatic Asylum. One purpose for this exposure was to engender public support for reform of these institutions, and the improvement of the condition of those dependent on the services or employment provided by those institutions. Muck-raking journalism was, itself, part of the larger Progressive Movement, an umbrella term for an array of initiatives organized to reform institutions and to correct social ills. Investigative journalism, like Bly's, was one tool that reformers could use to persuade not only the public, as mentioned, but also elected officials to take action.

Author Biography

Journalist Nellie Bly was born Elizabeth Cochran on May 5, 1864 outside Pittsburgh, Pennsylvania. Later, Elizabeth and her family would move into the city in 1880. In 1884, she read a letter to the *Pittsburgh Dispatch* titled "What Girls are Good For," in which the author argued that women were fit only for motherhood and that a Chinese-inspired practice of killing infant girls would save them from their pointless futures." The letter inspired Elizabeth to write a response in which she argued that the condition of women—particularly working class women who struggled to support their families was due to deep-seated inequalities between men and women and that women should be granted opportunities that were in line with their abilities.

The letter earned her a job at the paper and it was here that she received her pen name, Nellie Bly. Bly applied her skills to topics such as conditions women faced in factory work, but editors reassigned her to topics that were considered more appropriate for women such as gardening and fashion writing. She left Pittsburgh working as a correspondent in Mexico—she was forced to leave when she was threatened with arrest for criticizing the dictatorial regime of Porfirio Diaz.

In 1887, Bly moved to New York City, eventually landing a position with the *New York World*. It was here that she was assigned to the undercover investigation of the Women's Lunatic Asylum. Her reports were published as *Ten Days in a Mad-House*. She followed that success with an attempt to travel around the world in less than eighty days, beating the fictional record established in Jules Verne's novel. She completed the trip in seventy-two days. After marrying Robert Seaman in 1895, she took a hiatus from journalism and became the president of her husband's company, Iron Clad Manufacturing Company. During this time she was granted several patents for inventions such as the stacking garbage can. During World War I, she returned to journalism, reporting from the Eastern Front. She died in 1922.

HISTORICAL DOCUMENT

Chapter I: A Delicate Mission

On the 22d of September I was asked by the *World* if I could have myself committed to one of the asylums for the insane in New York, with a view to writing a plain and unvarnished narrative of the treatment of the patients therein and the methods of management, etc. Did I think I had the courage to go through such an ordeal as the mission would demand? Could I assume the characteristics of insanity to such a degree that I could pass the doctors, live for a week among the insane without the authorities there finding out that I was only a "chiel amang'em takin' notes?" I said I believed I could. I had some faith in my own ability as an actress and thought I could assume insanity long enough to accomplish any mission intrusted to me. Could I pass a week in the insane ward at Blackwell's Island? I said I could and I would. And I did.

My instructions were simply to go on with my work as soon as I felt that I was ready. I was to chronicle faithfully the experiences I underwent, and when once within the walls of the asylum to find out and describe its inside workings, which are always, so effectually hidden by white-capped nurses, as well as by bolts and bars, from the knowledge of the public. "We do not ask you to go there for the purpose of making sensational revelations. Write up things as you find them, good or bad; give praise or blame as you think best, and the truth all the time.... I went away to execute my delicate and, as I found out, difficult mission.

If I did get into the asylum, which I hardly hoped to do, I had no idea that my experiences would contain aught else than a simple tale of life in an asylum. That such an institution could be mismanaged, and that cruelties could exist 'neath its roof, I did not deem possible. I always had a desire to know asylum life more thoroughly—a desire to be convinced that the most helpless of God's creatures, the insane, were cared for kindly and properly. The many stories I had read of abuses in such institutions I had regarded as wildly exaggerated or else romances, yet there was a latent desire to know positively.

I shuddered to think how completely the insane were in the power of their keepers, and how one could weep and plead for release, and all of no avail, if the keepers were so minded. Eagerly I accepted the mission to learn the inside workings of the Blackwell Island Insane Asylum....

I succeeded in getting committed to the insane ward at Blackwell's Island, where I spent ten days and nights and had an experience which I shall never forget. I took upon myself to enact the part of a poor, unfortunate crazy girl, and felt it my duty not to shirk any of the disagreeable results that should follow. I became one of the city's insane wards for that length of time, experienced much, and saw and heard more of the treatment accorded to this helpless class of our population, and when I had seen and heard enough, my release was promptly secured. I left the insane ward with pleasure and regret—pleasure that I was once more able to enjoy the free breath of heaven; regret that I could not have brought with me some of the unfortunate women who lived and suffered with me, and who, I am convinced, are just as sane as I was and am now myself.

But here let me say one thing: From the moment I entered the insane ward on the Island, I made no attempt to keep up the assumed role of insanity. I talked and acted just as I do in ordinary life. Yet strange to say, the more sanely I talked and acted the crazier I was thought to be by all except one physician, whose kindness and gentle ways I shall not soon forget....

Chapter VIII: Inside the Madhouse

As the wagon was rapidly driven through the beautiful lawns up to the asylum my feelings of satisfaction at having attained the object of my work were greatly dampened by the look of distress on the faces of my companions. Poor women, they had no hopes of a speedy delivery. They were being driven to a prison, through no fault of their own, in all probability for life. In comparison, how much easier it would be to walk to the gallows than to this tomb of living horrors! On the wagon sped, and I, as well as my comrades, gave a despairing farewell glance at freedom as we came in sight of the long stone buildings. We passed one low building, and the stench was so horrible that I was compelled to hold my breath, and I mentally decided that it was the kitchen. I afterward found I was correct in my surmise, and smiled at the signboard at the end of the walk: "Visitors are not allowed on this road." I don't think the sign would be necessary if they once tried the road, especially on a warm day.

The wagon stopped, and the nurse and officer in charge told us to get out. The nurse added: "Thank God! they came quietly." We obeyed orders to go ahead up a flight of narrow, stone steps, which had evidently been built for the accommodation of people who climb stairs three at a time. I wondered if my companions knew where we were, so I said to Miss Tillie Mayard:

"Where are we?"

"At the Blackwell's Island Lunatic Asylum," she answered, sadly.

"Are you crazy?" I asked.

"No," she replied; "but as we have been sent here we will have to be quiet until we find some means of escape. They will be few, though, if all the doctors, as Dr. Field, refuse to listen to me or give me a chance to prove my sanity." We were ushered into a narrow vestibule, and the door was locked behind us.

In spite of the knowledge of my sanity and the assurance that I would be released in a few days, my heart gave a sharp twinge. Pronounced insane by four expert doctors and shut up behind the unmerciful bolts and bars of a madhouse! Not to be confined alone, but to be a companion, day and night, of senseless, chattering lunatics; to sleep with them, to eat with them, to be considered one of them, was an uncomfortable position. Timidly we followed the nurse up the long uncarpeted hall to a room filled by so-called crazy women. We were told to sit down, and some of the patients kindly made room for us. They looked at us curiously, and one came up to me and asked:

"Who sent you here?"

"The doctors," I answered.

"What for?" she persisted.

"Well, they say I am insane," I admitted.

"Insane!" she repeated, incredulously. "It cannot be seen in your face."

This woman was too clever, I concluded, and was glad to answer the roughly given orders to follow the nurse to see the doctor. This nurse, Miss Grupe, by the way, had a nice German face, and if I had not detected certain hard lines about the mouth I might have expected, as did my companions, to receive but kindness from her. She left us in a small waiting-room at the end of the hall, and left us alone while she went into a small office opening into the sitting or receiving-room.

"I like to go down in the wagon," she said to the invisible party on the inside. "It helps to break up the day." He answered her that the open air improved her looks, and she again appeared before us all smiles and simpers.

"Come here, Tillie Mayard," she said. Miss Mayard obeyed, and, though I could not see into the office, I could hear her gently but firmly pleading her case. All her remarks were as rational as any I ever heard, and I thought no good physician could help but be impressed with her story. She told of her recent illness, that she was suffering from nervous debility. She begged that they try all their tests for insanity, if they had any, and give her justice. Poor girl, how my heart ached for her! I determined then and there that I would try by every means to make my mission of benefit to my suffering sisters; that I would show how they are committed without ample trial. Without one word of sympathy or encouragement she was brought back to where we sat.

Mrs. Louise Schanz was taken into the presence of Dr. Kinier, the medical man.

"Your name?" he asked, loudly. She answered in German, saying she did not speak English nor could she understand it. However, when he said Mrs. Louise Schanz, she said "Yah, yah." Then he tried other questions, and when he found she could not understand one world of English, he said to Miss Grupe:

"You are German; speak to her for me."

Miss Grupe proved to be one of those people who are ashamed of their nationality, and she refused, saying she could understand but few worlds of her mother tongue.

"You know you speak German. Ask this woman what her husband does," and they both laughed as if they were enjoying a joke.

"I can't speak but a few words," she protested, but at last she managed to ascertain the occupation of Mr. Schanz.

"Now, what was the use of lying to me?" asked the doctor, with a laugh which dispelled the rudeness.

"I can't speak any more," she said, and she did not.

Thus was Mrs. Louise Schanz consigned to the asylum without a chance of making herself understood. Can such carelessness be excused, I wonder, when it is so easy to get an interpreter? If the confinement was but for a few days one might question the necessity. But here was a woman taken without her own consent from the free world to an asylum and there given no chance to prove her sanity. Confined most probably for life behind asylum bars, without even being told in her language the why and wherefore. Compare this with a criminal, who is given every chance to prove his innocence. Who would not rather be a murderer and take the chance for life than be declared insane, without hope of escape? Mrs. Schanz begged in German to know where she was, and pleaded for liberty. Her voice broken by sobs, she was led unheard out to us.

Mrs. Fox was then put through this weak, trifling examination and brought from the office, convicted. Miss Annie Neville took her turn, and I was again left to the last. I had by this time determined to act as I do when free, except that I would refuse to tell who I was or where my home was....

Chapter XII: Promenading with Lunatics

I shall never forget my first walk. When all the patients had donned the white straw hats, such as bathers wear at Coney Island, I could not but laugh at their comical appearances. I could not distinguish one woman from another. I lost Miss Neville, and had to take my hat off and search for her. When we met we put our hats on and laughed at one another. Two by two we formed in line, and guarded by the attendants we went out a back way on to the walks.

We had not gone many paces when I saw, proceeding from every walk, long lines of women guarded by nurses. How many there were! Every way I looked I could see them in the queer dresses, comical straw hats and shawls, marching slowly around. I eagerly watched the passing lines and a thrill of horror crept over me at the sight. Vacant eyes and meaningless faces, and their tongues uttered meaningless nonsense. One crowd passed and I noted by nose as well as eyes, that they were fearfully dirty.

"Who are they?" I asked of a patient near me.

"They are considered the most violent on the island," she replied. "They are from the Lodge, the first building with the high steps." Some were yelling, some were cursing, others were singing or praying or preaching, as the fancy struck them, and they made up the most miserable collection of humanity I had ever seen. As the din of their passing faded in the distance there came another sight I can never forget:

A long cable rope fastened to wide leather belts, and these belts locked around the waists of fifty-two women. At the end of the rope was a heavy iron cart, and in it two women—one nursing a sore foot, another screaming at some nurse, saying: "You beat me and I shall not forget it. You want to kill me," and then she would sob and cry. The women "on the rope," as the patients call it, were each busy on their individual freaks. Some were yelling all the while. One who had blue eyes saw me look at her, and she turned as far as she could, talking and smiling, with that terrible, horrifying look of absolute insanity stamped on her. The doctors might safely judge on her case. The horror of that sight to one who had never been near an insane person before, was something unspeakable.

"God help them!" breathed Miss Neville. "It is so dreadful I cannot look."

On they passed, but for their places to be filled by more. Can you imagine the sight? According to one of the physicians there are 1600 insane women on Blackwell's Island.

Mad! what can be half so horrible? My heart thrilled with pity when I looked on old, gray-haired women talking aimlessly to space. One woman had on a straightjacket, and two women had to drag her along. Crippled, blind, old, young, homely, and pretty; one senseless mass of humanity. No fate could be worse.

I looked at the pretty lawns, which I had once thought was such a comfort to the poor creatures confined on the Island, and laughed at my own notions. What enjoyment is it to them? They are not allowed on the grass–it is only to look at. I saw some patients eagerly and caressingly lift a nut or a colored leaf that had fallen on the path. But they were not permitted to keep them. The nurses would always compel them to throw their little bit of God's comfort away.

As I passed a low pavilion, where a crowd of helpless lunatics were confined, I read a motto on the wall, "While I live I hope." The absurdity of it struck me forcibly. I would have liked to put above the gates that open to the asylum, "He who enters here leaveth hope behind."…

It was not long until the dinner hour arrived and I was so hungry that I felt I could eat anything. The same old story of standing for a half and three-quarters of an hour in the hall was repeated before we got down to our dinners. The bowls in which we had had our tea were now filled with soup, and on a plate was one cold boiled potato and a chunk of beef, which on investigation, proved to be slightly spoiled. There were no knives or forks, and the patients looked fairly savage as they took the tough beef in their fingers and pulled in opposition to their teeth. Those toothless or with poor teeth could not eat it. One tablespoon was given for the soup, and a piece of bread was the final entree. Butter is never allowed at dinner nor coffee or tea. Miss Mayard could not eat, and I saw many of the sick ones turn away in disgust. I was getting very weak from the want of food and tried to eat a slice of bread. After the first few bites hunger asserted itself, and I was able to eat all but the crusts of the one slice.…

I have described my first day in the asylum, and as my other nine were exactly the same in the general run of things it would be tiresome to tell about each. In giving this story I expect to be contradicted by many who are exposed. I merely tell in common words, without exaggeration, of my life in a mad-house for ten days. The eating was one of the most horrible things. Excepting the first two days after I entered the asylum, there was no salt for the food. The hungry and even famishing women made an attempt to eat the horrible messes. Mustard and vinegar were put on meat and in soup to give it a taste, but it only helped to make it worse. Even that was all consumed after two days, and the patients had to try to choke down fresh fish, just boiled in water, without salt, pepper or butter; mutton, beef and potatoes without the faintest seasoning. The most insane refused to swallow the food and were threatened with punishment. In our short walks we passed the kitchen were food was prepared for the nurses and doctors. There we got glimpses of melons and grapes and all kinds of fruits, beautiful white bread and nice meats, and the hungry feeling would be increased tenfold. I spoke to some of the physicians, but it had no effect, and when I was taken away the food was yet unsalted.

My heart ached to see the sick patients grow sicker over the table. I saw Miss Tillie Mayard so suddenly overcome at a bite that she had to rush from the dining-room and then got a scolding for doing so. When the patients complained of the food they were told to shut up; that they would not have as good if they were at home, and that it was too good for charity patients.…

Chapter XIV: Some Unfortunate Stories

…

There is a Frenchwoman confined in hall 6, or was during my stay, whom I firmly believe to be perfectly sane. I watched her and talked with her every day, excepting the last three, and I was unable to find any delusion or mania in her. Her name is Josephine Despreau, if that is spelled correctly, and her husband and all her friends are in France. Josephine feels her position keenly. Her lips tremble, and she breaks down crying when she talks of her helpless condition. "How did you get here?" I asked.

"One morning as I was trying to get breakfast I grew deathly sick, and two officers were called in by the woman of the house, and I was taken to the station-house. I was unable to understand their proceedings, and they paid little attention to my story. Doings in this country were new to me, and before I realized it I was lodged as an insane woman in this asylum. When I first came I cried that I was here without hope of release, and for crying Miss Grady and her assistants choked me until they hurt my throat, for it has been sore ever since."

A pretty young Hebrew woman spoke so little English I could not get her story except as told by the nurses. They said her name is Sarah Fishbaum, and that her husband put her in the asylum because she had a fondness for other men than himself....

I had been watching and talking with a fair-complexioned woman for several days, and I was at a loss to see why she had been sent there, she was so sane.

"Why did you come here?" I asked her one day, after we had indulged in a long conversation.

"I was sick," she replied.

"Are you sick mentally?" I urged.

"Oh, no; what gave you such an idea? I had been overworking myself, and I broke down. Having some family trouble, and being penniless and nowhere to go, I applied to the commissioners to be sent to the poorhouse until I would be able to go to work."

"But they do not send poor people here unless they are insane," I said. "Don't you know there are only insane women, or those supposed to be so, sent here?"

"I knew after I got here that the majority of these women were insane, but then I believed them when they told me this was the place they sent all the poor who applied for aid as I had done."

"How have you been treated?" I asked. "Well, so far I have escaped a beating, although I have been sickened at the sight of many and the recital of more. When I was brought here they went to give me a bath, and the very disease for which I needed doctoring and from which I was suffering made it necessary that I should not bathe. But they put me in, and my sufferings were increased greatly for weeks thereafter."...

At first I could not sleep and did not want to so long as I could hear anything new. The night nurses may have complained of the fact. At any rate one night they came in and tried to make me take a dose of some mixture out of a glass "to make me sleep," they said. I told them I would do nothing of the sort and they left me, I hoped, for the night. My hopes were vain, for in a few minutes they returned with a doctor, the same that received us on our arrival. He insisted that I take it, but I was determined not to lose my wits even for a few hours. When he saw that I was not to be coaxed he grew rather rough, and said he had wasted too much time with me already. That if I did not take it he would put it into my arm with a needle. It occurred to me that if he put it into my arm I could not get rid of it, but if I swallowed it there was one hope, so I said I would take it. I smelt it and it smelt like laudanum, and it was a horrible dose. No sooner had they left the room and locked me in than I tried so see how far down my throat my finger would go, and the chloral was allowed to try its effect elsewhere....

Once a week the patients are given a bath, and that is the only time they see soap. A patient handed me a piece of soap one day about the size of a thimble, I considered it a great compliment in her wanting to be kind, but I thought she would appreciate the cheap soap more than I, so I thanked her but refused to take it. On bathing day the tub is filled with water, and the patients are washed, one after the other, without a change of water. This is done until the water is really thick, and then it is allowed to run out and the tub is refilled without being washed. The same towels are used on all the women, those with eruptions as well as those without. The healthy patients fight for a change of water, but they are compelled to submit to the dictates of the lazy, tyrannical nurses. The dresses are seldom changed oftener than once a month. If the patient has a visitor, I have seen the nurses hurry her out and change her dress before the visitor comes in. This keeps up the appearance of careful and good management.

The patients who are not able to take care of themselves get into beastly conditions, and the nurses never look after them, but order some of the patients to do so....

I made the acquaintance of Bridget McGuinness, who seems to be sane at the present time. She said she was sent to Retreat 4, and put on the "rope gang."

"The beating I got there were something dreadful. I was pulled around by the hair, held under the water until I strangled, and I was choked and kicked. The nurses would always keep a quiet patient stationed at the window to tell them when any of the doctors were approaching. It was hopeless to complain to the doctors, for they always said it was the imagination of our diseased brains, and besides we would get another beating for telling. They would hold patients under the water and threaten to leave them to die there if they did not promise not to tell the doctors. We would all promise, because we knew the doctors would not help us, and we would do anything to escape the punishment. After breaking a window I was transferred to the Lodge, the worst place on the island. It is dreadfully dirty in there, and the stench is awful. In the summer the flies swarm the place. The food is worse than we get in other wards and we are given only tin plates. Instead of the bars being on the outside, as in this ward, they are on the inside. There are many quiet patients there who have been there for years, but the nurses keep them to do the work. Among other beating I got there, the nurses jumped on me once and broke two of my ribs.

"While I was there a pretty young girl was brought in. She had been sick, and she fought against being put in that dirty place. One night the nurses took her and, after beating her, they held her naked in a cold bath, then they threw her on her bed. When morning came the girl was dead. The doctors said she died of convulsions, and that was all that was done about it.

"They inject so much morphine and chloral that the patients are made crazy. I have seen the patients wild for water from the effect of the drugs, and the nurses would refuse it to them. I have heard women beg for a whole night for one drop and it was not given them. I myself cried for water until my mouth was so parched and dry that I could not speak."...

Chapter XVII: The Grand Jury Investigation

Soon after I had bidden farewell to the Blackwell's Island Insane Asylum, I was summoned to appear before the Grand Jury. I answered the summons with pleasure, because I longed to help those of God's most unfortunate children whom I had left prisoners behind me. If I could not bring them that boon of all boons, liberty, I hoped at least to influence others to make life more bearable for them. I found the jurors to be gentlemen, and that I need not tremble before their twenty-three august presences.

I swore to the truth of my story, and then I related all—from my start at the Temporary Home until my release. Assistant District-Attorney Vernon M. Davis conducted the examination. The jurors then requested that I should accompany them on a visit to the Island. I was glad to consent.

No one was expected to know of the contemplated trip to the Island, yet we had not been there very long before one of the commissioners of charity and Dr. MacDonald, of Ward's Island, were with us. One of the jurors told me that in conversation with a man about the asylum, he heard that they were notified of our coming an hour before we reached the Island. This must have been done while the Grand Jury were examining the insane pavilion at Bellevue.

The trip to the island was vastly different to my first. This time we went on a clean new boat, while the one I had traveled in, they said, was laid up for repairs.

Some of the nurses were examined by the jury, and made contradictory statements to one another, as well as to my story. They confessed that the jury's contemplated visit had been talked over between them and the doctor. Dr. Dent confessed that he had no means by which to tell positively if the bath was cold and of the number of women put into the same water. He knew the food was not what it should be, but said it was due to the lack of funds.

If nurses were cruel to their patients, had he any positive means of ascertaining it? No, he had not. He said all the doctors were not competent, which was also due to the lack of means to secure good medical men. In the conversation with me, he said:

"I am glad you did this now, and had I known your purpose, I would have aided you. We have no means of learning the way things are going except to do as you did. Since your story was published I found a nurse at the Retreat who had watches set for our approach, just as you had stated. She was dismissed."

Miss Anne Neville was brought down, and I went into the hall to meet her, knowing that the sight of so many strange gentlemen would excite her, even if she be sane. It was as I feared. The attendants had told her she was going to be examined by a crowd of men, and she was shaking with fear. Although I had left her only two weeks before, yet she looked as if she had suffered a severe illness, in that time, so changed was her appearance. I asked her if she had taken any medicine, and she answered in the affirmative. I then told her that all I wanted her to do was tell the jury all we had done since I was brought with her to the asylum, so they would be convinced that I was sane. She only knew me as Miss Nellie Brown, and was wholly ignorant of my story.

She was not sworn, but her story must have convinced all hearers of the truth of my statements.

"When Miss Brown and I were brought here the nurses were cruel and the food was too bad to eat. We did not have enough clothing, and Miss Brown asked for more all the time. I thought she was very kind, for when a doctor promised her some clothing she said she would give it to me. Strange to say, ever since Miss Brown has been taken away everything is different. The nurses are very kind and we are given plenty to wear. The doctors come to see us often and the food is greatly improved."

Did we need more evidence?

The jurors then visited the kitchen. It was very clean, and two barrels of salt stood conspicuously open near the door! The bread on exhibition was beautifully white and wholly unlike what was given us to eat.

We found the halls in the finest order. The beds were improved, and in hall 7 the buckets in which we were compelled to wash had been replaced by bright new basins.

The institution was on exhibition, and no fault could be found.

But the women I had spoken of, where were they? Not one was to be found where I had left them. If my assertions were not true in regard to these patients, why should the latter be changed, so to make me unable to find them? Miss Neville complained before the jury of being changed several times. When we visited the hall later she was returned to her old place.

Mary Hughes, of whom I had spoken as appearing sane, was not to be found. Some relatives had taken her away. Where, they knew not. The fair woman I spoke of, who had been sent here because she was poor, they said had been transferred to another island. They denied all knowledge of the Mexican woman, and said there never had been such a patient. Mrs. Cotter had been discharged, and Bridget McGuinness and Rebecca Farron had been transferred to other quarters. The German girl, Margaret, was not to be found, and Louise had been sent elsewhere from hall 6. The Frenchwoman, Josephine, a great, healthy woman, they said was dying of paralysis, and we could not see her. If I was wrong in my judgment of these patients' sanity, why was all this done? I saw Tillie Mayard, and she had changed so much for the worse that I shuddered when I looked at her.

I hardly expected the grand jury to sustain me, after they saw everything different from what it had been while I was there. Yet they did, and their report to the court advises all the changes made that I had proposed.

I have one consolation for my work—on the strength of my story the committee of appropriation provides $1,000,000 more than was ever before given, for the benefit of the insane.

GLOSSARY

"a chiel amang'em": child among them

aught: anything

chloral: chloral hydrate, a drug used as a sedative

consolation: comfort

laudanum: medication containing opium

Document Analysis
Chapter I: A Delicate Mission

In Chapter I, "A Delicate Mission," Bly explains how she came to going undercover in the asylum and conveys the sense that her editors were skeptical of her ability to carry out the assignment. Her job was to report things accurately rather than sensationally. Bly describes how she acted "he part of a poor, unfortunate crazy girl" to gain entry into Blackwell's Island Insane Asylum but emphasizes that once she entered the asylum she did not keep up the pretense of mental illness.

Chapter VII, "Inside the Madhouse," begins with Bly recounting her conversation with Tillie Mayard, who was committed to the asylum despite having no discernible illness. Bly recounts Maynard's attempts to convict asylum officials that she had suffered from a physical ailment rather than a psychological one. Her struggle inspires Bly to use her reporting to ultimately help the women in the asylum if possible. Bly also tells the story of Louise Schanz, who could not respond to the questions because she spoke no English. Bly makes the point that a suspect in a criminal investigation would be give far more opportunity to defend him or herself than those sent to the asylum.

Bly provides a survey of the types of patients and the circumstances that brought them to (and kept them confined in) the asylum in Chapter XIV, "Some Unfortunate Stories." Josephine Despreau was sick. Her landlady called the police who transported her to the asylum. When she wept at her situation, she was choked until she stopped. Sarah Fishbaum's husband had her committed because he suspected her of infidelity. Another woman was committed because of her poverty and told the asylum "was the place they sent all the poor who applied for aid."

Bly also, in this chapter, describes her difficulties in sleeping (as well as her attempts to stay awake to gather information for her investigation). Nurses tried to drug her, but Bly was able to surreptitiously vomit up the sedative when the medical personnel had left. She describes the baths available, with cold water reused by multiple patients and insufficient soap. Clean clothing only appears once a month, unless the patient has a visitor—then she gets a clean dress. The nurses force patients to take care of women who were not able to care for themselves.

She talks to Bridget McGuinness who describes the physical abuse she suffered at the hands of the nurses, including choking and drowning. If the women complained, they would be told what they experienced was their imaginations. McGuinness also relates a story of a young girl who had brought in, beaten by the nurses and put in a cold bath. She died with no repercussions for any personnel involved. McGuinness claims that the drugs used in the asylum induce insanity and that patients are denied water.

The final chapter presented here, "The Grand Jury Investigation," details Bly's involvement in the wider investigation of conditions in the asylum. She testifies before a grand jury and accompanies them on an inspection of the asylum. Despite the trip being deemed a secret, officials at Blackwell's Island had been notified. Bly notes that the boat taken to the island was much cleaner than the one she had travelled on as a patient. The nurses, when questioned, gave conflicting stories both to each other and to Bly's testimony as well. They also acknowledged that they had talked to the doctors about the impending jury visit. One doctor claimed he had no way to tell how cold the bath water was, or how often it had been used. The food, he admitted, was bad but all the asylum could afford.

The jurors heard testimony from asylum patients and Bly describes how the asylum was "on exhibition": it had been cleaned and brought into line with optimal conditions. The women Bly had met during her stay were missing from the asylum before the jury's visit. Bly asserts that the transfer of these patients was proof that her claims about conditions and those women's stories had been true. Bly closes by ruefully relating that, if nothing else, her story had led to an increasing in the money granted "for the benefit of the insane."

Essential Themes
One of the most important issues that emerges in these excerpts from Bly's account is the incredible lack of agency, or control over their own lives and situations, that women experienced in the nineteenth century United States. While the lack of scrutiny of the patients who were committed to the asylum comes through in a number of the stories that Bly tells here, most striking are those in which women have been placed in the asylum for reasons that are profoundly unrelated to mental or physical health. Sarah Fishbaum, whose husband had her committed for having "a fondness for other men than himself" and Louise

Schanz, who could find no one who understood her German speech are just two of examples of the casual manner in which women's own will and words counted for very little in this world.

That fact makes Bly's own words and actions in attempting to bring public attention to the plight of women in the asylum all the more striking. While only a woman could have been given the job of infiltrating a woman's asylum, Bly's investigative skill and deft use of language presented here not only affected those who read the account of her investigation but also, to however slight a degree, influenced attempts to improve the conditions of treatment for those suffering from mental illness.

———*Aaron Gulyas, MA*

Bibliography and Additional Reading

Gamwell, Lynn and Nancy Tomes. Madness in America: Cultural and Medical Perceptions of Mental Illness Before 1914 (Ithaca, New York: Cornell University Press, 1995).

Grob, Gerald N. *Mental Illness and American Society: 1875-1940* (Princeton: Princeton University Press, 1987).

Kroeger, Brooke. *Nelly Bly: Daredevil, Reporter, Feminist* (New York: Crown, 1994).

Lutes, Jean Marie. Front-Page Girls: Women Journalists in American Culture and Fiction, 1880–1930 (Ithaca, New York: Cornell University Press, 2007).

Yanni, Carla. *The Architecture of Madness: Insane Asylums in the United States.* (Minneapolis: University of Minnesota Press, 2007).

How the Other Half Lives

Date: 1890
Author: Jacob Riis
Genre: Book chapter

Summary Overview

How the Other Half Lives: Studies among the Tenements of New York was published in 1890. The book shocked the conscience of Americans by showing in vivid detail the slum conditions of the Lower East Side of Manhattan, where Jewish, Bohemian, German, Italian, Chinese, and Irish immigrants were packed into tenements, many of them with no windows or ventilation, and waged a daily battle against overcrowding, crime, disease, filth, and poverty.

Riis's book was not merely a compendium of horror stories and heart-rending photographs. In the excerpts presented here, Riis does two things. The first is to provide a detailed history of working class housing in New York City, tracing the current problems back to the dawn of the American nation. He also discusses the current housing problems facing workers in New York City and the tenement system that developed to address it. The first of the chapters presented here closes with statistics on health issues in tenement buildings and an examination of the rapidly rising rents required of those who live in tenement rooms. Chapter 25, also produced here, details a number of solutions for the housing crisis that would improve the living conditions of those in the tenements as well as provide ports for those who undertake to build new housing.

Defining Moment

A number of developments enabled Riis's book—and Riis himself, later a confidant of President Theodore Roosevelt—to achieve prominence. One was technological. Riis was among the earliest journalists to take flash photographs, using a mixture of magnesium and potassium chlorate powder. Without this early kind of "flash bulb," developed in Germany in 1887, Riis would not have been able to illuminate the darkened, airless corridors and rooms of the slum tenements he visited, often at night.

The other developments were social. Of particular importance was the Progressive movement, which began as a social movement in the late nineteenth century and would evolve into a political movement in the early twentieth. The movement was a response to various factors, including the immense number of immigrants to the United States and the nation's rapid industrialization after the Civil War. Progressives attacked social ills—child labor, sweatshops, grinding poverty, racism, income inequality, corporate malfeasance, disease, ignorance—on many fronts. One was journalism, and during the late nineteenth century numerous writers began to document social and economic conditions that made the lives of the poor—particularly the urban poor—a misery. In time, the efforts of these journalists, later called "muckrakers," would lead to legislation designed to correct some of the social ills they witnessed. The growth of tenement housing, and the overcrowded, unhealthy, and hazardous conditions that soon typified them were a prime example of the type of damaging social change progressive reformers and their allies in the press targeted.

In *How the Other Half Lives*, Jacob Riis exposed tenement conditions in New York City. They book came out in subsequent editions and remained something of a best-seller.

Author Biography

Jacob Riis was born in Denmark in 1849. He was forced to move to the United States in 1870, at the age of 21, in order to find work. His first months in the US were difficult, moving from job to job. He, occasionally quit jobs during this time, attempting to enlist to fight against Prussia in the Franco-Prussian war, but he was unsuccessful. His poverty deepened as he was unable to find work. He was homeless, surviving on food scavenged from restaurants and garbage. Eventually, making his way to Philadelphia, Riis was taken in by the Danish Consul. The Consul found Riis work in Pennsylvania and, in his spare time, Riis began to write. His attempts to get his writing published were initially unsuccessful, he was able to make a good living selling flatirons.

His financial fortunes declined again, however, and Riis moved back to New York City, where his writing career started to blossom. He began with sporadic reporting assignments and, eventually, became the editor of a

How the Other Half Lives

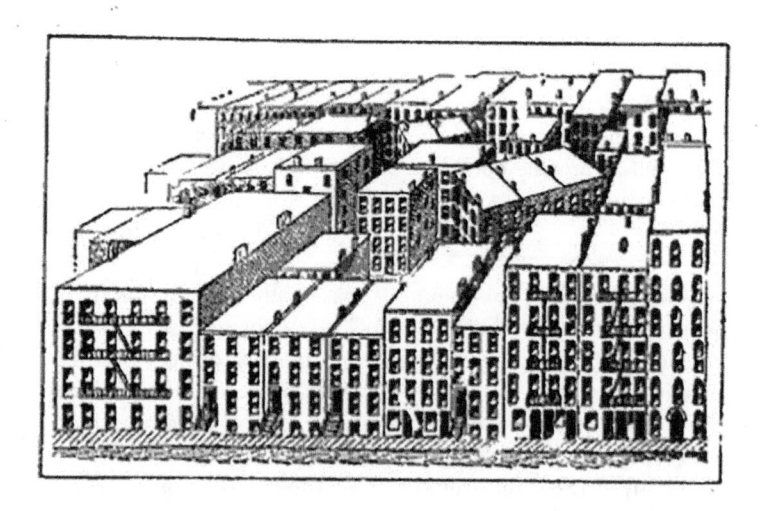

By Jacob A. Riis

weekly newspaper, which he purchased when it came into financial difficulty. He turned the paper, called the News, from a paper sponsored and controlled by politicians into a publication that scrutinized those politicians. Eventually, those same politicians bought the paper back from Riis and he made a handsome profit.

Riis then became a police reporter and, as a result, soon became exposed the the dangerous, impoverished New York City street life that would occupy much of his future writing and work. Exposed to the most poverty-stricken areas of the city. He began, also, to experiment with photography, especially some of the earliest uses of flash photography. With his photographs of the poverty of the city, Riis began to deliver public lectures, partnering with a public health official, W. L. Craig. From here, Riis penned an article, "How the Other Half Lives" in 1889 for Scribner's Magazine. Riis expanded this article into a book in 1890. Other books followed, including an autobiography in 1901. He died in 1914.

HISTORICAL DOCUMENT

CHAPTER I: GENESIS OF THE TENEMENT

THE first tenement New York knew bore the mark of Cain from its birth, though a generation passed before the waiting was deciphered. It was the "rear house," infamous ever after in our city's history. There had been tenant-houses before, but they were not built for the purpose. Nothing would probably have shocked their original owners more than the idea of their harboring a promiscuous crowd; for they were the decorous homes of the old Knickerbockers, the proud aristocracy of Manhattan in the early days. It was the stir and bustle of trade, together with the tremendous immigration that followed upon the war of 1812 that dislodged them. In thirty-five years the city of less than a hundred thousand came to harbor half a million souls, for whom homes had to be found.

It was thus the dark bedroom, prolific of untold depravities, came into the world. It was destined to survive the old houses. In their new role, says the old report, eloquent in its indignant denunciation of "evils more destructive than wars," "they were not intended to last. Rents were fixed high enough to cover damage and abuse from this class, from whom nothing was expected, and the most was made of them while they lasted. Neatness, order, cleanliness, were never dreamed of in connection with the tenant-house system, as it spread its localities from year to year; while redress slovenliness, discontent, privation, and ignorance were left to work out their invariable results, until the entire premises reached the level of tenant-house dilapidation, containing, but sheltering not, the miserable hordes that crowded beneath smouldering, water-rotted roofs or burrowed among the rats of clammy cellars." Yet so illogical is human greed that, at a later day, when called to account, "the proprietors frequently urged the filthy habits of the tenants as an excuse for the condition of their property, utterly losing sight of the fact that it was the tolerance of those habits which was the real evil, and that for this they themselves were alone responsible."

Within the memory of men not yet in their prime, Washington had moved from his house on Cherry Hill as too far out of town to be easily reached. Now the old residents followed his example; but they moved in a different direction and for a different reason. Their comfortable dwellings in the once fashionable streets along the East River front fell into the hands of real-estate agents and boarding-house keepers; and here, says the report to the Legislature of 1857, when the evils engendered had excited just alarm, "in its beginning, the tenant-house became a real blessing to that class of industrious poor whose small earnings limited their expenses, and whose employment in workshops, stores, or about the warehouses and thoroughfares, render a near residence of much importance." Not for long, however. As business increased, and the city grew with rapid strides, the necessities of the poor became the opportunity of their wealthier neighbors, and the stamp was set upon the old houses, suddenly become valuable, which the best thought and effort of a later age has vainly struggled to efface. Their "large rooms were partitioned into several smaller ones, without regard to light or ventilation, the rate of rent being lower in proportion to space or height from the street; and they soon became filled from cellar to garret with a class of tenantry living from hand to mouth, loose in morals, improvident in habits, degraded, and squalid as beggary itself."

Still the pressure of the crowds did not abate, and in the old garden where the stolid Dutch burgher grew his tulips or early cabbages a rear house was built, generally of wood, two stories high at first. Presently it was carried up another story, and another. Where two families had lived ten moved in. The front house followed suit, if the brick walls were strong enough. The question was not always asked, judging from complaints made by a contemporary witness, that the old buildings were "often carried up to a great height without regard to the strength of the foundation walls." It was rent the owner was after; nothing was said in the contract about either the safety or the comfort of the tenants. The garden gate no longer swung on its rusty hinges. The shell-paved walk had become an alley; what the rear house had left of the garden, a "court." Plenty such are yet to be found in the Fourth Ward, with here and there one of the original rear tenements.

Worse was to follow. It was "soon perceived by estate owners and agents of property that a greater percentage of profits could be realized by the conversion of houses and blocks into barracks, and dividing their space into smaller proportions capable of containing human life within four walls....Blocks were rented of real estate owners, or 'purchased on time,' or taken in charge at a percentage, and held for under-letting." With the appearance of the middleman, wholly irresponsible, and utterly reckless and unrestrained, began the era of tenement building which turned out such blocks as Gotham Court, where, in one cholera epidemic that scarcely touched the clean wards, the tenants died at the rate of one hundred and ninety-five to the thousand of population; which forced the general mortality of the city up from 1 in 41.83 in 1815, to 1 in 27.33 in 1855, a year of unusual freedom from epidemic disease, and which wrung from the early organizers of the Health Department this wail: "There are numerous examples of tenement-houses in which are lodged several hundred people that have a pro rata allotment of ground area scarcely equal to two-square yards upon the city lot, court-yards and all included." The tenement-house population had swelled to half a million souls by that time, and on the East Side, in what is still the most densely populated district in all the world, China not excluded, it was packed at the rate of 290,000 to the square mile, a state of affairs wholly unexampled. The utmost cupidity of other lands and other days had never contrived to herd much more than half that number within the same space. The greatest crowding of Old London was at the rate of 175,816. Swine roamed the streets and gutters as their principal scavengers.

The death of a child in a tenement was registered at the Bureau of Vital Statistics as "plainly due to suffocation in the foul air of an unventilated apartment," and the Senators, who had come down from Albany to find out what was the matter with New York, reported that "there are annually cut off from the population by disease and death enough human beings to people a city, and enough human labor to sustain it." And yet experts had testified that, as compared with uptown, rents were from twenty-five to thirty per cent. higher in the worst slums of the lower wards, with such accommodations as were enjoyed, for instance, by a "family with boarders" in Cedar Street, who fed hogs in the Stellar that contained eight or ten loads of manure; or "one room 12 x 19 with five families living in it, comprising twenty persons of both sexes and all ages, with only two beds, without partition, screen, chair, or table." The rate of rent has been successfully maintained to the present day, though the hog at least has been eliminated.

Lest anybody flatter himself with the notion that these were evils of a day that is happily past and may safely be forgotten, let me mention here three very recent instances of tenement-house life that came under my notice. One was the burning of a rear house in Mott Street, from appearances one of the original tenant-houses that made their owners rich. The fire made homeless ten families, who had paid an average of $5 a month for their mean little cubby-holes. The owner himself told me that it was fully insured for $800, though it brought him in $600 a year rent. He evidently considered himself especially entitled to be pitied for losing such valuable property. Another was the case of a hard-working family of man and wife, young people from the old country, who took poison together in a Crosby Street tenement because they were "tired." There was no other explanation, and none was needed when I stood in the room in which they had lived. It was in the attic with sloping ceiling and a single window so far out on the roof that it seemed not to belong to the place at all. With scarcely room enough to turn around in they had been compelled to pay five dollars and a half a month in advance. There were four such rooms in that attic, and together they brought in as much as many a handsome little cottage in a pleasant part of Brooklyn. The third instance was that of a colored family of husband, wife, and baby in a wretched rear rookery in West Third Street. Their rent was eight dollars and a half for a single room on the top-story, so small that I was unable to get a photograph of it even by placing the camera outside the open door. Three short steps across either way would have measured its full extent.

There was just one excuse for the early tenement house builders, and their successors may plead it with nearly as good right for what it is worth. "Such," says an official report, "is the lack of houseroom in the city that any kind of tenement can be immediately crowded with lodgers, if there is space offered." Thousands were living in cellars. There were three hundred underground lodging-houses in the city when the Health Department was organized. Some fifteen years before that the old Baptist Church in Mulberry Street, just off Chatham Street, had been sold, and the rear half of the frame structure had been converted into tenements that with their swarming population became the scandal even of that reckless age. The wretched pile harbored no less than forty families, and the annual rate of deaths to the population was officially stated to be 75 in 1,000. These tenements were an extreme type of very many, for the big barracks had by this time spread east and west and far up the island into the sparsely settled wards. Whether or not the title was clear to the land upon which they were built was of less account than that the rents were collected.

If there were damages to pay, the tenant had to foot them. Cases were "very frequent when property was in litigation, and two or three different parties were collecting rents." Of course under such circumstances "no repairs were ever made." The climax had been reached. The situation was summed up by the Society for the Improvement of the Condition of the Poor in these words: "Crazy old buildings, crowded rear tenements in filthy yards, dark, damp basements, leaking garrets, shops, outhouses, and stables [3] converted into dwellings, though scarcely fit to shelter brutes, are habitations of thousands of our fellow-beings in this wealthy, Christian city." "The city," says its historian, Mrs. Martha Lamb, commenting on the era of aqueduct building between 1835 and 1845, "was a general asylum for vagrants." Young vagabonds, the natural offspring of such "home" conditions, overran the streets. Juvenile crime increased fearfully year by year. The Children's Aid Society and kindred philanthropic organizations were yet unborn, but in the city directory was to be found the address of the "American Society for the Promotion of Education in Africa."...

CHAPTER XXV: HOW THE CASE STANDS

WHAT, then, are the bald facts with which we have to deal in New York?

I. That we have a tremendous, ever swelling crowd of wage-earners which it is our business to house decently.
II. That it is not housed decently.
III. That it must be so housed here for the present, and for a long time to come, all schemes of suburban relief being as yet utopian, impracticable.
IV. That it pays high enough rents to entitle it to be so housed, as a right.
V. That nothing but our own slothfulness is in the way of so housing it, since "the condition of the tenants is in advance of the condition of the houses which they occupy" (Report of Tenement-house Commission).
VI. That the security of the one no less than of the other half demands, on sanitary, moral, and economic grounds, that it be decently housed.

VII. That it will pay to do it. As an investment, I mean, and in hard cash. This I shall immediately proceed to prove.
VIII. That the tenement has come to stay, and must itself be the solution of the problem with which it confronts us.

This is the fact from which we cannot get away, however we may deplore it. Doubtless the best would be to get rid of it altogether; but as we cannot, all argument on that score may at this time be dismissed as idle. The practical question is what to do with the tenement. I watched a Mott Street landlord, the owner of a row of barracks that have made no end of trouble for the health authorities for twenty years, solve that question for himself the other day. His way was to give the wretched pile a coat of paint, and put a gorgeous tin cornice on with the year 1890 in letters a yard long. From where I stood watching the operation, I looked down upon the same dirty crowds camping on the roof, foremost among them an Italian mother with two stark-naked children who had apparently never made the acquaintance of a wash-tub. That was a landlord's way, and will not get us out of the mire.

The "flat" is another way that does not solve the problem. Rather, it extends it. The flat is not a model, though it is a modern, tenement. It gets rid of some of the nuisances of the low tenement, and of the worst of them, the overcrowding—if it gets rid of them at all—at a cost that takes it at once out of the catalogue of "homes for the poor," while imposing some of the evils from which they suffer upon those who ought to escape from them.

There are three effective ways of dealing with the tenements in New York:

I. By law.
II. By remodelling and making the most out of the old houses.
III. By building new, model tenements.

Private enterprise—conscience, to put it in the category of duties, where it belongs—must do the lion's share under these last two heads. Of what the law has effected I have spoken already. The drastic measures adopted in Paris, in Glasgow, and in London are not practicable here on anything like as large a scale. Still it can, under strong pressure of public opinion, rid us of tile worst plague-spots. The Mulberry Street Bend will go the way of the Five Points when all the red tape that binds the hands of municipal effort has been unwound. Prizes were offered in public competition, some years ago, for the best plans of modern tenement-houses. It may be that we shall see the day when the building of model tenements will be encouraged by subsidies in the way of a rebate of taxes. Meanwhile the arrest and summary punishment of landlords, or their agents, who persistently violate law and decency, will have a salutary effect. If a few of the wealthy absentee landlords, who are the worst offenders, could be got within the jurisdiction of the city, and by arrest be compelled to employ proper overseers, it would be a proud day for New York. To remedy the overcrowding, with which the night inspections of the sanitary police cannot keep step, tenements may eventually have to he licensed, as now the lodging-houses, to hold so many tenants, and no more; or the State may have to bring down the rents that cause the crowding, by assuming the right to regulate them as it regulates the fares on the elevated roads. I throw out the suggestion, knowing quite well that it is open to attack. It emanated originally from one of the brightest minds that have had to struggle officially with this tenement-house question in the last ten years. In any event, to succeed, reform by law must aim at making it unprofitable to own a bad tenement. At best, it is apt to travel at a snail's pace, while the enemy it pursues is putting the best foot foremost.

In this matter of profit the law ought to have its strongest ally in the landlord himself, though the reverse is the case. This condition of things I believe to rest on a monstrous error. It cannot be that tenement property that is worth preserving at all can continue to yield larger returns, if allowed to run down, than if properly cared for and kept in good repair. The point must be reached, and soon, where the cost of repairs, necessary with a house full of the lowest, most ignorant tenants, must overbalance the saving of the first few years of neglect; for this class is everywhere the most destructive, as well as the poorest paying. I have the experience of owners, who have found this out to their cost, to back me up in the assertion, even if it were not the statement of a plain business fact that proves itself. I do not include tenement property that is deliberately allowed to fall into decay because at some future time the ground will be valuable for business or other purposes. There is unfortunately enough of that kind in New York, often leasehold property owned by wealthy estates or soulless corporations that oppose all their great influence to the efforts of the law in behalf of their tenants.

...

From the managers of the two best-known experiments in model tenement building in the city, the Improved Dwellings Association and the Tenement-house Building Company, I have letters dated last August, declaring their enterprises eminently successful. There is no reason why their experience should not be conclusive. That the Philadelphia plan is not practicable in New York is not a good reason why our own plan, which is precisely the reverse of our neighbor's should not be. In fact it is an argument for its success. The very reason why we cannot house our working masses in cottages, as has been done in Philadelphia—viz., that they must live on Manhattan Island, where the land is too costly for small houses—is the best guarantee of the success of the model tenement house, properly located and managed. The drift in tenement building, as in everything else, is toward concentration, and helps smooth the way. Four families on the floor, twenty in the house, is the rule of to-day. As the crowds increase, the need of guiding this drift into safe channels becomes more urgent. The larger the scale upon which the model tenement is planned, the more certain the promise of success. The utmost ingenuity cannot build a house for sixteen or twenty families on a lot 25 × 100 feet in the middle of a block like it, that shall give them the amount of air and sunlight to be had by the erection of a dozen or twenty houses on a common plan around a central yard. This was the view of the committee that awarded the prizes for the best plan for the conventional tenement, ten years ago.

It coupled its verdict with the emphatic declaration that, in its view, it was "impossible to secure the requirements of physical and moral health within these narrow and arbitrary limits." Houses have been built since on better plans than any the committee saw, but its judgment stands unimpaired. A point, too, that is not to be overlooked, is the reduced cost of expert superintendence—the first condition of successful management—in the larger buildings.

The Improved Dwellings Association put up its block of thirteen houses in East Seventy-second Street nine years ago. Their cost, estimated at about $240,000 with the land, was increased to $285,000 by troubles with the contractor engaged to build them. Thus the Association's task did not begin under the happiest auspices. Unexpected expenses came to deplete its treasury. The neighborhood was new and not crowded at the start. No expense was spared, and the benefit of all the best and most recent experience in tenement building was given to the tenants. The families were provided with from two to four rooms, all "outer" rooms, of course, at rents ranging from $14 per month for the four on the ground floor, to $6.25 for two rooms on the top floor. Coal lifts, ash-chutes, common laundries in the basement, and free baths, are features of these buildings that were then new enough to be looked upon with suspicion by the doubting Thomases who predicted disaster. There are rooms in the block for 218 families, and when I looked in recently all but nine of the apartments were let. One of the nine was rented while I was in the building. The superintendent told me that he had little trouble with disorderly tenants, though the buildings shelter all sorts of people.

...

And so this task, too, has come to an end. Whatsoever a man soweth, that shall he also reap. I have aimed to tell the truth as I saw it. If this book shall have borne ever so feeble a hand in garnering a harvest of justice, it has served its purpose. While I was writing these lines I went down to the sea, where thousands from the city were enjoying their summer rest. The ocean slumbered under a cloudless sky. Gentle waves washed lazily over the white sand, where children fled before them with screams of laughter. Standing there and watching their play, I was told that during the fierce storms of winter it happened that this sea, now so calm, rose in rage and beat down, broke over the bluff, sweeping all before it. No barrier built by human hands had power to stay it then. The sea of a mighty population, held in galling fetters, heaves uneasily in the tenements. Once already our city, to which have come the duties and responsibilities of metropolitan greatness before it was able to fairly measure its task, has felt the swell of its resistless flood. If it rise once more, no human power may avail to check it. The gap between the classes in which it surges, unseen, unsuspected by the thoughtless, is widening day by day. No tardy enactment of law, no political expedient, can close it. Against all other dangers our system of government may offer defence and shelter; against this not. I know of but one bridge that will carry us over safe, a bridge founded upon justice and built of human hearts.

I believe that the danger of such conditions as are fast growing up around us is greater for the very freedom which they mock. The words of the poet, with whose lines I prefaced this book, are truer today, have far deeper meaning to us, than when they were penned forty years ago:

> "—Think ye that building shall endure
> Which shelters the noble and crushes the poor?"

GLOSSARY

bald: obvious

burgher: a city-dweller

Knickerbockers: wealthy Dutch merchants of colonial New York

mean: plain and humble

Document Analysis

Chapter I of *How the Other Half Lives* discusses the "genesis of the tenement." Riis describes the evolution of New York City from the days of the Knickerbockers (the Dutch aristocracy) and George Washington into the nineteenth century. Behind proud old homes were "rear houses" inhabited by the poor, and older homes were purchased and divided up into tenement apartments. In time, "neatness, order, cleanliness, were never dreamed of in connection with the tenant-house system, as it spread its localities from year to year." At the same time, "slovenliness, discontent, privation, and ignorance were left to work out their invariable results, until the entire premises reached the level of tenant-house dilapidation, containing, but sheltering not, the miserable hordes that crowded beneath smouldering, water-rotted roofs or burrowed among the rats of clammy cellars." Riis goes on to provide statistics concerning the overcrowding and deaths—deaths that were often the result of "suffocation in the foul air of an unventilated apartment." Significantly, the rate of death from the poor conditions in New York City grew during the nineteenth century. In an era where medical advances were being made and, in general, life expectancy increased, the residential conditions actively worked against that. He points out that the East Side of New York City was at the time the most densely populated district in the world—290,000 people per square mile. (To put that figure in perspective, the population density for all of New York City in 1890 was about 8,300 per square mile, and the population density of the borough of Manhattan in 2000 was just under 70,000 per square mile).

Riis then goes on to detail a state government investigation into conditions in the tenements, which was triggered by the death of a child due to suffocation. Rent, they found, was actually higher in the worst slums than in other areas of the city, with uptown twenty persons living one room. Thus, not only are the poorest New Yorkers subject to horrific living conditions, they are paying a premium for them. Riis informs his readers that these conditions exist in "recent" times. Overcrowding, conditions that literally induced suicide in one couple, and rooms that were too small to even photograph successfully still existed in the city.

In Chapter XXV, "How the Case Stands," Riis specifies conditions as they exist. These conditions include a rapidly growing population that need housing but a lack of decent housing. The workers need to be house now, and for the foreseeable future, so "utopian" suburban development schemes are not the solution. He also asserts that the rents are high enough in the tenements that these workers should receive much better housing. He goes on to explain that it will, in the long term, be profitable to invest in decent housing for the working class. Finally, the tenement itself "has come to stay" and must be a part of the solution to the housing crisis. One way in which he appeals to the sensitivities of more affluent Americans is by pointing out that the "security" of everyone demands, "on sanitary, moral, and economic grounds," that people be decently housed. He then makes specific proposals for ways to solve the tenement problem: the law, remodeling and making effective use of old houses, and building model tenements. Riis believes that promoting investment in new housing projects can be improved with incentives to those who would build them. Tax breaks, and freeing "private enterprise" from the shackles of bureaucratic red tap would encourage new building of decent housing. Riis also believes that, "the arrest and summary punishment of landlords, or their agents, who persistently violate law and decency, will have a salutary effect." But he also argues that "it can be made to pay to improve and make the most of the worst tenement property, even in the most wretched locality," and he gives examples, both of remodeling and of the construction of model tenements by such organizations as the Improved Dwellings Association and the Tenement House Building Company. Riis concludes by asserting that "if this book shall have borne ever so feeble a hand in garnering a harvest of justice, it has served its purpose."

Essential Themes

These two chapters from *How the Other Half Lives* provide an illustration of the methods of Progressive era reform journalism. Riis does not merely present the problem. He explains the historical roots of the problem as well as the present-day severity using both qualitative and quantitative data. Riis told the stories of the desperate, impoverished lives in New York City through words as well as through his photography. But he also used a variety of statistics to illustrate the increasingly dangerous and unhealthy environment of the tenements of New York City. Along with his thorough presentation of the current problems and their historical basis, Riis also presents a range of solutions for the housing crisis with his support for model tenements. Significantly, Riis is careful to discus the benefits of his plans not only for those whose quality of life would be improved by the superior housing but also the benefits to those who invest in the new projects and the cumulative economic effect that it would have.

——*Michael J. O'Neal, PhD*
with additional material by Aaron Gulyas, MA

Bibliography and Additional Reading

Buk-Swienty, Tom and Annette Buk-Swienty. *The Other Half: The Life of Jacob Riis and the World of Immigrant America* (New York: W. W. Norton, 2008).

Dowling, Robert M. *Slumming in New York: From the Waterfront to Mythic Harlem* (Urbana-Champaign: University of Illinois Press, 2008).

Pascal, Janet B. *Jacob Riis: Reporter and Reformer* (New York: Oxford University Press, 2005).

Yochelson, Bonnie and Daniel Czitrom. *Rediscovering Jacob Riis: Exposure Journalism and Photography in Turn-of-the-Century New York* (Chicago, University of Chicago Press, 2014).

■ "The Subjective Necessity for Social Settlements"

Date: 1892
Author: Jane Addams
Genre: Speech

Summary Overview

Jane Addams speech on "The Subjective Necessity for Social Settlements" has the impressive task of not only explaining the purpose of social settlements, or settlement houses but also of persuading the reader that thy are not only necessary but that they are, in fact, made necessary by the most fundamental realities of American urban and industrial development, explaining that they are "an experimental effort to aid in the solution of the social and industrial problems which are engendered by the modern conditions of life in a great city." She does this by explaining that the growing divide between the middle and working classes in the large industrial cities of the United States require solutions that are beneficial for members of both classes.

Addams's argument places the settlement house movement squarely in the realm of other Progressive era concerns. In particular, she addresses the rapidly widening gap between rich and poor and, more importantly, the breakdown of social cohesion that accompanies such divisions. Addams discusses the need for social settlements within the context of the ways they have worked well in Britain, providing a model for American urban and social development.

Defining Moment

Jane Addams was part of the Progressive movement, a broad and diverse middle-class coalition that, at the turn of the twentieth century, tried to reform American society and reconcile democracy with capitalism. The steady industrialization and urbanization of the 1880s and 1890s had deeply transformed American society, spurring harsh conflicts between labor and management. The middle class had supported the process of industrialization by espousing the Victorian values of laissez-faire individualism, domesticity, and self-control. Yet by the 1890s it was apparent that these values had trapped the middle class between the warring demands of big business and the working classes. Growing consumerism, a new wave of immigration, and tensions between the sexes further challenged bourgeois existence. In the face of these confrontations, the Progressives tried to reform the American capitalist system and its institutions from within, seeking to strike a compromise between radical demands and the preservation of established interests.

The expression of the Progressive movement's goals was incredibly varied, as was the range of Addams's own interests and passions. The settlement house movement, which she discusses here, was a crucial part of the ongoing concern about widening gaps between the richest and poorest Americans, often living in the same cities but in quite different worlds. The settlement movement, although it began in the United Kingdom, is often—at least in the United States—associated with Jane Addams. The main purpose of the movement was to establish "settlement houses" in low-income areas of cities. Volunteers, usually middle class, would live in the houses and provide services such as child care, education, and health services to the permanent residents of these areas. In 1889, Jane Addams and Ellen Gates Starr founded Hull House in Chicago, Illinois. It provided educational and recreational services for women and children recently arrived in the United States.

Author Biography

Jane Addams was born on September 6, 1860, in Cedarville, Illinois. She earned a bachelor's degree in 1881 from Rockford Female Seminary, in Illinois. In the 1880s Addams began studying medicine, but she had to suspend her work because of poor health. Despite her poor health, she visited Europe several times. During one of her voyages, Addams and her companion, Ellen Gates Starr, visited London's original settlement house of Toynbee Hall, established in 1884. The visit led the two women to establish the Chicago settlement house of Hull House in 1889, the second such house to be established in America. Through Hull House, Addams found a vocation for her adult life.

Addams campaigned for every major reform issue of her era, such as fairer workplace conditions for men and women, tenement regulation, juvenile-court law, women's suffrage, and women's rights. While in the first part of her life Addams was mainly involved in social work in Hull House, in the twentieth century she used her notoriety to advance political causes and became a well-known public figure. In 1910 she was the first woman president of the National Conference of Social Work, and in 1912 she actively campaigned for the Progressive presidential candidate, Theodore Roosevelt, becoming the first woman to give a nominating speech at a party convention. Addams was also a founding member of the National Association for the Advancement of Colored People.

In the 1920s, Addams concentrated many of her efforts on antiwar efforts, she became the president of the Woman's Peace Party in 1915 and chaired the International Women's Congress for Peace and Freedom at The Hague, Netherlands. Americans were not unanimous in their praise for Addams's campaigning for peace. Despite her unpopular views in the US, Addams's antiwar efforts won her the Nobel Peace Prize, which she shared with Nicholas Murray Butler. Addams died in Chicago on May 21, 1935, three days after being diagnosed with cancer.

HISTORICAL DOCUMENT

This paper is an attempt to analyze the motives which underlie a movement based, not only upon conviction, but upon genuine emotion, wherever educated young people are seeking an outlet for that sentiment for universal brotherhood, which the best spirit of our times is forcing from an emotion into a motive. These young people accomplish little toward the solution of this social problem, and bear the brunt of being cultivated into unnourished, oversensitive lives. They have been shut off from the common labor by which they live which is a great source of moral and physical health. They feel a fatal want of harmony between their theory and their lives, a lack of coördination between thought and action. I think it is hard for us to realize how seriously many of them are taking to the notion of human brotherhood, how eagerly they long to give tangible expression to the democratic ideal....

"It is true that there is nothing after disease, indigence and a sense of guilt, so fatal to health and to life itself as the want of a proper outlet for active faculties." I have seen young girls suffer and grow sensibly lowered in vitality in the first years after they leave school. In our attempt then to give a girl pleasure and freedom from care we succeed, for the most part, in making her pitifully miserable.... There is a heritage of noble obligation which young people accept and long to perpetuate. The desire for action, the wish to right wrong and alleviate suffering haunts them daily. Society smiles at it indulgently instead of making it of value to itself....

We have in America a fast-growing number of cultivated young people who have no recognized outlet for their active faculties. They hear constantly of the great social maladjustment, but no way is provided for them to change it, and their uselessness hangs about them heavily.... These young people have had advantages of college, of European travel, and of economic study, but they are sustaining this shock of inaction.... They tell their elders with all the bitterness of youth that if they expect success from them in business or politics or in whatever lines their ambition for them has run, they must let them consult all of humanity; that they must let them find out what the people want and how they want it. It is only the stronger young people, however, who formulate this. Many of them dissipate their energies in so-called enjoyment. Others not content with that, go on studying and go back to college for their second degrees; not that they are especially fond of study, but because they want something definite to do, and their powers have been trained in the direction of mental accumulation. Many are buried beneath this mental accumulation with lowered vitality and discontent....

This young life, so sincere in its emotion and good phrases and yet so undirected, seems to me as pitiful as the other great mass of destitute lives. One is supplementary to the other, and some method of communication can surely be devised. Mr. Barnett, who urged the first Settlement—Toynbee Hall, in East London,—recognized this need of outlet for the young men of Oxford and Cambridge, and hoped that the Settlement would supply the communication. It is easy to see why the Settlement movement originated in England, where the years of education are more constrained and definite than they are here, where class distinctions are more rigid....We are fast feeling the pressure of the need and meeting the necessity for Settlements in America. Our young people feel nervously the need of putting theory into action, and respond quickly to the Settlement form of activity....

The Settlement then, is an experimental effort to aid in the solution of the social and industrial problems which are engendered by the modern conditions of life in a great city. It insists that these problems are not confined to any one portion of a city. It is an attempt to relieve, at the same time, the overaccumulation at one end of society and the destitution at the other; but it assumes that this overaccumulation and destitution is most sorely felt in the things that pertain to social and educational privileges....The only thing to be dreaded in the Settlement is that it lose its flexibility, its power of quick adaptation, its readiness to change its methods as its environment may demand. It must be open to conviction and must have a deep and abiding sense of tolerance. It must be hospitable and ready for experiment....Its residents must be emptied of all conceit of opinion and all self-assertion, and ready to arouse and interpret the public opinion of their neighborhood. They must be content to live quietly side by side with their neighbors, until they grow into a sense of relationship and mutual interests.... In short, residents are pledged to devote themselves to the duties of good citizenship and to the arousing of the social energies which too largely lie dormant in every neighborhood given over to industrialism. They are bound to regard the entire life of their city as organic, to make an effort to unify it, and to protest against its over-differentiation

It is always easy to make all philosophy point one particular moral and all history adorn one particular tale; but I may be forgiven the reminder that the best speculative philosophy sets forth the solidarity of the human race; that the highest moralists have taught that without the advance and improvement of the whole, no man can hope for any lasting improvement in his own moral or material individual condition; and that the subjective necessity for Social Settlements is therefore identical with that necessity, which urges us on toward social and individual salvation.

GLOSSARY

emptied of all conceit of opinion: forced to give up one's own beliefs and preferences

Mr. Barnett: Samuel Barnett (1844–1919), who with his wife, Henrietta, founded the world's first settlement house in 1884

social settlements: settlement houses, or community centers that offer a variety of services in an economically disadvantaged area

Document Analysis

Like many other young, middle-class Progressives, Addams felt an urge to be useful and to find a vocation to occupy her adult life. For eight years following her father's death, Addams was unable to act and find such a purpose in her life: "During most of that time," she recalls in her autobiography, *Twenty Years at Hull-House*, "I was absolutely at sea so far as any moral purpose was concerned." This period of personal and professional insecurity ended when she found a way to couple her idealism with concrete action through the establishment of Hull House in Chicago's slum neighborhood around Halsted Street. The settlement house was one of the most ambitious aspects of urban reform movements. Settlement houses were located in slum neighborhoods densely populated by immigrants and were mainly directed by women. Young middle-class people worked in settlements to improve the living conditions of slum dwellers, encouraging them to improve their education, jobs, and housing as well as their understanding of American society and culture. Settlement workers soon became the leading personalities of the movement for social reform, progressively broadening their focus to campaign for school nurses, public playgrounds, and better working conditions.

As with other Progressive causes, the political relevance of the settlement movement should not obscure its middle-class basis. Such a basis clearly emerges in Addams's 1892 speech "The Subjective Necessity for Social Settlements," delivered at the summer school of the Ethical Culture Societies at Plymouth, Massachusetts, and later reprinted as the sixth chapter of *Twenty Years at Hull-House*. Addams makes clear that the settlement serves as a political solution to the personal malaise of young middle-class professionals who needed to find "an outlet for that sentiment of universal brotherhood" and must "give tangible expression to the democratic ideal." Settlements like Hull House, Addams indicates, thus benefit both the slum dwellers they aim to serve and the middle-class people, particularly women, who work in them, allowing them to find an outlet for their talents and compassions. Without the settlement houses, such talents would largely remain untapped by society, and those unable to work in such houses would feel a sense of aimlessness.

Building directly on her own experience, Addams indicts the domestic values of American Victorian culture for their negative impact on the lives of many women. Society restrains the desire to act to alleviate suffering that is part of the social obligation that human beings feel. While the aim of this culture may be to give women a life full of pleasure and free of worries, the corresponding social attitudes only make them unhappy. Addams claims that in America "a fast-growing number of cultivated young people...have no recognized outlet for their active faculties." To Addams, the fate of these young people who lack purpose is as pitiful as that of the destitute masses who occupy America's urban slums. Settlement houses can provide a medium of communication between the two groups and benefit both. Settlements are based on solidarity and the Christian impulse to better the lives of the poor.

The last part of the speech defines Hull House also as an experiment in urban sociology, designed to "relieve, at the same time, the overaccumulation at one end of society and the destitution at the other." According to Addams, this stark imbalance in the distribution of wealth is typical of the modern conditions of life in a great city. The activities of the settlement should be shaped by the conviction that solutions to urban problems can be achieved through cooperative efforts and reform. Settlement workers should have "a scientific patience in the accumulation of facts" about human life and should be tolerant, flexible, and keen to experiment with approaches. The goal of Hull House is not to highlight differences; on the contrary, the settlement should be built upon what workers and slum dwellers share. In Addams's conception, Hull House offers common ground where the working class and the middle class can meet and learn from one another.

Essential Themes

America, and the entire western world, was changing at a remarkable pace in the 1890s. The "social and industrial problems which are engendered by the modern conditions of life in a great city" would only increase. Within a year of Addams delivering this speech, the panic of 1893, one of the worst financial crises in American history, would increase the ranks of America's poor. The middle class, however, would continue to grow and continue to move further away—both geographically and culturally—from the working poor of American cities. Addams seeks, through the settlement movement, to "relieve" the increasing tension between over accumulation and destitution. The solution, provided through the settlement movement is to improve peoples' sense of citizenship, building "a sense of relationship and mutual interests." Like so much of the work of the progressive movement, this was about increasing social cohesion—bringing together different elements of society in order to improve the city (and nation) as a whole. Another crucial theme brought out in Addams's speech that is an echo of wider Progressive concerns is the reliance on the collection of data and the importance of approaching social issues with a scientific scrutiny.

——Luca Prono PhD

Bibliography and Additional Reading

Brown Victoria Bissell, *The Education of Jane Addams* (Philadelphia: University of Pennsylvania Press, 2007).

Knight, Louise W. *Citizen: Jane Addams and the Struggle for Democracy* (Chicago: University of Chicago Press, 2005).

——*Jane Addams: Spirit in Action* (New York: W.W. Norton, 2010).

McGerr, Michael. *A Fierce Discontent: The Rise and Fall of the Progressive Movement in America, 1870-1920*. (New York: Oxford University Press, 2005).

Editorial on the Pullman Strike

Date: 1894
Author: Samuel Gompers
Genre: Editorial

Summary Overview

In the wake of the Pullman strike of 1894, which failed to produce the wage increases demanded by the union, Samuel Gompers penned this brief editorial which publicly condemned Pullman both for the conditions in the company towns in which his employees had to live as well as Pullman's refusal to enter into arbitration with the American Railway Union over wages and conditions. Despite the fact that, as described below, Gompers did not want workers to engage in a general strike—that is a strike of all workers, not just the railway workers who had the grievance—he believed the union to be striking in a righteous cause and that Pullman's refusal to engage in arbitration talks with the union was disingenuous and proof of the company's greed.

Defining Moment

In response to the declining economic conditions during the Panic of 1893, the industrialist George Pullman reduced wages but failed to lower rents for the workers in his company town outside Chicago, where railway sleeping cars were produced. The wildcat strike of Pullman Palace Car Company workers that began on May 11, 1894, was supported by the American Railway Union and its leader, Eugene Debs. The ARU launched a boycott of trains containing Pullman cars, which disrupted national railroad traffic. Arguing that the boycott interfered with mail delivery, the administration of President Grover Cleveland obtained an injunction against the ARU leadership, and troops were dispatched to quash the strike. In desperation, Debs appealed to Gompers and the AFL for a general strike on behalf of the beleaguered union. But at a meeting of the AFL executive board in Chicago on July 12, 1894, Gompers refused to call for a general strike, arguing that the ARU strike was impulsive and that it was in the best interest of working people for sympathy work stoppages to be halted. Gompers also believed that it was foolhardy to involve the AFL in a doomed strike. Debs, however, perceived Gompers as betraying industrial unionism in favor of the elite interests of skilled craft unions. Debs and Gompers would continue their antagonistic relationship into the early twentieth century as Debs assumed a leadership role within the Socialist Party.

Author Biography

Samuel Gompers was born on January 27, 1850, in London, England. In July 1863, his family immigrated to the United States, where Gompers and his father found employment in New York City as skilled cigar rollers and he became active in the Cigar Makers' International Union. Along with his friend Adolph Strasser, who assumed the presidency of the union in 1877, Gompers fostered a more centralized union model for skilled craft workers in response to the fragility of the labor movement during such troubled economic times as the Panic of 1873—a financial depression that led to losses of jobs.

As a trade unionist, Gompers believed that political action was premature prior to workers' forming a sense of class consciousness. Accordingly, he opposed political alignments with the Democrats and Republicans or parties of the left, such as the Socialists, in favor of direct action that would increase a sense of labor solidarity. In 1886, Gompers and supporters among organized skilled workers formed the American Federation of Labor (AFL), and Gompers was elected president.

During the late 1880s, Gompers soon attempted to offset employer opposition to unionization by cooperating with the National Civic Federation, a reform group composed of the nation's corporate leadership. Although this alliance produced few tangible benefits for the AFL, the organization's membership continued to grow, numbering nearly two million workers by 1904. During the early twentieth century Gompers came to rethink his organization's avoidance of political entanglements, and in 1912 the AFL executive supported the presidential candidacy of the Democrat Woodrow Wilson, who prevailed. The Wilson administration honored labor's support by appointing a former coal miner, William B. Wilson, to head the Department of Labor and enacting legislation beneficial to labor.

Gompers died on December 13, 1924 in San Antonio, Texas. While labor was on the defensive in the 1920s, Gompers's leadership of the AFL from 1886 until his death established a strong foundation for craft unionism in the United States.

HISTORICAL DOCUMENT

It is a lamentable fact that success does not always attend the right or those who struggle to achieve it. If any doubt existed as to the truth of this statement, the strike at Pullman, and the strike of the American Railway Union in support of it, has dispelled that doubt.

It is indeed difficult to conceive a cause in which right was more on the side of those who were defeated as in the one under consideration.

We present to our readers the true story of this contest, and the cause which led up to it; and we hope to add to the contumely and contempt which every earnest, honest, liberty loving man, woman and child in the country must feel for the most consummate type of avaricious wealth absorber, tyrant and hypocrite this age, of that breed, has furnished—Pullman.

In the language of the picture drawn by Pullman, the *philanthropist* of Pullman, the town, he says: "That it is bordered with bright beds of flowers and green velvety stretches of land, that [it] is shaded with trees and dotted with parks and pretty water vistas and glimpses here and there of artistic sweeps and landscape gardening, a town where the homes even of the most modest are bright and wholesome and filled with pure air and light, a town, in a word, from which all that is ugly, discordant and demoralizing is eliminated and all that inspires to self-respect, to thrift and to cleanliness of person and of being is generally provided."

This description is unquestionably true so far as it refers to the view which the passer by sees upon the train; but back where the workers live and die, what a pitiful, horrible condition prevails. In whole blocks entire families have for years lived in one room in order that they might eke out an existence. In no community in the world, except possibly China, was there such a small proportion of families living in family privacy....

In Pullman there was always an indefinable something telling the workers that their presence was not wanted where the flowers and Fountains and velvety lawns are. The houses are not healthy and the records show an unusual number of deaths by zymotic diseases.

During the terrible suffering last winter the Company insisted that there was no destitution nor suffering in the place and with much nonchalance declared that "there could be none because it was not contemplated in the theory upon which the town was founded and controlled."

When a number of charitable ladies organized to relieve the destitution they were not permitted to carry on the work, for that would be an acknowledgment that there was need of relief.

The town of Pullman covers 350 acres estimated to be worth $10,000,000. Buildings occupied by the workers are congested as the most thickly settled residence districts of Chicago, yet Pullman pays but $15,000 on taxes. (Carnegie defrauds the government in his contracts; Pullman in taxes.)

Nor should it be imagined that the statement made by Pullman recently, that the reason he refused to arbitrate the matter in dispute with his employees was that the Company were producing cars at a loss. As a matter of fact last February, or two months before the strike commenced, the Company issued an official statement containing the following. "The day is near at hand when the $30,000,000 present capital of the Pullman Company will be covered and more than covered by the value of the 3,500 acres of land on which is built the town of Pullman." Coupled with this was the statement that the $30,000,000 capital stock had a market value of $60,000,000.

When the fact is borne in mind that Pullman has practically a monopoly in the building of his cars, is not the claim preposterous that he could not pay fair wages? Does anyone imagine that if Pullman's statement of his inability to pay the wage demanded was true that he would refuse to arbitrate? No arbitrator would make an award against him if he could prove his assertions; his refusal is the best evidence of his untruthfulness. In truth out of his own statements he convicts himself.

The end is not yet. Labor will not back down. It will triumph despite all the Pullmans combined; and as for Pullman, he has proven himself a public enemy. His name and memory are excoriated to-day and will be forever.

GLOSSARY

capital stock: the total of all shares in a particular company that are authorized for sale by that company's charter

Carnegie: Scottish-born industrial and philanthropist Andrew Carnegie (1835–1919)

contumely: insolence or arrogance

Pullman: George Pullman (1831–1897), inventor of the Pullman sleeping car, which made overnight rail travel more comfortable

Pullman, the town: Pullman, Illinois, founded in the 1880s for Pullman company workers and later annexed to the city of Chicago

zymotic: diseases a term, since outmoded, for diseases such as typhoid fever and smallpox that were thought to be caused by fermentation

Document Analysis

Gompers begins his editorial by explaining that the Pullman strike by the American Railway Union is an example of the fact that righteous causes are not always successful. He goes on to claim that what follows is "the true story" of the strike and why it happened, with the purpose of contributing to the negative public opinion that Pullman has acquired.

Pullman, who decreased wages while keeping the rents in his company town the same, is quoted by Gompers describing the Pullman company towns as idyllic places that uplift the workers and their families who live there. Gompers acknowledges that, to a passerby, this might be the case but for Pullman's workers, the conditions are "pitiful" and "horrible," with family often confined to a single room indoor to save costs and suffering from deadly diseases. The company denied that there were any problems and turned away charity that was offered to the workers.

While the properties of the Pullman company town are worth ten million dollars, Gompers explains, and densely populated with Pullman employees, the Pullman company pays only $15,000 in taxes, defrauding the government and, by extension, the American people. Gompers also disputes Pullman's claim that the company was operating at a loss, which was their stated reason for refusing to bargain with the striking workers. Rather, Gompers produces numbers to that show the company is in fine financial shape. It is almost beyond imagining, Gompers asserts, that given his near-monopoly in the railroad car manufacturing business, Pullman cannot pay the wages desired by his workers—if his company's losses were real, why was he afraid to enter into arbitration? The fact that he did not is proof that he is lying about his profits.

Despite this setback, however, Gompers pledges that the labor movement will continue and, eventually, be victorious. Pullman, on the other hand, has made himself into a "public enemy" and will be "forever" condemned.

Essential Themes

While he considered the tactics of the ARU rash, Gompers makes clear in his August 1894 editorial for the *American Federationist* his sympathy for the Pullman workers and his antipathy for the industrialist himself. Declaring his working-class sensibilities, Gompers describes George Pullman as "the most consummate type of avaricious wealth absorber, tyrant and hypocrite this age, of that breed, has produced." Discrediting Pullman's brand of welfare capitalism, Gompers proclaims the purported living and health conditions of the factory company town to be a charade for media consumption. The reality of life for Pullman workers was subpar housing standards and increased exposure to disease. As for the claim by Pullman that he was forced to reduce wages because of his declining profits, Gompers concludes that the industrialist simply refused to justly arbitrate the dispute, because he was certainly financially capable of providing more equitable compensation for his workers.

———Ron Briley

Bibliography and Additional Reading

Buhle, Paul, *Taking Care of Business: Samuel Gompers, George Meany, Lane Kirkland, and the Tragedy of American Labor*. (New York: Monthly Review Press, 1999).

Greene, Julie. *Pure and Simple Politics: The American Federation of Labor and Political Activism, 1881–1917*. (New York: Cambridge University Press, 1998).

Papke, David Ray. *The Pullman Case: The Clash of Labor and Capital in Industrial America*. (Lawrence, KS: University Press of Kansas, 1999).

Schneirov, Richard, et al. (eds.) *The Pullman Strike and the Crisis of the 1890s: Essays on Labor and Politics*. (Urbana, Illinois: University of Illinois Press, 1999).

Smith, Carl. *Urban Disorder and the Shape of Belief: The Great Chicago Fire, the Haymarket Bomb, and the Model Town of Pullman*. (Chicago: University of Chicago Press, 1995).

■ "Liberty"

Date: 1895
Author: Eugene V. Debs
Genre: Speech

Summary Overview

The American trade union leader, orator, and Socialist Party activist Eugene Debs was a master at making what might look today like radical political ideas seem as American as apple pie. A student of history as well as politics, Debs regularly invoked the memory of the Founding Fathers to make his policy suggestions seem more acceptable. Motivated by an unyielding sense of justice, he often tried to shame authorities to do what he thought was right. Whether addressing audiences at a labor rally or on the campaign trail, Debs invariably came back to a sharp critique of the American political system, touting the virtues of his brand of Socialism. His goal as a politician was not necessarily to win elections but instead to inspire listeners by his own example and to win converts to the Socialist cause. In a country with no Socialist legacy—unlike many European countries where Socialism was established—it is really quite remarkable that Debs had any success at all as a politician. That success was due in no small part to the power of Debs's oratory and prose. In his speech "Liberty," delivered in 1895 after his release from prison for support of the Pullman Palace Car strike, Debs connects the labor struggle with that of the Revolutionary era Patriots.

Defining Moment

The Pullman strike was an effort to organize workers at the Pullman Palace Car Company of Pullman, Illinois. As part of the strike, ARU members nationwide decided to boycott all trains that carried the company's famous sleeping cars in an effort to force them to recognize the union. As a result, rail traffic stopped nationwide. In response, railroad companies deliberately placed mail cars on trains with Pullman Palace Cars in order to encourage government intervention in the dispute. The legal injunction issued by a federal judge in response to the boycott essentially shut down the strike and destroyed the union. In 1895 Debs was convicted of interfering with the mail as a result of his refusal to abide by that injunction. Debs's political views were greatly affected by the Socialist literature he read during his short stay in jail. Indeed, this incarceration would prove to be the pivotal point of his entire life.

Upon his release Debs announced his conversion to Socialism.

Eugene Debs's fame began during his prison term following the Pullman strike. Countless people sought his opinion during his imprisonment. Since the jail was actually just a room in a local sheriff's house and his jailer gave him and the other ARU leaders imprisoned with him an incredible degree of freedom, Debs had the opportunity to read and to communicate with the outside world through correspondence and newspaper interviews. Upon his release, many newfound fans were excited to hear what he had to say about the modern world, especially about the government that had incarcerated him. While Debs had resisted adopting the Socialist label before his imprisonment, his embrace of the term at this juncture was extremely fortunate for the American Socialist movement. It not only gained a famous adherent, but it now also had its most eloquent spokesperson.

Author Biography

Eugene Victor Debs was a trade union leader, orator, and frequent Socialist Party candidate for the presidency of the United States. He was born in Terre Haute, Indiana, in 1855. While working his way up through the hierarchy of the Brotherhood of Locomotive Firemen, an important railroad union, he was elected city clerk in Terre Haute in 1879. He also served one term in the Indiana state legislature in 1885. In 1893 Debs cofounded the American Railway Union (ARU), an industrial union that, unlike most exclusive railroad brotherhoods of the era, admitted railroad workers of all skill levels. As the leader of that organization, Debs led the infamous Pullman strike of 1894, discussed above..

He also changed career paths from being a trade union leader to being a political leader. Debs would serve as a Socialist Party presidential candidate five times: 1900, 1904, 1908, 1912, and 1920. His best showing occurred in 1912 when he came close to garnering a million votes. That was 6 percent of the total votes cast in that election. In 1918 Debs was convicted of sedition for a speech he had given in Canton,

Ohio, earlier that year. Debs had to run his final campaign for president as a protest candidate from his jail cell. A famous campaign button from 1920 read "For President—Convict No. 9653." Between elections Debs toured the country giving speeches and writing articles that critiqued the American capitalist system and championed the cause of Socialism. Debs died in 1926 at the age of seventy.

Debs represented a vision of Socialism in America that got lost in the anti-Communist hysteria of the cold war era. His political beliefs, though Socialist, were grounded in American ideals like justice, equal rights, and Christianity. Debs's willingness to go to prison for the causes he championed greatly increased his appeal and the popularity of his ideas. While many other figures in American Socialism were immigrants from European countries like Germany, where Socialism was more in the mainstream, Debs attracted native-born Americans to the Socialist cause. His success as a politician came as the result of hundreds of thousands of Americans entertaining the possibility of radical change in American life in an era when the adverse effects of industrialization had made them unhappy with the existing political system.

HISTORICAL DOCUMENT

Manifestly the spirit of '76 still survives. The fires of liberty and noble aspirations are not yet extinguished. I greet you tonight as lovers of liberty and as despisers of despotism. I comprehend the significance of this demonstration and appreciate the honor that makes it possible for me to be your guest on such an occasion. The vindication and glorification of American principles of government, as proclaimed to the world in the Declaration of Independence, is the high purpose of this convocation.

Speaking for myself personally, I am not certain whether this is an occasion for rejoicing or lamentation. I confess to a serious doubt as to whether this day marks my deliverance from bondage to freedom or my doom from freedom to bondage. Certain it is, in the light of recent judicial proceedings, that I stand in your presence stripped of my constitutional rights as a freeman and shorn of the most sacred prerogatives of American citizenship, and what is true of myself is true of every other citizen who has the temerity to protest against corporation rule or question the absolute sway of the money power. It is not law nor the administration of law of which I complain. It is the flagrant violation of the constitution, the total abrogation of law and the usurpation of judicial and despotic power, by virtue of which my colleagues and myself were committed to jail, against which I enter my solemn protest; and any honest analysis of the proceedings must sustain the haggard truth of the indictment....

Dismissing this branch of the subject, permit me to assure you that I am not here to bemoan my lot. In my vocabulary there are no wails of despondency or despair. However gloomy the future may appear to others, I have an abiding faith in the ultimate triumph of the right....

Liberty is not a word of modern coinage. Liberty and slavery are primal worlds, like good and evil, right and wrong; they are opposites and coexistent....

The theme tonight is personal liberty; or giving it its full height, depth and breadth, American liberty, something that Americans have been accustomed to eulogize since the foundation of the Republic, and multiplied thousands of them continue in the habit to this day because they do not recognize the truth that in the imprisonment of one man in defiance of all constitutional guarantees, the liberties of all are invaded and placed in peril. In saying this, I conjecture I have struck the keynote of alarm that has convoked this vast audience....

Strike the fetters from the slave, give him liberty and he becomes an inhabitant of a new world. He looks abroad and beholds life and joy in all things around him. His soul expands beyond all boundaries. Emancipated by the genius of Liberty, he aspires to communion with all that is noble and beautiful, feels himself allied to all higher order of intelligence and superstition, a new being throbbing with glorious life....

It is in no spirit of laudation that I aver here tonight that it has fallen to the lot of the American Railway Union to arouse workingmen to a sense of the perils that environ their liberties.

In the great Pullman strike the American Railway Union challenged the power of corporations in a way that had not previously been done, and the analyzation of this fact serves to expand it to proportions that the most conservative men of the nation regard with alarm.

It must be borne in mind that the American Railway Union did not challenge the government. It threw down no gauntlet to courts or armies—it simply resisted the invasion of the rights of workingmen by corporations. It challenged and defied the power of corporations. Thrice armed with a just cause, the organization believed that justice would win for labor a notable victory; and the records proclaim that its confidence was not misplaced.

The corporations, left to their own resources of money, mendacity and malice, of thugs and ex-convicts, leeches and lawyers, would have been overwhelmed with defeat and the banners of organized labor would have floated triumphant in the breeze.

This the corporations saw and believed—hence the crowning act of infamy in which the federal courts and the federal armies participated, and which culminated in the defeat of labor....

From such reflections I turn to the practical lessons taught by this "Liberation Day" demonstration.

It means that American lovers of liberty are setting in operation forces to rescue their constitutional liberties from the grasp of monopoly and its mercenary hirelings. It means that the people are aroused in view of impending perils and that agitation, organization, and unification are to be the future battle cries of men who will not part with their birthrights and, like Patrick Henry, will have the courage to exclaim; "Give me liberty or give me death!"

I have borne with such composure as I could command the imprisonment which deprived me of my liberty. Were I a criminal; were I guilty of crimes meriting a prison cell; had I ever lifted my hand against the life or the liberty of my fellowmen; had I ever sought to filch their good name, I would not be here. I would have fled from the haunts of civilization and taken up my residence in some cave where the voice of my kindred is never heard. But I am standing here without a self-accusation of crime or criminal intent festering in my conscience, in the sunlight once more, among my fellowmen, contributing as best I can to make this "Liberation Day" from Woodstock prison a memorial day.

GLOSSARY

the haggard truth of the indictment: the ugly truth, as Debs sees it, behind the circumstances of his and others' imprisonment following the Pullman Strike

threw down no gauntlet: presented no challenge

usurpation: taking control from legitimate authority

Document Analysis

The speech begins with a tactic that was already a hundred years old when Debs used it, connecting modern labor struggles with the fight of the Patriots during the American Revolution. The idea was that modern workers struggled against the oppression of their employers in the same way that the American colonists fought the oppression of the British. Historians now call this concept "artisan republicanism." Since Debs believed that taking on rich corporations was a patriotic American thing to do, this tactic suited him well. He connects the American Revolution directly to his case later in the speech by equating his personal liberty to political liberty in the United States. At one point he even quotes the Revolutionary leader Patrick Henry, whose cry "Give me Liberty or give me death!" certainly fits the themes of Debs's career.

In the second paragraph, although being released form prison, Debs expresses concern that he might be plunging into a different kind of bondage—he is still living in a United States which condemned he and his fellow activists to imprisonment. "It is not law nor the administration of law of which I complain," says Debs, but rather "it is the flagrant violation of the constitution, the total abrogation of law and the usurpation of judicial and despotic power, by virtue of which my colleagues and myself were committed to jail. The entire Constitutional system on which the republic rests, he is saying, has been corrupted. But this is not a new thing.

This battle between the forces of good—in which Debs has "an abiding faith in the ultimate triumph of the right"—is as old as time itself. Debs persuaded people to entertain his views by connecting his politics to the teachings of the Bible, and he does this often in this speech. Debs relates the battle between liberty and slavery to the battle between good and evil in the world and suggests, as the Bible does, that the fate of humanity hangs in the balance. Christian imagery supplies the structure of Debs's vision of citizenship. More important, like Saul, who would become the apostle Paul after a conversion experience on the road to Damascus, Debs uses this occasion to suggest that in jail he had seen the light. Such Christian imagery served as a way for Debs to explain his ideals and inspire others to see the world as he now saw it.

Debs also speaks to the specific situation which the laboring forces of the United States find themselves and of the daunting forces arrayed against them. The American Railway Union took an unprecedented stand against corporate power, Debs explains. Crucially, he explains in the ninth paragraph, that the union, during the Pullman Strike did not challenge the government. Its enemy was the enemy of the working class—the corporations. If the battle had been between corporations and the power of the American workers, the workers would have prevailed. However, this "defeat of labor" was the culmination of the federal government—particularly the courts and the military—working in collusion with the railroad and other corporations that proved too steep a challenge for the workers.

This speech is important for understanding Debs's sense of justice and his willingness to take on what he deemed unjust laws. Debs makes no apologies for violating the injunction that led to his arrest. Indeed, in the course of his speech he directly attacks the judge and the institutions that supported him. This is in line with his readiness to criticize government in general whenever it supported corporations over the rights of its own citizens, as he did earlier in his speech. Debs deftly elevates the Constitution at the same time that he criticizes the forces he sees as a threat to the rights contained in that document, drawing a distinction between the principles at the foundation of the United States and the way those in power have corrupted those principles and misused their authority.. His main goal here is to rescue American liberty from domination by the forces of monopoly, a major political issue during this era.

Essential Themes

A key idea that emerges in Debs's 1895 speech on Liberty is that the workers of the United States—in the case of the Pullman Strike, railroad workers in particular—have been drawn into battle not only with the corporations that abuse their labor and their rights but also the federal government that supports its corporate citizens (the Supreme Court, in a number of cases, proclaimed that corporate entities had the same rights as individuals) over its laboring citizens. Thus, while the workers of the American Railway Union did not seek to be in conflict with the federal government, did not seek to take on the court system or the Army, this was the battle in which they now found themselves.

Here, Debs lays out not only the conflict between workers and corporations, but between American citizens and the dangerous combination of forces—corporate and political—that seeks to undermine the Constitution and citizenry's political freedom as well as their economic freedom. To the workers who participated in the Pullman Strike, who had to face the rifles and bayonets of American soldiers, this speech represents a call to further action.

———Jonathan Rees, PhD

Bibliography and Additional Reading

Burns, Dave. "The Soul of Socialism: Christianity, Civilization, and Citizenship in the Thought of Eugene Debs" in *Labor*, vol. 5, no. 2 (2008), pp. 83–116.

Ginger, Ray. *The Bending Cross: A Biography of Eugene Victor Debs*. (New Brunswick, New Jersey: Rutgers University Press: 1949).

Papke, David Ray. *The Pullman Case: The Clash of Labor and Capital in Industrial America*. (Lawrence, Kansas: University Press of Kansas, 1999).

Schneirov, Richard, et al. (eds.) *The Pullman Strike and the Crisis of the 1890s: Essays on Labor and Politics*. (Urbana, Illinois: University of Illinois Press, 1999).

The "Cross of Gold" Speech

Date: 1896
Author: William Jennings Bryan
Genre: Speech

Summary Overview

On July 8, 1896, at the Democratic National Convention in Chicago, William Jennings Bryan gave one of the most memorable political addresses in American history. Dubbed the "Cross of Gold" Speech because of its vivid image of crucifying humankind upon a golden cross, the oration propelled Bryan to the Democratic nomination for president of the United States. In the "Cross of Gold" Speech, Bryan articulated the feelings of Americans from the South and West who felt that the currency system and its effects had injured their financial and cultural interests. These sections saw a more flexible monetary system and some degree of inflation as a cure for the economic ills that afflicted farmers, miners, and industrial workers. Bryan captured their grievances and gave them eloquent expression in his "Cross of Gold" Speech.

Bryan's remarks, which he had given in earlier speeches, spoke to the specific discontent of Democratic leaders and their constituents in 1896. His words resonated because they summed up the feelings of alienation from the political system and from the emerging industrial society that so many Americans felt in that summer of a presidential election.

Defining Moment

The events that led to Bryan's oration grew out of the history of the Democratic Party during the 1890s. In 1892 the party had elected Grover Cleveland to a second term as president. After just a few weeks in office, the Panic of 1893 occurred, with bank failures, mass unemployment, and the bankruptcies of many businesses. This downturn exposed fault lines within the Democratic ranks. Cleveland and eastern party members believed that the solution lay in the "gold standard," meaning that the government should issue dollars based on the amount of gold bullion the nation held in its treasury. Because the world supply of gold was limited, the amount of dollars and credit in circulation would be restricted as well. Only in that way, Cleveland argued, could the nation regain its economic health.

Democrats in the West and South, however, countered that the problem lay elsewhere. These agricultural regions faced declining prices for staple crops such as wheat and cotton, which they produced. Farmers in these areas also had debts for land and equipment that they found more difficult to pay. As a result, they argued that the government should put more money into circulation, thereby raising prices and making debts easier to pay. They proposed to accomplish these ends through what was then known as "free silver," a shorthand phrase for the free and unlimited coinage of silver into money at a fixed ratio with gold. Bryan emerged a leader of the free silver wing of the party.

Violent protests and strikes followed during the 1890s and the Republicans made massive gains in the House and Senate against Democrats in 1894 elections. Now, free-silver Democrats resolved to control the nomination of a presidential candidate in 1896.

Bryan knew that if he could have a chance to address an audience of pro-silver Democrats, he could make a speech that would energize the crowd. During 1895 and 1896, he tested lines in his standard speeches to his fellow Democrats, perfecting the argument that he would advance in Chicago, where he sought an opportunity to make the speech of his life.

Author Biography

William Jennings Bryan was just thirty-six years old when he delivered the "Cross of Gold" Speech at the 1896 Democratic National Convention. He was born in Salem, Illinois, on March 19, 1860. During the late 1880s, after attending Whipple Academy and Illinois College, Bryan studied law and moved to Nebraska. He soon plunged into Democratic politics. Elected to Congress in 1890, he served two terms in the House before seeking a Senate seat in 1894. That campaign failed, and Bryan turned his attention to the Democratic presidential nomination in 1896, which was significant as it was a joint nomination with the Populist Party (who had Bryan as their presidential candidate but a different vice presidential candidate than the Democrats).

Bryan lost the 1896 general election to William McKinley, and he lost again to McKinley in 1900—an election in which Bryan voiced concerns over the American

The "Cross of Gold" Speech

acquisition of territory following the Spanish-American War—and to William Howard Taft in 1908. From 1913 to 1915, Bryan served as Secretary of State under President Woodrow Wilson, resigning over what he perceived as the President's lack of commitment to neutrality in the ongoing First World War. In 1925 he played a key role in the famed Scopes Trial in Tennessee, in which he argued that the teaching of evolution should be banned in public schools. He died in Dayton, Tennessee, on July 26, 1925, just five days after the Scopes trial ended.

HISTORICAL DOCUMENT

Mr. Chairman and Gentlemen of the convention: I would be presumptuous, indeed, to present myself against the distinguished gentlemen to whom you have listened if this was a mere measuring of abilities; but this is not a contest between persons. The humblest citizen in all the land, when clad in the armor of a righteous cause, is stronger than all the hosts of error. I come to speak to you in defense of a cause as holy as the cause of liberty, the cause of humanity.

When this debate is concluded a motion will be made to lay upon the table the resolution offered in commendation of the administration and also the resolution offered in condemnation of the administration. We object to bringing this question down to the level of persons. The individual is but an atom; he is born, he acts, he dies; but principles are eternal; and this has been a contest over a principle.

Never before in the history of this country has there been witnessed such a contest as that through which we have just passed. Never before in the history of American politics has a great issue been fought out, as this issue has been, by the voters of a great party. On the fourth of March, 1895, a few Democrats, most of them Members of Congress, issued an address to the Democrats of the nation, asserting that the money question was the paramount issue of the hour; declaring that a majority of the Democratic party had the right to control the action of the party on this paramount issue; and concluding with the request that the believers in the free coin age of silver in the Democratic party should organize, take charge of and control the policy of the Democratic party. Three months later, at Memphis, an organization was perfected, and the silver Democrats went forth openly and courageously proclaiming their belief, and declaring that, if successful, they would crystallize into a platform the declaration which they had made. Then began the conflict. With a zeal approaching the zeal which inspired the crusaders who followed Peter the Hermit, our silver Democrats went forth from victory unto victory until they are now assembled, not to discuss, not to debate, but to enter up the judgment already rendered by the plain people of this country. In this contest brother has been arrayed against brother, father against son. The warmest ties of love, acquaintance and association have been disregarded; old leaders have been cast aside when they have refused to give expression to the sentiments of those whom they would lead, and now leaders have sprung up to give direction to this cause of truth. Thus has the contest been waged, and we have assembled here under as binding and solemn instructions as were ever imposed upon representatives of the people.

We do not come as individuals. As individuals we might have been glad to compliment the gentleman from New York, but we know that the people for whom we speak would never be willing to put him in a position where he could thwart the will of the Democratic party. I say it was not a question of persons; it was a question of principle, and it is not with gladness, my friends, that we find ourselves brought into conflict with those who are now arrayed on the other side.

The gentleman who preceded me spoke of the State of Massachusetts; let me assure him that not one present in all this convention entertains the least hostility to the people of the State of Massachusetts, but we stand here representing people who are the equals before the law of the greatest citizens in the State of Massachusetts. When you come before us and tell us that we are about to disturb your business interests, we reply that you have disturbed our business interests by course.

We say to you that you have made the definition of a business man too limited in its application. The man who is employed for wages is as much a business man as his employer; the attorney in a country town is as much a business man as the corporation counsel in a great metropolis; the merchant at the crossroads store is as much a business man as the merchant of New York; the farmer who goes forth in the morning and toils all day—who begins in the spring and toils all summer—and who by the application of brain and muscle to the natural resources of the country creates wealth, is as much a business man as the man who goes upon the board of trade and bets upon the price of grain; the miners who go down a thousand feet into the earth, or climb two thousand feet upon the cliffs, and bring forth from their hiding-places the precious metals to be poured in the channels of trade, are as much business men as the few financial magnates who, in a back room, corner the money of the world. We come to speak for this broader class of business men.

Ah, my friends, we say not one word against those who live upon the Atlantic coast, but the hardy pioneers who have braved all the dangers of the wilderness, who have made the desert to blossom as the rose—the pioneers away out there, who rear their children near to Nature's heart, where they can mingle their voices with the voices of the birds—out there where they have erected schoolhouses for the education of their young, churches where they praise their Creator, and cemeteries where rest the ashes of their dead—these people, as we say, are as deserving of the consideration of our party as any people in this country. It is for these that we speak. We do not come as aggressors. Our war is not a war of conquest; we are fighting in the defense of our homes, our families, and posterity. We have petitioned, and out (sic) petitions have been scorned; we have entreated, and our entreaties have been disregarded; we have begged, and they have mocked when our calamity came. We beg no longer; we entreat no more; we petition no more. We defy them.

The gentleman from Wisconsin has said that he fears a Robespierre. My friends, in this land of the free you need not fear a tyrant that will spring up from among the people. What we need is an Andrew Jackson to stand, as Jackson stood, against the encroachments of organized wealth.

They tell us that this platform was made to catch votes. We reply to them that changing conditions make new issues; that the principles upon which democracy rests are as everlasting as the hills, but that they must be applied to new conditions as they arise. Conditions have arisen, and we are here to meet those conditions. They tell us that the income tax ought not to be brought in here; that it is a new idea. They criticize us for our criticism of the Supreme Court of the United States. My friends, we have not criticized; we have simply called attention to what you already know. If you want criticisms, read the dissenting opinions of the court. There you will find criticisms. They say that we passed an unconstitutional law; we deny it. The income-tax law was not unconstitutional when it went before the Supreme Court for the first time; it did not become unconstitutional until one of the judges changed his mind, and we cannot be expected to know when a judge will change his mind. The income tax is just. It simply intends to put the burdens of government justly upon the backs of the people. I am in favor of an income tax. When I find a man who is not willing to bear his share of the burdens of the government which protects him, I find a man who is unworthy to enjoy the blessings of a government like ours.

They say that we are opposing national bank currency; it is true. If you will read what Thomas Benton said, you will find he said that, in searching history, he could find but one parallel to Andrew Jackson; that was Cicero, who destroyed the conspiracy of Catiline and saved Rome. Benton said that Cicero only did for Rome what Jackson did for us when he destroyed the bank conspiracy and saved America. We say in our platform that we believe that the right to coin and issue money is a function of government. We believe it. We believe that it is a part of sovereignty, and can no more with safety be delegated to private individuals than we could afford to delegate private individuals the power to make penal statues or levy taxes. Mr. Jefferson, who was once regarded as good Democratic authority, seemed to have differed in opinion from the gentleman who has addressed us on the part of the minority. Those who are opposed to this proposition tell us that the issue of paper money is a function of the bank, and that the Government ought to go out of the banking business. I stand with Jefferson rather than with them, and tell them, as he did, that the issue of money is a function of government, and that banks ought to go out of the governing business.

They complain about the plank which declares against life tenure in office. They have tried to strain it to mean that which it does not mean. What we oppose by that plank is the life tenure which is being built up in Washington, and which excludes from participation in official benefits the humbler members of society.

Let me call your attention to two or three important things. The gentleman from New York says that he will propose an amendment to the platform providing that the proposed change in our monetary system shall not affect contracts already made. Let me remind you that there is no intention of affecting those contracts which according to present laws are made payable in god, but if he means to say that we cannot change our monetary system without protecting those who have loaned money before the change was made, I desire to ask him where, in law or in morals, he can find justification for not protecting the debtors when the act of 1873 was passed, if he now insists that we must protect the creditors.

He says he will also propose an amendment which will provide for the suspension of free coinage if we fail to maintain the parity within a year. We reply that when we advocate a policy which we believe will be successful, we are not compelled to raise a doubt as to our own sincerity by suggesting what we shall do if we fail. I ask him, if he would apply his logic to us, why he doesn't apply himself. He says he wants this country to try to secure an international agreement. Why does he not tell us what he is going to do if he fails to secure an international agreement? There is more reason for him to do that than there is for us to provide against the failure to maintain the parity. Our opponents have tried for twenty years to secure an international agreement, and those are waiting for it most patiently who do not want it at all.

And now, my friends, let me come to the paramount issue. If they ask us why it is that we say more on the money question than we say upon the tariff question, I reply that, if protection has slain its thousands, the gold standard has slain its tens of thousands. If they ask us why we do not embody in our platform all the things that we believe in, we reply that when we have restored the money of the Constitution all other necessary reforms will be possible; but that until this is done there is no other reform that can be accomplished.

Why is it that within three months such a change has come over the country? Three months ago, when it was confidently asserted that those who believe in the gold standard would frame our platform and nominate our candidates, even the advocates of the gold standard did not think that we could elect a president. And they had good reason for their doubt, because there is scarcely a State here today asking for the gold standard which is not in the absolute control of the Republican party. But note the change. Mr. McKinley was nominated as St. Louis upon a platform which declared for the maintenance of the gold standard until it can be changed into bimetallism by international agreement. Mr. McKinley was the most popular man among the Republicans, and three months ago everybody in the Republican party prophesied his election. How is it today? Why, the man who was once pleased to think that he looked like Napolean [sic]—that man shudders today when he remembers that he was nominated on the anniversary of the battle of Waterloo. Not only that, as he listens, he can hear with ever-increasing distinctness the sound of the waves as they beat upon the lonely shores of St. Helena.

Why this change? Ah, my friends, is not the reason for change evident to anyone who will look at the matter? No private character, however pure, no personal popularity, however great, can protect form the avenging wrath of an indignant people a man who will declare that he is in favor of fastening the gold standard upon this country or who is willing to surrender the right of self-government and place the legislative control of our affairs in the hands of foreign potentates and powers.

We go forth confident that we shall win. Why? Because upon the paramount issue of this campaign there is not a spot of ground upon which the enemy will dare to challenge battle. If they tell us that the gold standard is a good thing, we shall point to their platform and tell them that their platform pledges the party to get rid of the gold standard and substitute bimetallism. If the gold standard is a good thing, why try to get rid of it? I call your attention to the fact that some of the very people who are in this convention today and who tell us that we ought to declare in favor of international bimetallism—thereby declaring that the gold standard is wrong and that the principle of bimetallism is better—these very people four months ago were open and avowed advocates of the gold standard, and were then telling us that we could not legislate two metals together, even with the aid of all the world. If the gold standard is a good thing, we ought to declare it in favor of its retention and not in favor of abandoning it; and if the gold standard is a bad thing why should we wait until other nations are willing to help us to let go?

Here is the line of battle, and we care not upon which issue they force the fight; we are prepared to meet them on either issue or on both. If they tell us that the gold standard is the standard of civilization, we reply to them that this, the most enlightened of all the nations of the earth, has never declared for a gold standard and that both the great parties this year are declaring against it. If the gold standard is the standard of civilization, why, my friends, should we not have it? If they come to meet us on that issue we can present the history of our nation. More than that; we can tell them that they will search the pages of history in vain to find a single instance where the holders of fixed investments have declared for a gold standard, but not where the masses have.

Mr. Carlisle said in 1878 that this was a struggle between "the idle holders of capital" and "the struggling masses, who produce the wealth and pay the taxes of the country," and my friends, the question we are to decide is: Upon which side will the Democratic party fight: upon the side of the "idle holders of idle capital" or upon the side of "the struggling masses?" That is the question which the party must answer first, and then it must be answered by each individual hereafter. The sympathies of the Democratic party, as shown by the platform, are on the side of the struggling masses who have ever been the foundation of the Democratic party. There are two ideas of government. There are those who believe that, if you will only legislate to make the well-to-do prosperous, their prosperity will leak through on those below. The Democratic idea, however, has been that if you legislate to make the masses prosperous, their prosperity will find its way up through every class which rests upon them.

You come to us and tell us that the great cities are in favor of the gold standard; we reply that the great cities rest upon our broad and fertile prairies. Burn down your cities and leave our farms and your cities will spring up again as if by magic; but destroy our farms and the grass will grow in the streets of every city in the country.

My friends, we declare that this nation is able to legislate for its own people on every question, without waiting for the aid or consent of any other nation on earth; and upon that issue we expect to carry every state of New York by saying that, when they are confronted with the proposition, they will declare that this nation is not able to attend to its own business. It is the issue of 1776 over again. Our ancestors, when but three millions in number, had the courage to declare their political independence of every other nation; shall we, their descendants, when we have grown to seventy millions, declare that we are less independent than our forefathers? No, my friends, that will never be the verdict of our people. Therefore, we care not upon what lines the battle is fought. If they say bimetallism is good, but that we cannot have it until other nations help us, we reply that, instead of having a gold standard because England has, we will restore bimetallism, and then let England have bimetallism because the United States has it. If they dare to come out in the open field and defend the gold standard as a good thing, we will fight them to the uttermost. Having behind us the producing masses of this nation and the world, supported by the commercial interests, the laboring interests, and the toilers everywhere, we will answer their demand for a gold standard by saying to them: You shall not press down upon the brow of labor this crown of thorns; you shall not crucify mankind upon a cross of gold.

GLOSSARY

bimetallism: the use of gold and silver as the standards of value, within a fixed ratio to each other

counsel: attorney

encroachments: trespasses or transgressions

entreaties: pleas; requests

free coinage: the system by which the government coins either silver or gold into money at no charge or at cost.

instructions: in a political convention, binding orders to a delegation to vote for a candidate or platform plank

magnates: important business leaders

presumptuous: too bold or forward

protection: the policy of encouraging industry through customs duties on imported goods

Document Analysis

In the first paragraph, Bryan begins humbly with a disclaimer about his ability to measure up to previous speakers and notes that "this is not a contest between persons" but rather of eternal principles. By the third paragraph, Bryan moves into the heart of his oration. Bryan says that the debate over free silver has been divisive and intense but argues that the advocates of silver have prevailed. In the fourth paragraph, Bryan assures the former Massachusetts governor William Russell and the gold delegates that they have disturbed the business interests of the West as much as the silver men have caused dismay in the East.

In the sixth paragraph, Bryan reaches a key point in his speech. He says that the workers, farmers, and miners of the West are businessmen in the same sense that corporate officers, lawyers, and merchants in the East bear that title. Bryan's comments address sectional divisions and demonstrate that he is speaking for those who did as much labor as traditional business figures did in the East.

Bryan then advances the claims of those westerners who deserve better treatment from the rest of the country, asserting that their needs have been ignored by party elites in the east. Critics of Bryan accused him of being a radical, but Bryan associates himself with the aspirations of President Andrew Jackson, who, Bryan notes, resisted "the encroachments of organized wealth" in his fight against the Second Bank of the United States during the 1830s. He continues this comparison to the Age of Jackson in the tenth paragraph. In paragraph 12, Bryan reassures his opponents that the adoption of free silver would not undermine existing contracts that specified payment in gold.

Paragraph 13 brings Bryan into the substance of his argument for free silver. The market price of silver was low at this time, and raising it to a ratio of sixteen to one (which was what Bryan favored) would have required large subsidies from the treasury. Bryan brushes that argument aside. One of the devices that moderate thinkers on both sides of the issue advanced was the concept of an international agreement to use silver more widely. This was dubbed "international bimetallism." The large flaw in that proposal was the opposition of Great Britain, the leading champion of gold, to any such endeavor.

Bryan mocks William McKinley and the Republicans for their stand on the gold standard in his fifteenth paragraph. He contends that the political position has deteriorated since the Republican convention nominated McKinley on the gold standard and a promise to seek an international agreement on silver. The Republicans inserted that language at the behest of McKinley to placate silver supporters in the West. This alleged plunge in Republican fortunes, Bryan argues in his sixteenth paragraph, has occurred because McKinley and his party have become associated with the gold standard and the readiness to place American monetary affairs in the hands of other countries through an international bimetallic agreement. In paragraph 17, Bryan further ridicules the idea of international bimetallism and accuses his opponents of being willing to abandon the gold standard even as they say that he is doing the same thing. He adds that "the common people" had not come out for gold—only "the holders of the fixed investments."

John G. Carlisle, who is mentioned in the eighteenth paragraph, was Grover Cleveland's secretary of the treasury in 1896. When he was a member of the House of Representatives in 1878, Carlisle had made a pro-silver speech. Bryan uses Carlisle's words about "the idle holders of capital" and "the struggling masses" to ask where the Democrats would stand. He maintains that the party's sympathies "are on the side of the struggling masses who have ever been the foundation of the Democratic party."

The nineteenth paragraph is brief, but it contains some of the best expressions of the agrarian values that underlay the Democratic Party in 1896, arguing that the farms and ranches of the west are far more valuable than eastern business interests assume. In paragraph 20, he reiterates the point that free silver does not require international cooperation. He predicts victory across the country, and then he evokes the spirit of the American Revolution: "It is the issue of 1776 all over again." In 1896, as during the time of the battle against the British, the voters would display their political independence. The Democrats would institute bimetallism on their own without asking permission of England or other countries. If the fight was to be made over the gold standard itself, however, Bryan would welcome that as well.

As he prepared to utter his final words, Bryan turned to gestures he had practiced before. When he referred to "this crown of thorns," Bryan pressed his hands down on his forehead. When he ended with the words "crucify mankind upon a cross of gold," he spread his arms to make a cross of his own.

Essential Themes

In vintage rhetoric, arguing against factions within his own part as well as the opposition Republican Party, Bryan casts the issue as a moral struggle of the common citizen against wealthy interests. Free silver, as Bryan pictured it, was more than an economic issue. It was a way of life under siege. In the second-most-quoted passage of the speech, he returns to his agrarian theme that family farms were at the heart of American culture: "But destroy our farms and the grass will grow in the streets of every city in the country." The concluding words of the speech, cloaked in Christian symbolism and rhythmic intonation, are among the most quoted in modern history: "You shall not crucify mankind upon a cross of gold."

Bryan's speech was twenty minutes long, short by his standards. But the convention exploded in response. Both shouts of joy and tears were everywhere, and the demonstration that followed was unprecedented. By the fifth vote, Bryan had secured enough delegates to clinch the nomination. He was, at thirty-six, the youngest nominee of a major party in the country's history.

——Lewis L. Gould, PhD
with additional material by Charles Orson Cook, PhD

Bibliography and Additional Reading

Coletta, Paolo E. *William Jennings Bryan*, Vol. 1: *Political Evangelist, 1860–1908.* (Lincoln: University of Nebraska Press, 1964).

Jones, Stanley L. *The Presidential Election of 1896.* (Madison: University of Wisconsin Press, 1964).

Kazin, Michael. *A Godly Hero: The Life of William Jennings Bryan.* (New York: Knopf, 2006).

Koenig, Louis W. *Bryan: A Political Biography of William Jennings Bryan.* (New York: Putnam, 1971).

Morgan, H. Wayne. *William McKinley and His America*, rev. ed. (Kent, Ohio: Kent State University Press, 2003).

Williams, R. Hal. *Years of Decision: American Politics in the 1890s.* (Prospect Heights, Ill. Waveland Press, 1993).

Witcover, Jules. *Party of the People: A History of the Democrats.* (New York: Random House, 2003).

Speech Opposing the League of Nations

Date: 1919
Author: Henry Cabot Lodge
Genre: Speech

Summary Overview

Henry Cabot Lodge advocated a militant foreign policy, one based on the premise that the United States was a great power and should always act as such. At the same time he could also urge caution, as when he attacked President Woodrow Wilson in 1915 for engaging in a blundering and destructive intervention in Mexico. The president again met with Lodge's scorn in February 1917 when Lodge condemned Wilson's call for "peace without victory" in ending World War I and for seeking to create a binding league to enforce this peace; both policies, he claimed, were utterly unrealistic. Addressing his senatorial colleagues on February 28, 1919, in his Speech Opposing the League of Nations, Lodge critiques the Covenant of the League of Nations that Wilson had brought back from the Paris Peace Conference, stressing the dangers inherent in any indissoluble alliance.

Defining Moment

Although the United States had only been involved in the First World War since the spring of 1917, American contributions to the Allied victory and President Woodrow Wilson's commitment to forging a lasting peace in Europe and throughout the world led to him having a seat at the table during treaty negotiations following the November 11, 1918 Armistice. In December 1918, Wilson sailed to Europe to participate in the Paris Peace Conference that would draft treaties with the Central Powers (Germany, Austria-Hungary, the Ottoman Empire, and Bulgaria). On February 14 a special commission, over which the president presided, submitted a draft covenant for a proposed League of Nations to the conference's plenary session. The League of Nations was an example of a collective security arrangement, working to defuse volatile situations through diplomacy and, hopefully, prevent future wars. The United States had never been part of a treaty system so extensive or permanent. Ten days later Wilson briefly returned to the United States, in part to defuse anticipated Senate criticism. Arriving in Boston, he gave a speech in Mechanics Hall in which he claimed that peace could not last a single generation unless it was guaranteed by all the civilized world.

As a result of the 1918 congressional elections, the Republicans had gained control of both houses of Congress. Lodge, who had become chairman of the Senate Foreign Relations Committee, was quick to challenge the president.

Author Biography

Henry Cabot Lodge was born in Boston on May 12, 1850, the son of a wealthy Brahman merchant and shipowner. Lodge began his political career as a liberal independent, but finding such a reformist stance futile, he quickly became a Republican. In 1886 Lodge was elected to Congress, In 1893, the Massachusetts legislature elected Lodge to the Senate, where he backed such causes as immigration restriction, hard money, and economic protectionism. Yet when his close friend Theodore Roosevelt became president in 1901, Lodge went along with most of Roosevelt's more liberal domestic policies. Moderate change, he believed, was preferable to such radical measures as government ownership of public utilities.

Lodge was closer to Roosevelt on matters of foreign policy, which was always Lodge's primary focus. A staunch defender of what was called the "large policy" (control of the Caribbean and parts of the Pacific and seizure of strategic islands like Cuba, Hawaii, and the Philippines), Lodge supported the U.S. navy flag officer Alfred Thayer Mahan in his desire to maximize naval strength. He opposed President Woodrow Wilson's handling of relations with Mexico and when World War I broke out, Lodge strongly supported the allies (Britain, France, Italy, Russia, Serbia, Romania, and Belgium), so much so that in May 1915, when the *Lusitania* was sunk, he called for severing diplomatic relations with Germany.

Although Lodge backed Wilson's war measures when the United States entered the conflict, he bitterly fought the president once the war ended. As chairman of the Senate Foreign Relations Committee, he strongly objected to Article 10 of the League of Nations covenant, which called for members to respect and preserve the independence and territorial integrity of all members. He feared that this would tie America's hands to such a degree that vital decisions would be out of the control of Congress. Lodge died on November 9, 1924, in Cambridge, Massachusetts.

HISTORICAL DOCUMENT

Mr. President, all people, men and women alike, who are capable of connected thought abhor war and desire nothing so much as to make secure the future peace of the world....We ought to lay aside once and for all the unfounded and really evil suggestion that because men differ as to the best method of securing the world's peace in the future, anyone is against permanent peace, if it can be obtained, among all the nations of mankind....We all earnestly desire to advance toward the preservation of the world's peace, and difference in method makes no distinction in purpose....No question has ever confronted the United States Senate which equals in importance that which is involved in the league of nations intended to secure the future peace of the world. There should be no undue haste in considering it. My one desire is that not only the Senate, which is charged with responsibility, but that the press and the people of the country should investigate every proposal with the utmost thoroughness and weigh them all carefully before they make up their minds....

In the first place, the terms of the league...must be so plain and so explicit that no man can misunderstand them....The Senate can take no action upon it, but it lies open before us for criticism and discussion. What is said in the Senate ought to be placed before the peace conference and published in Paris, so that the foreign Governments may be informed as to the various views expressed here.

In this draft prepared for a constitution of a league of nations,...there is hardly a clause about the interpretation of which men do not already differ. As it stands there is serious danger that the very nations which sign the constitution of the league will quarrel about the meaning of the various articles before a twelvemonth has passed. It seems to have been very hastily drafted, and the result is crudeness and looseness of expression, unintentional, I hope. There are certainly many doubtful passages and open questions obvious in the articles which can not be settled by individual inference, but which must be made so clear and so distinct that we may all understand the exact meaning of the instrument to which we are asked to set our hands. The language of these articles does not appear to me to have the precision and unmistakable character which a constitution, a treaty, or a law ought to present....Arguments and historical facts have no place in a statute or a treaty. Statutory and legal language must assert and command, not argue and describe. I press this point because there is nothing so vital to the peace of the world as the sanctity of treaties. The suggestion that we can safely sign because we can always violate or abrogate is fatal not only to any league but to peace itself. You can not found world peace upon the cynical "scrap of paper" doctrine so dear to Germany. To whatever instrument the United States sets its hand it must carry out the provisions of that instrument to the last jot and tittle, and observe it absolutely both in letter and in spirit. If this is not done the instrument will become a source of controversy instead of agreement, of dissension instead of harmony. This is all the more essential because it is evident, although not expressly stated, that this league is intended to be indissoluble, for there is no provision for its termination or for the withdrawal of any signatory. We are left to infer that any nation withdrawing from the league exposes itself to penalties and probably to war. Therefore, before we ratify, the terms and language in which the terms are stated must be exact and precise, as free from any possibility of conflicting interpretations, as it is possible to make them.

The explanation or interpretation of any of these doubtful passages is not sufficient if made by one man, whether that man be the President of the United States, or a Senator, or anyone else. These questions and doubts must be answered and removed by the instrument itself.

It is to be remembered that if there is any dispute about the terms of this constitution there is no court provided that I can find to pass upon differences of opinion as to the terms of the constitution itself. There is no court to fulfill the function which our Supreme Court fulfills. There is provision for tribunals to decide questions submitted for arbitration, but there is no authority to decide differing interpretations as to the terms of the instrument itself....

I now come to questions of substance, which seem to me to demand the most careful thought of the entire American people, and particularly of those charged with the responsibility of ratification. We abandon entirely by the proposed constitution the policy laid down by Washington in his Farewell Address and the Monroe doctrine....I know that some of the ardent advocates of the plan submitted to us regard any suggestion of the importance of the Washington policy as foolish and irrelevant.... Perhaps the time has come when the policies of Washington should be abandoned; but if we are to cast them aside I think that at least it should be done respectfully and with a sense of gratitude to the great man who formulated them. For nearly a century and a quarter the policies laid down in the Farewell Address have been followed and adhered to by the Government of the United States and by the American people. I doubt if any purely political declaration has ever been observed by any people for so long a time. The principles of the Farewell Address in regard to our foreign relations have been sustained and acted upon by the American people down to the present moment. Washington declared against permanent alliances....He did not close the door on temporary alliances for particular purposes. Our entry in the great war just closed was entirely in accord with and violated in no respect the policy laid down by Washington. When we went to war with Germany we made no treaties with the nations engaged in the war against the German Government. The President was so careful in this direction that he did not permit himself ever to refer to the nations by whose side we fought as "allies," but always as "nations associated with us in the war."...Now, in the twinkling of an eye, while passion and emotion reign, the Washington policy is to be entirely laid aside and we are to enter upon a permanent and indissoluble alliance. That which we refuse to do in war we are to do in peace, deliberately, coolly, and with no war exigency. Let us not overlook the profound gravity of this step.

Washington was not only a very great man but he was also a very wise man. He looked far into the future and he never omitted human nature from his calculations....He was so great a man that the fact that this country had produced him was enough of itself to justify the Revolution and our existence as a Nation. Do not think that I overstate this in the fondness of patriotism and with the partiality of one of his countrymen. The opinion I have expressed is the opinion of the world....

But if we put aside forever the Washington policy in regard to our foreign relations we must always remember that it carries with it the corollary known as the Monroe doctrine. Under the terms of this league draft reported by the committee to the peace conference the Monroe doctrine disappears. It has been our cherished guide and guard for nearly a century. The Monroe doctrine is based on the principle of self-preservation. To say that it is a question of protecting the boundaries, the political integrity, or the American States, is not to state the Monroe doctrine....The real essence of that doctrine is that American questions shall be settled by Americans alone; that the Americas shall be separated from Europe in purely American questions. That is the vital principle of the doctrine.

I have seen it said that the Monroe doctrine is preserved under article 10; that we do not abandon the Monroe doctrine, we merely extend it to all the world. How anyone can say this passes my comprehension. The Monroe doctrine exists solely for the protection of the American Hemisphere, and to that hemisphere it was limited. If you extend it to all the world, it ceases to exist,...Under this draft of the constitution of the league of nations, American questions and European questions and Asian and African questions are all alike put within the control and jurisdiction of the league. Europe will have the right to take part in the settlement of all American questions, and we, of course, shall have the right to share in the settlement of all questions in Europe and Asia and Africa....Perhaps the time has come when it is necessary to do this, but it is a very grave step, and I wish now merely to point out that the American people ought never to abandon the Washington policy and the Monroe doctrine without being perfectly certain that they earnestly wish to do so. Standing always firmly by these great policies, we have thriven and prospered and have done more to preserve the world's peace than any nation, league, or alliance which ever existed. For this reason I ask the press and the public and, of course, the Senate to consider well the gravity of this proposition before it takes the heavy responsibility of finally casting aside these policies which we have adhered to for a century and more and under which we have greatly served the cause of peace both at home and abroad.

GLOSSARY

abrogate: renounce, go back on

"Article 10": Controversial part of the League of Nations charter that called for a collective security agreement among League members, potentially committing them to military action.

Monroe Doctrine: American foreign policy principle that the United States bore responsibility for protecting the western hemisphere from European influence.

Document Analysis

Addressing his senatorial colleagues on February 28, 1919, Lodge first concedes the universal desire for a lasting peace—regardless of whether leaders differ on the best way to establish peace. He also asserts that the issue of whether or not to join the League of Nations is the most important question that the Senate has ever addressed and urges a thorough examination of the document and its implications for the United States and other member nations, suggesting that the Senate debate be provided to other participants at the peace conference.

Lodge then begins his critique of the agreement, noting that a "there is hardly a clause about the interpretation of which men do not already differ," which carries with it the danger that the member nations will not even agree with each other about the meaning of the document. He points to its loose phrasing and equivocal language, which he finds inappropriate to what of necessity was a legal document. He also criticizes the charter's use of rhetorical arguments and "historical facts," asserting that this is not the language or style that should be used by a treaty. The greatest problem, however, is that the argument that the United States can "safely sign [the treaty] because we can always violate or abrogate" it later, if aspects are not to our liking. This kind of thinking, Lodge argues, undermines the entire purpose of a treaty and will create "dissension instead of harmony." This is especially dangerous, he points out, because there is no language in the treaty which allows for a nation to leave the League of Nations; if leaving the agreement leads to war, it might be best, he implies, to not agree at all. He urges his colleagues to only ratify an agreement whose terms are "exact and precise, as free from any possibility of conflicting interpretations, as it is possible to make them" especially since there is no body (like our Supreme Court, he suggests) that will serve to settle disputes about the meaning of parts the document itself.

Far more important, Lodge notes that the covenant reverses the policy of George Washington by committing the United States to a binding alliance. The Washington Administration (1789-1797) was beset by international intrigue as the young United States attempted by maintain a neutral stance, especially with regard to conflicts between England and France. Washington's parting advice to the nation was to avoid "entangling alliances" with foreign powers. Similarly, the Monroe Doctrine, with its stress upon the settling of American questions by Americans alone, was being violated. Of particular concern was Article 10 of the proposed league, which required members to preserve the integrity and independence of other member nations against acts of aggression. Article 10 frightened Lodge, since it committed the United States to involve itself in questions invoking Europe, Asia, and Africa. Article 10 carried with it the potential for the United States to be committed to overseas wars without the approval of Congress or orders of the President, superseding the Constitution. Also at issue for Lodge were matters involving Asia Minor, where there was soon talk of an American mandate for Constantinople and Armenia, and the Balkans, a region so full of ethnic and tribal rivalries that World War I itself had originated there. Similarly, European and Asian nations would be given the right to exercise police powers on the American continent, which authority even extended to the highly strategic Panama Canal. As Lodge saw it, the nation's very sovereignty was at stake.

After he delivered this speech, Lodge fought a rearguard action against Wilson's league. He drafted fourteen "reservations" to the covenant, the most important being one that Article 10 was inapplicable unless Congress were to uphold it by act or resolution Yet Lodge was not irreconcilable on the matter. He favored a society of nations; unlike the one envisioned by Wilson, however, Lodge's lacked coercive powers. Because Wilson refused to accept Lodge's reservations, the entire peace treaty went down to defeat, first in November 1919 and then again in March 1920.

Essential Themes
In many ways, Henry Cabot Lodge's speech to the Senate on the League of Nations was an example of a reaction against the overseas crusading that had brought the United States into the first World War and to the negotiating table at Versailles. While many, including Lodge, believed that it was in American interests to support the Allied cause, the post-war developments desired by Wilson and other internationalists were a step too far for many American leaders.

What comes through in this excerpt of Lodge's speech, however, is the degree to which his argument was based not only on the substance of the agreement (and the far flung adventures to which it might commit the United States) but also on the vague and unclear language of the document itself. "Statutory and legal language," Lodge argues, "must assert and command, not argue and describe." In connection with this, he raises the very practical question of who has the power to interpret this agreement. Lodge and his fellow Republican "irreconsilables" are often portrayed as "isolationist" but this speech makes clear that trepidation about American involvement abroad was only one of their concerns about the League of Nations.

———Justus D. Doenecke, PhD

Bibliography and Additional Reading
Cooper, John Milton. *Breaking the Heart of the World: Woodrow Wilson and the Fight for the League of Nations* (New York: Cambridge University Press, 2010).
Knock, Thomas J. *To End All Wars: Woodrow Wilson and the Quest for a New World Order.* (Princeton: Princeton University Press, 1995).
Thomas, Evan. *The War Lovers: Roosevelt, Lodge, Hearst, and the Rush to Empire, 1898* (New York: Hachette Digital, 2010).
Widenor, William C. *Henry Cabot Lodge and the search for an American foreign policy* (Los Angeles: University of California Press, 1983)

Auto Workers Strike

Date: 1933
Author: Walter Reuther
Genre: Magazine article

Summary Overview

The 1935 passage of the National Labor Relations Act, which established federal protections for labor organizing, and the subsequent sit-down strike and organization of General Motors workers in Flint, Michigan, is often the most visible and well-remembered example of automotive industry union activism during the era of the Great Depression. Attempts to unionize auto workers, however, had gone on for years and significant, if less well-remembered industrial actions paved the way for developments later in the decade.

In this 1933 article, labor activist Walter Reuther tells the story of the long, difficult effort to unionize the workers of the American automotive industry and the results of their efforts, a 1933 strike against the Briggs Manufacturing company in early 1933. Reuther imbues his account with praise for the efforts of the left-wing Auto Workers Union who succeeded where the more staid, less radical American Federation of Labor had failed.

Reuther also uses this article to discuss the methods used by factory owners to break strikes and turn members of the working class against each other. Despite these attempts, Reuther details the way in which the effects of the strike at the Briggs corporation spread throughout the automotive industry in the Detroit area. Reuther's account of the strike also notes the important role played in the picketing by leftist students from the local university, illustrating the broad appeal of the labor movement.

Defining Moment

This history of modern, industrial labor organization in the United States dates back to the formation of the Knights of Labor following the Great Railroad Strike of 1877. The notion of a labor union for all workers, skilled and unskilled proved unwieldy and less radical labor organizations like Samuel Gompers's American Federation of Labor focused on organizing workers who were employed in the skilled trades. Throughout the early twentieth century, the American labor movement had its ups and downs, but the 1920s were a particularly dark time for labor organizing. Three successive Republican presidential administrations, along with a Congress that was dominated by Republicans for most of the decade ensured that labor organizers had an uphill struggle. The onset of the Great Depression in 1929 led to a resurgence in attempts to widely organize American workers. the automotive industry, which employed millions of Americans had been a target of unionization attempts since the 1920s. As Reuther described in his article, those efforts were difficult.

The target of the strike discussed by Reuther in this article, the Briggs Manufacturing Company, was a coachwork company, which meant that they designed and built the bodies that automobile manufacturers would turn into complete cars. During the 1920s and 1930s, carmakers did not always make every part of the car in their own factories and would purchase vital components—even the entire car or truck body—from other manufacturers. At the time of the strike Reuther discusses in the article, Briggs was experiencing profitable business even during the Great Depression. In fact, 1932 was the only year during the Depression where the company lost money. Despite profits in the millions of dollars nearly every year, Briggs's employees were among the worst compensated in the industry. In the early 1930s, for example, Ford's assembly line workers earned a dollar an hour ($18-19 in 2016 dollars), Briggs paid their assembly workers ten cents per hour ($1-2 in 2016 dollars). These were conditions that made the Briggs Company ripe for labor unrest.

Author Biography

Born in Wheeling, West Virginia in 1907, Walter Reuther was raised by a socialist father, a brewery worker who had come to the United States from Germany and Reuther absorbed his father's ideas about union activism and socialism from a young age. Training as a tool-and-die worker, in 1927 Reuther moved to Detroit, Michigan and began working for the Ford Motor Company. He and his brothers were becoming known as socialist activists at the City College of Detroit (which, in 1933, became part of Wayne State University). As the economic decline of the Great Depression deepened, Reuther was laid off from Ford in 1932. Reuther would maintain later that he was laid off because of his socialist activism.

It was while he was laid off from Ford that he wrote this 1933 article for The Student Outlook. The Outlook was the magazine of the Student League for Industrial Democracy, an organization which at the time served as an unofficial student branch of the Socialist Party of America in the early 1930s. Reuther's interest in socialism and industrialization let him on an extensive overseas trip from 1933 to 1935, during which time he worked in an automotive plant in the Soviet Union. Upon his return to the United States, Reuther began working at General Motors and became an active part of the United Automobile Workers union. Reuther would leave the socialist party and, eventually, become part of the Democratic party. He would become one of the most significant figures in American labor history. Reuther died in a plane crash on May 9, 1970.

HISTORICAL DOCUMENT

One year ago a complacent public was shocked by the news of the Ford Riot in which four workers were killed and forty wounded. Added to this tragic method of education comes the latest Briggs' strike and the other related strikes which have all slowly and painfully had their effect in educating the public as to the true conditions in the auto industry.

The American Federation of Labor once made an effort to organize the auto workers through the Machinist's Union, but because of craft limitations in a craftless industry, the Machinist's Union did not scratch the surface of the nut it hoped to crack. Not until 1926 at their convention in Detroit did the A.F. of L. seriously consider the organization of the production workers of the industry. The hope that a militant and constructive program of unionization would grow out of the convention was shattered when the A.F. of L. strategists permitted their plans to degenerate into a plea to the "enlightened" capitalists to accept the leadership of a responsible labor group rather than be exposed to the dangers of radicals and agitators. The complete failure of the A.F. of L.'s attempt to organize the production workers resulted in its leadership voicing the attitude that the task of unionizing the auto workers was impossible.

The challenge to organize the production workers was taken up by the Auto Workers Union, which is organized on a broad industrial basis and is founded on the principle of the class struggle. At one time the union was affiliated with the A.F. of L., but its charter was revoked over a question of jurisdiction. During the years 1919 and 1920, when the auto industry was going through a period of rapid expansion, the membership in the union grew to 45,000 and many successful strikes were staged in some of the plants.

The success of the union, however, was short-lived, for the depression of 1921 so paralyzed the auto industry that the union was broken and it declined until in 1924 the membership numbered only about 1500. As the power of the union declined, the employers became more aggressive and wage cuts, speedups, and excessive hours were thrust upon the workers. The corporations, realizing that the union might come to life at some future date, inaugurated a period of personnel management and sham industrial democracy. The Chrysler Industrial Corporation, the welfare scheme of the Chrysler Corporation, in which the workers have a voice only in the management of the baseball team typifies the extent of industrial democracy afforded by this plan.

In the face of overwhelming odds, the remnants of the Auto Workers Union, under left wing leadership kept up an unceasing struggle to unionize the auto workers into a militant, class conscious industrial organization.

After years of constant and untiring propaganda work and agitation through the departmental committees, working secretly and under great pressure, and by selling and distributing small shop papers, such as the Ford Worker and the Briggs Worker, at the gates of the plants, the Auto Workers Union finally felt that it had sufficient strength and that the time was ripe for action. It called a strike at the Briggs Waterloo Plant. The strike, while it was consciously planned by the union was nevertheless the expression of the Briggs' workers en masse against the starvation wages, long hours and further wage cuts which have given the Briggs Corporation the reputation of being the most vicious sweat shop and hellhole in Detroit.

Threatened with a twenty percent wage cut, 600 tool-and-die makers of the Waterloo plant struck 100 percent strong against the Briggs industrial aristocracy.

A strategic moment had been selected for this first strike as the tools and dies for the new Ford car were about seventy-five percent complete and production could not begin on schedule without their completion.

The strike so completely paralyzed the Briggs Corporation that after three days of picketing, the company was compelled to withdraw the wage cut, recognize the union shop committees and furthermore, to reinstate the former wage rate in the other three Briggs plants where the cut had already gone into effect. The solidarity of the Briggs' workers in their successful strike caused the Hudson Motor Company to remove the signs in their factories announcing a ten percent wage cut and replacing them by notices announcing the withdrawal of the wage cut.

Instilled with confidence by the activities of the Briggs' workers, fifteen hundred men from the Motor Products Co. went out on strike against a fifteen percent wage cut levied several weeks before. As a result the Motor Products Co. was also forced, after three days of strike activity, to rescind the wage slash, to recognize shop committees, to establish a minimum wage rate of thirty cents for women and forty cents for men on production. In many cases this meant an actual increase of fifty percent in wages.

Two successful and well-organized strikes within one week filled the workers of Detroit with a spirit of revolt against capitalist feudalism and paved the way for a rapid succession of strikes unparalleled in the history of the auto industry.

Fired with enthusiasm by the success of the strike at the Briggs' Waterloo plant, and encouraged by the splendid display of solidarity among the ranks of the employed and unemployed, 10,000 Briggs' workers from the Highland Park and Mack Avenue plants walked out on strike on January 23rd against starvation wages and the "dead time" policy. So low were the wages at Briggs that some of the woman workers claimed that their pay ranged from five cents per hour upwards, while men on production were getting from thirteen cents upward per hour. The "dead time" policy of the company was the source of much grievance as some employees were compelled to wait as long as three hours for material without compensation for "dead time," the period they had to wait.

The workers of the Waterloo and Meldrum Avenue plants soon followed the action of the other plants and pledged their solidarity and agreed among themselves to go back to work only after their rights were recognized and their grievances settled. The strikers met, endorsed the leadership of the Auto Workers Union, outlined their demands, elected their department representatives to the general strike committee and immediately began the picketing of the various plants.

Insofar as the strike paralyzed all four Briggs' plants, the strike was one hundred percent successful. The workers instead of returning to their jobs, joined the others in the fast growing picket line, despite the fact that the press carried headlines to the effect that the strike was settled and urged the strikers to return to their jobs.

As a whole the strike was most orderly except for a few instances where strikers molested scabs who were leaving the plant and sent several of them to the hospital. In one case when bodies from Briggs were being transported on trucks, a group of strikers demolished the bodies. Further shipments ceased.

All day and all night the picketers marched in front of cold winds, disregarding their empty stomachs. The sight of these thousands of hungry and poorly clothed industrial workers carrying their protest banners; the inspired sound of their chants, urging the workers to "organize, unite and fight" had the usual effect upon the already frightened owners of industry who feared greatly this latest revolt of their machine-tenders. The police were there in full force. Dearborn's mounted of Ford Riot fame, Detroit's riot squads, Highland Park's police, Wayne County scout cars, and Governor

Comstock's state troopers were all on the spot, equipped with guns, tear gas and clubs. As many as 250 of them were stationed at one plant. Aside from arresting a few picketers, the police were very conservative in their activities. They did not seem eager to become violent with a crowd of desperate strikers. Perhaps they had learned their lesson from the Ford Riot.

At first the strikers were quite hostile toward the police, but soon became quite friendly with them (for they didn't desire violence either), and the picketers began singing to the effect that after they had won their own strike, they would organize the cops. Many of the "workers" in uniform stated they had already had too many salary cuts and would welcome a union that could secure for them a decent living.

Production at the Ford River Rouge plant, crippled by the Briggs' strike, was shut down completely. Workers were notified that they could not return until the strike at Briggs was over. Ford's strike-breaking role was one more demonstrated when he shut down his tool and die rooms which were not dependent upon production at Briggs. Ford's giving notice to his workers that it was the Briggs' strike that was responsible for their layoff was but another attempt by Ford to break the strike by making his workers and public antagonistic to the strikers. So interested was Ford in breaking the strike that he even closed his Highland Park Store.

The Murray Corporation using tactics similar to Ford's, and demonstrating along with Ford, capitalist solidarity with the Briggs' concern, locked out approximately 4,000 production workers in an attempt to break the strike, but to their surprise the tool and die division went out on a strike in support of the Briggs' strikers and the locked out workers.

In the meantime the Auto Workers Union had been carrying on a great deal of propaganda in the other auto plants in an attempt to secure the support of all auto workers. Through the formation of inside groups, 3,000 body workers of the Hudson Motor Body plant at Connors and Gratiot Avenues walked out on strike "against wage cuts and working conditions" as one of the workers' committee expressed it. While this committee which represents the Hudson strikers claims that their strike is independent of the Briggs' strike, it is quite evident that their strike was planned by the same union that called the one at Briggs. As a result of the Hudson walkout, both of the Hudson plants are shut down completely.

At the Mack Avenue plant of Briggs', one of the most encouraging features of the entire strike occurred when several thousand unemployed formed a picket line across the street from the picketing strikers and demonstrated their solidarity with their fellow workers.

As in many other present day strikes, the students also played their part. About twenty students from the College of the City of Detroit (both Communists and Socialists) marched in line with the Briggs' picketers, singing and carrying signs reading "City College Students Unite with Strikers."

The tremendous effect this cooperation from the "respectable young intellectuals" had in breaking down the antipathy of the bystanders and minimizing the "red scare" can best be illustrated by the fact that during the first few critical hours of the strike when it was most difficult to get the workers to fall in line with the picketers, this group of students through their songs and general militant activity aided in swelling the numbers of the picket line from fifty to four hundred in but a few hours. So effective was the work of the student group that it was not long before the company ordered the police to take the students off the picket line. The police surrounded the group and took them inside the plant for questioning. The school authorities were notified and a general attempt was made to intimidate the students. But the reply was a larger group of students on the line the next morning.

The present strikes in the automobile field are the most significant and encouraging developments in the history of the industry. The union claims it has the key men in the body plants organized 100 percent and production cannot be resumed without them. If the workers win it will be the beginning of a new era in the struggle of labor to emancipate itself.

> **GLOSSARY**
>
> **craft limitations:** rules within a skilled trades union that restrict who can be a member
>
> **"in so far as":** to the degree that
>
> **rescind:** to undo or withdraw a policy
>
> **scabs:** workers who defy a strike in order to work for the business being struck against
>
> **speedups:** increased production demands on workers

Document Analysis

Reuther begins his account by recalling the Ford Riot of a year before, characterizing that incident and the Briggs's strike as events that will educate the public about "the true conditions in the auto industry." He then provides an overview of attempts to unionize the automotive industry during the 1920s. The AFL's efforts (through the Machinists' union) failed because the organization focused on skilled labor and the automotive industry was largely made up of unskilled workers. In 1926, the AFL made another attempt however this attempt failed because, according to Reuther, the union did not maintain a radical enough attitude. The attempt to organize the auto industry was continued by the Auto Workers Union which was "founded on the principle of class struggle"—an indicator that they were much more politically radical than the AFL. This union grew rapidly and organized several successful strikes. An economic downturn in 1921, however, led to a drastic decline in union membership and power. Despite this, the union has continued on. Here, Reuther emphasizes the importance of "left wing leadership" to the union's continued work.

After laying groundwork for years, the union made the decision to call a strike at the Briggs Waterloo plant against "starvation wages" and miserable working conditions and the threat of further wage cuts. The strike shut down production across the corporation and management withdrew the wage cut. Reuther reported that the success of the strike convinced other companies and plants to restore wages or to cancel plans for wage cuts. Strikes occurred at other plants, inspired by the Briggs action. These successful efforts, according to Reuther "filled the workers of Detroit with a spirit of revolt against capitalist feudalism."

Strikes continued at other Briggs plants around Detroit, with women joining the strike effort. Violence, according to Reuther was confined to attacking scab workers and some damage to products. Reuther then continues to characterize the striking workers as self-sacrificial, facing bitterly cold weather and hunger in order to march on the picket lines. This frightened the factory owners who "feared greatly this latest revolt of their machine-tenders." Police—including mounted units, riot squads, and state troopers were stationed at plants. The police, however, did not initiate violence toward the strikers. In fact, the workers—despite initial hostilities—offered to organize the police. Reuther claims that many of the police said they would welcome unionization, but whether or not that was actually the case is unknown.

The strike affected more than just the Briggs factories. Ford's production was halted by the lack of product coming from Briggs plants. Ford, however, went further and—in what Reuther calls a "strike-breaking" attempt, shut down production even of those areas that were not idled by the Briggs strike, attempting to turn his workers against the labor movement by convincing them that the strike was the reason he had laid them off. The Murray corporation locked out 4000 workers, but found itself the victim of a strike by its own tool and die workers.

Reuther next discusses the work of the Auto Workers Union during the strike, spreading propaganda in plants, attempting to increase the number of organized workers. These attempts led to thousands more auto workers coming out on strike, shutting down, for example, the Hudson auto plant. The strike even extended to the unemployed who joined the picket line at the Briggs plant. College students also joined the picket lines, with Reuther identifying them as Communists and Socialists. Reuther credits the presence of the "respectable" students as easing public concerns about the radical politics of the labor uprising.

Reuther concludes by arguing that the Briggs strike was "the most significant and encouraging developments in the history of the industry" and would lead to the full unionization of auto workers in the United States, a crucial step toward the ultimate goal of the "emancipation" of labor.

Essential Themes

Walter Reuther's account of the Briggs strike is not merely a piece of thorough reporting on a significant industrial action. It is also a carefully presentation that Reuther uses to make a number of important arguments about the nature of the labor movement in the United States in the early 1930s. Reuther makes the case that the more traditional, craft-based skilled trades unionism of the AFL was not effective in organizing the auto industry. Rather, it was the broad-based union that was "organized on a broad industrial basis" and "founded on the principle of the class struggle" is the type of labor organization that was able to not only organize auto workers but also coordinate a number of effective strikes. Reuther is sure to note the Auto Workers Union had undertaken an "unceasing struggle to unionize the auto workers into a militant, class conscious industrial organization." Reuther's socialist/communist viewpoint comes through clearly in this article. Reuther is also very careful to explain how the actions of striking workers at one plant had cumulative effects of factories that may not even have been unionized at the time. The narrative he develops tells the story of factory owners attempting to play workers against each other but, in Reuther's telling, this is unsuccessful. Even the police brought into intimidate the striking workers are persuaded by the rhetoric of the auto industry's class warriors.

———Aaron Gulyas, MA

Bibliography and Additional Reading

Barnard, John. *American Vanguard: The United Auto Workers during the Reuther Years, 1935–1970.* (Detroit: Wayne State University Press, 2004).

Lichtenstein, Nelson. *The Most Dangerous Man in Detroit: Walter Reuther and the Fate of American Labor* (New York, Basic Books, 1995).

Peterson, Joyce Shaw. *American Automobile Workers: 1900-1933* (Albany: State University of New York Press, 1987).

Widick, B.J. *Detroit: City of Class and Race Violence* Revised Edition (Detroit: Wayne State University Press, 1989).

Website

Theobald, Mark. "Briggs Manufacturing Co., 1909-1954; Detroit, Michigan." Coachbuilt.com. Accessed February 17, 2017. http://www.coachbuilt.com/bui/b/briggs/briggs.htm

■ "Share Our Wealth" Address

Date: 1935
Author: Huey Long
Genre: Speech

Summary Overview
By all accounts Huey Long was a spellbinding speaker. No matter the platform—the radio, the Senate floor, or small towns and large cities alike during campaigns—Long was a consummate performer who could adjust the level of his talk to his audience. In rural Louisiana he was a common man, using plain and simple language. On the Senate floor he could be eloquent in tearing apart legislation by his colleagues that either ignored or did not do enough to relieve the economic plight of Americans. Over the radio, he appealed directly to depression-era audiences of millions who were looking for ways out of poverty, joblessness, and the growing influence of corporations and wealthy individuals who, in Long's view, prevented the "everyman" from becoming a king—that is, master of his own fate, on an equal playing field with every other man. In a 1934 radio address, "Share Our Wealth," Long sharply criticized Franklin D. Roosevelt and his New Deal and outlined his alternative populist program for redistributing wealth. This speech provides details of his plan and was delivered on radio in January, 1935. It was later printed in the *Congressional Record*.

Defining Moment
In 1934, when Long first introduced his Share Our Wealth program and 1935, when he delivered this address, US President Franklin Roosevelt's administration and the Democratic Party-led Congress had enacted a number of measures collectively referred to as the First New Deal. These measures generally fell into three broad categories: recovery, relief, and reform. The National Recovery Administration attempted to restore industrial capacity, consumer purchasing levels and jobs. Banking reforms and the Securities Act of 1933 sought to prevent similar economic disasters from happening again. The Agricultural Adjustment Act, the Rural Electrification Administration, and the Civilian Conservation Corps aimed to relieve economic suffering.

Despite the unprecedented level of government involvement in the economy and the federal dollars spent, Roosevelt's critics on the political left did not believe he and his fellow Democrats were doing enough to either undo the damage to the economy or to take the radical steps necessary to ensure economic equality—such as wide-scale redistribution of wealth. The most vocal of these critics was Louisiana Senator Huey Long. On the floor of the Senate, Long would lambaste the administration and conservative Democrats in Congress for their unwillingness to take the steps necessary to solve the nation's economic woes.

Long's radical positions and his bold, aggressive manner made him few friends in the Senate, and none of his proposed bills were passed. Among these were the 1933 "Long Plan," which created a new tax code that would heavily penalize the wealthiest Americans and limit the size of personal fortunes, annual incomes, and inheritances. When these bills went down in defeat, Long turned to the public at large, unveiling his Share Our Wealth program in February, 1934.

Author Biography
Born on August 30, 1893, Huey Pierce Long, Jr., was the seventh of nine children. Although he often spoke of his childhood as one of extreme poverty, in fact he grew up in comfortable, if not affluent, surroundings. A precocious and articulate child, he was also undisciplined and prone to rebel against the requirements of formal education. After desultory work as a traveling salesman, Long entered Tulane University Law School. Although he managed to finish less than a year of coursework, he persuaded state officials to give him a bar exam, which he passed, becoming a lawyer at the age of twenty-one.

Long admitted that for him the law was merely a means to a political career, which he began in 1918 with his election as a state railroad commissioner. A lifelong member of the Democratic Party, he established himself from the beginning as a populist—more specifically, as a crusading underdog who attacked corporations like Standard Oil and establishment politicians who did the bidding of big business. After serving on the Louisiana Public Service Commission and running unsuccessfully for governor in 1924, he won the governorship in 1928 on a platform promising free textbooks for schoolchildren and a massive highway-building program. Long consolidated his power quickly by putting his cronies in state offices and by establishing his own newspaper. His abuse of power led to impeachment proceedings, which he was able to quash by bribing and intimidating state legislators.

Called a dictator, Long retained and enhanced his power by winning a seat in the U.S. Senate in 1930 but holding his position as governor until 1932; in that election year, his close associate and chosen successor, O.K. Allen, won the governorship. Initially supporting Franklin Roosevelt in the 1932 election for president, Long became increasingly disenchanted with Roosevelt's unwillingness to implement the radical share-the-wealth program that Long advocated in national radio addresses and on the Senate floor. In 1933 he published his autobiography, *Every Man a King*. With a serious mass following throughout the country, Long might have mounted a vigorous challenge to Roosevelt's reelection campaign in 1936, but he was assassinated; Long was shot on September 8, 1935, and died two days later. His visionary work *My First Days in the White House* was published after his death.

HISTORICAL DOCUMENT

We are in our third year of the Roosevelt depression, with the conditions growing worse....

We must now become awakened! We must know the truth and speak the truth. There is no use to wait three more years. It is not Roosevelt or ruin; it is Roosevelt's ruin....

We ran Mr. Roosevelt for the presidency of the United States because he promised to us by word of mouth and in writing:

- That the size of the big man's fortune would be reduced so as to give the masses at the bottom enough to wipe out all poverty; and
- That the hours of labor would be so reduced that all would share in the work to be done and in consuming the abundance mankind produced.

Hundreds of words were used by Mr. Roosevelt to make these promises to the people, but they were made over and over again. He reiterated these pledges even after he took his oath as President. Summed up, what these promises meant was: "Share our wealth."

When I saw him spending all his time of ease and recreation with the business partners of Mr. John D. Rockefeller, Jr., with such men as the Astors, etc., maybe I ought to have had better sense than to have believed he would ever break down their big fortunes to give enough to the masses to end poverty—maybe some will think me weak for ever believing it all, but millions of other people were fooled the same as myself. I was like a drowning man grabbing at a straw, I guess. The face and eyes, the hungry forms of mothers and children, the aching hearts of students denied education were before our eyes, and when Roosevelt promised, we jumped for that ray of hope.

So therefore I call upon the men and women of America to immediately join in our work and movement to share our wealth.

There are thousands of share-our-wealth societies organized in the United States now. We want 100,000 such societies formed for every nook and corner of this country—societies that will meet, talk, and work, all for the purpose that the great wealth and abundance of this great land that belongs to us may be shared and enjoyed by all of us....

So in this land of God's abundance we propose laws, viz.:

1. The fortunes of the multimillionaires and billionaires shall be reduced so that no one person shall own more than a few million dollars to the person. We would do this by a capital levy tax. On the first million that a man was worth, we would not impose any tax. We would say, "All right for your first million dollars, but after you get that rich you will have to start helping the balance of us." So we would not levy any capital levy tax on the first million one owned. But on the second million a man owns, we would tax that 1 percent, so that every year the man owned the second million dollars he would be taxed $10,000. On the third million we would impose a tax of 2 percent. On the fourth million we would

impose a tax of 4 percent. On the fifth million we would impose a tax of 8 percent. On the sixth million we would impose a tax of 16 percent. On the seventh million we would impose a tax of 32 percent. On the eighth million we would impose a tax of 64 percent; and on all over the eighth million we would impose a tax of 100 percent....

2. We propose to limit the amount any one man can earn in one year or inherit to $1 million to the person.
3. Now, by limiting the size of the fortunes and incomes of the big men, we will throw into the government Treasury the money and property from which we will care for the millions of people who have nothing; and with this money we will provide a home and the comforts of home, with such common conveniences as radio and automobile, for every family in America, free of debt.
4. We guarantee food and clothing and employment for everyone who should work by shortening the hours of labor to thirty hours per week, maybe less, and to eleven months per year, maybe less. We would have the hours shortened just so much as would give work to everybody to produce enough for everybody; and if we were to get them down to where they were too short, then we would lengthen them again. As long as all the people working can produce enough of automobiles, radios, homes, schools, and theaters for everyone to have that kind of comfort and convenience, then let us all have work to do and have that much of heaven on earth.
5. We would provide education at the expense of the states and the United States for every child, not only through grammar school and high school but through to a college and vocational education. We would simply extend the Louisiana plan to apply to colleges and all people. Yes; we would have to build thousands of more colleges and employ 100,000 more teachers; but we have materials, men, and women who are ready and available for the work. Why have the right to a college education depend upon whether the father or mother is so well-to-do as to send a boy or girl to college? We would give every child the right to education and a living at birth.
6. We would give a pension to all persons above sixty years of age in an amount sufficient to support them in comfortable circumstances, excepting those who earn $1,000 per year or who are worth $10,000.
7. Until we could straighten things out—and we can straighten things out in two months under our program—we would grant a moratorium on all debts which people owe that they cannot pay. </numbered list>

And now you have our program, none too big, none too little, but every man a king....

Our plan would injure no one. It would not stop us from having millionaires—it would increase them tenfold, because so many more people could make $1 million if they had the chance our plan gives them. Our plan would not break up big concerns.

The only difference would be that maybe 10,000 people would own a concern instead of 10 people owning it.

But, my friends, unless we do share our wealth, unless we limit the size of the big man so as to give something to the little man, we can never have a happy or free people. God said so! He ordered it.

We have everything our people need. Too much of food, clothes, and houses—why not let all have their fill and lie down in the ease and comfort God has given us? Why not? Because a few own everything—the masses own nothing.

I wonder if any of you people who are listening to me were ever at a barbecue! We used to go there—sometimes 1,000 people or more. If there were 1,000 people, we would put enough meat and bread and everything else on the table for 1,000 people. Then everybody would be called and everyone would eat all they wanted. But suppose at one of these barbecues for 1,000 people that one man took 90 percent of the food and ran off with it and ate until he got sick and let the balance rot. Then 999 people would have only enough for 100 to eat and there would be many to starve because of the greed of just one person for something he couldn't eat himself.

Well, ladies and gentlemen, America, all the people of America, have been invited to a barbecue.

God invited us all to come and eat and drink all we wanted. He smiled on our land and we grew crops of plenty to eat and wear. He showed us in the earth the iron and other things to make everything we wanted. He unfolded to us the secrets of science so that our work might be easy. God called: "Come to my feast."

Then what happened? Rockefeller, Morgan, and their crowd stepped up and took enough for 120 million people and left only enough for 5 million for all the other 125 million to eat. And so many millions must go hungry and without these good things God gave us unless we call on them to put some of it back.

GLOSSARY

the Astors: one of the wealthiest families in America

capital levy tax: a tax on property

Morgan: a reference to John Pierpont Morgan Jr. (1867–1943), financier and one of the wealthiest men in America

to the person: per person

viz. abbreviation for the Latin videlicet, meaning "namely"

Document Analysis

Addressing a nationwide radio audience on January 14, 1935, Long wasted no time in attacking President Roosevelt. In the third year of the Roosevelt administration conditions had grown worse, Long argued. The president could no longer be regarded as the country's savior, or as Long put it pithily, "It is not Roosevelt or ruin; it is Roosevelt's ruin." The nation's leader had not acted on his promises to redistribute wealth and shorten the working hours of Americans who labored in a land of abundance.

Long personalizes the attack on Roosevelt by suggesting that the president prefers the companionship of rich men like John D. Rockefeller, Jr. Long even criticizes himself here, admitting that perhaps he should have known better than to trust Roosevelt to redistribute wealth, given the figures he befriended. As usual, Long presents himself as a simple man who has grown distrustful of the government's promises. Roosevelt, by implication, becomes the symbol of the politician who talks a good line but fails to deliver what he proposes. It is time, Long says, to begin an immediate program to share the country's wealth. And the vehicle for this program, he suggests, will be his Share Our Wealth societies. His expressed goal is to establish one hundred thousand societies that will meet and talk and work to ensure that the land produces everything that the nation's people need.

Long then sets out his seven-point program. The first aim would be to reduce individual fortunes to no more than a few million dollars. After the first million earned, a person would be taxed an increasing percentage of his income; after more than $8 million has been earned, the person's income would be taxed at 100 percent. Second, no person could inherit more than $1 million a year. Third, the taxes on the rich would be redistributed to every family so that all have "common conveniences," such as automobiles, radios, and freedom from debt. Fourth, a full-employment economy and a thirty-hour workweek would be instituted. Fifth, the Louisiana education program would be expanded to provide free education to all Americans, a plan that would also entail the employment of one hundred thousand new teachers. Sixth, pension plans would be put in place for those over sixty years of age. The final aspect of Long's program would be a moratorium on all unpayable debts.

Long believed that such a program could be instituted within two months. He provides few details about how such a massive redistribution of wealth would actually be administered, instead relying on basic language about his intentions, which are to "straighten things out." The phrase implies, of course, that the country is not governed fairly and that it is in the grip of crooked men. He reinforces this notion by suggesting that the wealth of the country has been "locked in a vise" by a few powerful and wealthy men.

Long emphasizes that he is not against wealth per se—that, in fact, his plan would increase the number of millionaires by redistributing the enormous wealth of the few. No one would really be injured, and millions would benefit from his plan. "The only difference," he contends in a memorable phrase, "would be that maybe 10,000 people would own a concern instead of 10 people owning it." As usual, Long uses elementary facts and figures to make his dramatic point that wealth should be held in common. And, as usual, Long invokes the Bible, suggesting that his plan is part of the divine economy: "But, my friends, unless we do share our wealth, unless we limit the size of the big man so as to give something to the little man, we can never have a happy or free people. God said so! He ordered it."

Near the very end of his address, Long resorts to one of his favorite ploys: presenting his plans as a kind of parable. In this case he presents an image of the country's wealth as a barbecue that could provide enough for everyone to eat, and yet 90 percent of the food is taken by one man, even though he cannot eat all of it and will have to abandon much of it to rot. This is Long's analogy for the functioning of a capitalist economy that produces goods in abundance and yet leaves people to starve. In his customary way, he presents the national depression in melodramatic terms, suggesting a sharp dichotomy between those who have all the wealth and those who are starving—the haves and the have-nots.

Finally, Long portrays America as God's paradise, a land of plenty—indeed, the site of a feast. It is the Rockefellers and their ilk who are despoiling this paradise, and it is now time, Long concludes, to demand that these thieves "put some of it back." Even more than in his "Every Man a King" address—a phrase Long also uses in this speech—he expresses outrage not only at the wealthy but also at President Roosevelt personally, who is treated as a man who has reneged on his assurances to help the American people. Consequently, Long's only hope is the people themselves. They must govern themselves when their leaders seem unwilling to do God's work, which should also be America's work.

Essential Themes

Long approached populism with religious fervor, claiming no special insight of his own but rather simply maintaining a dogged insistence on following the teachings of the Bible, the U.S. Constitution, and the Declaration of Independence. The latter document was his key authority for attacking the Roosevelt administration and politicians who did not heed what Long viewed as the radical egalitarian programs that should follow from the crucial statement that "all men are created equal." While Long played on people's emotions in portraying himself as a simple, plainspoken man, he also could cite facts and figures to buttress his arguments, demonstrating the legal training that enabled him to be a shrewd and relentless opponent of the status quo. These qualities are on full display in the "Share Our Wealth" speech. His plan to level the economic playing field for Americans was radical but reflected the deprivation and discontent that existed in Depression-era America even during the New Deal.

The essence of Long's plan was to "limit the size of the big man so as to give something to the little man." He ties this to the future happiness of the United States, suggesting that without radical measures discontent would grow. Better, perhaps, that the rich be slightly less rich than to risk the eruption of revolution, a point he would raise in speeches and debates as he pursued his vision of America.

——Carl Rollyson, PhD

Bibliography and Additional Reading

Brinkley, Alan. *Voices of Protest: Huey Long, Father Coughlin, and the Great Depression.* (New York: Knopf, 1982).

Jeansonne, Glen. *Messiah of the Masses: Huey P. Long and the Great Depression.* (Upper Saddle River, New Jersey: Pearson, 1997).

Shlaes, Amity. *The Forgotten Man: A New History of the Great Depression* (New York: Harper Collins, 2009).

Williams, Harry T. *Huey Long* (New York: Vintage, 1981).

Southern Manifesto

Date: 1956
Author: Strom Thurmond, et al
Genre: Public declaration

Summary Overview

On March 12, 1956, as the second anniversary of the U.S. Supreme Court case *Brown v. Board of Education* (1954) approached, Senator Walter F. George rose to the speaker's podium in the U.S. Senate to announce the creation of the latest weapon in the segregationist arsenal—the Southern Manifesto. It was a bold, brazen document, signed by 101 of the South's 128 congressional members. The Southern Manifesto, formally titled a Declaration of Constitutional Principles, denounced the Supreme Court's *Brown v. Board of Education* decision, calling it an "unwarranted exercise of power." The Southern Manifesto's signers pledged to "use all lawful means" to "bring about a reversal" of the *Brown v. Board of Education* decision.

The declaration of the Southern Manifesto was not the first act in the South's massive resistance campaign against school desegregation. It was, however, one of the most important. The Southern Manifesto's signers hoped to provide an ideological foundation for the white South's resistance movement. Rather than focusing on standard southern arguments about black racial inferiority or miscegenation, the Southern Manifesto concentrated on historical and constitutional issues. At base, it was a rear-guard action meant to preserve an entrenched but discriminatory system of education, which had existed in the South since the Supreme Court's *Plessy v. Ferguson* (1896) decision.

Defining Moment

In the mid-1950s white southern Democrats launched a legal and political campaign against the *Brown v. Board of Education* Supreme Court decision that ordered the desegregation of public schools. On May 17, 1954—the day that the decision appeared—Senator Harry F. Byrd of Virginia condemned the Supreme Court's school desegregation order. He warned of dangers that would result from racial mixing in the schools. Georgia's Governor Herman Talmadge took a different approach. He said that the Supreme Court had ignored precedent and overstepped the boundaries of its authority. As the South's white political leaders struggled to unite various segregationist organizations they drew on the region's deep-rooted political traditions. No one was more successful in this endeavor than Senator Byrd of Virginia, who in 1956 called for massive resistance to the *Brown* decision. Senator Strom Thurmond of South Carolina, an outspoken critic of *Brown v. Board of Education*, showed keen interest in the interposition doctrine. In February 1956 Thurmond approached Byrd with an idea for a Southern Manifesto that might unite the South. He suggested that the document be constitutional and historical in nature and that it emphasize interposition. He wrote three drafts of the document in February 1956. In uncompromising, bombastic tones, Thurmond spoke publicly against the Supreme Court for violating the Constitution and the principles of federalism.

Thurmond's work on the manifesto secured the support of Byrd, a soft-spoken Virginia reactionary who controlled his state's political system through an elaborate network known as the Byrd machine. With Byrd's assistance, Thurmond circulated drafts of the Southern Manifesto on Capitol Hill in the hope of winning support from other southern delegates. While a few die-hard segregationists were willing to sign on to Thurmond's initiative, it proved far too radical for most southern congressmen to approve. Undeterred, Thurmond and Byrd threatened to issue the document with as many signatures as they could get. After lengthy debates and drafts wherein the Senators tried to balance their opposition with some moderation, a committee of five senators including Strom Thurmond compiled a sixth and final draft of the manifesto in early March 1956.

Author Biography

The Southern Manifesto was the product of many minds including Harry F. Byrd (1887–1966) who, in February 1956, called for organized massive resistance in the South to fight integration; Sam Ervin, Jr. (1896–1985), who carefully cloaked his opposition to desegregation in terms of his dislike of big government. He thus avoided the blatantly racist argument commonly used by other southern politicians at the time to oppose civil rights initiatives; and J. William Fulbright (1905–1995), one of the most well-known, controversial figures in twentieth-century American political history. Fulbright, a native of Sumner, Mississippi was, early in his career, a dedicated supporter of segregation. He opposed the Supreme Court decision in *Brown v. Board of Education* but urged fellow southerners to pursue a moderate opposition to the civil rights movement. In 1956 he toned down much of the hyperbolic tone found in the first draft of the Southern Manifesto to produce a more moderate but still thoroughly pro-segregationist document. The document itself, however, was originally proposed by Senator Strom Thurmond of South Carolina, went through six revisions. Strom Thurmond (1902–2003) was the principal instigator behind the Southern Manifesto. He was born in Edgefield, South Carolina, and he graduated from Clemson College before serving as a school superintendent, a senator, a judge, and governor. In 1948 Thurmond rose to national prominence when he ran for president as head of the Dixiecrat Party. Although he won only four states and thirty-nine electoral votes, this was a remarkable showing for a third-party candidate. Thurmond's willingness to stand firm on racial segregation and his ability to muster inventive constitutional arguments in its defense made him a popular hero among many white South Carolinians. With their support, Thurmond won an election to the U.S. Senate in 1954 as a write-in candidate. He was the only person to accomplish such a feat. That same year, the Supreme Court helped define the course of Thurmond's early senatorial career with its *Brown v. Board of Education* decision. Thurmond opposed the decision and its enforcement. In 1956 he proposed the Southern Manifesto to resist the Court's decision.

HISTORICAL DOCUMENT

The unwarranted decision of the Supreme Court in the public school cases is now bearing the fruit always produced when men substitute naked power for established law.

The Founding Fathers gave us a Constitution of checks and balances because they realized the inescapable lesson of history that no man or group of men can be safely entrusted with unlimited power. They framed this Constitution with its provisions for change by amendment in order to secure the fundamentals of government against the dangers of temporary popular passion or the personal predilections of public officeholders.

We regard the decisions of the Supreme Court in the school cases as a clear abuse of judicial power. It climaxes a trend in the Federal Judiciary undertaking to legislate, in derogation of the authority of Congress, and to encroach upon the reserved rights of the States and the people.

The original Constitution does not mention education. Neither does the 14th Amendment nor any other amendment. The debates preceding the submission of the 14th Amendment clearly show that there was no intent that it should affect the system of education maintained by the States.

The very Congress which proposed the amendment subsequently provided for segregated schools in the District of Columbia.

When the amendment was adopted in 1868, there were 37 States of the Union....

Every one of the 26 States that had any substantial racial differences among its people, either approved the operation of segregated schools already in existence or subsequently established such schools by action of the same law-making body which considered the 14th Amendment.

As admitted by the Supreme Court in the public school case (*Brown v. Board of Education*), the doctrine of separate but equal schools "apparently originated in *Roberts v. City of Boston* (1849), upholding school segregation against attack as being violative of a State constitutional guarantee of equality." This constitutional doctrine began in the North, not in the South, and it was followed not only in Massachusetts, but in Connecticut, New York, Illinois, Indiana, Michigan, Minnesota, New Jersey, Ohio, Pennsylvania and other northern states until they, exercising their rights as states through the constitutional processes of local self-government, changed their school systems.

In the case of *Plessy v. Ferguson* in 1896 the Supreme Court expressly declared that under the 14th Amendment no person was denied any of his rights if the States provided separate but equal facilities. This decision has been followed in many other cases. It is notable that the Supreme Court, speaking through Chief Justice Taft, a former President of the United

States, unanimously declared in 1927 in *Lum v. Rice* that the "separate but equal" principle is "within the discretion of the State in regulating its public schools and does not conflict with the 14th Amendment."

This interpretation, restated time and again, became a part of the life of the people of many of the States and confirmed their habits, traditions, and way of life. It is founded on elemental humanity and commonsense, for parents should not be deprived by Government of the right to direct the lives and education of their own children.

Though there has been no constitutional amendment or act of Congress changing this established legal principle almost a century old, the Supreme Court of the United States, with no legal basis for such action, undertook to exercise their naked judicial power and substituted their personal political and social ideas for the established law of the land.

This unwarranted exercise of power by the Court, contrary to the Constitution, is creating chaos and confusion in the States principally affected. It is destroying the amicable relations between the white and Negro races that have been created through 90 years of patient effort by the good people of both races. It has planted hatred and suspicion where there has been heretofore friendship and understanding.

Without regard to the consent of the governed, outside mediators are threatening immediate and revolutionary changes in our public schools systems. If done, this is certain to destroy the system of public education in some of the States.

With the gravest concern for the explosive and dangerous condition created by this decision and inflamed by outside meddlers:

We reaffirm our reliance on the Constitution as the fundamental law of the land.

We decry the Supreme Court's encroachment on the rights reserved to the States and to the people, contrary to established law, and to the Constitution.

We commend the motives of those States which have declared the intention to resist forced integration by any lawful means.

We appeal to the States and people who are not directly affected by these decisions to consider the constitutional principles involved against the time when they too, on issues vital to them may be the victims of judicial encroachment.

Even though we constitute a minority in the present Congress, we have full faith that a majority of the American people believe in the dual system of government which has enabled us to achieve our greatness and will in time demand that the reserved rights of the States and of the people be made secure against judicial usurpation.

We pledge ourselves to use all lawful means to bring about a reversal of this decision which is contrary to the Constitution and to prevent the use of force in its implementation.

In this trying period, as we all seek to right this wrong, we appeal to our people not to be provoked by the agitators and troublemakers invading our States and to scrupulously refrain from disorder and lawless acts.

Signed by:

Members of the United States Senate
Walter F. George, Richard B. Russell, John Stennis, Sam J. Ervin, Jr., Strom Thurmond, Harry F. Byrd, A. Willis Robertson, John L. McClellan, Allen J. Ellender, Russell B. Long, Lister Hill, James O. Eastland, W. Kerr Scott, John Sparkman, Olin D. Johnston, Price Daniel, J.W. Fulbright, George A. Smathers, Spessard L. Holland.
Members of the United States House of Representatives
Alabama: Frank W. Boykin, George M. Grant, George W. Andrews, Kenneth A. Roberts, Albert Rains, Armistead I. Selden, Jr., Carl Elliott, Robert E. Jones, George Huddleston, Jr.
Arkansas: E.C. Gathings, Wilbur D. Mills, James W. Trimble, Oren Harris, Brooks Hays, W.F. Norrell.
Florida: Charles E. Bennett, Robert L.F. Sikes, A.S. Herlong, Jr., Paul G. Rogers, James A. Haley, D.R. Matthews.
Georgia: Prince H. Preston, John L. Pilcher, E.L. Forrester, John James Flynt, Jr., James C. Davis, Carl Vinson, Henderson Lanham, Iris F. Blitch, Phil M. Landrum, Paul Brown.
Louisiana: F. Edward Hebert, Hale Boggs, Edwin E. Willis, Overton Brooks, Otto E. Passman, James H. Morrison, T. Ashton Thompson, George S. Long.

Mississippi: Thomas G. Abernathy, Jamie L. Whitten, Frank E. Smith, John Bell Williams, Arthur Winstead, William M. Colmer.

North Carolina: Herbert C. Bonner, L.H. Fountain, Graham A. Barden, Carl T. Durham, F. Ertel Carlyle, Hugh Q. Alexander, Woodrow W. Jones, George A. Shuford.

South Carolina: L. Mendel Rivers, John J. Riley, W.J. Bryan Dorn, Robert T. Ashmore, James P. Richards, John L. McMillan.

Tennessee: James B. Frazier, Jr., Tom Murray, Jere Cooper, Clifford Davis.

GLOSSARY

checks and balances: the ability of separate federal branches to limit each other's powers

dual system of government: the division of sovereignty between the state and federal governments

rights reserved to the States: rights held exclusively by the states under a system of federalism and guaranteed by the Tenth Amendment to the Constitution

separate but equal: a phrase describing the system of segregated facilities in American society

Document Analysis

The Southern Manifesto, in the first three paragraphs of its "Declaration of Constitutional Principles," denounces the "unwarranted" decision in *Brown v. Board of Education* as a "clear abuse of judicial power." According to the manifesto, the Supreme Court ignored important constitutional precedents in the *Brown* decision. The manifesto states (in paragraph 11) that rather than following a traditional, strict-constructionist view of the Constitution, which had dominated school-segregation law for five decades, the Supreme Court justices "substituted their personal, political, and social ideas for the established law of the land." The manifesto declares that in doing so the justices overstepped their bounds and invaded the realm of states' rights.

The manifesto's signers challenge the *Brown* decision's most controversial finding: that segregated education deprives African Americans of their Fourteenth Amendment equal protection rights. The manifesto rejects this idea outright. It declares (in paragraph 4) that the Fourteenth Amendment's framers never intended to "affect the system of education maintained by the States." Indeed, the manifesto presents evidence to the contrary. It argues (in paragraphs 4–7) that the Fourteenth Amendment does not mention education. Indeed, the Congress that proposed it "subsequently provided for segregated schools in the District of Columbia," and twenty-six of the thirty-seven states that considered ratification of the amendment either possessed or developed segregated systems of public education. The manifesto's authors consider these points conclusive evidence that the Fourteenth Amendment does not provide legal justification for school desegregation.

The manifesto also claims (in paragraphs 8 and 9) that the *Brown* decision rejects a series of well-known legal precedents, including *Roberts v. City of Boston* (1849), *Plessy v. Ferguson* (1896), and *Gong Lum v. Rice* (1927). These cases each recognized the constitutionality of state-enforced segregation. *Gong Lum v. Rice* was perhaps the most powerful precedent in the group. In this case, the U.S. Supreme Court had declared that public school segregation was "within the discretion of the States…and does not conflict with the Fourteenth Amendment." The manifesto's authors argue in the following paragraphs that this decision and others like it confirm the "habits, traditions, and way of life" in the South. Now, however, without any "constitutional amendment or act of Congress," the Supreme Court was "changing this established legal principle," which had existed for almost a century. Southerners would not abide by the Court's decision. On the contrary, they would use "all lawful means to bring about a reversal of this decision."

The Southern Manifesto's constitutional argument sidesteps the base appeals to racism and violence that so many segregationists relied upon. In fact, the manifesto's authors blame (in paragraph 12) the Supreme Court for "destroying the amicable relations between the white and Negro races" in the South. This self-serving, fallacious interpretation of the Jim Crow era would become a standard political ploy in the segregationist argument against the *Brown* decision. Segregationists argued that it was the Supreme Court, not the white South, that treated African Americans unfairly. For in its *Brown* decision, the Court had "planted hatred and suspicion" where previously there had been "friendship and understanding."

Despite the manifesto's defiant tone, the document concludes with a hint of moderation. The document's signers "appeal to the States and people…to consider the constitutional principles involved" in the school desegregation debate. No program of interposition or nullification is proposed. On the contrary, the manifesto's signers pledge to use "lawful means" to seek a reversal of the *Brown* decision. In addition, they request the people of the South to "scrupulously refrain from disorder and lawless acts."

Essential Themes

As a statement read from the Senate floor and entered into the *Congressional Record*, the Southern Manifesto was aimed at all Americans but also appealed to some groups in particular. On a basic level the manifesto lent emotional support to southern white school board members, local governmental officials, and others actively opposing the desegregation of public schools. By adding the prestige of national political figures, the manifesto gave massive resistance a veneer of social legitimacy, at least in the southern political climate. It also invoked a common southern argument used since the antebellum period, namely, that the South was a distinct region that could settle its unique racial problems only without outside pressure.

The manifesto, more broadly, went through several rewrites specifically designed to appeal to nonsoutherners and moderates. By invoking history to place the segregationist cause on the same moral side as the Kentucky and Virginia Resolutions or as the political thought of James Madison, the manifesto's authors sought to appeal to conservatives and opponents of big government in all sections of the country. Furthermore, the manifesto sought to remind northern Democrats that the white South was united in its defiance of integration and would split the party if necessary to achieve this goal. By the same token, the Southern Manifesto's authors sent a strong message to the administration of Dwight Eisenhower (and presumably to all those who aspired to the White House in the future) that the Solid South would not back a presidential candidate that supported desegregation. The Southern Manifesto also reminded the U.S. Supreme Court to tread lightly on the issue of civil rights, as it needed the voluntary support of lower federal courts staffed by southern judges, as well as state and local government officials, to carry out its decisions.

———*Jeffrey L. Littlejohn, PhD*

Bibliography and Additional Reading

Aucoin, Brent. "The Southern Manifesto and Southern Opposition to Desegregation." *Arkansas Historical Quarterly* 55, no. 2 (1996): 173–193.

Badger, Tony. "The Southern Manifesto: White Southerners and Civil Rights, 1956." *European Contributions to American Studies* 15 (1988): 77–99.

Bartley, Numan. *The Rise of Massive Resistance: Race and Politics in the South During the 1950s.* Baton Rouge: Louisiana State University Press, 1969.

Cohodas, Nadine. *Strom Thurmond and the Politics of Southern Change.* New York: Simon and Schuster, 1993.

Commager, Henry, comp. *The Struggle for Racial Equality: A Documentary Record.* New York: Harper and Row, 1967.

Lassiter, Matthew D., and Andrew B. Lewis, eds. *The Moderates' Dilemma: Massive Resistance to School Desegregation in Virginia.* Charlottesville: University Press of Virginia, 1998.

Lewis, George. *Massive Resistance: The White Response to the Civil Rights Movement.* New York: Oxford University Press, 2006.

Patterson, James T. *Brown v. Board of Education: A Civil Rights Milestone and Its Troubled Legacy.* New York: Oxford University Press, 2001.

Webb, Clive, ed. *Massive Resistance: Southern Opposition to the Second Reconstruction.* New York: Oxford University Press, 2005.

Woods, Randall B. *Fulbright: A Biography.* New York: Cambridge University Press, 1995.

The Port Huron Statement

Date: 1962
Author: Tom Hayden
Genre: Public declaration

Summary Overview
"The Port Huron Statement" was the manifesto of the Students for a Democratic Society (SDS), an iconic 1960s student activist organization that called for participatory democracy, direct action and civil disobedience, an end to racial discrimination, and the enlargement of the public sector as a way to end economic inequality. The SDS was also highly critical of U.S. cold war policies, the arms race with the Soviet Union, and the proliferation of nuclear weapons. Presenting itself as an "Agenda for a Generation," the Port Huron Statement not only marked the political coming-of-age of the post-war, "baby boom" generation but it also signaled a shift in the American left, as radical ideologies no longer originated in entities like the Socialist Party or labor unions, but among middle-class, college educated young people. In later years, until it dissolved in 1969, Students for a Democratic Society led student protests of the war in Vietnam and was active in the civil rights movement.

Defining Moment
The historical context of the Port Huron Statement and the emergence of Students for Democratic Society is rooted in a number of political social and cultural developments in American history during the late 1940s and early 1950s.

Chief among these, of course, was the Cold War. Within domestic politics, the faintest hint of left-wing radicalism was, at worst, dangerous and, at best, unwise to promote lest your organization, movement, or political candidate be branded "communist" or "subversive" by your political opponents, rival organizations, or the news media. As a result of this incredibly harsh scrutiny of leftist politics in the United States, organizations, individuals and institutions that, since the 1930s, had been fairly open about their political orientation found themselves either disappearing or being forced to embrace some form of the anti-Communism prevalent at the time. Labor unions, media outlets, and civil rights organizations that had been comfortably left of center during the 1930s and during World War II loudly and publicly renounced communism and moved toward the political center. Thus, the coalition of organizations and institutions that had constituted the "old left" of previous decades lay in ruins. The Cold War also introduced changes to higher education in the United States, with an increasingly close relationship between the federal government and universities resulting from increased federal investment in scientific and technological research. This close relationship, and increased government funding and scrutiny led to the growing and complex bureaucracy in higher education that the Port Huron Statement decries.

Along with this political realignment, the civil rights movement had begun the process that would, by the mid-1960s, shatter the Democratic party as northern Democratic voters and politicians weakened in their solidarity with the segregationist states of the south.

Author Biography
The principal author of "The Port Huron Statement," adopted at the organization's first convention in June 1962 near Port Huron, Michigan, was Tom Hayden. Hayden was born in Detroit in 1939 and became involved in leftist activism while a student at the University of Michigan. It was during this time, when Hayden was just twenty-two years old and not well known outside student leftist circles, that he helped found the Students for a Democratic Society and drafted the Port Huron Statement. He served as President of the SDS from 1962 to 1963 and participated in civil rights protests such as the Freedom Rides to force desegregation of interstate bus lines in the American south. Moving to New Jersey in the mid-1960s, Hayden worked with community organizations in Newark. During the 1960s and 1970s, though, he would acquire considerably more notoriety as a staunch opponent of the Vietnam War including taking a trip to North Vietnam during the war alongside two other activists and wrote a book about his experiences there after his return to the US. Hayden was also one of the "Chicago Seven," along with such activists as Jerry Rubin and Abbie Hoffman, indicted for fomenting riots at the 1968 Democratic National Convention in Chicago, and as the husband of then-radical actress Jane Fonda, whom he accom-

panied on widely criticized peace missions to Vietnam and Cambodia. He later served in the California State Assembly from 1982 to 1992 and the California State Senate from 1992 to 2000.

HISTORICAL DOCUMENT

Introduction: Agenda for a Generation

We are people of this generation, bred in at least modest comfort, housed now in universities, looking uncomfortably to the world we inherit.

When we were kids the United States was the wealthiest and strongest country in the world: the only one with the atom bomb, the least scarred by modern war, an initiator of the United Nations that we thought would distribute Western influence throughout the world. Freedom and equality for each individual, government of, by, and for the people—these American values we found good, principles by which we could live as men. Many of us began maturing in complacency.

As we grew, however, our comfort was penetrated by events too troubling to dismiss. First, the permeating and victimizing fact of human degradation, symbolized by the Southern struggle against racial bigotry, compelled most of us from silence to activism. Second, the enclosing fact of the Cold War, symbolized by the presence of the Bomb, brought awareness that we ourselves, and our friends, and millions of abstract "others" we knew more directly because of our common peril, might die at any time. We might deliberately ignore, or avoid, or fail to feel all other human problems, but not these two, for these were too immediate and crushing in their impact, too challenging in the demand that we as individuals take the responsibility for encounter and resolution.

While these and other problems either directly oppressed us or rankled our consciences and became our own subjective concerns, we began to see complicated and disturbing paradoxes in our surrounding America. The declaration "all men are created equal...rang hollow before the facts of Negro life in the South and the big cities of the North. The proclaimed peaceful intentions of the United States contradicted its economic and military investments in the Cold War status quo.

We witnessed, and continue to witness, other paradoxes. With nuclear energy whole cities can easily be powered, yet the dominant nation-states seem more likely to unleash destruction greater than that incurred in all wars of human history. Although our own technology is destroying old and creating new forms of social organization, men still tolerate meaningless work and idleness. While two-thirds of mankind suffers undernourishment, our own upper classes revel amidst superfluous abundance. Although world population is expected to double in forty years, the nations still tolerate anarchy as a major principle of international conduct and uncontrolled exploitation governs the sapping of the earth's physical resources. Although mankind desperately needs revolutionary leadership, America rests in national stalemate, its goals ambiguous and tradition-bound instead of informed and clear, its democratic system apathetic and manipulated rather than "of, by, and for the people."

Not only did tarnish appear on our image of American virtue, not only did disillusion occur when the hypocrisy of American ideals was discovered, but we began to sense that what we had originally seen as the American Golden Age was actually the decline of an era. The worldwide outbreak of revolution against colonialism and imperialism, the entrenchment of totalitarian states, the menace of war, overpopulation, international disorder, super-technology—these trends were testing the tenacity of our own commitment to democracy and freedom and our abilities to visualize their application to a world in upheaval.

Our work is guided by the sense that we may be the last generation in the experiment with living. But we are a minority—the vast majority of our people regard the temporary equilibriums of our society and world as eternally-functional parts. In this is perhaps the outstanding paradox: we ourselves are imbued with urgency, yet the message of our society is that there is no viable alternative to the present. Beneath the reassuring tones of the politicians, beneath the common opinion that America will "muddle through," beneath the stagnation of those who have closed their minds to the future, is the pervading feeling that there simply are no alternatives, that our times have witnessed the exhaustion not only of Utopias, but of any new departures as well. Feeling the press of complexity upon the emptiness of life, people are fearful of the thought that at any moment things might thrust out of control. They fear change itself, since change might smash whatever invisible framework seems to hold back chaos for them now. For most Americans, all crusades are suspect, threatening. The fact that each individual sees apathy in his fellows perpetuates the common reluctance to organize for change. The dominant institutions are complex enough to blunt the minds of their potential critics, and entrenched enough to swiftly dissipate or entirely repel the energies of protest and reform, thus limiting human expectancies. Then, too, we are a materially improved society, and by our own improvements we seem to have weakened the case for further change.

Some would have us believe that Americans feel contentment amidst prosperity—but might it not better be called a glaze above deeply felt anxieties about their role in the new world? And if these anxieties produce a developed indifference to human affairs, do they not as well produce a yearning to believe there is an alternative to the present, that something can be done to change circumstances in the school, the workplaces, the bureaucracies, the government? It is to this latter yearning, at once the spark and engine of change, that we direct our present appeal. The search for truly democratic alternatives to the present, and a commitment to social experimentation with them, is a worthy and fulfilling human enterprise, one which moves us and, we hope, others today. On such a basis do we offer this document of our convictions and analysis: as an effort in understanding and changing the conditions of humanity in the late twentieth century, an effort rooted in the ancient, still unfulfilled conception of man attaining determining influence over his circumstances of life.

Values

Making values explicit—an initial task in establishing alternatives—is an activity that has been devalued and corrupted. The conventional moral terms of the age, the politician moralities—"free world," "people's democracies"—reflect realities poorly, if at all, and seem to function more as ruling myths than as descriptive principles. But neither has our experience in the universities brought as moral enlightenment. Our professors and administrators sacrifice controversy to public relations; their curriculums change more slowly than the living events of the world; their skills and silence are purchased by investors in the arms race; passion is called unscholastic. The questions we might want raised—what is really important? can we live in a different and better way? if we wanted to change society, how would we do it?—are not thought to be questions of a "fruitful, empirical nature," and thus are brushed aside.

Unlike youth in other countries we are used to moral leadership being exercised and moral dimensions being clarified by our elders. But today, for us, not even the liberal and socialist preachments of the past seem adequate to the forms of the present. Consider the old slogans; Capitalism Cannot Reform Itself, United Front Against Fascism, General Strike, All Out on May Day. Or, more recently, No Cooperation with Commies and Fellow Travelers, Ideologies Are Exhausted, Bipartisanship, No Utopias. These are incomplete, and there are few new prophets. It has been said that our liberal and socialist predecessors were plagued by vision without program, while our own generation is plagued by program without vision. All around us there is astute grasp of method, technique—the committee, the ad hoc group, the lobbyist, that hard and soft sell, the make, the projected image—but, if pressed critically, such expertise is incompetent to explain its implicit ideals. It is highly fashionable to identify oneself by old categories, or by naming a respected political figure, or by explaining "how we would vote" on various issues.

Theoretic chaos has replaced the idealistic thinking of old—and, unable to reconstitute theoretic order, men have condemned idealism itself. Doubt has replaced hopefulness—and men act out a defeatism that is labeled realistic. The decline of utopia and hope is in fact one of the defining features of social life today. The reasons are various: the dreams of the older left were perverted by Stalinism and never recreated; the congressional stalemate makes men narrow their view of the possible; the specialization of human activity leaves little room for sweeping thought; the horrors of the twentieth century, symbolized in the gas-ovens and concentration camps and atom bombs, have blasted hopefulness. To be idealistic is to be considered apocalyptic, deluded. To have no serious aspirations, on the contrary, is to be "tough-minded."

In suggesting social goals and values, therefore, we are aware of entering a sphere of some disrepute. Perhaps matured by the past, we have no sure formulas, no closed theories—but that does not mean values are beyond discussion and tentative determination. A first task of any social movement is to convenience people that the search for orienting theories and the creation of human values is complex but worthwhile. We are aware that to avoid platitudes we must analyze the concrete conditions of social order. But to direct such an analysis we must use the guideposts of basic principles. Our own social values involve conceptions of human beings, human relationships, and social systems.

We regard men as infinitely precious and possessed of unfulfilled capacities for reason, freedom, and love. In affirming these principles we are aware of countering perhaps the dominant conceptions of man in the twentieth century: that he is a thing to be manipulated, and that he is inherently incapable of directing his own affairs. We oppose the depersonalization that reduces human beings to the status of things—if anything, the brutalities of the twentieth century teach that means and ends are intimately related, that vague appeals to "posterity" cannot justify the mutilations of the present. We oppose, too, the doctrine of human incompetence because it rests essentially on the modern fact that men have been "competently" manipulated into incompetence—we see little reason why men cannot meet with increasing skill the complexities and responsibilities of their situation, if society is organized not for minority, but for majority, participation in decision-making.

Men have unrealized potential for self-cultivation, self-direction, self-understanding, and creativity. It is this potential that we regard as crucial and to which we appeal, not to the human potentiality for violence, unreason, and submission to authority. The goal of man and society should be human independence: a concern not with image of popularity but with finding a meaning in life that is personally authentic: a quality of mind not compulsively driven by a sense of powerlessness, nor one which unthinkingly adopts status values, nor one which represses all threats to its habits, but one which has full, spontaneous access to present and past experiences, one which easily unites the fragmented parts of personal history, one which openly faces problems which are troubling and unresolved: one with an intuitive awareness of possibilities, an active sense of curiosity, an ability and willingness to learn.

This kind of independence does not mean egoistic individualism—the object is not to have one's way so much as it is to have a way that is one's own. Nor do we deify man—we merely have faith in his potential.

Human relationships should involve fraternity and honesty. Human interdependence is contemporary fact; human brotherhood must be willed however, as a condition of future survival and as the most appropriate form of social relations. Personal links between man and man are needed, especially to go beyond the partial and fragmentary bonds of function that bind men only as worker to worker, employer to employee, teacher to student, American to Russian.

Loneliness, estrangement, isolation describe the vast distance between man and man today. These dominant tendencies cannot be overcome by better personnel management, nor by improved gadgets, but only when a love of man overcomes the idolatrous worship of things by man.

As the individualism we affirm is not egoism, the selflessness we affirm is not self-elimination. On the contrary, we believe in generosity of a kind that imprints one's unique individual qualities in the relation to other men, and to all human activity. Further, to dislike isolation is not to favor the abolition of privacy; the latter differs from isolation in that it occurs or is abolished according to individual will. Finally, we would replace power and personal uniqueness rooted in possession, privilege, or circumstance by power and uniqueness rooted in love, reflectiveness, reason, and creativity.

As a social system we seek the establishment of a democracy of individual participation, governed by two central aims: that the individual share in those social decisions determining the quality and direction of his life; that society be organized to encourage independence in men and provide the media for their common participation.

In a participatory democracy, the political life would be based in several root principles:

- that decision-making of basic social consequence be carried on by public groupings;
- that politics be seen positively, as the art of collectively creating an acceptable pattern of social relations;
- that politics has the function of bringing people out of isolation and into community, thus being a necessary, though not sufficient, means of finding meaning in personal life;
- that the political order should serve to clarify problems in a way instrumental to their solution; it should provide outlets for the expression of personal grievance and aspiration; opposing views should be organized so as to illuminate choices and facilities the attainment of goals; channels should be commonly available to related men to knowledge and to power so that private problems—from bad recreation facilities to personal alienation—are formulated as general issues.

The economic sphere would have as its basis the principles:

- that work should involve incentives worthier than money or survival. It should be educative, not stultifying; creative, not mechanical; self-directed, not manipulated, encouraging independence; a respect for others, a sense of dignity and a willingness to accept social responsibility, since it is this experience that has crucial influence on habits, perceptions and individual ethics;
- that the economic experience is so personally decisive that the individual must share in its full determination;
- that the economy itself is of such social importance that its major resources and means of production should be open to democratic participation and subject to democratic social regulation.

Like the political and economic ones, major social institutions—cultural, education, rehabilitative, and others—should be generally organized with the well-being and dignity of man as the essential measure of success.

In social change or interchange, we find violence to be abhorrent because it requires generally the transformation of the target, be it a human being or a community of people, into a depersonalized object of hate. It is imperative that the means of violence be abolished and the institutions—local, national, international—that encourage nonviolence as a condition of conflict be developed.

These are our central values, in skeletal form. It remains vital to understand their denial or attainment in the context of the modern world.

GLOSSARY

"free world": term used to refer to the United States and its allies

"people's democracies": term used to refer to the Soviet Union and its allies

"the Bomb": colloquial term for nuclear weapons, such as nuclear or hydrogen warheads

utopias: idealized realities that do not exist

Document Analysis

The excerpts reproduced here are the introduction to "The Port Huron Statement" and the organization's "Values" statement. In the introduction, Hayden articulates the principles and concerns of the SDS, beginning with the belief that many students have become disillusioned in recent years. They have grown up in relative comfort in a powerful and affluent nation, but they have come to recognize "events too troubling to dismiss." One is the struggle for racial equality, particularly in the American South. The other is the cold war (the state of tension between the United States and the Soviet Union) and the threat of nuclear annihilation—and, indeed, just four months later the Cuban Missile Crisis brought the United States and the Soviets to the brink of nuclear war. He calls these issues "paradoxes," for they undermine American ideals that "all men are created equal" and that the goal of American foreign policy is peace. He also calls attention to such problems as meaningless work, undernourishment, and the exploitation of the earth's resources. He places this disillusionment in the context of the decline of colonialism and imperialism, overpopulation, the threat of war, and the entrenchment of totalitarian states throughout the world.

Hayden then calls for change. He asserts that people in general are apathetic and fearful of change, unable to envision any alternatives to matters as they currently stand. He rejects the belief that anxiety and fearfulness necessarily result in paralysis, and he believes that under the glaze of indifference is a yearning for something better: "It is to this latter yearning, at once the spark and engine of change, that we direct our present appeal." Fundamentally, Hayden calls for a resurgence of idealism, a vision of a better future and a willingness to take action to make that future a reality. He takes a radically optimistic view of society: "We regard men as infinitely precious and possessed of unfulfilled capacities for reason, freedom, and love." Later, he states that "men have unrealized potential for self-cultivation, self-direction, self-understanding, and creativity." Hayden asserts that it is these qualities that their organization hopes to appeal to rather than its more common qualities of "violence, unreason, and submission to authority."

In Hayden's view, though, the events of the twentieth century have depersonalized human beings and rendered them incompetent because they have been treated as objects to be manipulated. On this basis, Hayden calls for a more participatory democracy, one that allows individuals to share in social decisions and encourages interdependence among people. One way to achieve these goals is to reform the economic system by recognizing that "work should involve incentives worthier than money or survival," that individuals must share in the determination of the shape of the "economic experience," and that the economy's major resources and means of production should "be open to democratic participation and subject to democratic social regulation." This emphasis on economic relations is undoubtedly a reflection of the SDS's roots in its predecessor organization, the Student League for Industrial Democracy, which was a branch of a socialist educational organization called the League for Industrial Democracy; the organization evolved into the SDS as a way of widening its appeal among college and university students.

Essential Themes

The Port Huron Statement established the basic agenda for the political and social counterculture of the 1960s. This manifesto has some specific statements about public policy concerns. The first was a push for nuclear disarmament as a necessary alternative to the nuclear arms race. The second and support for and acknowledgement for the African American civil rights movement and the necessity of remaking the Democratic party, stripping it of the remnants of racism and support for segregation. One of the most striking aspects of the Port Huron Statement, however, is its promotion of a fundamental change in American society; promoting a shift away from passive politics and toward "participatory democracy." One of the incubators for this participatory democracy should be universities. Before that could happen, however, universities must rid themselves of the bureaucratization that has come to typify many American institutions from government to education to business and politics. University reforms, the Statement argues in a portion not excerpted here, would necessitate "an alliance of students and faculty," which is a clear example of the was in which the SDS sought to break down what it saw as artificial constructed and imposed social distinctions and restrictions. The Port Huron Statement's proposals would lay the foundation for the development of student activism throughout the 1960s.

——*Michael J. O'Neal, PhD*

Bibliography and Additional Reading

Brick, Howard and Gregory Parker, *A New Insurgency: The Port Huron Statement and Its Times*. (Ann Arbor: Michigan Publishing, University of Michigan Library, 2015).

Isserman, Maurice. *If I Had a Hammer: The Death of the Old Left and the Birth of the New Left*. (New York: Basic Books, 1987).

Klatch, Rebecca E. *A Generation Divided: The New Left, the New Right, and the 1960s*. (Berkeley : University of California Press, 1999).

Miller, James. *Democracy is in the Streets: From Port Huron to the Siege of Chicago*. (Cambridge: Harvard University Press, 1994).

■ Gay Power Comes to Sheridan Square

Date: 1969
Author: Lucian Truscott IV
Genre: Newspaper article

Summary Overview

Lucian Truscott's account of the Stonewall Riots of 1969 appeared in *The Village Voice*, the first so-called "alternative weekly" newspaper in the United States. The story was more than a mere reporting of the events. Truscott presented the story in detail using colloquial language, some of which would be considered highly inappropriate today, actually triggered a subsequent protest, this time directed at the the offices of *The Village Voice* itself. He transcribed the chants of the crowed, followed the story to police stations and ensured that the language of power—in this case gay power—was given a prominent place in the narrative, highlighting the link to the wider civil rights movements of the late 1960s.

Truscott's recounting of the events of the Stonewall Riots brought the conflict—and the burgeoning gay rights movement—out of the subcultural shadows in which it had previously existed. While his writing in *The Village Voice* was initially directed at the urban, New York audience, his coverage spread throughout the country and world, demonstrating that the "rights revolution" of the time was not limited to racial or gender lines and became one of the definitive contemporary accounts of the event.

Defining Moment

Greenwich Village in Manhattan, where the Stonewall Inn was located, had been a haven for New York City's gay and lesbian population following the end of World War I in 1918. During the 1950s, a time when media and government forces promoted social and cultural conformity—particularly in regard to matters of sexuality and gender—Greenwich Village became one of he centers of subcultural resistance. Writers and poets such as the Beat movement's Allen Ginsburg and William S. Burroughs lived in the Village and wrote opening and, often, graphically about homosexuality. This cultural heyday, however, faded in the early 1960s as police and political forces desired to "clean up" the city. Gay bars faced bureaucratic hurdles (such as liquor licenses being revoked) and their patrons were the targets of entrapment operations by police. The result of these operations was that homosexuals faced increasing discrimination.

The owners of the Stonewall Inn, members of the Genovese crime family, reinvented it as a gay bar in 1966. Thanks to bribery of local police, the Stonewall operated without a liquor license or concern for health code compliance. On June 28, 1969, however, a police raid occurred—possibly ordered by the federal Bureau of Alcohol, Tobacco, and Firearms. The raid quickly became chaotic and when some patrons refused to identify themselves or otherwise comply with instructions, police made the decision to transport everyone present to the police station. As the crowd of over one hundred waited for the police wagons to arrive, the patrons as well as others in the area began to loudly protest police actions. The crowd witnessed a police officer strike a woman with a baton leading to violence between police and protesters. Truscott's coverage in *The Village Voice* described the scene outside the Stonewall Inn while another story, by *Voice* writer Howard Smith described police actions inside the Inn during the raid.

Author Biography

Lucian Truscott IV was born in Japan on April 11, 1947, where his father was stationed with the US Army. Not only Truscott's father, but also his Grandfather had held high ranks in the military, serving in World War II, the Korean War, and the Vietnam War. Truscott himself graduated from the US Military Academy at Westpoint in 1969. While at the Military Academy and during his short career as an Army officer, Truscott challenged the prevailing military culture and its traditions. As a cadet, he (along with several compatriots) protested rules about mandatory chapel attendance. As a young officer at Fort Carson, Colorado, he wrote articles about heroin addiction among soldiers and what he considered to be unjust court martial proceedings. When informed that he might be sent to Vietnam, he resigned from the Army, accepting a "general discharge under other than honorable conditions."

Truscott's career in journalism put him at the heart of cultural changes in America in the late 1960s and 1970s and he often wrote on topics often related to aspects of the countercultural scene in New York City.

Just weeks after graduating from West Point, he wrote this July 3, 1969 account of the June 28 police raid and subsequent riot at the Stonewall Inn, which referred to the protestors in derogatory terms, led—in September—to more unrest directed at the offices of The Village Voice.

Truscott would remain active in journalism as well as become a successful novelist.

HISTORICAL DOCUMENT

Sheridan Square this weekend looked like something from a William Burroughs novel as the sudden specter of "gay power" erected its brazen head and spat out a fairy tale the likes of which the area has never seen.

The forces of faggotry, spurred by a Friday night raid on one of the city's largest, most popular, and longest lived gay bars, the Stonewall Inn, rallied Saturday night in an unprecedented protest against the raid and continued Sunday night to assert presence, possibility, and pride until the early hours of Monday morning. "I'm a faggot, and I'm proud of it!" "Gay power!" "I like boys!"—these and many other slogans were heard all three nights as the show of force by the city's finery met the force of the city's finest. The result was a kind of liberation, as the gay brigade emerged from the bars, back rooms, and bedrooms of the Village and became street people.

Cops entered the Stonewall for the second time in a week just before midnight on Friday. It began as a small raid—only two patrolmen, two detectives, and two policewomen were involved. But as the patrons trapped inside were released one by one, a crowd started to gather on the street. It was initially a festive gathering, composed mostly of Stonewall boys who were waiting around for friends still inside or to see what was going to happen. Cheers would go up as favorites would emerge from the door, strike a pose and swish by the detective with a "Hello there, fella." The stars were in their element. Wrists were limp, hair was primped, and reactions to the applause were classic. "I gave them the gay power bit, and they loved it, girls." "Have you seen Maxine? Where is my wife—I told her not to go far."

Suddenly the paddywagon arrived and the mood of the crowd changed. Three of the more blatant queens—in full drag—were loaded inside, along with the bartender and doorman, to a chorus of catcalls and boos from the crowd. A cry went up to push the paddywagon over, but it drove away before anything could happen. With its exit, the action waned momentarily. The next person to come out was a dyke, and she put up a struggle—from car to door to car again. It was at that moment that the scene became explosive. Limp wrists were forgotten. Beer cans and bottles were heaved at the windows, and a rain of coins descended on the cops. At the height of the action, a bearded figure was plucked from the crowd and dragged inside. It was Dave Van Ronk, who had come from the Lion's Head to see what was going on. He was charged with throwing an object at the police.

Three cops were necessary to get Van Ronk away from the crowd and into the Stonewall. The exit left no cops on the street, and almost by signal the crowd erupted into cobblestone and bottle heaving. The reaction was solid: they were pissed. The trashcan I was standing on was nearly yanked out from under me as a kid tried to grab it for use in the window smashing melee. From nowhere came an uprooted parking meter—used as a battering ram on the Stonewall door. I heard several cries of "Let's get some gas," but the blaze of flame which soon appeared in the window of the Stonewall was still a shock. As the wood barrier behind the glass was beaten open, the cops inside turned a firehose on the crowd. Several kids took the opportunity to cavort in the spray, and their momentary glee served to stave off what was rapidly becoming a full-scale attack. By the time the fags were able to regroup forces and come up with another assault, several carloads of police reinforcements had arrived, and in minutes the streets were cleared.

A visit to the Sixth Precinct revealed the fact that 13 persons had been arrested on charges that ranged from Van Ronk's felonious assault of a police officer to the owners' illegal sale and storage of alcoholic beverages without a license. Two police officers had been injured in the battle with the crowd. By the time the last cop was off the street Saturday morning, a sign was going up announcing that the Stonewall would reopen that night. It did.

Protest set the tone for "gay power" activities on Saturday. The afternoon was spent boarding up the windows of the Stonewall and chalking them with signs of the new revolution: "We are Open," "There is all college boys and girls in here," "Support Gay Power—C'mon in, girls." "Insp. Smyth looted our: money, jukebox, cigarette mach, telephones, safe, cash register, and the boys tips." Among the slogans were two carefully clipped and bordered copies of the Daily News story about the previous night's events, which was anything but kind to the gay cause.

The real action Saturday was that night in the street. Friday night's crowd had returned and was being led in "gay power" cheers by a group of gay cheerleaders. "We are the Stonewall girls / We wear our hair in curls / We have no underwear / We show our pubic hairs!" The crowd was gathered across the street from the Stonewall and was growing with additions of onlookers, Eastsiders, and rough street people who saw a chance for a little action. Though dress had changed from Friday night's gayery to Saturday night street clothes, the scene was a command performance for queers. If Friday night had been pick-up night, Saturday was date night. Hand-holding, kissing, and posing accented each of the cheers with a homosexual liberation that had appeared only fleetingly on the street before. One-liners were as practiced as if they had been used for years. "I just want you all to know," quipped a platinum blond with obvious glee, "that sometimes being homosexual is a big pain in the ass." Another allowed as how he had become a "left-deviationist." And on and on.

The quasi-political tone of the street scene was looked upon with disdain by some, for radio news announcements about the previous night's "gay power" chaos had brought half of Fire Island's Cherry Grove running back to see what they had left behind. The generation gap existed even here. Older boys had strained looks on their faces and talked in concerned whispers as they watched the up-and-coming generation take being gay and flaunt it.

As the "gay power" chants on the street rose in frequency and volume, the crowd grew restless. The front of the Stonewall was losing its attraction, despite efforts by the owners to talk the crowd back into the club. "C'mon in and see what da pigs done to us," they growled. "We're honest businessmen here. We're American-born boys. We run a legitimate joint here. There ain't nuttin bein' done wrong in the dis place. Everybody come and see."

The people on the street were not to be coerced. "Let's go down the street and see what's happening, girls," someone yelled. And down the street went the crowd, smack into the Tactical Patrol Force, who had been called earlier to disperse the crowd and were walking west on Christopher from Sixth Avenue. Formed in a line, the TPF swept the crowd back to the corner of Waverly Place where they stopped. A stagnant situation there brought on some gay tomfoolery in the form of a chorus line facing the helmeted and club-carrying cops. Just as the line got into a full kick routine, the TPF advanced again and cleared the crowd of screaming gay powerites down Christopher to Seventh Avenue. The street and park were then held from both ends, and no one was allowed to enter—naturally causing a fall-off in normal Saturday night business, even at the straight Lion's Head and 55. The TPF positions in and around the square were held with only minor incident—one busted head and a number of scattered arrest—while the cops amused themselves by arbitrarily breaking up small groups of people up and down the avenue. The crowd finally dispersed around 3:30 A.M. The TPF had come and they had conquered, but Sunday was already there, and it was to be another story.

Sunday night was a time for watching and rapping. Gone were the "gay power" chants of Saturday, but not the new and open brand of exhibitionism. Steps, curbs, and the park provided props for what amounted to the Sunday fag follies as returning stars from the previous night's performances stopped by to close the show for the weekend.

It was slow going. Around 1 am a non-helmeted version of the TPF arrived and made a controlled and very cool sweep of the area, getting everyone moving and out of the park. That put a damper on posing and primping, and as the last buses were leaving Jerseyward, the crowd grew thin. Allen Ginsberg and Taylor Mead walked by to see what was happening and were filled in on the previous evenings' activities by some of the gay activists. "Gay power! Isn't that great!" Allen said. "We're one of the largest minorities in the country—10 per cent, you know. It's about time we did something to express ourselves."

Ginsberg expressed a desire to visit the Stonewall—"You know, I've never been in there"—and ambled on down the street, flashing peace signs and helloing the TPF. It was a relief and a kind of joy to see him on the street. He lent an extra umbrella of serenity of the scene with his laughter and quiet commentary on consciousness, "gay power" as a new movement, and the various implications of what had happened. I followed him into the Stonewall, where rock music blared from speakers all around a room that might have come right from a Hollywood set of a gay bar. He was immediately bouncing and dancing wherever he moved.

He left, and I walked east with him. Along the way, he described how things used to be. "You know, the guys there were so beautiful -- they've lost that wounded look that fags all had 10 years ago." It was the first time I had heard this crowd described as beautiful.

We reached Cooper Square, and as Ginsberg turned to head toward home, he waved and yelled, "Defend the fairies!" and bounced on across the square. He enjoyed the prospect of "gay power" and is probably working on a manifesto for the movement right now. Watch out. The liberation is under way.

GLOSSARY

Allen Ginsburg: American poet usually identified with the Beat movement of the 1950s

Dave von Ronk: American folk singer

paddywagon: Armored truck used by police for mass arrests

William Burroughs: American novelist known for subversive political and sexual themes

Document Analysis

Truscott begins his account of the Stonewall Riot by comparing it to a scene from the pen of Beat writer William Burroughs. From the outset, the phrase "gay power" is prominent, although Truscott ominously characterizes the notion as a "specter." He starts the next paragraph with one of the phrases that would, later, incite anger from those who had been involved in the protest: "forces of faggotry." This would not be the only epithet used by Truscott. While some of the derogatory terms he uses are quotations from participants in the event, others (like "forces of faggotry," "dyke," and "fags,") were his own. While recounting the events in a manner that is, in general, sympathetic to the cause of equal treatment and gay rights, Truscott does so while parroting the language of oppression. Truscott closes the second paragraph by explaining that the movement was larger than the one by the patrons of the bar itself, as participants "emerged from the bars, back rooms, and bedrooms of the Village and became street people."

Truscott then moves to the detailed account of the incident at the Stonewall Inn, describing the manner in which a crowd gathered in the street outside the Stonewall during the police raid. Using several quotations from the crowd, Truscott attempts to convey the sense that this was, at first "a festive gathering" of those who were regulars at the Stonewall and their friends. Things changed, however, when the police arrived. Truscott describes the darkening mood of the crowd as patrons and employees were hustled into the police vans. The crowd attempts to push over the van but were unsuccessful. As a woman is brought out from the bar, the crowd sees her struck by a police baton as she struggles. At this point, Truscott relates, "Beer cans and bottles were heaved at the windows, and a rain of coins descended on the cops." The crowd tried to beat down the door and set a fire using some nearby gasoline while the police responded by turning a firehose on the crowd. As additional police arrived, a total of thirteen were arrested.

Protests continued the next night. In describing the scene on Saturday, Truscott highlights the manner in which the protesters opening displayed their sexuality in a way that had not previously been done. "Hand-holding, kissing, and posing," he wrote, "accented each of the cheers with a homosexual liberation that had appeared only fleetingly on the street before." Despite the misgivings of "older boys," the younger generation was determined to make a statement, to " take being gay and flaunt it."

Truscott then describes the way that the crowd began to move down Christopher Street, colliding with the New York Police Department's "Tactical Patrol Force." This led to a series of movements by police and protesters as the authorities attempted to control the size and movements of the crowd. While there were few injuries. Protests continued on Sunday night but, as Truscott describes, "was a time for watching and rapping." While the "gay power" rhetoric of the previous night was absent, the flamboyant displays by the protesters continued until the police broke up the last groups of protesters.

Truscott concluded his report by describing the reaction of Beat poet and Greenwich Village resident Allen Ginsberg. Ginsberg—who, in the 1950s, had been prosecuted on obscenity charges for the vivid homosexual imagery in his poem "Howl"—expressed support for the notion of "gay power." Describing the gay community as "one of the largest minorities in the country," he argues that the time is right for the movement to "express" itself. After describing his brief encounter with the poet, Truscott concludes by predicting that "the liberation is under way."

Essential Themes

In a fairly subtle way, Lucian Truscott's account of the several days of rioting and protesting at the Stonewall Inn highlights two important ways in which the emerging gay power movement was developing in a similar direction as other civil rights efforts in the United States. The first was that one of the crucial ways that the protesters expressed themselves was by flaunting their sexuality in a display that Truscott described as "quasi-political." The use of "quasi-" gives the impression of diminishing the very real political statement that was being made. The exaggerated sexual display was a political act—a more overt continuation of the actions of those who, the night before had "emerged from the bars, back rooms, and bedrooms." Much like the Black Power movement emphasized the unique position and contributions of African American culture, the events at Stonewall created an opening for a fuller and more public expression of gay life and culture.

The second important factor that Truscott describes is the "generation gap." highlighted by the actions of the crowd. Older gay activists in New York—such as those who belonged to the Mattachine Society—felt that the actions of the protesters were too confrontational and might undo some of the work they had done during the 1950s and 1960s. This is not too different from the generational split that developed in the African American civil rights movement or the women's rights movement during the same era.

———*Aaron Gulyas, MA*

Bibliography and Additional Reading

Carter, David. *Stonewall: The Riots that Sparked the Gay Revolution*, (New York: St. Martin's Press, 2004).

Duberman, Martin. *Stonewall* (New York: Penguin Books, 1993).

Edsall, Nicholas. *Toward Stonewall: Homosexuality and Society in the Modern Western World* (Charlottesville: University of Virginia Press, 2003).

Williams, Walter and Retter, Yolanda, eds. *Gay and Lesbian Rights in the United States: A Documentary History* (Westport, Connecticut: Greenwood Press, 2003).

Steal This Book

Date: 1971
Author: Abbie Hoffman
Genre: Book excerpt

Summary Overview

Steal This Book was, in effect, a manual for dissidence and rebellion against government and corporate authority as well as an assertion that individual, personal liberty should, perhaps, not be bounded even by law. The very title is self-reflexive, suggesting that one way to rebel against legal and social norms is to steal the very book that advocates such action; ironically, many bookstores refused to carry the book because so many people took Hoffman literally and stole it. The book provided dissidents with advice on how to make explosive devices, grow marijuana, create a pirate (unlicensed) radio station, steal food, live in a commune, shoplift, find weapons, obtain free medical care, steal credit cards, and—in the excerpt here—find free or low-cost transportation.

Defining Moment

The late 1960s and early 1970s saw an enormous amount of social, political, and cultural turmoil in the United States. While the catalyst for much of this unrest were resistance to US involvement in the ongoing and escalating Vietnam War as well as issues such as racial and gender equality there were also even larger and more systemic issues that concerned young people in the United States. While the image of the coutercultural protest movements of the later 1960s is usually dominated by stereotypical "hippies," more radical elements existed and it is to this part of the counter cultural spectrum that Hoffman belongs.

The Youth International Party (or Yippies), founded by Abbie Hoffman, Anita Hoffman, Jerry Rubin, Nancy Kurshan, and Paul Krassner was one example of the more radically anti-authoritarian groups of the time. In addition pointing out the flaws and inequality in America's political and economic systems, they advocated for a "new nation," which would grow from countercultural institutions such as communes, food cooperatives, free or low-cost health clinics and an underground press and media network. In time, they claimed, this radicalized "new nation" could replace the old. It is this mindset—rather than a more generalized anti-war or anti-establishment one—that provides an intellectual foundation for the very practical techniques Hoffman presents in *Steal This Book*. The commercial, corporate, and civil institutions that readers would take advantage of were illegitimate and on the way out. In a way, following Hoffman's instructions could provide a path toward the new nation the Yippies foresaw.

Author Biography

Abbot ("Abbie") Howard Hoffman (1936–1989) was one of the most widely known political and social activists of the 1960s, as much for his theatrics and flamboyant personality as for his viewpoints. He began his career in the civil rights movement, participated in the activities of the Student Nonviolent Coordinating Committee, and cofounded the Youth International Party, commonly called the Yippies. He also became a prominent leader of the anti–Vietnam War movement. In 1967 he helped organize a mass demonstration in which 50,000 protesters attempted to use psychic energy to levitate the Pentagon, which, in their view, would bring the war to an end. He gained considerable notoriety as a member of the Chicago Seven, a group of activists tried for conspiracy and inciting riot in connection with the turmoil surrounding the 1968 Democratic National Convention in Chicago. (The group was originally called the Chicago Eight, but the trial of one of the accused was severed from that of the others). Through these and other activities, Hoffman became an icon of the 1960s counterculture.

During the 1970s, when *Steal This Book* was published, Hoffman continued to have encounters with law enforcement, inlcuding a 1973 arrest for his alleged intent to sell and distribute cocaine. Skipping bail, Hoffman disappeared from the public eye, surfacing occasionally to write articles, coordinate political activities. He surrendered to authorities in late 1980. He continued his political activism and writing throughout the decade, until his death by suicide on April 12, 1989.

HISTORICAL DOCUMENT

Free Transportation

HITCH-HIKING

Certainly one of the neatest ways of getting where you want to go for nothing is to hitch. In the city it's a real snap. Just position yourself at a busy intersection and ask the drivers for a lift when they stop for the red light. If you're hitching on a road where the traffic zooms by pretty fast, be sure to stand where the car will have room to safely pull off the road. Traveling long distances, even cross-country, can be easy if you have some sense of what you are doing.

A lone hitch-hiker will do much better than two or more. A man and woman will do very well together. Single women are certain to get propositioned and possibly worse. Amerikan males have endless sexual fantasies about picking up a poor lonesome damsel in distress. Unless your karate and head are in top form, women should avoid hitching alone. Telling men you have V.D. might help in difficult situations.

New England and the entire West Coast are the best sections for easy hitches. The South and Midwest can sometimes be a real hassle. *Easy Rider* and all that. The best season to hitch is in the summer. Daytime is much better than night. If you have to hitch at night, get under some type of illumination where you'll be seen.

Hitch-hiking is legal in most states, but remember you always can get a "say-so" bust. A "say-so" arrest is to police what Catch-22 is to the Army. When you ask why you're under arrest, the pig answers, "cause I say-so." If you stand on the shoulder of the road, the pigs won't give you too bad a time. If you've got long hair, cops will often stop to play games. You can wear a hat with your hair tucked under to avoid hassles. However this might hurt your ability to get rides, since many straights will pick up hippies out of curiosity who would not pick up a straight scruffy looking kid. Freak drivers usually only pick up other freaks.

Once in a while you hear stories of fines levied or even a few arrests for hitching (Flagstaff, Arizona is notorious), but even in the states where it is illegal, the law is rarely enforced. If you're stopped by the pigs, play dumb and they'll just tell you to move along. You can wait until they leave and then let your thumb hang out again.

Hitching on super highways is really far out. It's illegal but you won't get hassled if you hitch at the entrances. On a fucked-up exit, take your chances hitching right on the road, but keep a sharp eye out for porkers. When you get a ride be discriminating. Find out where the driver is headed. If you are at a good spot, don't take a ride under a hundred miles that won't end up in a location just as good. When the driver is headed to an out-of-the-way place, ask him to let you off where you can get the best rides. If he's going to a particularly small town, ask him to drive you to the other side of the town line. It's usually only a mile or two. Small towns often enforce all sorts of "say-so" ordinances. If you get stuck on the wrong side of town, it would be wise to even hoof it through the place. Getting to a point on the road where the cars are inter-city rather than local traffic is always preferable.

When you hit the road you should have a good idea of how to get where you are going. You can pick up a free map at any gas station. Long distance routes, road conditions, weather and all sorts of information can be gotten free by calling the American Automobile Association in any city. Say that you are a member driving to Phoenix, Arizona or wherever your destination is, and find out what you want to know. Always carry a sign indicating where you are going. If you get stranded on the road without one, ask in a diner or gas station for a piece of cardboard and a magic marker. Make the letters bold and fill them in so they can be seen by drivers from a distance. If your destination is a small town, the sign should indicate the state. For really long distances, EAST or WEST is best. Unless, of course, you're going north or south. A phony foreign flag sewed on your pack also helps.

Carrying dope is not advisable, and although searching you is illegal, few pigs can read the Constitution. If you are carrying when the patrol car pulls up, tell them you are Kanadian and hitching through Amerika. Highway patrols are very uptight about promoting incidents with foreigners. The foreign bit goes over especially well with small-town types, and is also amazingly good for avoiding hassles with greasers. If you can't hack this one, tell them you are a reporter for a newspaper writing a feature story on hitching around the country. This story has averted many a bust.

Don't be shy when you hitch. Go into diners and gas stations and ask people if they're heading East or to Texas. Sometimes gas station attendants will help. When in the car be friendly as hell. Offer to share the driving if you've got a license. If you're broke, you can usually bum a meal or a few bucks, maybe even a free night's lodging. Never be intimidated into giving money for a ride.

As for what to carry when hitching, the advice is to travel light. The rule is to make up a pack of the absolute minimum, then cut that in half. Hitching is an art form as is all survival. Master it and you'll travel on a free trip forever.

FREIGHTING
There is a way to hitch long distances that has certain advantages over letting your thumb hang out for hours on some two-laner. Learn about riding the trains and you'll always have that alternative. Hitchhiking at night can be impossible, but hopping a train is easier at night than by day. By hitchhiking days and hopping freights and sleeping on them at night, you can cover incredible distances rapidly and stay well rested. Every city and most large towns have a freight yard. You can find it by following the tracks or asking where the freight yard is located.

When you get to the yard, ask the workmen when the next train leaving in your direction will be pulling out. Unlike the phony Hollywood image, railroad men are nice to folks who drop by to grab a ride. Most yards don't have a guard or a "bull" as they are called. Even if they do, he is generally not around. If there is a bull around, the most he's going to do is tell you it's private property and ask you to leave. There are exceptions to this rule, such as the notorious Lincoln, Nebraska, and Las Vegas, Nevada, but by asking you can find out. Even if he asks you to leave or throws you out, sneak back when your train is pulling out and jump aboard.

After you've located the right train for your trip, hunt for an empty boxcar to ride. The men in the yards will generally point one out if you ask. Pig-sties, flat cars and coal cars are definitely third class due to exposure to the elements. Boxcars are by far the best. They are clean and the roof over your head helps in bad weather and cuts down the wind. Boxcars with a hydro-cushion suspension system used for carrying fragile cargo make for the smoothest ride. Unless you get one, you should be prepared for a pretty bumpy and noisy voyage.

You should avoid cars with only one door open, because the pin may break, locking you in. A car with both doors open gives you one free chance. Pig-backs (trailers on flatcars) are generally considered unsafe. Most trains make a number of short hops, so if time is an important factor try to get on a "hot shot" express. A hot shot travels faster and has priority over other trains in crowded yards. You should favor a hot shot even if you have to wait an extra hour or two or more to get one going your way.

If you're traveling at night, be sure to dress warmly. You can freeze your ass off. Trains might not offer the most comfortable ride, but they go through beautiful countryside that you'd never see from the highway or airway. There are no billboards, road signs, cops, Jack-in-the-Boxes, gas stations or other artifacts of honky culture. You'll get dirty on the trains so wear old clothes. Don't pass up this great way to travel cause some bullshit western scared you out of it.

CARS
If you know how to drive and want to travel long distances, the auto transportation agencies are a good deal. Look in the Yellow Pages under Automobile Transportation and Trucking or Driveway. Rules vary, but normally you must be over 21 and have a valid license. Call up and tell them when and where you want to go and they will let you know if they have a car available. They give you the car and a tank of gas free. You pay the rest. Go to pick up the car alone, then get some people to ride along and help with the driving and expenses. You can make New York to San Francisco for about eighty dollars in tolls and gas in four days without pushing. Usually you have the car for longer and can make a whole thing out of it. You must look straight when you go to the agency. This can be simply be done by wetting down your hair and shoving it under a cap.

Another good way to travel cheaply is to find somebody who has a car and is going your way. Usually underground newspapers list people who either want rides or riders. Another excellent place to find information is your local campus. Every campus has a bulletin board for rides. Head shops and other community-minded stores have notices up on the wall.

GAS

If you have a car and need some gas late at night you can get a quart and then some by emptying the hoses from the pumps into your tank. There is always a fair amount of surplus gas left when the pumps are shut off.

If your [sic] traveling in a car and don't have enough money for gas and tolls, stop at the bus station and see if anybody wants a lift. If you find someone, explain your money situation and make a deal with him. Hitch-hikers also can be asked to chip in on the gas.

You can carry a piece of tubing in the trunk of your car and when the gas indicator gets low, pull up to a nice looking Cadillac on some dark street and syphon off some of his gas. Just park your car so the gas tank is next to the Caddy's, or use a large can. Stick the hose into his tank, suck up enough to get things flowing, and stick the other end into your tank. Having a lower level of liquid, you tank will draw gas until you and the Caddy are equal. "To each according to his need, from each according to his ability," wrote Marx. Bet you hadn't realized until now that the law of gravity affects economics.

Another way is to park in a service station over their filler hole. Lift off one lid (like a small manhole cover), run down twenty feet of rubber tubing thru the hole you've cut in your floorboard, then turn on the electric pump which you have installed to feed into your gas tank. All they ever see is a parked car. This technique is especially rewarding when you have a bus.

BUSES

If you'd rather leave the driving and the paying to them, try swiping a ride on the bus. Here's a method that has worked well. Get a rough idea of where the bus has stopped before it arrived at your station. If you are not at the beginning or final stop on the route, wait until the bus you want pulls in and then out of the station. Make like the bus just pulled off without you while you went to the bathroom. If there is a station master, complain like crazy to him. Tell him you're going to sue the company if your luggage gets stolen. He'll put you on the next bus for free. If there is no station master, lay your sad tale on the next driver that comes along. If you know when the last bus left, just tell the driver you've been stranded there for eight hours and you left your kid sleeping on the other bus. Tell him you called ahead to the company and they said to grab the next bus and they would take care of it.

The next method isn't totally free but close enough. It's called the hopper-bopper. Find a bus that makes a few stops before it gets to where you want to go. The more stops with people getting in or out the better. Buy a ticket for the short hop and stay on the bus until you end up at your destination. You must develop a whole style in order to pull this off because the driver has to forget you are connected with the ticket you gave him. Dress unobtrusively or make sure the driver hasn't seen your face. Pretend to be asleep when the short hop station is reached. If you get questioned, just act upset about sleeping through the stop you "really" want and ask if it's possible to get a ride back.

AIRLINES

Up and away, junior outlaws! If you really want to get where you're going in a hurry, don't forget skyjacker's paradise. Don't forget the airlines. They make an unbelievable amount of bread on their inflated prices, ruin the land with incredible amounts of polluting wastes and noise, and deliberately hold back aviation advances that would reduce prices and time of flight. We know two foolproof methods to fly free, but unfortunately we feel publishing them would cause the airlines to change their policy. The following methods have been talked about enough, so the time seems right to make them known to a larger circle of friends.

A word should be said right off about stolen tickets. Literally millions of dollars worth of airline tickets are stolen each year. If you have good underworld contacts, you can get a ticket to anywhere you want at one-fourth the regular price. If you are charged more, you are getting a slight rooking. In any case, you can get a ticket for any flight or date and just trade it in. They are actually as good as cash, except that it takes 30 days to get a refund, and by then they might have traced the stolen tickets. If you can get a stolen ticket, exchange or use it as soon as possible, and always fly under a phony name. A stolen ticket for a trip around the world currently goes for one hundred and fifty dollars in New York.

One successful scheme requires access to the mailbox of a person listed in the local phone book. Let's use the name Ron Davis as an example. A woman calls one of the airlines with a very efficient sounding rap such as: "Hello, this is Mr. Davis' secretary at Allied Chemical. He and his wife would like to fly to Chicago on Friday. Could you mail two first-class tickets to his home and bill us here at Allied?" Every major corporation probably has a Ron Davis, and the airlines rarely bother checking anyway. Order your tickets two days before you wish to travel, and pick them up at the mailbox or address you had them sent to. If you are uptight in the airport about the tickets, just go up to another airline and have the tickets exchanged.

One gutsy way to hitch a free ride is to board the plane without a ticket. This is how it works. Locate the flight you want and rummage through a wastebasket until you find an envelope for that particular airline. Shuffle by the counter men (which is fairly easy if it's busy). When the boarding call is made, stand in line and get on the plane. Flash the empty envelope at the stewardess as you board the plane. Carry a number of packages as a decoy, so the stewardess won't ask you to open the envelope. If she does, which is rare, and sees you have no ticket, act surprised. "Oh my gosh, it must have fallen out in the wash room," will do fine. Run back down the ramp as if you're going to retrieve the ticket. Disappear and try later on a different airline. Nine out of ten revolutionaries say it's the only way to fly. This trick works only on airlines that don't use the boarding pass system.

If you want to be covered completely, use the hopper-bopper method described in the section on Buses, with this added security precaution. Buy two tickets from different cashiers, or better still, one from an agent in town. Both will be on the same flight. Only one ticket will be under a phony name and for the short hop, white the ticket under your real name will be for your actual destination. At the boarding counter, present the short hop ticket. You will be given an envelope with a white receipt in it. Actually, the white receipt is the last leaf in your ticket. Once you are securely seated and aloft, take out the ticket with your name and final destination. Gently peel away everything but the white receipt. Place the still valid ticket back in your pocket. Now remove from the envelope and destroy the short hop receipt. In its place, put the receipt for the ticket you have in your pocket.

When you land at the short hop airport, stay on the plane. Usually the stewardesses just ask you if you are remaining on the flight. If you have to, you can actually show her your authentic receipt. When you get to your destination, you merely put the receipt back on the bonafide ticket that you still have in your pocket. It isn't necessary that they be glued together. Present the ticket for a refund or exchange it for another ticket. This method works well even in foreign countries. You can actually fly around the world for $88.00 using the hopper-bopper method and switching receipts.

If you can't hack these shucks you should at least get a Youth Card and travel for half fare. If you are over twenty-two but still in your twenties, you can easily pass. Get a card from a friend who has similar color hair and eyes. Your friend can easily get one from another airline. You can master your friend's signature and get a supporting piece of identification from him to back up your youth card if you find it necessary. If you have a friend who works for an airline or travel agency, just get a card under your own name and an age below the limit. Your friend can validate the card. Flying youth fare is on stand-by, so it's always a good idea to call ahead and book a number of reservations under fictitious names on the flight you'll be taking. This will fuck up the booking of regular passengers and insure you a seat.

By the way, if you fly cross-country a number of times, swipe one of the plug-in head sets. Always remember to pack it in your traveling bag. This way you'll save a two dollar fee charged for the in-flight movie. The headsets are interchangeable on all airlines.

One way to fly free is to actually hitch a ride. Look for the private plane area located at every airport, usually in some remote part of the field. You can find it by noticing where the small planes without airline markings take off and land. Go over to the runways and ask around. Often the mechanics will let you know when someone is leaving for your destination and point out a pilot. Tell him you lost your ticket and have to get back to school. Single pilots often like to have a passenger along and it's a real gas flying in a small plane.

Some foreign countries have special arrangements for free air travel to visiting writers, artists or reporters. Brazil and Argentina are two we know of for sure. Call or write the embassy of the country you wish to visit in Washington or their mission to the United Nations in New York. Writing works best, especially if you can cop some stationery from a newspaper or publishing house. Tell them you will be writing a feature story for some magazine on the tourist spots or handcrafts of the country. The embassy will arrange for you to travel gratis aboard one of their air force planes. The planes leave only from Washington and New York at unscheduled times. Once you have the O.K. letter from the embassy you're all set. This is definitely worth checking out if you want to vacation in a foreign country with all sorts of free bonuses thrown in.

A one-way ride is easy if you want to get into skyjacking. Keep the piece or knife in your shoe to avoid possible detection with the "metal scanner," a long black tube that acts like a geiger counter. Or use a plastic knife or bomb. It's also advisable to wrap your dope in a non-metallic material. Avoid tinfoil.

The crews have instructions to take you wherever you want to go even if they have to refuel, but watch out for air marshals. To avoid air marshals and searches pick an airline which flies short domestic hops. You should plan to end up in a country hostile to the United States or you'll end up right back where you came from in some sturdy handcuffs. One dude wanted to travel in style so he demanded $100,000 as a going-away gift. The airlines quickly paid off. The guy then got greedy and demanded a hundred million dollars. When he returned to pick up the extra pocket money, he got nabbed. None the less, skyjacking appears to be the cheapest, fastest way to get away from it all.

IN CITY TRAVEL

Any of the public means of transportation can be ripped off easily. Get on the bus with a large bill and present it after the bus has left the stop. If the bus is crowded, slip in the back door when it opens to dispatch passengers.

Two people can easily get through the turnstile in a subway on one token by doubling up. In some subway systems cards are given out to high school kids or senior citizens or employees of the city. The next time you are in a subway station notice people flashing cards to the man in the booth and entering through the "exit" door. Notice the color of the card used by people in your age group. Get a piece of colored paper in a stationery store or find some card of the same color you need. Put this "card" in a plastic window of your wallet and flash it in the same way those with a bona fide pass do.

Before entering a turnstile, always test the swing bar. If someone during the day put in an extra token, it's still in the machine waiting for you to enter free.

For every token and coin deposited in an automatic turnstile, there is a foreign coin the same size for much less that will work in the machine. ...Buy a cheap bag of assorted foreign coins from a dealer that you can locate in the Yellow Pages. Size up the coins with a token from your subway system. You can get any of these coins in bulk from a large dealer. Generally they are about 1,000 for five dollars. Tell him you make jewelry out of them if he gets suspicious. Giving what almost amounts to free subway rides away is a communal act of love. The best outlaws in the world rip-off shit for a lot more people than just themselves. Robin Hood lives!

GLOSSARY

Pigs/Porkers: Derogatory term for law enforcement officers.

To "look straight": Not appearing to be a member of the counterculture; to appear well-groomed and "conventional."

V.D.: Venereal Disease, another term for a sexually transmitted disease.

term: definition

Document Analysis
Steal This Book is written in simple language and adopts much of the slang of the 1960s counterculture in its appeal to dissident youth. Hoffman's overall point is that stealing from the government and corporations is not only easy but also a moral imperative for those who reject the nation's social and economic system. In the excerpt reproduced here, Hoffman offers specific advice on traveling for little or no cost—though many of the techniques he describes would be virtually impossible today because of changes in technology and because of heightened security in response to the threat of terrorist attacks. He begins with a discussion of hitchhiking and ways to avoid having to deal with the police, commonly called "pigs" by 1960s dissidents—a term that caught on during and after the 1968 Democratic National Convention, when the Yippies, led by Hoffman, carried around a pig that, they said, they were nominating as a candidate for president. One tactic Hoffman advocates in police encounters is for the hitchhiker to claim that he or she is "Kanadian and hitching through Amerika." The use of the letter K in America was commonplace among 1960s radicals and continues to be used as a satiric misspelling; it is the German spelling of America and used sardonically in the United States to suggest Fascism and Nazism.

Hoffman also advocates riding in train boxcars ("Freighting"), noting that for all its discomforts, it provides a way to avoid the "artifacts of honky [white] culture" along roadways, a comment designed to denigrate the increasing commercial presence, on interstate highways, of increasingly homogenous restaurant and lodging options. Another method of transportation is to offer to transport a car, and he outlines ways to obtain free gasoline. One way to travel cheaply by bus is the "hopper-bopper"—that is, buying a ticket for a short hop but staying on the bus for a longer distance. Hoffman then describes ways to obtain free or low-cost plane tickets, usually by illegal means. At the time it was possible to use stolen tickets or to buy tickets in the name of a corporation, for airport security was lax and it was possible to travel by air without showing identification. Hoffman also claims that it is possible to sneak onto a plane by flashing a ticket envelope. Similarly, Hoffman explains that it is possible to travel virtually for free within a city by, for example, using low-value coins that are the same size as bus tokens.

Essential Themes
This brief excerpt from *Steal This Book* is typical of the entire volume. Looking beyond the 1960s-1970s countercultural slang and putting aside the present-day unworkability of many of these scams and schemes, there is a consistent message thats appear in this excerpt as well as in the book as a whole. In Hoffman's world, there is clearly an ideological element to these instructions on theft, stowing away, or other activities. This is not simply a grifter's guidebook. One example of this is somewhat blithe comment when discussion siphoning gas out of "a nice looking Cadillac": " 'To each according to his need, from each according to his ability,' wrote Marx. Bet you hadn't realized until now that the law of gravity affects economics." There is an ideological imperative to even the playing field between the haves and the have-nots. Most of the techniques Hoffman describes in *Steal This Book* have corporations or government agencies as their victims. Those that do not often target those Hoffman believes are wealthy enough to absorb a loss (such as one who owns "a nice looking Cadillac.").

The other side to this ideology is the notion that if the reader has an abundance of an item—such as foreign coins that can be fraudulently used as subway tokens—the reader should share them with those who might need them. He describes this as a "communal act of love" and such guidance is in keeping with the broader work of the Youth International Party and similar organizations. The creation of a new nation to supplant the old would not occur if people used these tools and techniques only to enrich or benefit themselves. Rather, it is incumbent on indiviudals to work for the collective good.

——Michael J. O'Neal, PhD

Bibliography and Additional Reading
Hoffman, Jack, and Daniel Simon. *Run Run Run: The Lives of Abbie Hoffman*. New York: Tarcher/Putnam, 1994.

Raskin, Jonah. *For the Hell of It: The Life and Times of Abbie Hoffman*. Los Angeles: University of California Press, 1996.

Web Sites
The Realist Archive Project. Abbie Hoffman articles in *The Realist* http://www.ep.tc/realist/abbiehoffman.html

Federal Bureau of Investigation. *FBI Records:Abbie Hoffman*. https://vault.fbi.gov/abbie-hoffman

■ Commonwealth Address

Date: 1984
Author: César Chávez
Genre: Speech

Summary Overview

César Chávez, the leader of the United Farm Workers of America, saw the hopes for better lives for Mexican, Mexican American, and Hispanic workers in the United States repeatedly raised, sunk, and revived again. Many factors contributed to this seemingly unending pendulum swing from hopefulness to despair, and his Commonwealth Address highlights some of these factors. The address offers a window into Chávez's keen awareness of the plights of the farmworkers whom he represented as well as of Latinos in general.

Chávez delivered the speech to the Commonwealth Club of California on November 9, 1984. Among the several issues addressed in this speech are the blunt disregard of growers for the provision of safe vehicles to transport farmworkers, the intimidation tactics used by growers to discourage unionization among farmworkers, child labor concerns, union survival, pesticides and environmental concerns, Chávez's nonviolence philosophy, and the role of the boycott in pressuring growers to acknowledge workers' needs. Chávez also highlights his view of how the political climate created by California's governor, George Deukmejian, discouraged and nearly prevented farmworkers from fulfilling the American dream of enjoying equal rights. Throughout his Commonwealth Address, Chávez's main drive to fulfill the tenets of La Causa—the farmworkers' movement he founded—resounds loud and clear.

Defining Moment

César Chávez's Commonwealth Address was delivered at the Commonwealth Club of California in San Francisco. The Commonwealth Club of California is a nonprofit, nonpartisan organization that was founded in 1903 with the principal goal of supporting independent thought, particularly cultural thought. The club has a program called Voices of Reform, aimed at fomenting understanding among policy makers in California. Many famous leaders have spoken at club events, including President Franklin Delano Roosevelt. The actress Shirley Temple Black was the president of the club in 1984. That year, an admirer who very much respected what Chávez stood for sought him out to speak to members of the club in San Francisco. In this speech, given on November 9, 1984, Chávez discussed the changes that he underwent as a leader of farmworkers and as a man who advocated the causes of the oppressed of all races and walks of life.

At the time of this address, Chávez's peak years of grape boycotts, strikes, and marches of protest had diminished. However, according to the biographer Dan La Botz, Chávez knew that this was no time to retreat, especially since his "archenemy [had] moved into the White House." As governor of California, Ronald Reagan was a forthright opponent of the United Farm Workers of America. César Chávez's speech to the audience of the Commonwealth Club of California should be placed in the context of what the historians Richard J. Jensen and John C. Hammerback call "the difficult years": the period from 1984 to 1993 and its "conservative reaction," which saw Ronald Reagan and George H.W. Bush as President and George Deukmejian and Pete Wilson serving as governors of California. Reagan and Deukmejian in particular were friends of the powerful growers' lobby in California.

Author Biography

César Estrada Chávez was born on March 31, 1927, near Yuma, Arizona. Chávez's parents were originally from Mexico, where his grandfather had lived under the dictator Porfirio Díaz which motivated him to move his family to the United States. Chávez's father's hard work enabled him to homestead a large farm in Yuma, Arizona, but he was eventually denied the continuation of this homesteading. As they were unable to find another way to sustain a living, the Chávez family began the common practice of wandering from farm to farm for work, following the crops. In 1937 the family moved to California.

In 1962, Chávez organized the National Farm Workers Association, the precursor organization to the United Farm Workers of America. Chávez always asserted that he sought improvements in the lives of the oppressed regardless of race. This philosophy ultimately made Chávez very appealing to people of all ethnicities and walks of life. Chávez opposed the bracero program, through which Mexican workers were admitted to the United States from the years 1942 to 1964, seeing the program as granting legal sanction to the exploitation of farmworkers. During the 1960s, 1970s, and 1980s, Chávez continued to fight for the civil rights of farmworkers and against the use of pesticides on the fields of California, which extended his appeal to environmentalists.

In 1968 Chávez embraced the teachings of the Indian nationalist leader Mahatma Gandhi in a more concrete way by beginning a fast, so as to emphasize the notion that victory for the farmworkers needed to be won by peaceful means. Through this fast, which lasted twenty-five days, Chávez lost thirty-five pounds. Afterward, his message was deemed ethically stronger, and his reputation as a serious nonviolent labor leader was reinforced. In 1984 Chávez began a new boycott on grapes to protest the harmful effects of the pesticides on farmworkers and on the people who consumed the grapes. Chávez fasted again in 1988, for thirty-six days, further protesting the use of pesticides.

Chávez died on April 23, 1993. In 1994, President Bill Clinton posthumously awarded Chávez the Presidential Medal of Freedom.

HISTORICAL DOCUMENT

Twenty-one years ago last September, on a lonely stretch of railroad track paralleling U.S. Highway 101 near Salinas, 32 Bracero farm workers lost their lives in a tragic accident.

The Braceros had been imported from Mexico to work on California farms. They died when their bus, which was converted from a flatbed truck, drove in front of a freight train.

Conversion of the bus had not been approved by any government agency. The driver had "tunnel" vision.

Most of the bodies lay unidentified for days. No one, including the grower who employed the workers, even knew their names.

Today, thousands of farm workers live under savage conditions—beneath trees and amid garbage and human excrement—near tomato fields in San Diego County, tomato fields which use the most modern farm technology.

Vicious rats gnaw on them as they sleep. They walk miles to buy food at inflated prices. And they carry in water from irrigation pumps.

Child labor is still common in many farm areas.

As much as 30 percent of Northern California's garlic harvesters are under-aged children. Kids as young as six years old have voted in state-conducted union elections since they qualified as workers.

Some 800,000 under-aged children work with their families harvesting crops across America. Babies born to migrant workers suffer 25 percent higher infant mortality than the rest of the population.

Malnutrition among migrant worker children is 10 times higher than the national rate.

Farm workers' average life expectancy is still 49 years—compared to 73 years for the average American.

All my life, I have been driven by one dream, one goal, one vision: To overthrow a farm labor system in this nation which treats farm workers as if they were not important human beings.

Farm workers are not agricultural implements. They are not beasts of burden—to be used and discarded.

That dream was born in my youth. It was nurtured in my early days of organizing. It has flourished. It has been attacked.

I'm not very different from anyone else who has ever tried to accomplish something with his life. My motivation comes from my personal life—from watching what my mother and father went through when I was growing up; from what we experienced as migrant farm workers in California.

That dream, that vision, grew from my own experience with racism, with hope, with the desire to be treated fairly and to see my people treated as human beings and not as chattel.

It grew from anger and rage—emotions I felt 40 years ago when people of my color were denied the right to see a movie or eat at a restaurant in many parts of California.

It grew from the frustration and humiliation I felt as a boy who couldn't understand how the growers could abuse and exploit farm workers when there were so many of us and so few of them.

Later, in the '50s, I experienced a different kind of exploitation. In San Jose, in Los Angeles and in other urban communities, we—the Mexican American people—were dominated by a majority that was Anglo.

I began to realize what other minority people had discovered: That the only answer—the only hope—was in organizing. More of us had to become citizens. We had to register to vote. And people like me had to develop the skills it would take to organize, to educate, to help empower the Chicano people.

I spent many years—before we founded the union—learning how to work with people.

We experienced some successes in voter registration, in politics, in battling racial discrimination—successes in an era when Black Americans were just beginning to assert their civil rights and when political awareness among Hispanics was almost non-existent.

But deep in my heart, I knew I could never be happy unless I tried organizing the farm workers. I didn't know if I would succeed. But I had to try.

All Hispanics—urban and rural, young and old—are connected to the farm workers' experience. We had all lived through the fields—or our parents had. We shared that common humiliation.

How could we progress as a people, even if we lived in the cities, while the farm workers—men and women of our color—were condemned to a life without pride?

How could we progress as a people while the farm workers—who symbolized our history in this land—were denied self-respect?

How could our people believe that their children could become lawyers and doctors and judges and business people while this shame, this injustice was permitted to continue?

Those who attack our union often say, "It's not really a union. It's something else: A social movement. A civil rights movement. It's something dangerous."

They're half right. The United Farm Workers is first and foremost a union. A union like any other. A union that either produces for its members on the bread and butter issues or doesn't survive.

But the UFW has always been something more than a union—although it's never been dangerous if you believe in the Bill of Rights.

The UFW was the beginning! We attacked that historical source of shame and infamy that our people in this country lived with. We attacked that injustice, not by complaining; not by seeking handouts; not by becoming soldiers in the War on Poverty.

We organized!

Farm workers acknowledged we had allowed ourselves to become victims in a democratic society—a society where majority rule and collective bargaining are supposed to be more than academic theories or political rhetoric. And by addressing this historical problem, we created confidence and pride and hope in an entire people's ability to create the future.

The UFW's survival—its existence—was not in doubt in my mind when the time began to come—after the union became visible—when Chicanos started entering college in greater numbers, when Hispanics began running for public office in greater numbers—when our people started asserting their rights on a broad range of issues and in many communities across the country.

The union's survival—its very existence—sent out a signal to all Hispanics that we were fighting for our dignity, that we were challenging and overcoming injustice, that we were empowering the least educated among us—the poorest among us.

The message was clear: If it could happen in the fields, it could happen anywhere—in the cities, in the courts, in the city councils, in the state legislatures.

I didn't really appreciate it at the time, but the coming of our union signaled the start of great changes among Hispanics that are only now beginning to be seen.

I've travelled to every part of this nation. I have met and spoken with thousands of Hispanics from every walk of life—from every social and economic class.

One thing I hear most often from Hispanics, regardless of age or position—and from many non-Hispanics as well—is that the farm workers gave them hope that they could succeed and the inspiration to work for change.

From time to time you will hear our opponents declare that the union is weak, that the union has no support, that the union has not grown fast enough. Our obituary has been written many times.

How ironic it is that the same forces which argue so passionately that the union is not influential are the same forces that continue to fight us so hard.

The union's power in agriculture has nothing to do with the number of farm workers under union contract. It has nothing to do with the farm workers' ability to contribute to Democratic politicians. It doesn't even have much to do with our ability to conduct successful boycotts.

The very fact of our existence forces an entire industry—unionized and non-unionized—to spend millions of dollars year after year on improved wages, on improved working conditions, on benefits for workers.

If we're so weak and unsuccessful, why do the growers continue to fight us with such passion?

Because so long as we continue to exist, farm workers will benefit from our existence—even if they don't work under union contract.

It doesn't really matter whether we have 100,000 members or 500,000 members. In truth, hundreds of thousands of farm workers in California—and in other states—are better off today because of our work.

And Hispanics across California and the nation who don't work in agriculture are better off today because of what the farm workers taught people about organization, about pride and strength, about seizing control over their own lives.

Tens of thousands of the children and grandchildren of farm workers and the children and grandchildren of poor Hispanics are moving out of the fields and out of the barrios—and into the professions and into business and into politics. And that movement cannot be reversed!

Our union will forever exist as an empowering force among Chicanos in the Southwest. And that means our power and our influence will grow and not diminish.

Two major trends give us hope and encouragement.

First, our union has returned to a tried and tested weapon in the farm workers' non-violent arsenal—the boycott!

After the Agricultural Labor Relations Act became law in California in 1975, we dismantled our boycott to work with the law.

During the early- and mid-'70s, millions of Americans supported our boycotts. After 1975, we redirected our efforts from the boycott to organizing and winning elections under the law.

The law helped farm workers make progress in overcoming poverty and injustice. At companies where farm workers are protected by union contracts, we have made progress in overcoming child labor, in overcoming miserable wages and working conditions, in overcoming sexual harassment of women workers, in overcoming dangerous pesticides which poison our people and poison the food we all eat.

Where we have organized, these injustices soon pass into history.

But under Republican Governor George Deukmejian, the law that guarantees our right to organize no longer protects farm workers. It doesn't work anymore.

In 1982, corporate growers gave Deukmejian one million dollars to run for governor of California. Since he took office, Deukmejian has paid back his debt to the growers with the blood and sweat of California farm workers.

Instead of enforcing the law as it was written against those who break it, Deukmejian invites growers who break the law to seek relief from the governor's appointees.

What does all this mean for farm workers?

It means that the right to vote in free elections is a sham. It means that the right to talk freely about the union among your fellow workers on the job is a cruel hoax. It means the right to be free from threats and intimidation by growers is an empty promise.

It means the right to sit down and negotiate with your employer as equals across the bargaining table—and not as peons in the field—is a fraud. It means that thousands of farm workers—who are owed millions of dollars in back pay because their employers broke the law—are still waiting for their checks.

It means that 36,000 farm workers—who voted to be represented by the United Farm Workers in free elections—are still waiting for contracts from growers who refuse to bargain in good faith.

It means that, for farm workers, child labor will continue. It means that infant mortality will continue. It means malnutrition among our children will continue. It means the short life expectancy and the inhuman living and working conditions will continue.

Are these make-believe threats? Are they exaggerations?

Ask the farm workers who are still waiting for growers to bargain in good faith and sign contracts. Ask the farm workers who've been fired from their jobs because they spoke out for the union. Ask the farm workers who've been threatened with physical violence because they support the UFW.

Ask the family of Rene Lopez, the young farm worker from Fresno who was shot to death last year because he supported the union.

These tragic events forced farm workers to declare a new international boycott of California table grapes. That's why we are asking Americans once again to join the farm workers by boycotting California grapes.

The Louis Harris poll revealed that 17 million American adults boycotted grapes. We are convinced that those people and that good will have not disappeared.

That segment of the population which makes our boycotts work are the Hispanics, the Blacks, the other minorities and our allies in labor and the church. But it is also an entire generation of young Americans who matured politically and socially in the 1960s and '70s—millions of people for whom boycotting grapes and other products became a socially accepted pattern of behavior.

If you were young, Anglo and on or near campus during the late '60s and early '70s, chances are you supported farm workers.

Fifteen years later, the men and women of that generation of are alive and well. They are in their mid-30s and '40s. They are pursuing professional careers. Their disposable income is relatively high. But they are still inclined to respond to an appeal from farm workers. The union's mission still has meaning for them.

Only today we must translate the importance of a union for farm workers into the language of the 1980s. Instead of talking about the right to organize, we must talk about protection against sexual harassment in the fields. We must speak about the right to quality food—and food that is safe to eat.

I can tell you that the new language is working; the 17 million are still there. They are responding—not to picket-lines and leafletting alone, but to the high-tech boycott of today—a boycott that uses computers and direct mail and advertising techniques which have revolutionized business and politics in recent years.

We have achieved more success with the boycott in the first 11 months of 1984 that we achieved in the 14 years since 1970.

The other trend that gives us hope is the monumental growth of Hispanic influence in this country and what that means in increased population, increased social and economic clout, and increased political influence.

South of the Sacramento River in California, Hispanics now make up more than 25 percent of the population. That figure will top 30 percent by the year 2000.

There are 1.1 million Spanish-surnamed registered voters in California; 85 percent are Democrats; only 13 percent are Republicans.

In 1975, there were 200 Hispanic elected officials at all levels of government. In ·1984, there are over 400 elected judges, city council members, mayors and legislators.

In light of these trends, it is absurd to believe or suggest that we are going to go back in time—as a union or as a people!

The growers often try to blame the union for their problems—to lay their sins off on us—sins for which they only have themselves to blame.

The growers only have themselves to blame as they begin to reap the harvest from decades of environmental damage they have brought upon the land—the pesticides, the herbicides, the soil fumigants, the fertilizers, the salt deposits from thoughtless irrigation—the ravages from years of unrestrained poisoning of our soil and water.

Thousands of acres of land in California have already been irrevocably damaged by this wanton abuse of nature. Thousands more will be lost unless growers understand that dumping more poisons on the soil won't solve their problems—on the short term or the long term.

Health authorities in many San Joaquin Valley towns already warn young children and pregnant women not to drink the water because of nitrates from fertilizers which have contaminated the groundwater.

The growers only have themselves to blame for an increasing demand by consumers for higher quality food—food that isn't tainted by toxics; food that doesn't result from plant mutations or chemicals which produce red, luscious-looking tomatoes—that taste like alfalfa.

The growers are making the same mistake American automakers made in the '60s and '70s when they refused to produce small economical cars—and opened the door to increased foreign competition.

Growers only have themselves to blame for increasing attacks on their publicly-financed hand-outs and government welfare: Water subsidies; mechanization research; huge subsidies for not growing crops.

These special privileges came into being before the Supreme Court's one-person, one-vote decision—at a time when rural lawmakers dominated the Legislature and the Congress. Soon, those hand-outs could be in jeopardy as government searches for more revenue and as urban taxpayers take a closer look at farm programs—and who they really benefit.

The growers only have themselves to blame for the humiliation they have brought upon succeeding waves of immigrant groups which have sweated and sacrificed for 100 years to make this industry rich. For generations, they have subjugated entire races of dark-skinned farm workers.

These are the sins of the growers, not the farm workers. We didn't poison the land. We didn't open the door to imported produce. We didn't covet billions of dollars in government hand-outs. We didn't abuse and exploit the people who work the land.

Today, the growers are like a punch-drunk old boxer who doesn't know he's past his prime. The times are changing. The political and social environment has changed. The chickens are coming home to roost—and the time to account for past sins is approaching.

I am told, these days, why farm workers should be discouraged and pessimistic: The Republicans control the governor's office and the White House. They say there is a conservative trend in the nation.

Yet we are filled with hope and encouragement. We have looked into the future and the future is ours!

History and inevitability are on our side. The farm workers and their children—and the Hispanics and their children—are the future in California. And corporate growers are the past!

Those politicians who ally themselves with the corporate growers and against the farm workers and the Hispanics are in for a big surprise. They want to make their careers in politics. They want to hold power 20 and 30 years from now.

But 20 and 30 years from now—in Modesto, in Salinas, in Fresno, in Bakersfield, in the Imperial Valley, and in many of the great cities of California—those communities will be dominated by farm workers and not by growers, by the children and grandchildren of farm workers and not by the children and grandchildren of growers.

These trends are part of the forces of history that cannot be stopped. No person and no organization can resist them for very long. They are inevitable.

Once social change begins, it cannot be reversed. You cannot uneducate the person who has learned to read. You cannot humiliate the person who feels pride. You cannot oppress the people who are not afraid anymore.

Our opponents must understand that it's not just a union we have built. Unions, like other institutions, can come and go.

But we're more than an institution. For nearly 20 years, our union has been on the cutting edge of a people's cause—and you cannot do away with an entire people; you cannot stamp out a people's cause.

Regardless of what the future holds for the union, regardless of what the future holds for farm workers, our accomplishments cannot be undone. "La Causa"—our cause—doesn't have to be experienced twice.

The consciousness and pride that were raised by our union are alive and thriving inside millions of young Hispanics who will never work on a farm!

Like the other immigrant groups, the day will come when we win the economic and political rewards which are in keeping with our numbers in society. The day will come when the politicians do the right thing by our people out of political necessity and not out of charity or idealism.

That day may not come this year. That day may not come during this decade. But it will come, someday!

And when that day comes, we shall see the fulfillment of that passage from the Book of Matthew in the New Testament, "That the last shall be first and the first shall be last."

And on that day, our nation shall fulfill its creed—and that fulfillment shall enrich us all.

Thank you very much.

GLOSSARY

braceros: Mexican workers, primarily peasants, imported by the U.S. government to fill the need for manual labor in crop fields in a program that ended in 1964

"Organize": In this context, the process of workers forming a labor union for the purposes of collective bargaining.

Document Analysis

From the opening, Chávez captures the attention and sympathy of his audience by relating the story of the 1963 truck accident which killed 32 braceros, vividly presenting the plight of the farmworker, establishing the humanity of these workers in a very emotional way. He continues to humanize farmworkers by remarking, "The Braceros had been imported from Mexico," saying that while human beings are not cattle, farmworkers are often transported as cattle, with little regard for their lives.

In the fifth paragraph, Chávez continues his appeal to sympathy by contrasting the state-of-the-art farm technologies in the fields with the appalling conditions that farmworkers live under. His description is graphic and persuasive. Chávez does not spare his sophisticated audience the harsh details of the farmworkers' lives making his description both graphic and persuasive. Chávez next addresses child labor and other facts of farmworkers' lives: malnutrition, a high infant mortality rate, and short life expectancy.

In the twelfth paragraph he makes the appeal personal, detailing his dream of justice for the lowest of the low, the farmworker. He dreams that someday farmworkers will be treated like "human beings" and Chávez defines his dream as a form of resistance to oppression, stating that he and his people were treated like "chattel"—like slaves. Chávez next addresses the need for farmworkers to become citizens and the importance of civic education and notes that the fate of Hispanics in America, regardless of socioeconomic status, is linked to the fate of the farmworkers. According to Chávez, just as free African Americans in the antebellum period felt a bond with their brothers and sisters under the yoke of slavery, Hispanics in the twentieth century could not enjoy freedom and advancement in society while their farmworker brothers and sisters suffered humiliation and defeat. The answer to the dilemma was civic education, which would allow farmworkers to exercise citizenship. As citizens, farmworkers could, without fear, enjoy their rights to free speech and to labor organizing.

Paragraphs 28 through 37 offer a defense of the UFW and of his approach to unionizing. Here Chávez wants his audience to see that his primary concern is the betterment of the farmworker community. His core efforts were aimed at ensuring that collective bargaining became a reality and that Hispanics gained positions of leadership through which they could help bring about positive outcomes for Hispanics in general.

In the next segment of the address, beginning with paragraph 40, Chávez delivers a series of statements aimed at defending the position of the UFW in the 1980s. He addresses the accusation that the numbers of workers belonging to the UFW had decreased significantly since that time. He states that the mere fact that the union was under attack, with agribusiness spending millions of dollars in this attack, testified to its strength. He wants his audience to become aware of the full relevance of the union: All farmworkers, unionized or not, are directly or indirectly benefiting from union efforts to better their lives. Chávez sees his clarification of the vitality of the union as a fundamental point.

Chávez begins by reporting on the successes that UFW has accomplished such as the boycott of 1970, which, among other benefits, brought about regulations to protect workers from pesticides. He explains that in the companies where workers were unionized, child labor had been abolished, and miserable wages and living conditions had been ameliorated. He also relates what is impeding progress in 1984, detailing the actions both of the conservative state government of California as well as other labor organizations such as the Teamsters.

Chávez next nother call to boycott grapes, to protest both environmental issues and the violations of human rights that agribusiness is continuing to commit. Here he acknowledges the importance of help from environmentally conscious nonminority people. His allies also included members of the baby boom generation who had supported civil rights and environmental consciousness twenty years earlier and who continued to fight for those causes. Chávez next focuses on new forms of violations of farmworkers' rights, including sexual harassment and pesticides found to be carcinogenic. He wants his audience to know, however, that change is on the horizon.

Close to the end of his speech, Chávez's tone changes markedly, from one of hope to one of unapologetic indictment of agribusiness. He addresses the environmental damage that has been done to the land and the consequences of this damage, identifying the growers as clearly responsible. But the last segment of Chávez's speech is optimistic and uplifting, as he predicts that social change is unstoppable. Chávez harks back to a statement he made at the beginning of his speech, when he recalled that while farmworkers were great in number, a select few were dictating their lot. At the end of his speech, Chávez declares that farmworkers have learned what representation means and will let their numbers speak of their political power. Reminiscent of Martin Luther King, Jr., Chávez ends his speech by describing what he sees as the promised land—the land where equal rights reign.

Essential Themes

The immediate significance of César Chávez's Commonwealth Address partly lay in the speaker's deep introspection, which allowed listeners a closer look not just at his philosophy but also at his feelings as a leader and as a man. Chávez offered a bold denunciation of some of the practices of right-wing conservatives in the nation and more particularly in California, which served to prepare the public to understand the coming grape boycott.

Throughout his rhetoric, Chávez reiterates his basic principle, namely, that all human beings owe respect to one another as human beings. While he uses the specific example and situation of the workers represented by the United Farm Workers of America, Chávez uses the language and imagery common to other racial and economic social justice campaigns throughout the American post-war era. In particular, it is crucial to note that Chávez is attempting to connect—for an audience that is, in general, affluent—the efforts and gains made in the 1960s and 1970s to the political realities of the 1980s.

In addition to explaining the danger to existing laws presented by conservative state and federal politicians, Chávez, through his use of examples such as environmental degradation and sexual harassment farmworkers, demonstrate to his audience that the trials Of farm workers for protection continues into the 1980s, compounding the still existing concerns that his movement had been battling for decades.

———Alicia J. Rivera, MA

Bibliography and Additional Reading

García, Richard A. "César Chávez: A Personal and Historical Testimony." *Pacific Historical Review* 63, no. 2 (May 1994): 225–233.

Gordon, Robert. "Poisons in the Fields: The United Farm Workers, Pesticides, and Environmental Politics." *Pacific Historical Review* 68, no. 1 (February 1999): 51–77.

"Gov. Brown Orders Full Probe of Train Bus Crash." *Salinas Californian*, September 18, 1963.

La Botz, Dan. *César Chávez and La Causa*. New York: Pearson Longman, 2006.

Matthiessen, Peter. *Sal Si Puedes (Escape If You Can): Cesar Chavez and the New American Revolution*. Berkeley: University of California Press, 2000.

Stavans, Ilan. "Reading Cesar." *Transition* 9, no. 4 (2000): 62–76.

Walsh, Edward J. "On the Interaction between a Movement and Its Environment." *American Sociological Review* 43, no. 1 (February 1978): 110–112.

Zompetti, Joseph P. "César Chávez's Rhetorical Strategies of Resistance." PhD dissertation, Wayne State University, 1998.

Kushner, Sam. *Long Road to Delano*. New York: International Publishers, 1975.

Anti-War Activism

Pacifism and anti-war activism in the United States has a long history. The documents we present in this section provide an overview of opinions that span the twentieth century and reach into the twenty-first. We have gathered expressions of opposition to American military activities from three divisive conflicts. The earliest of these conflicts is the First World War, which began in 1914, but which the United States did not enter until 1917. Opposition from the war came from a number of quarters, but all three of these documents are concerned with the threat American participation in the conflict—and war in general—pose to the working classes of the United States. While all three share this common point of protest, the figures who presented them represent a spectrum of political thought. Robert La Follette was solidly a member of the political establishment, serving as a Senator from Wisconsin and one of the most prominent Progressive voices in the United States. His Speech Opposing War with Germany, delivered shortly before the American declaration of war, presents his case that the war has been devastating for the working classes of the nations involved, that it would be equally devastating to the workers of America, and that the majority of Americans oppose getting involved. Following the declaration of war, labor activist Eugene V. Debs's Antiwar Speech and anarchist Emma Goldman's Speech against Conscription and War not only criticized the war but also encouraged American men to not enlist and to resist conscription. Advocating these positions placed Goldman and Debs outside the bounds of the restrictive limitations on free speech and dissent that the federal government had imposed to promote national unity during wartime.

The Vietnam War, which dominated the 1960s and early 1970s, heavily contributed to the increasing divisions that were emerging in the United States. These fault lines, which were political, generational, and racial, were exacerbated not only by the government's decision to pursue war in Southeast Asia but also by the manner in which that war was conducted. Civil rights leader Martin Luther King, Jr., in his 1967 speech "Beyond Vietnam: A Time to Break Silence" criticizes the war's effects on impoverished and minority communities in the United States as well as the effects of the war on America's standing among developing, postcolonial nations. Future Senator and Secretary of State John Kerry, representing thousands of his comrades in his Testimony of the Vietnam Veterans against the War before the Senate Foreign Relations Committee in 1971, after serving in Vietnam for four months, harshly criticizes the policies that led to horrific atrocities against civilians in Southeast Asia, the treatment of returning veterans, and the Cold War worldview that has led to the United States allowing its fear of communist expansion to override every other consideration. Like King, Kerry draws connections between the war in Vietnam and the racial strife dividing the United States.

This section concludes in the twenty-first century, with West Virginia Senator Robert C Byrd and his 2004 speech centered on the well-known fable in which The Emperor Has No Clothes. This is only one of the over twenty speeches against the 2003 invasion of Iraq and subsequent war. Byrd opposition to the war does not come from a place of pacifism but, rather, because of what he argues is the blatant dishonesty of the George W. Bush administration—particularly its lies to the American people as well as the international community about the threat that Sadaam Hussein's regime posed to the region. Byrd's questioning of the legitimacy of the war echoes the concerns raised by Kerry, King, Debs, and Goldman in the previous century.

■ Speech against Conscription and War

Date: 1917
Author: Emma Goldman
Genre: Speech

Summary Overview
From 1893 to 1917 Emma Goldman delivered numerous and controversial lectures regarding anarchism, women's rights, patriotism, and labor conditions. In addition to her efforts on the lecture circuit, in 1906 Goldman established the anarchist journal *Mother Earth*, which she edited in New York City's bohemian center of Greenwich Village. In 1910 several of Goldman's *Mother Earth* pieces were collected in the anthology *Anarchism and Other Essays*.

American entrance into World War I was opposed by Goldman as a capitalist conflict enriching bankers and munitions makers at the expense of the international working class. Her opposition to the war and conscription is well represented by her Speech against Conscription and War at Forward Hall in New York City, delivered on June 14, 1917. In her speech she not only opposes US entry into the war but also critiques the constitutional and political means by which it occurred, arguing that the people of the nation rather than their leaders should make such decisions. This is fully in keeping with Goldman's radical politics.

Goldman's antiwar activities resulted in her arrest and sentence to a two-year prison term under the Espionage Act. Following her imprisonment, Goldman was exiled to Russia, but she left the workers' paradise in 1921, settling in London three years later. Her denunciation of capitalism, as well as Bolshevism, led to increasing political isolation.

Defining Moment
By the time the United States entered the first World War in April, 1917, the conflict had been raging for several years. American involvement was a contentious topic in the years leading up to the declaration of war. American declarations of neutrality had not stopped—indeed, had enabled—American financial and industrial interests to provide loans and materiel to both sides, although as the war wore on, the Allies (particularly Britain and France) were the greatest recipients. These economics connections in America—along with the supposed war profiteering in European nations—fueled the suspicions of radicals such as Emma Goldman.

Along with entry into the war came new laws that targeted those who opposed the war or who might be suspected of aiding enemy forces or their cause. The most significant of these was the Espionage Act of 1917 which, in addition to outlawing activities which could reasonably be considered "espionage" (such as conveying information to enemy personnel with intent to harm the US war effort), it included a prohibition on causing or attempting to cause "insubordination, disloyalty, mutiny, refusal of duty, in the military or naval forces of the United States, or to willfully obstruct the recruiting or enlistment service of the United States."

The arrival of war and the enactment of laws suppressing free speech intersected with the increasing popularity of radical political movements in the United States, often heavily influenced by similar movements in Europe. As can be seen form the brief biography of Emma Goldman below, she and her fellow radicals had been active in causes supporting the working class. For socialists and anarchists like Goldman, the war was not primarily a geopolitical issue but, rather, an example of capitalist exploitation of the working class, as the poor were sent to fight and die in a cause in which they had no stake.

Author Biography
Emma Goldman was born June 27, 1869, in Kovno, Lithuania, which was then part of the Russian Empire. The Goldman family moved to St. Petersburg, Russia where Emma's father experienced a series of business failures. eIn 1885 Goldman and her older sister Helena left Russia for the United States and settled with other family members in Rochester, New York, where Goldman began factory work as a seamstress, moving to New York City in 1889.

Upon her arrival met the anarchist Alexander Berkman, with whom she began a political and romantic relationship. In 1892 Pennsylvania authorities violently suppressed a labor uprising in the steel plants of Andrew Carnegie in Homestead, Pennsylvania. Following the violent suppression of the steel strike, Berkman was imprisoned for his attempted assassination of the plant manager, Henry Clay Frick. Although no evidence was

THE SENTIMENT OF EVERY AMERICAN MOTHER
AMERICA
HERE'S MY BOY
WORDS BY
ANDREW B. STERLING
JOE MORRIS MUSIC CO.
NEW YORK
MUSIC BY
ARTHUR LANGE

established linking Goldman to the act, she later acknowledged her involvement.

On September 6, 1901, President William McKinley was assassinated by the anarchist Leon Czolgosz. Goldman was arrested for her alleged association with the assassin but freed for lack of evidence. In 1906 Berkman was released from prison, and the couple began publication of the anarchist journal *Mother Earth*. In the pages of *Mother Earth* and in her public speeches over the next decade, Goldman addressed issues of anarchism, women's rights, patriotism, and labor organization.

In 1917 Berkman and Goldman were arrested for their opposition to conscription and American participation in World War I. Charged under the newly enacted Espionage Act, Goldman and Berkman were sentenced to two years in prison. Released during the zenith of America's "red scare"—a period of anti-Communism that followed World War I, in reaction to the Russian Revolution—Berkman and Goldman were deported to Russia.

Although she initially supported the Bolshevik seizure of power in Russia in 1917, Goldman expressed disillusionment with the centralized state evolving there. In 1921 she left Russia, living briefly in Germany before settling in London. Suffering from a stroke, Goldman died in Toronto on May 14, 1940.

HISTORICAL DOCUMENT

This is not the place to applaud or shout Hurrah for Emma Goldman. We have more serious things to talk about and some serious things to do. First of all I wish to say to you, all of you, workers, men and women from the East Side, that I regret deeply that I cannot speak to you in the language I have always spoken from this platform; that I cannot speak to you tonight in Yiddish. I shall speak English because I want those representing the State and Militarism and the Courts and Prisons to understand what I have to say....

Evidently, America has to learn a salutary lesson and it is going to pay a terrible price. It is going to shed oceans of blood, it is going to heap mountains of human sacrifices of men of this country who are able to create and produce, to whom the future belongs. They are to be slaughtered in blood and in sacrifice in the name of a thing which has never yet existed in the United States of America, in the name of democracy and liberty.

My friends, there are people who say and tell you that when they prophesy something the prophecy comes true. I am sorry to say that I am one such and I have to say the same. For thirty years we have pointed out to you that this democratic State which is a government supposedly of the people, by the people and for the people has now become one of the most Imperialistic that the world has ever laid its eyes upon....

If war is necessary, only the people must decide whether they want war or not, and as long as the people have not given their consent I deny that the President of the United States has any right to declare it; I deny that the President or those who back the President have any right to tell the people that they shall take their sons and husbands and brothers and lovers and shall conscript them in order to ship them across the seas for the conquest of militarism and the support of wealth and power in the United States. You say that is a law. I deny your law. I don't believe in it.

The only law that I recognize is the law which ministers to the needs of humanity, which makes men and women finer and better and more humane, the kind of law which teaches children that human life is sacred, and that those who arm for the purpose of taking human life are going to be called before the bar of human justice and not before a wretched little court which is called your law of the United States. And so, friends, the people have not yet decided whether they want war and the people are going to say, ultimately, whether they want war or not....

If the framers of the Declaration of Independence, if Jefferson or Henry or the others, if they could look down upon the country and see what their offspring has done to it, how they have outraged it, how they have robbed it, how they have polluted it—why, my friends, they would turn in their graves. They would rise again and they would cleanse this country from its internal enemies, and that is the ruling class of the United States. There is a lesson you are going to learn and terrible as it is for us we nevertheless are glad that you will have to learn that lesson.

And now we come down to the tragedy that was committed in the United States Court in the State of New York yesterday, when two boys were sentenced. It is not only a tragedy because they were sentenced. Such things happen every day, hundreds, thousands of innocent working men are sent to the prison and the penitentiary, thousands of unfortunates throughout the world as well as here in so-called free America and nobody ever hears anything about it. It is an ordinary, commonplace thing to do. But the tragedy of yesterday is in the fact that a Judge, supported as you have been told by your money, protected by public opinion, protected by the President, the tragedy of it is that that Judge had the impudence and audacity to insult Kramer and Becker after he gave them the sentence of such horrible dimensions. Think of a man like that who sits there in judgment on other human beings. Think what must be his character, what must be his mind, what must be his soul, if he can spit human beings in the face, only because he has got the power....

I wish to say here, and I don't say it with any authority and I don't say it as a prophet, I merely tell you—I merely tell you the more people you lock up, the more will be the idealists who will take their place; the more of the human voice you suppress, the greater and louder and the profounder will be the human voice. At present it is a mere rumbling, but that rumbling is increasing in volume, it is growing in depth, it is spreading all over the country until it will be raised into a thunder and people of America will rise and say, we want to be a democracy, to be sure, but we want the kind of democracy which means liberty and opportunity to every man and woman in America.

GLOSSARY

Salutary lesson: A valuable benefit from something generally seen as negative or unwelcome

Yiddish: a language, whose name literally means "Jewish," that is based in German but uses elements of Hebrew and Aramaic

Document Analysis

On April 2, 1917, President Woodrow Wilson asked the Congress for a declaration of war against Germany, asserting that American participation in World War I would make the world "safe for democracy." Anarchists such as Emma Goldman denounced American entrance into the conflict, arguing that the powers of the state would be increased in pursuit of a war that would benefit bankers and munitions makers at the expense of the international working class whose blood would be shed to further imperialist and capitalist goals. Accompanying the declaration of war was a conscription act that forced young men into military service—the very sort of government oppression that Goldman proclaims led immigrants to flee the tyranny of czarist Russia.

Despite threats against her life, Goldman delivered a forceful speech on June 14, 1917, in Forward Hall in New York City, articulating her opposition to conscription and war. The meeting was convened following the convictions of two young anarchists, Morris Becker and Louis Kramer, for refusing conscription. Goldman began her address by telling her working-class immigrant audience that she would speak in English rather than her customary Yiddish so that the repressive forces of the state would understand her words. Appealing to the aspirations of immigrants who flocked to America's shores feeling the tyranny of European despotism, she scolds Americans for deserting the principles of liberty symbolized by the Statue of Liberty. She condemns President Wilson for sacrificing American lives in pursuit of a democracy "which has never yet existed in the United States of America."

Goldman asserts that the coercion pursued by the Wilson administration is yet another example of the imperialist and capitalist exploitation practiced by the American state. In her challenge to the nature of American democracy, she notes that Wilson was reelected to the presidency in 1916 for keeping the nation out of war, yet a year later Wilson led the country into war without the consent of the American people. In response to those who argued that Congress approved the declaration of war and conscription law, Goldman proclaims that she will only accept a legal order in which those "taking human life are going to be called before the bar of human justice and not before a wretched little court which is called your law of the United States."

Maintaining that conscription is unnecessary because Americans will support a war in which they believe, Goldman evokes the example of the Spanish-American War, seemingly ignoring the imperialistic ramifications of that conflict. Nevertheless, she continues to employ American history in the construction of her argument, insisting that the ruling class of the United States, in forcing war upon the American people, has departed from the principles enunciated by the nation's founders and contained in the Declaration of Independence.

In her conclusion, Goldman comes close to advocating revolution, asserting that the oppressive powers of prison and the state will not silence the anarchists. Warning Woodrow Wilson of the fate suffered by the ruling classes of Bourbon France and czarist Russia, Goldman proclaims that government suppression will only fan the flames of discontent and encourage the American people to establish a true democracy. While Goldman's call to action was unable to halt application of the conscription laws, she and other radicals certainly threatened the Wilson administration, which used the war emergency as an opportunity to silence the Industrial Workers of the World, anarchists, and Socialists. The day following her speech at Forward Hall, Goldman was arrested for violating the Espionage Act by inducing eligible young man to refuse registration for conscription.

Essential Themes

Essential to fully understanding Goldman's speech are her contentions about the nature of the American government. She goes beyond asserting that the Congress and President Wilson erred by committing the United States to the war in Europe. Rather, she argues that the system whereby the Congress votes to declare war is unjust, as the decision of going to war should be left up to the people who will be doing the fighting or sending their sons abroad to fight. She proclaims, "You say that is a law. I deny your law. I don't believe in it. The only law that I recognize is the law which ministers to the needs of humanity."

it is important to see Goldman's speech within the wider context of radical political causes like socialism and anarchism, not just the context of the first World War. Like others both persecuted and prosecuted for their opposition like Eugene V. Debs, the war—and war in general—was an example of the oppression of the working class, justified and motivated by nationalist sentiment. The workers of the world would never "unite," as Marx had called on them to do in 1848, while the working masses were forced into fighting each other for the financial and political benefit of others.

———Ron Briley
with additional material by Aaron Gulyas, MA

Bibliography and Additional Reading

Kohn, Stephen M. *American Political Prisoners: Prosecutions under the Espionage and Sedition Acts*. (Westport, CT: Praeger, 1994).

Marshall, Peter. *Demanding the Impossible: A History of Anarchism*. (London: HarperCollins, 1992).

Moritz, Theresa. *The World's Most Dangerous Woman: A New Biography of Emma Goldman*. (Vancouver: Subway Books, 2001).

Wexler, Alice. *Emma Goldman in America*. (Boston: Beacon Press, 1984).

Speech Opposing War with Germany

Date: 1917
Author: Robert La Follette
Genre: Speech

Summary Overview

Throughout much of his adult life, Robert M. La Follette was known as "Fighting Bob," and the appellation was most apt. He was admittedly by nature combative and suspicious. At the same time, he was an indefatigable researcher who could often intimidate opponents with mounds of supporting data. In April 1917, in his Speech Opposing War with Germany, he addressed the Senate when they met to vote on President Woodrow Wilson's call for a declaration of war. In his address, La Follette sought to parry Wilson's call for war by denying that the United States had ever been neutral. He cited the extravagant costs of war in terms of its effects on the poor of both countries, and he warns against binding the United States to the war aims and methods of Britain.

Defining Moment

On April 2, 1917, President Woodrow Wilson asked Congress for a declaration of war against Germany. On January 31, the imperial German government had announced that on the following day its submarines would sink without warning all ships, including those belonging to neutral nations, in a broad war zone that covered the seas around Britain, France, Italy, and the eastern Mediterranean. Then, in late February, it became known that Arthur Zimmermann, the German foreign minister, had proposed an alliance with Mexico in the event that Kaiser Wilhelm's government went to war against the United States. In return, Mexico would receive vast territories lost in the Mexican-American War of 1846–1848. Wilson sought to keep U.S. involvement limited to "armed neutrality" but found his hand forced on March 18 by the German sinking of three American ships.

On April 4, the Senate met to vote upon Wilson's call for a war declaration. Debate began at ten in the morning and lasted until late that night. Only five senators spoke against the declaration—the first four being James K. Vardaman (D-Miss.), William J. Stone (D-Mo.), George Norris (R-Nebr.), and Asle Gronna (R-N.D.). Then, in the afternoon, La Follette addressed his colleagues.

Author Biography

Robert Marion La Follette was born on June 14, 1855. At age twenty he entered the University of Wisconsin, graduating in 1879. In 1880, after briefly attending law school, he was elected district attorney of Dane County, where Madison, the capital of Wisconsin, is located. In 1884 he was elected as the youngest member of U.S. House of Representatives. The victim of a Democratic landslide in 1890, he resumed his law practice in Madison.

La Follette was elected governor of Wisconsin in 1900 and was reelected in both 1902 and 1904. While still governor, he was chosen in January 1905 by the state legislature to represent Wisconsin in the U.S. Senate, where he would serve until his death in 1925. Although he was nominally a Republican, he broke with the presidency of William Howard Taft over the high Payne-Aldrich Tariff and over alleged corruption in the Department of the Interior. He sought to gain the Republican presidential nomination of 1912, but his major supporters abandoned him once former President Theodore Roosevelt entered the race.

When Woodrow Wilson became president in 1913, La Follette backed such "New Freedom" proposals as the Underwood Tariff and the Federal Reserve System. Always a foe of military intervention, he spoke forcefully against armed involvement in Mexico and the Caribbean. In March 1917 he led a filibuster against Wilson's proposal to arm American merchant ships in the aftermath of Germany's declaration of unrestricted submarine warfare and was equally outspoken in his opposition to American entrance into World War I, conscription, the curbing of the freedoms of speech and the press, the Treaty of Versailles, and entry into the League of Nations. In 1924 he ran for president on an independent Progressive Party ticket, gaining 4.8 million votes. His platform included collective bargaining, public ownership of water power and railroads, aid to farmers, a ban on child labor, and the recall of federal judges. On June 18, 1925, he died of heart failure in Washington, D.C.

HISTORICAL DOCUMENT

Mr. President, I had supposed until recently that it was the duty of senators and representatives in congress to vote and act according to their convictions on all public matters that came before them for consideration and decision....

For myself I shall support the president in the measures he proposes when I believe them to be right. I shall oppose measures proposed by the president when I believe them to be wrong....

If, unhappily, on such momentous questions the most patient research and conscientious consideration we could give to them leave us in disagreement with this president, I know of no course to take except to oppose, regretfully but not the less firmly, the demands of the executive....

The poor, sir, who are the ones called upon to get in the trenches, have no organized power, have no press to voice their will upon this question of peace or war but, oh, Mr. President, at some time they will be heard.

I hope and I believe they will be heard in an orderly and a peaceful way. I think they may be heard from before long. I think, sir, if we take this step, when the people today who are staggering under the burden of supporting families at the present prices of the necessaries of life find those prices multiplied, when they are raised a hundred percent, or 300 per cent, as they will be quickly, aye, sir, when beyond that those who pay taxes come to have their taxes doubled and again doubled to pay the interest on the nontaxable bonds held by Morgan and his combinations, which have been issued to meet this war, there will come an awakening: they will have their day and they will be heard.

It will be as certain and as inevitable as the return of the tides, and as resistless, too....

In his message of April 2, the president said:

We have no quarrel with the German people—it was not upon their impulse that their government acted in entering this war; it was not with their previous knowledge or approval....

At least, the German people, then, are not outlaws. What is the thing the president asks us to do to these German people of whom he speaks so highly and whose sincere friend he declares us to be?

Here is what he declares we shall do in this war. We shall undertake, he says—

The utmost practicable cooperation in counsel and action with the governments now at war with Germany, and as an incident to that, the extension to these governments of the most liberal financial credits in order that our resources may, so far as possible, be added to theirs.

"Practical cooperation!" Practicable cooperation with England and her allies in starving to death the old men and women, the children, the sick and maimed of Germany. The thing we are asked to do is the thing I have stated.

It is idle to talk of a war upon a government only. We are leagued in this war, or it is the president's proposition that we shall be so leagued, with the hereditary enemies of Germany. Any war with Germany, or any other country for that matter, would be bad enough, but there are not words strong enough to voice my protest against the proposed combination with the entente allies.

When we cooperate with those governments we endorse their methods, we endorse the violations of international law, we endorse the shameful methods of warfare against which we have again and again protested in this war....

Finally when the end comes, whatever it may be, we find ourselves in cooperation with our ally, Great Britain, and if we cannot resist now the pressure she is exerting to carry us into the war, how can we hope to resist, then, the thousandfold greater pressure she will exert to bend us to her purposes and compel compliance with her demands?...

Once enlisted, once in the co-partnership, we will be carried through with the purposes, whatever they may be, of which we know nothing.

Sir, if we are to enter upon this war in the manner the president demands, let us throw pretense to the winds, let us be honest, let us admit that this is a ruthless war against not only Germany's army and navy but against her civilian population as well, and frankly state that the purpose of Germany's hereditary European enemies has become our purpose....

Just a word of comment more upon one of the points in the president's address. He says that this is a war "for the things we have always carried nearest to our hearts—for democracy, for the right of those who submit to authority to have a voice in their own government."...

It is a sentiment peculiarly calculated to appeal to American hearts and, when accompanied by acts consistent with it, is certain to receive our support; but in this same connection, and strangely enough, the president says that we have become convinced that the German government as it now exists—"Prussian autocracy" he calls it—can never again maintain friendly relations with us....

Who has registered the knowledge or approval of the American people of the course this congress is called upon to take in declaring war upon Germany? Submit the question to the people, you who support it. You who support it dare not do it, for you know that by a vote of more than 10 to one the American people as a body would register their declaration against it....

The espionage bills, the conscription bills, and other forcible military measures which we understand are being ground out of the war machine in this country is the complete proof that those responsible for this war fear that it has no popular support and that armies sufficient to satisfy the demand of the entente allies cannot be recruited by voluntary enlistments....

I have said that with the causes of the present war we have nothing to do. That is true. We certainly are not responsible for it. It originated from causes beyond the sphere of our influence and outside the realm of our responsibility. It is not inadmissible, however, to say that no responsible narrator of the events which have led up to this greatest of all wars has failed to hold that the government of each country engaged in it is at fault for it.

For my own part, I believe that this war, like nearly all others, originated in the selfish ambition and cruel greed of a comparatively few men in each government who saw in war an opportunity for profit and power for themselves, and who were wholly indifferent to the awful suffering they knew that war would bring to the masses....

The offenses of Great Britain and Germany against us can not be treated as they might be treated if those nations were not at war with each other. Undoubtedly, if those nations were not at war with each other we could suffer one to violate international law to our injury and make no protest and take no action against the nations so offending and hold the other to strict accountability and compel her to respect to the limit our rights under international law, and if she refused we would be justified in going to war about it.

But when we are dealing with Germany and Great Britain, warring against each other, so evenly balanced in strength that a little help to one or a little hindrance to the other turns the scale and spells victory for one and defeat for the other, in that situation I say the principle of international law steps in which declares that any failure on our part to enforce our rights equally against both is a gross act of un-neutrality....

There can be no greater violation of our neutrality than the requirement that one of two belligerents shall adhere to the settled principles of law and that the other shall have the advantage of not doing so. The respect that German naval authorities were required to pay to the rights of our people upon the high seas would depend upon the question whether we had exacted the same rights from Germany's enemies.

If we had not done so we lost our character as a neutral nation, and our people unfortunately had lost the protection that belongs to neutrals. Our responsibility was joint in the sense that we must exact the same conduct from both belligerents....

Had the plain principle of international law announced by Jefferson been followed by us, we would not be called on today to declare war upon any of the belligerents. The failure to treat the belligerent nations of Europe alike, the failure to reject the unlawful "war zones" of both Germany and Great Britain, is wholly accountable for our present dilemma.

We should not seek to hide our blunder behind the smoke of battle, to inflame the mind of our people by half truths into the frenzy of war, in order that they may never appreciate the real cause of it until it is too late. I do not believe that our national honor is served by such a course. The right way is the honorable way.

One alternative is to admit our initial blunder to enforce our rights against Great Britain as we have enforced our rights against Germany; demand that both those nations shall respect our neutral rights upon the high seas to the letters and give notice that we will enforce those rights from that time forth against both belligerents and then live up to that notice.

The other alternative is to withdraw our commerce from both. The mere suggestion that food supplies would be withheld from both sides impartially would compel belligerents to observe the principle of freedom of the seas for neutral commerce.

GLOSSARY

autocracy: a political system in which power is concentrated in the hands of a single person

belligerents: warring parties

entente allies: the Triple Entente allies—Great Britain, France, and Russia—opposed to the Central Powers, led by Germany and Austria-Hungary, in World War I

Morgan: James Pierpont Morgan, American financier in the steel industry

Prussian: referring to the leading state in the nineteenth- and early-twentieth-century German empire

Document Analysis

In the record of the speech, La Follette begins by claiming that senators have the duty to vote their convictions, irrespective of whether they are backing the president, saying the he will back the president when he thinks the president is right, and oppose the president when he thinks the president is wrong. He then defends his opposition to the armed-ship bill, claiming that polls revealed strong opposition to entrance into the European war and portraying himself as representing "the poor," that is, those powerless Americans who would be making the major sacrifices. Once such people experienced 300 percent price increases in life's necessities and a quadrupling of taxes to enrich J. P. Morgan, they would be heard—though, of course, in a peaceful manner.

La Follette then turns his attention to the President's April 2 call for a declaration of war against Germany. Citing Wilson's call for "practicable cooperation" with Germany's foes, La Follette warns that the United States would thereby be embracing Britain's "shameful methods of warfare," against which he had continually protested. Such "practicable cooperation" would, in fact, mean the starving of children, the aged, and the infirm in Germany—people, La Follette points out, that President Wilson has said "We have no quarrel with." Furthermore, the United States would be binding itself to British war aims, "of which we know nothing." He was certain, however, of one thing: Britain was a hereditary monarchy based on restricted suffrage and the grinding exploitation of its laborers. Indeed, with the exception of France and Russia (where, he states, democracy had just been established), America's new allies all represented the old order, one that had not even kept pace with the municipal and social reforms of the new German enemy. Furthermore, the United States had not even made its support of Britain conditional upon home rule for the rebellious nations of Ireland, Egypt, and India. La Follette notes that Wilson had called the war one for democracy, which the president defined as a condition wherein "those who submit to authority" possess "a voice in their own government." La Follette cynically notes that this is "a sentiment peculiarly calculated to appeal to American hearts." He also asks if such were really the case, why was the very issue of entering the war not being presented directly to the American people? The senator then answers his own question, claiming that the public would vote ten to one against entering any such conflict. Instead of permitting a popular referendum, the government was considering forced conscription and "espionage" bills, both of which, he asserts, would violate traditional American liberties.

La Follette also, in this portion of the speech, voices a concern about the war that would echo down the decades which followed it, stating his belief that "that this war, like nearly all others, originated in the selfish ambition and cruel greed of a comparatively few men in each government who saw in war an opportunity for profit and power for themselves."

La Follette points to centuries of American tension with Britain, which he contrasts to long-standing friendly relations with Germany. He blames the outbreak of the current conflict on a small minority of greedy and ambitious men who sought profit and power while being indifferent to any suffering inflicted on the masses. He finds much credence in the German claim that France, Britain, and Russia had long been secret allies. The senator goes on at length, quoting various documents to support his claim that the United States acquiesced in Britain's continued violation of neutral rights, in particular, British efforts to prevent American goods from reaching Germany. Making an even more serious accusation, La Follette calls the United States itself highly non-neutral, for applying one standard to Britain and a far more rigorous one to Germany. Rather than go to war, he asserts, the United States should demand that both belligerents respect American commercial rights and should furthermore enforce these rights against the two major powers. If the nation did not choose this option, it could withdraw food supplies to both sides, which would force them to honor American commerce.

Essential Themes

La Follette's argument against American entry into World War I was deeply rooted in his concern for the working classes not only of the United States but of other nations as well. This is in keeping with his career of championing progressive causes and the rights of working people. Several times in his speech, he highlights the dangers to the civilians in Germany and the suffering they face due to the war. At the same time, La Follette presents himself as the voice of America's working people who would be the ones who would have to fight if Congress declares war. He maintains that, if the decision were put in the hands of the American people, there would be no war.

He also points out the inconsistency of Wilson declaring that the war is being fought to preserve democracy while, at the same time, cooperating with Britain—a nation of whose goals La Follette seems suspicious. "If we cannot resist now the pressure she is exerting to carry us into the war," he asks, "how can we hope to resist, then, the thousandfold greater pressure she will exert to bend us to her purposes and compel compliance with her demands?" A long tradition of American neutrality in European affairs was at stake and La Follette did not want to see it sacrificed in this manner.

———*Justus D. Doenecke, PhD*

Bibliography and Additional Reading

Drake, Richard. *The Education of an Anti-Imperialist Robert La Follette and U.S. Expansion* (University of Wisconsin Press; 2013).

Miller, Karen A. J., *Populist Nationalism: Republican Insurgency and American Foreign Policy Making, 1918–1925* (Westport, Connecticut: Greenwood Press, 1999).

Doenecke, Justus D. *Nothing Less Than War: A New History of America's Entry into World War I* (Lexington: University Press of Kentucky, 2011)

Unger, Nancy C. *Fighting Bob La Follette: The Righteous Reformer* Chapel Hill: University of North Carolina Press, 2000.

■ Antiwar Speech

Date: 1918
Author: Eugene V. Debs
Genre: Speech

Summary Overview

The American trade union leader, orator, and Socialist Party activist Eugene Debs was a master at making what might look today like radical political ideas seem as American as apple pie. A student of history as well as politics, Debs regularly invoked the memory of the Founding Fathers to make his policy suggestions seem more acceptable. Motivated by an unyielding sense of justice, he often tried to shame authorities to do what he thought was right. Whether addressing audiences at a labor rally or on the campaign trail, Debs invariably came back to a sharp critique of the American political system, touting the virtues of his brand of Socialism. His goal as a politician was not necessarily to win elections but instead to inspire listeners by his own example and to win converts to the Socialist cause. In a country with no Socialist legacy—unlike many European countries where Socialism was established—it is really quite remarkable that Debs had any success at all as a politician. That success was due in no small part to the power of Debs's oratory and prose. In his 1918 Antiwar Speech, Debs associates military warfare with class warfare.

Defining Moment

American entry into the First World War brought with it unprecedented efforts by the federal government to limit speech and actions it deemed detrimental to the war effort. The Espionage Act of 1917 outlawed interference with military recruitment and military activities or operations. President Woodrow Wilson had asked Congress to pass such a law in 1915 (before the United States was involved in the war). In 1918, Congress passed the Sedition Act, which extended prohibited activities to criticism of of the government or war effort including "disloyal, profane, scurrilous, or abusive language." A number of anti-war publications and writers, particularly socialist ones, were targeted under these laws.

Debs began a speaking tour because the Socialist press that he had depended upon to distribute his writings was wiped out by the government censorship enabled by the Espionage and Sedition Acts. Debs knew he was risking his already failing health and his freedom by speaking out. He toured anyway. The words that Debs spoke at Nimisilla Park in Canton, Ohio, before twelve hundred people were little different from the ones he had spoken at earlier stops on his tour. What made this speech different was the presence of a government stenographer and the willingness of the local U.S. attorney, E. S. Wertz, to prosecute Debs (against the advice of Wertz's superiors) for what he said.

Author Biography

Eugene Victor Debs was a trade union leader, orator, and frequent Socialist Party candidate for the presidency of the United States. He was born in Terre Haute, Indiana, in 1855. While working his way up through the hierarchy of the Brotherhood of Locomotive Firemen, an important railroad union, he was elected city clerk in Terre Haute in 1879. He also served one term in the Indiana state legislature in 1885. In 1893 Debs cofounded the American Railway Union (ARU), an industrial union that, unlike most exclusive railroad brotherhoods of the era, admitted railroad workers of all skill levels. As the leader of that organization, Debs led the infamous Pullman strike of 1894.

In 1895 Debs was convicted of interfering with the mail as a result of his refusal to abide by that injunction. Debs's political views were greatly affected by the Socialist literature he read during his short stay in jail. Indeed, this incarceration would prove to be the pivotal point of his entire life. 4Upon his release Debs announced his conversion to Socialism. He also changed career paths from being a trade union leader to being a political leader. Debs would serve as a Socialist Party presidential candidate five times: 1900, 1904, 1908, 1912, and 1920. His best showing occurred in 1912 when he came close to garnering a million votes. That was 6 percent of the total votes cast in that election. In 1918 Debs was convicted of sedition for this Canton, Ohio, anti-war speech. Debs had to run his final campaign for president as a protest candidate from his jail cell. Between elections Debs toured the country giving speeches and writing articles that critiqued the American capitalist system and championed the cause of Socialism. Debs died in 1926 at the age of seventy.

HISTORICAL DOCUMENT

Comrades, friends and fellow-workers, for this very cordial greeting, this very hearty reception, I thank you all with the fullest appreciation of your interest in and your devotion to the cause for which I am to speak to you this afternoon.

To speak for labor; to plead the cause of the men and women and children who toil; to serve the working class, has always been to me a high privilege; a duty of love....

I realize that, in speaking to you this afternoon, there are certain limitations placed upon the right of free speech. I must be exceedingly careful, prudent, as to what I say, and even more careful and prudent as to how I say it. I may not be able to say all I think; but I am not going to say anything that I do not think. I would rather a thousand times be a free soul in jail than to be a sycophant and coward in the streets....

If it had not been for the men and women who, in the past, have had the moral courage to go to jail, we would still be in the jungles....

There is but one thing you have to be concerned about, and that is that you keep foursquare with the principles of the international Socialist movement. It is only when you begin to compromise that trouble begins. So far as I am concerned, it does not matter what others may say, or think, or do, as long as I am sure that I am right with myself and the cause. There are so many who seek refuge in the popular side of a great question. As a Socialist, I have long since learned how to stand alone. For the last month I have been traveling over the Hoosier State; and, let me say to you, that, in all my connection with the Socialist movement, I have never seen such meetings, such enthusiasm, such unity of purpose; never have I seen such a promising outlook as there is today, notwithstanding the statement published repeatedly that our leaders have deserted us. Well, for myself, I never had much faith in leaders. I am willing to be charged with almost anything, rather than to be charged with being a leader. I am suspicious of leaders, and especially of the intellectual variety. Give me the rank and file every day in the week. If you go to the city of Washington, and you examine the pages of the Congressional Directory, you will find that almost all of those corporation lawyers and cowardly politicians, members of Congress, and misrepresentatives of the masses—you will find that almost all of them claim, in glowing terms, that they have risen from the ranks to places of eminence and distinction. I am very glad I cannot make that claim for myself. I would be ashamed to admit that I had risen from the ranks. When I rise it will be with the ranks, and not from the ranks....

They tell us that we live in a great free republic; that our institutions are democratic; that we are a free and self-governing people. This is too much, even for a joke. But it is not a subject for levity; it is an exceedingly serious matter....

Wars throughout history have been waged for conquest and plunder. In the Middle Ages when the feudal lords who inhabited the castles whose towers may still be seen along the Rhine concluded to enlarge their domains, to increase their power, their prestige and their wealth they declared war upon one another. But they themselves did not go to war any more than the modern feudal lords, the barons of Wall Street go to war. The feudal barons of the Middle Ages, the economic predecessors of the capitalists of our day, declared all wars. And their miserable serfs fought all the battles. The poor, ignorant serfs had been taught to revere their masters; to believe that when their masters declared war upon one another, it was their patriotic duty to fall upon one another and to cut one another's throats for the profit and glory of the lords and barons who held them in contempt. And that is war in a nutshell. The master class has always declared the wars; the subject class has always fought the battles. The master class has had all to gain and nothing to lose, while the subject class has had nothing to gain and all to lose—especially their lives.

They have always taught and trained you to believe it to be your patriotic duty to go to war and to have yourselves slaughtered at their command. But in all the history of the world you, the people, have never had a voice in declaring war, and strange as it certainly appears, no war by any nation in any age has ever been declared by the people.

And here let me emphasize the fact—and it cannot be repeated too often—that the working class who fight all the battles, the working class who make the supreme sacrifices, the working class who freely shed their blood and furnish the corpses, have never yet had a voice in either declaring war or making peace. It is the ruling class that invariably does both. They alone declare war and they alone make peace....

If war is right let it be declared by the people. You who have your lives to lose, you certainly above all others have the right to decide the momentous issue of war or peace....

The heart of the international Socialist never beats a retreat.

They are pressing forward, here, there and everywhere, in all the zones that girdle the globe. Everywhere these awakening workers, these class-conscious proletarians, these hardy sons and daughters of honest toil are proclaiming the glad tidings of the coming emancipation, everywhere their hearts are attuned to the most sacred cause that ever challenged men and women to action in all the history of the world. Everywhere they are moving toward democracy and the dawn; marching toward the sunrise, their faces all aglow with the light of the coming day. These are the Socialists, the most zealous and enthusiastic crusaders the world has ever known. They are making history that will light up the horizon of coming generations, for their mission is the emancipation of the human race. They have been reviled; they have been ridiculed, persecuted, imprisoned and have suffered death, but they have been sufficient to themselves and their cause, and their final triumph is but a question of time.

Do you wish to hasten the day of victory? Join the Socialist Party! Don't wait for the morrow. Join now! Enroll your name without fear and take your place where you belong. You cannot do your duty by proxy. You have got to do it yourself and do it squarely and then as you look yourself in the face you will have no occasion to blush. You will know what it is to be a real man or woman. You will lose nothing; you will gain everything. Not only will you lose nothing but you will find something of infinite value, and that something will be yourself. And that is your supreme need—to find yourself—to really know yourself and your purpose in life.

You need at this time especially to know that you are fit for something better than slavery and cannon fodder. You need to know that you were not created to work and produce and impoverish yourself to enrich an idle exploiter. You need to know that you have a mind to improve, a soul to develop, and a manhood to sustain....

To turn your back on the corrupt Republican Party and the still more corrupt Democratic Party—the gold-dust lackeys of the ruling class—counts for still more after you have stepped out of those popular and corrupt capitalist parties to join a minority party that has an ideal, that stands for a principle, and fights for a cause. This will be the most important change you have ever made and the time will come when you will thank me for having made the suggestion....

There are few men who have the courage to say a word in favor of the I.W.W. I have. Let me say here that I have great respect for the I.W.W. Far greater than I have for their infamous detractors.... It is only necessary to label a man "I.W.W." to have him lynched as they did Praeger, an absolutely innocent man. He was a Socialist and bore a German name, and that was his crime. A rumor was started that he was disloyal and he was promptly seized and lynched by the cowardly mob of so-called "patriots."

War makes possible all such crimes and outrages. And war comes in spite of the people. When Wall Street says war the press says war and the pulpit promptly follows with its Amen. In every age the pulpit has been on the side of the rulers and not on the side of the people. That is one reason why the preachers so fiercely denounce the I.W.W....

Political action and industrial action must supplement and sustain each other. You will never vote the Socialist republic into existence. You will have to lay its foundations in industrial organization. The industrial union is the forerunner of industrial democracy. In the shop where the workers are associated is where industrial democracy has its beginning. Organize according to your industries! Get together in every department of industrial service! United and acting together for the common good your power is invincible.

When you have organized industrially you will soon learn that you can manage as well as operate industry. You will soon realize that you do not need the idle masters and exploiters. They are simply parasites. They do not employ you as you imagine but you employ them to take from you what you produce, and that is how they function in industry. You can certainly dispense with them in that capacity. You do not need them to depend upon for your jobs. You can never be free while you work and live by their sufferance. You must own your own tools and then you will control your own jobs, enjoy the products of your own labor and be free men instead of industrial slaves.

Organize industrially and make your organization complete. Then unite in the Socialist Party. Vote as you strike and strike as you vote.

Your union and your party embrace the working class. The Socialist Party expresses the interests, hopes and aspirations of the toilers of all the world.

GLOSSARY

bore a German name, and that was his crime: reference to the widespread paranoia of the time regarding Germans and eastern Europeans, seen by many to be terrorists and spies

class-conscious: aware of one's role in what Debs saw as the historic struggle between the workers and the capitalists

comrades: a term used at the time by a wide spectrum on the far left to indicate brotherhood in the international workers' movement

industrial democracy: a system of government whereby the workers act as a single union and thereby effectively control the government

proletarians: industrial workers

sycophant: someone who plays up to the rich and powerful

Document Analysis

Much of the speech deals with specific controversies, like the case of the jailed trade unionist Tom Mooney, that do not resonate down to this day, but there are many passages in the text that demonstrate Debs's ability to inspire. For example, near the beginning of the speech, Debs jokes openly about the possibility of getting arrested. Indeed, he suggests that he would rather be arrested than remain silent about the injustice around him. His willingness to speak under threat of arrest was undoubtedly as important in inspiring his listeners as any particular phrase he spoke that day. Notably, much of the speech is devoted to attacks not just on the government but also on Wall Street. He attacks Wall Street for greed and shortsightedness in the exploitation of its employees. Debs is arguing that the worse conditions get, the better Socialism will do. In fact, Debs suggests that the triumph of Socialism in America is near, an argument that might have seemed strange at a time when Socialists and Socialism had been largely silenced by government repression.

In the speech, Debs repeats his long-standing critique of the two-party system. He calls both the Democratic and Republican parties corrupt, presumably because of their mutual embrace of the war. He recommends organizing along industrial lines, meaning workers from all skill levels, just as the ARU had done. He then suggests that joining the Socialist Party is the political equivalent of industrial organization. If your union embraces the working class, he suggests, your political party should too. While the positions of the Socialist Party were unpopular at the time, Debs argues that a brighter day would come as long as his listeners remained true to themselves.

It is also worth noting that Debs defended the IWW during his speech, despite his differences with the organization. "Let me say here that I have great respect for the I.W.W.," he told the crowd. "Far greater than I have for their infamous detractors." This is an excellent illustration of how the Left came together in the face of a common enemy, in this case the Wilson administration. In September 1917, months before Debs spoke, the U.S. Justice Department had simultaneously raided forty-eight IWW meeting halls across the country, arresting 165 leaders. While this did not destroy the organization entirely, it certainly rendered it incapable of effectively opposing the war. The example of the Wobblies could not have been far from Debs's mind when he spoke in Canton. That Debs spoke there (and elsewhere beforehand) is a testament to his courage. He would arrested and tried for his violation of the sedition act.

As was the case after the Pullman strike, Debs did not deny the charges against him. "I wish to admit the truth of all that has been testified to in this proceeding," he told the jury that eventually convicted him. "I would not retract a word that I have uttered that I believe to be true to save myself from going to the penitentiary for the rest of my days." Indeed, Debs refused to mount any defense at all. Although he was convicted, he did not die in prison or even serve his entire ten-year sentence. Combat in World War I ended in 1918, but the United States did not sign a peace treaty to end the war formally until after Warren Harding became president in 1921. With peace officially at hand, Harding pardoned Debs and other political prisoners who had opposed the war, effective that Christmas. Debs was in poor health before he ever went to jail. His time in prison undoubtedly accelerated his decline.

Essential Themes

In his two-hour speech, Debs made no direct reference to World War I, which raged in Europe at the time. Instead, he attacks war in general, most notably in this famous passage: "The master class has always declared the wars; the subject class has always fought the battles. The master class has had all to gain and nothing to lose, while the subject class has had nothing to gain and all to lose—especially their lives." That quotation is nothing but an eloquent way of associating military warfare with class warfare, a point that has been made many times since. Unfortunately for Debs, the government and much of the public were unwilling to accept any public opposition to a conflict that was, in fact, fairly unpopular compared with other wars throughout American history. Simply pointing out that different social classes are affected differently by war was enough to get Debs arrested.

———*Jonathan Rees, PhD*

Bibliography and Additional Reading

Kennedy, David M., *Over Here: The First World War and American Society* (New York : Oxford University Press, 2004).

Kohn, Stephen M., *American Political Prisoners: Prosecutions under the Espionage and Sedition Acts* (Westport, Connecticut: Praeger, 1994).

Murphy, Paul L., *World War I and the Origin of Civil Liberties in the United States* (New York: W. W. Norton, 1979).

Stone, Geoffrey R., *Perilous Times: Free Speech in Wartime from the Sedition Act of 1798 to the War on Terrorism* (New York: W. W. Norton & Company, 2004).

Thomas, William H., Jr. *Unsafe for Democracy: World War I and the U.S. Justice Department's Covert Campaign to Suppress Dissent.* (Madison: University of Wisconsin Press, 2008).

"Beyond Vietnam: A Time to Break Silence"

Date: 1967
Author: Martin Luther King, Jr.
Genre: Speech

Summary Overview

On April 4, 1967, one of America's greatest orators gave a speech on a subject he had previously been reluctant to address. Martin Luther King, Jr., was the preeminent civil rights leader of the 1960s, but as he stood in the pulpit of Riverside Church in New York City his topic was the Vietnam War. King had been an eloquent advocate of African American civil rights and a fearless opponent of racial bigotry. His words and deeds helped secure passage of the Civil Rights Act of 1964 and the Voting Rights Act of 1965. King, however, had said little in public about the Vietnam War, where large numbers of Americans troops were fighting and dying during 1965 and 1966. When he raised questions about the war or called for peace talks, critics replied that he was not qualified to speak about foreign policy. Friends counseled him to keep his distance from the controversies over the war lest he jeopardize support for the civil rights movement.

By 1967, however, King felt compelled to speak out. In "Beyond Vietnam: A Time to Break Silence," King denounced the war for deepening the problems of African Americans and poor people. His critique went farther, as he condemned the "madness" of Vietnam as a "symptom of a far deeper malady" that put the United States at odds with the aspirations for social justice of people in the developing world. King endured hostile rebukes for his sweeping and radical criticisms of America's role in Vietnam and in other emerging nations. He insisted, however, that the civil rights movement was part of a global struggle against "racism, materialism, and militarism."

Defining Moment

When King delivered his "Beyond Vietnam" speech, the Vietnam War was a growing source of global controversy. More than four hundred thousand Americans in uniform were fighting in South Vietnam. President Lyndon B. Johnson had sent the first U.S. combat troops to that nation little more than two years earlier, in March 1965, transforming a conflict that the South Vietnamese had previously fought with U.S. advice and armaments into an American war. As more U.S. troops poured into South Vietnam, however, public discontent with the war increased. By January 1967, polls showed that more Americans disapproved of the president's war policies than supported them. By the spring of 1967, Johnson was feeling considerable pressure from this public discontent over a war that was growing larger but had no end in sight.

Vietnam, however, became an urgent issue for King in early 1967 after he read a magazine article with horrifying pictures of children injured in the war. King declared that he could not ignore his conscience and felt obligated to campaign for an end to a war that was devastating Vietnamese and destroying hopes of Americans for a Great Society. He had heated arguments with other African American leaders, who warned that his antiwar activities would alienate many supporters who had contributed to his campaigns for civil rights, but King was adamantly unconcerned about the loss of financial backing. On February 25, 1967, he spoke to an antiwar conference in Los Angeles, California. In late March, in Chicago, Illinois, he participated in his first march against the war. Ten days later, he came to New York's Riverside Church to deliver a major address on the reasons he had decided to break his silence on Vietnam.

Author Biography

Born on January 15, 1929, King's grandfather and father were pastors of Atlanta's Ebenezer Baptist Church and leaders of the local branch of the National Association for the Advancement of Colored People. After graduating from Morehouse College in 1948, he earned a divinity degree in 1951 at Crozier Theological Seminary, where he finished first in his class. Three years later, he graduated from Boston University with a PhD in theology.

King gained national recognition as a civil rights activist during the Montgomery bus boycott that began in December 1955. King, who was pastor of a local Baptist church, became the most eloquent voice of the boycott movement, urging supporters to protest in a Christian fashion—that is, with courage but also dignity and love. Although King faced intimidation and violence, including the bombing of his house, he insisted on nonviolent protest. In 1957, King founded the Southern Christian Leadership Conference to promote civil rights.

In spring 1963, he organized demonstrations in Birmingham, Alabama, to challenge racial segregation. When television cameras showed local authorities using fire hoses and police dogs against the nonviolent demonstrators national outrage led to increased public support for civil rights legislation. On August 28, 1963, King spoke at a huge rally in Washington, D.C., to mobilize support for the legislation, delivering his famed "I Have a Dream" address. In March 1965, King helped organize demonstrations against discriminatory voting practices in Selma, Alabama. When these produced another ugly incident of police violence, the resulting national outcry contributed to the passage of the Voting Rights Act of 1965.

After 1965, King began to call for "a new turn toward greater economic justice. His activism shifted in this direction. In November 1967, he announced the beginning of a "Poor People's Campaign" aimed at boosting federal efforts to reduce poverty. In March 1968, he led a march of striking sanitation workers in Memphis, Tennessee. King delivered his final speech in that city on the evening of April 3, 1968. The next evening, he was shot dead by James Earl Ray as he stood on a Memphis motel balcony.

HISTORICAL DOCUMENT

I come to this magnificent house of worship tonight because my conscience leaves me no other choice. I join with you in this meeting because I am in deepest agreement with the aims and work of the organization which has brought us together: Clergy and Laymen Concerned about Vietnam. The recent statements of your executive committee are the sentiments of my own heart and I found myself in full accord when I read its opening lines: "A time comes when silence is betrayal." That time has come for us in relation to Vietnam.

The truth of these words is beyond doubt but the mission to which they call us is a most difficult one. Even when pressed by the demands of inner truth, men do not easily assume the task of opposing their government's policy, especially in time of war. Nor does the human spirit move without great difficulty against all the apathy of conformist thought within one's own bosom and in the surrounding world. Moreover when the issues at hand seem as perplexed as they often do in the case of this dreadful conflict we are always on the verge of being mesmerized by uncertainty; but we must move on.

Some of us who have already begun to break the silence of the night have found that the calling to speak is often a vocation of agony, but we must speak. We must speak with all the humility that is appropriate to our limited vision, but we must speak. And we must rejoice as well, for surely this is the first time in our nation's history that a significant number of its religious leaders have chosen to move beyond the prophesying of smooth patriotism to the high grounds of a firm dissent based upon the mandates of conscience and the reading of history. Perhaps a new spirit is rising among us. If it is, let us trace its movement well and pray that our own inner being may be sensitive to its guidance, for we are deeply in need of a new way beyond the darkness that seems so close around us.

Over the past two years, as I have moved to break the betrayal of my own silences and to speak from the burnings of my own heart, as I have called for radical departures from the destruction of Vietnam, many persons have questioned me about the wisdom of my path. At the heart of their concerns this query has often loomed large and loud: Why are you speaking about war, Dr. King? Why are you joining the voices of dissent? Peace and civil rights don't mix, they say. Aren't you hurting the cause of your people, they ask? And when I hear them, though I often understand the source of their concern, I am nevertheless greatly saddened, for such questions mean that the inquirers have not really known me, my commitment or my calling. Indeed, their questions suggest that they do not know the world in which they live.

In the light of such tragic misunderstandings, I deem it of signal importance to try to state clearly, and I trust concisely, why I believe that the path from Dexter Avenue Baptist Church—the church in Montgomery, Alabama, where I began my pastorate—leads clearly to this sanctuary tonight.

I come to this platform tonight to make a passionate plea to my beloved nation. This speech is not addressed to Hanoi or to the National Liberation Front. It is not addressed to China or to Russia.

Nor is it an attempt to overlook the ambiguity of the total situation and the need for a collective solution to the tragedy of Vietnam. Neither is it an attempt to make North Vietnam or the National Liberation Front paragons of virtue, nor to overlook the role they can play in a successful resolution of the problem. While they both may have justifiable reason to be suspicious of the good faith of the United States, life and history give eloquent testimony to the fact that conflicts are never resolved without trustful give and take on both sides.

Tonight, however, I wish not to speak with Hanoi and the NLF, but rather to my fellow Americans, who, with me, bear the greatest responsibility in ending a conflict that has exacted a heavy price on both continents.

The Importance of Vietnam
Since I am a preacher by trade, I suppose it is not surprising that I have seven major reasons for bringing Vietnam into the field of my moral vision. There is at the outset a very obvious and almost facile connection between the war in Vietnam and the struggle I, and others, have been waging in America. A few years ago there was a shining moment in that struggle. It seemed as if there was a real promise of hope for the poor—both black and white—through the poverty program. There were experiments, hopes, new beginnings. Then came the buildup in Vietnam and I watched the program broken and eviscerated as if it were some idle political plaything of a society gone mad on war, and I knew that America would never invest the necessary funds or energies in rehabilitation of its poor so long as adventures like Vietnam continued to draw men and skills and money like some demonic destructive suction tube. So I was increasingly compelled to see the war as an enemy of the poor and to attack it as such.

Perhaps the more tragic recognition of reality took place when it became clear to me that the war was doing far more than devastating the hopes of the poor at home. It was sending their sons and their brothers and their husbands to fight and to die in extraordinarily high proportions relative to the rest of the population. We were taking the black young men who had been crippled by our society and sending them eight thousand miles away to guarantee liberties in Southeast Asia which they had not found in southwest Georgia and East Harlem. So we have been repeatedly faced with the cruel irony of watching Negro and white boys on TV screens as they kill and die together for a nation that has been unable to seat them together in the same schools. So we watch them in brutal solidarity burning the huts of a poor village, but we realize that they would never live on the same block in Detroit. I could not be silent in the face of such cruel manipulation of the poor.

My third reason moves to an even deeper level of awareness, for it grows out of my experience in the ghettoes of the North over the last three years—especially the last three summers. As I have walked among the desperate, rejected and angry young men I have told them that Molotov cocktails and rifles would not solve their problems. I have tried to offer them my deepest compassion while maintaining my conviction that social change comes most meaningfully through nonviolent action. But they asked—and rightly so—what about Vietnam? They asked if our own nation wasn't using massive doses of violence to solve its problems, to bring about the changes it wanted. Their questions hit home, and I knew that I could never again raise my voice against the violence of the oppressed in the ghettos without having first spoken clearly to the greatest purveyor of violence in the world today—my own government. For the sake of those boys, for the sake of this government, for the sake of hundreds of thousands trembling under our violence, I cannot be silent.

For those who ask the question, "Aren't you a civil rights leader?" and thereby mean to exclude me from the movement for peace, I have this further answer. In 1957 when a group of us formed the Southern Christian Leadership Conference, we chose as our motto: "To save the soul of America." We were convinced that we could not limit our vision to certain rights for black people, but instead affirmed the conviction that America would never be free or saved from itself unless the descendants of its slaves were loosed completely from the shackles they still wear. In a way we were agreeing with Langston Hughes, that black bard of Harlem, who had written earlier:

> O, yes,
> I say it plain,
> America never was America to me,
> And yet I swear this oath—
> America will be!

Now, it should be incandescently clear that no one who has any concern for the integrity and life of America today can ignore the present war. If America's soul becomes totally poisoned, part of the autopsy must read Vietnam. It can never be saved so long as it destroys the deepest hopes of men the world over. So it is that those of us who are yet determined that America will be are led down the path of protest and dissent, working for the health of our land.

As if the weight of such a commitment to the life and health of America were not enough, another burden of responsibility was placed upon me in 1964; and I cannot forget that the Nobel Prize for Peace was also a commission—a commission to work harder than I had ever worked before for "the brotherhood of man." This is a calling that takes me beyond national allegiances, but even if it were not present I would yet have to live with the meaning of my commitment to the ministry of Jesus Christ. To me the relationship of this ministry to the making of peace is so obvious that I sometimes marvel at those who ask me why I am speaking against the war. Could it be that they do not know that the good news was meant for all men—for Communist and capitalist, for their children and ours, for black and for white, for revolutionary and conservative? Have they forgotten that my ministry is in obedience to the one who loved his enemies so fully that he died for them? What then can I say to the "Vietcong" or to Castro or to Mao as a faithful minister of this one? Can I threaten them with death or must I not share with them my life?

Finally, as I try to delineate for you and for myself the road that leads from Montgomery to this place I would have offered all that was most valid if I simply said that I must be true to my conviction that I share with all men the calling to be a son of the living God. Beyond the calling of race or nation or creed is this vocation of sonship and brotherhood, and because I believe that the Father is deeply concerned especially for his suffering and helpless and outcast children, I come tonight to speak for them.

This I believe to be the privilege and the burden of all of us who deem ourselves bound by allegiances and loyalties which are broader and deeper than nationalism and which go beyond our nation's self-defined goals and positions. We are called to speak for the weak, for the voiceless, for victims of our nation and for those it calls enemy, for no document from human hands can make these humans any less our brothers.

Strange Liberators

And as I ponder the madness of Vietnam and search within myself for ways to understand and respond to compassion my mind goes constantly to the people of that peninsula. I speak now not of the soldiers of each side, not of the junta in Saigon, but simply of the people who have been living under the curse of war for almost three continuous decades now. I think of them too because it is clear to me that there will be no meaningful solution there until some attempt is made to know them and hear their broken cries.

They must see Americans as strange liberators. The Vietnamese people proclaimed their own independence in 1945 after a combined French and Japanese occupation, and before the Communist revolution in China. They were led by Ho Chi Minh. Even though they quoted the American Declaration of Independence in their own document of freedom, we refused to recognize them. Instead, we decided to support France in its reconquest of her former colony.

Our government felt then that the Vietnamese people were not "ready" for independence, and we again fell victim to the deadly Western arrogance that has poisoned the international atmosphere for so long. With that tragic decision we rejected a revolutionary government seeking self-determination, and a government that had been established not by China (for whom the Vietnamese have no great love) but by clearly indigenous forces that included some Communists. For the peasants this new government meant real land reform, one of the most important needs in their lives.

For nine years following 1945 we denied the people of Vietnam the right of independence. For nine years we vigorously supported the French in their abortive effort to recolonize Vietnam.

Before the end of the war we were meeting eighty percent of the French war costs. Even before the French were defeated at Dien Bien Phu, they began to despair of the reckless action, but we did not. We encouraged them with our huge financial and military supplies to continue the war even after they had lost the will. Soon we would be paying almost the full costs of this tragic attempt at recolonization.

After the French were defeated it looked as if independence and land reform would come again through the Geneva agreements. But instead there came the United States, determined that Ho should not unify the temporarily divided nation, and the peasants watched again as we supported one of the most vicious modern dictators—our chosen man, Premier Diem. The peasants watched and cringed as Diem ruthlessly routed out all opposition, supported their extortionist landlords and refused even to discuss reunification with the north. The peasants watched as all this was presided over by U.S. influence and then by increasing numbers of U.S. troops who came to help quell the insurgency that Diem's methods had aroused. When Diem was overthrown they may have been happy, but the long line of military dictatorships seemed to offer no real change—especially in terms of their need for land and peace.

The only change came from America as we increased our troop commitments in support of governments which were singularly corrupt, inept and without popular support. All the while the people read our leaflets and received regular promises of peace and democracy—and land reform. Now they languish under our bombs and consider us—not their fellow Vietnamese—the real enemy. They move sadly and apathetically as we herd them off the land of their fathers into concentration camps where minimal social needs are rarely met. They know they must move or be destroyed by our bombs. So they go—primarily women and children and the aged.

They watch as we poison their water, as we kill a million acres of their crops. They must weep as the bulldozers roar through their areas preparing to destroy the precious trees. They wander into the hospitals, with at least twenty casualties from American firepower for one "Vietcong"-inflicted injury. So far we may have killed a million of them—mostly children. They wander into the towns and see thousands of the children, homeless, without clothes, running in packs on the streets like animals. They see the children, degraded by our soldiers as they beg for food. They see the children selling their sisters to our soldiers, soliciting for their mothers.

What do the peasants think as we ally ourselves with the landlords and as we refuse to put any action into our many words concerning land reform? What do they think as we test our latest weapons on them, just as the Germans tested out new medicine and new tortures in the concentration camps of Europe? Where are the roots of the independent Vietnam we claim to be building? Is it among these voiceless ones?

We have destroyed their two most cherished institutions: the family and the village. We have destroyed their land and their crops. We have cooperated in the crushing of the nation's only non-Communist revolutionary political force—the unified Buddhist church. We have supported the enemies of the peasants of Saigon. We have corrupted their women and children and killed their men. What liberators?

Now there is little left to build on—save bitterness. Soon the only solid physical foundations remaining will be found at our military bases and in the concrete of the concentration camps we call fortified hamlets. The peasants may well wonder if we plan to build our new Vietnam on such grounds as these? Could we blame them for such thoughts? We must speak for them and raise the questions they cannot raise. These too are our brothers.

Perhaps the more difficult but no less necessary task is to speak for those who have been designated as our enemies. What of the National Liberation Front—that strangely anonymous group we call VC or Communists? What must they think of us in America when they realize that we permitted the repression and cruelty of Diem which helped to bring them into being as a resistance group in the south? What do they think of our condoning the violence which led to their own taking up of arms? How can they believe in our integrity when now we speak of "aggression from the north" as if there were nothing more essential to the war? How can they trust us when now we charge them with violence after the murderous reign of Diem and charge them with violence while we pour every new weapon of death into their land? Surely we must understand their feelings even if we do not condone their actions. Surely we must see that the men we supported pressed them to their violence. Surely we must see that our own computerized plans of destruction simply dwarf their greatest acts.

How do they judge us when our officials know that their membership is less than twenty-five percent Communist and yet insist on giving them the blanket name? What must they be thinking when they know that we are aware of their control of major sections of Vietnam and yet we appear ready to allow national elections in which this highly organized political parallel government will have no part? They ask how we can speak of free elections when the Saigon press is censored and controlled by the military junta. And they are surely right to wonder what kind of new government we plan to help form without them—the only party in real touch with the peasants. They question our political goals and they deny the reality of a peace settlement from which they will be excluded. Their questions are frighteningly relevant. Is our nation planning to build on political myth again and then shore it up with the power of new violence?

Here is the true meaning and value of compassion and nonviolence when it helps us to see the enemy's point of view, to hear his questions, to know his assessment of ourselves. For from his view we may indeed see the basic weaknesses of our own condition, and if we are mature, we may learn and grow and profit from the wisdom of the brothers who are called the opposition.

So, too, with Hanoi. In the north, where our bombs now pummel the land, and our mines endanger the waterways, we are met by a deep but understandable mistrust. To speak for them is to explain this lack of confidence in Western words, and especially their distrust of American intentions now. In Hanoi are the men who led the nation to independence against the Japanese and the French, the men who sought membership in the French commonwealth and were betrayed by the weakness of Paris and the willfulness of the colonial armies. It was they who led a second struggle against French domination at tremendous costs, and then were persuaded to give up the land they controlled between the thirteenth and seventeenth parallel as a temporary measure at Geneva. After 1954 they watched us conspire with Diem to prevent elections which would have surely brought Ho Chi Minh to power over a united Vietnam, and they realized they had been betrayed again.

When we ask why they do not leap to negotiate, these things must be remembered. Also it must be clear that the leaders of Hanoi considered the presence of American troops in support of the Diem regime to have been the initial military breach of the Geneva agreements concerning foreign troops, and they remind us that they did not begin to send in any large number of supplies or men until American forces had moved into the tens of thousands.

Hanoi remembers how our leaders refused to tell us the truth about the earlier North Vietnamese overtures for peace, how the president claimed that none existed when they had clearly been made. Ho Chi Minh has watched as America has spoken of peace and built up its forces, and now he has surely heard of the increasing international rumors of American plans for an invasion of the north. He knows the bombing and shelling and mining we are doing are part of traditional pre-invasion strategy. Perhaps only his sense of humor and of irony can save him when he hears the most powerful nation of the world speaking of aggression as it drops thousands of bombs on a poor weak nation more than eight thousand miles away from its shores.

At this point I should make it clear that while I have tried in these last few minutes to give a voice to the voiceless on Vietnam and to understand the arguments of those who are called enemy, I am as deeply concerned about our troops there as anything else. For it occurs to me that what we are submitting them to in Vietnam is not simply the brutalizing process that goes on in any war where armies face each other and seek to destroy. We are adding cynicism to the process of death, for they must know after a short period there that none of the things we claim to be fighting for are really involved. Before long they must know that their government has sent them into a struggle among Vietnamese, and the more sophisticated surely realize that we are on the side of the wealthy and the secure while we create hell for the poor.

This Madness Must Cease
Somehow this madness must cease. We must stop now. I speak as a child of God and brother to the suffering poor of Vietnam. I speak for those whose land is being laid waste, whose homes are being destroyed, whose culture is being subverted. I speak for the poor of America who are paying the double price of smashed hopes at home and death and corruption in Vietnam. I speak as a citizen of the world, for the world as it stands aghast at the path we have taken. I speak as an American to the leaders of my own nation. The great initiative in this war is ours. The initiative to stop it must be ours.

This is the message of the great Buddhist leaders of Vietnam. Recently one of them wrote these words:

"Each day the war goes on the hatred increases in the heart of the Vietnamese and in the hearts of those of humanitarian instinct. The Americans are forcing even their friends into becoming their enemies. It is curious that the Americans, who calculate so carefully on the possibilities of military victory, do not realize that in the process they are incurring deep psychological and political defeat. The image of America will never again be the image of revolution, freedom and democracy, but the image of violence and militarism."

If we continue, there will be no doubt in my mind and in the mind of the world that we have no honorable intentions in Vietnam. It will become clear that our minimal expectation is to occupy it as an American colony and men will not refrain from thinking that our maximum hope is to goad China into a war so that we may bomb her nuclear installations. If we do not stop our war against the people of Vietnam immediately the world will be left with no other alternative than to see this as some horribly clumsy and deadly game we have decided to play.

The world now demands a maturity of America that we may not be able to achieve. It demands that we admit that we have been wrong from the beginning of our adventure in Vietnam, that we have been detrimental to the life of the Vietnamese people. The situation is one in which we must be ready to turn sharply from our present ways.

In order to atone for our sins and errors in Vietnam, we should take the initiative in bringing a halt to this tragic war. I would like to suggest five concrete things that our government should do immediately to begin the long and difficult process of extricating ourselves from this nightmarish conflict:

1. End all bombing in North and South Vietnam.
2. Declare a unilateral cease-fire in the hope that such action will create the atmosphere for negotiation.
3. Take immediate steps to prevent other battlegrounds in Southeast Asia by curtailing our military buildup in Thailand and our interference in Laos.
4. Realistically accept the fact that the National Liberation Front has substantial support in South Vietnam and must thereby play a role in any meaningful negotiations and in any future Vietnam government.
5. Set a date that we will remove all foreign troops from Vietnam in accordance with the 1954 Geneva agreement.

Part of our ongoing commitment might well express itself in an offer to grant asylum to any Vietnamese who fears for his life under a new regime which included the Liberation Front. Then we must make what reparations we can for the damage we have done. We must provide the medical aid that is badly needed, making it available in this country if necessary.

Protesting the War
Meanwhile we in the churches and synagogues have a continuing task while we urge our government to disengage itself from a disgraceful commitment. We must continue to raise our voices if our

nation persists in its perverse ways in Vietnam. We must be prepared to match actions with words by seeking out every creative means of protest possible.

As we counsel young men concerning military service we must clarify for them our nation's role in Vietnam and challenge them with the alternative of conscientious objection. I am pleased to say that this is the path now being chosen by more than seventy students at my own alma mater, Morehouse College, and I recommend it to all who find the American course in Vietnam a dishonorable and unjust one. Moreover I would encourage all ministers of draft age to give up their ministerial exemptions and seek status as conscientious objectors. These are the times for real choices and not false ones. We are at the moment when our lives must be placed on the line if our nation is to survive its own folly. Every man of humane convictions must decide on the protest that best suits his convictions, but we must all protest.

There is something seductively tempting about stopping there and sending us all off on what in some circles has become a popular crusade against the war in Vietnam. I say we must enter the struggle, but I wish to go on now to say something even more disturbing. The war in Vietnam is but a symptom of a far deeper malady within the American spirit, and if we ignore this sobering reality we will find ourselves organizing clergy- and laymen-concerned committees for the next generation. They will be concerned about Guatemala and Peru. They will be concerned about Thailand and Cambodia. They will be concerned about Mozambique and South Africa. We will be marching for these and a dozen other names and attending rallies without end unless there is a significant and profound change in American life and policy. Such thoughts take us beyond Vietnam, but not beyond our calling as sons of the living God.

In 1957 a sensitive American official overseas said that it seemed to him that our nation was on the wrong side of a world revolution. During the past ten years we have seen emerge a pattern of suppression which now has justified the presence of U.S. military "advisors" in Venezuela. This need to maintain social stability for our investments accounts for the counter-revolutionary action of American forces in Guatemala. It tells why American helicopters are being used against guerrillas in Colombia and why American napalm and green beret forces have already been active against rebels in Peru. It is with such activity in mind that the words of the late John F. Kennedy come back to haunt us. Five years ago he said, "Those who make peaceful revolution impossible will make violent revolution inevitable."

Increasingly, by choice or by accident, this is the role our nation has taken—the role of those who make peaceful revolution impossible by refusing to give up the privileges and the pleasures that come from the immense profits of overseas investment.

I am convinced that if we are to get on the right side of the world revolution, we as a nation must undergo a radical revolution of values. We must rapidly begin the shift from a "thing-oriented" society to a "person-oriented" society. When machines and computers, profit motives and property rights are considered more important than people, the giant triplets of racism, materialism, and militarism are incapable of being conquered.

A true revolution of values will soon cause us to question the fairness and justice of many of our past and present policies. On the one hand we are called to play the good Samaritan on life's roadside; but that will be only an initial act. One day we must come to see that the whole Jericho road must be transformed so that men and women will not be constantly beaten and robbed as they make their journey on life's highway. True compassion is more than flinging a coin to a beggar; it is not haphazard and superficial. It comes to see that an edifice which produces beggars needs restructuring. A true revolution of values will soon look uneasily on the glaring contrast of poverty and wealth. With righteous indignation, it will look across the seas and see individual capitalists of the West investing huge sums of money in Asia, Africa and South America, only to take the profits out with no concern for the social betterment of the countries, and say: "This is not just." It will look at our alliance with the landed gentry of Latin America and say: "This is not just." The Western arrogance of feeling that it has everything to teach others and nothing to learn from them is not just. A true revolution of values will lay hands on the world order and say of war: "This way of settling differences is not just." This business of burning human beings with napalm, of filling our nation's homes with orphans and widows, of injecting poisonous drugs of hate into veins of people normally humane, of sending men home from dark and bloody battlefields physically handicapped and psychologically deranged, cannot be reconciled with wisdom, justice and love. A nation that continues year after year to spend more money on military defense than on programs of social uplift is approaching spiritual death.

America, the richest and most powerful nation in the world, can well lead the way in this revolution of values. There is nothing, except a tragic death wish, to prevent us from reordering our priorities, so that the pursuit of peace will take precedence over the pursuit of war. There is nothing to keep us from molding a recalcitrant status quo with bruised hands until we have fashioned it into a brotherhood.

This kind of positive revolution of values is our best defense against communism. War is not the answer. Communism will never be defeated by the use of atomic bombs or nuclear weapons. Let us not join those who shout war and through their misguided passions urge the United States to relinquish its participation in the United Nations. These are days which demand wise restraint and calm reasonableness. We must not call everyone a Communist or an appeaser who advocates the seating of Red China in the United Nations and who recognizes that hate and hysteria are not the final answers to the problem of these turbulent days. We must not engage in a negative anti-communism, but rather in a positive thrust for democracy, realizing that our greatest defense against communism is to take offensive action in behalf of justice. We must with positive action seek to remove those conditions of poverty, insecurity and injustice which are the fertile soil in which the seed of communism grows and develops.

The People Are Important

These are revolutionary times. All over the globe men are revolting against old systems of exploitation and oppression and out of the wombs of a frail world new systems of justice and equality are being born. The shirtless and barefoot people of the land are rising up as never before. "The people who sat in darkness have seen a great light." We in the West must support these revolutions. It is a sad fact that, because of comfort, complacency, a morbid fear of communism, and our proneness to adjust to injustice, the Western nations that initiated so much of the revolutionary spirit of the modern world have now become the arch anti-revolutionaries. This has driven many to feel that only Marxism has the revolutionary spirit. Therefore, communism is a judgment against our failure to make democracy real and follow through on the revolutions we initiated. Our only hope today lies in our ability to recapture the revolutionary spirit and go out into a sometimes hostile world declaring eternal hostility to poverty, racism, and militarism. With this powerful commitment we shall boldly challenge the status quo and unjust mores and thereby speed the day when "every valley shall be exalted, and every mountain and hill shall be made low, and the crooked shall be made straight and the rough places plain."

A genuine revolution of values means in the final analysis that our loyalties must become ecumenical rather than sectional. Every nation must now develop an overriding loyalty to mankind as a whole in order to preserve the best in their individual societies.

This call for a world-wide fellowship that lifts neighborly concern beyond one's tribe, race, class and nation is in reality a call for an all-embracing and unconditional love for all men. This oft misunderstood and misinterpreted concept—so readily dismissed by the Nietzsches of the world as a weak and cowardly force—has now become an absolute necessity for the survival of man. When I speak of love I am not speaking of some sentimental and weak response. I am speaking of that force which all of the great religions have seen as the supreme unifying principle of life. Love is somehow the key that unlocks the door which leads to ultimate reality. This Hindu-Moslem-Christian-Jewish-Buddhist belief about ultimate reality is beautifully summed up in the first epistle of Saint John:

Let us love one another; for love is God and everyone that loveth is born of God and knoweth God. He that loveth not knoweth not God; for God is love. If we love one another God dwelleth in us, and his love is perfected in us.

Let us hope that this spirit will become the order of the day. We can no longer afford to worship the god of hate or bow before the altar of retaliation. The oceans of history are made turbulent by the ever-rising tides of hate. History is cluttered with the wreckage of nations and individuals that pursued this self-defeating path of hate. As Arnold Toynbee says: "Love is the ultimate force that makes for the saving choice of life and good against the damning choice of death and evil. Therefore the first hope in our inventory must be the hope that love is going to have the last word."

We are now faced with the fact that tomorrow is today. We are confronted with the fierce urgency of now. In this unfolding conundrum of life and history there is such a thing as being too late. Procrastination is still the thief of time. Life often leaves us standing bare, naked and dejected with a lost opportunity. The "tide in the affairs of men" does not remain at the flood; it ebbs. We may cry out desperately for time to pause in her passage, but time is deaf to every plea and rushes on. Over the bleached bones and jumbled residue of numerous civilizations are written the pathetic words: "Too late." There is an invisible book of life that faithfully records our vigilance or our neglect. "The moving finger writes, and having writ moves on...." We still have a choice today; nonviolent coexistence or violent co-annihilation.

We must move past indecision to action. We must find new ways to speak for peace in Vietnam and justice throughout the developing world—a world that borders on our doors. If we do not act we shall surely be dragged down the long dark and shameful corridors of time reserved for those who possess power without compassion, might without morality, and strength without sight.

Now let us begin. Now let us rededicate ourselves to the long and bitter—but beautiful—struggle for a new world. This is the calling of the sons of God, and our brothers wait eagerly for our response. Shall we say the odds are too great? Shall we tell them the struggle is too hard? Will our message be that the forces of American life militate against their arrival as full men, and we send our deepest regrets? Or will there be another message, of longing, of hope, of solidarity with their yearnings, of commitment to their cause, whatever the cost? The choice is ours, and though we might prefer it otherwise we must choose in this crucial moment of human history.

As that noble bard of yesterday, James Russell Lowell, eloquently stated:

> Once to every man and nation
> Comes the moment to decide,
> In the strife of truth and falsehood,
> For the good or evil side;
> Some great cause, God's new Messiah,
> Off'ring each the bloom or blight,
> And the choice goes by forever
> Twixt that darkness and that light.
> Though the cause of evil prosper,
> Yet 'tis truth alone is strong;
> Though her portion be the scaffold,
> And upon the throne be wrong:
> Yet that scaffold sways the future,
> And behind the dim unknown,
> Standeth God within the shadow
> Keeping watch above his own.

GLOSSARY

Arnold Toynbee: a twentieth-century British historian who examined the rise and fall of civilizations

Castro: Fidel Castro, who was then the Communist dictator of Cuba

Dien Bien Phu: a town in North Vietnam, the site of a decisive battle between the Communists and the French in 1954

648 • ANTI-WAR ACTIVISM

Hanoi: the capital of North Vietnam

Ho Chi Minh: the leader of the Communist forces during the Vietnam War

James Russell Lowell: nineteenth-century American poet; the quotation is from his 1845 poem "Once to Every Man and Nation."

junta: a dictatorship run by a group of military officers

Langston Hughes: a prominent African American poet of the Harlem Renaissance; the quote is from his 1939 poem "Let America Be America Again."

Mao: Mao Zedong, the Communist dictator of China

Marxism: the philosophy of Karl Marx, the nineteenth-century German writer whose name is often used synonymously with Communism

Molotov cocktails: improvised bombs, usually made with gasoline and a bottle; named after Vyacheslav Molotov, Soviet foreign minister during World War II, by the Finns, who used them to resist the Soviet Union

napalm: a highly flammable explosive often used to burn forested areas thought to hold troops during the Vietnam War

National Liberation Front: Communists who led the insurgency in Vietnam

Nietzsches: a reference to Friedrich Nietzsche, a nineteenth-century German philosopher

"The people who sat in darkness ...": quotation from the Gospel of Matthew, chapter 4, verse 16

Premier Diem: Ngo Dinh Diem, the first president of South Vietnam, who was assassinated in 1963

VC: abbreviation for Vietcong, the Western name for the Communist insurgents in Vietnam

Document Analysis

Anticipating criticism, King begins by declaring that his position on the Vietnam War is a matter of "conscience." To remain silent would be "a betrayal" of principle. He acknowledges that it would be much easier to express "conformist thought" rather than "inner truth," especially when conviction leads to denunciation of government policies during wartime. King asserts that his dissent from U.S. policies in Vietnam conforms to the principles that have guided him since he became a civil rights leader during the Montgomery bus boycott. King also maintains that while there is no simple way to stop the war, the United States has "the greatest responsibility" for "ending a conflict that has exacted a heavy price on both continents."

In the next section of his address, King enumerates specific reasons for opposing the Vietnam War, while emphasizing that the basis of his criticism is his "moral vision." Especially important to King are the detrimental effects of the war on America's poor. He condemns the war for draining funds from the Johnson administration's War on Poverty. Also troubling to King are the disproportionate numbers of poor and black soldiers who are fighting and dying in Vietnam. King then explains that his belief in nonviolence also accounts for his opposition to the war, asserting that he cannot invoke his commitment to nonviolence selectively. King's responsibilities as a civil rights leader, a Nobel Peace Prize recipient, and a Christian also lead him to question the war. King deftly rebuts the charge that his work in the civil rights movement disqualifies him from speaking on issues of war and peace.

King next reviews the history of the Vietnam War in order to challenge the Johnson administration's position that the United States was fighting to halt aggression and advance democracy. King adopts the perspective of the Vietnamese who "have been living under the curse of the war for almost three continuous decades." His use of the term *madness* at the beginning of this section indicates how strongly he disagrees with President Johnson that the war is serving either U.S. or Vietnamese interests. King goes on to detail the ways in which American policy has support the repression of the Vietnamese people and encourages support for the Ho Chi Minh regime, leading to his characterization American troops as "strange liberators."

King offers five proposals that require drastic changes in U.S. Policy. His views are not those of a mediator who is encouraging all major parties to make concessions for peace but of a moral critic who believes that Americans should "atone for our sins and errors in Vietnam." He speaks as a brother to the suffering poor in Vietnam and the United States, a citizen of the world who is "aghast" at U.S. actions, and an American citizen who holds his nation accountable for expanding the war and for stopping it.

King next advocates protest against the war, including counseling young men to become conscientious objectors as an alternative to military service. Vietnam, however, is only a symptom of "a far deeper malady within the American spirit." King charges that the United States has become an imperialist nation, exploiting overseas investments while stifling the ambitions of people in developing nations for peaceful change.

King calls for "a true revolution of values" that will transform America's world role, favoring economic restructuring that will end "the glaring contrast" between poverty and wealth. His prescriptions for international reform mirror his vision for domestic change. He also believes that a revolution in values will provide enormous benefits in America's cold war contest with Communism. King argues that U.S. policymakers' fears of Communist takeovers in other countries led them to pursue "negative anti-communism," including a resort to war. King instead favors "positive action" to "remove those conditions of poverty, insecurity and injustice" that lead to the spread of Communism.

In this closing section, King tells his fellow Americans that they face revolutionary times and that they must find new ways to cooperate with people in developing nations, concentrating on the worldwide challenges to "old systems of exploitation and oppression" and the necessity of aligning the United States with "the shirtless and barefoot people" who "are rising up as never before." He believes that Western nations made essential contributions to this revolutionary spirit but that they have become rich, complacent, and reactionary. "Our only hope today," he declares, "lies in our ability to recapture the revolutionary spirit and go out into a sometimes hostile world declaring eternal hostility to poverty, racism, and militarism." Success requires thinking beyond one's community, race, or nation. Instead, he calls for "an overriding loyalty to mankind as a whole" based on the idea—which "all of the great religions have seen as the supreme unifying principle of life"—of love.

Essential Themes

As a recipient of the Nobel Peace Prize, King felt a special responsibility to strive for peace. His duty to work for "'the brotherhood of man'" is universal, he says; it requires him to disregard national boundaries. Ultimately, however, King's dedication to the cause of peace was rooted in his Christian faith. He believes that all men are sons of the same God who cares for His children regardless of "race or nation or creed." King boldly declares, "Somehow this madness must cease." He speaks on behalf of Vietnamese victims of the war and poor Americans who bear the burden of the fighting. He speaks both as a citizen of the world and as a patriotic American. He calls upon leaders of the United States to stop the conflict. What America needs, King maintains, is a "radical revolution of values." The country must move away from racism, materialism, and militarism to become a more "person-oriented society." If this revolution occurs, Americans will question the wisdom of many national policies; they will realize that true compassion requires basic changes in the structure of society. King calls on American capitalists to stop extracting profits from overseas investments with no concern for the welfare of third world people. He urges world leaders to end the awful human cost of modern warfare. He calls on American leaders to embrace this revolution of values so that the pursuit of peace becomes the highest national priority. In conclusion, King asks his audience to dedicate themselves to the struggle for a new world order. Despite many difficulties, the choice is clear. As sons of God, they must embrace the cause of peace.

———*Chester Pach, PhD and Paul Murray, PhD*

Bibliography and Additional Reading

Dallek, Robert. *Flawed Giant: Lyndon Johnson and His Times, 1961–1973.* (New York: Oxford University Press, 1998).

DeBenedetti, Charles. *An American Ordeal: The Antiwar Movement of the Vietnam Era.* (Syracuse, N.Y. Syracuse University Press, 1990).

Garrow, David J. *Bearing the Cross: Martin Luther King, Jr., and the Southern Christian Leadership Conference.* (New York: William Morrow, 1986).

Jackson, Thomas F. *From Civil Rights to Human Rights: Martin Luther King, Jr., and the Struggle for Economic Justice.* (Philadelphia: University of Pennsylvania Press, 2007).

Lewis, David Levering. *King: A Biography.* 2nd ed. (Urbana: University of Illinois Press, 1978).

Oates, Stephen B. *Let the Trumpet Sound: The Life of Martin Luther King, Jr..* (New York: Harper & Row, 1982).

Sitkoff, Harvard. *King: Pilgrimage to the Mountaintop.* (New York: Hill and Wang, 2008).

Washington, James M., ed. *A Testament of Hope: The Essential Writings and Speeches of Martin Luther King, Jr.* (New York: HarperCollins, 1986).

Woods, Randall B. *LBJ: Architect of American Ambition.* (New York: Free Press, 2006).

Web site

"Liberation Curriculum." The Martin Luther King, Jr. Research and Education Institute Web site. https://kinginstitute.stanford.edu/liberation-curriculum.

Testimony of the Vietnam Veterans against the War

Date: 1971
Author: John Kerry
Genre: Congressional testimony

Summary Overview

In 1971, John Kerry, representing thousands of veterans through the organization Vietnam Veterans Against the War, testified before the US Senate Foreign Affairs Committee as part of its lengthy hearings on formulating a legislative plan for the Vietnam War. In the six years since heavy American troop involvement began, thousands had been killed and wounded, thousands of Americans had taken to the streets in protest and Americans began to speak of a "credibility gap" between what President Lyndon Johnson and his advisers had said about the progress of the war and what was rapidly becoming known to the public about the reality. President Richard Nixon had taken office in January, 1969, promising "peace with honor."

Kerry's heartfelt testimony about American treatment of civilians and prisoners in Vietnam and his charge that American policies were at least partially to blame for the excessive brutality. On a wider scale his critique of the war is also a critique of the entire post-1945, Cold War approach to American foreign policy. The relentless drive to confront and roll back Communism wherever it may be found has been, Kerry argues, unsuccessful: "we cannot fight communism all over the world." Kerry combines this criticism of the American war effort and international relations with equally harsh criticism of the manner in which the veterans of the actions in Vietnam had been treated by the military and Veterans Administration bureaucracy.

Defining Moment

By the early 1970s, American involvement in the Vietnam war had—seemingly—declined from its high point in 1968. However, despite a lower number of troops on the ground in Southeast Asia, American military might was still on display though increased bombing campaigns, including secretly bombing targets in Cambodia. In the United States, opposition to the war, always prominent on college campuses, began to spread to other sectors of society. One of these was returning veterans of combat in Vietnam. In New York City in 1967, Vietnam Veterans Against the War was formally established "to voice the growing opposition among returning servicemen and women to the still-raging war in Indochina." One of the VVAW's efforts was dubbed the Winter Soldier Investigation. This was an independent series of testimonies by combat veterans designed to publicize atrocities and war crimes committed by American troops. This took place from January 31 to February 2, 1971 in Detroit.

Public attention had been drawn to war crimes and atrocities in Vietnam by, among other events, the My Lai Massacre. On March 16, 1968, American troops led by Second Lieutenant William Calley. During this event, American troops murdered at least 347 (according to US Army records) and possibly more than 400 civilians, including elderly men, women, and children. Additional, the troops raped women and mutilated the bodies of the some of the dead. When the incident became public in late 1969, it sparked protest as well as debate. Some argued, as Kerry does in his testimony, that American policies on how the war in Vietnam should be prosecuted were responsible for events like the My Lai Massacre.

In response to the continuing war and to increasing anti-war sentiment, the US Senate Foreign Relations Committee held a number of hearings on future US policy (including the possibly of ending the war) in Vietnam chaired by Senator William Fulbright. The hearings took place between April 20 and May 27, 1971. The various witnesses included both those in favor of continuing the war as well as those opposed to it. John Kerry, representing Vietnam Veterans Against the War was the eight witness to testify, making his statement on April 22, 1971.

Author Biography

John Forbes Kerry was born on December 11, 1943 in Colorado. After attending boarding schools in New England, he attended Yale University, graduating in 1966. Joining the Naval Reserved that same year, he served four months during 1968 and 1969 in South Vietnam in command of a Swift Boat (technically called a "Patrol Craft Fast"), a river patrol and combat vessel used for transport, intercepting enemy transportation of weapons and ammunition, and other similar operations during the Vietnam War. During his brief tour of duty, he was decorated several times, including the Silver Star and three Purple Hearts. After his service, he joined Vietnam Veterans Against the War, serving as one of their most prominent spokesmen against continued American involvement in the Vietnam War as well as participating in the "Winter Soldier Investigation" into atrocities committed by American troops in Vietnam. It was in this capacity that he provided this testimony to the Senate Foreign Relations Committee in 1971. The day after this testimony, Kerry and other veterans participated in an anti-war demonstration during which he and a thousand others threw their medals, uniform, and other militaria over a fence at the capitol building in protest.

Later, Kerry lose a highly publicized congressional election in 1972 and spend several years in various jobs, often for humanitarian organizations. He would later attend law school at Boston College and serve as a prosecutor in Massachusetts. He entered politics, serving as Lieutenant Governor of Massachusetts under Michael Dukakis from 1983 to 1985 and as a Senator from Massachusetts from 1985 to 2013. He ran a losing campaign as the Democratic nominee for President in 2004 and, from 2013 to 2017 served as Secretary of State under President Barack Obama.

HISTORICAL DOCUMENT

I would like to say for the record, and also for the men behind me who are also wearing the uniforms and their medals, that my sitting here is really symbolic. I am not here as John Kerry. I am here as one member of the group of one thousand, which is a small representation of a very much larger group of veterans in this country, and were it possible for all of them to sit at this table they would be here and have the same kind of testimony.

I would simply like to speak in very general terms. I apologize if my statement is general because I received notification yesterday you would hear me and I am afraid because of the injunction I was up most of the night and haven't had a great deal of chance to prepare.

I would like to talk, representing all those veterans, and say that several months ago in Detroit, we had an investigation at which over 150 honorably discharged and many very highly decorated veterans testified to war crimes committed in Southeast Asia, not isolated incidents but crimes committed on a day-to-day basis with the full awareness of officers at all levels of command.

It is impossible to describe to you exactly what did happen in Detroit, the emotions in the room, the feelings of the men who were reliving their experiences in Vietnam, but they did. They relived the absolute horror of what this country, in a sense, made them do.

They told the stories at times they had personally raped, cut off ears, cut off heads, taped wires from portable telephones to human genitals and turned up the power, cut off limbs, blown up bodies, randomly shot at civilians, razed villages in fashion reminiscent of Ghengis Khan, shot cattle and dogs for fun, poisoned food stocks, and generally ravaged the country side of South Vietnam in addition to the normal ravage of war, and the normal and very particular ravaging which is done by the applied bombing power of this country.

We call this investigation the "Winter Soldier Investigation." The term "Winter Soldier" is a play on words of Thomas Paine in 1776 when he spoke of the Sunshine Patriot and summertime soldiers who deserted at Valley Forge because the going was rough.

We who have come here to Washington have come here because we feel we have to be winter soldiers now. We could come back to this country; we could be quiet; we could hold our silence; we could not tell what went on in Vietnam, but we feel because of what threatens this country, the fact that the crimes threaten it, not reds, and not redcoats but the crimes which we are committing that threaten it, that we have to speak out.

I would like to talk to you a little bit about what the result is of the feelings these men carry with them after coming back from Vietnam. The country doesn't know it yet, but it has created a monster, a monster in the form of millions of men who have been taught to deal and to trade in violence, and who are given the chance to die for the biggest nothing in history; men who have returned with a sense of anger and a sense of betrayal which no one has yet grasped.

As a veteran and one who feels this anger, I would like to talk about it. We are angry because we feel we have been used in the worst fashion by the administration of this country.

In 1970 at West Point, Vice President [Spiro] Agnew said "some glamorize the criminal misfits of society while our best men die in Asian rice paddies to preserve the freedom which most of those misfits abuse" and this was used as a rallying point for our effort in Vietnam.

But for us, as boys in Asia, whom the country was supposed to support, his statement is a terrible distortion from which we can only draw a very deep sense of revulsion. Hence the anger of some of the men who are here in Washington today. It is a distortion because we in no way consider ourselves the best men of this country, because those he calls misfits were standing up for us in a way that nobody else in this country dated to, because so many who have died would have returned to this country to join the misfits in their efforts to ask for an immediate withdrawal from South Vietnam, because so many of those best men have returned as quadriplegics and amputees, and they lie forgotten in Veterans' Administration hospitals in this country which fly the flag which so many have chosen as their own personal symbol. And we cannot consider ourselves America's best men when we are ashamed of and hated what we were called on to do in Southeast Asia.

In our opinion, and from our experience, there is nothing in South Vietnam, nothing which could happen that realistically threatens the United States of America. And to attempt to justify the loss of one American life in Vietnam, Cambodia or Laos by linking such loss to the preservation of freedom, which those misfits supposedly abuse, is to use the height of criminal hypocrisy, and it is that kind of hypocrisy which we feel has torn this country apart.

We are probably much more angry than that and I don't want to go into the foreign policy aspects because I am outclassed here. I know that all of you talk about every possible alternative of getting out of Vietnam. We understand that. We know you have considered the seriousness of the aspects to the utmost level and I am not going to try to dwell on that, but I want to relate to you the feeling that many of the men who have returned to this country express because we are probably angriest about all that we were told about Vietnam and about the mystical war against communism.

We found that not only was it a civil war, an effort by a people who had for years been seeking their liberation from any colonial influence whatsoever, but also we found that the Vietnamese whom we had enthusiastically molded after our own image were hard put to take up the fight against the threat we were supposedly saving them from.

We found most people didn't even know the difference between communism and democracy. They only wanted to work in rice paddies without helicopters strafing them and bombs with napalm burning their villages and tearing their country apart. They wanted everything to do with the war, particularly with this foreign presence of the United States of America, to leave them alone in peace, and they practiced the art of survival by siding with whichever military force was present at a particular time, be it Vietcong, North Vietnamese, or American.

We found also that all too often American men were dying in those rice paddies for want of support from their allies. We saw first hand how money from American taxes was used for a corrupt dictatorial regime. We saw that many people in this country had a one-sided idea of who was kept free by our flag, as blacks provided the highest percentage of casualties. We saw Vietnam ravaged equally by American bombs as well as by search and destroy missions, as well as by Vietcong terrorism, and yet we listened while this country tried to blame all of the havoc on the Vietcong.

We rationalized destroying villages in order to save them. We saw America lose her sense of morality as she accepted very coolly a My Lai and refused to give up the image of American soldiers who hand out chocolate bars and chewing gum.

We learned the meaning of free fire zones, shooting anything that moves, and we watched while

America placed a cheapness on the lives of Orientals.

We watched the U.S. falsification of body counts, in fact the glorification of body counts. We listened while month after month we were told the back of the enemy was about to break. We fought using weapons against "oriental human beings," with quotation marks around that. We fought using weapons against those people which I do not believe this country would dream of using were we fighting in the European theater or let us say a non-third-world people theater, and so we watched while men charged up hills because a general said that hill has to be taken, and after losing one platoon or two platoons they marched away to leave the high for the reoccupation by the North Vietnamese because we watched pride allow the most unimportant of battles to be blown into extravaganzas, because we couldn't lose, and we couldn't retreat, and because it didn't matter how many American bodies were lost to prove that point. And so there were Hamburger Hills and Khe Sanhs and Hill 881's and Fire Base 6's and so many others.

Now we are told that the men who fought there must watch quietly while American lives are lost so that we can exercise the incredible arrogance of Vietnamizing the Vietnamese. Each day to facilitate the process by which the United States washes her hands of Vietnam someone has to give up his life so that the United States doesn't have to admit something that the entire world already knows, so that we can't say that we have made a mistake. Someone has to die so that President Nixon won't be, and these are his words, "the first President to lose a war."

We are asking Americans to think about that because how do you ask a man to be the last man to die in Vietnam? How do ask a man to be the last man to die for a mistake? But we are trying to do that, and we are doing it with thousands of rationalizations, and if you read carefully the President's last speech to the people of this country, you can see that he says, and says clearly: "But the issue, gentlemen, the issue is communism, and the question is whether or not we will leave that country to the communists or whether or not we will try to give it hope to be a free people."

But the point is they are not a free people now under us. They are not a free people, and we cannot fight communism all over the world, and I think we should have learned that lesson by now.

But the problem of veterans goes beyond this personal problem, because you think about a poster in this country with a picture of Uncle Sam and the picture says "I want you." And a young man comes out of high school and says, "That is fine. I am going to serve my country." And he goes to Vietnam and he shoots and he kills and he does his job or maybe he doesn't kill, maybe he just goes and he comes back, and when he gets back to this country he finds that he isn't really wanted, because the largest unemployment figure in the country- it varies depending on who you get it from, the VA Administration 15 percent, various other sources 22 percent. But the largest corps of unemployed in this country are veterans of this war, and of those veterans 33 percent of the unemployed are black. That means 1 out of every 10 of the Nation's unemployed is a veteran of Vietnam.

The hospitals across the country won't, or can't meet their demands. It is not a question of not trying. They don't have the appropriations. A man recently died after he had a tracheotomy in California, not because of the operation but because there weren't enough personnel to clean the mucous out of his tube and he suffocated to death.

Another young man just died in a New York VA hospital the other day. A friend of mine was lying in a bed two beds away and tried to help him, but he couldn't. He rang a bell and there was nobody there to service that man and so he died of convulsions.

I understand 57 percent of all those entering the VA hospitals talk about suicide. Some 27 percent have tried, and they try because they come back to this country and they have to face what they did in Vietnam, and then they come back and find the indifference of a country that doesn't really care, that doesn't really care.

Suddenly we are faced with a very sickening situation in this country, because there is no moral indignation and, if there is, it comes from people who are almost exhausted by their past indignations, and I know that may of them are sitting in front of me.

The country seems to have lain down and shrugged off something as serious as Laos, just as we calmly shrugged off the loss of 700,000 lives in Pakistan, the so-called greatest disaster of all times.

But we are here as veterans to say we think we are in the midst of the greatest disaster of all times now because they are still dying over there, and not just Americans, Vietnamese, and we are rationalizing leaving that country so that those people can go on killing each other for years to come.

Americans seems to have accepted the idea that the war is winding down, at least for Americans, and they have also allowed the bodies which were once used by a President for statistics to prove that we were winning that war, to be used as evidence against a man who followed orders and who interpreted those orders no differently than hundreds of other men in Vietnam.

We veterans can only look with amazement on the fact that this country has been unable to see there is absolutely no difference between ground troops and a helicopter crew, and yet people have accepted a differentiation fed them by the administration.

No ground troops are in Laos, so it is all right to kill Laotians by remote control. But believe me the helicopter crews fill the same body bags and they wreak the same kind of damage on the Vietnamese and Laotian countryside as anybody else, and the President is talking about allowing that to go on for many years to come. One can only ask if we will really be satisfied only when the troops march into Hanoi.

We are asking here in Washington for some action, action from the Congress of the United States of America which has the power to raise and maintain armies, and which by the Constitution also has the power to declare war.

We have come here, not to the President, because we believe that this body can be responsive to the will of the people, and we believe that the will of the people says that we should be out of Vietnam now.

We are here in Washington also to say that the problem of this war is not just a question of war and diplomacy. It is part and parcel of everything that we are trying as human beings to communicate to people in this country, the question of racism, which is rampant in the military, and so many other questions also, the use of weapons, the hypocrisy in our taking umbrage in the Geneva Conventions and using that as justification for a continuation of this war, when we are more guilty than any other body of violations of those Geneva Conventions, in the use of free fire zones, harassment interdiction fire, search and destroy missions, the bombings, the torture of prisoners, the killing of prisoners, accepted policy by many units in South Vietnam. That is what we are trying to say. It is part and parcel of everything.

An American Indian friend of mine who lives in the Indian Nation of Alcatraz put it to me very succinctly. He told me how as a boy on an Indian reservation he had watched television and he used to cheer the cowboys when they came in and shot the Indians, and then suddenly one day he stopped in Vietnam and he said "My God, I am doing to these people the very same thing that was done to my people." And he stopped. And that is what we are trying to say, that we think this thing has to end.

We are also here to ask, and we are here to ask vehemently, where are the leaders of our country? Where is the leadership? We are here to ask where are [Robert] McNamara, [Walt] Rostow, [George] Bundy, [Roswell] Gilpatrick and so many others. Where are they now that we, the men whom they sent off to war, have returned? These are commanders who have deserted their troops, and there is no more serious crime in the law of war. The Army says they never leave their wounded.

The Marines say they never leave even their dead. These men have left all the casualties and retreated behind a pious shield of public rectitude. They have left the real stuff of their reputation bleaching behind them in the sun in this country.

Finally, this administration has done us the ultimate dishonor. They have attempted to disown us and the sacrifice we made for this country. In their blindness and fear they have tried to deny that we are veterans or that we served in Nam. We do not need their testimony. Our own scars and stumps of limbs are witnesses enough for others and for ourselves.

We wish that a merciful God could wipe away our own memories of that service as easily as this administration has wiped their memories of us. But all that they have done and all that they can do by this denial is to make more clear than ever our own determination to undertake one last mission, to search out and destroy the last vestige of this barbarous war, to pacify our own hearts, to conquer the hate and the fear that have driven this country these last 10 years and more and so when, in 30 years from now, our brothers go down the street without a leg, without an arm or a face, and small boys ask why, we will be able to say "Vietnam" and not mean a desert, not a filthy obscene memory but mean instead the place where America finally turned and where soldiers like us helped it in the turning.

Thank you.

GLOSSARY

body counts: total number of enemy dead reported to headquarters

Ghengis Khan: Mongol leader notorious for his brutality

napalm: incendiary substance used as a weapon in the Vietnam war

Vietcong: guerilla forces that operated in South Vietnam on behalf of the communist North Vietnamese

"Vietnamizing the Vietnamese": reference to the Nixon administration's policy of "Vietnamization," which called for the South Vietnamese military to take a greater role in the conflict

Document Analysis

Kerry prefaces his remarks by telling the members of the Foreign Relations committee that he is testifying as representative of the thousands of veterans who would "have the same kind of testimony." He also refers to the Vietnam Veterans Against the War investigation into war crimes, which took place from January 31 to February 2, 1971 and recites a litany of atrocity discussed by the Vietnam veterans. Kerry goes on to explain that, while the group could have shifted back into civilian society after coming back from Vietnam, they felt that they had a duty to share the truth because the crimes committed in Southeast Asia are more of a threat to the United States than the Communism that is the nominal danger.

Part of this danger, Kerry asserts, is that the experience of the war has "created a monster…in the form of millions of men who have been taught to deal and to trade in violence" who died for "nothing" and who have returned with a sense of anger and a sense of betrayal which no one has yet grasped." Kerry then recounts a 1970 speech by Vice President Agnew and dismisses his characterization of anti-war protesters as "misfits." Rather, Kerry argues, the protesters stood up for the soldiers when the nation would not.

Kerry moves into a detailed critique of American war aims in Vietnam and the motivations behind them. He argues that there is no real threat to the United States from what is, essentially, a civil war as well as an anti-imperialist movement and that most of the Vietnamese couldn't distinguish between democracy and communism. They survived the best way they could, even if that meant siding with more than one of the belligerent forces in the area. Kerry also denounces the behavior of America's South Vietnamese allies, whom he characterizes as "a corrupt dictatorial regime."

Kerry then attacks the policies and practices that contributed to the normalization of incidents like the My Lai massacre. Policies such as "free fire zones" in which any person was considered a viable target and the practice of overemphasizing enemy body count, Kerry argued, led to a dehumanization of the enemy that was uncommon even in a time of war.

Kerry's also critiques the ongoing prosecution of the war under President Richard Nixon, including the policy of Vietnamization, which increased American bombing raids while leaving more of the ground battles to the South Vietnamese Army. He attacks Nixon's contention that the issue is still "communism" and the need to preserve the freedom of the Vietnamese people. Those people, Kerry argues, are not free under the American-supported government. Further, he asserts that "we cannot fight communism all over the world."

Kerry transitions from his criticism of policies behind the war and the practice of the war to the treatment of the war's returning veterans. He cites statistics on unemployment among veterans as well as the sometimes fatal difficulties veterans encounter trying to obtain medical care. A particularly troubling fact Kerry relates is the high rate of suicidal thoughts and suicide attempts among Vietnam veterans. Kerry attributes this directly to "the indifference of a country that doesn't really care."

Despite the number of lives lost of all nationalities, Americans seem content to allow the war to continue, even after American withdrawal. Kerry is concerned also because of the willingness of the American public to prosecute soldiers in hypocritical war crimes trials while authorizing the killing of people "by remote control" in bombing raids.

After presenting these narratives and statistics, Kerry begins to detail what he and his fellow veterans want Congress to do. He asks Congress to take leadership and address issues not only of "war and diplomacy" but also of the racism prevalent in the military, including the conduct of the war, bombing of civilians, mistreatment of prisoners and other activities.

Kerry closes his testimony by denouncing the administration for denigrating the anti-war veterans' service and sacrifices and by expressing again their determination to work for peace in Vietnam and in their own hearts.

Essential Themes
John Kerry's 1971 testimony to the Senate Foreign Relations Committed bristles with the anger and frustration of the men who feel that they have been used, abused, and discarded by a government that wishes to ignore the horrific consequences of their policies and of the methods they have authorized to carry out those policies. Kerry's statement addresses a range of issues related to the war in Vietnam. These include the body-count driven statistical analysis that encourages soldiers to treat any Vietnamese person as a potentially-viable target to the military justice system that punishes soldiers "who followed orders and who interpreted those orders no differently than hundreds of other men in Vietnam." Kerry ties American policy in Southeast Asia to a pervasive culture of racism and links this policy to the same discredited imperialist practices that the Vietnamese people are fighting against. The United States, Kerry explained, has subjugated its ideals to the specter of communism; the Vietnamese people and American soldiers are paying the price for that decision.

Kerry also emphasizes the need for long-term, quality medical and psychiatric care for Vietnam veterans. His discussion of the high level of suicidal thought and the horrific examples of veterans who have died from simple injuries and ailments due to the neglect and incompetence of the Veterans Administration conveys a palpable sense of deep betrayal.

———Aaron Gulyas, MA

Bibliography and Additional Reading
Brinkley, Douglas. *Tour of Duty: John Kerry and the Vietnam War*. (New York: William Morrow & Company, 2004).

Kerry, John, and Vietnam Veterans Against the War. *The New Soldier*. (New York: MacMillan Publishing Company: October 1971).

Nicosia, Gerald. *Home to War: A History of the Vietnam Veterans' Movement*. (New York: Crown Publishers: 2001).

Hunt, Andrew E. *The Turning: A History of Vietnam Veterans Against the War*. (New York: New York University Press, 2001).

Website
"VVAW: Where We Came From, Who We Are." Vietnam Veterans Against the War. Accessed January 5, 2017. http://www.vvaw.org/about/

"The Emperor Has No Clothes" Speech

Date: 2003
Author: Robert C. Byrd
Genre: Speech

Summary Overview

Senator Robert Byrd's speeches before the Senate exhibited the oratorical skills of nineteenth-century statesmen, complete with flowery rhetoric and grand gestures. He recited poems; quoted historical figures, particularly the Roman statesman and orator Cicero; and frequently cited parables from history and classical fairy tales to make his point—his use of the Danish writer Hans Christian Andersen's 1837 fairy story is typical in this regard. "The Emperor Has No Clothes" Speech, one of the U.S. senator's twenty-seven speeches on the war in Iraq given between October 2002 and April 2004, summarized his belief that Iraq posed no direct threat to the United States. The "emperor" George W. Bush, he believed, had promoted a war based on nonexistent weapons of mass destruction and no records that established that Iraq's leader, Saddam Hussein, was involved in the terrorist attacks of September 11, 2001. He criticizes President Bush for trying to take power from the Senate and for attacking the civil liberties of Americans.

Defining Moment

Byrd was a former defense hawk who voted in favor of President Lyndon B. Johnson's Gulf of Tonkin Resolution in August 1964. This resolution broadened presidential power to wage war without a formal declaration. Byrd, however, became the Senate's most outspoken critic of the 2003 Iraqi war. He believed that giving the president such broad authority to engage in war gave away power that belonged to the legislative branch of government. He insisted that Congress alone had the right to declare war under the U.S. Constitution and that presidential usurpation of that power, particularly under the administration of George W. Bush, disrupted the Constitution's system of checks and balances among the judicial, legislative, and executive branches of government.

Author Biography

Robert C. Byrd was born Cornelius Calvin Sale, Jr., in North Carolina in 1917. Adopted and raised by his aunt and uncle, Byrd grew up in the coalfields of West Virginia, where his father worked as a teamster, farmer, and coal miner. The Byrd family was poor, and Robert Byrd frequently did his homework by the light of oil lamps because their home had no electricity. After Byrd graduated from high school in 1934, he worked as a gas station attendant and a produce boy. After taking welding classes, he helped build cargo ships during World War II.

In 1946 Byrd ran for the West Virginia House of Delegates and won. In 1950 he ran for a seat in the West Virginia Senate and won. Then, halfway through his Senate term, he ran for a seat in the U.S. House of Representatives and was elected in 1952. In 1958, he won the first of nine consecutive terms in the U.S. Senate.

Byrd remained a traditionalist throughout his career. He always carried a copy of the U.S. Constitution in his pocket and often waved it on the Senate floor while he spoke. His strong defense of constitutional law resulted in his adamant opposition to proposed changes to the Constitution, such as line-item veto or balanced-budget amendments. Still, during his fifty years in the Senate, he became increasingly liberal, focusing on government spending for social programs that improved education and health care and voting for civil rights.

Byrd's congressional career spanned numerous presidential administrations. On June 21, 2007, he became the first senator ever to cast eighteen thousand roll call votes in American history, and in November 2006 he was elected to an unprecedented ninth consecutive term in the U.S. Senate. Over the years, he served as majority leader, majority whip, minority leader, and president pro tempore of the Senate as well as on such key committees as the Senate Appropriations Committee, which he chaired. While still in office, Byrd died at the age of ninety-two, in June 2010.

HISTORICAL DOCUMENT

In 1837, Danish author, Hans Christian Andersen, wrote a wonderful fairy tale which he titled *The Emperor's New Clothes*. It may be the very first example of the power of political correctness. It is the story of the Ruler of a distant land who was so enamored of his appearance and his clothing that he had a different suit for every hour of the day.

One day two rogues arrived in town, claiming to be gifted weavers. They convinced the Emperor that they could weave the most wonderful cloth, which had a magical property. The clothes were only visible to those who were completely pure in heart and spirit.

The Emperor was impressed and ordered the weavers to begin work immediately. The rogues, who had a deep understanding of human nature, began to feign work on empty looms.

Minister after minister went to view the new clothes and all came back exhorting the beauty of the cloth on the looms even though none of them could see a thing.

Finally a grand procession was planned for the Emperor to display his new finery. The Emperor went to view his clothes and was shocked to see absolutely nothing, but he pretended to admire the fabulous cloth, inspect the clothes with awe, and, after disrobing, go through the motions of carefully putting on a suit of the new garments.

Under a royal canopy, the Emperor appeared to the admiring throng of his people—all of whom cheered and clapped because they all knew the rogue weavers' tale and did not want to be seen as less than pure of heart.

But, the bubble burst when an innocent child loudly exclaimed, for the whole kingdom to hear, that the Emperor had nothing on at all. He had no clothes.

That tale seems to me very like the way this nation was led to war.

We were told that we were threatened by weapons of mass destruction in Iraq, but they have not been seen.

We were told that the throngs of Iraqi's would welcome our troops with flowers, but no throngs or flowers appeared.

We were led to believe that Saddam Hussein was connected to the attack on the Twin Towers and the Pentagon, but no evidence has ever been produced.

We were told in 16 words that Saddam Hussein tried to buy "yellow cake" from Africa for the production of nuclear weapons, but the story has turned into empty air.

We were frightened with visions of mushroom clouds, but they turned out to be only vapors of the mind.

We were told that major combat was over but 101 [as of October 17] Americans have died in combat since that proclamation from the deck of an aircraft carrier by our very own Emperor in his new clothes.

Our emperor says that we are not occupiers, yet we show no inclination to relinquish the country of Iraq to its people.

Those who have dared to expose the nakedness of the Administration's policies in Iraq have been subjected to scorn. Those who have noticed the elephant in the room—that is, the fact that this war was based on falsehoods—have had our patriotism questioned. Those who have spoken aloud the thought shared by hundreds of thousands of military families across this country, that our troops should return quickly and safely from the dangers half a world away, have been accused of cowardice. We have then seen the untruths, the dissembling, the fabrication, the misleading inferences surrounding this rush to war in Iraq wrapped quickly in the flag....

The Emperor has no clothes. This entire adventure in Iraq has been based on propaganda and manipulation. Eighty-seven billion dollars is too much to pay for the continuation of a war based on falsehoods.

Taking the nation to war based on misleading rhetoric and hyped intelligence is a travesty and a tragedy. It is the most cynical of all cynical acts. It is dangerous to manipulate the truth. It is dangerous because once having lied, it is difficult to ever be believed again. Having misled the American people and stampeded them to war, this Administration must now attempt to sustain a policy predicated on falsehoods. The President asks for billions from those same citizens who know that they were misled about the need to go to war. We misinformed and insulted our friends and allies and now this Administration is having more than a little trouble getting help from the international community. It is perilous to mislead....

I cannot support the continuation of a policy that unwisely ties down 150,000 American troops for the foreseeable future, with no end in sight.

I cannot support a President who refuses to authorize the reasonable change in course that would bring traditional allies to our side in Iraq.

I cannot support the politics of zeal and "might makes right" that created the new American arrogance and unilateralism which passes for foreign policy in this Administration.

I cannot support this foolish manifestation of the dangerous and destabilizing doctrine of preemption that changes the image of America into that of a reckless bully.

The emperor has no clothes. And our former allies around the world were the first to loudly observe it.

I shall vote against this bill because I cannot support a policy based on prevarication. I cannot support doling out 87 billion of our hard-earned tax dollars when I have so many doubts about the wisdom of its use.

I began my remarks with a fairy tale. I shall close my remarks with a horror story, in the form of a quote from the book *Nuremberg Diaries*, written by G. M. Gilbert, in which the author interviews Hermann Goering:

"We got around to the subject of war again and I said that, contrary to his attitude, I did not think that the common people are very thankful for leaders who bring them war and destruction.

"...But, after all, it is the *leaders* of the country who determine the policy and it is always a simple matter to drag the people along, whether it is a democracy or a fascist dictatorship or a Parliament or a Communist dictatorship.

"There is one difference," I pointed out. "In a democracy the people have some say in the matter through their elected representatives, and in the United States only Congress can declare wars."

"Oh, that is all well and good, but, voice or no voice, the people can always be brought to the bidding of the leaders. That is easy. All you have to do is tell them they are being attacked and denounce the pacifists for lack of patriotism and exposing the country to danger. It works the same way in any country."

GLOSSARY

unilateralism: a policy of taking action without consulting or considering the reactions of others

we were told in 16 words: reference to George W. Bush's statement, in his 2003 State of the Union speech, "The British government has learned that Saddam Hussein recently sought significant quantities of uranium from Africa."

weapons of mass destruction: nuclear, biological, radiological, chemical, or other forms of weaponry capable of killing large populations in a short time

yellow cake: a form of uranium that can be used for making nuclear weaponry

Document Analysis

One of Byrd's twenty-seven speeches on the Iraq War, referred to as "The Emperor Has No Clothes" Speech, summarized his belief that there was no direct or imminent threat from Iraq. Byrd used Hans Christian Andersen's classic 1837 fairy tale to make his point. In the story, an emperor decks himself out in a suit of clothes thought to be visible only to those pure of heart and mind. All the townspeople exclaim over the beauty of the raiment as the emperor appears before them—except one child, who proclaims the truth of the emperor's nakedness.

On October 17, 2003, Byrd gave his speech prior to the Senate's vote on the Iraqi Supplemental Bill, an $87 billion presidential bill that would provide additional funding for the U.S. military in Iraq and for the reconstruction of the country. Continued military force, it was argued, would make Iraq more secure from outside terrorists groups and provide for the training of a new Iraqi military, and more funding was needed to rebuild needed public services such as electricity and water systems. Byrd pressed for improvements in the bill at least twelve times, calling for more accountability and congressional oversight of the money. Each time, President Bush garnered enough support to override Byrd's amendments to the proposed legislation.

In this speech, the "emperor" is President Bush, who, according to Byrd, promoted a war on the basis of something that was not there. Before the war, Bush claimed the war was necessary because Iraq had weapons of mass destruction, but no weapons of mass destruction were found during the months and years after the invasion. Bush also claimed that Iraqis were oppressed under Saddam Hussein's regime and that American troops would be seen as liberators, yet, Byrd insists, American troops were not welcomed with open arms. Despite the belief that Hussein's Iraq sponsored terrorism in America and was collecting materials from other countries to build nuclear weapons, Byrd says that no records were found to indicate that Hussein was involved in the terrorist attacks on September 11, 2001, and no evidence shows that he bought material to produce nuclear weapons from other nations. Bush told Americans that the conflict was over two months after the initial invasion while standing on the deck of an aircraft carrier, the USS *Abraham Lincoln*. Dressed in his "new" clothes, a flight suit worn by U.S. military pilots, Bush gave a speech in front of a large banner that proclaimed "Mission Accomplished." However, the mission was not over. The war dragged on, and, Byrd notes, more soldiers died after Bush declared the war over than during the invasion. Byrd claims that although the emperor knew nothing was there, he continued to insist Iraq was a threat to America. Since these threats, like the emperor's clothes, could be seen only by those who were "pure of heart," or patriotic, many Americans agreed with the "emperor."

Byrd maintains that by stirring up fears of imminent danger and denouncing those who did not believe in the danger as unpatriotic, Bush persuaded Americans to believe in something that was not there. Byrd ends the speech by comparing Bush's leadership to that of the Nazi Hermann Goering, the second man in Adolf Hitler's Third Reich, Germany's Fascist and racist government during World War II. Goering believed that leaders determined policy in any society and could always sway people to follow their policy by telling them they were being attacked and then denouncing pacifists for their lack of patriotism. Goering's belief led millions of innocent people to their deaths during the war. Byrd attracted widespread criticism for these remarks.

Essential Themes

In his "The Emperor Has No Clothes" speech, Senator Robert Byrd has a very clear message for the American people: "you are being deceived." This deception is coming from the highest levels of the government of the United States. In particular, he attacks the Bush administrations misuse of patriotism to persuade Americans to support the war in Iraq. He argues that in his arrogance Bush created a war based on falsehoods and that he lied to the American people as well as to America's allies throughout the world.

Many of Byrd's criticisms of President Bush stemmed from his belief that Bush had little regard for the Constitution. He accuses Bush of trying to usurp the power of the Senate, particularly the power to declare war, and he insists that Bush abused the civil liberties of Americans as established in the Constitution through the creation and passage of laws such as the USA Patriot Act (October 26, 2001), a law that expanded the authority of U.S. law-enforcement agencies. Intended to provide agencies with widespread power to fight terrorism, the act authorized the search of telephone and e-mail communications and medical and financial records and redefined "terrorism" to include domestic terrorism.

——*Connie Park Rice, PhD*

Bibliography and Additional Reading

Isikoff, Michael and David Corn. *Hubris: The Inside Story of Spin, Scandal, and the Selling of the Iraq War.* (New York: Crown, 2006).

Roberts, Paul William. A War Against Truth: An Intimate Account of the Invasion of Iraq. (Vancouver: Raincoast Books, 2005).

Thomas E. Ricks (2006). *Fiasco: The American Military Adventure in Iraq*. Penguin.

Woodward, Bob. Plan of Attack: The Definitive Account of the Decision to Invade Iraq. (New York: Simon and Schuster, 2004).

APPENDIXES

Chronological List

1637: Excerpts from the Massachusetts Bay Colony Trial against Anne Hutchinson. .3
1688: A Minute against Slavery, From the Germantown Monthly Meeting, Addressed to the Monthly Meeting in Dublin. 83
1689: Declaration of Protestant Subjects in Maryland. 10
1739: An Account of the Negroe Insurrection in South Carolina 90
1764: The Rights of the British Colonies Asserted and Proved. 17
1765: Declaration of Rights of the Stamp Act Congress 22
1767–1768: Letters from a Farmer in Pennsylvania. 27
1768: Boston Non-Importation Agreement. 35
1771: Samuel Adams Writing as Candidus. 39
1773: Rules by Which a Great Empire May Be Reduced to a Small One. 43
1774: Boston Massacre Oration 49
1775: "Liberty or Death" Speech. 56
1776: *Common Sense* 62
1777: Petition of Prince Hall and Other African Americans to the Massachusetts General Court. 94
1780: Petition to the Assembly of Pennsylvania against the Slave Trade 99
1792: Petition against the Excise Tax by Inhabitants of Western Pennsylvania. 76
1794: An Address to Those Who Keep Slaves, and Approve the Practice 101
1811: Appeal to Choctaws and Chickasaws. 289
1829: Appeal to the Coloured Citizens of the World 105
1829: Memorial to Congress. 294
1831: *The Confessions of Nat Turner*. 118
1832: South Carolina Ordinance of Nullification 227
1833: Declaration of Sentiments of the American Anti-Slavery Convention. 129
1833: Prejudices against People of Color, and Our Duties in Relation to This Subject 135
1843: "An Address to the Slaves of the United States of America". 143
1843: Speech Opposing the Kansas-Nebraska Act. 232
1848: Seneca Falls Convention Declaration of Sentiments. 483
1852: "What to the Slave is the Fourth of July?". 151
1852: *The Condition, Elevation, Emigration, and Destiny of the Colored People of the United States, Politically Considered*. 165
1853: *Twelve Years a Slave: Narrative of Solomon Northup*. 176
1858: Provisional Constitution and Ordinances for the People of the United States 184
1860: South Carolina Declaration of Causes of Secession 237
1861: "Cornerstone Speech". 195

1861: "Under the Flag" 209
1861: *A Voice from Harper's Ferry* 216
1861: Farewell Address to the U.S. Senate 245
1861: *Incidents in the Life of a Slave Girl* 251
1861: Speech on His Refusal to Take the Oath of Loyalty to the Confederacy .. 254
1864-1865: Battle of Sand Creek: Editorials and Congressional Testimony ... 298
1865: Valedictory Editorial of the *Liberator* 220
1868: Speech on His Expulsion from the Georgia Legislature 263
1868: Treaty of Fort Laramie 316
1871: Lecture on Constitutional Equality 488
1873: "Is It a Crime for a Citizen of the United States to Vote?" 494
1874: "All That We Ask Is Equal Laws, Equal Legislation, and Equal Rights" .. 272
1881: Preface to *The Rise and Fall of the Confederate Government* 281
1887: Dawes Severalty Act 325
1887: *Ten Days in a Mad-House* 535
1890: *How the Other Half Lives* 545
1891: Wounded Knee Massacre: Statements and Eyewitness Accounts 333
1892: "The Subjective Necessity for Social Settlements" 554
1894: Editorial on the Pullman Strike 558
1895: "Liberty" 357
1895: "The Status of Woman, Past, Present, and Future" 562
1895: Atlanta Exposition Address 566
1896: The "Cross of Gold" Speech 501
1905: Niagara Movement Declaration of Principles 363
1909: "Lynching: Our National Crime" 369
1910: "Agitation" 375
1910: "Why Women Should Vote" 508
1914: William Monroe Trotter's Protest to Woodrow Wilson 378
1915: Testimony before the House Judiciary Committee 514
1917: Speech against Conscription and War 623
1917: Speech Opposing War with Germany 628
1918: Antiwar Speech 633
1919: Speech Opposing the League of Nations 574
1921: "The Eruption of Tulsa" 383
1933: Auto Workers Strike 579
1935: "A Black Inventory of the New Deal" 390
1935: "Share Our Wealth" Address 397

1935: "U.S. Department of (White) Justice" 585
1941: Call to Negro America to March on Washington 405
1947: *An Appeal to the World*. 410
1956: Southern Manifesto 590
1960: Student Nonviolent Coordinating Committee Statement of Purpose. 416
1962: The Port Huron Statement 595
1963: "I Have a Dream". 419
1963: "Message to the Grass Roots". 433
1963: Letter from Birmingham Jail 439
1964: "The Ballot or the Bullet" 446
1966: "Black Power". 453
1966: "What We Want, What We Believe" 461
1966: What We Want. 474
1967: "Beyond Vietnam: A Time to Break Silence" 638
1968: The SCUM Manifesto. 520
1969: Gay Power Comes To Sheridan Square. 343
1969: Indians of All Tribes Occupation of Alcatraz: Proclamation 601
1971: *Steal This Book* 606
1971: Testimony of the Vietnam Veterans against the War 651
1984: Commonwealth Address. 613
2003: "The Emperor Has No Clothes" Speech. 658
2016: Summary of Letter Requesting Further Review of the Dakota Access Pipeline (DAPL). 347
2017: Women's March on Washington 529

Web Resources

The documents we present in this volume are a great starting point for understanding dissent and protest in American history through historical sources. There are a number of outstanding resources on the Internet that you can use to continue your journey through the past. Whether you are a teacher or a student, a well-seasoned investigator of historical evidence or someone who is coming to these materials for the first time, these internet resources have materials that will enable you to expand your knowledge of dissent and protest in the history of the United States.

While these web sites were operation when this volume went to press, it is possible that they might not be when you try to visit them. We recommend the Wayback Machine at the Internet Archive (http://www.archive.org) as an excellent tool for exploring vanished online materials.

The American Social History Project (https://ashp.cuny.edu) is sponsored by the City University of New York and provides a wealth of multimedia and print resources centered on the history of the United States from the bottom up.

History Matters (http://historymatters.gmu.edu) bills itself as "The U.S. History Survey Course on the Web), providing lesson plans, assignments, historical documents, teaching tips and strategies, and more. It is hosted by the American Social History Project.

The Early Americas Digital Archive (http://eada.lib.umd.edu), sponsored by the University of Maryland Libraries' e-Publishing Initiative, provides historical documents and commentary from and about the Americas from 1492 to the 1820s.

The American Abolitionism Project (http://americanabolitionist.liberalarts.iupui.edu) is hosted by Indiana University-Purdue University, Indianapolis and provides overviews and analysis of the Abolition Movement, biographies of key historical figures, and primary sources.

The Race and Slavery Petitions Project (http://library.uncg.edu/slavery/petitions/) is hosted by the University of North Carolina at Greensboro. It is a database of petitions submitted to southern state legislatures by slaves between 1775 and 1867.

The Black Panthers Digital Collection (http://www.lib.msu.edu/branches/dmc/collectionbrowse/?coll=20). Hosted by the Michigan State University Libraries, this collection includes digital reproductions of posters, pamphlets and other documents from the Black Panther Party.

Discovering American Women's History Online (http://digital.mtsu.edu/cdm/landingpage/collection/women) provides, among other resources, links and descriptions for over 700 online primary source collections relating to the history of women in America.

Documents from Students for a Democratic Society (http://www.sds-1960s.org/documents.htm) provides an archive of speeches and publications from the political revolution of the 1960s.

Antiwar and Radical History Project-Pacific Northwest (https://depts.washington.edu/antiwar/photosdocs.shtml) provides a wealth of historical documents and background information on the antiwar movement in this region during the era of the Vietnam War.

The Farmerworker Movement Documentation Project (https://libraries.ucsd.edu/farmworkermovement/) hosts oral histories, essays, and primary sources from the history of the United Farm Workers.

Bibliography

Abernethy, Graeme. *The Iconography of Malcolm X*. Lawrence, Kan.: University Press of Kansas, 2013.

Abzug, Robert H. *Cosmos Crumbling: American Reform and the Religious Imagination*. New York: Oxford University Press, 1994.

Adams, Katherine H.; Keene, Michael L. *Alice Paul and the American Suffrage Campaign*. Chicago: University of Illinois Press, 2008.

Adeleke, Tunde. *Without Regard to Race: The Other Martin Robison Delany*. Jackson: University Press of Mississippi, 2003.

Aisèrithe, A.J. and Donald Yacovone, eds. *Wendell Phillips, Social Justice, and the Power of the Past*. Baton Rouge: Louisiana State University Press, 2016.

Alkebulan, Paul. *Survival Pending Revolution: The History of the Black Panther Party*. Tuscaloosa: University of Alabama Press, 2007.

Alvarez, Alexandra. "Martin Luther King's 'I Have a Dream': The Speech Event as Metaphor." *Journal of Black Studies* 18, no. 3. March 1988: 337–357.

Anderson, Jervis. *A. Philip Randolph: A Biographical Portrait*. Berkeley: University of California Press, 1986.

Andersson, Rani-Henrik. *The Lakota Ghost Dance of 1890*. Lincoln, NE: University of Nebraska Press, 2009.

Andrews, William L., ed. *The North Carolina Roots of African American Literature: An Anthology*. Chapel Hill: University of North Carolina Press, 2006.

Angell, Stephen Ward. *Bishop Henry McNeal Turner and African-American Religion in the South*. Knoxville: University of Tennessee Press, 1992.

Aptheker, Herbert. "The Quakers and Negro Slavery." *Journal of Negro History* 25, no. 3. July 1940: 331–362.

Aptheker, Herbert. *Nat Turner's Slave Rebellion*. New York: Humanities Press, 1966.

———. *American Negro Slave Revolts*. 5th ed. New York: International Publishers, 1983.

Armstrong, Thomas F. "From Task Labor to Free Labor: The Transition along Georgia's Rice Coast, 1820–1880."*Georgia Historical Quarterly* 64. Fall 1980: 432–447.

Asante, Molefi Kete. *100 Greatest African Americans: A Biographical Encyclopedia*. Amherst, N.Y. Prometheus Books, 2002.

Assensoh, A. B.; Alex-Assensoh, Yvette M. *Malcolm X and Africa*. Amherst, N.Y.: Cambria Press, 2016.

Aucoin, Brent. "The Southern Manifesto and Southern Opposition to Desegregation." *Arkansas Historical Quarterly* 55, no. 2 (1996: 173–193.

Austin, Curtis J. *Up Against the Wall: Violence in the Making and Unmaking of the Black Panther Party*. Fayetteville: University of Arkansas Press, 2006.

Badger, Tony. "The Southern Manifesto: White Southerners and Civil Rights, 1956." *European Contributions to American Studies* 15 (1988: 77–99.

Baer, Helene Gilbert *The Heart is Like Heaven: The Life of Lydia Maria Child*. Philadelphia: University of Pennsylvania Press, 1964.

Bailey, N. Louise, et al. *Biographical Directory of the South Carolina Senate, 1776–1985*. Columbia: University of South Carolina Press, 1986.

Bailyn, Bernard. *The Ideological Origins of the American Revolution*, Enlarged Edition. New York: Belknap Press, 1992.

Baker, Jean H., ed. *Votes for Women: The Struggle for Suffrage Revisited*. New York: Oxford University Press, 2002.

Barnard, John. *American Vanguard: The United Auto Workers during the Reuther Years, 1935–1970*. Detroit: Wayne State University Press, 2004.

Barnhill, J. Herschel. "Civil Rights in the 1940s." *Negro History Bulletin* 45, no. 1. January–March 1982: 21–22.

Barry, Kathleen (1988). *Susan B. Anthony: A Biography of a Singular Feminist*. New York: Ballantine Books.

Barry, Kathleen. *Susan B. Anthony: A Biography of a Singular Feminist*. New York: Ballantine Books, 1988.

Bartlett, Bruce. *Wrong on Race: The Democratic Party's Buried Past*. New York: Palgrave Macmillan, 2008.

Bartley, Numan. *The Rise of Massive Resistance: Race and Politics in the South During the 1950s*. Baton Rouge: Louisiana State University Press, 1969.

Bass, S. Jonathan. *Blessed Are the Peacemakers: Martin Luther King, Jr., Eight White Clergymen, and the "Letter from Birmingham Jail."* Baton Rouge: Louisiana State University Press, 2001.

Battis, Emery. *Saints and Sectaries: Anne Hutchinson and the Antinomian Controversy in the Massachusetts Bay Colony*. Chapel Hill: University of North Carolina Press, 1962.

Baum, Dale. *The Shattering of Texas Unionism: Politics in the Lone Star State during the Civil War Era*. Boton Rouge: Louisiana State University Press, 1998.

Bay, Mia. *To Tell the Truth Freely: the life of Ida B. Wells*. New York: Hill & Wang, 2009.

Beeman, Richard R. *Patrick Henry: A Biography*. New York: McGraw-Hill, 1974.

Bennett, Lerone, Jr. *Pioneers in Protest*. Baltimore, Md. Penguin, 1969.

———. *Confrontation: Black and White*. Chicago: Johnson Publishing, 1965.

Berlin, Ira. *Generations of Captivity: A History of African-American Slaves*. Cambridge: Harvard University Press, 2004.

Binder-Johnson, Hildegard. "The Germantown Protest of 1688 against Negro Slavery." *Pennsylvania Magazine of History and Biography* 65, no. 2. April 1941: 145–156.

Black Americans in Congress, 1870–2007. Washington, D.C. U.S. Government Printing Office, 2008.

Blassingame, John W., et al., eds. *The Frederick Douglass Papers*, Series One: *Speeches, Debates, and In terviews*, Vol. 2: *1847–54*. New Haven, Conn. Yale University Press, 1982.

Bodnar, John E. *Remaking America: Public Memory, Commemoration, and Patriotism in the Twentieth Century*. Princeton, N.J. Princeton University Press, 1991.

Bolt, William K. "Founding Father and Rebellious Son: James Madison, John C. Calhoun, and the Use of Precedents." *American Nineteenth Century History* 53, no. 3. Fall 2004: 1–27.

Boyd, Steven R. "The Whiskey Rebellion, Popular Rights, and the Meaning of the First Amendment." In W. Thomas Mainwaring, ed. *The Whiskey Rebellion and the Trans-Appalachian Frontier*, 73–84. Washington, Pennsylvania: Washington and Jefferson College, 1994.

Bradley, Patricia. *Slavery, Propaganda, and the American Revolution*. Jackson: University of Mississippi Press, 1999.

Branch, Taylor. *Parting the Waters: America in the King Years, 1954–63*. New York: Simon & Schuster, 1988.

Breen, T. H. "Subjecthood and Citizenship: The Context of James Otis's Radical Critique of John Locke," *New England Quarterly*. Sep., 1998) 71 #3, 378–403.

Brick, Howard and Gregory Parker, *A New Insurgency: The Port Huron Statement and Its Times*. Ann Arbor: Michigan Publishing, University of Michigan Library, 2015.

Brinkley, Alan. *Voices of Protest: Huey Long, Father Coughlin, and the Great Depression*. New York: Knopf, 1982.

Brinkley, Douglas. *Tour of Duty: John Kerry and the Vietnam War*. New York: William Morrow & Company, 2004.

Brodhead, Richard H. "Millennium, Prophecy and the Energies of Social Transformation: The Case of Nat Turner." In *Imagining the End: Visions of Apocalypse from the Ancient Middle East to Modern America*, eds. Abbas Amanat and Magnus Bernhardsson. London: I. B. Tauris, 2002.

Brophy, Alfred L. *Reconstructing the Dreamland: The Tulsa Race Riot of 1921: Race, Reparations, and Reconciliation*. New York: Oxford University Press, 2002.

Brown Victoria Bissell, *The Education of Jane Addams*. Philadelphia: University of Pennsylvania Press, 2007.

Brown, Dee. *Bury My Heart at Wounded Knee: An Indian History of the American West*. New York: Picador, 2007)

Brugger, Robert J., *Maryland, a Middle Temperament 1634-1980*. Baltimore: Johns Hopkins University Press, 1988.

Brundage, W. Fitzhugh, ed. *Booker T. Washington and Black Progress: Up from Slavery 100 Years Later*. Gainesville: University of Florida Press, 2003.

Buchanan, Paul D. *Radical Feminists: A Guide to an American Subculture*. Santa Barbara: Greenwood, 2011.

Buenger, Walter L. *Secession and the Union in Texas*. Austin: University of Texas Press, 1984.

Buhle, Paul, *Taking Care of Business: Samuel Gompers, George Meany, Lane Kirkland, and the Tragedy of American Labor*. New York: Monthly Review Press, 1999.

Buk-Swienty, Tom and Annette Buk-Swienty. *The Other Half: The Life of Jacob Riis and the World of Immigrant America*. New York: W. W. Norton, 2008.

Burns, Dave. "The Soul of Socialism: Christianity, Civilization, and Citizenship in the Thought of Eugene Debs" in *Labor*, vol. 5, no. 2 (2008), pp. 83–116.

Butterfield, L. H., et al. eds. *Adams Family Correspondence*. Vol.1: *December 1761–May 1776*. Cambridge: Belknap Press of Harvard University Press, 1963.

Cadbury, Henry J. "An Early Quaker Anti-Slavery Statement." *Journal of Negro History* 22, no. 4. October 1937: 488–493.

Calvert, Jane E. July 2007). "Liberty Without Tumult: Understanding the Politics of John Dickinson". *The Pennsylvania Magazine of History and Biography*. Philadelphia: Historical Society of Pennsylvania. CXXXI (3: 233–62.

———. *Quaker Constitutionalism and the Political Thought of John Dickinson*. Cambridge and New York: Cambridge University Press, 2008.

Caplan, Sheri J. *Petticoats and Pinstripes: Portraits of Women in Wall Street's History*. Westport, Connecticut: Praeger, 2013.

Carlson, Leonard A. "The Dawes Act and Indian Farming." *Journal of Economic History* 38, no. 1. March 1978: 274–276.

Carmichael, Stokely. *Stokely Speaks: Black Power Back to Pan-Africanism*. New York, Random House, 1971.

———, and Charles V. Hamilton. *Black Power: The Politics of Liberation in America*. New York: Random House, 1967.

———, and Ekwueme Michael Thelwell. *Ready for Revolution: The Life and Struggles of Stokely Carmichael*. New York: Scribner, 2003.

Carr, Lois Green and David William Jordan. *Maryland's Revolution of Government, 1689-1692*. Ithaca, New York: Cornell University Press, 1974.

Carson, Clayborne. *In Struggle : SNCC and the Black Awakening of the 1960s*. Cambridge: Harvard University Press, 1995.

Carson, Clayborne. *In Struggle: SNCC and the Black Awakening of the 1960s*. Cambridge, Mass. Harvard University Press, 1981.

Carson, Roberta F. "The Loyalty Leagues in Georgia." *Georgia Historical Society* 20. June 1936: 125–153.

Carter, David. *Stonewall: The Riots that Sparked the Gay Revolution,*. New York: St. Martin's Press, 2004.

Cashin, Joan E. *First Lady of the Confederacy: Varina Davis's Civil War*. Cambridge, Mass. Belknap Press of Harvard University Press, 2006.

Catton, Bruce. *The Coming Fury*. Vol. 1. Garden City, N.Y. Doubleday, 1961.

Cimbala, Paul A. "The Freedmen's Bureau, the Freedmen, and Sherman's Grant in Reconstruction Georgia, 1865–1867."*Journal of Southern History* 55. November 1989: 597–632.

Cohodas, Nadine. *Strom Thurmond and the Politics of Southern Change*. New York: Simon and Schuster, 1993.

Colaiaco, James A. "The American Dream Unfulfilled: Martin Luther King, Jr., and the 'Letter from Birmingham Jail.'" *Phylon* 45 (1984: 1–18.

Colaiaco, James A. *Frederick Douglass and the Fourth of July*. New York: Palgrave Macmillan, 2006.

Coleman, William S.E. *Voices of Wounded Knee*. Lincoln: University of Nebraska Press, 2000.

Coletta, Paolo E. *William Jennings Bryan*, Vol. 1: *Political Evangelist, 1860–1908*. Lincoln: University of Nebraska Press, 1964.

Commager, Henry, comp. *The Struggle for Racial Equality: A Documentary Record*. New York: Harper and Row, 1967.

Conway, Alan. *The Reconstruction of Georgia*. Minneapolis: University of Minnesota Press, 1966.

Conyers Jr., James L.; Smallwood, Andrew P., eds. *Malcolm X: A Historical Reader*. Durham, N.C.: Carolina Academic Press, 2008.

Cooper, John Milton. *Breaking the Heart of the World: Woodrow Wilson and the Fight for the League of Nations*. New York: Cambridge University Press, 2010.

———. *Reconsidering Woodrow Wilson: Progressivism, Internationalism, War, and Peace*. Baltimore, Md. Johns Hopkins University Press, 2008.

———. *Woodrow Wilson: A Biography*. New York: Alfred A. Knopf, 2009.

Cooper, William J., Jr. *Jefferson Davis, American*. New York: Knopf, 2000.

———. *Jefferson Davis and the Civil War Era*. Baton Rouge: Louisiana State University Press, 2009.

Corrigan, Mary Beth. "Imaginary Cruelties? A History of the Slave Trade in Washington, D.C." *Washington History* 13, no. 2. Fall/Winter 2001–2002: 4–27.

Cotroneo, Ross R., and Jack Dozier. "A Time of Disintegration: The Coeur d'Alene and the Dawes Act." *Western Historical Quarterly* 5, no. 4. October 1974: 405–419.

Cottrol, Robert J. *The Afro-Yankees: Providence's Black Community in the Antebellum Era*. Westport, Conn. Greenwood Press, 1982.

Coulter, E. Merton "Henry M. Turner: Georgia Negro Preacher-Politician during the Reconstruction Era." *Georgia Historical Quarterly* 48. December 1964: 371–410.

Cwiklik, Robert. *Stokely Carmichael and Black Power*. Brookfield, Conn. Millbrook Press, 1993.

Dallek, Robert. *Flawed Giant: Lyndon Johnson and His Times, 1961–1973*. New York: Oxford University Press, 1998.

Davis, Charles Twitchell, and Henry Louis Gates. *The Slave's Narrative*. New York. Oxford University Press, 1985.

Davis, Varina. *Jefferson Davis: Ex-President of the Confederate States of America—A Memoir by His Wife.* 1890. Reprinted with an introduction by Craig L. Symonds. Baltimore: Nautical and Aviation Publishing Company of America, 1990.

Davis, William C. *Jefferson Davis: The Man and His Hour.* New York: HarperCollins Publishers, 1991.

———. *Look Away! A History of the Confederate States of America.* New York: The Free Press, 2002.

———. *The Union that Shaped the Confederacy: Robert Toombs & Alexander H. Stephens.* Lawrence: University Press of Kansas, 2001.

DeBenedetti, Charles. *An American Ordeal: The Antiwar Movement of the Vietnam Era.* Syracuse, N.Y. Syracuse University Press, 1990.

DeMallie, Raymond J. "Touching the Pen: Plains Indian Treaty Councils in Ethnohistorical Perspective." In *Ethnicity on the Great Plains*, ed. Frederick C. Luebke. Lincoln: University of Nebraska Press, 1980.

Ditmore, Michael G. (2000). "A Prophetess in Her Own Country: an Exegesis of Anne Hutchinson's 'Immediate Revelation'". *William and Mary Quarterly.* 57 (2: 349–392.

Doenecke, Justus D. *Nothing Less Than War: A New History of America's Entry into World War I.* Lexington: University Press of Kentucky, 2011)

Douglass, Frederick. *Oration, Delivered in Corinthian Hall, Rochester, July 5, 1852.* Rochester, New York, 1852.

Dowd, Gregory Evans. *A Spirited Resistance: The North American Indian Struggle for Unity, 1745-1815.* Baltimore: Johns Hopkins University Press, 1992.

Dowling, Robert M. *Slumming in New York: From the Waterfront to Mythic Harlem.* Urbana-Champaign: University of Illinois Press, 2008.

Drago, Edmund L. *Black Politicians and Reconstruction in Georgia: A Splendid Failure.* Baton Rouge: Louisiana State University Press, 1982.

Drake, Richard. *The Education of an Anti-Imperialist Robert La Follette and U.S. Expansion.* University of Wisconsin Press; 2013.

Dray, Philip. *At the Hands of Persons Unknown: The Lynching of Black America.* New York: Random House, 2002.

Du Bois, W. E. B. *John Brown.* New York: International Publishers, 1962.

Duberman, Martin. *Stonewall.* New York: Penguin Books, 1993.

DuBois, Ellen Carol. *Feminism and Suffrage: The Emergence of an Independent Women's Movement in the United States, 1848–1869.* Revised edition. Ithaca, N.Y. Cornell University Press, 1999.

———. *Women's Suffrage and Women's Rights.* New York: New York University Press, 1998.

Dudden, Faye E. *Fighting Chance: The Struggle over Woman Suffrage and Black Suffrage in Reconstruction America.* New York: Oxford University Press, 2011.

Duncan, Russell. *Freedom's Shore: Tunis Campbell and the Georgia Freedman.* Athens: University of Georgia Press, 1986.

Dungan, Nicholas. *Gallatin: America's Swiss Founding Father.* New York University Press, 2010.

Durham, Michael S. *Powerful Days: The Civil Rights Photography of Charles Moore.* New York: Stewart, Tabori & Chang, 1991.

Dyja, Thomas. *Walter White: The Dilemma of Black Identity in America.* Chicago: Ivan R. Dee, 2008.

Eckert, Allan. *A Sorrow in Our Hearts: The Life of Tecumseh.* New York: Bantam Books, 1992.

Edmunds, R. David. *Tecumseh and the Quest for Indian Leadership.* Boston: Little Brown, 1984.

———. (December 1987 – January 1988). "The Thin Red Line. Tecumseh, The Prophet, and Shawnee Resistance." *Timeline.* Ohio Historical Society. 4 (6: 3).

Edsall, Nicholas. *Toward Stonewall: Homosexuality and Society in the Modern Western World.* Charlottesville: University of Virginia Press, 2003.

Egerton, Douglas. *Death or Liberty: African Americans and Revolutionary America.* New York: Oxford University Press, 2008.

Eichhoff, Jürgen. "The Three Hundredth Anniversary of the Germantown Protest against Slavery." *Monatshefte* 80, no. 3. Fall 1988: 265–267.

Ellis, Richard E. *The Union at Risk: Jacksonian Democracy, States' Rights and the Nullification Crisis.* New York: Oxford University Press, 1987.

Ellsworth, Scott. *Death in a Promised Land: The Tulsa Race Riot of 1921.* Baton Rouge: Louisiana State University Press, 1982.

Ericson, David F. "The Nullification Crisis, American Republicanism, and the Force Bill Debate." *Journal of Southern History* 61, no. 2 (1995: 249–270.

———. *The Shaping of American Liberalism: The Debates over Ratification, Nullification, and Slavery.* Chicago: University of Chicago Press, 1993.

Eskew, Glenn T. *But for Birmingham: The Local and National Movements in the Civil Rights Struggle*. Chapel Hill: University of North Carolina Press, 1997.

Etchison, Jessica. *Bleeding Kansas: Contested Liberty in the Civil War Era*. Lawrence: University of Kansas Press, 2004.

Evans, Sara M. *Born for Liberty: A History of Women in America*. New York: The Free Press, 1989.

Fabricant, Daniel S. "Thomas R. Gray and William Styron: Finally, a Critical Look at the 1831 *Confessions of Nat Turner*." *American Journal of Legal History* 37. July 1993: 332–361.

Farber, Daniel. *Lincoln's Constitution*. Chicago: University of Chicago Press, 2003.

Farrell, James M. "The Writs of Assistance and Public Memory: John Adams and the Legacy of James Otis," *New England Quarterly* (2006) 79 #4 533–556.

Ferguson, James R. "Reason in Madness: The Political Thought of James Otis," *William and Mary Quarterly*, (1979: 36:194–214.

Finkelman, Paul, ed. *His Soul Goes Marching On: Responses to John Brown and the Harpers Ferry Raid*. Charlottesville: University Press of Virginia, 1995.

Fisch, Audrey, ed. *The Cambridge Companion to the African American Slave Narrative*. Cambridge, U.K. Cambridge University Press, 2007.

Fishel, Leslie H., Jr. "The Negro in the New Deal Era." *Wisconsin Magazine of History* 8, no. 2. Winter 1964–1965: 111–126.

Fitzgerald, Michael W. "Reconstruction Politics and the Politics of Reconstruction." In *Reconstructions: New Perspectives of the Postbellum United States*, ed. Thomas J. Brown. New York: Oxford University Press, 2006.

Fitzpatrick, Ellen. *The Highest Glass Ceiling : Women's Quest for the American Presidency*. Cambridge: Harvard University Press, 2016.

Flexner, Eleanor, and Ellen Fitzpatrick. *Century of Struggle: The Woman's Rights Movement in the United States*. Enlarged edition. Cambridge, Mass. Belknap Press of Harvard University Press, 1996.

Flower, Milton E. *John Dickinson – Conservative Revolutionary*. Charlottesville, Virginia: University Press of Virginia, 1983.

Foner, Eric. *Reconstruction, America's Unfinished Revolution, 1863–1877*. New York: Harper and Row, 1988.

Foner, Eric. *Tom Paine and Revolutionary America*. New York: Oxford University Press, 1976.

Fowler, William M., Jr. *Samuel Adams: Radical Puritan*. New York: Longman, 1997.

Fox, Stephen R. *The Guardian of Boston: William Monroe Trotter*. New York: Atheneum, 1970.

Franklin, John Hope. "The Enforcement of the Civil Rights Act of 1875." In *African Americans and the Emergence of Segregation, 1865–1900*. Donald G. Nieman, ed.. New York: Garland, 1994.

French, Scot. *The Rebellious Slave: Nat Turner in American Memory*.(Boston: Houghton Mifflin, 2004.

Fruchtman, Jack, Jr. *Thomas Paine: Apostle of Freedom*. New York: Four Walls Eight Windows, 1994.

Gabriel, Mary. *Notorious Victoria: The Life of Victoria Woodhull Uncensored*. Chapel Hill: Algonquin Books, 1998)

Gamwell, Lynn and Nancy Tomes. Madness in America: Cultural and Medical Perceptions of Mental Illness Before 1914. Ithaca, New York: Cornell University Press, 1995.

García, Richard A. "César Chávez: A Personal and Historical Testimony." *Pacific Historical Review* 63, no. 2. May 1994: 225–233.

Garfinkel, Herbert. *When Negroes March: The March on Washington Movement in the Organizational Politics for FEPC*. New York: Atheneum, 1969.

Garrow, David J. "King: The Man, the March, the Dream." *American History* 38, no. 3. August 2003: 26–35.

Garrow, David J. *Bearing the Cross: Martin Luther King, Jr., and the Southern Christian Leadership Conference, 1955–1968*. New York: William Morrow, 1986.

———, ed. *Birmingham, Alabama, 1956–1963: The Black Struggle for Civil Rights*. New York: Carlson Publishing, 1989.

Gellman, David. *Emancipating New York: The Politics of Slavery and Freedom, 1777–1827*. Baton Rouge: Louisiana State University Press, 2006.

Giddings, P. J. *Ida, A Sword Among Lions: Ida B. Wells and the Campaign Against Lynching*. New York: Amistad/HarperCollins, 2008.

Ginger, Ray. *The Bending Cross: A Biography of Eugene Victor Debs*. New Brunswick, New Jersey: Rutgers University Press: 1949.

Ginzberg, Lori D. *Women in Antebellum Reform*. Hoboken, New Jersey: Wiley-Blackwell, 2000.

———. *Untidy Origins: A Story of Woman's Rights in Antebellum New York*. Chapel Hill: University of North Carolina Press, 2005.

Gipson, Lawrence Henry. "The Great Debate in the Committee of the Whole House of Commons on the Stamp Act, as Reported by Nathaniel Ryder." *Pennsylvania Magazine of History and Biography* 86, no. 1 (1962: 10–41.

Goldman, Peter. *The Death and Life of Malcolm X* (2nd ed.). Urbana, Ill.: University of Illinois Press, 1979.

Goldsmith, Barbara. *Other Powers: The Age of Suffrage, Spiritualism, and the Scandalous Victoria Woodhull.* New York: Harper Perennial, 1998.

Gordon, Robert. "Poisons in the Fields: The United Farm Workers, Pesticides, and Environmental Politics." *Pacific Historical Review* 68, no. 1. February 1999: 51–77.

Gottlieb, Manuel. "The Land Question in Georgia." *Science and Society* 3. Summer 1939: 356–388.

Graham, Sara Hunter. *Woman Suffrage and the New Democracy.* New Haven: Yale University Press, 1996.

Greenberg, Kenneth S., ed. *Nat Turner: A Slave Rebellion in History and Memory.* New York: Oxford University Press, 2003(.

Greene, Jerome A. *American Carnage: Wounded Knee, 1890.* Norman, OK: University of Oklahoma Press, 2014.

Greene, Julie. *Pure and Simple Politics: The American Federation of Labor and Political Activism, 1881–1917.* New York: Cambridge University Press, 1998.

Gregory, Jack and Rennard Strickland. *Sam Houston with the Cherokees, 1829-1933.* Norman: University of Oklahoma Press, 1996.

Griffith, Cyril E. *The African Dream: Martin R. Delany and the Emergence of Pan-African Thought.* University Park: Pennsylvania State University Press, 1975.

Griffith, Elisabeth. *In Her Own Right: The Life of Elizabeth Cady Stanton.* New York: Oxford University Press, 1985.

Grob, Gerald N. *Mental Illness and American Society: 1875-1940.* Princeton: Princeton University Press, 1987.

Gura, Philip F. *A Glimpse of Sion's Glory: Puritan Radicalism in New England, 1620–1660.* Middletown, Connecticut: Wesleyan University Press, 1984.

Halberstam, David. *The Children.* New York: Fawcett, 1999.

Halliburton, R. *The Tulsa Race War of 1921.* San Francisco: R and E Research Associates, 1975.

Hamilton, Donna Cooper. "The National Association for the Advancement of Colored People and New Deal Reform Legislation: A Dual Agenda." *Social Service Review* 68, no. 4. December 1994: 488–502.

Hansen, Drew D. *The Dream: Martin Luther King, Jr., and the Speech That Inspired a Nation.* New York: HarperCollins, 2003.

Harlan, Louis R. *Booker T. Washington: The Making of a Black Leader, 1856–1901.* New York: Oxford University Press, 1972.

Harris, William H. *The Harder We Run: Black Workers since the Civil War.* New York: Oxford University Press, 1982.

Hattaway, Herman, and Richard E. Beringer. *Jefferson Davis: Confederate President.* Lawrence: University Press of Kansas, 2002.

Hauptman, Laurence M., and L. Gordon McLester, III. *The Oneida Indians in the Age of Allotment, 1860–1920.* Norman: University of Oklahoma Press, 2006.

Heglar, Charles J. *Rethinking the Slave Narrative: Slave Marriage and the Narratives of Henry Bibb and William and Ellen Craft.* Westport, Conn. Greenwood Press, 2001.

Heller, Dana (2008). "Shooting Solanas: radical feminist history and the technology of failure". In Victoria Hesford & Lisa Diedrich. *Feminist Time against Nation Time: Gender, Politics, and the Nation-State in an Age of Permanent War.* Lanham, Maryland: Lexington Books, 2008). pp. 151–168.

Hicks, Brian. *Toward the Setting Sun: John Ross, the Cherokees, and the Trail of Tears.* New York: Atlantic Monthly Press, 2011.

Hine, Robert V. and John Mack Faragher. *The American West: A New Interpretive History.* New Haven, Connecticut: Yale University Press, 2000)

Hinks, Peter P, John R. McKivigan, and R. Owen Williams. Encyclopedia of Antislavery and Abolition: Greenwood Milestones in African American History. Westport, Connecticut: Greenwood Press, 2007.

Hinks, Peter P. *To Awaken My Afflicted Brethren: David Walker and the Problem of Antebellum Slave Resistance.* University Park: Pennsylvania State University Press, 1997.

Hinton, Richard J. *John Brown and His Men: With Some Account of the Roads They Traveled to Reach Harper's Ferry.* 1894. Reprint. New York: Arno Press, 1968.

Hirsch, James S. *Riot and Remembrance: The Tulsa Race War and Its Legacy.* Boston: Houghton Mifflin, 2002.

Hoffer, Peter Charles: *Cry Liberty. The Great Stono River Slave Rebellion of 1739.* New York: Oxford University Press, 2010.

Hoffman, Jack, and Daniel Simon. *Run Run Run: The Lives of Abbie Hoffman.* New York: Tarcher/Putnam, 1994.

Hoffman, Ronald, *Princes of Ireland, Planters of Maryland: A Carroll Saga, 1500-1782.* Chapel Hill: University of North Carolina Press, 2000.

Hogeland, William. *The Whiskey Rebellion: George Washington, Alexander Hamilton, and the Frontier Rebels Who Challenged America's Newfound Sovereignty.* New York: Scribner, 2006.

Hoig, Stan. *White Man's Paper Trail: Grand Councils and Treaty-Making on the Central Plains.* Boulder: University of Colorado Press, 2006.

Holsaert, Faith S., et al, ed. *Hands on the Freedom Plow: Personal Accounts by Women in SNCC.* Urbana-Champaign: University of Illinois Press, 2010.

Holton, Woody, ed. *Black Americans in the Revolutionary Era: A Brief History with Documents.* New York: Bedford/St. Martin's, 2009.

Horton, James Oliver, and Lois E. Horton. *Black Bostonians: Family Life and Community Struggle in the Antebellum North.* New York: Holmes & Meier Publishers, 1979.

———. *In Hope of Liberty: Culture, Community, and Protest among Northern Free Blacks, 1700–1860.* New York: Oxford University Press, 1997.

Horwitz, Tony. *Midnight Rising: John Brown and the Raid That Sparked the Civil War.* New York: Henry Holt & Co., 2011.

Hower, Bob, and Maurice Willows. *1921 Tulsa Race Riot and the American Red Cross, "Angels of Mercy.".* Tulsa: Homestead Press, 1993.

Hull, N. E. H. *The Woman Who Dared to Vote: The Trial of Susan B. Anthony.* University Press of Kansas, 2012.

Hunt, Andrew E. *The Turning: A History of Vietnam Veterans Against the War.* New York: New York University Press, 2001.

Hutchinson, Earl Ofari. *Let Your Motto Be Resistance: The Life and Thought of Henry Highland Garnet.* Boston: Beacon Press, 1972.

Hyman, Harold M., and William M. Wiecek. *Equal Justice under Law: Constitutional Development, 1835–1875.* New York: Harper & Row, 1982.

Inskeep, Steve. *Jacksonland: President Andrew Jackson, Cherokee Chief John Ross, and a Great American Land Grab.* Penguin Press, 2015.

Isenberg, Nancy. *Sex and Citizenship in Antebellum America.* Chapel Hill: University of North Carolina Press, 1998.

Isikoff, Michael and David Corn. *Hubris: The Inside Story of Spin, Scandal, and the Selling of the Iraq War.* New York: Crown, 2006.

Isserman, Maurice. *If I Had a Hammer: The Death of the Old Left and the Birth of the New Left.* New York: Basic Books, 1987.

Jackson, Maurice and Susan Kozel, eds. *Quakers and Their Allies in the Abolitionist Cause, 1754-1808.* London: Routledge: 2015.

Jackson, Thomas F. *From Civil Rights to Human Rights: Martin Luther King, Jr., and the Struggle for Economic Justice.* Philadelphia: University of Pennsylvania Press, 2007.

James, Marquis. *The Raven: A Biography of Sam Houston.* Austin: University of Texas Press, 1988.

Jeansonne, Glen. *Messiah of the Masses: Huey P. Long and the Great Depression.* Upper Saddle River, New Jersey: Pearson, 1997.

Johnson, Charles, and Bob Adelman. *King: The Photobiography of Martin Luther King, Jr.* New York: Viking Studio, 2000.

Johnson, Hannibal B. *Black Wall Street: From Riot to Renaissance in Tulsa's Historic Greenwood District.* Austin: Eakin Press, 1998.

Johnson, Jacqueline. *Stokely Carmichael: The Story of Black Power.* Englewood Cliffs, N.J. Silver Burdett, 1990.

Johnson, Troy R. "Roots of Contemporary Native American Activism," *American Indian Culture and Research Journal,* 20(2):127–154.

———. *The Occupation of Alcatraz Island: Indian Self-determination and the Rise of Indian Activism.* University of Illinois Press, 1996.

Johnson, Yvonne. *The Voices of African American Women: The Use of Narrative and Authorial Voice in the Works of Harriet Jacobs, Zora Neale Hurston, and Alice Walker.* New York: Peter Lang, 1998.

Johnston, Robert D., and Catherine McNicol Stock, eds. *The Countryside in the Age of the Modern State: Political Histories of Rural America.* Ithaca, N.Y. Cornell University Press, 2001.

Jones, Stanley L. *The Presidential Election of 1896.* Madison: University of Wisconsin Press, 1964.

Jordan, Winthrop D. *White over Black: American Attitudes toward the Negro, 1550–1812.* New York: W. W. Norton, 1977.

Kaplan, Sidney, and Emma Nogrady Kaplan. *The Black Presence in the Era of the American Revolution.* Rev. ed. Amherst: University of Massachusetts Press, 1989.

Kappler, Charles J., ed. *Indian Treaties*. New York: Interland, 1972.

Karcher, Carolyn L. *The First Woman in the Republic: A Cultural Biography of Lydia Maria Child*. Durham: Duke University Press, 1994.

Kaye, Harvey J. *Thomas Paine and the Promise of America*. New York: Hill and Wang, 2005.

Kazin, Michael. *A Godly Hero: The Life of William Jennings Bryan*. New York: Knopf, 2006.

Kelly, Casey Ryan (2014). "Détournement, Decolonization, and the American Indian Occupation of Alcatraz Island (1969–1971)". *Rhetoric Society Quarterly*. 44 (2: 168.

Kelman, Ari. *A Misplaced Massacre: Struggling Over the Memory of Sand Creek*. Cambridge, MA: Harvard University Press, 2013.

Kennedy, David M., *Over Here: The First World War and American Society*. New York : Oxford University Press, 2004.

Kerber, Linda K. No Constitutional Right to Be Ladies: Women and the Obligations of Citizenship. New York: Hill and Wang, 1998.

Kerry, John, and Vietnam Veterans Against the War. *The New Soldier*. New York: MacMillan Publishing Company: October 1971.

Kersten, Andrew E. *A. Philip Randolph: A Life in the Vanguard*. Lanham, Md. Rowman and Littlefield, 2007.

Klatch, Rebecca E. *A Generation Divided: The New Left, the New Right, and the 1960s*. Berkeley : University of California Press, 1999.

Knight, Louise W. *Citizen: Jane Addams and the Struggle for Democracy*. Chicago: University of Chicago Press, 2005.

———*Jane Addams: Spirit in Action*. New York: W.W. Norton, 2010.

Knock, Thomas J. *To End All Wars: Woodrow Wilson and the Quest for a New World Order*. Princeton: Princeton University Press, 1995.

Knollenberg, Bernhard. *Growth of the American Revolution: 1766–1775*. New York: Free Press, 1975.

Koenig, Louis W. *Bryan: A Political Biography of William Jennings Bryan*. New York: Putnam, 1971.

Kohn, Richard H. "The Washington Administration's Decision to Crush the Whiskey Rebellion." *Journal of American History* 59. December 1972), 567–84.

Kohn, Stephen M., *American Political Prisoners: Prosecutions under the Espionage and Sedition Acts*. Westport, Connecticut: Praeger, 1994.

Kroeger, Brooke. *Nelly Bly: Daredevil, Reporter, Feminist*. New York: Crown, 1994.

Kushner, Sam. *Long Road to Delano*. New York: International Publishers, 1975.

La Botz, Dan. *César Chávez and La Causa*. New York: Pearson Longman, 2006.

Lampe, Gregory P. *Frederick Douglass: Freedom's Voice*. Rhetoric and Public Affairs Series. East Lansing: Michigan State University Press, 1998.

LaPlante, Eve. American Jezebel: The Uncommon Life of Anne Hutchinson, the Woman Who Defied the Puritans. New York: HarperOne, 2004.

Laprade, William T. "The Stamp Act in British Politics." *American Historical Review* 35, no. 4 (1930: 735–757.

Lassiter, Matthew D., and Andrew B. Lewis, eds. *The Moderates' Dilemma: Massive Resistance to School Desegregation in Virginia*. Charlottesville: University Press of Virginia, 1998.

Laurie, Bruce *Beyond Garrison*. New York: Cambridge University Press, 2005.

Lazerow, Jama and Yohuru Williams, Yohuru, ed. *In Search of the Black Panther Party: New Perspectives on a Revolutionary Movement*. Durham, North Carolina: Duke University Press, 2006.

Leibhardt, Barbara. "Allotment Policy in an Incongruous Legal System: The Yakima Indian Nation as a Case Study, 1887–1934." *Agricultural History* 65, no. 4. Autumn 1991: 78–103

Levine, Robert S., ed. *Martin R. Delany: A Documentary Reader*. Chapel Hill: University of North Carolina Press, 2003.

Lewis, David Levering. *King: A Biography*. 2nd ed. Urbana: University of Illinois Press, 1978.

———. *W. E. B. Du Bois: Biography of a Race, 1868–1919*. New York: Henry Holt, 1993.

Lewis, George. *Massive Resistance: The White Response to the Civil Rights Movement*. New York: Oxford University Press, 2006.

Libby, Jean. *Black Voices from Harpers Ferry: Osborne Anderson and the John Brown Raid*. Palo Alto, Calif. Libby, 1979.

Lichtenstein, Nelson. *The Most Dangerous Man in Detroit: Walter Reuther and the Fate of American Labor*. New York, Basic Books, 1995.

Lischer, Richard. *The Preacher King: Martin Luther King, Jr. and the Word That Moved America*. New York: Oxford University Press, 1995.

Logan, Rayford W. *The Betrayal of the Negro: From Rutherford B. Hayes to Woodrow Wilson.* New York: Da Capo Press, 1997.

Lunardini, Christine. "Standing Firm: William Monroe Trotter's Meetings with Woodrow Wilson, 1913–1914." *Journal of Negro History* 64, no. 3. Summer 1979: 244–264.

Lutes, Jean Marie. *Front-Page Girls: Women Journalists in American Culture and Fiction, 1880–1930.* Ithaca, New York: Cornell University Press, 2007.

Madigan, Tim. *The Burning: Massacre, Destruction, and the Tulsa Race Riot of 1921.* New York: St. Martin's Press, 2001.

Maier, Pauline. "The Road Not Taken: Nullification, John C. Calhoun, and the Revolutionary Tradition in South Carolina." *South Carolina Historical Magazine* 82, no. 1 (1981: 1–19.

———. *From Resistance to Revolution: Colonial Radicals and the Development of American Opposition to Britain, 1765–1776.* New York: Alfred A. Knopf, 1972.

Mandell, Daniel. "Shifting Boundaries of Race and Ethnicity: Indian-Black Intermarriage in Southern New England, 1760–1880." *Journal of American History* 85, no. 2. September 1998: 466–501.

Manis, Andrew M. *A Fire You Can't Put Out: The Civil Rights Life of Birmingham's Reverend Fred Shuttlesworth.* Tuscaloosa: University of Alabama Press, 1999.

Marable, Manning. *W. E. B. Du Bois: Black Radical Democrat.* Boston: Twayne, 1986.

Marshall, Peter. *Demanding the Impossible: A History of Anarchism.* London: HarperCollins, 1992.

Marten, James. *Texas Divided: Loyalty and Dissent in the Lone Star State, 1856-1874.* Lexington: University Press of Kentucky, 1990.

Mathews, L. K. "Benjamin Franklin's Plans for a Colonial Union, 1750–1775." *American Political Science Review* 8. August 1914: 393–412.

Matthews, John M. "Negro Republicans in the Reconstruction of Georgia." *Georgia Historical Quarterly* 60. Summer 1976: 145–164.

Matthiessen, Peter. *Sal Si Puedes. Escape If You Can): Cesar Chavez and the New American Revolution.* Berkeley: University of California Press, 2000.

Mayer, Henry. *A Son of Thunder: Patrick Henry and the American Republic.* New York: Franklin Watts, 1986.

———. *All on Fire: William Lloyd Garrison and the Abolition of Slavery.* New York: St. Martin's Press, 1998.

Maynard, William Barksdale. *Woodrow Wilson: Princeton to the Presidency.* New Haven, Conn. Yale University Press, 2008.

Mayo, Bernard. *Myths and Men: Patrick Henry, George Washington, Thomas Jefferson.* Athens: University of Georgia Press, 1959.

McCarthy, Timothy P., and John Stauffer, eds. *Prophets of Protest: Reconsidering the History of American Abolitionism.* New York: New Press, 2006.

McDaniel, W. Caleb. *The Problem of Democracy in the Age of Slavery: Garrisonian Abolitionists and Transatlantic Reform.* Baton Rouge, Louisiana: Louisiana State University Press, 2013.

McDonnell, Janet A. *The Dispossession of the American Indian, 1887–1934.* Bloomington: Indiana University Press, 1991.

McFeely, William S. *Frederick Douglass.* New York: W.W. Norton, 1991)

McGerr, Michael. *A Fierce Discontent: The Rise and Fall of the Progressive Movement in America, 1870-1920.* New York: Oxford University Press, 2005.

McGinty, Brian. *John Brown's Trial.* Cambridge, Massachusetts: Harvard University Press, 2009.

McGlone, Robert E. *John Brown's War against Slavery.* Cambridge, Cambridge University Press, 2009.

McPherson, James M. *Ordeal by Fire: The Civil War and Reconstruction.* New York:Knopf, 1982.

McWhorter, Diane. *Carry Me Home: Birmingham, Alabama—The Climactic Battle of the Civil Rights Revolution.* New York: Simon & Schuster, 2001.

Meade, Robert D. *Patrick Henry.* 2 vols. Philadelphia: Lippincott, 1957–1969.

Meier, August. *Negro Thought in America, 1880–1915: Racial Ideologies in the Age of Booker T. Washington.* Ann Arbor: University of Michigan Press, 1968.

Michno, Gregory. *The Three Battles of Sand Creek: The Cheyenne Massacre in Blood, in Court, and as the End of History.* El Dorado Hills, California: Savas Beatie, 2017.

Miller, Calvin Craig. *A. Philip Randolph and the African American Labor Movement.* Greensboro, N.C. Morgan Reynolds, 2005.

Miller, James. *Democracy is in the Streets: From Port Huron to the Siege of Chicago.* Cambridge: Harvard University Press, 1994.

Miller, John C. *Origins of the American Revolution.* Stanford, California: Stanford University Press, 1959.

Miller, Karen A. J., *Populist Nationalism: Republican Insurgency and American Foreign Policy Making, 1918–1925*. Westport, Connecticut: Greenwood Press, 1999.

Miller, Keith D. *Voice of Deliverance: The Language of Martin Luther King, Jr., and Its Sources*. New York: Free Press, 1992.

Mills, Nicholas. "Heard and Unheard Speeches: What Really Happened at the March on Washington?" *Dissent* 35. Summer 1988: 285–291.

Moore, George H. *Notes on the History of Slavery in Massachusetts*. New York: D. Appleton, 1866.

Moore, Jacqueline H. *Booker T. Washington, W. E. B. Du Bois, and the Struggle for Racial Uplift*. Wilmington, Del. Scholarly Resources, 2003.

Morgan, Edmund S. *The Birth of the Republic, 1763–1789*. Chicago: University of Chicago Press, 1977.

Morgan, Edmund S., and Helen M. Morgan. *The Stamp Act Crisis: Prologue to Revolution*. New York: Collier Books, 1963.

Morgan, H. Wayne. *William McKinley and His America*, rev. ed. Kent, Ohio: Kent State University Press, 2003.

Moritz, Theresa. *The World's Most Dangerous Woman: A New Biography of Emma Goldman*. Vancouver: Subway Books, 2001.

Mott, Wesley T. "The Rhetoric of Martin Luther King, Jr. Letter from Birmingham Jail." *Phylon* 36 (1975: 411–421.

Moulton, Gary E. *John Ross Cherokee Chief*. Athens: The University of Georgia Press, 1978.

Munroe, John A. *Philadelawareans*. Newark, Delaware: University of Delaware Press, 2004.

Murch, Donna. *Living for the City: Migration, Education, and the Rise of the Black Panther Party in Oakland, California*. Chapel Hill: University of North Carolina Press, 2010.

Murphy, Paul L. *World War I and the Origin of Civil Liberties in the United States*. New York: W. W. Norton, 1979.

Nash, Gary B. *Forging Freedom: The Formation of Philadelphia's African American Community, 1720–1840*. Cambridge, Mass. Harvard University Press, 1991.

———. *Race and Revolution*. Lanham, Md. Rowan and Littlefield, 2001.

Nathans, Elizabeth S. *Losing the Peace: Georgia Republicans and Reconstruction, 1865–1871*. Baton Rouge: Louisiana State University Press, 1968.

Nelson, Craig. *Thomas Paine: Enlightenment, Revolution, and the Birth of Modern Nations*. New York: Viking, 2006.

Newman, Richard, et al., eds. *Pamphlets of Protest: An Anthology of Early African-American Protest Literature, 1790–1860*. New York: Routledge, 2001.

Newman, Richard. *Freedom's Prophet: Bishop Richard Allen, the AME Church, and the Black Founding Fathers*. New York: New York University Press, 2008.

Nichols, Roy F. "United States vs. Jefferson Davis, 1865–1869." *American Historical Review* 31(January 1926: 266–284.

Nichols, William W. "Slave Narratives: Dismissed Evidence in the Writing of Southern History." *Phylon* 32, no. 4 (1971: 403–409.

Nicosia, Gerald. *Home to War: A History of the Vietnam Veterans' Movement*. New York: Crown Publishers: 2001.

Niven, John. *John C. Calhoun and the Price of Union*. Baton Rouge: Louisiana State University Press, 1988.

Nobles, Gregory. "Yet the Old Republicans Still Persevere: Samuel Adams, John Hancock, and the Crisis of Popular Leadership in Revolutionary Massachusetts, 1775–90". In Hoffman, Ronald; Albert, Peter J. *The Transforming Hand of Revolution: Reconsidering the American Revolution as a Social Movement*. Charlottesville: University Press of Virginia, 1995). pp. 258–85.

Oates, Stephen B. *Let the Trumpet Sound: The Life of Martin Luther King, Jr.*. New York: Harper & Row, 1982.

———. *The Fires of Jubilee: Nat Turner's Fierce Rebellion*. New York: HarperPerennial, 1990.

———. *To Purge This Land with Blood: A Biography of John Brown*. 2nd ed. Amherst: University of Massachusetts Press, 1985.

Olson, James C. *Red Cloud and the Sioux Problem*. Lincoln: University of Nebraska Press, 1965.

Osofsky, Gilbert, ed. *Puttin' on Ole Massa: The Slave Narratives of Henry Bibb, William Wells Brown, and Solomon Northup*. New York: Harper & Row, 1969.

———. "Wendell Phillips and the Quest for a New American National Identity" *Canadian Review of Studies in Nationalism* 1973. 1: 15-46.

Ostler, Jeffrey. *The Plains Sioux and U.S. Colonialism from Lewis and Clark to Wounded Knee*. New York: Cambridge University Press, 2004.

Otis, D. S. *The Dawes Act and the Allotment of Indian Lands*, ed. Francis Paul Prucha. Norman: University of Oklahoma Press, 1973.

Otis, James. *The Rights of British Colonies Asserted and Proved*. Boston: Edes and Gill, 1764.Piersen, William D. *Black Yankees: The Development of an Afro- American Subculture in Eighteenth-Century New England*. Amherst: University of Massachusetts Press, 1988.

Papke, David Ray. *The Pullman Case: The Clash of Labor and Capital in Industrial America*. Lawrence, Kansas: University Press of Kansas, 1999.

Parrish, Mary E. Jones. *Race Riot 1921: Events of the Tulsa Disaster*. Tulsa: Out on a Limb Publishers, 1998.

Pascal, Janet B. *Jacob Riis: Reporter and Reformer*. New York: Oxford University Press, 2005.

Patterson, James T. Brown v. Board of Education: *A Civil Rights Milestone and Its Troubled Legacy*. New York: Oxford University Press, 2001.

Pease, Jane H., and William H. Pease. "The Economics and Politics of Charleston's Nullification Crisis." *Journal of Southern History* 47, no. 3. August 1981: 335–362.

Pennypacker, Samuel W. "The Settlement of Germantown, and the Causes Which Led to It." *Pennsylvania Magazine of History and Biography* 4, no. 1 (1880: 1–41.

Peterson, Joyce Shaw. *American Automobile Workers: 1900-1933*. Albany: State University of New York Press, 1987.

Peterson, Merrill D. *Olive Branch and Sword: The Compromise of 1833*. Baton Rouge: Louisiana State University Press, 1982.

Pfeffer, Paula F. *A. Philip Randolph, Pioneer of the Civil Rights Movement*. Baton Rouge: Louisiana State University Press, 1996.

Pfeifer, Michael J. ed.), *Lynching Beyond Dixie: American Mob Violence Outside the South*. Urbana, IL: University of Illinois Press, 2013.

Pfeifer, Michael J. *Rough Justice: Lynching and American Society, 1874–1947*. Urbana: University of Illinois Press, 2004.

Pinn, Anthony B., ed. *Moral Evil and Redemptive Suffering: A History of Theodicy in African-American Religious Thought*. Gainesville: University Press of Florida, 2002.

Potter, David M. *The Impending Crisis, 1848–1861*. New York: Harper & Row, 1976.

Powers, Richard Gid. "The FBI Marches on the Dreamer." *American History* 38, no. 3. August 2003: 42–47.

Prucha, Francis Paul. *The Great Father: The United States Government and the American Indian*. 2 vols. Lincoln: University of Nebraska Press, 1995.

Puls, Mark. *Samuel Adams: Father of the American Revolution*. New York: Palgrave Macmillan, 2006.

Quarles, Benjamin. *Allies for Freedom: Blacks and John Brown*. New York: Oxford University Press, 1974.

———. *Black Abolitionists*. New York: Da Capo Press, 1991.

Raskin, Jonah. *For the Hell of It: The Life and Times of Abbie Hoffman*. Los Angeles: University of California Press, 1996.

Ratcliffe, Donald J. "The Nullification Crisis, Southern Discontents, and the American Political Process." *American Nineteenth Century History* 1, no. 2. Summer 2000: 1.

Redkey, Edwin S.*Respect Black: The Writings and Speeches of Henry McNeal Turner*. New York: Arno Press, 1971.

Reed, Harry A. "Martin Luther King, Jr. History and Memory, Reflections on Dreams and Silences." *Journal of Negro History* 84, no. 2. Spring 1999: 150–166.

Reid, John Phillip. *Constitutional History of the American Revolution, II: The Authority to Tax*. Madison: University of Wisconsin Press, 1987)

Rich, B. Ruby (1993). "Manifesto destiny: drawing a bead on Valerie Solanas". *Voice Literary Supplement*. New York, NY: The Village Voice. 119: 16–17.

Ritter, Kurt W (1977). "Confrontation as Moral Drama: the Boston Massacre in Rhetorical Perspective". *Southern Speech Communication Journal*. Volume 42, No. 1: 114–136.

Roberts, Paul William. A War Against Truth: An Intimate Account of the Invasion of Iraq. Vancouver: Raincoast Books, 2005.

Rugeley, Terry (1989). "Savage and Statesman: Changing Historical Interpretations of Tecumseh". *Indiana Magazine of History*. 85. 4: 289–311.

Russo, Peggy A., and Paul Finkelman, eds. *Terrible Swift Sword: The Legacy of John Brown*. Athens: Ohio University Press, 2005.

Salerno, Beth A. *Sister Societies: Women's Antislavery Societies in Antebellum America*. DeKalb, Illinois: Northern Illinois University Press, 2005.

Samuelson, Richard A. "The Constitutional Sanity of James Otis: Resistance Leader and Loyal Subject," *Review of Politics*. Summer, 1999), 61 #3 493–523.

Sanborn, Franklin B. *The Life and Letters of John Brown: Liberator of Kansas and Martyr of Virginia.* 1885. Reprint. New York: Negro Universities Press, 1969.

Schechter, Patricia A. Ida B. Wells-Barnett and American Reform, 1880-1930. Chapel Hill: University of North Carolina Press, 2001)

Schneirov, Richard, et al. eds.) *The Pullman Strike and the Crisis of the 1890s: Essays on Labor and Politics.* Urbana, Illinois: University of Illinois Press, 1999.

Schor, Joel. *Henry Highland Garnet: A Voice of Black Radicalism in the Nineteenth Century.* Westport, Conn. Greenwood Publishing, 1977.

Schott, Thomas E. *Alexander H. Stephens of Georgia: A Biography.* Baton Rogue: Louisiana State University Press, 1988.

Sellers, Cleveland, and Robert Terrell. *The River of No Return: The Autobiography of a Black Militant in the Life and Death of SNCC.* New York: Morrow, 1973.

Sewall, Samuel. *The Selling of Joseph: A Memorial.* Boston: Green and Allen, 1700.

Shay, Allison. "Remembering Ida B. Wells-Barnett". University of North Carolina at Chapel Hill. https://lcrm.lib.unc.edu/blog/index.php/2012/07/16/remembering-ida-b-wells-barnett/ Retrieved 1-23-201

Shelby, Tommie. "Two Conceptions of Black Nationalism: Martin Delany on the Meaning of Black Political Solidarity." *Political Theory* 31, no. 5. October 2003: 664–692.

Sheridan, R. (1960). The British Credit Crisis of 1772 and The American Colonies. *The Journal of Economic History,* 20. 2), 161-186.

Shields, John, ed. *The Collected Works of Phillis Wheatley.* New York: Oxford University Press, 1988.

Shlaes, Amity. *The Forgotten Man: A New History of the Great Depression.* New York: Harper Collins, 2009.

Shuffelton, Frank, ed. *A Mixed Race: Ethnicity in Early America.* New York: Oxford University Press, 1993.

Shuler, Jack. *Calling Out Liberty: The Stono Rebellion and the Universal Struggle for Human Rights.* Jackson, MS: University Press of Mississippi, 2009.

Simmons, William J. *Men of Mark: Eminent, Progressive and Rising.* 1887. Reprint. New York: Arno Press, 1968.

Sitkoff, Harvard. *A New Deal for Blacks: The Emergence of Civil Rights as a National Issue during the Depression Decade.* New York: Oxford University Press, 1978.

———. *King: Pilgrimage to the Mountaintop.* New York: Hill and Wang, 2008.

Smith, Carl. *Urban Disorder and the Shape of Belief: The Great Chicago Fire, the Haymarket Bomb, and the Model Town of Pullman.* Chicago: University of Chicago Press, 1995.

Smith, Jessie Carney. "William Monroe Trotter." In *Notable Black American Men.* Detroit: Gale Research, 1999.

Smith, Mark M., *Stono: Documenting and Interpreting a Southern Slave Revolt,* Columbia, SC: University of South Carolina Press, 2005.

Smith, Paul Chaar and Robert Allen Warrior. *Like a Hurricane: The Indian Movement from Alcatraz to Wounded Knee.* New York: The New Press, 1996)

Stampp, Kenneth M. *The Imperiled Union: Essays on the Background of the Civil War.* New York: Oxford University Press, 1980.

Stauffer, John and Zoe Trodd, eds. *The Tribunal: Responses to John Brown and the Harpers Ferry Raid.* Cambridge, Massachusetts, Belknap Press, 2012.

Stavans, Ilan. "Reading Cesar." *Transition* 9, no. 4. 2000: 62–76.

Sterling, Dorothy. *The Making of an Afro-American: Martin Robison Delany, 1812–1885.* New York: Da Capo Press, 1996.

Sternsher, Bernard, ed. *The Negro in Depression and War: Prelude to Revolution, 1930–1945.* Chicago, Ill. Quadrangle Books, 1969.

Stewart, James B. "Heroes, Villains, Liberty, and License: the Abolitionist Vision of Wendell Phillips" in *Antislavery Reconsidered: New Perspectives on the Abolitionists.* Louisiana State U. Press, 1979: 168-191.

Stoll, Ira. *Samuel Adams: A Life.* New York: The Free Press, 2008.

Stone, Geoffrey R., *Perilous Times: Free Speech in Wartime from the Sedition Act of 1798 to the War on Terrorism.* New York: W. W. Norton & Company, 2004.

Stowe, Harriet Beecher. *Uncle Tom's Cabin.* New York: Signet Classics, 2008.

Stuckey, Sterling. "A Last Stern Struggle: Henry Highland Garnet and Liberation Theory." In *Black Leaders of the Nineteenth Century,* eds. Leon Litwack and August Meier. Chicago: University of Illinois Press, 1988.

Sullivan, Patricia. *Days of Hope: Race and Democracy in the New Deal Era.* Chapel Hill: University of North Carolina Press, 1996.

Taylor, Cynthia. *A. Philip Randolph: The Religious Journey of an African American Labor Leader.* New York: New York University Press, 2006.

Tetrault, Lisa. *The Myth of Seneca Falls: Memory and the Women's Suffrage Movement, 1848-1898*. University of North Carolina Press, 2014.

Third, Amanda (2006). "'Shooting from the hip': Valerie Solanas, SCUM and the apocalyptic politics of radical feminism". *Hecate*. 32. 2: 104–132. 2006.

Thomas E. Ricks (2006). *Fiasco: The American Military Adventure in Iraq*. Penguin.

Thomas, Emory M. *The Confederate Nation: 1861-1865*. New York: Harper Perennial, 2011.

Thomas, Evan. *The War Lovers: Roosevelt, Lodge, Hearst, and the Rush to Empire, 1898*. New York: Hachette Digital, 2010.

Thomas, Hugh. The Slave Trade: The Story of the Atlantic Slave Trade: 1440 - 1870. New York: Simon and Schuster, 1999.

Thomas, Peter D. G. *The Townshend Duties Crisis: The Second Phase of the American Revolution, 1767–1773*. Oxford: Oxford University Press, 1987.

Thomas, William H., Jr. *Unsafe for Democracy: World War I and the U.S. Justice Department's Covert Campaign to Suppress Dissent*. Madison: University of Wisconsin Press, 2008.

Thompson, C. Mildred. *Reconstruction in Georgia: Economic, Social, Political, 1865–1872*. New York: Columbia University Press, 1915.

Thornton, John. October 1991). "African Dimensions of the Stono Rebellion". *The American Historical Review*. 4. 96. 4: 1101–1113.

Tolles, Frederick. *Meeting House and Counting House: The Quaker Merchants of Colonial Philadelphia, 1682–1763*. New York: W. W. Norton, 1948.

Tragle, Henry Irving, ed. *The Southampton Slave Revolt of 1831: A Compilation of Source Material*. Amherst: University of Massachusetts Press, 1971.

Tsai, Robert L. *John Brown's Constitution*, 51 B.C.L. Rev. 151 (2010). Available online at http://lawdigitalcommons.bc.edu/bclr/vol51/iss1/4

Tyler, John W. *Smugglers & Patriots: Boston Merchants and the Advent of the American Revolution*. Boston: Northeastern University Press 1986.

Unger, Harlow Giles. *John Hancock: Merchant King and American Patriot*. New York: Wiley & Sons, 2000.

Unger, Nancy C. *Fighting Bob La Follette: The Righteous Reformer* Chapel Hill: University of North Carolina Press, 2000.

Utley, Robert M. *The Indian Frontier 1846–1890*. Albuquerque: University of New Mexico Press, 2003.

Vaughan, Alden T., ed. *Chronicles of the American Revolution*. New York: Grosset and Dunlap, 1965.

Villard, Oswald Garrison. *John Brown, 1800–1859: A Biography Fifty Years After*. New York: Alfred A. Knopf, 1943.

Walsh, Edward J. "On the Interaction between a Movement and Its Environment." *American Sociological Review* 43, no. 1. February 1978: 110–112.

Walton, Mary. *A Woman's Crusade: Alice Paul and the Battle for the Ballot*. New York: Palgrave Macmillan, 2010

Ward, Geoffrey C., with essays by Martha Saxton, Ann D. Gordon and Ellen Carol DuBois. *Not for Ourselves Alone: The Story of Elizabeth Cady Stanton and Susan B. Anthony*. New York: Alfred Knopf, 1999.

Ware, Susan (2012). "The book I couldn't write: Alice Paul and the challenge of feminist biography". *Journal of Women's History*. 24 (2: 13–36.

Washington, James M., ed. *A Testament of Hope: The Essential Writings of Martin Luther King, Jr.* San Francisco: Harper & Row, 1986.

Washington, Mary Helen. "Meditations on History: The Slave Narrative of Linda Brent." In *Invented Lives: Narratives of Black Women, 1860–1960*, ed. Mary Helen Washington. New York: Doubleday, 1987.

Webb, Clive, ed. *Massive Resistance: Southern Opposition to the Second Reconstruction*. New York: Oxford University Press, 2005.

Weeks, Philip. *Farewell, My Nation: The American Indian and the United States, 1820–1890*. Arlington Heights, Ill. Harlan Davidson, 1990.

Wellman, Judith. *The Road to Seneca Falls: Elizabeth Cady Stanton and the First Woman's Rights Convention*. Urbana: University of Illinois Press, 2004.

Wells, Ida B. Alfreda M. Duster. ed. *Crusade For Justice: The Autobiography of Ida B. Wells*. Negro American Biographies and Autobiographies Series. John Hope Franklin, Series Editor. Chicago: University of Chicago Press, 1970.

Weslager, Clinton A. *The Stamp Act Congress*. Newark: University of Delaware Press, 1976.

West, Michael Rudolph. *The Education of Booker T. Washington: American Democracy and the Idea of Race Relations*. New York: Columbia University Press, 2006.

Wexler, Alice. *Emma Goldman in America*. Boston: Beacon Press, 1984.

White, Richard. "The Winning of the West: The Expansion of the Western Sioux in the Eighteenth and

Nineteenth Centuries." *Journal of American History* 65. September 1978: 319–343.

White, Walter. *A Man Called White: The Autobiography of Walter White*. Athens, Georgia: University of Georgia Press, 1995.

Widenor, William C. *Henry Cabot Lodge and the search for an American foreign policy*. Los Angeles: University of California Press, 1983)

Widick, B.J. *Detroit: City of Class and Race Violence* Revised Edition. Detroit: Wayne State University Press, 1989.

Williams, David. *The Georgia Gold Rush: Twenty-Niners, Cherokees, and Gold Fever*. Columbia: University of South Carolina Press, 1993.

Williams, Harry T. *Huey Long*. New York: Vintage, 1981.

Williams, Lee E., and Lee E. Williams II. *Anatomy of Four Race Riots: Racial Conflict in Knoxville, Elaine, Arkansas), Tulsa, and Chicago, 1919–1921*. Hattiesburg: University and College Press of Mississippi, 1972.

Williams, R. Hal. *Years of Decision: American Politics in the 1890s*. Prospect Heights, Ill. Waveland Press, 1993.

Williams, Selma R. Divine Rebel: The Life of Anne Marbury Hutchinson. New York: Henry Holt, 1981.

Williams, Walter and Retter, Yolanda, eds. *Gay and Lesbian Rights in the United States: A Documentary History*. Westport, Connecticut: Greenwood Press, 2003.

Willison, George F. *Patrick Henry and His World*. Garden City, N.Y. Doubleday, 1969.

Winship, Michael Paul. *Making Heretics: Militant Protestantism and Free Grace in Massachusetts, 1636–1641*. Princeton, New Jersey: Princeton University Press, 2002.

Witcover, Jules. *Party of the People: A History of the Democrats*. New York: Random House, 2003.

Wolf, Eva Sheppard. *Race and Liberty in the New Nation: Emancipation in Virginia from the Revolution to Nat Turner's Rebellion*. Baton Rouge: Louisiana State University Press, 2006.

Wolf, Stephanie Grauman. *Urban Village: Population, Community, and Family Structure in Germantown, Pennsylvania, 1683–1800*. Princeton, N.J.: Princeton University Press, 1976.

Wolters, Raymond. *Du Bois and His Rivals*. Columbia: University of Missouri Press, 2002.

———. *Negroes and the Great Depression: The Problem of Economic Recovery*. Westport, Conn. Greenwood Press, 1970.

Wood, W. Kirk. "In Defense of the Republic: John C. Calhoun and State Interposition in South Carolina, 1776–1833." *Southern Studies* 10, nos. 1–2 (2003: 9–48.

Woods, Randall B. *Fulbright: A Biography*. New York: Cambridge University Press, 1995.

———. *LBJ: Architect of American Ambition*. New York: Free Press, 2006.

Woodward, Bob. Plan of Attack: The Definitive Account of the Decision to Invade Iraq. New York: Simon and Schuster, 2004.

Worley, Sam. "Solomon Northup and the Sly Philosophy of the Slave Pen." *Callaloo* 20, no. 1. Winter 1997: 243–259.

Wright, Sarah E. *A. Philip Randolph: Integration in the Workplace*. Englewood Cliffs, N.J. Silver Burdett Press, 1990.

Wunder, John R. *"Retained by the People": A History of American Indians and the Bill of Rights*. New York: Oxford University Press, 1994.

Yanni, Carla. *The Architecture of Madness: Insane Asylums in the United States*. Minneapolis: University of Minnesota Press, 2007.

Yellin, Jean Fagan. *Harriet Jacobs: A Life*. Cambridge, Mass. Basic Civitas Books, 2004.

Yochelson, Bonnie and Daniel Czitrom. *Rediscovering Jacob Riis: Exposure Journalism and Photography in Turn-of-the-Century New York*. Chicago, University of Chicago Press, 2014.

York, Neil Longley (2009). "Rival Truths, Political Accommodation, and the Boston 'Massacre'". *Massachusetts Historical Review*. Volume 11: 57–95.

———. *The Boston Massacre: a History with Documents*. New York: Taylor & Francis, 2010.

Zahniser, J. D.; Fry, Amelia R. (2014). *Alice Paul: Claiming Power*. New York: Oxford University Press, 2014.

Zinn, Howard. *SNCC: The New Abolitionists*. Reprint Edition. Chicago: Haymarket Books, 2013.

Zompetti, Joseph P. "César Chávez's Rhetorical Strategies of Resistance." PhD dissertation, Wayne State University, 1998.

Index

A
Adams, Samuel, 39–42
Addams, Jane, 508–512, 554–557
"An Address to the Slaves of the United States of America," 143–150
an address to those who keep slaves, and approve the practice, 101–104
"Agitation," 375–377
Allen, Richard, 101–104
"All That We Ask Is Equal Laws, Equal Legislation, and Equal Rights," 272–280
American Anti-Slavery Convention, declaration of sentiments, 129–134
Anderson, Osborne P., 195–207
Anthony, Susan B., 494–500, 501–507
Antiwar Speech, 633–637
appeal to Choctaws and Chickasaws, 289–293
appeal to the coloured citizens of the world, 105–116
An Appeal to the World, 410–415
Atlanta Exposition Address, 357–362
Auto Workers Strike, 579–584

B
"The Ballot or the Bullet," 446–452
Battle of Sand Creek: editorials and congressional testimony, 298–315
"Beyond Vietnam: A Time to Break Silence," 638–649
"A Black Inventory of the New Deal," 397–404
The Black Panther Party, 474–479
"Black Power," 461–473
Bly, Nellie, 535–544
Book
   Incidents in the Life of a Slave Girl, 209–215
   Twelve Years a Slave: Narrative of Solomon Northup, 176–183
book chapter
   How the Other Half Lives, 545–553
book excerpt
   The Condition, Elevation, Emigration, and Destiny of the Colored People of the United States, Politically Considered, 165–175
   prejudices against people of color, and our duties, 135–142
   Steal This Book, 606–612
   Ten Days in a Mad-House, 535–544
Boston Massacre Oration, 49–55
Boston Non-Importation Agreement, 35–38

Brown, John, 184–194
Bryan, William Jennings, 566–573
Byrd, Robert C., 658–661

C
Cain, Richard Harvey, 272–280
call to Negro America to March on Washington, 405–409
CANDIDUS, 39–42
Carmichael, Stokely, 453–460, 461–473
chapter
   preface to *The Rise and Fall of the Confederate Government*, 281–285
Chávez, César, 613–620
Child, Lydia Marie, 135–142
Chivington, John M., 298–315
Common Sense, 62–75
Commonwealth Address, 613–620
The Condition, Elevation, Emigration, and Destiny of the Colored People of the United States, Politically Considered, 165–175
The Confessions of Nat Turner, 118–128
congressional testimony
   Battle of Sand Creek: editorials and congressional testimony, 298–315
   testimony before the House Judiciary Committee, 514–519
   Testimony of the Vietnam Veterans against the War, 651–657
"Cornerstone Speech," 254–262
court transcript
   excerpts from the Massachusetts Bay Colony Trial against Anne Hutchinson, 3–9
The "Cross of Gold" Speech, 566–573

D
Davis, Angela, 529–532
Davis, Jefferson, 245–250, 281–285
Davis, John P., 397–404
Dawes, Henry L., 325–332
Dawes Severalty Act, 325–332
Debs, Eugene V., 562–565, 633–637
declaration
   of protestant subjects in Maryland, 10–16
   of rights of the Stamp Act Congress, 22–26
   of sentiments of the American Anti-Slavery Convention, 129–134

Delany, Martin, 165–175
delegates to the Stamp Act Congress, 22–26
Dickinson, John, 27–34
Douglass, Frederick, 151–164
Du Bois, W. E. B., 363–368, 375–377, 410–415

E
editorial
    Battle of Sand Creek: editorials and congressional testimony, 298–315
    editorial on the Pullman Strike, 558–560
    Valedictory Editorial of the *Liberator,* 220–223
    "Why Women Should Vote," 508–512
editorial on the Pullman Strike, 558–560
"The Emperor Has No Clothes" Speech, 658–661
"The Eruption of Tulsa," 383–389
essay
    an account of the Negroe insurrection in South Carolina, 90–93
    an address to those who keep slaves, and approve the practice, 101–104
    "Agitation," 375–377
    "A Black Inventory of the New Deal," 397–404
    letters from a farmer in Pennsylvania, 27–34
    A minute against slavery, from the Germantown monthly meeting, addressed to the monthly meeting in Dublin, 83–89
    rules by which a great empire may be reduced to a small one, 43–48
Excerpts from the Massachusetts Bay Colony Trial against Anne Hutchinson, 3–9

F
farewell address to the U.S. Senate, 245–250
Follettey, Robert La, 628–632
formal document
    provisional constitution and ordinances for the people of the United States, 184–194
    summary of letter requesting further review of the Dakota Access Pipeline (DAPL), 347–354
Franklin, Benjamin, 43–48

G
Gallatin, Albert, 76–79
Garnet, Henry Highland, 143–150
Garrison, William Lloyd, 129–134, 220–223
Gay Power Comes To Sheridan Square, 601–605
Goldman, Emma, 623–627

Gompers, Samuel, 558–560
government proclamation
    South Carolina Declaration of Causes of Secession, 237–244
Graff, Abram Opden, 83–89
Graff, Derick Opden, 83–89
Gray, Thomas Ruffin, 118–128

H
Hall, Prince, 94–97
Hancock, John, 49–55
Hayden, Tom, 595–600
Henderich, Gerhard, 83–89
Henry, Patrick, 56–61
Hoffman, Abbie, 606–612
Honor the Earth, 347–354
Houston, Sam, 232–236, 251–253
How the Other Half Lives, 545–553
Hutchinson, Anne Marbury, 3–9

I
Incidents in the Life of a Slave Girl (Book), 209–215
Indian Peace Commission, 316–323
Indians of All Tribes Occupation of Alcatraz: proclamation, 343–346
Indigenous Environmental Network, 347–354
"Is It a Crime for a Citizen of the United States to Vote?," 494–500

J
Jacobs, Harriet, 209–215

K
Kerry, John, 651–657
King, Martin Luther, Jr., 419–432, 638–649

L
law
    Dawes Severalty Act, 325–332
Lawson, James, Jr., 416–418
Lecture on Constitutional Equality, 488–493
letter from Birmingham Jail, 419–432
letters from a farmer in Pennsylvania, 27–34
"Liberty," 562–565
"Liberty or Death" speech, 56–61
Lodge, Henry Cabot, 574–578
Long, Huey, 585–589
"Lynching: Our National Crime," 369–374

M

magazine article
- Auto Workers Strike, 579–584
- "The Eruption of Tulsa," 383–389
- "The Status of Woman, Past, Present, and Future," 501–507
- "U.S. Department of (White) Justice," 390–396
- What We Want, 453–460

Malcolm X, 439–445, 446–452
Memminger, Christopher, 237–244
Memorial to Congress, 294–297
merchants and traders of Boston, 35–38
message to congress
- Memorial to Congress, 294–297
- "Message to the Grass Roots," 439–445

A minute against slavery, from the Germantown monthly meeting, addressed to the monthly meeting in Dublin, 83–89

N

Negroe insurrection in South Carolina, account of, 90–93
newspaper article
- Gay Power Comes To Sheridan Square, 601–605

Niagara Movement Declaration of Principles, 363–368
Northup, Solomon, 176–183

O

Oakes, Richard, 343–346
Oglethorpe, James, 90–93
Otis, James, Jr., 17–20

P

Paine, Thomas, 62–75
pamphlet
- *appeal to the coloured citizens of the world,* 105–116
- *Common Sense,* 62–75
- *The Confessions of Nat Turner,* 118–128
- *The Rights of the British Colonies Asserted and Proved,* 17–20
- *Samuel Adams writing as Candidus,* 39–42
- *A Voice from Harper's Ferry,* 195–207

Pastorius, Francis Daniell, 83–89
Paul, Alice, 514–519
petition
- An Appeal to the World, 410–415
- declaration of protestant subjects in Maryland, 10–16
- petition against the excise tax by inhabitants of Western Pennsylvania, 76–79
- petition of Prince Hall and other African Americans to the Massachusetts General Court, 94–97
- petition to the Assembly of Pennsylvania against the slave trade, 99–100

petition against the excise tax by inhabitants of Western Pennsylvania, 76–79
petition of Prince Hall and other African Americans to the Massachusetts General Court, 94–97
petition to the Assembly of Pennsylvania against the slave trade, 99–100
Phillips, Wendell, 216–219
political manifesto
- The SCUM Manifesto, 520–528
- The Port Huron Statement, 595–600

preface to *The Rise and Fall of the Confederate Government,* 281–285
prejudices against people of color, and our duties, 135–142
press release
- call to Negro America to March on Washington, 405–409

provisional constitution and ordinances for the people of the United States, 184–194
public declaration
- Boston Non-Importation Agreement, 35–38
- declaration of sentiments of the American Anti-Slavery Convention, 129–134
- Indians of All Tribes Occupation of Alcatraz: proclamation, 343–346
- Niagara Movement Declaration of Principles, 363–368
- The Port Huron Statement, 595–600
- Seneca Falls Convention Declaration of Sentiments, 483–487
- South Carolina Ordinance of Nullification, 227–231
- Southern Manifesto, 590–594
- Student Nonviolent Coordinating Committee Statement of Purpose, 416–418
- "What We Want, What We Believe," 474–479

public statement
- declaration of rights of the Stamp Act Congress, 22–26

R

Randolph, A. Phillip, 405–409
Reuther, Walter, 579–584
The Rights of the British Colonies Asserted and Proved, 17–20
Riis, Jacob, 545–553
Ross, John, 294–297

rules by which a great empire may be reduced to a small one, 43–48

S
Samuel Adams writing as Candidus, 39–42
The SCUM Manifesto, 520–528
Seneca Falls Convention Declaration of Sentiments, 483–487
"Share Our Wealth" Address, 585–589
Sierra Club, 347–354
Smith, John S., 298–315
Solanas, Valerie, 520–528
South Carolina Declaration of Causes of Secession, 237–244
South Carolina Nullification Convention, 227–231
South Carolina Ordinance of Nullification, 227–231
Southern Manifesto, 590–594
speech
    "An Address to the Slaves of the United States of America," 143–150
    "All That We Ask Is Equal Laws, Equal Legislation, and Equal Rights," 272–280
    Antiwar Speech, 633–637
    appeal to Choctaws and Chickasaws, 289–293
    Atlanta Exposition Address, 357–362
    "The Ballot or the Bullet," 446–452
    "Beyond Vietnam: A Time to Break Silence," 638–649
    "Black Power," 461–473
    Boston Massacre Oration, 49–55
    Commonwealth Address, 613–620
    "Cornerstone Speech," 254–262
    The "Cross of Gold" Speech, 566–573
    "The Emperor Has No Clothes" Speech, 658–661
    farewell address to the U.S. Senate, 245–250
    "Is It a Crime for a Citizen of the United States to Vote?," 494–500
    Lecture on Constitutional Equality, 488–493
    "Liberty," 562–565
    "Liberty or Death" speech, 56–61
    "Lynching: Our National Crime," 369–374
    "Message to the Grass Roots," 439–445
    "Share Our Wealth" Address, 585–589
    Speech against Conscription and War, 623–627
    speech on his expulsion from the Georgia Legislature, 263–271
    Speech on His Refusal to Take the Oath of Loyalty to the Confederacy, 251–253
    speech opposing the Kansas-Nebraska Act, 232–236
    speech opposing the League of Nations, 574–578
    Speech Opposing War with Germany, 628–632
    "The Subjective Necessity for Social Settlements," 554–557
    "Under the Flag," 216–219
    "What to the Slave is the Fourth of July?," 151–164
    William Monroe Trotter's Protest to Woodrow Wilson, 378–382
    Women's March on Washington, 529–532
Speech against Conscription and War, 623–627
speech on his expulsion from the Georgia Legislature, 263–271
Speech on His Refusal to Take the Oath of Loyalty to the Confederacy, 251–253
speech opposing the Kansas-Nebraska Act, 232–236
speech opposing the League of Nations, 574–578
Speech Opposing War with Germany, 628–632
Stamp Act Congress, 22–26
Stanton, Elizabeth Cady, 483–487
"The Status of Woman, Past, Present, and Future," 501–507
Steal This Book, 606–612
Stephens, Alexander, 254–262
Student Nonviolent Coordinating Committee Statement of Purpose, 416–418
"The Subjective Necessity for Social Settlements," 554–557
summary of letter requesting further review of the Dakota Access Pipeline (DAPL), 347–354

T
Tecumseh, 289–293
Ten Days in a Mad-House, 535–544
testimony
    Wounded Knee Massacre: statements and eyewitness accounts, 333–342
testimony before the House Judiciary Committee, 514–519
Testimony of the Vietnam Veterans against the War, 651–657
Thurmond, Strom, 590–594
treaty
    Treaty of Fort Laramie, 316–323
Treaty of Fort Laramie, 316–323
Trotter, William Monroe, 363–368, 378–382
Truscott IV, Lucian, 601–605
Turner, Henry McNeal, 263–271
Turner, Nat, 118–128
Twelve Years a Slave: Narrative of Solomon Northup (Book), 176–183

U
"Under the Flag," 216–219
"U.S. Department of (White) Justice," 390–396

V
Valedictory Editorial of the *Liberator*, 220–223
A Voice from Harper's Ferry, 195–207

W
Walker, David, 105–116
Washington, Booker T., 357–362
Wells, Ida B., 369–374
"What to the Slave is the Fourth of July?," 151–164
What We Want, 453–460
"What We Want, What We Believe," 474–479
White, Walter F., 383–389, 390–396
"Why Women Should Vote," 508–512
William Monroe Trotter's Protest to Woodrow Wilson, 378–382
Women's March on Washington, 529–532
Woodhull, Victoria, 488–493
Wounded Knee Massacre: statements and eyewitness accounts, 333–342

Photo Credits

Photo Credits: p. 23, Printed copy of the Stamp Act of 1765 (Library of Congress, Gwillhickers via Wikimedia Commons) [Public domain]; p. 44, Franklin's The General Magazine and Historical Chronicle (Jan. 1741) By B. Franklin ("The Cooper Collections" via Wikimedia Commons) [Public domain]; p. 57, A Hue & Cry, Virginia broadside, 1775 (via Wikimedia Commons) [Public domain]; p. 84, Petition against slavery (via Wikimedia Commons) [Public domain]; p. 177, Sketch of Solomon Northup (By Frederick M. Coffin (engraved by Nathaniel Orr], via Wikimedia Commons) [Public domain]; p. 238, The first published imprint of secession. By Charleston Mercury (Heritage Auctions, via Wikimedia Commons) [Public domain]; p. 326, A 1911 ad offering "allotted Indian land" for sale (By United States Department of the Interior, via Wikimedia Commons) [Public domain]; p. 334, Map of Wounded Knee (Wounded_Knee_mapa.jpg: via Wikimedia Commons) [Public domain]; p. 370, Cover of Southern Horrors: Lynch Law in All Its Phases (via Wikimedia Commons) [Public domain]; p. 420, Recreation of Martin Luther King's cell in Birmingham Jail at the National Civil Rights Museum (By Adam Jones, Ph.D. via Wikimedia Commons) [CC BY-SA 3.0 (http://creativecommons.org/licenses/by-sa/3.0)]; p. 475, Black Power logo (By Mangokeylime (Own work), via Wikimedia Commons) [CC BY-SA 4.0 (http://creativecommons.org/licenses/by-sa/4.0)]; p. 509, "Kaiser Wilson" banner held by a woman who picketed the White House (By Harris &Ewing, Photographer (NARA record: 1123803) (U.S. National Archives and Records Administration], via Wikimedia Commons) [Public domain]; p. 524, Sheet music cover for patriotic song, 1917 (By Joe Morris Music Co., via Wikimedia Commons) [Public domain]; p. 546, Original Cover of 1890 edition of *How the Other Half Lives* .(via Wikimedia Commons) [Public domain]; p. 567, Artist's conception of William Jennings Bryan after the Cross of Gold speech at the 1896 Democratic National Convention .(William Robinson Leigh, via Wikimedia Commons) [Public domain].